Visual Guide to

Options

Since 1996, Bloomberg Press has published books for finance professionals on investing, economics, and policy affecting investors. Titles are written by leading practitioners and authorities, and have been translated into more than 20 languages.

The Bloomberg Financial Series provides both core reference knowledge and actionable information for finance professionals. The books are written by experts familiar with the work flows, challenges, and demands of investment professionals who trade the markets, manage money, and analyze investments in their capacity of growing and protecting wealth, hedging risk, and generating revenue.

Books in the series include:

Visual Guide to Candlestick Charting by Michael Thomsett
Visual Guide to Municipal Bonds by Robert Doty
Visual Guide to Financial Markets by David Wilson
Visual Guide to Chart Patterns by Thomas N. Bulkowski
Visual Guide to ETFs by David Abner
Visual Guide to Options by Jared Levy

For more information, please visit our Web site at www.wiley.com/go/bloombergpress.

Visual Guide to
Options

Jared A. Levy

Cover image: Waves © Peter Firus/ istockphoto, chart courtesy of Jared Levy
Cover design: C. Wallace

Published by John Wiley & Sons, Inc., Hoboken, New Jersey.
Published simultaneously in Canada.

For general information on our other products and services or for technical support, please contact our Customer Care Department within the United States at (800) 762-2974, outside the United States at (317) 572-3993 or fax (317) 572-4002.

Wiley publishes in a variety of print and electronic formats and by print-on-demand. Some material included with standard print versions of this book may not be included in e-books or in print-on-demand. If this book refers to media such as a CD or DVD that is not included in the version you purchased, you may download this material at http://booksupport.wiley.com. For more information about Wiley products, visit www.wiley.com.

Library of Congress Cataloging-in-Publication Data:

Levy, Jared, 1976
Visual guide to options/Jared A. Levy.
p. cm. — (Bloomberg press series)
Includes index.
ISBN 978-1-118-19666-3 (pbk.); 978-1-118-22774-9 (ebk); 978-1-118-26531-4 (ebk);
978-1-118-24062-5 (ebk)
1. Options (Finance). I. Title.
HG6024.A3L484 2013
332.64' 53—dc23

2012030699

Printed in the United States of America

10 9 8 7 6 5 4 3 2 1

Don't Be Afraid to Take Risks

Load the ship and set out. No one knows for certain whether the vessel will sink or reach the harbor. Cautious people say, "I'll do nothing until I can be sure." Merchants know better. If you do nothing, you lose. Don't be one of those merchants who won't risk the ocean.

—Rumi

Think Outside the Box

. . . a new type of thinking is essential if mankind is to survive and move toward higher levels.

—Albert Einstein

Be Prepared

If you know the enemy and know yourself, you need not fear the result of a hundred battles. If you know yourself but not the enemy, for every victory gained you will also suffer a defeat. If you know neither the enemy nor yourself, you will succumb in every battle.

—Sun Tzu

Ask Questions

A wise man can learn more from a foolish question than a fool can learn from a wise answer.

—Bruce Lee

Don't Give Up

The world ain't all sunshine and rainbows. It's a very mean and nasty place and I don't care how tough you are it will beat you to your knees and keep you there permanently if you let it. You, me, or nobody is gonna hit as hard as life. But it ain't about how hard ya hit. It's about how hard you can get hit and keep moving forward; how much you can take and keep moving forward. That's how winning is done!

—Rocky

Contents

How to Use This Book

The *Visual Guide* series is meant to serve as the all-encompassing, yet easy-to-follow, guide on today's most relevant finance and trading topics. The content truly lives up to the series name by being highly visual; all charts are in color and presented in a large format for ease of use and readability. Other strong visual attributes include consistent elements that function as additional learning aids for the reader:

- Key Points: Primary ideas and takeaways, designed to help the reader skim through definitions and text.
- Definitions: Terminology and technical concepts that arise in the discussion.
- Step-by-Step: Tutorials designed to ensure that readers understand and can execute each section of a multiphase process.
- Do It Yourself: Worksheets, formulas, and calculations.
- Bloomberg Functionality Cheat Sheet: For Bloomberg terminal users, a back-of-the-book summary of relevant functions for the topics and tools discussed.

For e-reader users, the *Visual Guide* series is available as an enhanced e-book and offers special features, like an interactive Test Yourself section where readers can test their newly honed knowledge and skills. The enhanced e-book version also includes video tutorials and special pop-up features. It can be purchased wherever e-books are sold.

Acknowledgments

Nothing truly meaningful in life is created or even possible if not for the trials and tribulations that shape us as humans.

I'm most gracious to life's mountains that have stood before me, challenged me, and ultimately given me a chance to get a better view of the beautiful existence I have been fortunate enough to live.

Thank you.

Introduction

My goal for this guide is to allow you to open to just about any point in the book and find a useful tip, method, or actionable idea that you can apply immediately, without having to go back and read too far.

Most of us believe we are free thinkers, but it's important to realize that on some level, information flows into our minds through filters or biased channels. The specific publications you read or websites you browse dictate your information sources. As you structure your investment thesis and strategy, don't ever be afraid to break your normal pattern and look for alternative methods of gathering information, statistics, and strategy.

Depending on your particular exposure or experience with trading options, you are going to have preconceived notions about how useful they are to you. Even if you have been an extremely successful options trader, keep your mind open to looking at the option markets and their risk in a different way. The ideas, techniques, and processes in this book are not the only solution, but they have worked for me for many years and may make a good addition to your existing repertoire. No one has "the secret sauce"; you simply need a viable action plan and a sound risk and psychological management system.

Although there is no perfect way to trade options, there are many wrong ways to do it. I learned some valuable (and costly) lessons along the way; I hope to show you where I screwed it up so that you can avoid the major pitfalls of *bad* options trading.

This book expands on the focus of my first book, *Your Options Handbook*, and details more of the nuanced techniques and analysis that professionals use to get an edge on the market. The goal of this text is to help you to truly understand risk, order flow, and volume as well as execution and strategy.

Even with Bloomberg being one of the best information sources out there, don't be discouraged if you don't have access to a terminal. The bulk of strategies, tools, and techniques contained in these pages can be utilized and applied in many forms.

Also realize that this book couldn't possibly contain every single thing you need to know about options, so if you have a question or if you don't feel completely comfortable with a concept or strategy, be sure to research it further and ask questions! I am available at www.jaredlevy.com if you need a helping hand or if you are looking for further depth on a subject.

Visual Guide to
Options

CHAPTER 1

The World of Options

There are infinite ways that options can be utilized in your investment portfolio. Whether you are an individual writing covered calls on 200 shares of IBM, a hedge fund manager with billions in assets that need to be protected against volatility or "tail risk," or anywhere in between, there is a place for options in your account, period.

To get the most from the options markets, it is best to fully understand the underlying securities from which they are valued and then take on the options themselves. The trends, abnormalities, and patterns that emerge in the options markets get their cues from their underlying security. Because of this, you must never look at an option (strategy) in a vacuum.

When I was trading on the floor, I tended to end my trading day delta-neutral—or not having a "directional bet"—going into the next morning. Market makers, like I was, have to deal with a constant flow of orders without preparation. By ending delta-neutral the previous day, I could reset and remain flexible in my strategy.

Option traders tend to have an "if, then" attitude because of our ability to be elastic with our hypothesis and adjust positions as events, news, and data change. This mind-set is usually in stark contrast to a regular stock trader, who needs to be more rigid in predictions and theses. I certainly prefer the flexibility options offer, because I still have yet to meet a person who knows exactly where a stock is going, not to mention that I always like contingency plans. As an option trader you always have the choice of getting or giving odds depending on the situation.

As a professional with a trained eye I can look at an option chain on just about any security and surmise a general hypothesis about the condition of the stock; but I am learning more and more that it's actually easier—and more profitable in the long run—to make sense of the nuances of the underlying detail first and

KEY POINT:

Options traders can use certain strategies to take a neutral position in a stock or can employ protective tactics to increase their probability of becoming profitable, even on the fly.

use the options markets as your microscope and scalpel as opposed to your looking glass.

But we all get that wild streak from time to time. I remember looking at Apple's upside call skew in early 2011 (see Exhibit 1.1) and thinking that it might be a good idea to sell some out-of-the-money call spreads because they were so expensive. Little did I know that they had planned a conference call to announce a special dividend and the stock started screaming higher (those calls were pricey for a reason), putting me in an uncomfortable spot; always take time to do your homework!

Have a Checklist

I believe that the most effective method of trading starts with a checklist or filter of sorts that gets you to a specific quantitative, objective target on which you can add your subjective twist. Start from the outside (macro) and work inward (details of a stock's fundamentals and technicals).

Optimally, your checklist should consist of fundamental, technical, and statistical parameters that narrow your potential candidates to a manageable field.

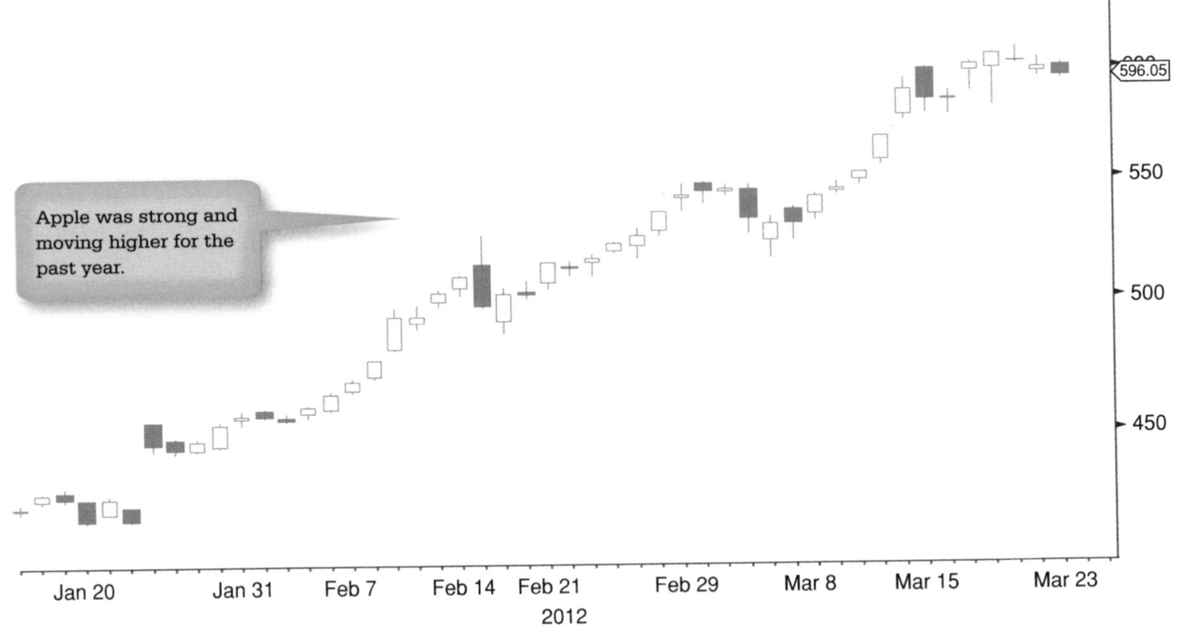

Exhibit 1.1

Bloomberg's OSRCH screen is a quick and dirty way to cut through some of the basic fundamental, technical, and statistical noise that exists. Once the noise is out of the way, you can more effectively review only the top contenders without wasting too much time on research and missing your timing.

There are many ways of finding candidates. Running scans and filters at different times will help you to screen for stocks that meet certain criteria. Another method I favor is to form a thesis around a general social, technological, political, or global trend and find the stocks that stand to benefit (or falter) from it. Form a timeline and potential path in your head of how you think these events will unfold and then overlay an option strategy on top of that thesis.

In addition to all this, when you are forming a forward thesis, consider the effects of news, earnings, macroeconomic climate, seasonal effects, and even political developments. I can't stress this enough! The emotional waves of the masses often override corporate fundamentals and technical formations at least in the short term. Don't get stuck with blinders on in your own bullish or bearish mind. It's the worst place to be.

In the longer term, earnings strength and a viable, thriving business structure with a popular good or service is what I believe motivates the markets. Most analysts, especially those using the Discounted Cash Flow (DCF) methodology and the like, agree.

The core of the options universe revolves around volatility and time. Many of the strategies, techniques, and methods I cover in this book are related to volatility/time in some form or fashion. You must understand both the volatility of the stock and the volatility of the option or spread that you are trading. An intimate knowledge of volatility in the underlying asset and subsequent manifestation in the derivative is essential to generating consistent profits and becoming a professional trader.

We explore volatility in detail in Chapter 7 and reference it throughout this book. You also see the Bloomberg screens used to analyze it. At the end of the day, everything comes back to volatility; make its comprehension your number one priority. Just when you think you get it, you are just getting started.

The volatility conundrum haunts every good option trader. It is a question that cannot be solved, at least not fully. But you can make "realistic assumptions" about it and often that is good enough.

If you get what I am saying then you probably have some experience under your belt; if you do not, then you have a long journey ahead of you—take it slow.

Exhibit 1.2 shows the growth of puts and calls separately over the last 20 years (calls in yellow).

Options traders are growing in record numbers. Their cumulative experience and growing selection of strategies continue to increase liquidity and flexibility in the option markets, which is beneficial for all of us. See Exhibit 1.3 for totals in annual options volume. It is also the reason why indicators such as the Chicago Board Options Exchange (CBOE) put-call ratio are becoming antiquated and obsolete. I discuss this later.

Don't be a sucker—learn as much as you can before taking big risks in the option markets.

Smart Investor Tip!

The checklist is a major step in preventing mistakes and overlooking key information. It also helps with trade consistency and keeps scatterbrains like me focused.

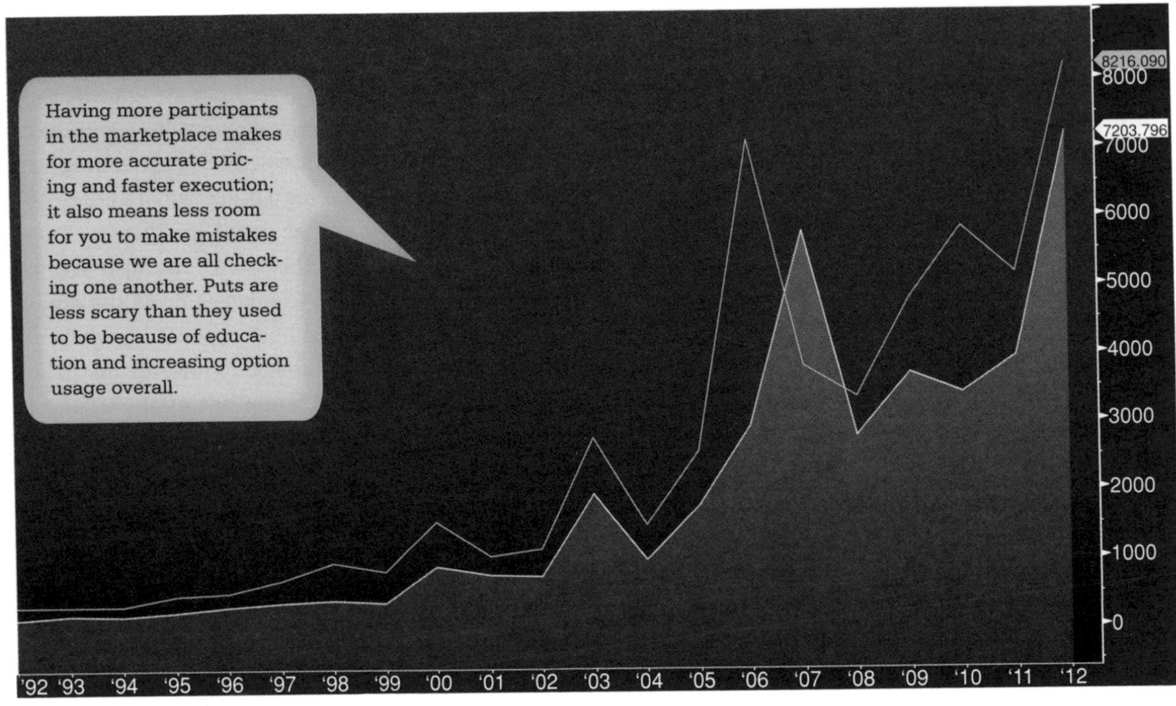

Exhibit 1.2

The Basics

Thales of Miletus used options to lock in a low and set price for olive presses ahead of Greek harvests back in 600 BC. In the 1600s, the Dojima Rice exchange, which started on the front lawn of Yodoya Keian, arguably became the world's first futures exchange.

Even though options in some form or fashion have been around for thousands of years, the modern standardized world of options came about in 1973 when the Chicago Board of Trade (CBOT) gave birth to the CBOE. The CBOE became home to the first equity and index exchange in the United States.

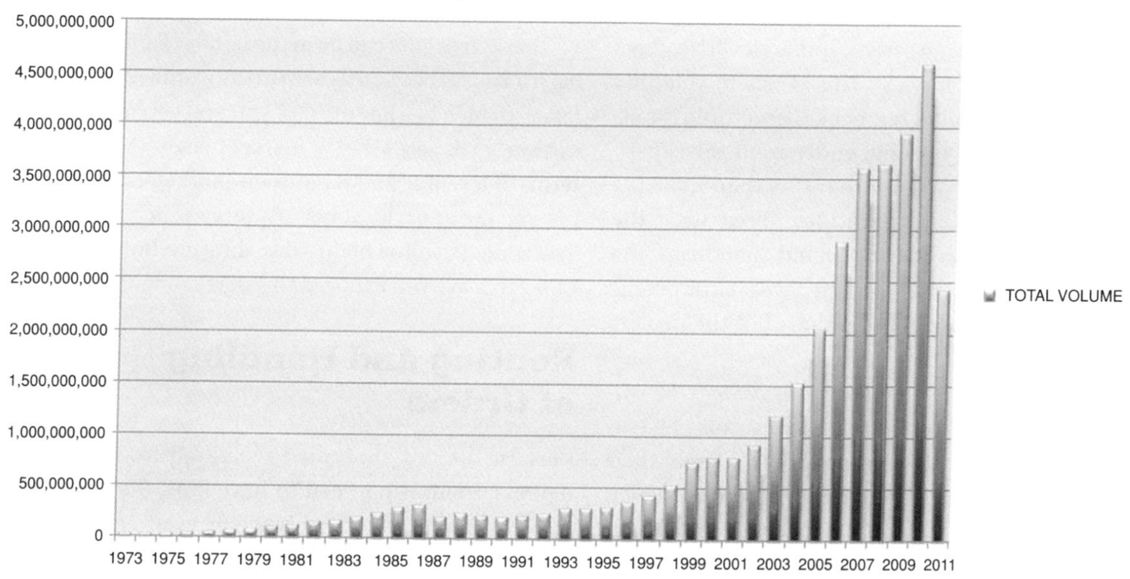

Exhibit 1.3

This was about the time the Black-Scholes model was created as a means of calculating options prices using standardized, measurable, objective integers as opposed to random price quotes that often favored the dealer, not the customer.

Prior to that, the option market was fragmented and if you wanted to buy or sell an option, you went directly to a dealer as opposed to everyone meeting on the exchange to create the most efficient price. Because of this fragmentation, there were major price discrepancies.

You see, without a standard formula there was no accurate way to price an option anyway. It was simply a random price driven market, with little rationale as to the correct price to buy or sell.

When you think about it, the underlying asset has its own set of random forces pushing and pulling on the price. Quantifying and finding a price to buy or sell an asset is hard enough. For a derivative to have no structure, you simply end up magnifying variables and making things more complicated and random.

KEY POINT:

The underlying securities themselves can also be flawed; think back to the Credit Default Swap (CDS) or Mortgage Backed Securities (MBS) vehicles.

Dealers (called *Bucket Shops*) would publish static quotes with not only wide bid-ask spreads, but prices that sometimes made no sense compared with today's pricing systems and models. This is where volatility and time come into play, but back then it didn't matter because not many people understood this. These shops operated more like horse tracks than financial firms. The dealers had a good idea about what the options were really worth and would "handicap" the prices (odds) many times in their favor. Sure people won some money from time to time, but the dealers were in control.

Jesse Livermore (*Reminiscences of a Stock Operator,* 1923) made a killing with options because he had the uncommon knowledge about how to derive their value. Perhaps he had a knack for knowing which way the market was moving, too, because the Bucket Shops banned him when he won so much money; he was certainly the exception.

Exhibit 1.4 shows the early twentieth century, which was no doubt the dark ages of the option markets.

But even in the early 1970s, trading and quote technology was still in its infancy. Quotes for options and commodity prices were updates on chalkboards such as the one you see in Exhibit 1.5 in 1971 at the CBOT.

Option prices were still slow to update and the markets were wide and illiquid in many cases.

Fast-forward 40 years and the technology has advanced by an order of magnitude that even Gordon E. Moore could have never imagined. The advantage now lies in knowing behavior and strategy, and having the ability to analyze and execute quickly and efficiently. These tools are at *everyone's* disposal.

These strengths can lie in the hands of anyone working from just about anywhere in the world. As a "market taker" (which is what most of you are) you may not get certain small perks that a "market maker" (MM) gets in terms of leverage and rebates on short stock positions, but you are at parity, if not advantaged in comparison. Trust me. (I will explain why, showing how being an MM can leave you exposed to smart money.)

Routing and Handling of Orders

Because options are traded separately from their underliers, there is no need to have both the stock and option trade at the same place or even on the same exchange. Like stocks, options trade on several exchanges, which are somewhat linked together when it comes to disseminating prices.

This can be good and bad when it comes to getting executions in the options that you trade.

One detriment is that exchanges do *not* share orders with one another! If you send an order to buy calls on the Philadelphia Stock Exchange (PHLX) they are not going to be filled at the International Stock Exchange (ISE) unless PHLX sends the order away. The exchanges do, however, have rules that help ensure the best pricing for the customer. If one exchange is priced better than another, the exchange with the order needs to either fill it at the better price or send it away! See Exhibit 1.6.

CLEMENT, PARKER & COMPANY.

Exhibit 1.4

One of the biggest "problems" with completely electronic exchanges is the handling of spread orders. When you send a two-, three-, four- or more legged spread to a certain exchange, it may not be represented in the best way possible to market participants as it would be in a physical crowd. Exchanges like the ISE disseminate data as quickly as possible and market markers use different types of software interfaces to see and trade on that data.

In other words, if you are trying to buy an iron condor that has a market of $1 to $2 and you are bidding

Exhibit 1.5
Source: Pat Arnow Photography, arnow.org.

$1.80, your order may not be filled, even though it should be. Sometimes you may even bid the full $2 and not see your order filled on the spot, because of the varying prices of each individual option and the way the orders are presented to market makers. In theory, as technology improves so does execution speed and efficiency, but highly efficient markets also mean that the market makers are less willing to make errors themselves or stick their necks out just to get an order completed. So be wary when using AON (all or none)

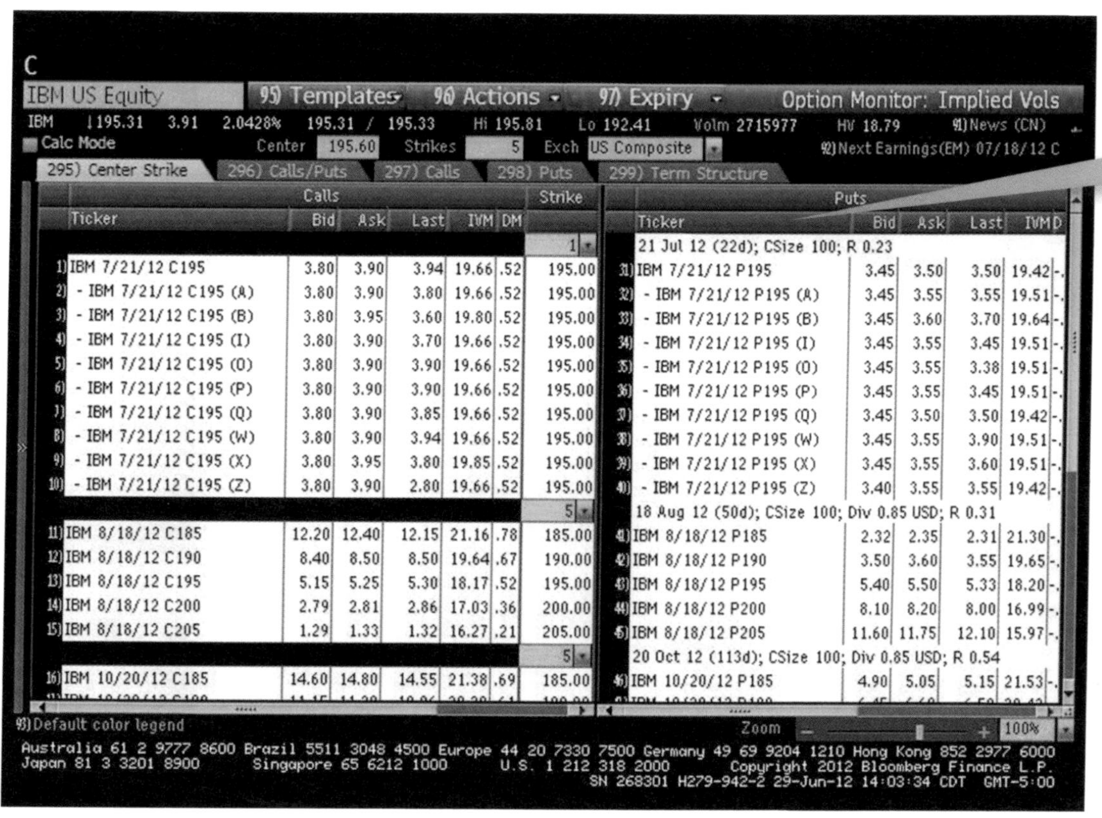

C

IBM US Equity | 95) Templates | 96) Actions | 97) Expiry | Option Monitor: Implied Vols

IBM ↓195.31 3.91 2.0428% 195.31 / 195.33 Hi 195.81 Lo 192.41 Volm 2715977 HV 18.79 91)News (CN)

Calc Mode Center 195.60 Strikes 5 Exch US Composite 92)Next Earnings(EM) 07/18/12 C

295) Center Strike | 296) Calls/Puts | 297) Calls | 298) Puts | 299) Term Structure

	Calls Ticker	Bid	Ask	Last	IVM	DM	Strike
							1
1)	IBM 7/21/12 C195	3.80	3.90	3.94	19.66	.52	195.00
2)	- IBM 7/21/12 C195 (A)	3.80	3.90	3.80	19.66	.52	195.00
3)	- IBM 7/21/12 C195 (B)	3.80	3.95	3.60	19.80	.52	195.00
4)	- IBM 7/21/12 C195 (I)	3.80	3.90	3.70	19.66	.52	195.00
5)	- IBM 7/21/12 C195 (O)	3.80	3.90	3.90	19.66	.52	195.00
6)	- IBM 7/21/12 C195 (P)	3.80	3.90	3.90	19.66	.52	195.00
7)	- IBM 7/21/12 C195 (Q)	3.80	3.90	3.85	19.66	.52	195.00
8)	- IBM 7/21/12 C195 (W)	3.80	3.90	3.94	19.66	.52	195.00
9)	- IBM 7/21/12 C195 (X)	3.80	3.95	3.80	19.85	.52	195.00
10)	- IBM 7/21/12 C195 (Z)	3.80	3.90	2.80	19.66	.52	195.00
							5
11)	IBM 8/18/12 C185	12.20	12.40	12.15	21.16	.78	185.00
12)	IBM 8/18/12 C190	8.40	8.50	8.50	19.64	.67	190.00
13)	IBM 8/18/12 C195	5.15	5.25	5.30	18.17	.52	195.00
14)	IBM 8/18/12 C200	2.79	2.81	2.86	17.03	.36	200.00
15)	IBM 8/18/12 C205	1.29	1.33	1.32	16.27	.21	205.00
							5
16)	IBM 10/20/12 C185	14.60	14.80	14.55	21.38	.69	185.00

	Puts Ticker	Bid	Ask	Last	IVM	D
	21 Jul 12 (22d); CSize 100; R 0.23					
31)	IBM 7/21/12 P195	3.45	3.50	3.50	19.42	-.
32)	- IBM 7/21/12 P195 (A)	3.45	3.55	3.55	19.51	-.
33)	- IBM 7/21/12 P195 (B)	3.45	3.60	3.70	19.64	-.
34)	- IBM 7/21/12 P195 (I)	3.45	3.55	3.45	19.51	-.
35)	- IBM 7/21/12 P195 (O)	3.45	3.55	3.38	19.51	-.
36)	- IBM 7/21/12 P195 (P)	3.45	3.55	3.45	19.51	-.
37)	- IBM 7/21/12 P195 (Q)	3.45	3.50	3.50	19.42	-.
38)	- IBM 7/21/12 P195 (W)	3.45	3.55	3.90	19.51	-.
39)	- IBM 7/21/12 P195 (X)	3.45	3.55	3.60	19.51	-.
40)	- IBM 7/21/12 P195 (Z)	3.40	3.55	3.55	19.42	-.
	18 Aug 12 (50d); CSize 100; Div 0.85 USD; R 0.31					
41)	IBM 8/18/12 P185	2.32	2.35	2.31	21.30	-.
42)	IBM 8/18/12 P190	3.50	3.60	3.55	19.65	-.
43)	IBM 8/18/12 P195	5.40	5.50	5.33	18.20	-.
44)	IBM 8/18/12 P200	8.10	8.20	8.00	16.99	-.
45)	IBM 8/18/12 P205	11.60	11.75	12.10	15.97	-.
	20 Oct 12 (113d); CSize 100; Div 0.85 USD; R 0.54					
46)	IBM 10/20/12 P185	4.90	5.05	5.15	21.53	-.

93) Default color legend Zoom 100%

Australia 61 2 9777 8600 Brazil 5511 3048 4500 Europe 44 20 7330 7500 Germany 49 69 9204 1210 Hong Kong 852 2977 6000
Japan 81 3 3201 8900 Singapore 65 6212 1000 U.S. 1 212 318 2000 Copyright 2012 Bloomberg Finance L.P.
SN 268301 H279-942-2 29-Jun-12 14:03:34 CDT GMT-5:00

The Level 2 screen for IBM shows the different exchanges' bids and offers for each option represented by different letters (in parentheses).

Exhibit 1.6

orders or if you need to get into or out of a position in between the markets. There is nothing worse than a partial fill where you tried to save a couple of pennies, but end up losing thousands. It has happened to me many times, trust me.

When it comes to executing spreads effectively, there are three things you need:

1. An understanding of the theoretical value and risk of the options themselves.

In the early days, IBM would have had its options listed on only one exchange. Since one exchange controlled all the order flow and, in some respects, implied volatility and pricing, it could easily alter pricing by making adjustments to this model.

Exhibit 1.7

2. The ability to watch the underlying instrument's price change.
3. An understanding of how various changes in market conditions are affecting your spread's value (skew, option pricing model, etc.).

These three things are an integral part of being an effective order execution trader. It can also save you money and reduce risk. See Exhibit 1.7.

At the end of the twentieth century, the options markets began to change again with the introduction of multiple listings, where a company's options were now listed on more than one exchange. This enabled investors to trade options just about anywhere they wanted. But more important, this created competition among exchanges to earn business through cheaper transaction prices and tighter bid-ask spreads.

Initially, it was a war over technology and liquidity—who could provide the fastest, most liquid markets with the best price. Exchanges were sometimes paying to have orders routed through their systems. Even today, there are still multiple exchanges trading and flourishing, although many exchanges have either closed for good or have changed the way they conduct business to keep up with the times. There are currently eight exchanges where options can be traded, all of which are fighting for your business. The days of the pit trader (my former profession) are numbered, if not already gone entirely.

Higher volume and concentrated order flow naturally improves prices, so I would expect further consolidation within the exchanges to the extent that the Securities and Exchange Commission (SEC) and other regulatory bodies will allow.

The Options Exchanges

There are agreements that some brokers have with certain exchanges to send them order flow, which may or may not be to your advantage. There is little you need to do as a retail trader to most efficiently execute your orders. As a professional, you may develop relationships with certain exchanges or even specialists to get your orders executed efficiently and at the best price.

Bloomberg has a platform (as do some brokers) that allows you to "shop" off floor liquidity providers for options and spreads if you trade in size. This may help you to execute large trades at one price.

List of Exchanges and Their Acronyms

AMEX	American Stock Exchange, housed on the NYSE
BOX	Boston Stock Exchange
CBOE	Chicago Board Options Exchange
ISE	International Stock Exchange
BATS	BATS Exchange founded in June 2005 as an ECN (electronic communication network)
PCST	Pacific Coast Stock Exchange, absorbed by NYSE (see Exhibit 1.8)
PHLX	Philadelphia Stock Exchange, part of Nasdaq OMX
NASDAQ OMX	Nasdaq Options Market

Each of the exchanges disseminates quotes dynamically throughout the day, which are determined both electronically and via open outcry.

Note that some exchanges may have higher bids or lower offers with more or less size (number of contracts). This means that they may be better buyers or sellers at any given moment or that you are seeing standing customer limit orders. This again may also be related to different market maker positions. If the bid or offer size tends to follow the price, it's most likely a market maker leaning one way or the other. If the size of the market doesn't move when the price moves, you may have a standing order on the specialist's books.

Smart Investor Tip!

As a general rule, your broker will typically route your order to the best-priced exchange, or that exchange will match the best price.

	Ticker	Bid	Ask	Last	IVM	DM
1)	IBM 7/21/12 C195	3.80	3.90	3.94	19.66	.52
2)	- IBM 7/21/12 C195 (A)	3.80	3.90	3.80	19.66	[illegible]
3)	- IBM 7/21/12 C195 (B)	3.80	3.95	3.60	[illegible]	.52
4)	- IBM 7/21/12 C195 (I)	3.80	3.90	[illegible]	19.66	.52
5)	- IBM 7/21/12 C195 (O)	3.80	3.90	[illegible]	19.66	.52
6)	- IBM 7/21/12 C195 (P)	3.80	[illegible]	3.90	19.66	.52
7)	- IBM 7/21/12 C195 (Q)	3.80	3.90	3.85	19.66	.52
8)	- IBM 7/21/12 C195 (W)	3.80	3.90	3.94	19.66	.52
9)	- IBM 7/21/12 C195 (X)	3.80	3.95	3.80	19.85	.52
10)	- IBM 7/21/12 C195 (Z)	3.80	3.90	2.80	19.66	.52

If you were to notice that the PHLX is a better seller of a group of calls when compared to theoretical value, it might be an indication that the market makers have an overly long position or a bearish bias. Here they are all lined up nicely.

Exhibit 1.8

KEY POINT:

While the option is trading, you have the right to buy or sell it as long as you have the money.

DEFINITION:

Standardized

Standardized means that the trading rules and strike prices are guaranteed by the Options Clearing Corporation (www.occ.com).

A stock that trades more than 1 million shares a day on average and is a member of the S&P 500 will generally have ample liquidity for you to get into and out of positions up to 50 contracts fairly easily. But there are still many thinly traded securities that you will struggle with to get executed. If you notice bid-ask spreads of $1 or more on a stock that is $50 or less and the stock has volume less than 750,000 shares traded on average a day, it might be best to avoid that all together. See Exhibit 1.9.

Standardized

Listed options contracts are **standardized**. If you are buying or selling an option, the Options Clearing Corporation ensures that your counterparty will perform its obligations.

The OCC, along with clearinghouses like Goldman Sachs and even the Chicago Mercantile Exchange (which is both an exchange and a clearinghouse), reduce counterparty risk in options trading.

So if you buy a call and the stock goes up $100, that contract will still be good for sale even though the seller who originally did the trade with you may be in some serious financial pain. Understand that you will seldom be buying an option from and selling it back to the same person; the fluid markets move money around quite efficiently.

ATK US $ ↑ 50.64 +2.46 Z50.63/50.65N 2x5
At 14:23 d Vol 282,957 O 49.18T H 50.66N L 48.96B Val 14.164M
ATK US Equity 95) Templates 96) Actions 97) Expiry Option Monitor: Eqty/Indx Trading
ALLIANT TECHSYS ↑50.64 2.46 5.1059% 50.63 / 50.65 Hi 50.66 Lo 48.96 Volm 282457 HV 31.10 91) News (CN)
Calc Mode Center 50.65 Strikes 10 Exch US Composite 92) Next Earnings(EM) 08/03/12 E
295) Center Strike 296) Calls/Puts 297) Calls 298) Puts 299) Term Structure

Calls								Strike	Puts							
Ticker	BSze	Bid	Ask	ASze	BASp	Volm	OInt		Ticker	BSze	Bid	Ask	ASze	BASp	Volm	OInt
21 Jul 12 (22d); CSize 100; R 0.23								10	21 Jul 12 (22d); CSize 100; R 0.23							
1) ATK 7 C30	21	18.80	20.90	10	2.10			30.00	41) ATK 7 P30			.15	247	.15		
2) ATK 7 C35	51	14.50	16.00	31	1.50			35.00	42) ATK 7 P35			.15	105	.15		
3) ATK 7 C40	52	9.60	10.80	51	1.20			40.00	43) ATK 7 P40			.15	264	.15		
4) ATK 7 C45	290	4.90	5.80	205	.90	2	16	45.00	44) ATK 7 P45	393	.05	.10	530	.05		20
5) ATK 7 C50	145	1.35	1.50	204	.15	20	184	50.00	45) ATK 7 P50	73	.70	1.35	106	.65		41
6) ATK 7 C55			.15	406	.15		87	55.00	46) ATK 7 P55	51	4.20	5.50	102	1.30		
7) ATK 7 C60			.15	207	.15			60.00	47) ATK 7 P60	10	9.10	11.20	20	2.10		
8) ATK 7 C65			.15	207	.15			65.00	48) ATK 7 P65	20	13.50	16.80	20	3.30		
9) ATK 7 C70			.15	247	.15			70.00	49) ATK 7 P70	10	18.50	21.70	31	3.20		
10) ATK 7 C75			.15	247	.15			75.00	50) ATK 7 P75	10	23.50	26.80	31	3.30		
18 Aug 12 (50d); CSize 100; R 0.31								10	18 Aug 12 (50d); CSize 100; R 0.31							
11) ATK 8 C30	21	18.30	21.60	72	3.30		5	30.00	51) ATK 8 P30			.15	127	.15		
12) ATK 8 C35	31	13.30	16.50	21	3.20			35.00	52) ATK 8 P35			.10	428	.10		12
13) ATK 8 C40	153	9.20	10.90	51	1.70	1	2	40.00	53) ATK 8 P40	307	.05	.15	218	.10		43
14) ATK 8 C45	103	5.60	6.20	40	.60	5	2	45.00	54) ATK 8 P45	252	.35	.50	231	.15		188
15) ATK 8 C50	516	2.20	2.30	175	.10	37	117	50.00	55) ATK 8 P50	92	1.55	2.45	317	.90		35
16) ATK 8 C55	475	.40	.50	110	.10		219	55.00	56) ATK 8 P55	51	4.60	5.20	106	.60	4	31
17) ATK 8 C60			.15	127	.15		116	60.00	57) ATK 8 P60	22	8.50	11.70	31	3.20		
18) ATK 8 C65			.10	120	.10		145	65.00	58) ATK 8 P65	10	13.50	16.80	20	3.30		5

Low volume and/or volatility can lead to wide bid-ask spreads. Abnormal spreads as expressed in Exhibit 1.9 can hinder or even prohibit you from making consistent profits.

Exhibit 1.9

If you buy a put and the stock drops to a nickel from $100, the person who originally sold you that put may have bought it back from someone else when the stock started to drop, or that original trader was short stock and was selling puts to collect some extra income. The bottom line is that as long as the stock is still trading on a major exchange, the options should be trading as well, which means that you can enter or exit your position as you see fit. I will get into what happens during expiration later, because there are nuances to each and every strategy and security that can help or harm you if you don't know them.

DEFINITION:

Employee stock options

Employee stock options, which you may hear about in the news or even receive from the company you work for, are call options that are not traded on an exchange. There are some similarities, but generally speaking stock options given by a company are illiquid and not tradable or standardized like the equity options listed on exchanges. They can be turned into stock and dilute the outstanding shares of a company.

Puts and Calls

There are only two types of options: puts and calls. All the spreads and strategies that have ever been created are simply combinations of one, two, or more of these options.

You must thoroughly understand the basic fundamentals, behavioral characteristics, and laws surrounding both types of options. In a perfect world, I would not bend on this. I know that many newbies just learn calls or puts enough to either be dangerous to themselves or slightly successful, but you are doing yourself a great disservice if you don't understand all the basics of both types.

That includes risk, Greeks, direction, margin requirements, behavior, credit versus debit, and their general behavior in the marketplace.

There are five basic components that make up an options price:

1. Stock price
2. Strike price
3. Interest rate
4. Dividend
5. Implied volatility

From these inputs, we can determine an option's theoretical value at any point in time on any security.

The OVME screen allows you to synthetically value any option on any security by plugging in the factors above.

In a more advanced scenario, this screen can be used to simulate different market changes (like dividends, stock price and volatility) and monetary factors influencing your trade over time, such as changing interest rates. You can also analyze more complicated spreads, which I discuss in later chapters.

In later chapters I also discuss the Greeks, forward prices, different pricing models, and volatility, which all play a role in finding the theoretical value of an option. Many times they can explain any abnormalities you may find when comparing calls and puts in the same class or series.

Here you can see how these factors influence option prices.

Let's take a look at the basics of pricing, trading, and execution in a real-life scenario. (See Exhibit 1.10.)

The Options Monitor (OMON) is easiest way to view option prices on any option-able security. This screen can be fully customized, so you can view a plethora of data points and measurements. I prefer to keep it limited to the following fields in the option chains (see Exhibit 1.11):

- Strike
- Bid
- Ask
- Mark
- Theoretical val
- Implied vol (theoretical change)

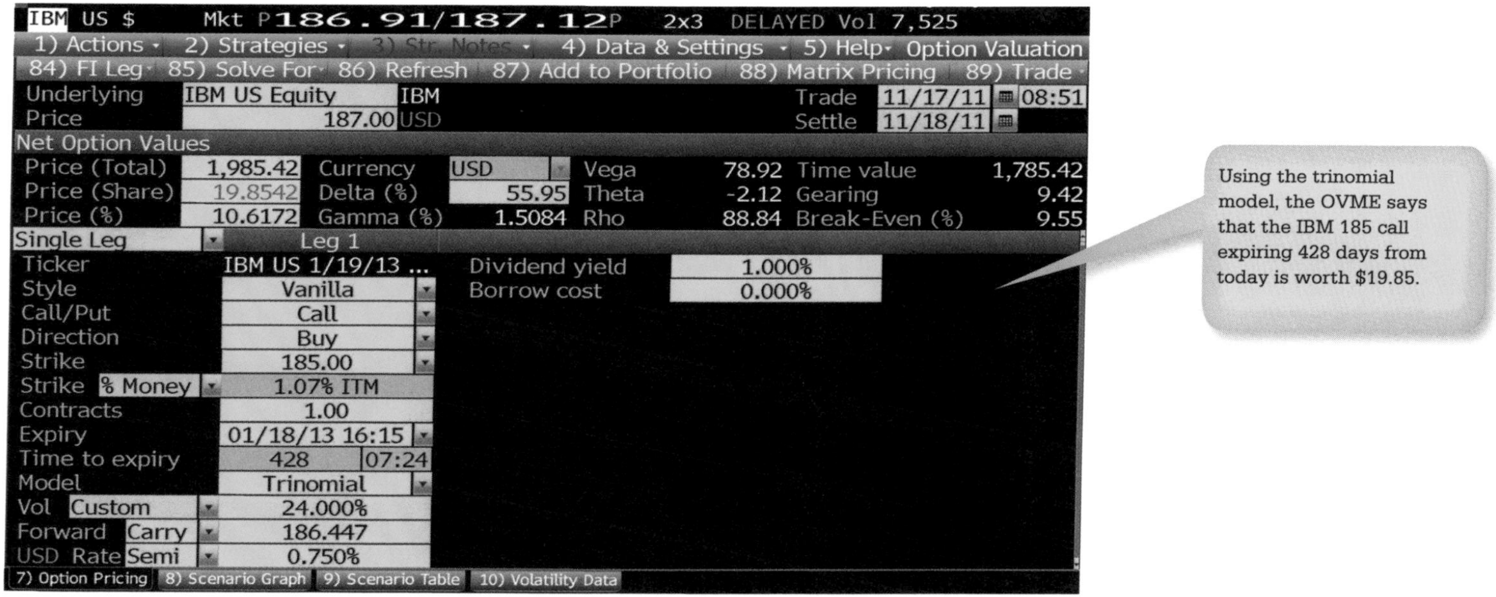

IBM US $ Mkt P186.91/187.12P 2x3 DELAYED Vol 7,525
1) Actions 2) Strategies 3) Str. Notes 4) Data & Settings 5) Help Option Valuation
84) FI Leg 85) Solve For 86) Refresh 87) Add to Portfolio 88) Matrix Pricing 89) Trade

Underlying	IBM US Equity	IBM	Trade	11/17/11	08:51
Price	187.00	USD	Settle	11/18/11	

Net Option Values

Price (Total)	1,985.42	Currency	USD	Vega	78.92	Time value	1,785.42
Price (Share)	19.8542	Delta (%)	55.95	Theta	-2.12	Gearing	9.42
Price (%)	10.6172	Gamma (%)	1.5084	Rho	88.84	Break-Even (%)	9.55

Single Leg — Leg 1

Ticker	IBM US 1/19/13 ...	Dividend yield	1.000%
Style	Vanilla	Borrow cost	0.000%
Call/Put	Call		
Direction	Buy		
Strike	185.00		
Strike % Money	1.07% ITM		
Contracts	1.00		
Expiry	01/18/13 16:15		
Time to expiry	428 07:24		
Model	Trinomial		
Vol Custom	24.000%		
Forward Carry	186.447		
USD Rate Semi	0.750%		

7) Option Pricing 8) Scenario Graph 9) Scenario Table 10) Volatility Data

Using the trinomial model, the OVME says that the IBM 185 call expiring 428 days from today is worth $19.85.

Exhibit 1.10

- Delta
- Gamma
- Theta
- Vega

You can also see the basic pricing and analysis I need to begin my study. If I were to buy the IBM December 180 calls, what price would I have to pay? How many contracts could I theoretically buy at that price? What exchange would I get executed on? Who would route my order to the proper exchange?

Make sure that you can answer these questions before moving on!

Remember that puts and calls can be bought or sold, just like stocks. But unlike stocks, the bid-ask spread of an option can and often will be fairly wide, with the average spread coming in around 10 cents ($0.10) or so. High volume, low volatility, and lower

IBM US $ ↓ 195.25 +3.85 Z195.25 / 195.27T 3 x 2
At 14:26 d Vol 3,064,322 O 194.55T H 195.81Z L 192.41D Val 596.598M
IBM US Equity 95) Templates 96) Actions 97) Expiry Option Monitor: Greeks Mid
IBM ↓195.25 3.85 2.0115% 195.25 / 195.27 Hi 195.81 Lo 192.41 Volm 3064322 HV 18.68 91) News (CN)
Calc Mode Center 195.15 Strikes 6 Exch US Composite 92) Next Earnings(EM) 07/18/12 C
295) Center Strike 296) Calls/Puts 297) Calls 298) Puts 299) Term Structure

Calls											
Strike	Ticker	ThPx	sIVM	Bid	IVal	Ask	Last	DM	GM	VM	TM
6	21 Jul 12 (22d); CSize 100; R 0.23										
185.00	IBM 7/21/12 C185	11.28	23.73	11.15	10.26	11.40	11.55	.84	.0222	.1180	.0664
190.00	IBM 7/21/12 C190	7.17	21.63	7.10	5.26	7.25	7.30	.71	.0338	.1613	.0840
195.00	IBM 7/21/12 C195	3.83	19.70	3.80	.26	3.85	3.75	.52	.0431	.1867	.0892
200.00	IBM 7/21/12 C200	1.61	18.31	1.60		1.61	1.59	.30	.0406	.1645	.0720
205.00	IBM 7/21/12 C205	.53	17.65	.52		.54	.53	.13	.0256	.1029	.0416
210.00	IBM 7/21/12 C210	.17	18.16	.17		.18	.17	.05	.0121	.0520	.0205
6	18 Aug 12 (50d); CSize 100; Div 0.85 USD; R 0.31										
185.00	IBM 8/18/12 C185	12.23	21.00	12.15	10.26	12.30	12.15	.78	.0207	.2121	.0484
190.00	IBM 8/18/12 C190	8.37	19.50	8.30	5.26	8.45	8.40	.67	.0270	.2571	.0546
195.00	IBM 8/18/12 C195	5.15	18.12	5.10	.26	5.20	5.20	.52	.0324	.2810	.0553
200.00	IBM 8/18/12 C200	2.76	16.95	2.74		2.77	2.76	.36	.0317	.2644	.0480
205.00	IBM 8/18/12 C205	1.28	16.16	1.25		1.30	1.30	.21	.0254	.2060	.0347
210.00	IBM 8/18/12 C210	.53	15.78	.53		.55	.55	.10	.0162	.1345	.0213
6	20 Oct 12 (113d); CSize 100; Div 0.85 USD; R 0.54										
185.00	IBM 10/20/12 C185	14.60	21.19	14.50	10.26	14.70	14.55	.70	.0160	.3773	.0390
190.00	IBM 10/20/12 C190	11.13	20.13	11.05	5.26	11.20	11.18	.61	.0181	.4121	.0397
195.00	IBM 10/20/12 C195	8.07	19.08	8.00	.26	8.15	8.25	.52	.0197	.4287	.0385
200.00	IBM 10/20/12 C200	5.53	18.09	5.45		5.60	5.50	.42	.0201	.4204	.0353
205.00	IBM 10/20/12 C205	3.55	17.25	3.50		3.60	3.65	.31	.0191	.3841	.0303
210.00	IBM 10/20/12 C210	2.13	16.54	2.09		2.17	2.14	.22	.0166	.3237	.0241
6	19 Jan 13 (204d); CSize 100; Div 1.70 USD; R 0.78										
185.00	IBM 1/19/13 C185	17.52	21.61	17.40	10.26	17.65	16.60y	.65	.0120	.5245	.0313
190.00	IBM 1/19/13 C190	14.28	20.80	14.15	5.26	14.40	11.49y	.59	.0130	.5573	.0316
195.00	IBM 1/19/13 C195	11.33	19.99	11.25	.26	11.40	11.37	.52	.0139	.5756	.0311

Exhibit 1.11

priced stocks will generally have tight bid-ask spreads and thinly traded, high volatility, high price stocks will tend to have options with wide spreads, sometimes greater than $1. See Exhibit 1.12.

To help pinpoint an option's theoretical value and get a better sense of the true value of a particular option, Bloomberg offers the ThPx column ("calc" mode), which uses Bloomberg's pricing models to display the theoretical value of an option. You can use this value to shave the bid-ask spread down while increasing your chances of getting filled on your single option or spread orders.

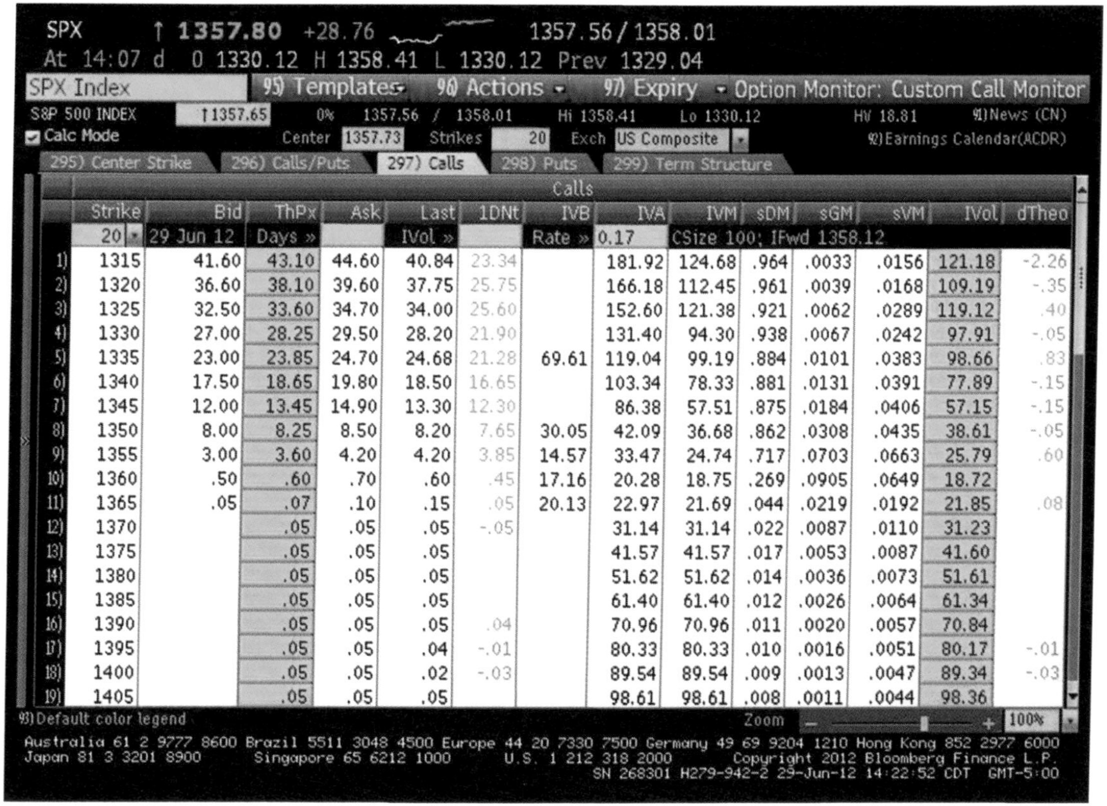

SPX ↑ 1357.80 +28.76 1357.56 / 1358.01
At 14:07 d O 1330.12 H 1358.41 L 1330.12 Prev 1329.04
SPX Index 95) Templates 96) Actions 97) Expiry Option Monitor: Custom Call Monitor
S&P 500 INDEX ↑1357.65 0% 1357.56 / 1358.01 Hi 1358.41 Lo 1330.12 HV 18.81 91) News (CN)
Calc Mode Center 1357.73 Strikes 20 Exch US Composite 92) Earnings Calendar(ACDR)
295) Center Strike 296) Calls/Puts 297) Calls 298) Puts 299) Term Structure

Calls

	Strike	Bid	ThPx	Ask	Last	1DNt	IVB	IVA	IVM	sDM	sGM	sVM	IVol	dTheo
	20	29 Jun 12	Days »		IVol »		Rate »	0.17	CSize 100; IFwd 1358.12					
1)	1315	41.60	43.10	44.60	40.84	23.34		181.92	124.68	.964	.0033	.0156	121.18	-2.26
2)	1320	36.60	38.10	39.60	37.75	25.75		166.18	112.45	.961	.0039	.0168	109.19	-.35
3)	1325	32.50	33.60	34.70	34.00	25.60		152.60	121.38	.921	.0062	.0289	119.12	.40
4)	1330	27.00	28.25	29.50	28.20	21.90		131.40	94.30	.938	.0067	.0242	97.91	-.05
5)	1335	23.00	23.85	24.70	24.68	21.28	69.61	119.04	99.19	.884	.0101	.0383	98.66	.83
6)	1340	17.50	18.65	19.80	18.50	16.65		103.34	78.33	.881	.0131	.0391	77.89	-.15
7)	1345	12.00	13.45	14.90	13.30	12.30		86.38	57.51	.875	.0184	.0406	57.15	-.15
8)	1350	8.00	8.25	8.50	8.20	7.65	30.05	42.09	36.68	.862	.0308	.0435	38.61	-.05
9)	1355	3.00	3.60	4.20	4.20	3.85	14.57	33.47	24.74	.717	.0703	.0663	25.79	.60
10)	1360	.50	.60	.70	.60	.45	17.16	20.28	18.75	.269	.0905	.0649	18.72	
11)	1365	.05	.07	.10	.15	.05	20.13	22.97	21.69	.044	.0219	.0192	21.85	.08
12)	1370		.05	.05	.05	-.05		31.14	31.14	.022	.0087	.0110	31.23	
13)	1375		.05	.05	.05			41.57	41.57	.017	.0053	.0087	41.60	
14)	1380		.05	.05	.05			51.62	51.62	.014	.0036	.0073	51.61	
15)	1385		.05	.05	.05			61.40	61.40	.012	.0026	.0064	61.34	
16)	1390		.05	.05	.05	.04		70.96	70.96	.011	.0020	.0057	70.84	
17)	1395		.05	.05	.04	-.01		80.33	80.33	.010	.0016	.0051	80.17	-.01
18)	1400		.05	.05	.02	-.03		89.54	89.54	.009	.0013	.0047	89.34	-.03
19)	1405		.05	.05	.05			98.61	98.61	.008	.0011	.0044	98.36	

93) Default color legend Zoom 100%
Australia 61 2 9777 8600 Brazil 5511 3048 4500 Europe 44 20 7330 7500 Germany 49 69 9204 1210 Hong Kong 852 2977 6000
Japan 81 3 3201 8900 Singapore 65 6212 1000 U.S. 1 212 318 2000 Copyright 2012 Bloomberg Finance L.P.
SN 268301 H279-942-2 29-Jun-12 14:22:52 CDT GMT-5:00

Exhibit 1.12

Essentially it's like having an inside look at what the market makers are using to find the value of an option. When you know the "market value" of something you will be able to execute your orders more efficiently and at the best price. It's almost like knowing what a group of people at an auction are willing to pay for your vehicle. If you know that the crowd will pay $10,000 for it, why would you settle for selling it

DEFINITION:

An option "series"

An option "series" denotes options with the same strike and expiration date on a particular security, whereas an option "class" includes *all* the options, strikes, and expirations on a particular security.

Ticker	Bid	ThPx	Ask
		Calls	
30 Dec 11	Days »	4	IVol »
1) SPXQ 12/30/11 C1250	18.90y	20.50	22.10y
2) SPXQ 12/30/11 C1255	15.40y	16.80	18.20y
3) SPXQ 12/30/11 C1260	12.40y	13.75	15.10y
4) SPXQ 12/30/11 C1265	9.80y	10.80	11.80y
5) SPXQ 12/30/11 C1270	7.40y	8.35	9.30y
6) SPXQ 12/30/11 C1275	5.20y	5.90	6.60y
7) SPXQ 12/30/11 C1280	3.70y	4.45	5.20y

Would you pay $11.80 for the SPX 1265 calls, when you might be able to get them for $11.20? If they are worth $10.80 to the market maker, he probably wouldn't mind selling them for $0.40 worth of "edge" or theoretical profit.

Exhibit 1.13

at $9,700? The option world works the same way. Just because an option has a market of $4 bid to $5 ask, doesn't mean the theoretical value is always $4.50.

Exhibit 1.13 illustrates some SPX (S&P 500 cash index) calls. Notice the ThPx value for the 1265 call. With a theoretical value, you have a guide from which to price your buy and sell orders without getting left in the dust.

Taking Value a Step Further—General Knowledge and Nomenclature

When you buy (to open) an option (paying a debit), you are said to be long that option and have rights as the owner.

When you sell (to open) an option (collecting a credit), you have a short position on or can be "short that option," and in that case you have obligations, not rights, and typically higher risk.

Calls

The scenario or risk graph illustrates the long call in the OVME screen. See Exhibit 1.14.

A call gives the owner (long-call buyer) the right, but not the obligation, to **buy** 100 shares of a stock at a specified price on or before a specified date.

As a call buyer you will always be bullish on the stock and may realize a profit if the stock rises in value, but not always.

The breakeven of a long call will almost always be greater than the underlying price because of the time value component.

Puts

The scenario or risk graph illustrates the long put in the OVME screen. See Exhibit 1.15.

A put gives the owner (long-put buyer) the right, but not the obligation to **sell** 100 shares of a stock at a specified price on or before a specified date.

Smart Investor Tip!

The "Mark" is *not* the same at the theoretical value. The Mark is generally the midpoint between the bid-ask, and it is what most brokerages use to calculate your profit/loss at the end of each day.

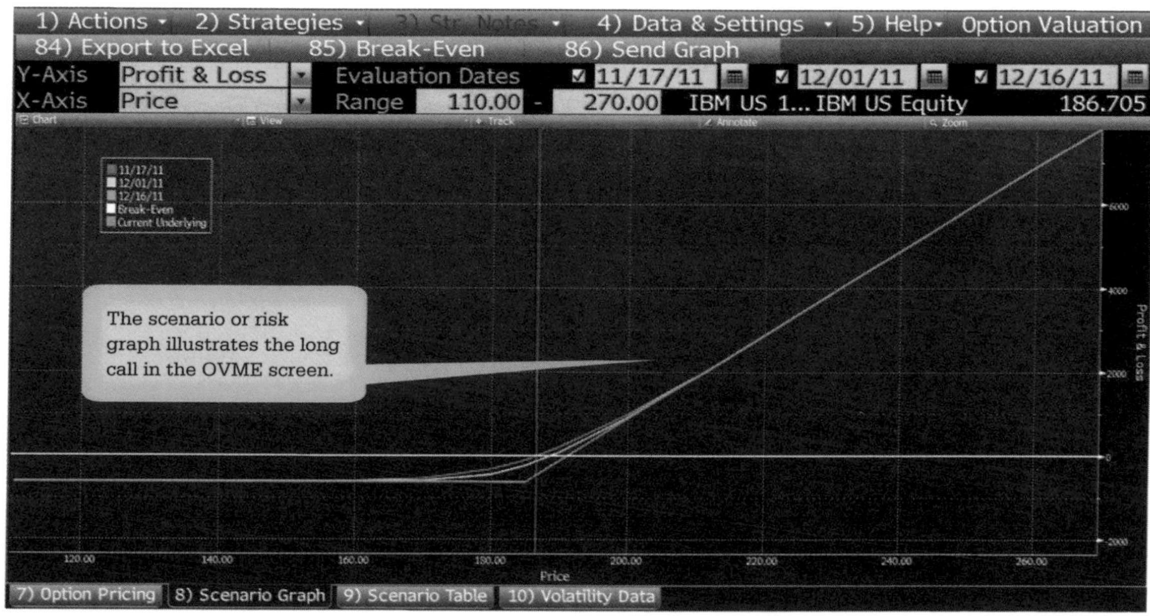

Exhibit 1.14

As a put buyer, you will always be bearish on the stock and may realize a profit if the stock falls in value.

The breakeven of a long put will almost always be *less* than the underlying price because of the time-value component.

In, At, and Out of the Money

- In the money

In the money means that the call or put option has intrinsic or real value. In-the-money calls have a strike price that is less than the current stock price; in-the-money puts have a strike price above the current stock price.

Deeper in-the-money calls (those with a delta of 0.70 or greater) tend to behave more like the stock, mimicking its moves with greater accuracy. (See Exhibit 1.16.)

Deep in-the-money puts (those with a delta of –0.70 to –1) tend to behave more like short stock.

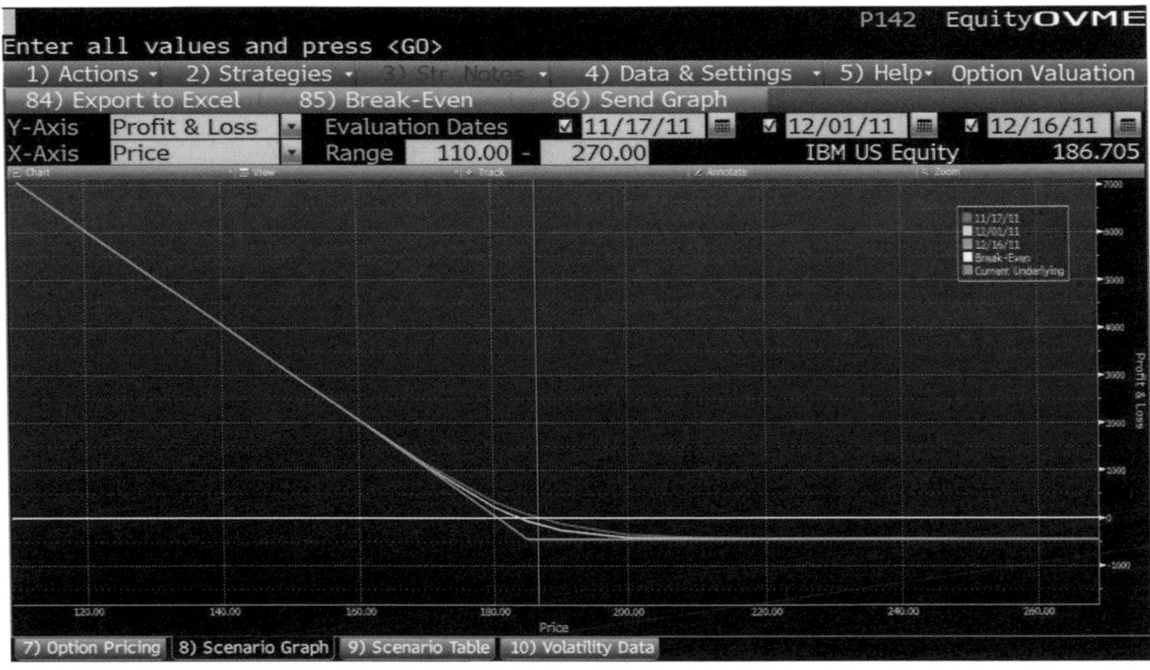

Exhibit 1.15

These options provide you with less leverage and cost more than cheaper, lower-delta options. They are a good choice if you believe that the stock will move higher or lower, but you aren't anticipating a large fast move in the stock.

They also are the least sensitive to changes in time and implied volatility on a percentage basis compared to at-the-money and out-of-the-money options. In-the-money options are more expensive than at- or out-of-the-money options.

- At the money

These options have a strike price that is at or very close to the stock price. Typically the delta of these options is around 0.40 to 0.60 or –0.40 to –0.60 for puts. At-the-money options generally have the most amount of time value relative to other options in the chain.

Because of their high level of time value, at-the-money options have the highest time decay, or

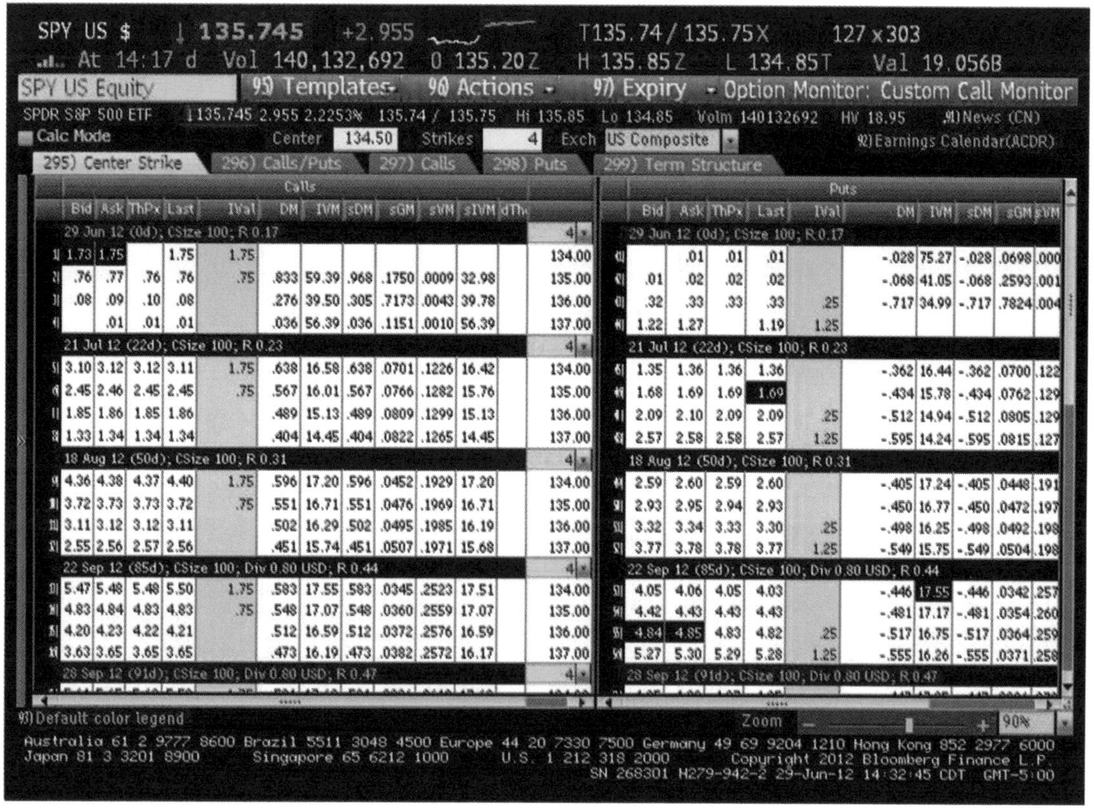

SPY US $ ↓ 135.745 +2.955 T135.74 / 135.75X 127 x 303
At 14:17 d Vol 140,132,692 O 135.20Z H 135.85Z L 134.85T Val 19.056B
SPY US Equity 95) Templates 96) Actions 97) Expiry Option Monitor: Custom Call Monitor
SPDR S&P 500 ETF ↓135.745 2.955 2.2253% 135.74 / 135.75 Hi 135.85 Lo 134.85 Volm 140132692 HV 18.95 91) News (CN)
Calc Mode Center 134.50 Strikes 4 Exch US Composite 92) Earnings Calendar(ACDR)
295) Center Strike 296) Calls/Puts 297) Calls 298) Puts 299) Term Structure

Calls Bid	Ask	ThPx	Last	IVal	DM	IVM	sDM	sGM	sVM	sIVM	dTh	Strike	Puts Bid	Ask	ThPx	Last	IVal	DM	IVM	sDM	sGM	sVM
29 Jun 12 (0d); CSize 100; R 0.17												4	29 Jun 12 (0d); CSize 100; R 0.17									
1.73	1.75		1.75	1.75								134.00		.01	.01	.01		-.028	75.27	-.028	.0698	.000
.76	.77	.76	.76	.75	.833	59.39	.968	.1750	.0009	32.98		135.00	.01	.02	.02	.02		-.068	41.05	-.068	.2593	.001
.08	.09	.10	.08		.276	39.50	.305	.7173	.0043	39.78		136.00	.32	.33	.33	.33	.25	-.717	34.99	-.717	.7824	.004
	.01	.01	.01		.036	56.39	.036	.1151	.0010	56.39		137.00	1.22	1.27		1.19	1.25					
21 Jul 12 (22d); CSize 100; R 0.23												4	21 Jul 12 (22d); CSize 100; R 0.23									
3.10	3.12	3.12	3.11	1.75	.638	16.58	.638	.0701	.1226	16.42		134.00	1.35	1.36	1.36	1.36		-.362	16.44	-.362	.0700	.122
2.45	2.46	2.45	2.45	.75	.567	16.01	.567	.0766	.1282	15.76		135.00	1.68	1.69	1.69	1.69		-.434	15.78	-.434	.0762	.129
1.85	1.86	1.85	1.86		.489	15.13	.489	.0809	.1299	15.13		136.00	2.09	2.10	2.09	2.09	.25	-.512	14.94	-.512	.0805	.129
1.33	1.34	1.34	1.34		.404	14.45	.404	.0822	.1265	14.45		137.00	2.57	2.58	2.58	2.57	1.25	-.595	14.24	-.595	.0815	.127
18 Aug 12 (50d); CSize 100; R 0.31												4	18 Aug 12 (50d); CSize 100; R 0.31									
4.36	4.38	4.37	4.40	1.75	.596	17.20	.596	.0452	.1929	17.20		134.00	2.59	2.60	2.59	2.60		-.405	17.24	-.405	.0448	.191
3.72	3.73	3.73	3.72	.75	.551	16.71	.551	.0476	.1969	16.71		135.00	2.93	2.95	2.94	2.93		-.450	16.77	-.450	.0472	.197
3.11	3.12	3.12	3.11		.502	16.29	.502	.0495	.1985	16.19		136.00	3.32	3.34	3.33	3.30	.25	-.498	16.25	-.498	.0492	.198
2.55	2.56	2.57	2.56		.451	15.74	.451	.0507	.1971	15.68		137.00	3.77	3.78	3.78	3.77	1.25	-.549	15.75	-.549	.0504	.198
22 Sep 12 (85d); CSize 100; Div 0.80 USD; R 0.44												4	22 Sep 12 (85d); CSize 100; Div 0.80 USD; R 0.44									
5.47	5.48	5.48	5.50	1.75	.583	17.55	.583	.0345	.2523	17.51		134.00	4.05	4.06	4.05	4.03		-.446	17.55	-.446	.0342	.257
4.83	4.84	4.83	4.83	.75	.548	17.07	.548	.0360	.2559	17.07		135.00	4.42	4.43	4.43	4.43		-.481	17.17	-.481	.0354	.260
4.20	4.23	4.22	4.21		.512	16.59	.512	.0372	.2576	16.59		136.00	4.84	4.85	4.83	4.82	.25	-.517	16.75	-.517	.0364	.259
3.63	3.65	3.65	3.65		.473	16.19	.473	.0382	.2572	16.17		137.00	5.27	5.30	5.29	5.28	1.25	-.555	16.26	-.555	.0371	.258
28 Sep 12 (91d); CSize 100; Div 0.80 USD; R 0.47												4	28 Sep 12 (91d); CSize 100; Div 0.80 USD; R 0.47									

93) Default color legend Zoom 90%
Australia 61 2 9777 8600 Brazil 5511 3048 4500 Europe 44 20 7330 7500 Germany 49 69 9204 1210 Hong Kong 852 2977 6000
Japan 81 3 3201 8900 Singapore 65 6212 1000 U.S. 1 212 318 2000 Copyright 2012 Bloomberg Finance L.P.
SN 268301 H279-942-2 29-Jun-12 14:32:45 CDT GMT-5:00

Exhibit 1.16

theta, and the most sensitivity to volatility changes, or vega, as well as changes in time. They also have the most gamma, meaning that the delta will change faster than in- or out-of-the-money options, especially as you come closer to expiration.

If you feel volatility is low and you believe that the underlying stock is going to make a very fast, big move, at-the-money options can be considered; however, remember that you will be paying the most time value and losing the most theta with these options, so I do not typically recommend that traders *buy* options at the money.

- Out of the money

  Out-of-the-money (OTM) options are the cheapest of the three. OTM calls have a strike price that is higher than the stock price. OTM puts have a strike price that's lower than the stock price. They are comprised completely of time value with no intrinsic value at all.

  Out-of-the-money options do have their place in trading and there are certain times when they are appropriate.

  Buying them as a hedge, as part of a spread, or as a bonus for "extra upside" are all rationales for purchasing an OTM option.

  Since they are lower in delta, OTM options tend to be less correlated with the movements of the underlying. This means that you will have to pay close attention to all the Greeks, especially time decay (theta), if you are buying them.

  If you buy a 0.15 delta call, you have a 15 percent shot, statistically, of that option being worth *anything* at expiration. Anything is the key word; 0.000001 is something, and the delta is telling us that there is a 15 percent shot that this option will be worth less than zero. It is not very promising if you think about it like that. Out-of-the-money options can be used if you have a *very* strong belief that the stock will move very far, very fast. It helps to have a price target in mind and buy your call accordingly. In other words, if IBM is currently at $120 and you believe that it will be at $135 in two months, then buying the $130 call for $0.60 might be an option for you. However, remember that it is impossible for any person to predict a stock's movement with accuracy. Just be sure that your price target is realistic, based not only on the stock's volatility history, but also on an upcoming catalyst of some sort, especially if you are making a short-term trade. (See Exhibit 1.17.)

DEFINITION:

The strike price

The strike price is the price at which the option owner can either buy (call) or sell (put) the underlying stock.

Strike Price and Selection

The options seller is obligated to fulfill the owner's rights at the strike price of the option. The strike price is also called the *exercise price* and for the owner is the price at which the owner can purchase (in the case of a call) or sell (in the case of a put) the underlying security or commodity as long as that option has not expired.

There is no absolute when it comes to selecting a strike price. It will vary with the sentiments and needs of the trader. Every thesis you form, combined with the strategy and time horizon you choose will determine what strike price(s) you select. There is no one right answer.

Option Seller Commitment

An argument could be made that option sellers are going to be a bit more cautious when it comes to strike selection because the call seller must *sell* 100 shares of stock (or other security) at the strike price

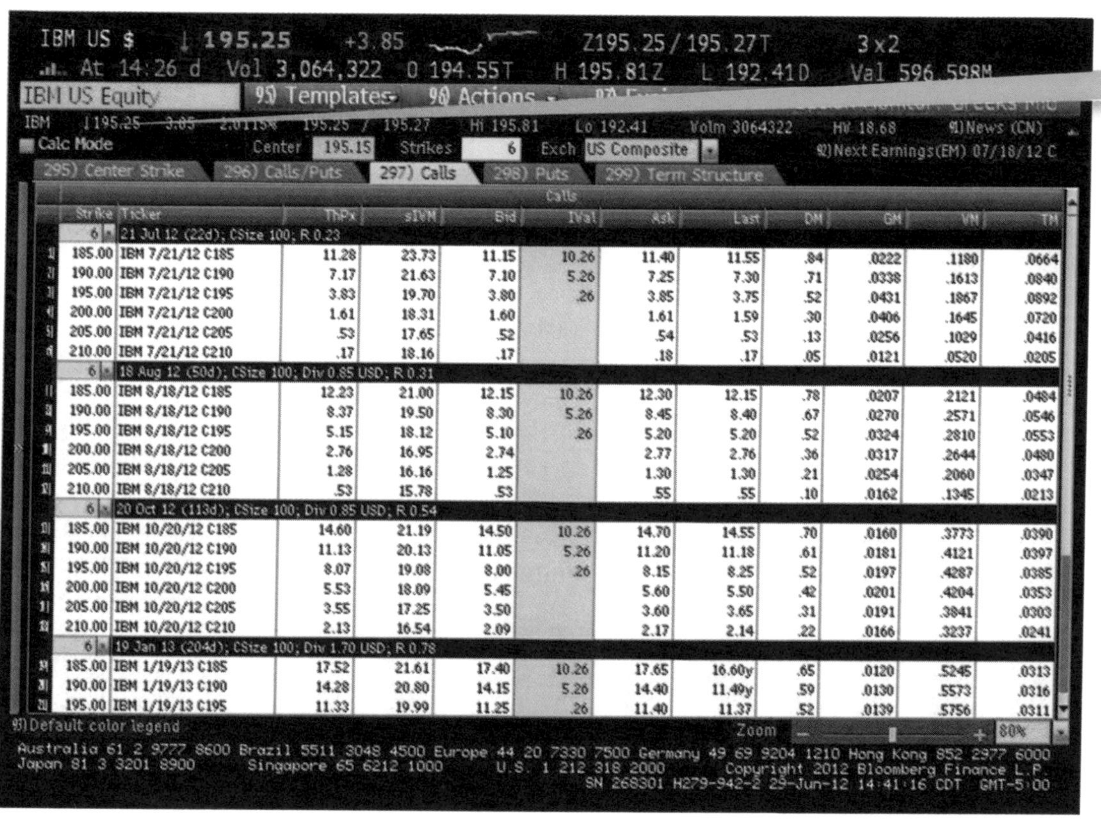

Strike	Ticker	ThPx	sIVM	Bid	IVal	Ask	Last	DM	GM	VM	TM
6	21 Jul 12 (22d); CSize 100; R 0.23										
185.00	IBM 7/21/12 C185	11.28	23.73	11.15	10.26	11.40	11.55	.84	.0222	.1180	.0664
190.00	IBM 7/21/12 C190	7.17	21.63	7.10	5.26	7.25	7.30	.71	.0338	.1613	.0840
195.00	IBM 7/21/12 C195	3.83	19.70	3.80	.26	3.85	3.75	.52	.0431	.1867	.0892
200.00	IBM 7/21/12 C200	1.61	18.31	1.60		1.61	1.59	.30	.0406	.1645	.0720
205.00	IBM 7/21/12 C205	.53	17.65	.52		.54	.53	.13	.0256	.1029	.0416
210.00	IBM 7/21/12 C210	.17	18.16	.17		.18	.17	.05	.0121	.0520	.0205
6	18 Aug 12 (50d); CSize 100; Div 0.85 USD; R 0.31										
185.00	IBM 8/18/12 C185	12.23	21.00	12.15	10.26	12.30	12.15	.78	.0207	.2121	.0484
190.00	IBM 8/18/12 C190	8.37	19.50	8.30	5.26	8.45	8.40	.67	.0270	.2571	.0546
195.00	IBM 8/18/12 C195	5.15	18.12	5.10	.26	5.20	5.20	.52	.0324	.2810	.0553
200.00	IBM 8/18/12 C200	2.76	16.95	2.74		2.77	2.76	.36	.0317	.2644	.0480
205.00	IBM 8/18/12 C205	1.28	16.16	1.25		1.30	1.30	.21	.0254	.2060	.0347
210.00	IBM 8/18/12 C210	.53	15.78	.53		.55	.55	.10	.0162	.1345	.0213
6	20 Oct 12 (113d); CSize 100; Div 0.85 USD; R 0.54										
185.00	IBM 10/20/12 C185	14.60	21.19	14.50	10.26	14.70	14.55	.70	.0160	.3773	.0390
190.00	IBM 10/20/12 C190	11.13	20.13	11.05	5.26	11.20	11.18	.61	.0181	.4121	.0397
195.00	IBM 10/20/12 C195	8.07	19.08	8.00	.26	8.15	8.25	.52	.0197	.4287	.0385
200.00	IBM 10/20/12 C200	5.53	18.09	5.45		5.60	5.50	.42	.0201	.4204	.0353
205.00	IBM 10/20/12 C205	3.55	17.25	3.50		3.60	3.65	.31	.0191	.3841	.0303
210.00	IBM 10/20/12 C210	2.13	16.54	2.09		2.17	2.14	.22	.0166	.3237	.0241
6	19 Jan 13 (204d); CSize 100; Div 1.70 USD; R 0.78										
185.00	IBM 1/19/13 C185	17.52	21.61	17.40	10.26	17.65	16.60y	.65	.0120	.5245	.0313
190.00	IBM 1/19/13 C190	14.28	20.80	14.15	5.26	14.40	11.49y	.59	.0130	.5573	.0316
195.00	IBM 1/19/13 C195	11.33	19.99	11.25	.26	11.40	11.37	.52	.0139	.5756	.0311

This option chain contains in-, at-, and out-of-the-money options. Remember that the relationship varies from puts to calls.

Exhibit 1.17

for every contract that is sold on or sometime before expiration.

The put seller must *buy* 100 shares of stock (or other security) at the strike price for every contract that is sold on or sometime before expiration.

Generally speaking, when I sell naked options, or options for which I do not own shares of the underlying stock, I am most likely doing so to establish an improved stock position (long or short) in an underlying that has elevated volatility. To sell an option naked

KEY POINT:

When you are talking options, a trader might reference a "June" option, which would expire the third Friday of June; if it were an October option then it would cease to exist on the third Friday of October, and so on. When an option expires, it is said to be at "parity," which is essentially what it is really worth or its intrinsic value.

DEFINITION:

Expiration

Expiration is the date and time at which that option ceases to exist.

I better damn sure have a good reason and firm thesis that backs up my willingness to take on more risk. I may also choose to sell an option naked if I am offsetting risk from another trade.

I almost always sell options with less than 30 days until expiration to limit exposure and collect theta as quickly as possible. You can examine the theta of different months, but you will learn later that time decay is not linear and what looks one way today might be very different in a week or month from now.

Expiration Date

All options (and warrants) have an expiration date and a date at which they stop trading; yes, there is a difference between the two and not all securities expire on the same cycles; check CBOE.com for most equity, index, or exchange-traded fund (ETF) product expirations or talk to your broker.

Standard equity options typically cease trading at 4 p.m. Eastern Time on the third Friday of the month and actually expire Saturday, giving you time as the owner to exercise, or if you are a seller, to be assigned. Talk to your brokers about their process and cutoff times for exercise and assignment, as it can vary.

Cash index options will cease trading at 4:15 p.m. on the third Thursday of the month and expire the following morning. Some index ETFs such as the SPY and QQQ trade until 4:15 p.m. on Friday and expire on Saturday.

On expiration, the option cannot be assigned or exercised. The time between when the option stops trading and when the option expires gives the long option holder time to decide to exercise the option.

The value of an option at expiration is determined by the amount it is "in the money." If it doesn't have any intrinsic value it will not be worth anything on expiration, but that does not mean that it cannot be exercised.

Premium (Cost)

In essence, an option's premium can be broken down into two separate values: intrinsic (parity or real value, related to the price of the underlying stock, index, or ETF), and time (volatility) value. Both of these values make up the total price you pay. The total premium is determined by the five factors we discussed earlier in this chapter.

Bid-Ask Spreads in All Strategies

In every trade you do, from the very basic to the very advanced, you will have to consider the risks of the bid-ask spread as part of your analysis. See Exhibit 1.18.

I like to think of the spread as another commission you have to pay to do business in options. Most traders buy on the ask and sell on the bid, which I think is *only* appropriate when you must get in at that moment in time.

You can always enter a limit order and get filled in between the market, but this is not a guarantee. Think about it like this: If you are trading a put with a bid-ask spread of $1 (yes, there are many of those out there)

VIX ↓ 17.77 -1.94
At 14:29 d O 17.52 H 18.31 L 17.50 Prev 19.71

VIX Index | 95) Templates | 96) Actions | 97) Expiry | Option Monitor: jared intrinsic

CBOE SPX VOLATILITY INDX ↓17.77 -1.94 -9.8427% / Hi 18.31 Lo 17.50 HV 130.49 91) News (CN)
Calc Mode Center 17.78 Strikes 10 Exch US Composite 92) Earnings Calendar(ACDR)

295) Center Strike | 296) Calls/Puts | 297) Calls | 298) Puts | 299) Term Structure

Calls

Strike	Ticker	ThPx	sIVM	Bid	IVal	Ask	Last	DM	GM	VM	TM
10	18 Jul 12 (19d); CSize 100; R 0.23; IFwd 19.98										
14.0	VIX 7 C14	5.95	51.43	5.80	5.95	6.00	8.70y	1.00	.0015	.0002	.0002
15.0	VIX 7 C15	5.00	72.84	4.90	4.95	5.10	5.00	.96	.0239	.0037	.0067
16.0	VIX 7 C16	4.10	76.15	4.00	3.95	4.20	4.30	.91	.0459	.0073	.0143
17.0	VIX 7 C17	3.30	79.87	3.20	2.95	3.40	3.20	.83	.0686	.0114	.0239
18.0	VIX 7 C18	2.65	85.55	2.60	1.95	2.70	2.70	.73	.0843	.0150	.0339
19.0	VIX 7 C19	2.15	92.17	2.10	.95	2.20	2.10	.63	.0898	.0172	.0421
20.0	VIX 7 C20	1.73	96.40	1.70		1.75	1.75	.54	.0904	.0181	.0464
21.0	VIX 7 C21	1.40	100.99	1.35		1.45	1.40	.46	.0862	.0181	.0486
22.0	VIX 7 C22	1.15	105.62	1.10		1.20	1.15	.39	.0796	.0175	.0490
23.0	VIX 7 C23	.95	109.78	.90		1.00	1.00	.33	.0723	.0165	.0480
10	22 Aug 12 (54d); CSize 100; R 0.33; IFwd 22.20										
14.0	VIX 8 C14	8.25	56.87	8.10	8.23	8.40	9.32y	.99	.0069	.0030	.0014
15.0	VIX 8 C15	7.30	59.63	7.20	7.23	7.40	7.30	.97	.0147	.0066	.0034
16.0	VIX 8 C16	6.40	62.10	6.30	6.23	6.50	7.83y	.93	.0245	.0113	.0063
17.0	VIX 8 C17	5.60	66.33	5.50	5.23	5.70	5.70	.88	.0351	.0172	.0104
18.0	VIX 8 C18	4.90	70.43	4.80	4.23	5.00	5.00	.82	.0436	.0225	.0146
19.0	VIX 8 C19	4.30	74.40	4.20	3.23	4.40	4.30	.76	.0493	.0269	.0185
20.0	VIX 8 C20	3.80	78.51	3.70	2.23	3.90	3.80	.69	.0524	.0301	.0219
21.0	VIX 8 C21	3.35	81.50	3.30	1.23	3.40	3.35	.63	.0540	.0322	.0244
22.0	VIX 8 C22	2.95	83.89	2.90	.23	3.00	2.96	.58	.0546	.0335	.0261
23.0	VIX 8 C23	2.65	87.45	2.60		2.70	2.70	.53	.0532	.0340	.0276
10	19 Sep 12 (82d); CSize 100; R 0.43; IFwd 24.09										
10.0	VIX 9 C10			13.60	13.78	13.90	13.88				
15.0	VIX 9 C15	8.85	55.36	8.70	8.78	9.00	9.90y	.97	.0108	.0078	.0024

93) Default color legend Zoom 80%

Australia 61 2 9777 8600 Brazil 5511 3048 4500 Europe 44 20 7330 7500 Germany 49 69 9204 1210 Hong Kong 852 2977 6000
Japan 81 3 3201 8900 Singapore 65 6212 1000 U.S. 1 212 318 2000
SN 268301 H279-942-2 29-Jun-12 14:44:39 CDT GMT-5:00

Exhibit 1.18

KEY POINT:
Spreads are usually wide for a reason. Either the stock is thinly traded, it has a high relative volatility, or it is very expensive ($200 or more).

DEFINITION:
Intrinsic value or "real value" of that option
Intrinsic value or "real value" of that option is what you are going to be left with on expiration.

KEY POINT:
Intrinsic value is more than just a measurement. You can think of it as the only absolute connection that the option has to the underlying. In essence the intrinsic value can be the saving grace for the beginner or a key part of the strategy for the expert.

and you buy just 10 contracts, you are immediately marked at a $1,000 loss (excluding commission). Psychologically, the loss may be a blow for some traders. Now imagine that you bought a –0.70 delta put and the stock falls $1, you may still be at a loss in your trade, which can certainly be disheartening—pay attention to them!

Volatile and expensive stocks are just fine to trade, but trading stocks with poor volume isn't the soundest strategy (although some more advanced traders are successful at trading low volume stocks). In my opinion, try to find options with spreads less than $0.20, if possible. You can find these lower spreads in the bigger stock names that trade heavy volume (1mm plus), stocks like AAPL, QQQ (ETF), IBM, and others. Sometimes higher spreads will be inevitable; just be aware of them and be sure to look up and down the option chain to get an idea of the average spread size. Remember, the lower the spread, the less your immediate loss will be in a trade. I prefer to trade options with spreads less than $0.20; however, you can choose a number that you feel comfortable with.

I am waiting for the stock to rally a bit for the perfect entry, but for demonstration's sake, I placed a limit order "buy to open" of 10 contracts at $13.50. Remember, placing a limit order allows you to set the purchase or sale price, but not a fill. At the time I placed my bid, the asking price was $14.50, one dollar away from my bid. I was waiting for the stock to rally (put then gets cheaper).

Intrinsic Value (aka Moneyness)

In-the-money options have **intrinsic value**; out-of-the-money options do not. The amount of intrinsic value in an option is determined by the strike price of the option and the price of the underlying stock price only, plus or minus any dividends until expiration. Nothing else can influence intrinsic value.

So if you have a call option with a strike price of $50 and the stock is at $52, you would have $2 of intrinsic value. Whereas the $50 strike price put with the stock at $52 would have *no* intrinsic value.

You can customize the OMON screen to display intrinsic value as a column. (I personally like to look at time value on my monitor, but more on that in a minute.) See Exhibit 1.19.

As a novice tactic, if you are not yet comfortable with the Greeks, consider using the intrinsic value of an option compared to its price to help select your strikes.

For example, if a $60 call strike price were trading for 25 cents and I thought for sure the stock would be trading $65 by the time this particular option expired, I might not even care about the other effects that are influencing the price of the option because in my case it's all about intrinsic value. My ultimate goal is to make $4.75 on this trade. That said, don't be foolish and buy tons of cheap options thinking that they are going to jump in price.

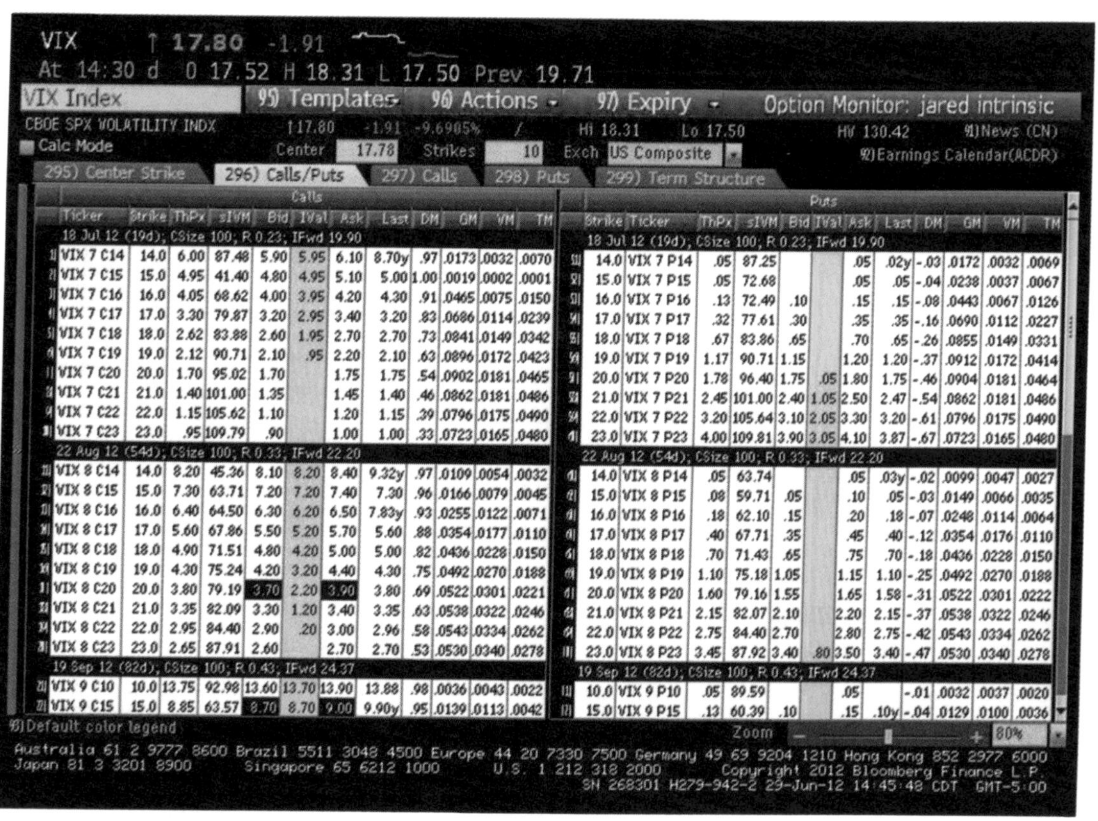

VIX ↑ 17.80 -1.91
At 14:30 d O 17.52 H 18.31 L 17.50 Prev 19.71
VIX Index 95) Templates 96) Actions 97) Expiry Option Monitor: jared intrinsic
CBOE SPX VOLATILITY INDX ↑17.80 -1.91 -9.6905% / Hi 18.31 Lo 17.50 HV 130.42 91) News (CN)
Calc Mode Center 17.78 Strikes 10 Exch US Composite 92) Earnings Calendar(ACDR)
295) Center Strike 296) Calls/Puts 297) Calls 298) Puts 299) Term Structure

Calls

Ticker	Strike	ThPx	sIVM	Bid	IVal	Ask	Last	DM	GM	VM	TM
18 Jul 12 (19d); CSize 100; R 0.23; IFwd 19.90											
VIX 7 C14	14.0	6.00	87.48	5.90	5.95	6.10	8.70y	.97	.0173	.0032	.0070
VIX 7 C15	15.0	4.95	41.40	4.80	4.95	5.10	5.00	1.00	.0019	.0002	.0001
VIX 7 C16	16.0	4.05	68.62	4.00	3.95	4.20	4.30	.91	.0465	.0075	.0150
VIX 7 C17	17.0	3.30	79.87	3.20	2.95	3.40	3.20	.83	.0686	.0114	.0239
VIX 7 C18	18.0	2.62	83.88	2.60	1.95	2.70	2.70	.73	.0841	.0149	.0342
VIX 7 C19	19.0	2.12	90.71	2.10	.95	2.20	2.10	.63	.0896	.0172	.0423
VIX 7 C20	20.0	1.70	95.02	1.70		1.75	1.75	.54	.0902	.0181	.0465
VIX 7 C21	21.0	1.40	101.00	1.35		1.45	1.40	.46	.0862	.0181	.0486
VIX 7 C22	22.0	1.15	105.62	1.10		1.20	1.15	.39	.0796	.0175	.0490
VIX 7 C23	23.0	.95	109.79	.90		1.00	1.00	.33	.0723	.0165	.0480
22 Aug 12 (54d); CSize 100; R 0.33; IFwd 22.20											
VIX 8 C14	14.0	8.20	45.36	8.10	8.20	8.40	9.32y	.97	.0109	.0054	.0032
VIX 8 C15	15.0	7.30	63.71	7.20	7.20	7.40	7.30	.96	.0166	.0079	.0045
VIX 8 C16	16.0	6.40	64.50	6.30	6.20	6.50	7.83y	.93	.0255	.0122	.0071
VIX 8 C17	17.0	5.60	67.86	5.50	5.20	5.70	5.60	.88	.0354	.0177	.0110
VIX 8 C18	18.0	4.90	71.51	4.80	4.20	5.00	5.00	.82	.0436	.0228	.0150
VIX 8 C19	19.0	4.30	75.24	4.20	3.20	4.40	4.30	.75	.0492	.0270	.0188
VIX 8 C20	20.0	3.80	79.19	3.70	2.20	3.90	3.80	.69	.0522	.0301	.0221
VIX 8 C21	21.0	3.35	82.09	3.30	1.20	3.40	3.35	.63	.0538	.0322	.0246
VIX 8 C22	22.0	2.95	84.40	2.90	.20	3.00	2.96	.58	.0543	.0334	.0262
VIX 8 C23	23.0	2.65	87.91	2.60		2.70	2.70	.53	.0530	.0340	.0278
19 Sep 12 (82d); CSize 100; R 0.43; IFwd 24.37											
VIX 9 C10	10.0	13.75	92.98	13.60	13.70	13.90	13.88	.98	.0036	.0043	.0022
VIX 9 C15	15.0	8.85	63.57	8.70	8.70	9.00	9.90y	.95	.0139	.0113	.0042

Puts

Strike	Ticker	ThPx	sIVM	Bid	IVal	Ask	Last	DM	GM	VM	TM
18 Jul 12 (19d); CSize 100; R 0.23; IFwd 19.90											
14.0	VIX 7 P14	.05	87.25			.05	.02y	-.03	.0172	.0032	.0069
15.0	VIX 7 P15	.05	72.68			.05	.05	-.04	.0238	.0037	.0067
16.0	VIX 7 P16	.13	72.49	.10		.15	.15	-.08	.0443	.0067	.0126
17.0	VIX 7 P17	.32	77.61	.30		.35	.35	-.16	.0690	.0112	.0227
18.0	VIX 7 P18	.67	83.86	.65		.70	.65	-.26	.0855	.0149	.0331
19.0	VIX 7 P19	1.17	90.71	1.15		1.20	1.20	-.37	.0912	.0172	.0414
20.0	VIX 7 P20	1.78	96.40	1.75	.05	1.80	1.75	-.46	.0904	.0181	.0464
21.0	VIX 7 P21	2.45	101.00	2.40	1.05	2.50	2.47	-.54	.0862	.0181	.0486
22.0	VIX 7 P22	3.20	105.64	3.10	2.05	3.30	3.20	-.61	.0796	.0175	.0490
23.0	VIX 7 P23	4.00	109.81	3.90	3.05	4.10	3.87	-.67	.0723	.0165	.0480
22 Aug 12 (54d); CSize 100; R 0.33; IFwd 22.20											
14.0	VIX 8 P14	.05	63.74			.05	.03y	-.02	.0099	.0047	.0027
15.0	VIX 8 P15	.08	59.71	.05		.10	.05	-.03	.0149	.0066	.0035
16.0	VIX 8 P16	.18	62.10	.15		.20	.18	-.07	.0248	.0114	.0064
17.0	VIX 8 P17	.40	67.71	.35		.45	.40	-.12	.0354	.0176	.0110
18.0	VIX 8 P18	.70	71.43	.65		.75	.70	-.18	.0436	.0228	.0150
19.0	VIX 8 P19	1.10	75.18	1.05		1.15	1.10	-.25	.0492	.0270	.0188
20.0	VIX 8 P20	1.60	79.16	1.55		1.65	1.58	-.31	.0522	.0301	.0222
21.0	VIX 8 P21	2.15	82.07	2.10		2.20	2.15	-.37	.0538	.0322	.0246
22.0	VIX 8 P22	2.75	84.40	2.70		2.80	2.75	-.42	.0543	.0334	.0262
23.0	VIX 8 P23	3.45	87.92	3.40	.80	3.50	3.40	-.47	.0530	.0340	.0278
19 Sep 12 (82d); CSize 100; R 0.43; IFwd 24.37											
10.0	VIX 9 P10	.05	89.59			.05		-.01	.0032	.0037	.0020
15.0	VIX 9 P15	.13	60.39	.10		.15	.10y	-.04	.0129	.0100	.0036

93) Default color legend Zoom 80%
Australia 61 2 9777 8600 Brazil 5511 3048 4500 Europe 44 20 7330 7500 Germany 49 69 9204 1210 Hong Kong 852 2977 6000
Japan 81 3 3201 8900 Singapore 65 6212 1000 U.S. 1 212 318 2000 Copyright 2012 Bloomberg Finance L.P.
SN 268301 H279-942-2 29-Jun-12 14:45:48 CDT GMT-5:00

Exhibit 1.19

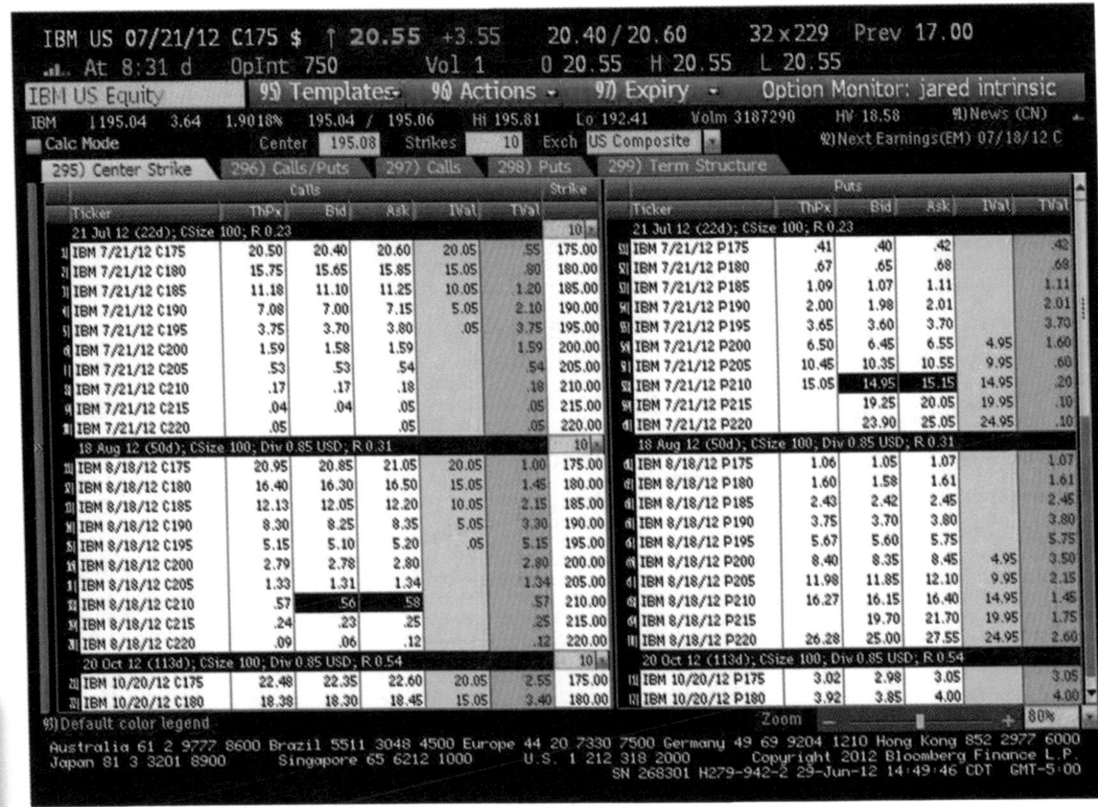

IBM US 07/21/12 C175 $ ↑ 20.55 +3.55 20.40 / 20.60 32 x 229 Prev 17.00
At 8:31 d OpInt 750 Vol 1 O 20.55 H 20.55 L 20.55
IBM US Equity 95) Templates 96) Actions 97) Expiry Option Monitor: jared intrinsic
IBM ↓195.04 3.64 1.9018% 195.04 / 195.06 Hi 195.81 Lo 192.41 Volm 3187290 HV 18.58 91) News (CN)
Calc Mode Center 195.08 Strikes 10 Exch US Composite 92) Next Earnings(EM) 07/18/12 C
295) Center Strike 296) Calls/Puts 297) Calls 298) Puts 299) Term Structure

Calls Ticker	ThPx	Bid	Ask	IVal	TVal	Strike	Puts Ticker	ThPx	Bid	Ask	IVal	TVal
21 Jul 12 (22d); CSize 100; R 0.23						10	21 Jul 12 (22d); CSize 100; R 0.23					
IBM 7/21/12 C175	20.50	20.40	20.60	20.05	.55	175.00	IBM 7/21/12 P175	.41	.40	.42		.42
IBM 7/21/12 C180	15.75	15.65	15.85	15.05	.80	180.00	IBM 7/21/12 P180	.67	.65	.68		.68
IBM 7/21/12 C185	11.18	11.10	11.25	10.05	1.20	185.00	IBM 7/21/12 P185	1.09	1.07	1.11		1.11
IBM 7/21/12 C190	7.08	7.00	7.15	5.05	2.10	190.00	IBM 7/21/12 P190	2.00	1.98	2.01		2.01
IBM 7/21/12 C195	3.75	3.70	3.80	.05	3.75	195.00	IBM 7/21/12 P195	3.65	3.60	3.70		3.70
IBM 7/21/12 C200	1.59	1.58	1.59		1.59	200.00	IBM 7/21/12 P200	6.50	6.45	6.55	4.95	1.60
IBM 7/21/12 C205	.53	.53	.54		.54	205.00	IBM 7/21/12 P205	10.45	10.35	10.55	9.95	.60
IBM 7/21/12 C210	.17	.17	.18		.18	210.00	IBM 7/21/12 P210	15.05	14.95	15.15	14.95	.20
IBM 7/21/12 C215	.04	.04	.05		.05	215.00	IBM 7/21/12 P215		19.25	20.05	19.95	.10
IBM 7/21/12 C220	.05		.05		.05	220.00	IBM 7/21/12 P220		23.90	25.05	24.95	.10
18 Aug 12 (50d); CSize 100; Div 0.85 USD; R 0.31						10	18 Aug 12 (50d); CSize 100; Div 0.85 USD; R 0.31					
IBM 8/18/12 C175	20.95	20.85	21.05	20.05	1.00	175.00	IBM 8/18/12 P175	1.06	1.05	1.07		1.07
IBM 8/18/12 C180	16.40	16.30	16.50	15.05	1.45	180.00	IBM 8/18/12 P180	1.60	1.58	1.61		1.61
IBM 8/18/12 C185	12.13	12.05	12.20	10.05	2.15	185.00	IBM 8/18/12 P185	2.43	2.42	2.45		2.45
IBM 8/18/12 C190	8.30	8.25	8.35	5.05	3.30	190.00	IBM 8/18/12 P190	3.75	3.70	3.80		3.80
IBM 8/18/12 C195	5.15	5.10	5.20	.05	5.15	195.00	IBM 8/18/12 P195	5.67	5.60	5.75		5.75
IBM 8/18/12 C200	2.79	2.78	2.80		2.80	200.00	IBM 8/18/12 P200	8.40	8.35	8.45	4.95	3.50
IBM 8/18/12 C205	1.33	1.31	1.34		1.34	205.00	IBM 8/18/12 P205	11.98	11.85	12.10	9.95	2.15
IBM 8/18/12 C210	.57	.56	.58		.57	210.00	IBM 8/18/12 P210	16.27	16.15	16.40	14.95	1.45
IBM 8/18/12 C215	.24	.23	.25		.25	215.00	IBM 8/18/12 P215		19.70	21.70	19.95	1.75
IBM 8/18/12 C220	.09	.06	.12		.12	220.00	IBM 8/18/12 P220	26.28	25.00	27.55	24.95	2.60
20 Oct 12 (113d); CSize 100; Div 0.85 USD; R 0.54						10	20 Oct 12 (113d); CSize 100; Div 0.85 USD; R 0.54					
IBM 10/20/12 C175	22.48	22.35	22.60	20.05	2.55	175.00	IBM 10/20/12 P175	3.02	2.98	3.05		3.05
IBM 10/20/12 C180	18.38	18.30	18.45	15.05	3.40	180.00	IBM 10/20/12 P180	3.92	3.85	4.00		4.00

93) Default color legend Zoom 80%
Australia 61 2 9777 8600 Brazil 5511 3048 4500 Europe 44 20 7330 7500 Germany 49 69 9204 1210 Hong Kong 852 2977 6000
Japan 81 3 3201 8900 Singapore 65 6212 1000 U.S. 1 212 318 2000 Copyright 2012 Bloomberg Finance L.P.
SN 268301 H279-942-2 29-Jun-12 14:49:46 CDT GMT-5:00

Exhibit 1.20

DEFINITION:
Dividends

When a company returns cash to investors in the form of a dividend, this lowers the forward price of a security and makes calls look cheap and puts expensive. Option buyers are *not* entitled to receive dividends; because of this, the price of the option is compensated.

Options will always trade for their intrinsic value plus a certain amount of time value barring any special situations such as a hard-to-borrow stock (big short interest or unshortable), put-call parity not holding up (i.e., VIX options), or in the case of a huge dividend between now and expiration. All of these factors can create a scenario where an option will trade for less than intrinsic value. See Exhibit 1.20.

Anticipating the intrinsic value of an option at expiration based on your forward thesis of the underlying security can help you determine theoretical P&L at that time. Using the Greeks can help quantify the day-to-day influences with accuracy.

Time Value

The time value of an option is determined both by the amount of time it has until expiration and the volatility of the corresponding underlying, coupled with demand for the option(s) themselves.

All options are losing time value as they approach expiration. The speed at which they decay is not linear and is determined by several forces including changes in time, volatility, and even changes in dividends and interest rates.

Time value should be a focus when you are trading, but it is only a piece of the entire puzzle. Time value and implied volatility go hand in hand. The more volatile a stock is or is going to be, the more time value it will have.

Some beginners may separate intrinsic from time value and/or just focus on the delta of an option. As traders become more advanced they understand the need to focus on the total value of the option and how that value will morph with changes in the marketplace.

Because out-of-the-money options are *completely* comprised of time value (which will eventually dwindle to zero by expiration) they can only become profitable on expiration if the stock moves above your break-even level, which may be much higher than the current stock price. That's not to say that they cannot gain value beforehand, but beginners who use the "stock price at expiration" trick to select strikes may find themselves frustrated.

In-the-money options prices are a combination of both intrinsic value plus time value and generally will have lower break-even points than their out-of-the-money counterparts.

The concept of time value is both objective and subjective, with a ton of gray in between. The reality is that it takes a trained eye to spot minute abnormalities in time value and take advantage of it. Time value *at that moment* is what the market believes that it should be. This doesn't mean that it's 100 percent accurate or that it won't change, because obviously it will.

What you find is that you have to layer on multiple lines of analysis to come to the best solution for your thesis. In the beginning, you may make money, but as you become more experienced, the same strategy could make you even more money (or lose less) because you have an educated eye for time value and volatility separate from what you see in the stock.

Until that time comes, simply be aware of the time value and/or implied volatility that you are buying or selling and record it in your journal or screen captures to see what you could have done differently, if anything, to improve your trades.

KEY POINT:

An option will typically trade for its intrinsic value, plus an amount of time value. Some options are comprised of completely time value (have no real value) and some may be trading for only their intrinsic value (typically these options are very deep in the money and close to expiration).

In- At- Out-of-the-Money Recap

In the money, *at the money*, and *out of the money* are terms that options traders use to express where the option strike price is in relation to the stock price. To find whether an option is in or out of the money you simply need to know if that option has intrinsic value or not. If a put is in the money the same strike call *must* be out of the money. A put and a call with the same strike can never both be in or out of the money, but they can be *at* the money, which basically means that the strike price is equal to the stock price.

- In the money—Has intrinsic value.
- Out of the money—Does *not* have intrinsic value.
- At the money—Strike price is at or very close to the stock price (may have intrinsic value or not).
- In-the-money *calls* have a *strike price* that is *below* the *stock* price.
  - If the call strike price is above the stock price, it's always out of the money.
- In-the-money *puts* have a *strike price* that is *above* the *stock* price.
  - If the put strike price is below the stock price, it's always out of the money.

KEY POINT:

To find the amount of time value for an in-the-money option, simply subtract the amount the option is in the money from the total value of the option. For a quick and dirty method, just look at the corresponding out-of-the-money option's value.

I use the same example as I used earlier to determine time value. If there were a dividend, the call prices would be cheaper by the dividend amount.

ABC Stock Is $50.

Calls	Puts
60 call $1.50—Out of the money	60 put $11.50—In the money
50 call $4—At the money	50 put $4—At the money
40 call $11.50—In the money	40 put $1.50—Out of the money

Options to Control Risk

All options are derivatives of an underlying asset such as a stock, ETF, bond, future, or other security. The rules that govern options prices (Greeks, pricing models, etc.) are applicable for just about every security that has options listed on them. This means that you can essentially price and trade an option on just about any security that has value (or perceived value) and another party that is willing to trade with you. If you understand how a particular asset behaves, you simply need to employ the option strategy that best suits your belief.

Generally speaking, the cost of carry and the implied volatility component of an asset are the most important variables when it comes to pricing options on securities other than vanilla equities or simple ETFs.

Compared to the underlying asset, an option can have much less risk. When you buy or short a stock, future, bond, or ETF by itself you have 100 percent of that underlier's price times the number of shares at risk at all times! You are also exposed to 100 percent of that asset's volatility and therefore its risk. By taking this action you are also limited to direction and com-

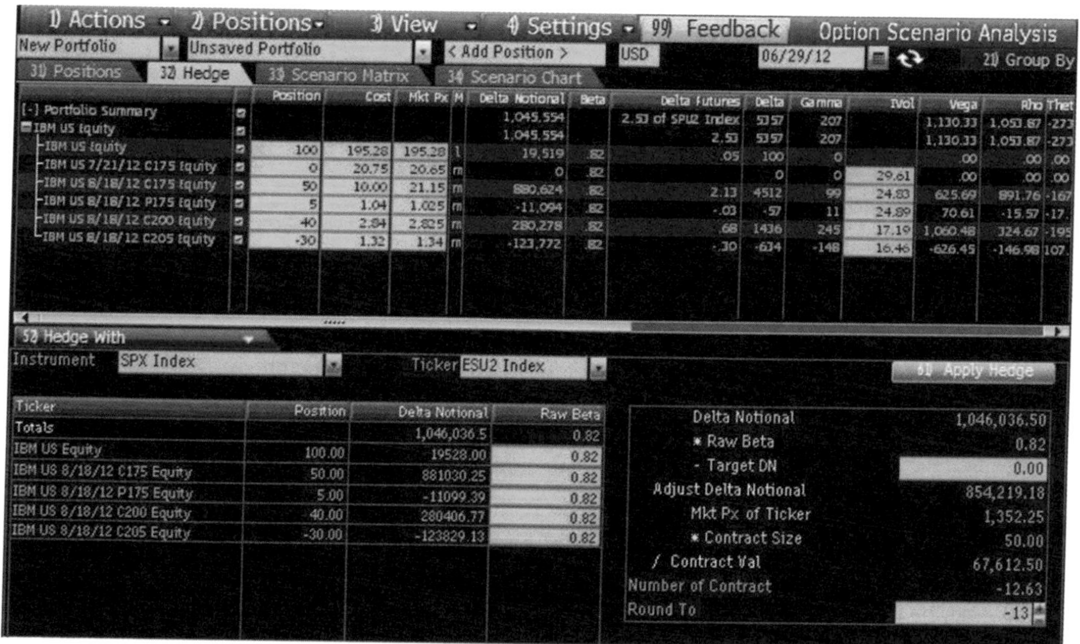

Exhibit 1.21

pletely sensitive to moves in the underlier. A simple example would be the purchase of 100 shares of stock at $100. For each dollar move up or down, you are gaining or losing 100 bucks, no exceptions. See Exhibit 1.21.

Augment Risk

Options can be used to enhance, amplify, or reduce exposure to a stock's movement. They can increase or decrease your P&L (profit and loss) correlation with the underlying asset. For most stock, index, or futures traders, options would probably be best used as a simply leveraged proxy for the underlying asset. This would simply mean buying a high delta put or call with close to the same net deltas that you would have bought in the underlying, but for a fraction of the price.

This reduces most types of risk and allows for an amplification of returns if the trade moves in your favor.

> KEY POINT:
>
> **Focus not only on the option's position relative to spot, but on its break-even, delta, cost, and theta. Selecting a singular, unhedged option has everything to do with your thesis in the movement of the stock and the speed and distance at which you think it will move.**

Smart Investor Tip!

Risk can be controlled by using a number of techniques and strategies with or without stock positions.

KEY POINT:

The models that professionals use to determine a theoretical value of an option at any moment in time come with a big caveat: *constant delta-neutral hedging.*

Because most nonoption investors really only have one, maybe two choices when it comes to investing direction—buy a stock long or go short—they are highly disadvantaged. In fact, shorting stock can be extremely risky and not suitable or tolerable for some, so non-option investors are extremely limited in how they can play the market.

In my first book, *Your Options Handbook*, I noted that the ability to hold a stock for an unlimited period of time doesn't benefit an investor because it doesn't force him or her to be as strict in preparation, thesis, and risk management.

Some stock traders become married to their positions, they don't have an end to the trade, they just buy it, it goes up, then they hold it, then it drops down, hold it, it becomes a horrible losing trade and they continue to hold it some more, in some cases until the stock dwindles to a fraction of where they bought it.

The missed opportunities in this sort of mind-set are enough to drive me mad! When used properly, options force traders into thinking about the future in more detail; we are also required to think about risk and reward and set a true, realistic time horizon for our trades, with a beginning, middle, and end. In most cases option traders have a more specific and what I believe to be superior plan.

With options, you can control with precision the amount of risk, and type of risk for that matter, you wish to take in any given trade in any situation. This can be achieved through a myriad of call and put combinations, and by adjusting the number of contracts bought or sold either in balance or on a rationed basis.

I remember trading thousands of contracts an hour on the floor of the exchange and being forced into positions I did not want to be in. While this was happening, I had to be creative. I had to come up with ways to protect the bad position that I was being put in, while efficiently and quietly controlling risk. I frequently used nonstandard spreads and ratios, or looked for cheap options to buy if I needed to get long some or expensive options to sell if I needed to get short. For me, my primary objective was being able to get an "edge" (better price) to that theoretical price I discussed earlier and then manage the risk on the fly from being forced into so many positions.

For most of you, the objectives are opposite. Sure you want to get a good price for the strategy that you are using, but it's more about the movement in the underlying security that will bring you profits.

Most of you will not operate your accounts using that technique, so don't get too hung up on the whole theoretical price thing, just use it to get a good execution on entry and exit and manage your trade with the information you gather.

Remember that the word *risk* carries many meanings and can be used to describe many different areas of exposure. Think of everything that could possibly go wrong for each type of risk. Also think of every individual Greek measurement as a form of risk and be sure that you can quantify that risk at any point during your trade.

Basics of Hedging

Hedging can be thought of as any form of risk reduction. For all traders, hedges are used to control runaway losses or simply reduce the beta of a portfolio.

When trading only stocks, risk tends to be associated with straight dollars (price) and volatility (beta, ATR, etc.). These specific risks can be partially offset by diversification, hedging with an index, or moving in and out of cash or stock positions at the appropriate times.

Hedging an equity portfolio by diversification may mitigate volatility, but if the entire market were to roll over in your long-only portfolio, chances are you will keep losing money, albeit slower than your nondiversified friends. See Exhibit 1.22.

To better balance this portfolio you might look at the correlations and beta of each stock in the portfolio to the hedging index and perhaps the weighing of the stocks in the index itself to get a more accurate relationship.

I discuss both these techniques later when I get into risk management in detail.

To make life easier for those of you who don't want to hedge with options, there is a nice feature in the OSA screen where Bloomberg can quickly figure the deltas (futures contracts or shares) of a specific index or ETF that are needed to gain the desired hedge based on the raw beta and shares of your stock positions. (See Exhibit 1.23.)

In addition, stop losses can be used to control catastrophic occurrences, but they are inefficient and useless in a gap situation, where the underlying security makes a large price move while the market is closed.

This example of a stock/futures hedge has its limits and would not necessarily protect you if one or more stocks in the portfolio were to experience a catastrophic event such as a major earnings miss, FDA denial, or bankruptcy. Again, this is why stock-only traders have far fewer "risk controls" than option traders.

A Little More Homework

Option traders have many more ways to control price and volatility risk as well as the ability to place an absolutely effective stop loss that will perform its function even in a gap scenario.

1) Actions · 2) Positions · 3) View · 4) Settings · 99) Feedback Option Scenario Analysis

New Portfolio | <Untitled Portfolio> | < Add Position > | USD | 08/11/12 | 21) Group By

31) Positions | 32) Hedge | 33) Scenario Matrix | 34) Scenario Chart

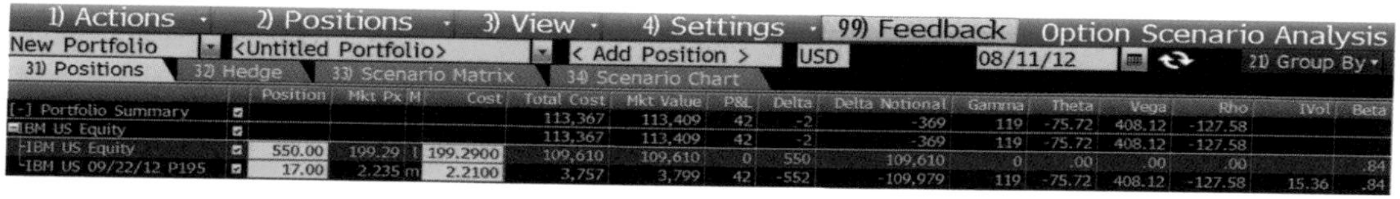

	Position	Mkt Px	M	Cost	Total Cost	Mkt Value	P&L	Delta	Delta Notional	Gamma	Theta	Vega	Rho	IVol	Beta
[-] Portfolio Summary					113,367	113,409	42	-2	-369	119	-75.72	408.12	-127.58		
IBM US Equity					113,367	113,409	42	-2	-369	119	-75.72	408.12	-127.58		
IBM US Equity	550.00	199.29	l	199.2900	109,610	109,610	0	550	109,610	0	.00	.00	.00		.84
IBM US 09/22/12 P195	17.00	2.235	m	2.2100	3,757	3,799	42	-552	-109,979	119	-75.72	408.12	-127.58	15.36	.84

Exhibit 1.22

KEY POINT:

Delta is how option traders measure price risk compared to the stock. It can also be thought of as the amount of "dollars" you are long or short compared to the underlying stock.

Delta Notional	1,046,036.50
* Raw Beta	0.82
- Target DN	0.00
Adjust Delta Notional	854,219.18
Mkt Px of Ticker	1,352.25
* Contract Size	50.00
/ Contract Val	67,612.50
Number of Contract	-12.63
Round To	-13

Exhibit 1.23

To obtain these advanced risk controls, option traders must monitor a couple more indicators. The way to think about it is that trading a stock could be likened to flying a single engine Cessna, whereas a professional option trader is piloting a Gulfstream jet, which is faster, more agile, more comfortable, and able to fly above most of the weather. The trade-off is the more advanced systems that pilots would need to learn and the nuances that they would have to be aware of while in flight, or in this case, in a trade. (See Exhibit 1.24.)

That's what this book is designed to help you with. It's the manual for all those advanced systems.

An option trader's "heads-up display" should be a combination of everything that a seasoned stock investor should use along with several other tools:

- Risk viewer
- Portfolio manager
- Strategy simulator
- Option chain
- Volatility chart
- Calendar

Bloomberg has these tools as part of their offering, so all you need now is the knowledge.

Smart Investor Tip!

These are the basic tools that you need to manage your position effectively. You can layer on a plethora of other tools that can make your trading more productive and efficient, but when you combine these basic tools with your primary checklist to analyze whatever security you are trading, you have everything you need.

Options as a Hedge

Assume that stock traders are bullish on tech stocks and buy 100 shares of IBM for $200, their risk is quite clear. Even if they sell 75 shares of the DIA for $130 as a hedge, they may get minimal protection if IBM were to go bankrupt. That's an extreme example, but what if the price got cut by 20 percent?

Exhibit 1.24

If it were a company-specific event, let's say the Dow might be down only 4 percent with the move in IBM. That means that they would lose approximately $40 × 100 or $4,000 in their IBM positions and make about $390 in their DIA positions.

That's a net loss of $3,610. *Was the hedge effective?*

Sure, they could have sold 100 shares in the SPDR Dow Jones Industrial Average ETF (DIA), but then how are they going to make any money with IBM having a beta of 0.75? That one-to-one hedge still would have only brought in another couple hundred bucks.

Sometimes you must assume the unexpected.

If you were foolish enough to get short Apple at the beginning of the 2012 and even if you used the SPX as a one-to-one hedge, your short position in Apple just ran 50 percent, while your one-to-one SPX hedge only protected about 12 percent. Even if you used the Nasdaq as your hedge, it was only up 20 percent!

An ineffective hedge can be extremely frustrating.

More Accurate Risk Reduction

Let's go back to IBM for a second and assume that instead of trading the 100 shares of IBM and

75 shares short of DIA, I just use a basic bull-put spread in IBM.

Perhaps I could sell a 190/180 bull-put spread (which is an option strategy that bets the stock to stay above 190) for $1.50 credit ($8.50 is max risk). This bull-put spread caps my risk and gives me similar risk exposure, but at a much lower margin cost.

I am only trading 100 shares of IBM, so I will do one spread (because each option controls 100 shares of stock and this spread has about a 30 delta, which was the same as my hedged stock/index position).

Let's first assume IBM experiences catastrophe and drops 20 percent, which puts the shares $40 lower, how much would I lose?

In this case, the max risk on one spread would be $850, a far cry from the $3,600 in the stock, but with the same delta! What's even better is that if the stock dropped, but stayed above $190, I would still make 18 percent in my spread while the hedged stock trader would be losing.

As you can see my "probability of success" is greater using the spread, but for that advantage, I cap my return at 18 percent. This may seem like a large sacrifice, but think about it—an 18 percent move in a $200 stock would be $36. Chances are that IBM may not get that far in 30 days, especially given the fact that the monthly average true range (ATR) is less than $13. The reality is that if IBM rallied 10 percent in that time, you would probably take profit on your stock position anyway.

The bull-put spread is just one of many risk reduction strategies we examine in this book.

Combining Stock and Option Hedges

You don't have to completely use either options or stock to create a hedge or reduce risk. There are many ways you can combine and harmonize stock and options together to customize a risk profile and control your risk. Strategies such as covered calls, married puts, and collars are all ways to protect long stock. Obviously you can do the same with short stock positions, just using different options. Finding the most appropriate strategy will be highly correlated with how profitable or not profitable you are in an existing position or portfolio in addition to how you want to protect yourself.

Why Doesn't Everyone Trade Options?

Options get a bad rap, mostly because they are vastly misunderstood and misused by inexperienced traders. In some cases, with certain strategies the inherent greed in most investors deters them from capping their profits and using a spread strategy; even if it increases their chances of success by tenfold, they are still reluctant because there is always that chance of striking it filthy rich on one trade. I detail all of this in later chapters and compare the different strategies and their applications.

Depending on your choice of strategy, positioning, and risk profile of the option strategy you select, you could be knocking out singles and doubles with a high rate of success, hitting home runs that pay for all your losses and then some, or find yourself somewhere in between.

Options—Leverage and Probability

Options, unlike stocks, can allow traders to truly customize and trade in harmony with their time horizons, reduce risk, and make bets/investments with odds better than 1:1 and probability better than 50/50. If I can place a bet using a certain option strategy with an 80 percent statistical probability of winning on a company that has great fundamentals, all the while limiting my risk to just 10 percent of what I could potentially lose in the stock to achieve the same return, I would take that any day over just buying stock. See Exhibit 1.25.

What drew me to options is the fact that I can basically trade them on any company I choose, not to mention apply a strategy with a set risk, reward, and probability, and at the same time still have a major advantage over the regular stock trader. Essentially, options allow you to be "sort of right" and still make more than a comparable stock trade. And, if you were to simply follow my methods when trading long-call or long-put options, generally your cost will be about 10 to 15 percent of what you would have to pay for the stock.

As much as I loathe the markets being compared to the casino, it just so happens to be the perfect analogy. In many respects, options markets are closely tied to the games you find on the Las Vegas Strip. The question is whether you want to be Steve Wynn or the guy who calls 1-800-GAMBLER after your pockets and bank account are finally empty.

It's important not to generalize here. Each game played in the casino has different objectives, odds, risk, costs, speed, behavior, and so on. The same is true of the markets, stocks, options, and the strategies or games you select.

I remember taking my "non-gambling" girlfriend to Las Vegas and walking the floor for hours explaining all the different games, their odds, advantages and disadvantages. What interested her more was not the games themselves, but why people choose to play certain games in certain ways.

Take roulette for example (see Exhibit 1.26).

In America, there are 38 slots on the wheel and 38 different places to lay a chip that will generally pay you 35 on your money. Right there was the casino's edge in this game, but we get to that later. Why do some people lay 35 chips on the table inside to only win 35, which would only bring them to even? Is it the fear of losing? Do they not understand the game? Maybe both? Some lay 38 chips only to win 35.

There are others who keep betting the same number or cluster on the table, hoping that that one number or small group of numbers hits eventually, trying to win before they lose it all or get into a negative position. They even look for "sticky" numbers that tend to repeat themselves.

KEY POINT:

Even selling a put or a put spread at a level at which you would not mind owning the stock is a method you can employ to lower your risk.

Here is a simple comparison of a move in IBM stock and a call option that fit my parameters; which would you want to own?

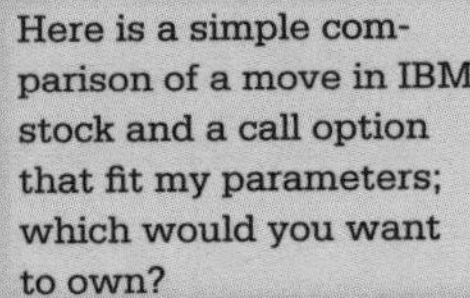

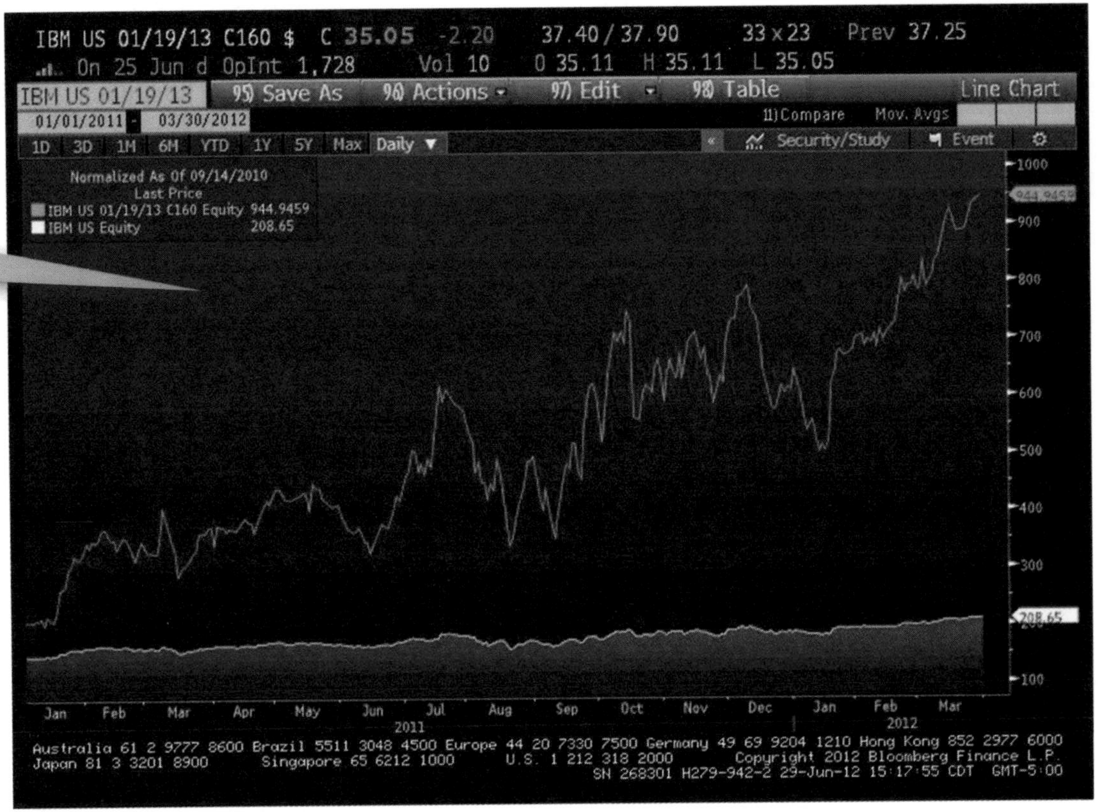

Exhibit 1.25

Then there are the statistical nuts who bet the outside, praying for black or red and doubling their bet each time they lose, praying for that mean reversion and their number to hit. The casino limits this action by capping the amount you can bet in certain areas.

Generally, most casual gamblers don't have a "system" or intimate knowledge of the game they are playing, which almost always leads to disaster.

The bet that you would take is both dependent on your personality and your knowledge of the game and opinion on where you think the ball (or trade) will land.

Double-Zero Roulette			
Bet	Pays	Probability Win	House Edge
Red	1	47.37%	5.26%
Black	1	47.37%	5.26%
Odd	1	47.37%	5.26%
Even	1	47.37%	5.26%
1 to 18	1	47.37%	5.26%
19 to 36	1	47.37%	5.26%
1 to 12	2	31.58%	5.26%
13 to 24	2	31.58%	5.26%
25 to 36	2	31.58%	5.26%
Sixline (6 numbers)	5	15.79%	5.26%
First five (5 numbers)	6	13.16%	7.89%
Corner (4 numbers)	8	10.53%	5.26%
Street (3 numbers)	11	7.89%	5.26%
Split (2 numbers)	17	5.26%	5.26%
Any one number	35	2.63%	5.26%

Exhibit 1.26
Source: www.wizardofodds.com.

While you play, the casino takes a certain percent in edge in just about every bet in the game of roulette. Think of that 5.26 percent as a commission of sorts.

In the world of options, singles, or spreads, leverage can be your best friend or worst enemy. Just like in the casino you have the ability to make a lot of money with a little—it just depends on how much you want to win, want to spend, and what you want your likelihood of winning to be.

In the stock market, the main difference is that you have this third party (the stock), which has a mind of its own in a sense. It's kind of like playing craps but adding weight to a specific side of the die to coax them into landing on six more often than any other number. If it weren't illegal and you could do such a thing, it would be prudent to bet on the six more often than other numbers.

I bring all this up because it's the way you should be thinking if you are going to be a true options trader. What is the probability of my being right/wrong in my trade and for that probability, what am I willing to risk?

Options strategies are universal and can be used to place "bets" on direction, time, volatility, interest rates, and so on, on just about any security in any market anytime, anywhere, no matter the situation. With them, I have much more control over the position than if I just went long or short the underlying instrument. (See Exhibit 1.27.)

Options strategies reduce volatility in your portfolio so you don't have to be a slave to the irrational crowd behavior that is often seen in the stock market. You will be able to create your own odds, which is not only empowering, but the only way you should want to trade.

Try to think outside your normal "box," because once you learn options, you can trade just about anything that is presented to you and choose the appropriate strategy that not only truly matches your opinion on that stock but offers you a hedge against the sometimes irrational world we live in.

Options for Strategy

Your strategy should be developed through a combination of your thoughts on the underlying asset, leverage, probability, risk, protection, and anything else you deem appropriate all rolled into one. But there's an important step you shouldn't forget in your calculations.

Your research should include a realistic theoretical path that you feel the underlying security will take in the time frame you select. (This doesn't have to be perfect, just a realistic expectation.)

Building a strategy based on that and the ultimate price the security will be at the end of your time horizon enables you to make sense of your investment plan from all angles, such as volatility, risk, earnings, news, economy, and probability. This will also be the strategy that will allow you to capture the most profits.

What I mean is that you don't want to pick a strategy that will make you 20 percent on your investment if you see a high probability of the security experiencing a 70 percent drawdown before reaching your goal.

Here's what I'm talking about: Imagine that your research determined that XYZ oil and gas stock was going to finish right around $110 on June expiration, which is in 90 days. It's currently trading at $95. In that time frame the stock will release an earnings report and four oil and gas inventory reports . . . and there is a war brewing in the Middle East.

In this complex situation, a stock trader would have no choice but to bear the full brunt of all

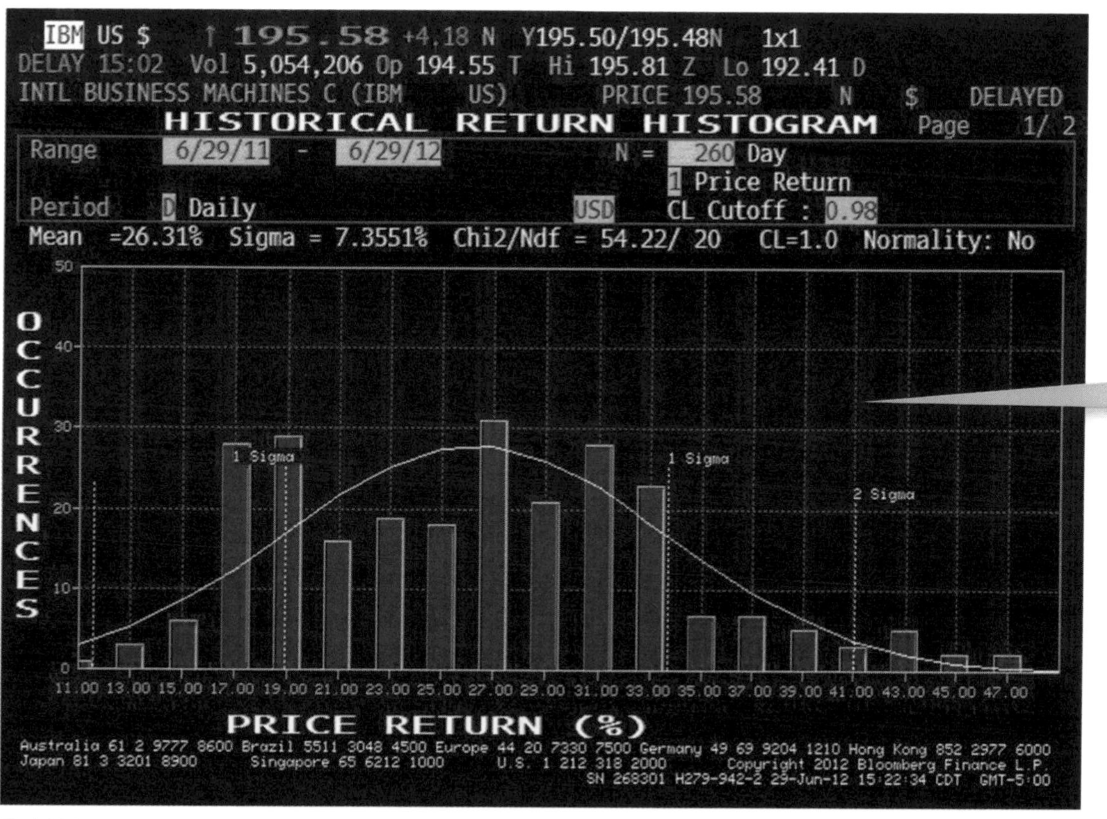

The historical return histogram is one of the many tools to quantify price distribution (volatility) over a given period of time.

Exhibit 1.27

KEY POINT:

Try to let your market/stock thesis determine the appropriate strategy as opposed to locking yourself into one "signature" strategy. Certain market conditions are better suited for specific strategies.

those market events and their probable volatility, basically praying for the stock to get through unscathed.

As an option strategist, you have your choice of strategies that take into account all the data. You get to choose an options strategy that allows you to profit from the rise in the stock, but maybe tone down all the bumps on the road. For example, in this case, a simple in-the-money bull-call spread might help decrease all that volatility while still giving you a superior return on investment (ROI) compared to the stock.

Or if you thought it was going to be an "all or nothing" sort of event, you might position that bull-call spread out of the money, so it was much cheaper—heck, while you're at it, if you weren't sure about direction at all, you might combine that bull-call spread with a bear-call spread and form an iron condor.

Again, it's all about compound thinking and getting out of your mind's normal boundaries that have been set by years of routines, beliefs, and fears.

Technical Patterns

For this guide, I choose to focus more on techniques, strategies, and nuances of the option markets themselves. That said, all of the strategies in this guide utilize some form of technical analysis so that you can quantify volatility with price points in the stock as well as identify patterns and trends that are important to your trade.

I don't care what you think about technicals—love 'em or hate 'em, you should at the very least take a quick glance at a chart and find some basic levels and trends.

In my 16 years trading stocks and options I have found it next to impossible to trade derivatives without having knowledge of technical and volatility trends on top of my fundamental analysis.

Technicals also narrow down the sheer number of option strategies and strikes to just one. The only strategies that might not require technical analysis are the deep-in-the-money long call and long put because they are limited in risk and tend to only have slightly worse breakevens than the stock itself.

If you are completely anti-technical for whatever reason, at least find basic support and resistance levels in a chart using major moving averages, trend lines, or other big-picture tools. See if those points coincide with the 52-week high or low as it may add more or less weight to that level and help you choose the best strategy.

Basic moving averages (levels) and the most popular indicators (MACD, Fibonacci, Bollinger bands, etc.) can also give you a reference point for your profit targets, stop losses, and, most important, to select the best strategy, strikes, and expiration.

I reference certain extremely common technical indicators throughout this book when I am discussing strategy. All of them are basic and fairly easy to learn in a short time.

In my first book, *Your Options Handbook*, I spent quite a bit of time on the subject of technicals, fundamentals, and general market and option knowledge. The book no doubt complements this guide. You can also pick up a copy of the *Visual Guide to Technical Analysis* as another reference.

The bottom line is that you should at least understand the basics!

Volume Trends

Volume is the cause and price is the effect. Think of volume as a river's current flowing into or out of a stock. If you are depending on a strong stream of current to carry your stock along the river at a certain pace and that current dries up, you may have a problem on your hands.

Just like water building up behind a dam, high levels of volume pouring into a stock can cause an explosion of price movement. If you can spot the tsunami before it hits the shore or identify an undertow you can exploit this underutilized indicator.

Consistent volume trends observed over time will help you anticipate the "real" trend in volume at the current moment in time. A rising tide on an ocean beach doesn't just flood in; it is a series of ebbs and flows that gradually move the water up the beach. (See Exhibit 1.28.)

Volume trends have gotten a bit clouded with the introduction of high frequency trading (HFT), which is basically bogus volume that is occurring in large quantities between normal trades and prices.

You can think of HFT as an amplifier of normal variations in volume; unfortunately that amplification, like sound, can cause distortion. It takes practice to see through it all.

HFT strategies vary, but are generally favored and utilized when markets widen out and become irrational or scared. In those instances, HFT algorithms can generate tremendous profits and perhaps exacerbate price and volume movements. It can also make your analysis a bit more difficult. See Exhibit 1.29.

Obviously, volume trends are important to the downside as well, but generally volume tends to be higher when stocks are dropping because of the effects of fear, so you must account for this to an extent. Use past history to give you a sense of normal volume, but don't go back too far and be sure that you correlate news and economic events with high- or low-volume periods to normalize the data.

Volume changes influence stocks, and that means they can have a direct effect on derivatives. I am going to share a couple of volume hints and tricks to help you make the best use of this market current.

Is the CBOE Put-Call Ratio Useful or Relevant Anymore?

The CBOE.com posts put and call volume for the entire exchange, equity market, index, VIX, and the S&P

Smart Investor Tip!

Reading volume properly and understanding how to compare and contrast them to one another can be like getting a "free look" into the psyche of the market participants.

A rising volume trend in one direction or another will let you know if that stock's overall tide is rising or falling and which direction is really favored.

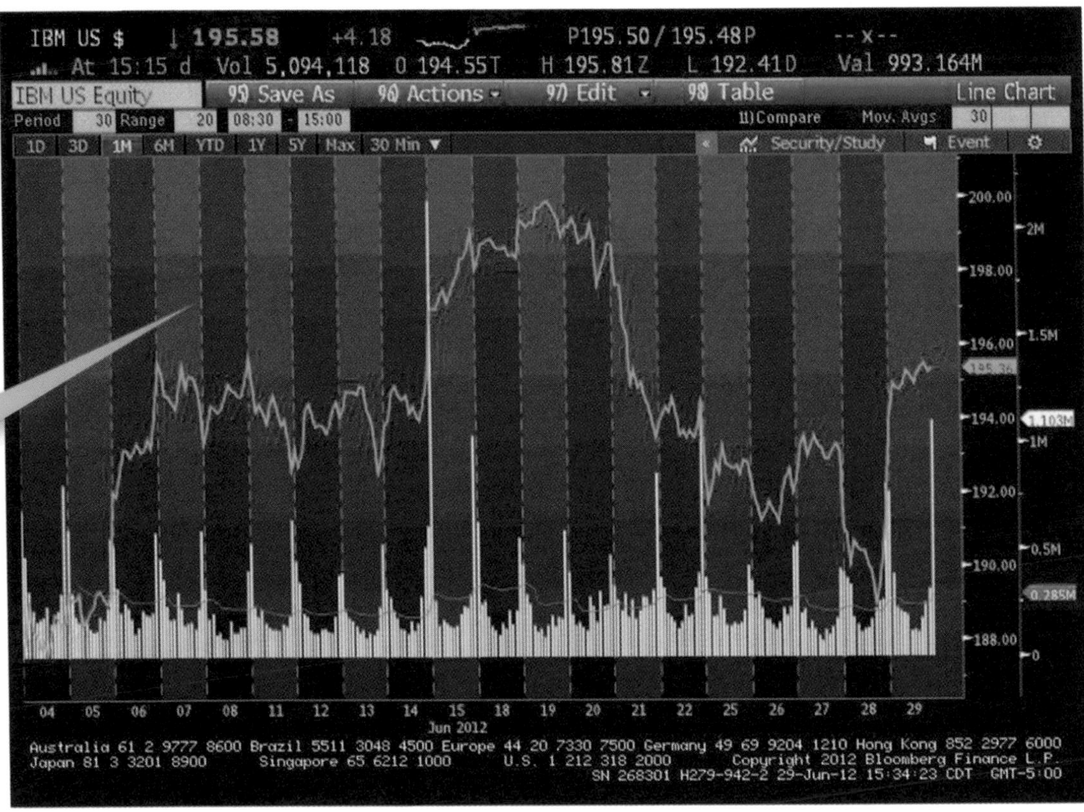

Exhibit 1.28

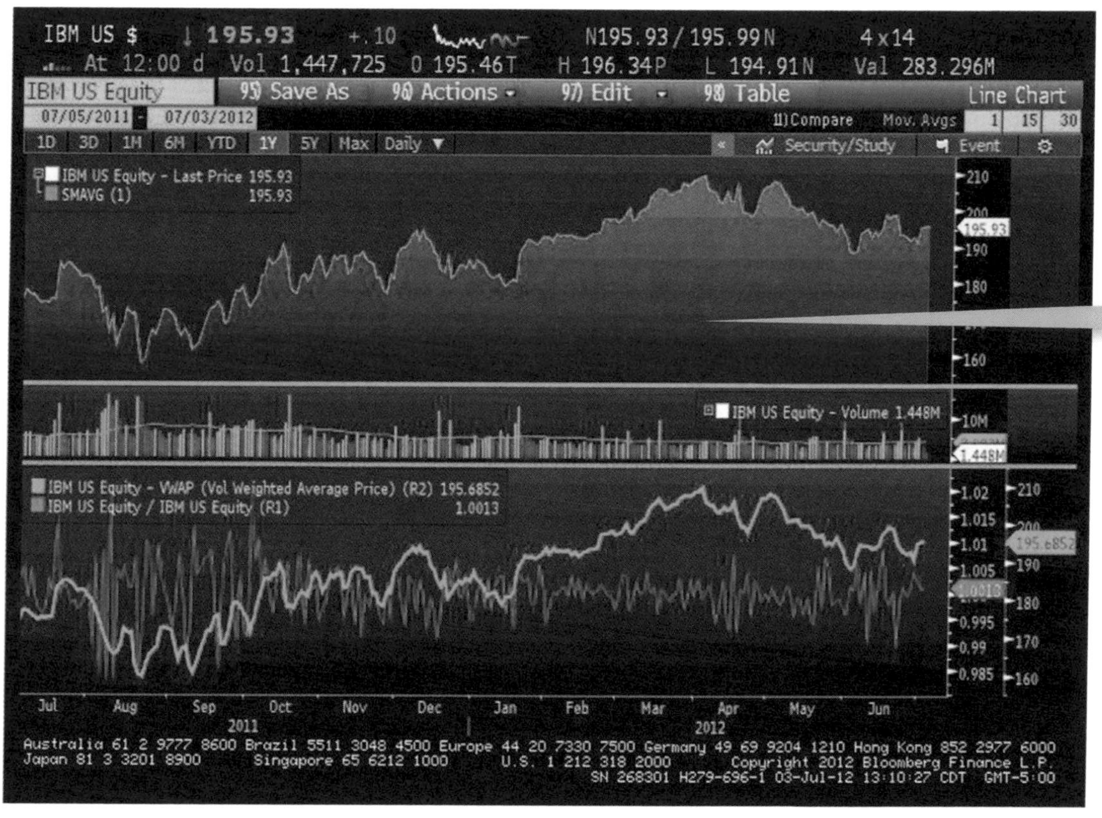

VWAP basically is the ratio of value (price) to volume; it lets you see where the bulk of trades are occurring.

Exhibit 1.29

500 specifically. Based on this overall volume, the site also displays a ratio of the puts and calls separately.

This question of its significance and usefulness is obviously debatable. My theory is that with the rise of option volume, education, and sophistication, the imbalance between call and put usage is on the decline. This means that there is more equal usage between puts and calls and they are used not only for bullish and bearish tactics, but also as parts of spreads, which may skew the data (no pun intended). All that leads to a less helpful indicator.

I took all the data from the total exchange put-call ratio since inception and you can see that the trend line shows the average increasing, which helps to prove my thesis.

But that doesn't mean the put-call ratio is completely useless. To get a more reliable signal, you can combine a low put-call ratio, decreasing volume in the SPY, DIA, QQQQ, or market as whole, and a low relative VIX (general implied volatility reading) if you are looking to identify an overbought, complacent market. Thus this takes the bearish contrarian stance or vice versa if the markets have been selling off.

Finding Abnormalities

Volume spikes in a security are often a telltale sign of an event. Usually there is a dramatic change in price during that spike, and that is the giveaway. But what if there is increased volume for no apparent reason? Or what if there is no abnormal price movement in the security itself? (See Exhibit 1.30.)

The option markets can play a vital role in identifying the bias of the abnormality (bullish or bearish) as well as gauging whether that volatility is expected to continue.

If you notice volume to be unusually high a certain day or over a short period of time, take a look at the implied volatility of the options as well as their volume. Here's why.

First, if you notice elevated volume in the stock and one or more options with volume, but no major change in the stock price or implied volatility of the option, chances are that the trade may have been previously made and simply crossed on the exchange. Professionals sometimes arrange a trade off the floor, then send it to the floor with a buyer and seller already lined up.

Shares may also change hands because one or both sides wants to remain delta-neutral (we discuss this more later) and therefore agrees to a price at which to trade the stock.

Because the trade isn't sent down as a straight buy or sell, the stock price may not be influenced.

If it has changed more than the delta says it should have and there is a spike in implied volatility, then you might have a buyer on your hands. If the option is an out-of-the-money call close to expiration and the volume is much higher than the average volume traded, it could be a sign that someone either knows something or has done some serious research to anticipate a move higher.

There are instances where the trade is simply a protective move or a hedge against a bigger position.

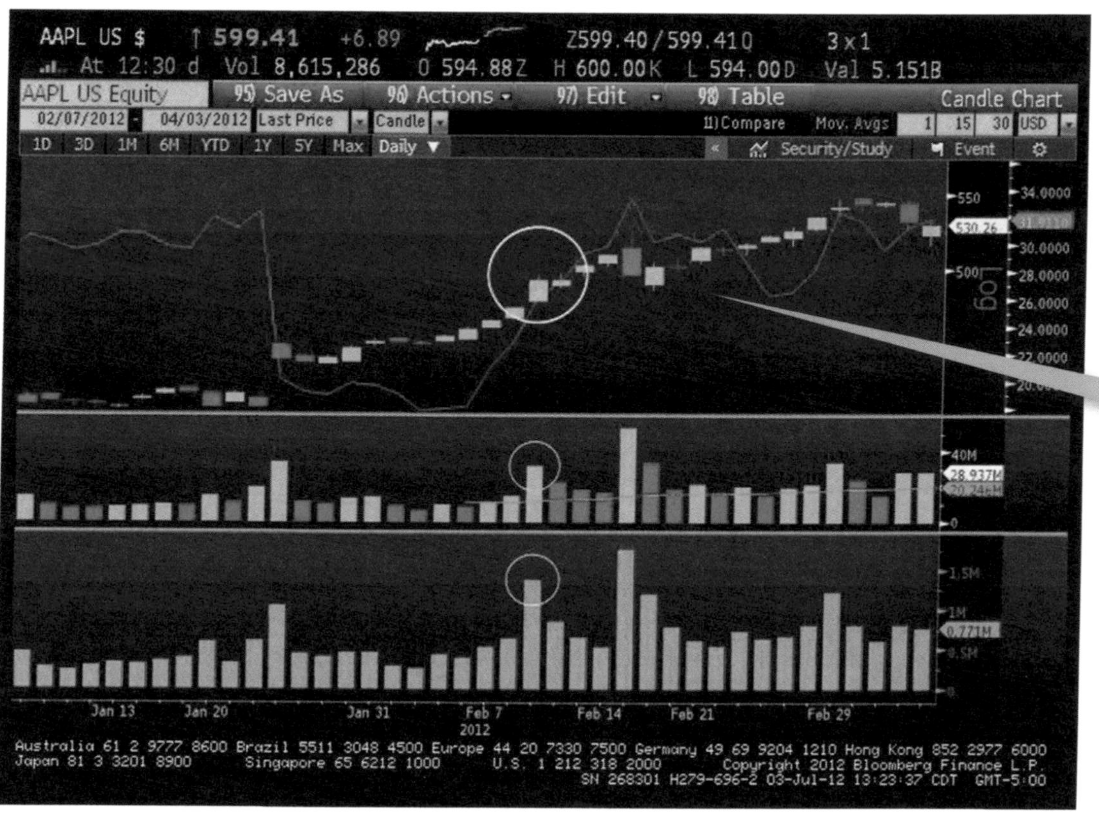

If you notice a big volume spike in the stock and minimal change in the stock price, but a large change (up or down) in the implied volatility combined with abnormal volume in one or more options, then there may be a large buyer or seller of that particular option executing a trade to speculate or protect a position.

Exhibit 1.30

The MOST screen is a great tool to scan for stock volume in any time frame; you can also use options volume search to scan for anomalies there.

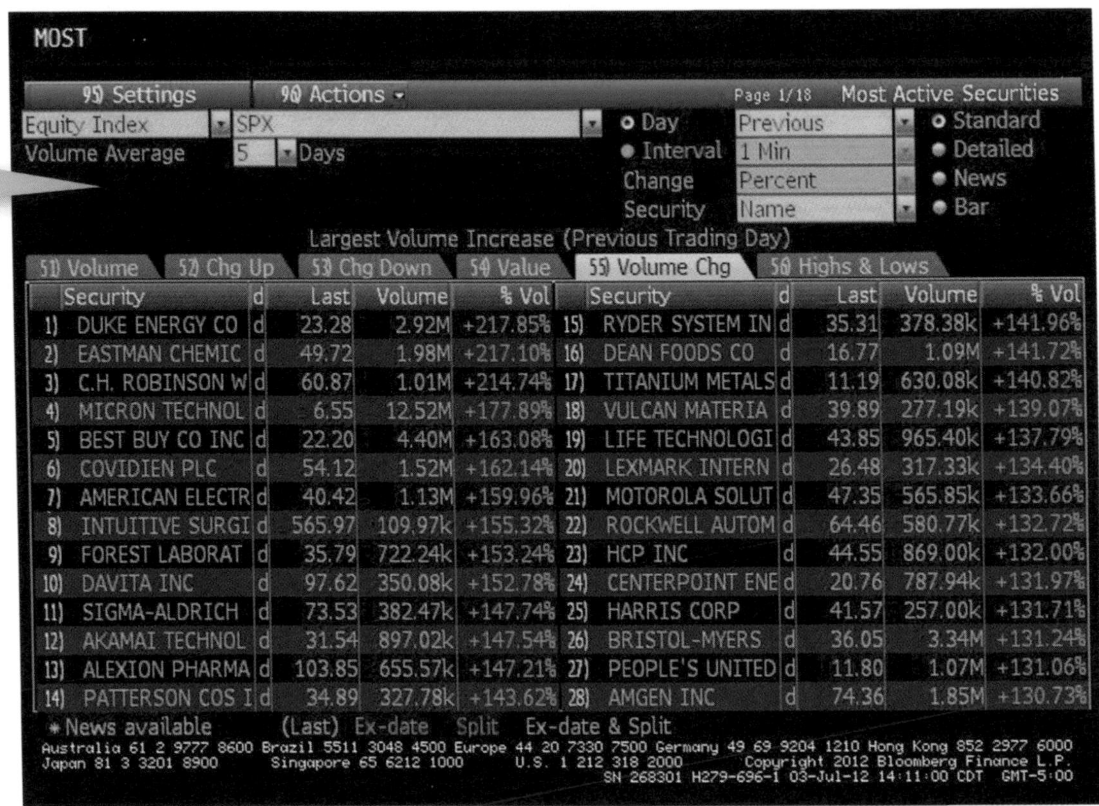

	Security	d	Last	Volume	% Vol		Security	d	Last	Volume	% Vol
1)	DUKE ENERGY CO	d	23.28	2.92M	+217.85%	15)	RYDER SYSTEM IN	d	35.31	378.38k	+141.96%
2)	EASTMAN CHEMIC	d	49.72	1.98M	+217.10%	16)	DEAN FOODS CO	d	16.77	1.09M	+141.72%
3)	C.H. ROBINSON W	d	60.87	1.01M	+214.74%	17)	TITANIUM METALS	d	11.19	630.08k	+140.82%
4)	MICRON TECHNOL	d	6.55	12.52M	+177.89%	18)	VULCAN MATERIA	d	39.89	277.19k	+139.07%
5)	BEST BUY CO INC	d	22.20	4.40M	+163.08%	19)	LIFE TECHNOLOGI	d	43.85	965.40k	+137.79%
6)	COVIDIEN PLC	d	54.12	1.52M	+162.14%	20)	LEXMARK INTERN	d	26.48	317.33k	+134.40%
7)	AMERICAN ELECTR	d	40.42	1.13M	+159.96%	21)	MOTOROLA SOLUT	d	47.35	565.85k	+133.66%
8)	INTUITIVE SURGI	d	565.97	109.97k	+155.32%	22)	ROCKWELL AUTOM	d	64.46	580.77k	+132.72%
9)	FOREST LABORAT	d	35.79	722.24k	+153.24%	23)	HCP INC	d	44.55	869.00k	+132.00%
10)	DAVITA INC	d	97.62	350.08k	+152.78%	24)	CENTERPOINT ENE	d	20.76	787.94k	+131.97%
11)	SIGMA-ALDRICH	d	73.53	382.47k	+147.74%	25)	HARRIS CORP	d	41.57	257.00k	+131.71%
12)	AKAMAI TECHNOL	d	31.54	897.02k	+147.54%	26)	BRISTOL-MYERS	d	36.05	3.34M	+131.24%
13)	ALEXION PHARMA	d	103.85	655.57k	+147.21%	27)	PEOPLE'S UNITED	d	11.80	1.07M	+131.06%
14)	PATTERSON COS I	d	34.89	327.78k	+143.62%	28)	AMGEN INC	d	74.36	1.85M	+130.73%

Exhibit 1.31

At any rate, the information can be useful, especially if it is a level that you are concerned with or are hoping the stock can get to.

This technique works in both directions, with puts and calls, and is most effective when looking to identify quiet smart money trends. I usually look for minimum trades of 500 to 1,000 lots.

Be sure to scan the entire option chain in all months and strikes and look for similar volume in one or more options to help identify spreads and perhaps explain a bit more about direction. For example: You might see 5,000 of the May 50 calls being sold, which looks bearish, but if you look out in time, you might notice that 5,000 of the June 45 calls were bought. This changes the entire dynamic of the trade.

Second, if you notice a big volume spike in the stock, abnormal movement in the share price, and large changes in implied volatility coupled with abnormal volume in the options, it may also be a sign that the smart money is doing something, but also may be more reactionary than anticipatory.

In this instance, you really have to be good at identifying just normal daily noise and trading to get to the good stuff. When there is a price anomaly in a stock, stop orders and trigger orders often flood the market and that gets the attention of a bunch of active traders who just want to scalp the mean reversion or momentum. These types of traders and their volume are typically useless for gaining any real knowledge in future direction other than a day or two out.

If the price movement is not that extreme and perhaps influenced by a broad market movement, then you might have an easier time finding the options that are being accumulated or sold and thus get an idea of the bets being made.

Scanning for Volume Anomalies

Volume anomalies can be used as a means to initiate a trade. The "MOST" screen allows you to scan the markets for abnormal options volume. (See Exhibit 1.31.)

Usually I run a generic scan for high volume relative to average volume and then filter down to industries and stocks. While I am filtering I search the news to find reasoning behind the volume. If there is no news or the news is counter to what the volume and price action are initially telling me, I start to look deeper, as those situations can often yield the best results.

Sounds counterintuitive, but here's why it works: If the event is completely obvious, that often means that everyone is doing the obvious thing and the pros might just be selling into the euphoria or buying into the panic, which doesn't do much for my strategies unless again I am just looking for a mean reversion intraday or swing trade.

Smart Investor Tip!

The most active options, or MOST screen, is one way to see a snapshot of where the biggest option volume is and to seek out potential trade. Big option volume should only be used as an initial catalyst or red flag to signal further research. It may help you to find volatility abnormalities or to identify buyers or sellers ahead of an event.

KEY POINT:

Big money managers often use abnormal market conditions to get into and out of their big trades. They may also use options to do so. Some use a big sell-off to accumulate shares or a rally to sell. Although it can be hard to detect all their movements, the option markets will often reveal their hand if you know what to look for.

CHAPTER 2

Tools and Knowledge for Trading Options Professionally

Option traders come in all shapes, sizes, and disciplines. I want to offer just some quick advice on forming your investment thesis and then overlaying the proper option strategy on top of it.

When I was asked to write this book, I was extremely excited because I feel that Bloomberg is the epicenter of detailed, quality information that is organized in an efficient way. In my book *Your Options Handbook*, I spent a great amount of time detailing the process that traders and investors should go through to come to the most accurate conclusion for their investment decisions. This *Visual Guide to Options* offers you a simple checklist for each strategy along with the best Bloomberg screens to utilize in obtaining the data you need.

Once you have created a basic investment idea based on whatever research, indicators, or methods you choose, you should have a general idea of the trajectory of the market and of your stock.

When you establish that broad asset trajectory, your next step is to plot your "investment trajectory" for the strategy you select. While you are plotting this trajectory, adjust your strike price choices and your risk, if needed, or change to a more appropriate strategy.

It's like drawing a map of the direction, duration, and terrain of a trip you are about to take and then deciding on the best vehicle to get you there. If your trip takes you over water, you obviously cannot use a car. If your trade takes you into a volatile scenario, it doesn't make sense to use a strategy that performs best with low volatility.

Plotting a trajectory means visualizing several scenarios that the asset(s) may take and examining what the corresponding effects that will have on your

Smart Investor Tip!

Form your thesis, find your acceptable risk, and place your trade.

portfolio. These scenarios should obviously incorporate the possible movement of the asset itself, but more specifically should include the external variables you found during your research.

This may sound like overkill, but running through several different variations can help you to pinpoint the strategy you want to use, its specifics (risk/strikes/ratio), and your allocation to that strategy by itself and in relation to your portfolio.

Experienced traders often do this in their heads in a matter of minutes, maybe by using some scrap paper to jot down any notes or ideas they think of. It may take novice traders an extra hour or two to envision, test, interpret, and analyze different scenarios, but I can assure you that it will make a marked difference in your trading.

KEY POINT:

In early 2011, the global economic environment was slowly improving. Analysts seemed to believe that growth would be slow, but positive. The biggest real risks were a disorderly default by Greece and a Chinese hard landing. Commodities were under general bullish pressure because of global QE (Quantitative Easing), with oil prices supported by unrest between Israel and Iran, and gold supported by fear of another crisis and weak dollar. All in all, volatility for the next three months seemed slightly elevated and major catastrophic risk seemed minimal.

Steps to Forming Your Basic Thesis

Depending on your time horizon, existing knowledge of the security you are trading, and the complexity of your strategy, there are varying steps taken to form your thesis that we discuss in detail throughout this book. No matter where on the scale you find yourself, these four steps should be a starting foundation.

Step 1: Gauge Macroeconomic Conditions and Upcoming Events

The first step in creating your investment thesis is to quantify and understand the current global economic situation and the most likely direction it is headed for the duration of your trade. This includes studying economic analyst reports from major houses such as Goldman Sachs, JPMorgan, Morgan Stanley, and Bloomberg. They will help you consolidate your thoughts and snag the highlights. See Exhibit 2.1.

Research reports are available from several sources; on the Bloomberg Terminal; simply type "Research."

It helps to quickly correlate your particular stock or sector with the events that are currently unfolding and those brewing on the horizon. I find it helpful to assign a couple of basic adjectives to my thesis.

See my thesis in the Key Point on this page. It is really all you need to start, with perhaps a couple more details. I like to think of it as the two-minute elevator pitch you would give a colleague in the business if he asked you how the world was doing.

You should also select a fair volatility range expectation in that same time frame and check out any major global events that could impact your trade. Take this, for example: If you were buying a Euro/USD exchange-traded fund (ETF), you might want to be aware of any European Union (EU) meetings or monetary events.

I continue to aggregate several trusted opinions to find common threads along with time horizons for each of their projections to add into mine. This is done on a daily or weekly basis even while I am in trade. You can also combine your ideas with observations in the general media from both major outlets as well as popular blogs.

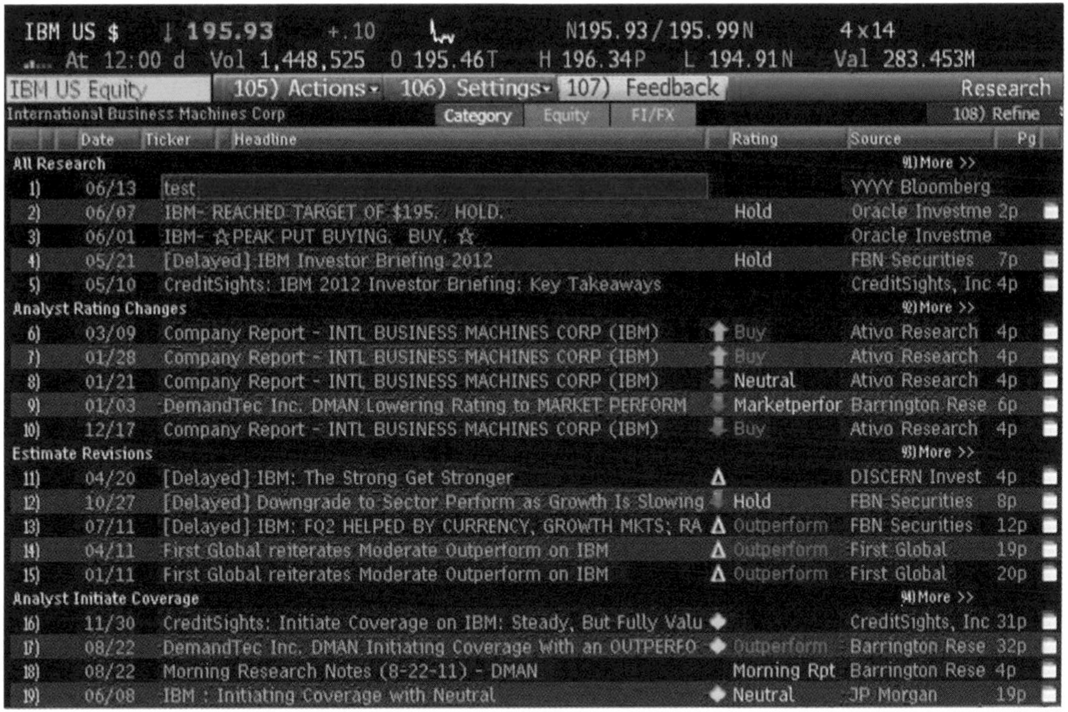

IBM US $ ↓ 195.93 +.10 N195.93/195.99N 4x14
At 12:00 d Vol 1,448,525 O 195.46T H 196.34P L 194.91N Val 283.453M

IBM US Equity | 105) Actions | 106) Settings | 107) Feedback | Research

International Business Machines Corp | Category | Equity | FI/FX | 108) Refine

	Date	Ticker	Headline	Rating	Source	Pg
All Research					91) More >>	
1)	06/13		test		YYYY Bloomberg	
2)	06/07		IBM- REACHED TARGET OF $195. HOLD.	Hold	Oracle Investme	2p
3)	06/01		IBM- ☆PEAK PUT BUYING. BUY. ☆		Oracle Investme	
4)	05/21		[Delayed] IBM Investor Briefing 2012	Hold	FBN Securities	7p
5)	05/10		CreditSights: IBM 2012 Investor Briefing: Key Takeaways		CreditSights, Inc	4p
Analyst Rating Changes					92) More >>	
6)	03/09		Company Report - INTL BUSINESS MACHINES CORP (IBM)	Buy	Ativo Research	4p
7)	01/28		Company Report - INTL BUSINESS MACHINES CORP (IBM)	Buy	Ativo Research	4p
8)	01/21		Company Report - INTL BUSINESS MACHINES CORP (IBM)	Neutral	Ativo Research	4p
9)	01/03		DemandTec Inc. DMAN Lowering Rating to MARKET PERFORM	Marketperfor	Barrington Rese	6p
10)	12/17		Company Report - INTL BUSINESS MACHINES CORP (IBM)	Buy	Ativo Research	4p
Estimate Revisions					93) More >>	
11)	04/20		[Delayed] IBM: The Strong Get Stronger	Δ	DISCERN Invest	4p
12)	10/27		[Delayed] Downgrade to Sector Perform as Growth Is Slowing	Hold	FBN Securities	8p
13)	07/11		[Delayed] IBM: FQ2 HELPED BY CURRENCY, GROWTH MKTS; RA	Δ Outperform	FBN Securities	12p
14)	04/11		First Global reiterates Moderate Outperform on IBM	Δ Outperform	First Global	19p
15)	01/11		First Global reiterates Moderate Outperform on IBM	Δ Outperform	First Global	20p
Analyst Initiate Coverage					94) More >>	
16)	11/30		CreditSights: Initiate Coverage on IBM: Steady, But Fully Valu	◆	CreditSights, Inc	31p
17)	08/22		DemandTec Inc. DMAN Initiating Coverage With an OUTPERFO	◆ Outperform	Barrington Rese	32p
18)	08/22		Morning Research Notes (8-22-11) - DMAN	Morning Rpt	Barrington Rese	4p
19)	06/08		IBM : Initiating Coverage with Neutral	◆ Neutral	JP Morgan	19p

Exhibit 2.1

Step 2: Quantify Economic Data in Your Country of Focus (Including Mind-Related Economies)

The three types of economic indicators and their timing are:

1. **Leading:** Leading economic indicators are indicators that tend to change before the economy changes.

   The stock market itself is generally a leading indicator, as it usually begins to decline before

Smart Investor Tip!

Don't forget to mind the relationship that the data has to the current market environment. If a lagging indicator doesn't seem to be in line with the others, do be afraid to give it more time.

the economy declines and it improves before the economy begins to pull out of a recession. Building permits and money supply also are considered leading indicators. Leading economic indicators are the most important type for investors as they help predict what the economy will be like in the future.

2. **Lagging:** A lagging economic indicator is one that may not change direction until a few quarters after the economy does or there has been a change in the other leading indicators. The unemployment rate is a lagging economic indicator as the unemployment rate may take several quarters to reflect improvement after the economy really starts to improve. The prime rate is also a lagging indicator.
3. **Coincident:** A coincident economic indicator is one that simply moves at the same time the economy does. The gross domestic product, retail sales, and consumer confidence are all coincident indicators.

Smart Investor Tip!

For a quick and dirty way to find out what professionals believe the FED will do you can check out both the FED fund futures on screen "FDTR" and the yield curve of government debt on screen "YCRV."

I tend to look at the charts and identify the trends of the major data sets in addition to analyzing what the top firms say about future expectations. I want to see how they compare to my ideas. If the trends complement them, then things are straightforward. If they are contrary to my opinions, I want to know why, and who is more right. If you have strong convictions that the general consensus is wrong, than incorporate your ideas into your thesis.

If you are focusing your investments on a U.S.-based company or a company with considerable exposure to the U.S. economy, then added attention and research should be placed on U.S. economic indicators and trends. Obviously, do the same for companies/securities that are more sensitive to foreign economies. You should examine data like sales numbers (retail, durable and nondurable goods, housing, etc.), industrial production (ISM, PMI, etc.), inflation and price trends (CPI, PPI, etc.), consumer sentiment (consumer sentiment and activity), consumer spending/savings habits, and the jobs situation (unemployment, job creation, wages, etc.). See Exhibit 2.2.

The ECO screen can give you a quick snapshot of upcoming data. Then you can drill down to find trends in each. Strong, bullish trends in these data sets allow you to be more aggressive in your strategy. Mixed trends within the major economic data should guide you to more neutral, less aggressive bullish strategies and obviously weakening trends may deter you from being bullish altogether. Negative trends may be best traded with a neutral or bearish strategy. See Exhibit 2.3.

Monetary policy changes and trends should also be included in this part of your thesis.

Step 3: Relative Value in the Marketplace

Before you dig down into an individual security, you need to look at the broad market and the sector you

Exhibit 2.2

are trading and determine its relative value and trend. There are a multitude of methods and indicators that can be used to gauge market and sector health as well as expansion or contraction trends in both. This book would be another 200 pages if I were to detail all of them. As an investor, you must have a method that includes several different ways to measure both quantifiable objective data, as well as subjective views on news, relative data trends, and sentiment. The *Visual Guide to Financial Markets*, another installment in this series, may help.

A quick and dirty way to determine the overall "value" of the S&P 500 is to take a look at the price-to-earnings ratio (P/E) of the SPX itself, which has

By clicking on any of the items in the calendar, you can further analyze that data set. Here you can spot trends and gather details about expectations, revisions, and so on.

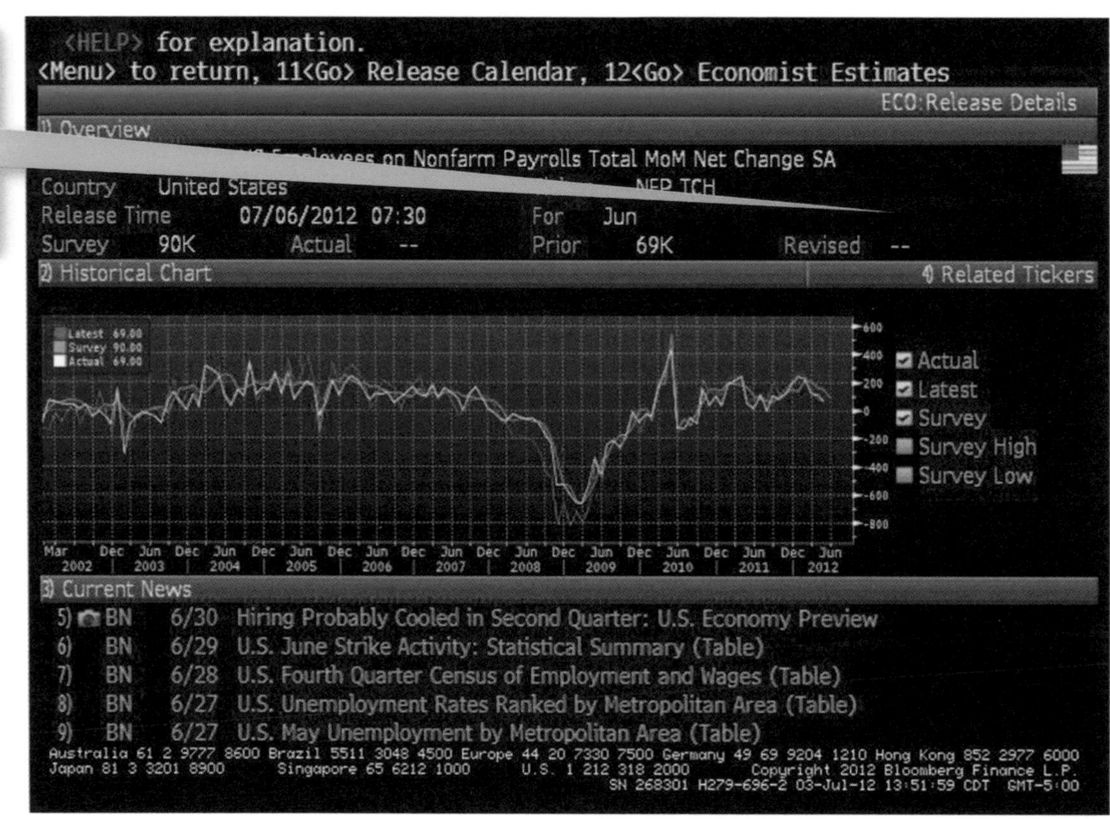

Exhibit 2.3

When this was taken, the trailing P/E of the SPX was about 13.2 and the forward P/E (BEST) is 12.566. Average range is between 13 and 18.

Exhibit 2.4

historically (from 1990 to 2010) ranged from about 13 times earnings on the low end to 19 on the high end. This simple data set can give you a quick look and give you something to compare to when you drill deeper into the stocks within. See Exhibit 2.4.

Using the trailing P/E as well as the forward will help you determine both current and future expected value. You can also gauge expectations and ensure that the market's expectations are in line with current earnings growth trends. This helps eliminate surprises. If the forward P/E is not too different from the trailing P/E, expectations for growth (or contraction) are minimal. That tells me that the bar is set low and there should be fewer negative surprises, which is good for bulls. If there is a wide gap between the two, the economy and corporate earnings growth had better be strong or there could be disappointments.

If you see a wide gap between the two numbers (Bloomberg can plot the average distance for you) and you believe that the economy is not extremely healthy, you should reduce your risk or rethink your bullish strategy.

If the P/E of the market is 13, which is on the low side historically, you can assume that stocks in general are relatively cheap based on what they are earning. You have to make sure that the future is looking brighter not dimmer for business.

Step 4: Analyze the Security's Fundamental and Technicals

This is the final step before you select a strategy; it may also be the most difficult because you have to get a bit more specific with your ideas and research. I recommend that you follow the same routine over and over again. That way it becomes habit and you'll know subconsciously if you're missing something.

Find Relative Value

The best way to determine if a stock (or anything for that matter) is cheap, expensive, or a good value is to compare it to something. Without comparison, precedent, or a price history, value can be hard to justify. If someone walked up to you wanting to sell a Rolex (assuming it was real) for $8,000, the first thing you might do is check on eBay to see what similar watches are selling for, maybe a call a watch dealer or two, then offer to pay less to the seller (or take his offer if the market tells you said watch is worth $13,000). This is a form of value discovery that should be done in the marketplace, but often it's not or it's completed hastily or incorrectly.

DO IT YOURSELF

Imagine you're reviewing a stock and notice that the stock is trading 30 percent lower than its average range over the past 10 years. The price seems cheap. But is it cheap for a reason? Are similar stocks in its sector also trading for a discount as well and if so, why? Is it a sector or industry that is maturing or dying out? Or is there real *value* there?

Cheap versus Value

When you are scanning the markets and come across a stock that looks extremely "cheap," take pause for just a second before firing off a bullish trade. Some stocks are cheap from both a price and/or a price-to-earnings perspective, but have little or no value because there is nothing of worth to unlock within the business and therefore minimal chance that the marketplace will ever perceive value in the future. In that case it's just cheap for a reason and shouldn't take up too much of your time. If you were to look at the options, they would most likely reflect a flat-to-negative skew going out in time and up the options chain.

Stocks that are valuable are experiencing what I would call a *temporary setback* in price, recognition, or sector rotation. Valuable stocks may also be at the center of a negative news frenzy that sends their shares abnormally lower. In any of these cases, as long as the news isn't bankruptcy or something that would have a long-lasting negative effect, value can be one of the bull's strongest allies and a catalyst for future price appreciation.

It's imperative to recognize the difference between both and the nuances that determine them. Be careful when you think a stock is "cheap." Are you referring to price and/or to its price relative to its earnings? Just because a stock is cheap both in price and even from a price to earnings standpoint, it is not always valuable; look deeper.

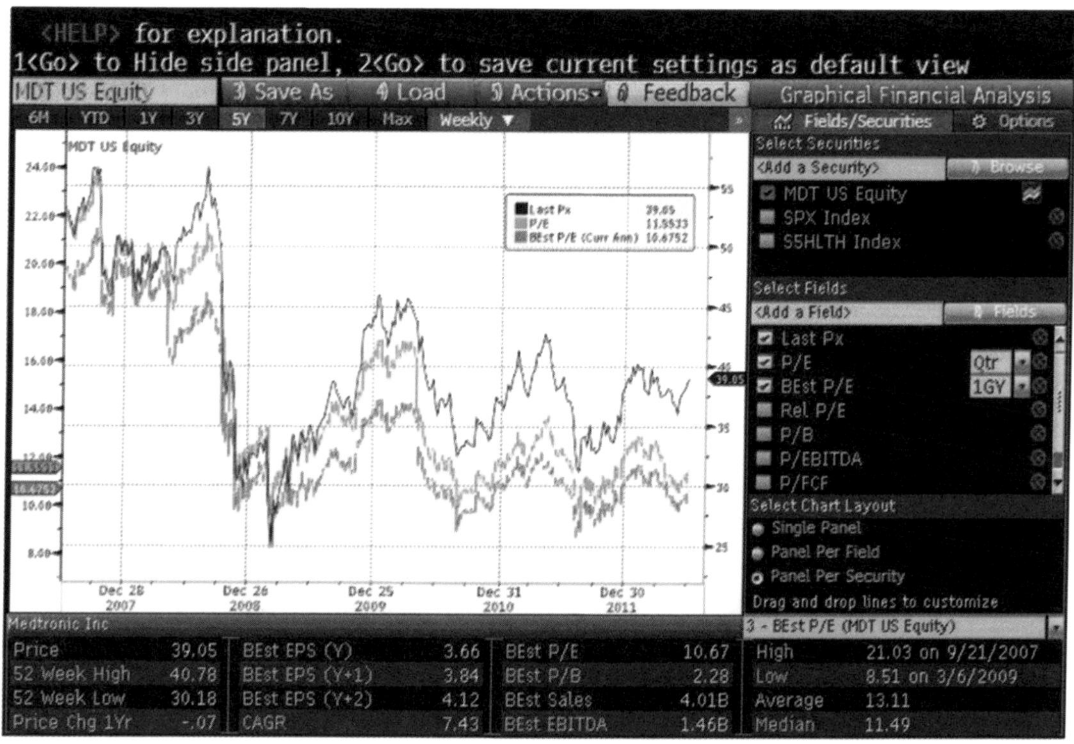

Exhibit 2.5

I'm sure that somewhere along the line, someone has told you that things are cheap for a reason, this applies to stocks as well! See Exhibit 2.5.

Other Guidelines for Finding Value

Many value investors also consider dividends, book value, cash flow, PEG, and debt-to-equity ratios.

There are many more considerations, and different investors put different weight in each, but here are some general guidelines that value investors follow for determining five fundamentals:

1. Price-to-earnings ratio
2. Price-to-book ratio

Smart Investor Tip!

Being more of a visual learner, I find it easier to see anomalies in a chart than when reading just a bank of numbers.

3. Debt equity
4. Free cash flow
5. PEG (price/earnings to growth) ratio

- **P/E ratio:** Traditionally, a value company will have a P/E ratio that should be in the bottom 10 percent of all equity securities. Nowadays, a P/E ratio should at the very least be well below the industry average.
- **P/B ratio:** This price-to-book ratio should be below 1.5 for the stock to be considered a value stock. It's the amount investors are willing to pay for a company's assets found by dividing the share price by net assets. Obviously in turbulent markets, share prices fluctuate, so keep that in mind when you're comparing P/B ratios.
- **Debt to equity:** Ideally, this figure should be less than one. With an overleveraged market, which caused the great financial crisis, finding a company with a debt-to-equity ratio below one is a rare thing.
- **Free cash flow:** FCF accounts for how much money a company has left after any capital investments. A negative cash flow isn't bad per se. It could just mean that the company's made some big investments. A huge FCF, however, might mean the company's not investing enough.
- **PEG ratio:** This ratio is the P/E ratio divided by the annual earnings per share growth. Like debt to equity, the ideal number for PEG is less than one. In general, though, a lower PEG compared to the industry average may indicate the company is a good value.

None of these guidelines should be considered in a vacuum. They each make up a piece of the whole picture, and that picture is just one of many you will have to draw up as part of your investment thesis.

Let's look at how to use other important guidelines to find value. See Exhibit 2.6.

You also need to know what you're looking for in each of these data. Some standard guidelines say that the P/E ratio of a "value" company should be at the lowest 10 percent of all equity securities. Another guideline is that the PEG should be less than one, as should the debt-to-equity ratio.

There are others who talk about share prices being no more than two thirds of the company's intrinsic worth, assets at two times current liabilities, and earnings growth of at least 7 percent a year over the past decade.

There are many parameters, and applying them all in today's market really narrows your possibilities of finding the perfect candidate. Sometimes you just have to choose a limited number of data points to analyze; if not, you may have a hard time making a trade, because rarely is everything perfect—especially after the revaluation of global stock markets during the financial crisis.

Starting with the fundamentals, I usually focus on a couple of key measurements, looking for any measurements that are out of "normal" relative ranges. Price to earnings (P/E) is obviously the most common and widely accepted form of value. You should look both at trailing and forward projections and put it in

These fundamental data can be accessed in numerical table form in the graphical financial analysis (GFA); they can also be plotted visually on the CA screen.

Exhibit 2.6

a chart. The GE screen is where I begin to plot my fundamental measurements.

Once you have gathered and analyzed the data, you should then plot several "trade trajectories." These different paths should be based on a combination of objective and subjective data that enables you to realistically plot the stock or option position over the life of the trade. You should run at least three different scenarios (assuming best, base, and worst) and make sure that you are prepared for each.

KEY POINT:

Stocks do not go straight up or down for extended periods of time. They generally move in one direction, stabilize, and regroup, and then continue on or correct in the other direction if the markets don't feel "good" about the value at that moment in time. As you are building your fundamental and technical thesis, you need to be aware of and find justification for abnormal unilateral stock price movements.

KEY POINT:

Trading and investing is about finding reasons *not* to invest. Think about walking into an Apple store that was packed with people, then getting home and realizing you alone have more than 10 Apple products. You then turn on Bloomberg or CNBC and hear the pundits pumping Apple stock, calling for it to double in a year's time. Your son walks in the door and tells you that his school just adopted the iPad to replace all paper books . . . and then your broker calls you.

The investor would probably be thinking that he should sell the house and buy Apple; he at the very least needs a system to quantify and measure risk. This sort of irrational exuberance occurs every day for buyers and sellers alike. That is why it's paramount to put everything in perspective.

To form these trajectories, you use a combination of the fundamental and technical data that you have gathered, coupled with forward price, time, and volatility considerations for your selected strategy.

Rating/Grading System

I developed a simple grading system that can be used when evaluating a specific strategy to find its relative risk. Once you have developed your different hypotheses on the broad market down to the stock, you can use this system to uncover issues and compare and contrast the strategies you are thinking of utilizing.

Every trade starts with a hypothetical "A." From there, it's all about working your way lower on the grading system until you find a reason(s) to reduce risk or not to trade it at all.

Top-Down Approach

As you go through the following list, you will gradually uncover the "flaws" or risks in your trade. As you uncover more flaws in your thesis or the perceived strength of the trade, you should adjust risk or strategy specifics accordingly.

You can use trade simulation tools like the OSA screen that enable you to run hypothetical scenarios. Remember that no matter how good a trade looks, you shouldn't be investing more than 10 to 15 percent of your portfolio in any one position; so be as strict as possible when reducing your allocation using this system.

1. **What direction is the market in (sentiment) and is it in line with your trade?**

   If your trade's overall direction is in stark contrast to the overall trend, then reduce one grade level. This rule also applies to trades that are betting against analyst consensus; so if you are buying QCOM when the analysts are saying it's a sell, you should reduce grade one level, even if the market is generally bullish.

   Neutral trades (straddles, strangles, butterflies, condors, etc.) do not apply here, but be sure to compare the costs/breakevens of these trades to the observed volatility of the underlying security.

   A–C good for bullish trades; D–F is preferred if you are bearish.

2. **Fundamentals**
   a. Knowledge of the stock? Do you have a good basic knowledge of what the company does and its sector?
   b. Is there sufficient volume (750k traded per day minimum)?
   c. Is the overall business direction in line with your trade?
   d. Would you consider this stock to be in the top 20% of its sector?

   If the answers to any of the above questions are not in line with the direction of your trade, reduce grade one level for each.

3. **Charts:** Do all the criteria fit for your strategy? Here you will analyze patterns, trends, and indicators.

a. Overall trend of the stock (6 months plus)
   i. Is the overall trend neutral or in line with your strategy?
b. Current trend (past 30 days)
   i. Is the stock overextended (would you be buying or selling after a run)?
   ii. Is the stock overbought or oversold (Bollinger bands)?
   iii. Are the major moving averages (20-, 50-, 200-day) in a favorable position for your strategy? (Are they below the share price for bullish trades, above for bearish, etc.?)
c. Is volume favoring your desired trend?
d. Does MACD have fresh crosses in the direction of trade (within three bars) and are stocastics showing an overextension or new strong trend?

For each of the chart criteria that are not met, reduce grade one level.

4. **Options:** Examine the nuances of the option chains, volatility, and more.
   a. Does there look to be sufficient volume in options?
      i. If there are less than 50 contracts in open interest and the option has been listed for at least a week, reduce.
      ii. If the stock trades more than 750k shares per day, but options volume is less than 1,000, reduce.
   b. Are the bid-ask spreads normal? (More than $0.20 to $0.30 on average is abnormal, but for stocks over $200 expect $0.20 to $0.30.)
      i. If a stock is extra volatile, spreads may be wider—this is still a detriment.
   c. Does the relative implied volatility of the options fit your strategy?
      i. Relatively low if you are a net buyer, high if you are a net seller.
      ii. Compare different months to find the best one to trade. (This will be more strategy-specific.) If you are forced to trade a month that is not favorable, reduce.
      iii. Use skew to examine volatility.

   For each of the option criteria that are not met, reduce grade one level.
5. **Trade-specific criteria:** Options and other variables.

   This part of the list is specific to each strategy. I give you a couple of examples here, but you are essentially looking for flaws or characteristics of the options and their positions relative to the stock that add risk to your trade.
   a. When selling an out-of-the-money vertical spread, be sure that your short strike is at least one standard deviation away from the stock for the expiration that you are trading. This will give you a statistical edge, but doesn't have to reduce your grade necessarily.
      i. To find what a one standard deviation move would be over the life of the trade, use the HRH or GV screen and input the asset and end date of the trade. Remember

Exhibit 2.7

that one standard deviation is about 70 percent. See Exhibit 2.7.

b. Make sure that the vertical spread you are selling will yield at least 12 to 15 percent minimum profit.

   i. ***Don't do trade if not yielding at least 10 percent.**

If any of the strategy criteria does not fit—reduce grade.

6. **Timing:** The actual point at which you enter your trade can have technical, fundamental, and even seasonal risks.

   a. Has the stock moved more than its average true range (ATR) in your desired direction that day?

b. If trading commodities, are you buying in a historically bad season?
c. Are you executing your trade just ahead of a major market event?
   i. Neutral trades are okay here.
d. Does the entry make sense from a chart perspective? Are the technicals favoring another level?
e. How is your mental state? Are you frustrated, angry, in a rush, drinking (don't laugh, it happens)?

For each of the timing criteria that are not met, reduce grade one level.

Grade-Level Risk Adjustments

- Once a trade has been assigned a grade level, you now have an objective means of risk control, the most basic of which is portfolio allocation and strategy selection. **A-rated trade** is risk up to 10 percent or more of your total portfolio.
  - Okay to use riskier strategies (risk reversal, synthetic, double vertical spread, etc.).
  - Have high flexibility in losses and trades gone wrong for recovery.
- **B-rated trade:** Risk between 5 percent and 9 percent of account, but use more caution.
  - Okay to use basic verticals and limited risk, higher probability trades.
  - Might use a split strike risk reversal.
  - Try to sell vertical spreads further—increases probability.
- **C-rated trade:** Risk between 2 percent and 5 percent of account, use high caution and only low risk, high probability trades (out-of-the-money verticals).
  - Exit quicker than usual.
- **D-rated trade:** Risk less than 2 percent of your total portfolio.
  - This trade is more high risk or what we call a *flier*. Trades with lower probability can generate a profit, but probability will generally be less because there are more than a couple of issues.
  - You don't want to execute too many of these in succession; it's better to "pepper" them in between better-rated trades.
  - Try to use statistically advantaged strategy to help offset the reduced probability of success and other risks.
  - Use only if you have very strong hunch or have had great past success!
- **F-rated trade:** Don't do it if at all possible.
  - If you feel that you must make the trade, keep allocation extremely low and take profits quickly.
  - It is advisable to only execute this type of trade after a string of winners or a period of high returns so that a loss won't have a compounding effect or feel as bad psychologically.
  - Do not execute these types of trades if you are in a bad mental state or trying to fight your way back from a deficit in your account.

Smart Investor Tip!

When you are giving your trade a final grade and you are feeling rather confident in the trade, it's okay to give yourself a mulligan on one or two of the criteria, but that's it!

Smart Investor Tip!

If a stock pays no dividends and interest rates are stable or increasing, call prices should always be more expensive than put prices with the same strike and expiration, when you remove any intrinsic (parity) value from the comparison.

Forward Pricing

The balance in price between calls and puts is a tug of war between interest and dividends (sometimes other factors can play a role as well). Both can have a profound effect on options prices especially the farther out in time you go. You will learn that call and put prices are related and one technique to find the put-call parity or price difference between the same strike call and put would be to use the forward value of a stock or ETF at a certain point in the future.

To find the specific forward or future value of a stock or ETF you must first find the appropriate risk-free interest rate for the time to expiry you are trying to price (forward date) and then simply subtract from that the dividends that would be paid up until that date as the final step.

Let's look at the forces that determine a stock's forward price.

Interest rates increase the forward price of a security. In a rising interest rate environment, you may notice favorable price action in your long calls.

Typically, treasuries with the corresponding expiration date are used to find this "risk-free" rate for the term of the trade. See Exhibit 2.8.

Dividends affect forward price in a negative way.

Remember that call owners do not receive dividends and put owners don't have to pay them. Option prices are simply adjusted for upcoming dividends until their expiration date. They can also be adjusted on the fly for unexpected special dividends.

For each dividend that is paid, the forward price (of the stock) drops by that amount, and since call prices are reduced for dividends, call prices on high dividend-paying stocks will be less than a comparable nondividend-paying stock.

Generally speaking, call options are more expensive in stocks without dividends and can borrow easily because of interest rates. This also means that all calls have positive rho or are positively correlated to the changes in interest rates. We discuss rho in the next chapter.

The next thing you want to find is the **Cost of Carry**, or how much it costs to take an investment position, and hold for your specified time frame. Find the amount of interest that would be collected based on the current stock price and appropriate risk-free interest rate for the time to expiry (forward date). Take that dollar amount and the dividends that would be paid up until that date. What you're left with is the **Cost of Carry.** (It's important to note that this figure can be negative.)

If you add the **Cost of Carry** to the current stock price, you now have a **Forward Price**!

If you don't want to do the math, the NOVM screen shows you synthetic forwards at a glance using the treasury yield curve to forecast future rate changes. All of this can change with the ebbs and flows of global monetary policy changes. See Exhibit 2.9.

Let's assume that IBM stock is trading for $200 and we are examining the January 2013 200-strike call and 200-strike put. I am going to give you two ways to look

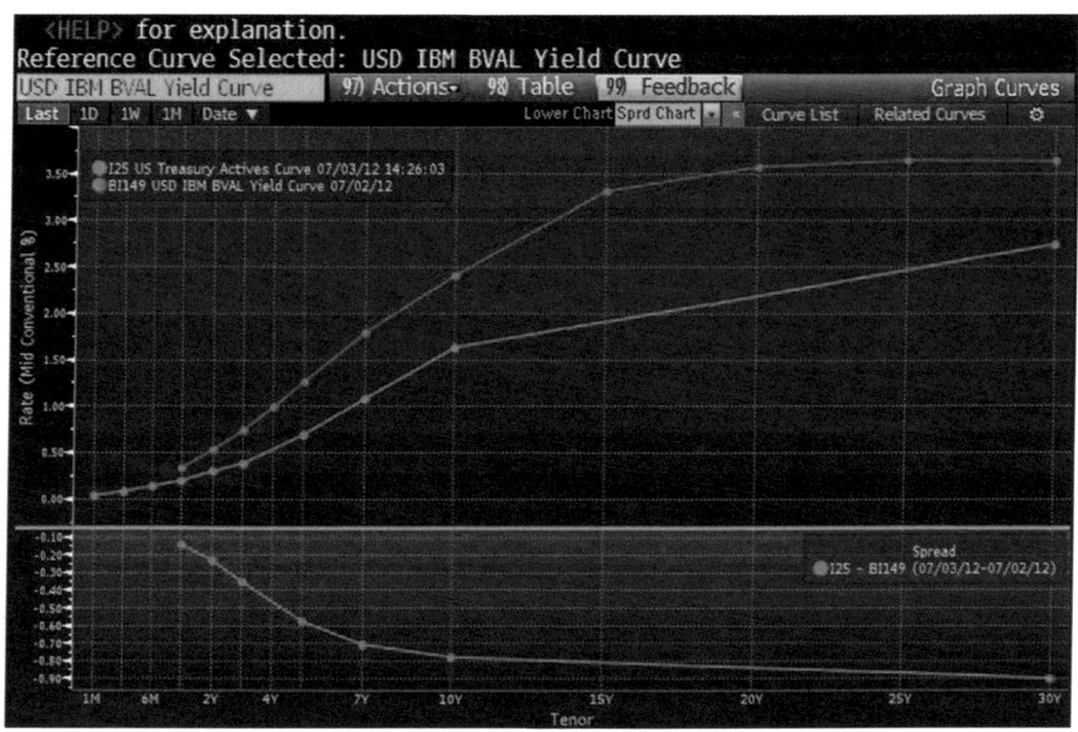

Exhibit 2.8

at the relationship between the stock and these options. First, we have to be sure that we are using the correct rate (this can vary from person to person).

Assume for this example that January LEAPS options expire exactly 469 days from today. The current yield on the 12-month treasury is 0.35 percent.

Now divide 469 (days until expiration) by 365 (days in a year) = 1.28 (our interest multiplier).

When finding our forward price, we multiply the stock price of IBM by the interest we *would* have received if we had invested that money in a risk-free asset.

KEY POINT:

Some futures contracts (like crude oil) and other securities may have unique carry costs that can influence future prices. Check the contract specifications and with the exchange that they are traded on to verify these costs.

KEY POINT:

Forward price, basis, put-call parity, and synthetics are all interconnected. The forward price allows the trader to come up with a future value of an asset, while the basis or carry cost tells the trader what it will cost (debit or credit) to hold that position for a specific period of time. Put-call parity is the relationship that the call, put, stock, and carry costs all have with one another. And synthetics allow the trader to enter into the most profitable trade or morph a real position into a synthetic position to gain advantage.

<HELP> for explanation. P142 EquityNOVM

Enter all values and press <GO>

1) User Settings 2) Rate Source 3) Export to Excel 4) Refresh Option Valuation Matrix

Underlying IBM US Equity IBM | Trade 11/17/11 10:54

Und. Price 188.48 USD | Direction Buy Call | Expiry 12/16/11 Days 29

Strike 190.00 USD | Exercise American

Calculations:

X-Axis Maturity | Output (1) Option Price | Output (2) Volatility

Y-Axis Moneyness | Output (3) Delta

Y-Axis: Moneyness	X-Axis: Maturity	1M	3M	6M	9M	1Y	2Y
	Option Price	20.02	23.04	26.23	28.60	30.77	37.69
	Volatility	32.964%	31.217%	30.347%	29.538%	29.304%	29.258%
90.00%	Delta	87.70%	77.72%	72.59%	70.33%	68.93%	66.76%
	Option Price	11.88	15.77	19.52	22.20	24.63	32.14
	Volatility	28.454%	28.288%	28.226%	27.787%	27.810%	28.184%
95.00%	Delta	74.85%	67.06%	63.82%	62.69%	62.05%	61.64%
	Option Price	5.44	9.68	13.69	16.57	19.18	27.09
	Volatility	25.083%	25.742%	26.246%	26.168%	26.457%	27.194%
100.00%	Delta	51.55%	52.75%	53.42%	53.96%	54.50%	56.23%
	Option Price	1.55	5.14	8.94	11.80	14.45	22.34
	Volatility	21.960%	23.619%	24.490%	24.686%	25.172%	26.085%
105.00%	Delta	23.04%	36.27%	41.92%	44.56%	46.44%	50.62%
	Option Price	0.2720	2.31	5.42	8.00	10.52	18.45
	Volatility	20.643%	21.987%	23.072%	23.401%	24.033%	25.362%
110.00%	Delta	5.80%	20.82%	30.32%	34.96%	38.26%	45.06%
	Option Price	0.0755	0.8837	3.06	5.17	7.39	15.10
	Volatility	22.625%	20.907%	22.004%	22.369%	23.029%	24.746%
115.00%	Delta	1.73%	9.93%	20.19%	25.97%	30.31%	39.62%

Exhibit 2.9

So that is $200 (stock price) * .0035 (annual rate) * 1.28 (interest multiplier) = $0.90.

This interest will *raise* the forward price of IBM to $200.90.

We are not finished. Now we have to subtract any dividends, as that would lower the forward price of the stock.

Let's say that IBM has several dividends scheduled between September 2011 and January 2013 expiration: 11/11: $0.55, 2/12: $0.55, 5/12: $0.59, 8/12: $0.59, 11/12: $0.59. That is a grand total of $2.87.

If I subtract the total dividends ($2.87) from $200.90, I get $198.03, which would be the expected forward price for IBM on January 2013 expiration. See Exhibit 2.10.

Finding the forward price also tells me that if IBM is trading at $200, the January 2013 200 puts (currently

IBM US Equity | 90) Actions | 91) Settings | 92) Refresh | Page 6/6 | Option Horizon Analysis

INTL BUSINESS MACHINES CORP | Expiry 18-JAN-2014

Valuation Date: 07/06/2012 | 560 Days | Rate 0.515% | Underlying 200.00s | Center 200.00

Horizon Date: 01/18/2013 | 196 Days Later | Rate 0.520% | Underlying 200.00s | Delta/IVol

	Calls			Puts			Calls			Puts		
Pricing	Close Price			Close Price			Vol Shift +0			Vol Shift +0		
Strike	Price	Delta	IVol %	Price	Delta	IVol %	Price	Change	Chng %	Price	Change	Chng %
160	39.50	N.A.	N.A.	11.65	-23.18	29.27		N.A.	N.A.	7.256	-4.394	-37.71
165	39.49	80.23	21.75	12.50	-25.37	28.00	37.435	-2.055	-5.20	8.026	-4.474	-35.80
170	35.40	77.20	20.91	14.00	-28.00	27.46	33.18	-2.22	-6.27	9.325	-4.675	-33.40
175	29.00	76.99	16.85	18.00	-31.30	29.68	27.291	-1.709	-5.89	12.629	-5.371	-29.84
180	29.80	68.77	21.84	19.00	-33.91	28.20	26.815	-2.985	-10.02	13.666	-5.334	-28.07
185	26.60	64.98	21.41	21.05	-36.82	27.79	23.466	-3.134	-11.78	15.587	-5.463	-25.95
190	24.00	60.97	21.43	22.50	-39.88	26.60	20.678	-3.322	-13.84	17.086	-5.414	-24.06
195	20.25	56.89	20.03	24.50	-43.08	25.86	17.045	-3.205	-15.83	19.089	-5.411	-22.08
200	18.40	52.81	20.43	26.15	-46.57	24.63	15.034	-3.366	-18.29	20.875	-5.275	-20.17
205	15.85	48.57	19.89	28.70	-50.01	24.18	12.543	-3.307	-20.87	23.46	-5.24	-18.26
210	13.80	44.43	19.67	34.15	-51.79	26.55	10.541	-3.259	-23.62	28.45	-5.70	-16.69
215	11.93	40.37	19.44	34.35	-56.86	23.37	8.766	-3.164	-26.52	29.288	-5.062	-14.74
220	10.05	36.21	19.00	45.80	-53.82	31.72	7.065	-2.985	-29.70	39.142	-6.658	-14.54
225	8.70	32.56	18.95				5.848	-2.852	-32.78			
230	7.35	28.95	18.71	47.75	-62.70	26.33	4.698	-2.652	-36.09	42.331	-5.419	-11.35

Exhibit 2.10

at the money) should be trading about \$1.97 over the 200 calls, because the 200 puts have \$1.97 more value based on the forward pricing calculations. (Current price of \$200 – forward price of \$198.03 = \$1.97.)

This is a basic example of put-call parity. The above method is a bit more quick and dirty as opposed to using the NOVM screen and it gets your mind working to understand the relationships.

This is an example where the dividends overtake interest rates to bring the forward price lower and make the puts more expensive than the calls.

Put-Call Parity

You can actually know for certain what the value of the call is if we know what the put is trading for and

> DEFINITION:
>
> **The VIX index value**
>
> **is derived from an amalgam of the first two months of options on the SPX. It is quoted in percentage points and is intended to represent the expected annualized movement in the S&P 500 index over the next 30-day period. This means that if the VIX is 20, the expected annualized change over the next 30 days is 20 percent.**

DO IT YOURSELF

Without using a forward price calculator, try and find the forward price for GOOG (Google stock) going out about a year. See if the options are telling you that your math is correct. Here's a tip: Google doesn't pay a dividend, so the calls should be more expensive.

Smart Investor Tip!

Put-call parity is the balance that exists between the prices of calls and puts. It is the fundamental law that you *must* understand before trading your first option or even attempting to comprehend the Greeks.

KEY POINT:

The law of put-call parity tells us that if a stock is trading for *X* and the call is trading for *Y*, the put with the same strike and expiration must be trading for *Z*, if put-call parity is holding.

the other way around. Many professionals in the early days used this to their advantage to find markets that were "out of line." These days, finding mispriced options is much more difficult, especially with the advent of computerized trading and black box systems that scan the market looking for possible arbitrage opportunities between calls and puts or even spreads.

You often hear traders say calls are puts and puts are calls, meaning that they are completely interchangeable and with a little help can morph into one or the other. There are ways to combine calls, puts, and stock to create entirely new risk characteristics. You can augment your call position to imitate a put position and vice versa; this procedure of combining an option with stock is known as *creating a synthetic*, which I discuss shortly.

Basically if we know the price of two, we can figure out the third variable. If there is a violation in this equation, then either arbitrage exists or there is an imbalance or abnormality in the underlying security. It could also mean that the options are not basing themselves on the security that you think they are. This is the case with VIX options; they are based on VIX futures, not the cash index they are listed on.

See Exhibit 2.11.

In a hard-to-borrow stock the puts are bought and the calls are sold to create synthetic short position as a substitute for short stock. Sometimes when this risk reversal (sell call, buy put, same month, and strike) is done on an extreme scale it forces put prices through the roof.

It gets worse if market makers, who have to hedge their long positions, not only stop collecting their "short stock rebate," but begin paying to be short stock when they would normally collect interest. This adds to the price of the puts. When puts become more expensive than their same-strike calls and there is no dividend to account for this deficit, put-call parity does not hold and certain trades like buying puts may be disadvantaged.

The most important thing to remember is that there is no real arbitrage here, because traders who sell puts, buy calls, and sell stock (called a reversal) to try to capture this excess may be *unable* to short the stock as a hedge and will then be exposed. Amateurs and pros alike sometimes make this mistake. They do the reversal but then get "bought in" when their broker forces them to buy back the shares at any price. The brokers will often do it for you (sometimes overnight) and leave you twisting in the wind with a synthetic long position just as the stock is tanking . . . ouch!

In the synthetics section of this chapter, you learn how we can create a synthetic long or short stock position using options. Usually there are only minor differences in the cost of creating a synthetic versus just going out and buying the stock (other than commissions of course). The reason for this is put-call parity, which is the natural three-sided relationship between a call and put and the underlying instrument.

Here are the three characteristics that are referred to as *put-call parity*:

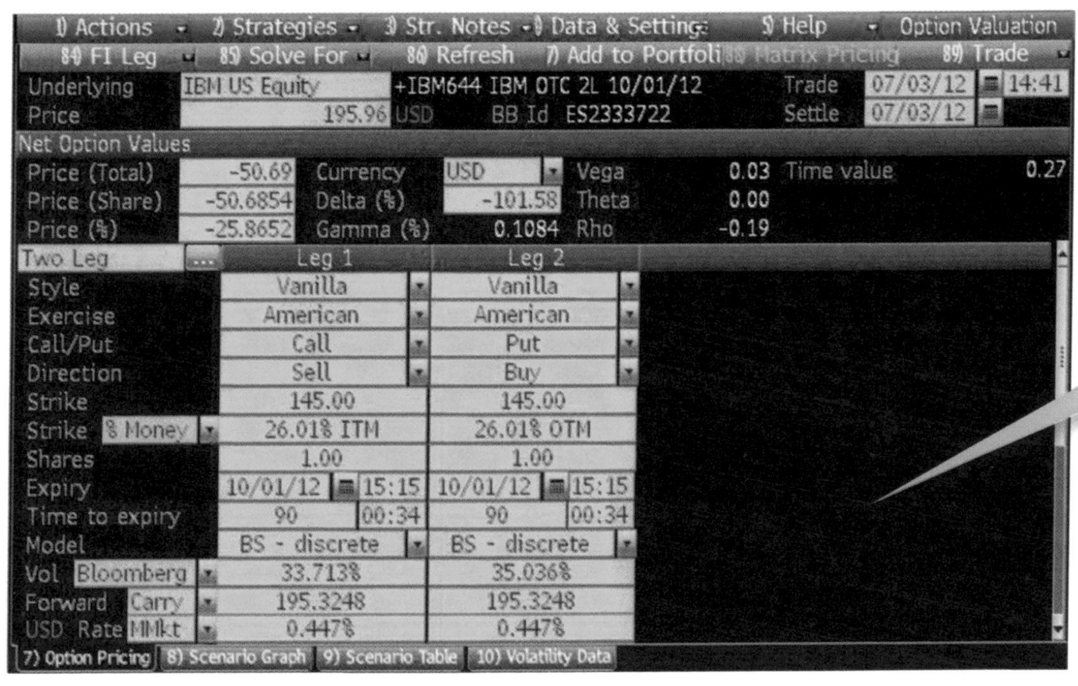

Exhibit 2.11

1. Underlying price = call price – put price + exercise price.
2. Put price = call price – underlying price + exercise price.
3. Call price = put price + underlying price – exercise price.

If the time value for the put is different than the call, there will be a difference in the synthetic position compared to a real stock position, making the synthetic either too cheap or too expensive.

By the way, if these concepts make absolutely no sense to you, don't worry. Understanding put-call parity and synthetics in gross detail is not a prerequisite to making money with options. Also keep in mind that in today's highly technological and computer-driven marketplace, you will be hard-pressed to find a market that is out of balance without reason. Basically, it is extremely difficult to find risk-free arbitrage as a retail trader. So if you use some of the techniques that I'm about to teach you and find that the put or call seem mispriced, there is probably a reason for it. Don't go firing off trades thinking that you're capturing risk-free arbitrage, because it's probably not true. Several factors, like a changing interest rate environment, a stock that is hard to borrow (or is getting even harder to borrow), changing dividend rates, or other reasons can throw put and call parity (or what you think it should be) out of balance.

The importance of the put-call parity, however, is twofold. Finding this parity out of balance could mean there's something else going on that might affect what strategy you choose. Understanding this parity is essential before understanding Greeks.

The good news is that technology is also on your side. Companies like Bloomberg do all they can to ensure the integrity and timeliness of their data.

Smart Investor Tip!

If put-call parity does not hold then there is an extenuating circumstance causing this abnormality. It is up to you to find it and decide if it changes your original thesis, but it doesn't have to completely deter you from making the trade.

Synthetics

Synthetics enable you to adapt one position into a completely different— sometimes opposite—position by adding another option or stock. Synthetics can transform option spreads as well. It is even more useful when you are trying to find the most efficient way to express a bias. Because there are different variables in every stock and its options there may be certain price risk or tax advantages when a trade is done in a certain way.

In the modern world, markets are extremely efficient, but that doesn't mean that a certain arbitrage doesn't exist for you to take advantage of. Let's examine the rules and then look at an example.

Following are the six basic synthetic positions. They show you how a combination of calls, puts, and stock can be assembled with one or more of each to create a completely different strategy and risk profile. The synthetic should behave almost identical to the actual position it synthesizes. It's just a way to substitute risk. Sometimes certain transactions can be cheaper or more expensive than others, which is why a professional looks at the most efficient way to take risk.

The six synthetics are:

1. Long call = 1 long put and 100 shares long stock.
2. Long put = 1 long call and 100 shares short stock.
3. Short call = 1 short put and 100 shares short stock.
4. Short put = 1 short call and 100 shares long stock.
5. Long stock = 1 long call and 1 short put (same strike).
6. Short stock =1 long put and 1 short call (same strike).

The synthetic (options) will always have the same expiration month and strike price. Remember that when you complete a synthetic, you have made the trade, without having to actually place another order. So if I were to buy a call and sell stock, I have synthetically bought a put, which doesn't mean that I will actually have a long put in my account.

Example of a Synthetic Position

If I wanted to have the same risk as being short stock, I could buy a put and sell a call with the same month and strike. By doing this, I create an identical risk position to short stock.

Now why would anyone want to have the same risk as short stock? Well, as options traders, we want to buy what is cheap and sell what is expensive.

If you were to create a September 145 short stock synthetic position by purchasing a 145 put and selling a 145 call for a $0.55 credit, it would be essentially the same taking a short position in the stock at $145.55, which would also be your profit and loss (P&L) breakeven in the underlying stock.

There are interest and dividend considerations to think about when creating synthetics. Remember that call owners are *not* entitled to the dividend and interest rates can change, which may affect your synthetic position's value. Exhibit 2.12 proves that the synthetic market above the breakeven, and the look of the risk graph are identical to being short the stock at $145.55.

Again, the term *synthetics* relates to combining options with options or options with stock to create an entirely different position or risk profile altogether. Traders use synthetics for many reasons; some look for arbitrage or find a better or cheaper way to hedge themselves. The more you trade options, the more you begin to notice the relationships that exist between them and the stocks that they are associated with. For the beginner, it is paramount that you understand what you are creating when you are combining different strategies. There are many strategies and relationships that may suit the situation better. Keep your eyes open.

A professional wants to find the cheapest things to buy and the most expensive things to sell; therefore, instead of just buying a put, the trader may opt to buy the call and sell the stock because it will him cost less over time.

Obviously, finding arbitrage situations or severe imbalances in that marketplace are much harder to come by these days. However, the retail trader should understand these relationships and synthetics as it pertains to risk.

Smart Investor Tip!

If you are *buying* an option, the synthetic will always come out to *buying* the other option. In other words, if you are long a put and create the synthetic by buying stock against, you are *long* a call. If you are selling an option, the synthetic will always come out to *selling* the other option.

Synthetic Twist

Let's assume that IBM stock is trading at $208.50, the January 210 call is trading for $14.90 and the January 210 put is trading for $15.95. You would think that if you buy stock at $208.50, and create a short stock synthetic @ 210 for a $1.05 debit, you have a "guaranteed" winner on your hands (you'd make $1.50 on the synthetic trade and you only paid out $1.05).

Look closer: In the earlier example you bought the stock at $208.50, sold it synthetically at $210, and had to pay $1.05 to do so. The short synthetic cost money, but there was $2 of parity (profit in this case) built in. This means that this trade would guarantee the trader a credit of 45 cents at expiration, with no directional risk in the stock. Or would it?

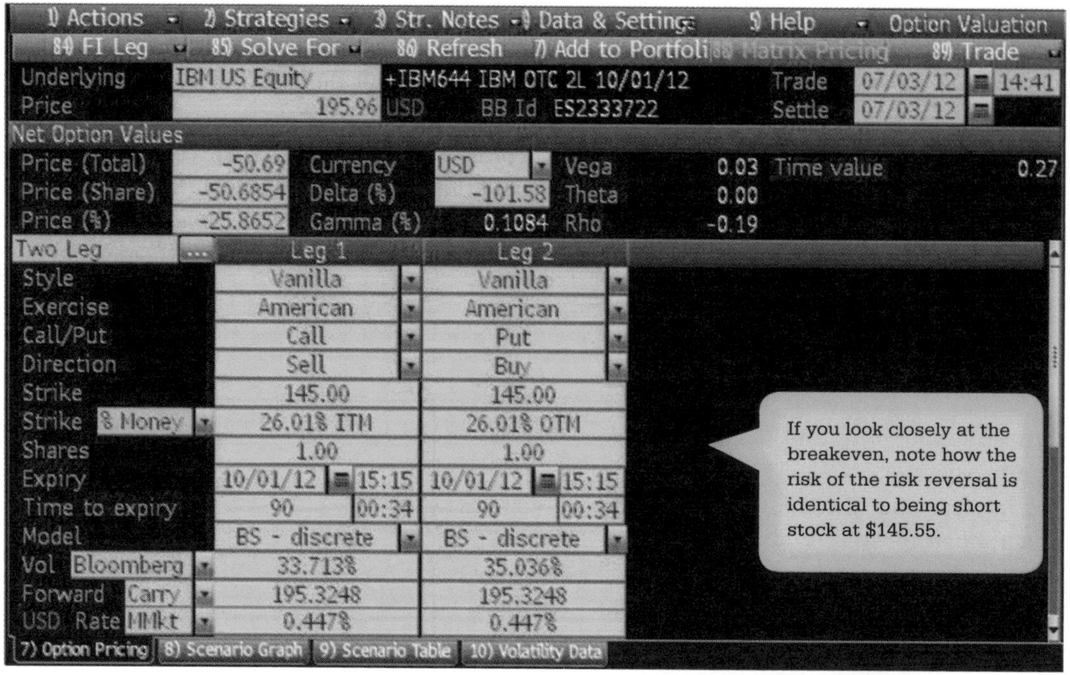

1) Actions 2) Strategies 3) Str. Notes 4) Data & Settings 5) Help Option Valuation

84) FI Leg 85) Solve For 86) Refresh 7) Add to Portfolio 88) Matrix Pricing 89) Trade

Underlying	IBM US Equity	+IBM644 IBM OTC 2L 10/01/12	Trade	07/03/12	14:41
Price	195.96 USD	BB Id ES2333722	Settle	07/03/12	

Net Option Values

Price (Total)	-50.69	Currency	USD	Vega	0.03	Time value	0.27
Price (Share)	-50.6854	Delta (%)	-101.58	Theta	0.00		
Price (%)	-25.8652	Gamma (%)	0.1084	Rho	-0.19		

Two Leg	Leg 1	Leg 2
Style	Vanilla	Vanilla
Exercise	American	American
Call/Put	Call	Put
Direction	Sell	Buy
Strike	145.00	145.00
Strike % Money	26.01% ITM	26.01% OTM
Shares	1.00	1.00
Expiry	10/01/12 15:15	10/01/12 15:15
Time to expiry	90 00:34	90 00:34
Model	BS - discrete	BS - discrete
Vol Bloomberg	33.713%	35.036%
Forward Carry	195.3248	195.3248
USD Rate MMkt	0.447%	0.447%

7) Option Pricing 8) Scenario Graph 9) Scenario Table 10) Volatility Data

If you look closely at the breakeven, note how the risk of the risk reversal is identical to being short stock at $145.55.

Exhibit 2.12

At first glance it seems all good, but what if interest rates were 3 percent and January expiration is 600 days away . . . still a good deal?

There are interest considerations and risk here; suppose the stock was bought on margin. What if the trader has to pay interest on his long stock position? The cost of the interest paid on the long stock position may equal or exceed the $0.45 credit received.

Dividends would *help* this position.

If something seems too good to be true, it probably is and rarely does a retail trader find "free money." The reality is that arbitrage opportunities like this rarely surface for anyone for more than a millisecond, given the speed at which the markets move and the technology driving them. Prevailing interest rates determine call and put prices and the subsequent credits and debits in trades like this. I discuss this more in the section on put-call parity.

For most of you, being aware of these relationships and having fun with them is about the extent of how you will use them in the real world. I wouldn't be out there searching for put-call parity discrepancies and out-of-balance synthetic markets.

But they are useful in helping you understand the relationships between options, and between options and stocks, and in seeing where risk lies.

Risk in Synthetics

Notice the shape of the risk graphs below and the maximum loss when we compare the purchase of 100 shares of IBM stock and the purchase of the 200 put. Both are exactly the same when it comes to risk, with the maximum loss being right around $*** and the upside being unlimited. (There may a slight difference in P&L because the bid ask spreads can have an effect.) Typically the call would be a bit more expensive than the put, unless there was a dividend. This is addressed in the put-call parity section. But other than the slight difference in interest, the synthetic is proven. You can and should try this on your own for all of the synthetics. See Exhibits 2.13 and 2.14.

Visualizing Synthetics

Risk graphs are an excellent way to visualize risk and to find and prove the synthetics discussed in this chapter.

A call's risk profile is quite simple: the most you can lose is the premium you pay for it, period. No matter how low the stock plummets, your risk is completely capped at the premium paid. However, the most you can make with a rise in the stock is theoretically unlimited, because the stock, in theory, can rise to infinity. See Exhibit 2.15.

A put's risk profile is also similar, just in the opposite direction and with one catch—that a stock can only fall to zero. When you buy a put, your risk is limited to the premium paid.

If you sell a put, your risk is also limited to the stock going to zero. Your profit is also limited to the premium (credit) you received. So if you sold a 100 strike put for $4, the most you can make is $4 (or $400, as contracts are bundles of 100)—and only if the stock goes to zero. The short put's P&L graph is always flat to the right of the strike price then falls at a 45-degree angle to the left, showing losses as the stock falls. Use risk graphs to help you understand and experiment with synthetics and risk. See Exhibit 2.16.

See the graphical representation of the long stock synthetics. This works the same for the short stock synthetic, where the short call adds the unlimited upside risk that the long put does *not* have, thus creating synthetic short stock. See Exhibit 2.17.

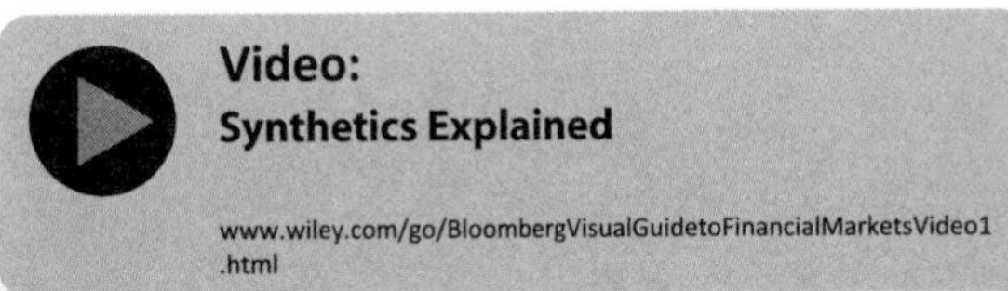

Smart Investor Tip!

To create a short stock synthetic, you're buying a put and selling a call of the same strike price. Although it is true that when you sell an option, you receive a credit, not all short synthetics are done for a credit.

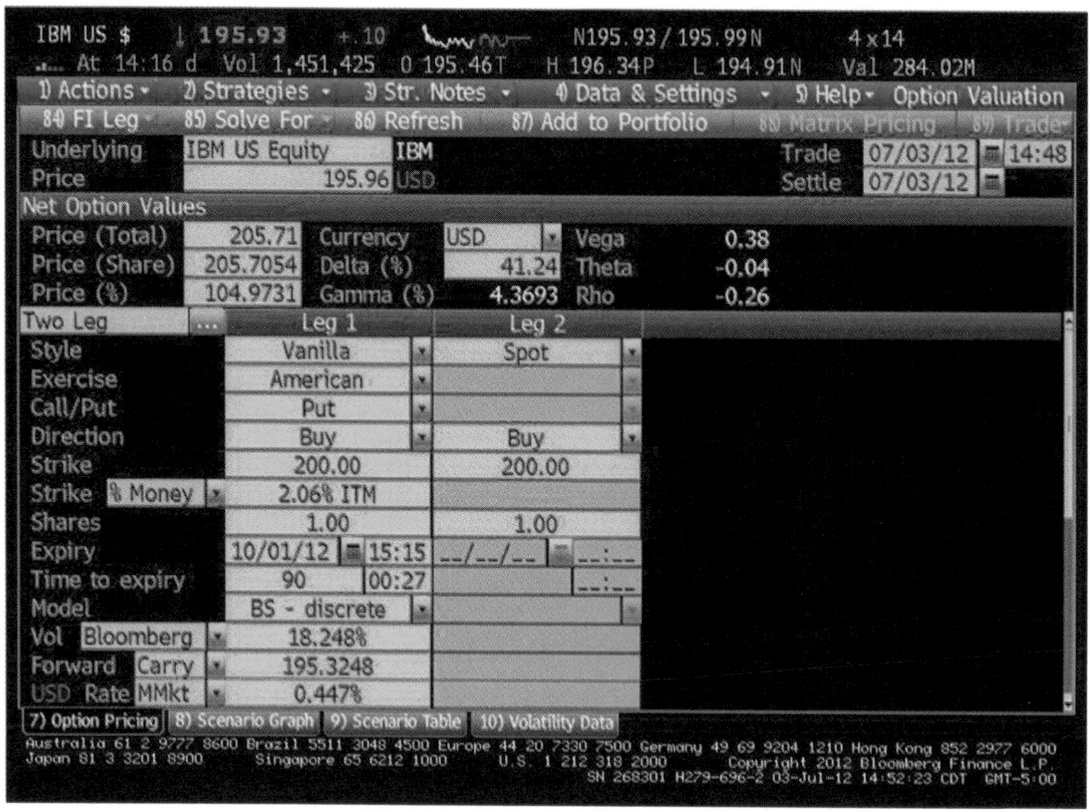
IBM US $ ↓195.93 +.10 N195.93/195.99N 4x14
At 14:16 d Vol 1,451,425 O 195.46T H 196.34P L 194.91N Val 284.02M
1) Actions 2) Strategies 3) Str. Notes 4) Data & Settings 5) Help Option Valuation
84) FI Leg 85) Solve For 86) Refresh 87) Add to Portfolio 88) Matrix Pricing 89) Trade
Underlying IBM US Equity IBM
Price 195.96 USD
Trade 07/03/12 14:48
Settle 07/03/12
Net Option Values
Price (Total) 205.71 Currency USD Vega 0.38
Price (Share) 205.7054 Delta (%) 41.24 Theta -0.04
Price (%) 104.9731 Gamma (%) 4.3693 Rho -0.26
Two Leg Leg 1 Leg 2
Style Vanilla Spot
Exercise American
Call/Put Put
Direction Buy Buy
Strike 200.00 200.00
Strike % Money 2.06% ITM
Shares 1.00 1.00
Expiry 10/01/12 15:15
Time to expiry 90 00:27
Model BS - discrete
Vol Bloomberg 18.248%
Forward Carry 195.3248
USD Rate MMkt 0.447%
7) Option Pricing 8) Scenario Graph 9) Scenario Table 10) Volatility Data
Australia 61 2 9777 8600 Brazil 5511 3048 4500 Europe 44 20 7330 7500 Germany 49 69 9204 1210 Hong Kong 852 2977 6000
Japan 81 3 3201 8900 Singapore 65 6212 1000 U.S. 1 212 318 2000 Copyright 2012 Bloomberg Finance L.P.
SN 268301 H279-696-2 03-Jul-12 14:52:23 CDT GMT-5:00

Exhibit 2.13

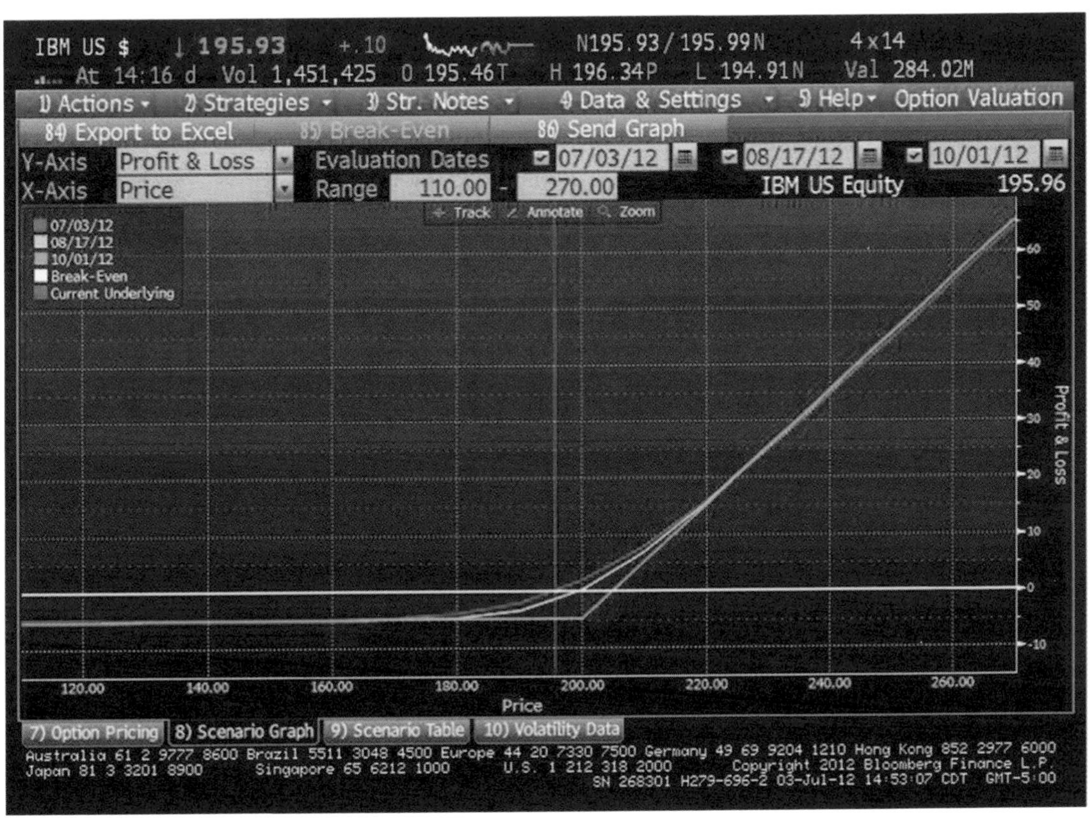
IBM US $ ↓195.93 +.10 N195.93/195.99N 4x14
At 14:16 d Vol 1,451,425 O 195.46T H 196.34P L 194.91N Val 284.02M
1) Actions 2) Strategies 3) Str. Notes 4) Data & Settings 5) Help Option Valuation
84) Export to Excel 85) Break-Even 86) Send Graph
Y-Axis Profit & Loss Evaluation Dates 07/03/12 08/17/12 10/01/12
X-Axis Price Range 110.00 - 270.00 IBM US Equity 195.96
Track Annotate Zoom
07/03/12
08/17/12
10/01/12
Break-Even
Current Underlying
60
50
40
30
20
10
0
-10
Profit & Loss
120.00 140.00 160.00 180.00 200.00 220.00 240.00 260.00
Price
7) Option Pricing 8) Scenario Graph 9) Scenario Table 10) Volatility Data
Australia 61 2 9777 8600 Brazil 5511 3048 4500 Europe 44 20 7330 7500 Germany 49 69 9204 1210 Hong Kong 852 2977 6000
Japan 81 3 3201 8900 Singapore 65 6212 1000 U.S. 1 212 318 2000 Copyright 2012 Bloomberg Finance L.P.
SN 268301 H279-696-2 03-Jul-12 14:53:07 CDT GMT-5:00

Exhibit 2.14

The call's P&L graph is always flat to the left of the strike price and rises at a 45-degree angle to the right, showing profitability with the rise of the stock price.

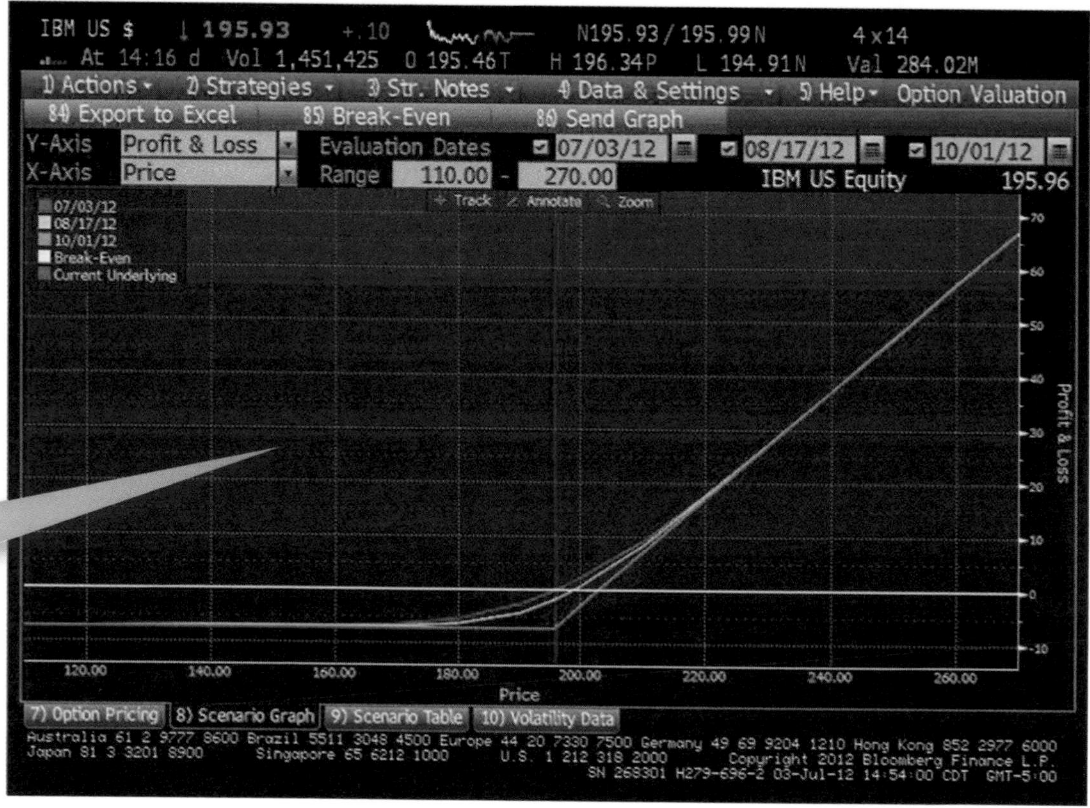

Exhibit 2.15

Strategy Sneak-Peek

Let's take a look at how options can be used to circumvent a hard-to-borrow stock's shorting restrictions.

Hard-to-Borrow Short Stock Synthetic Substitution

If you understand put-call parity, you can not only find abnormalities in the security or options, but also

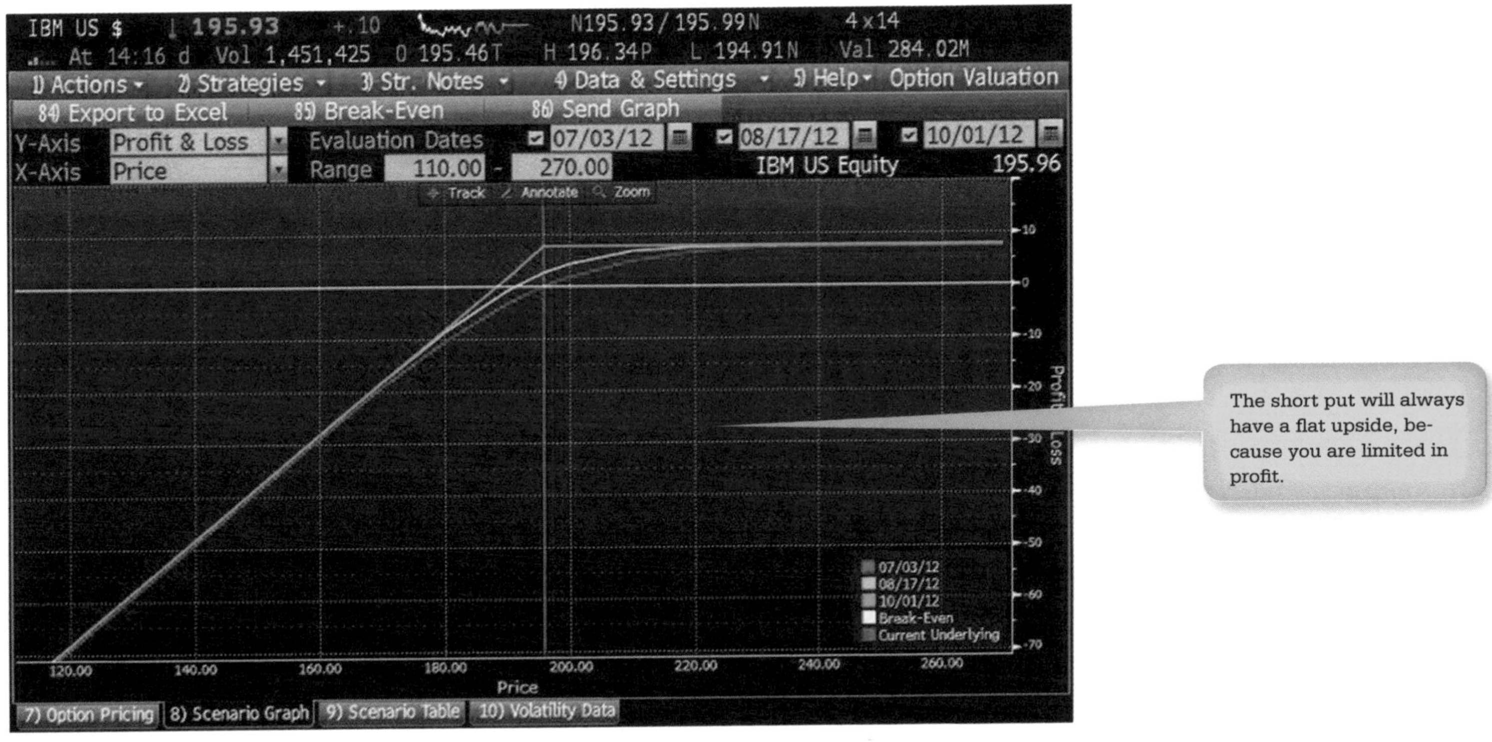

Exhibit 2.16

identify hard-to-borrow. Just because a stock is hard to borrow doesn't mean that you can't get short stock (at least synthetically) if you want to.

Just from synthetics, you know that if you buy a put and sell a call, you are synthetically short stock. This means that you will essentially have the same risk as selling the stock short in the open market.

Furthermore, before you even create the synthetic short stock positions you will know exactly just how much interest you have to pay to be short by the prices

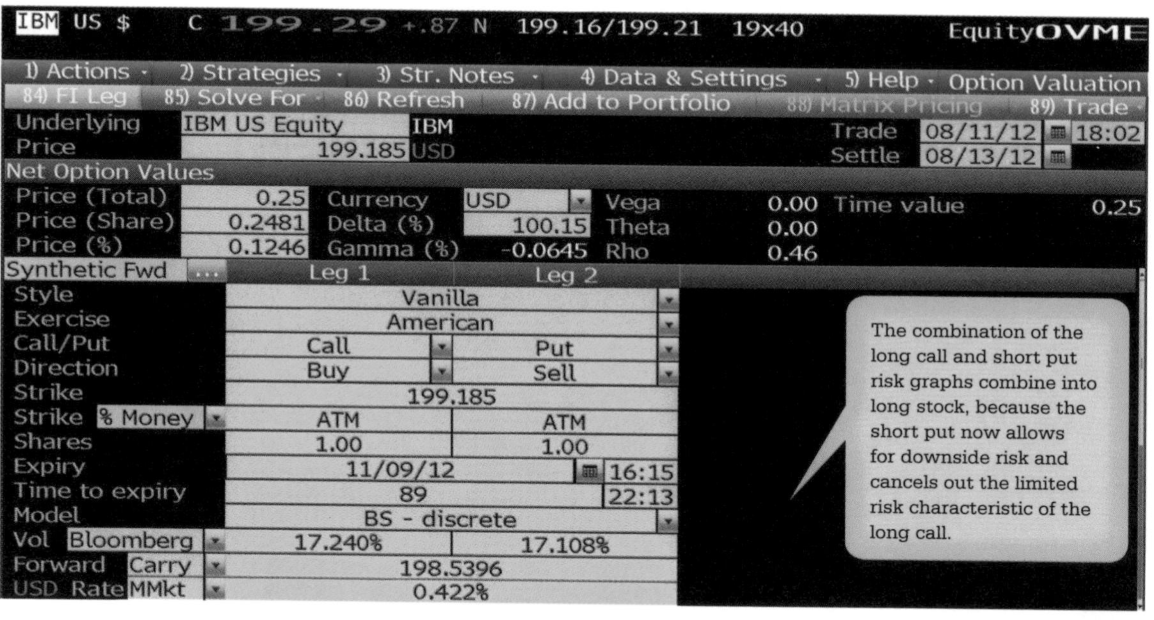

Exhibit 2.17

of the options. This puts you ahead of the gaggle of stock traders who may be unable to short a stock at all!

Since investors can't short some stocks, it's probably fair that you pay a little something if you are using options to create a short stock synthetic.

When a stock is hard to borrow, your breakeven will always be lower than the current stock price. If you want to put the odds further in your favor you can execute a risk reversal, which is also called a split strike conversion. This enables you to create modified synthetic short or long positions all while reducing risk with two out of the money options. If done correctly it can give you an advantageous breakeven and when done for a credit can increasing your probability of making a profit.

If you want to put the odds further in your favor you can execute a risk reversal, which is also called a *split strike conversion*. This enables you to create modified synthetic short or long positions all while reducing

<HELP> for explanation. EquitySIA
Enter value(s) and hit <Go>, <Menu> to Return
95) Edit Defaults 96) Output to Excel 97) Update Schedule Short Interest Analysis
Source Exchange Name NYSE Periodicity Bi-Monthly
GICS > All Securities > All Securities 07/31/12

	Ticker		Company Name	Short Interest	% SI Change	SI Ratio	SIR Change	% Float	% Float Change
1)	TU	UN	TELUS Corp	19,669,0...	-1.07	177.97	-11.40	13.10	-0.14
2)	PRIS	UN	Promotora de Informaciones SA	697,355	-1.15	97.31	-231....		
3)	STN	UN	Stantec Inc	353,106	-11.98	86.65	-24.96	0.80	-0.11
4)	JW/B	UN	John Wiley & Sons Inc	17,606	-0.54	65.69	35.59	1.46	-0.01
5)	RC	UN	Grupo Radio Centro SAB de CV	4,975		64.61	-387....		
6)	IHC	UN	Independence Holding Co	326,057	-0.47	61.92	32.07	4.13	-0.02
7)	ETM	UN	Entercom Communications Corp	3,923,512	-1.18	56.95	-3.22	19.37	-0.24
8)	BBX	UN	BBX Capital Corp	922,018	0.60	56.43	-19.22	13.28	0.08
9)	KH	UN	China Kanghui Holdings Inc	1,891,047	-0.03	54.90	-56.95		
10)	JOE	UN	St Joe Co/The	15,906,4...	-0.63	53.47	9.44	24.11	-0.15
11)	GTN/A	UN	Gray Television Inc	7,841	55.95	52.27	47.84	0.53	0.19
12)	ZZ	UN	Sealy Corp	14,688,2...	0.82	50.76	20.31	28.44	0.23
13)	GSH	UN	Guangshen Railway Co Ltd	1,207,049	-0.78	48.75	-10.43		
14)	FMD	UN	First Marblehead Corp/The	3,120,130	-2.00	48.57	7.35	4.94	-0.10
15)	MNI	UN	McClatchy Co/The	17,068,6...	-0.65	48.27	-23.64	30.03	1.45
16)	BOXC	UN	Brookfield Canada Office Pro...	15,198	-26.39	48.25	-123....		

Stocks with high short interest may be at risk of, or already be unshortable. You can find these stocks in the SIA screen.

Exhibit 2.18

risk with two out-of-the-money options. If done correctly it can give you an advantageous breakeven and when done for a credit can increase your probability of making a profit.

Risk reversals and split strike conversions are generally formed by using an out-of-the-money call and an out-of-the-money put just around the current stock price. I prefer to do them for credits or no cost if at all possible so that my breakeven is favorable. See Exhibit 2.19.

Synthetics and combos like what I just showed you are simple ways that professional option traders can get near the same delta exposure as they would have with short stock, but with a lower volatility factor and a favorable break-even point.

Another way to think about it would be that because the delta in this case is ****, the synthetic stock will have a beta of roughly *** to the stock. That means that if the stock dives below the put strike or rallies

Notice how the break-evens are favorable in the credit trade and the minor difference in the delta of the trades.

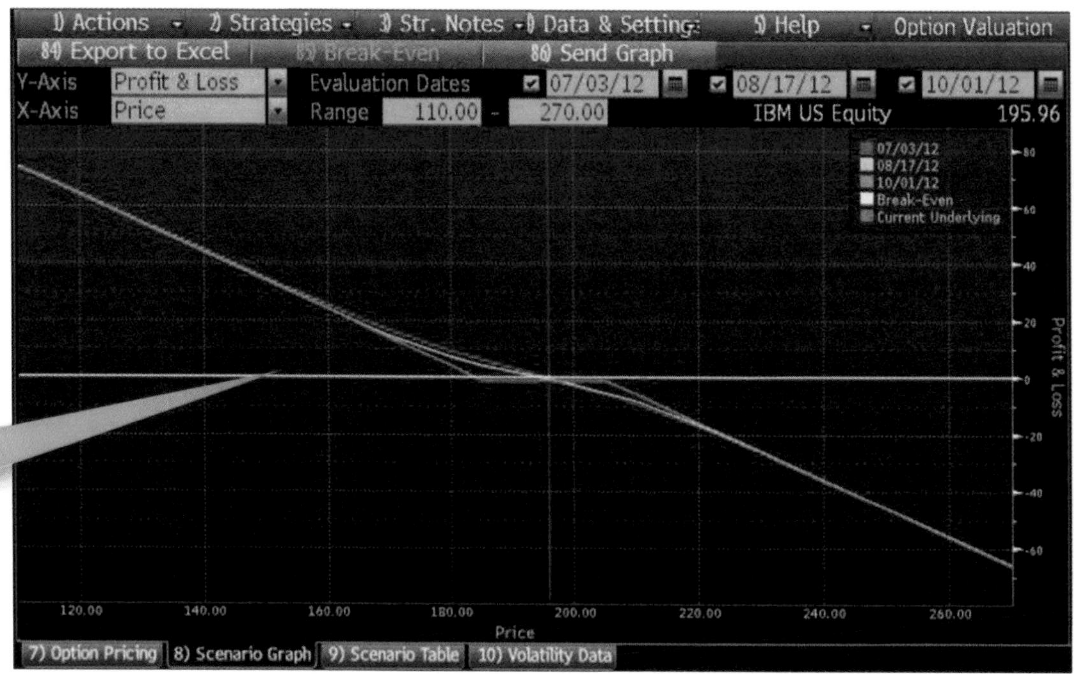

Exhibit 2.19

above the call strike, then the correlation will increase and the delta will move closer to 1.

Basis

Basis is another way of expressing carrying costs or quantifying the value differential between a call and a put. You calculate basis by determining the costs of being long or short the underlying security versus the option. It's also known as the *reversal/conversion rate*.

Traders can use the reversal or conversion rate to calculate the value differential between a call option and a put option with the same strike in the same month and find whether it's best to be long stock, short the synthetic, or short the stock, long the synthetic.

Think of basis as the theoretical value for the conversion or reversal (credit or debit).

Basis can also be figured backward by looking at the credit or debit you would get by buying call, selling put (same month and strike), and selling stock; or by selling call, buying put, and buying stock using the midprices. These trades are called *reversals* and *conversions* respectively, and are completely delta-neutral (not susceptible to changes in stock price), but they are not completely riskless.

For some market participants, things are a bit different. When professional market makers hold short stock in their accounts some are collecting what is called a *short stock rebate*. They are getting paid interest to be short stock. On the flip side, maintaining a long stock position will cost the pro traders money, though they are still entitled to dividends.

There are also variables between different traders at different firms. A major variable is that every trader can borrow money at slightly different rates and receive different amounts of interest on short stock. This changes their own personal basis, which may or may not be the same as what's in the option chains. If traders can wiggle their way into a position like a conversion for a great price and their rates are favorable, they just completed a riskless transaction and simply have to sit tight and wait for expiration for them to realize profit.

Exhibit 2.20 is an example of a typical reversal/conversion market along with breakevens in the trade.

In a retail trader's account, short stock positions usually cost money and effecting a conversion or reversal is not really a smart option unless you are able to leg into the trade.

- You can find basis (or the conversion/reversal rate) for any strike in any month.
- The conversion/reversal rate may be slightly different from a professional's actual basis.

Multiply the strike price by the interest until expiration (using appropriate risk-free rate), then subtract the dividends. This amount is your basis. You can use the basis to find where the put should be trading at in relation to the call and vice versa, but instead of using the forward price, you would simply have the basis (which can be negative) that you would add to the put to get the price of the call.

More Uses for Options

Options are for more than just speculating on changes in asset prices or protection of assets. Over the years, there have been several alternative uses for options. One of those uses is to get around usury laws or to make OTC loans where the parties can simply agree to an interest rate, term, and use stock and options to make the agreement and postcollateral.

I wouldn't recommend trying this with your friends unless you really know what you are doing.

KEY POINT:

Reversals and conversions are subject to dividend and interest rate risk! Just because it seems like you captured 20 cents in free money, it doesn't prevent the company from declaring a 50 cent special dividend. If you were short stock and long the synthetic, you would automatically lose 30 cents!

Smart Investor Tip!

If the call price is known, you subtract basis from the amount the call is trading over parity to find the put's value. If the put price is known, you will add basis. (If the call has parity value or intrinsic value, the same-strike put will not, and vice versa.)

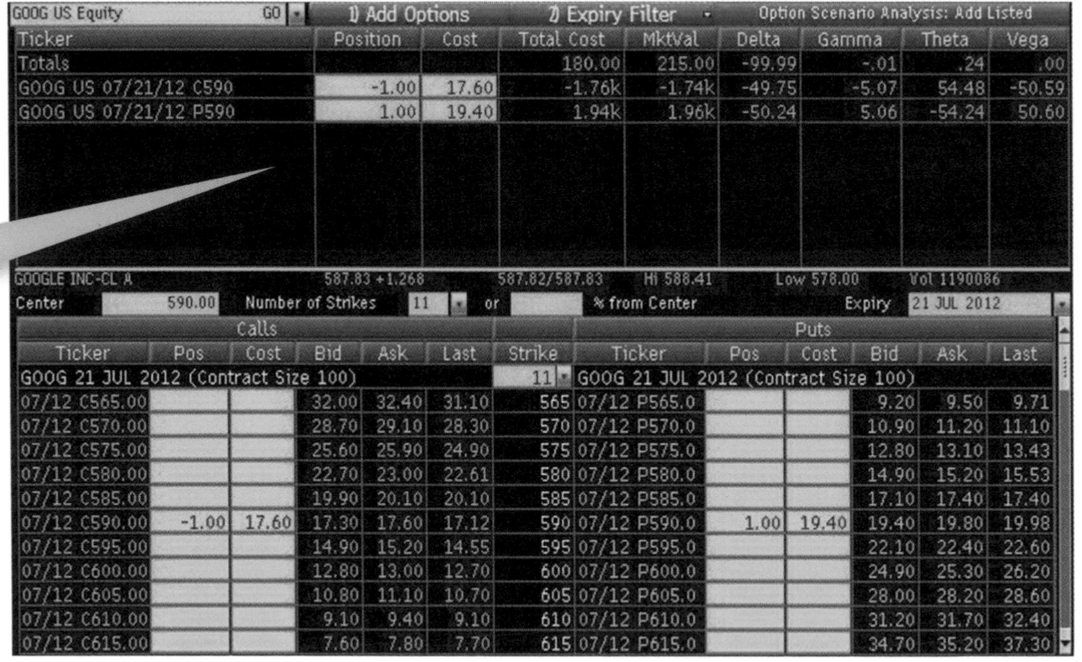

GOOG US Equity GO | 1) Add Options | 2) Expiry Filter | Option Scenario Analysis: Add Listed

Ticker	Position	Cost	Total Cost	MktVal	Delta	Gamma	Theta	Vega
Totals			180.00	215.00	-99.99	-.01	.24	.00
GOOG US 07/21/12 C590	-1.00	17.60	-1.76k	-1.74k	-49.75	-5.07	54.48	-50.59
GOOG US 07/21/12 P590	1.00	19.40	1.94k	1.96k	-50.24	5.06	-54.24	50.60

GOOGLE INC-CL A 587.83 +1.268 587.82/587.83 Hi 588.41 Low 578.00 Vol 1190086

Center 590.00 Number of Strikes 11 or % from Center Expiry 21 JUL 2012

Calls							Puts					
Ticker	Pos	Cost	Bid	Ask	Last	Strike	Ticker	Pos	Cost	Bid	Ask	Last
GOOG 21 JUL 2012 (Contract Size 100)						11	GOOG 21 JUL 2012 (Contract Size 100)					
07/12 C565.00			32.00	32.40	31.10	565	07/12 P565.0			9.20	9.50	9.71
07/12 C570.00			28.70	29.10	28.30	570	07/12 P570.0			10.90	11.20	11.10
07/12 C575.00			25.60	25.90	24.90	575	07/12 P575.0			12.80	13.10	13.43
07/12 C580.00			22.70	23.00	22.61	580	07/12 P580.0			14.90	15.20	15.53
07/12 C585.00			19.90	20.10	20.10	585	07/12 P585.0			17.10	17.40	17.40
07/12 C590.00	-1.00	17.60	17.30	17.60	17.12	590	07/12 P590.0	1.00	19.40	19.40	19.80	19.98
07/12 C595.00			14.90	15.20	14.55	595	07/12 P595.0			22.10	22.40	22.60
07/12 C600.00			12.80	13.00	12.70	600	07/12 P600.0			24.90	25.30	26.20
07/12 C605.00			10.80	11.10	10.70	605	07/12 P605.0			28.00	28.20	28.60
07/12 C610.00			9.10	9.40	9.10	610	07/12 P610.0			31.20	31.70	32.40
07/12 C615.00			7.60	7.80	7.70	615	07/12 P615.0			34.70	35.20	37.30

Here you can say basis is +1.80 and the conversion/reversal market might be $2.00 debit to reverse and $1.60 credit to convert. There is $2.17 of parity to the put, since the stock is trading $587.

Exhibit 2.20

Using Options to Lend or Borrow Money

The concepts that we have been discussing in this chapter all revolve around the forward price of a stock and the value of the options that expire at a specific period of time on that stock. See Exhibit 2.21.

If stock basis is simply interest minus dividends, then one could assume that if you had a stock with no dividends all you are accounting for is interest. I also said that conversions and reversals have no directional risk, only risk from interest and dividends.

Don't forget the formula:

Basis (or Cost of Carry) = Interest Collected – Dividends Paid, Until Expiration

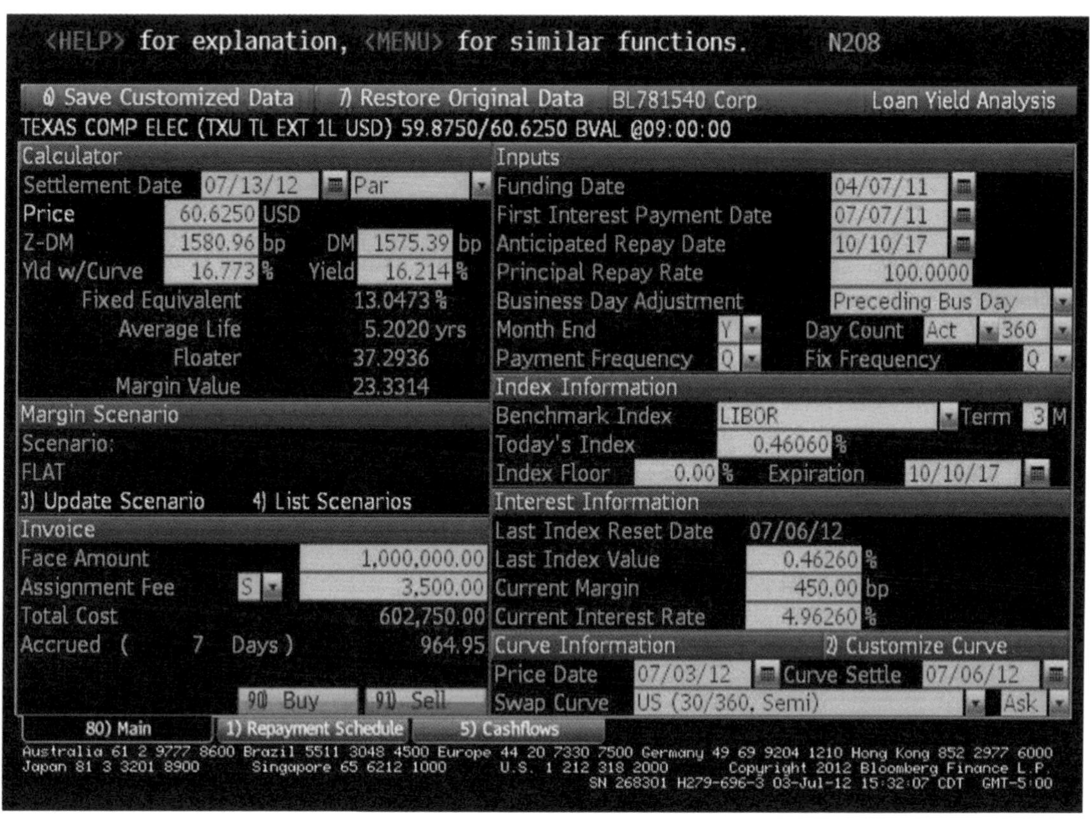
<HELP> for explanation, <MENU> for similar functions. N208
6) Save Customized Data
7) Restore Original Data
BL781540 Corp
Loan Yield Analysis
TEXAS COMP ELEC (TXU TL EXT 1L USD) 59.8750/60.6250 BVAL @09:00:00
Calculator
Settlement Date 07/13/12 Par
Price 60.6250 USD
Z-DM 1580.96 bp DM 1575.39 bp
Yld w/Curve 16.773 % Yield 16.214 %
Fixed Equivalent 13.0473 %
Average Life 5.2020 yrs
Floater 37.2936
Margin Value 23.3314
Margin Scenario
Scenario:
FLAT
3) Update Scenario
4) List Scenarios
Invoice
Face Amount 1,000,000.00
Assignment Fee S 3,500.00
Total Cost 602,750.00
Accrued (7 Days) 964.95
90) Buy
91) Sell
Inputs
Funding Date 04/07/11
First Interest Payment Date 07/07/11
Anticipated Repay Date 10/10/17
Principal Repay Rate 100.0000
Business Day Adjustment Preceding Bus Day
Month End Y
Day Count Act 360
Payment Frequency Q
Fix Frequency Q
Index Information
Benchmark Index LIBOR Term 3 M
Today's Index 0.46060 %
Index Floor 0.00 % Expiration 10/10/17
Interest Information
Last Index Reset Date 07/06/12
Last Index Value 0.46260 %
Current Margin 450.00 bp
Current Interest Rate 4.96260 %
Curve Information
2) Customize Curve
Price Date 07/03/12
Curve Settle 07/06/12
Swap Curve US (30/360, Semi) Ask
80) Main
1) Repayment Schedule
5) Cashflows
Australia 61 2 9777 8600 Brazil 5511 3048 4500 Europe 44 20 7330 7500 Germany 49 69 9204 1210 Hong Kong 852 2977 6000
Japan 81 3 3201 8900 Singapore 65 6212 1000 U.S. 1 212 318 2000 Copyright 2012 Bloomberg Finance L.P.
SN 268301 H279-696-3 03-Jul-12 15:32:07 CDT GMT-5:00

Exhibit 2.21

So if you have a stock with no dividend and can agree with another party on an interest rate, options can be used to borrow and lend money!

If you wanted to lend money to a friend for one year, you could buy shares of a nondividend-paying stock at a specific price from a person who needed to borrow money from you. He would at that point have a short stock position. There is the initial loan.

You would then simultaneously sell the call and buy the put for a credit and he would do the opposite (buy call/sell put). The expiration date of the options would be selected to mark the end of the loan.

The amount that you two come up with is the interest amount, and because the stock you selected doesn't have a dividend, it's also the basis. Since he would have to buy a call and sell a put and for a debit, you are getting the credit and thus getting paid. As long as you keep your position intact, you have no risk. It would also be foolish for him to remove his trade because at that point he would have directional exposure. I've seen these types of trades done in big indexes with wide bid-ask spreads, so there was little or no risk of the stock going hard-to-borrow.

In the real world, prevailing risk-free rates dictate what your conversion is going to cost (or credit) you. But if you make your own market in those options (do the trade OTC) and agree with the borrower that he would have to pay you an amount equal to 20 percent in interest for the trade per year, then you could theoretically do so. Remember that there is no risk in the stock and it's a closed transaction.

This was the way that Russell Sage, a crafty businessman in the 1800s, got around usury laws and lent money (secured) to people at high rates of interest. Using options, he got around the law. He wasn't the first; in fact, there is evidence of using options (in some form) and put-call parity to bypass religious usury laws dating back 2,000 years.

Now that we have proven that we can create synthetic calls by using puts and stock and synthetic puts by using calls and stock and even synthetic stock by using calls and puts, there has to be more to the relationship between calls and puts. In fact, there is a balance between the two—an equilibrium that is dependent on a couple of simple inputs, interest, and dividends.

A conversion or reversal is essentially an arbitrage strategy when a trader believes that there is a mispriced marketplace.

In both strategies you would need to use basis to find where the options should be trading in relation to each other and the stock and determine if there is any arbitrage in the marketplace.

Professional traders use the terms *conversion* and *reversal*, which basically translates to interest minus dividends.

A *conversion* means getting long stock and synthetically short stock by using a short call and long put. By doing this trade for more of a credit than what it may cost you in interest on your long stock, you can lock in a nearly riskless profit. If the stock pays a dividend in the time you are in the trade, the trade will cost more to put on compared to a nondividend stock because the dividend is paid to owners of the stock, not to the options.

A *reversal* means selling stock short and at the same time creating a synthetic long stock position by purchasing a call and selling a put. Because professionals collect interest on short stock positions, this trade is generally done for a debit. The professional trader will be collecting interest on his short stock position. If there is a dividend being paid in the time you are in the trade, you should expect to be compensated for the dividend as you will be required to pay that dividend because you are *short* stock.

Professional traders may choose to convert or reverse for many reasons, including the neutralization of existing positions. This might happen because of expiration or perhaps they are making a bet on interest rates increasing or decreasing. Maybe there is an arbitrage opportunity, but because of current technology and increased market efficiencies and participants, real easy arbitrage is hard to come by. Most retail traders do not employ these strategies due to trading costs and complexity and efficient markets.

Implied and Historical Volatility

This section is brief, but the ramifications of all types of volatility are extremely important, perhaps the most important part of option traders' lives. They should be continually studied and mastered over time. Most professional traders form their strategy and determine their risk based on opinions about volatility.

Obviously there are strategies that can benefit from changes in volatility, which I discuss shortly, but perhaps more important for most traders is the analytical edge that volatility can give you.

I start with historical or observed volatility. I define it, and offer you some tactical uses for it. Historical volatility is an objective volatility and has no other gauge than its ability to measure how a stock tends to move. Implied volatility is subjective and is open to interpretation and opinions, which can vary greatly.

Historical Volatility

Historical or observed volatility (vol or Hvol) is just that—it is a measurement of the actual movements of a stock over a given period of time, *annualized*. In the equity options world, when volatility is referenced it is generally understood to be a percentage and to be annualized.

If I were to say that a stock was moving at a 30 Hvol in the past month, my models are telling me that over the past 30 days, the observed volatility would be extrapolated to equal 30 percent, one standard deviation move in a year's time.

Volatility should actually be thought of as the speed at which the market is moving, not necessarily the distance a price travels. In lay terms, you might look at the past 30 days of a stock's *close-to-close prices* and, by observing those price movements, determine

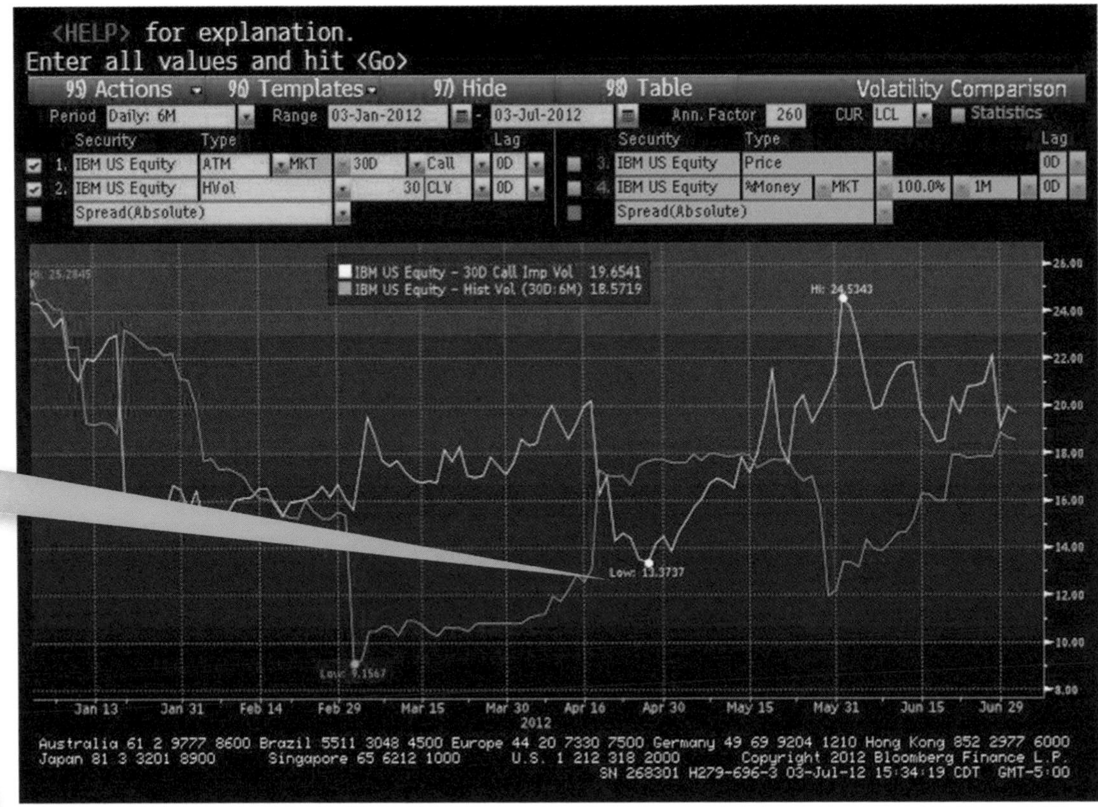

The chart shows you what IBM 30-day Hvol stock looks like visually; it has fluctuated between 25 percent and 9 percent over the past seven months.

Exhibit 2.22

Smart Investor Tip!

Hvol must be identified by a time frame such as 10, 30, or 90 days. Many traders do tend to look at 30-day volatility, so if you read or watch commentary on unidentified Hvol, you can assume they are referencing 30-day Hvol.

that it has been moving at 30 percent volatility. Again this is done by a calculator simply extrapolating those movements into an annual number and is usually observed best in graphic form so you can spot trends. See Exhibits 2.22 and 2.23.

Time Frames

Just looking at 30 days of data doesn't give us a very accurate or typical measurement of how a stock moves, so we might look back at a year or more of data to get a more "typical" reading. I generally observe different

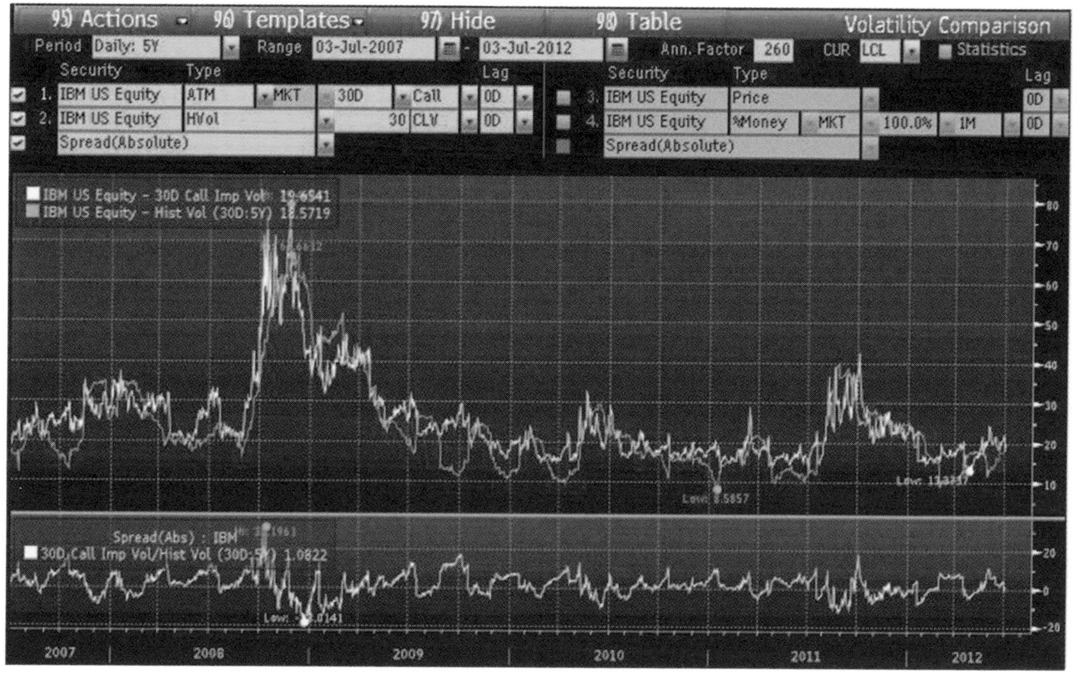

Exhibit 2.23

time frames of data and relate them to one another. Typically I use 90-, 60-, 30-, and 10-day vols. Think of different time frame Hvols as moving averages and not that you are only looking back 10 to 90 days. See Exhibit 2.24.

Be aware of "normal' or "typical" Hvol. Although you should have an idea of the normal range of Hvol in a certain security, don't pigeonhole yourself into a certain level, just buying when it's low or selling when it's high.

The word *typical* is a tough one to use in the land of volatility, because in 2008 and early 2009, when stocks were dropping like rocks, their typical volatility observations were probably much higher than their five-year volatility averages. If you were a volatility seller in September 2008, you got a rude awakening in

A 90-day Hvol chart will generally be smoother and give you a better idea of the mean Hvol, whereas a 10-day chart will jump around a bit more and allow you to spot short-term anomalies.

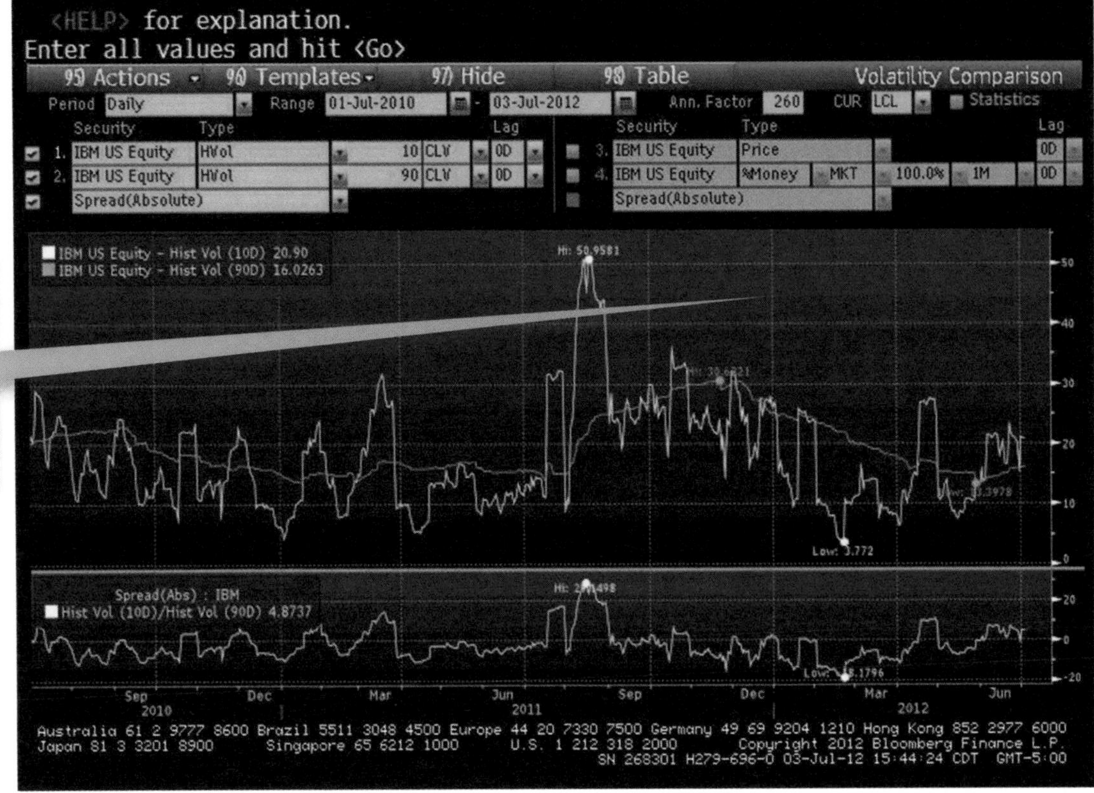

Exhibit 2.24

early 2009. So it is important to not only look at how volatile the stock has been recently, but to look even further back in time and try to associate relatively high- and low-volatility periods with fundamental, economic, and geopolitical data and trends.

Historical volatility can be used in conjunction with indicators like ATR to find realistic price movements for a particular stock. For each strategy I indicate the optimal volatility scenario, which varies depending on the objective.

Option prices (implied volatility) should be relatively commensurate with historical volatility, but will generally be higher because the future is unknown.

Implied Volatility

Implied volatility (Ivol) is what the option market implies the volatility will be for a particular security in the future. In other words, if a stock has an Hvol of 30, but the at-the-money options are averaging an Ivol of 40, the market participants believe that volatility will increase over the life of that option.

Implied volatility can be calculated backward from an options price. In other words, in general, if investors are paying more for options, implied volatility is rising and vice versa if investors are selling options. When you understand option strategies it makes sense. If you think the market is going to move fast and in one direction or the other, you may buy a straddle, strangle, call, or put. On the flip side, if you were thinking the market was going to move slower, you may choose to sell one of those options strategies.

This is where the conundrum and questions begin:

- Are Ivols correct?
- Does an Ivol of 40 predict the future?
- Are Ivols typically higher than Hvol because Hvol doesn't look at full intraday volatility and is therefore missing a piece of the real volatility picture?

These questions and many more will be streaming through your mind if you are a good option trader. You not only need to question just about everything, but have a reasonable rationale to address those questions.

Typically, market participants are scared of unknowns. That generally means higher implied volatility. Another reason for high Ivol versus Hvol is because traders are buying protection in the form of puts and/or speculating on a rise in stock by buying calls. There are more "market-taking" buyers than market-taking sellers.

Sometimes, in a panic, with little information, traders tend to disregard trends, prices, and fundamental data and either oversell or overbuy (relative to normal movement) a stock or option. This is more common if there is an unknown event like an earnings report or Food and Drug Administration (FDA) decision occurring or on the horizon. That panic can cause abnormal volume and changes in implied volatility in the options markets.

Smart Investor Tip!

Hvol calculations only account for close-to-close prices. Average true range (ATR) accounts for total movement in a security; ATR is quoted in dollars, not percentages.

KEY POINT:

Each and every option has an implied volatility that is constantly changing. Without Ivol, an option would have no time value.

DEFINITION:

A "market taker"

is initiating a transaction and generally removing liquidity from the markets; whereas a "market maker" is facilitating transaction and adding liquidity.

Informed options traders can literally see fear being built into or taken out of options, without any change in the underlying stock price. This fear is represented by increasing implied volatility (rising options prices) usually with volume increases, but not always.

This can be both a warning and opportunity! Rising or abnormal Ivol can warn you of an impending event. However, if you think that the expectations of the options markets are way higher than what the real outcome of the stock is going to be, then you should look to execute a strategy that is short vega (profits from a decrease in Ivol) and allows the stock some movement. Maybe a short straddle or strangle or perhaps a short iron condor, and so on.

If you thought that implied volatility was low, you could affect a long vega strategy (which profits from a rally in Ivol). Strategies like the long straddle or strangle, long iron condor, or short butterfly may benefit.

An increase in implied volatility generally translates into actual movement in the underlying security, so when you are forming opinions about volatility, you must also form an opinion about prices and combine the two into selecting the best strategy and strikes.

Can the Straddle Guide You?

Look at the charts the three-month and two-year UV/HV charts. In the three-month chart, Ivol looks low, which might incline you to buy the $XXX straddle; but does the price of the straddle fall in line with how far you think the stock will move? Always check your breakevens at different points in the trade. After periods of high volatility in the overall market followed by quick calming, straddles may drop in price very quickly, but it's all relative.

If the stock just came out of three months of high-observed volatility (where Hvol was between 40 and 50), but the straddle is trading at 35 Ivol, is it a buy? Perhaps, but you may want to take a look back a couple of years and see just how volatile this stock is and if a 35 Ivol is really cheap or pricey. Options markets can be good general guides, but like the rest of us, they are not always right. We discuss this more in the chapters on strategy. See Exhibits 2.25 and 2.26.

The specific inputs that we enter into our models to find an options price—stock price, time to expiration, strike price, dividend rate, interest rate—are all known, or can at least be calculated to some degree. The unknown input is what implied volatility amount to use. We extrapolate implied volatility from the live option price, to see what the *market* is assigning to a particular option at that moment in time.

If you want to see what the option would be worth at a different point in time with a 15 percent jump in implied volatility, use the option calculator on the OV screen.

It's not a magic wand that changes Ivol. Supply and demand change options prices, and the greater the demand, the higher the price and the greater the *implied* (*predicted*) volatility. The same is true in the opposite direction. For thinly traded stocks, you may

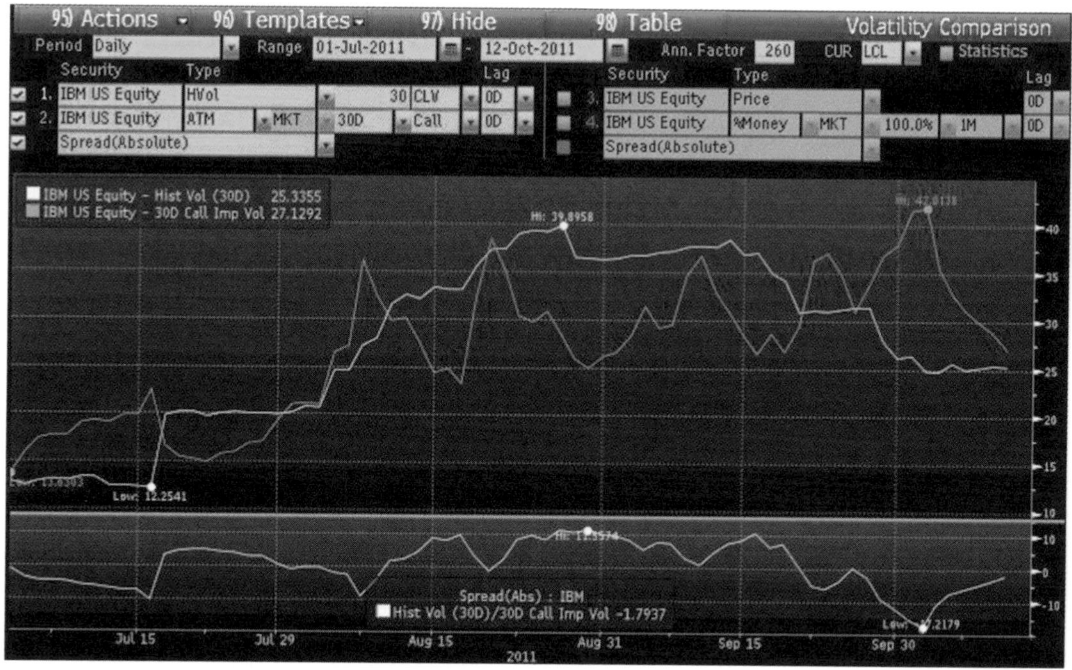

Exhibit 2.25

notice greater fluctuations in Ivol because there are fewer participants.

Professional traders can make *pure* trades on Ivol. They can buy implied volatility when it's relatively low and sell implied volatility when it's relatively high. As a retail trader, the majority of the risk you have has more to do with volatility levels in the stock or its direction. But that doesn't mean you should turn a blind eye to volatility trends. They can only help you.

If you want to get a quick glance at the current general state of implied volatility in the market, look to the Chicago Board Options Exchange Market Volatility Index (VIX or VXX) products. Both the VIX and the VXX are a general measurement of implied volatility on the S&P 500. The VIX cash index is a synthetic blend of all

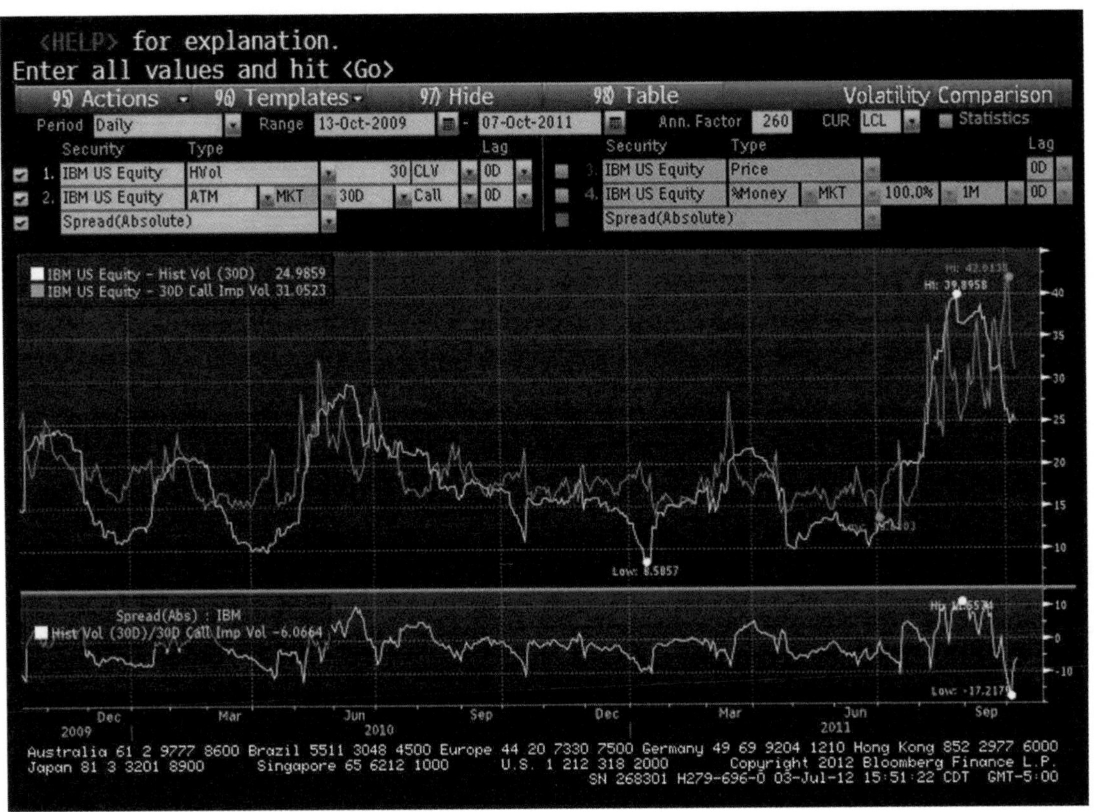
<HELP> for explanation.
Enter all values and hit <Go>
95) Actions
96) Templates
97) Hide
98) Table
Volatility Comparison
Period Daily
Range 13-Oct-2009 - 07-Oct-2011
Ann. Factor 260
CUR LCL
Statistics
Security Type Lag
1. IBM US Equity HVol 30 CLV 0D
2. IBM US Equity ATM MKT 30D Call 0D
Spread(Absolute)
3. IBM US Equity Price 0D
4. IBM US Equity %Money MKT 100.0% 1M 0D
Spread(Absolute)
IBM US Equity - Hist Vol (30D) 24.9859
IBM US Equity - 30D Call Imp Vol 31.0523
Hi: 39.8958
Low: 8.5857
Spread(Abs) : IBM
Hist Vol (30D)/30D Call Imp Vol -6.0664
Low: -17.2179
Dec Mar Jun Sep Dec Mar Jun Sep
2009 2010 2011
Australia 61 2 9777 8600 Brazil 5511 3048 4500 Europe 44 20 7330 7500 Germany 49 69 9204 1210 Hong Kong 852 2977 6000
Japan 81 3 3201 8900 Singapore 65 6212 1000 U.S. 1 212 318 2000 Copyright 2012 Bloomberg Finance L.P.
SN 268301 H279-696-0 03-Jul-12 15:51:22 CDT GMT-5:00

Exhibit 2.26

the options in the SPX index. The goal of the VIX is to create a continuous, rolling 30-day forward value of option volatility. You cannot own or short shares of the VIX.

The VXX on the other hand is actually an index that blends the first two months of *futures* on the VIX index itself and has nothing to do with the actual options on the VIX. You *can* own or short shares of the VXX.

By comparing the VIX (or VXX—use one or the other) to the historical volatility in the S&P 500, you can get a gauge of how complacent or fearful the market is as compared to the average state of volatility.

Let's dig a bit deeper into volatility.

SKEW

Skew is used to describe the variations in volatility both vertically in the option chain (price) and horizontally in the chain (time). Most traders look at vertical skew or the difference in the implied volatility moving up and down the chain. Professionals often describe skew as the implied volatility smile, which is what you see in the image of the SKEW screen in Exhibit 2.27.

Vertical Skew

The steepness of the smile or curvature of the graph identifies just how expensive the out-of-the-money options are compared to at-the-money options. When a colleague asks me what the Ivol is for GLD in the January 12 options, I would usually quote at the money Ivol for the ATM GLD options, which was about 25 at the time of writing. I wouldn't go up and down the strikes averaging them all out. This is because it's typical to have some serious variations in the Ivol of options as you go away from the at-the-money strikes. There are several reasons for this:

- Flaws in pricing models as you approach expiration
  - If IBM (trading at $200) options normally trade at an Ivol of 20 and it is two days to expiration, the pricing models may give the 202 strike a value of zero. But if people are paying an extremely cheap price—like 25 cents—for that option, the Ivol might be at 60!
- Takeover rumor
  - If a stock is rumored to be taken over, the upside (out-of-the-money) calls may be abnormally expensive (elevated Ivol), which would increase the angle of the right hand side of the smile.
- Put protection
  - It's common to see the out-of-the-money puts in a high-flying stock get more expensive as traders buy them to protect their profitable long positions. This buying frenzy sends Ivol higher. Because put-call parity needs to hold, market makers will often widen the bid-ask spreads of the in-the-money calls so there is no

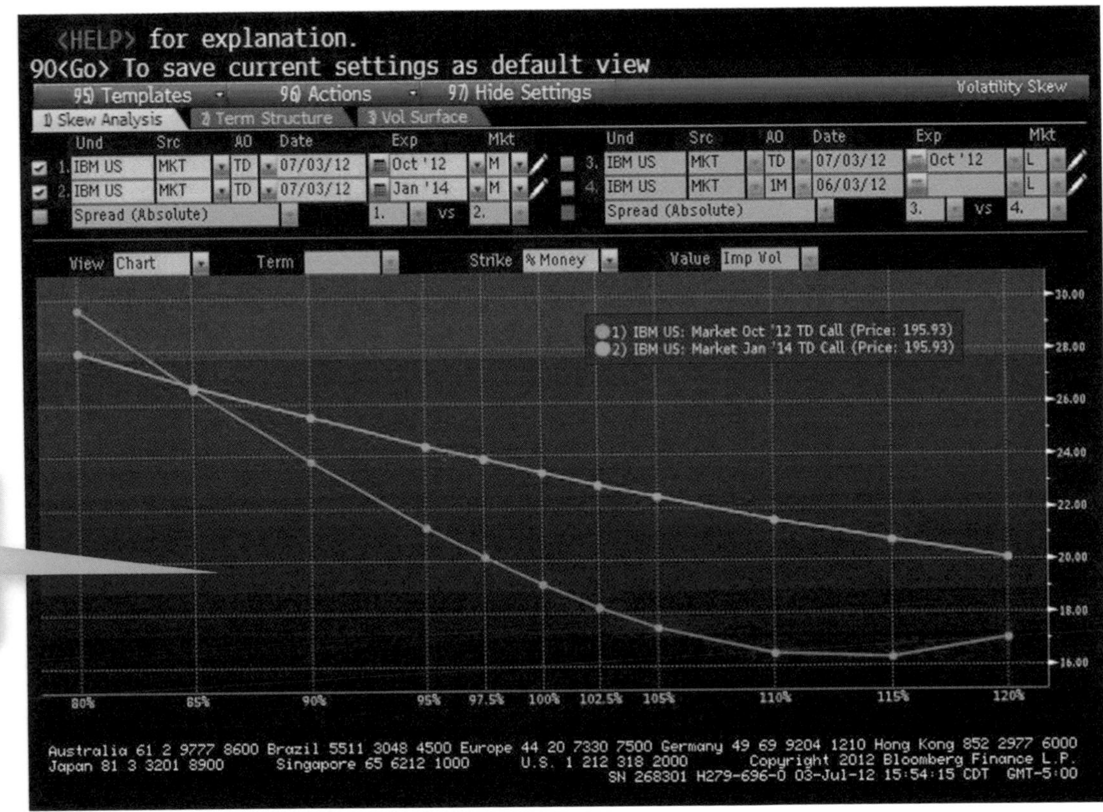

The SKEW screen allows you to plot implied volatility for all the strikes (calls or puts) and all the months in an option class.

Exhibit 2.27

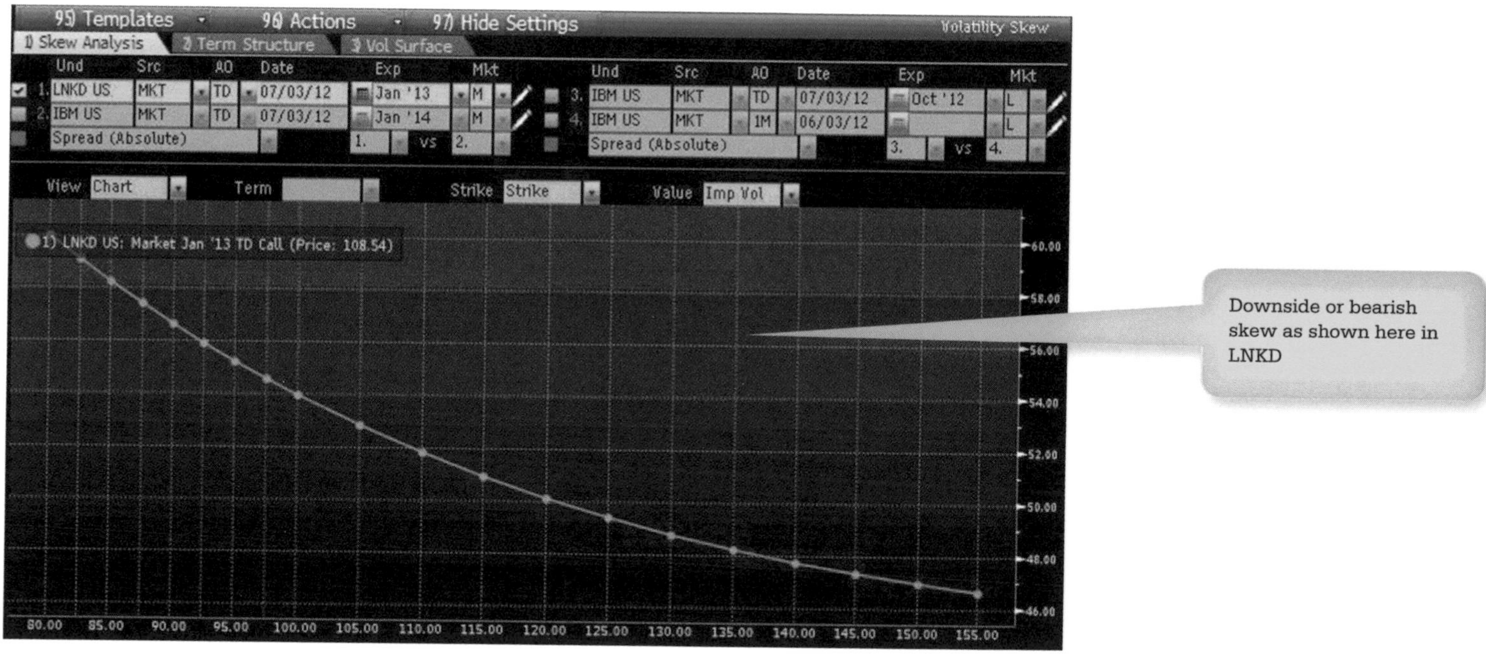

Exhibit 2.28

easy arbitrage opportunity in the conversion/reversal market.

- Covered call writing
  - It is common to see upside calls less expensive than their out-of-the-money puts at the same distance away from the center. This is due to the high incidence of investors selling calls against long stock and buying puts as protection. You may see this skew pattern increase as a stock rallies without a break. See Exhibit 2.28.

Supply and demand generally determine implied volatility and option prices. Because option values are derived from an underlying security, market participants who are buying OTM puts en masse will typically increase implied volatilities even if the stock itself isn't moving. These abnormalities can bring opportunity to the savvy trader. I remember when Apple was screaming higher in the first part of 2011 and everyone and their mother was buying upside calls to both protect themselves and to speculate on the Cupertino rocket ship.

Because of this phenomenon, calls that were expiring in four days that were $50 out of the money had value even though the statistical probably of Apple getting that far was about 1 percent.

Skew also occurs in part because of natural sentiments and emotions. Think about the average investor. Most tend to be long-side players, buying puts for protection against their long stock. Typically the put options bought as protection for stock are OTM, which is why we typically see OTM put Ivol skewed higher.

The most popular option strategy is the covered call, which again involves long common stock, but now with the sale of an OTM call. These actions tend to drive down the price of ATM and slightly OTM calls and skew them lower.

Further out OTM calls tend to see a slight increase in implied volatility because of short stock sellers buying calls for protection and because of speculators, but usually not as much as an equally spaced OTM put. This tends to create the look of a "smile" when looking at the SKEW screen. See Exhibit 2.29.

Just because an option is priced a certain way doesn't mean that the price is "correct" or better yet, justified. In other words, don't assume that the Ivol assigned to an option "should" be that way. Over time, you will be able to quickly identify the things that "don't fit." The most efficient way to do this is to examine skew to find anomalies, which in turn create an advantageous buying or selling opportunity. You can also incorporate those strikes into a spread strategy that takes advantage of the pricing anomaly (cheap or expensive) but also fits into your thesis on the stock.

Extreme Skew Example

The UVXY may be one of the best examples of extreme skew with serious manipulation.

There are reasons why this product and others have such abnormal volatility curves. For UVXY, we have to look at the asset to get the story. In this case, there are several assets and derivatives to consider. See Exhibit 2.30.

Complex and Flawed Products

The **UVXY** is a leveraged ETF that is created by using a blend of futures, swaps, and other instruments to offer investors a high correlation with the VIX index only with double the daily percentage movement when compared to the index itself. In theory, if the VIX moves 5 percent in a day the UVXY should move 10 percent in the same direction.

The main problem is that the VIX itself is not a tradable asset and is rather esoteric in value, its price being derived from a complex blend of the first two months of options expiring in the SPX index.

Even the options that are listed as "VIX" options have little or nothing to do with the VIX itself; they are actually

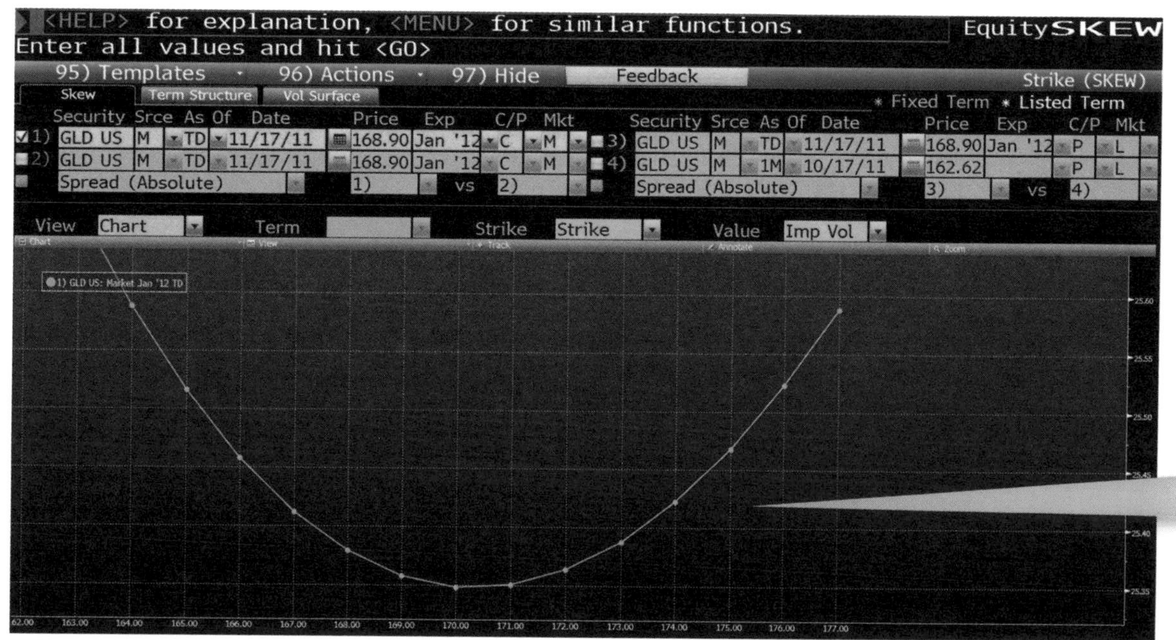

An example of a nice smile is illustrated in the chart of GLD (SPDR Gold Shares ETF), a product that tends to skew OTM calls higher.

Exhibit 2.29

based off a synthetic blend of the first two months of futures that are traded on the VIX index. If the options on the VIX were truly related to the index than put-call parity would exist in the option chain in Exhibit 2.30. As you can see it does *not*. In fact, the options on the VIX at the time of writing imply an underlying value of 19.

So the UVXY is not derived from the VIX at all; its price has more to do with a 30-day synthetic forward price in the futures.

As you can see, this is just the start of the problem.

Decaying Asset That's Hard to Trade

Another issue with the UVXY is that it can have erratic moves that are hard to measure. Those oscillations are not only contrary to what the market is doing, but they are not accurately quantifiable because the underlying asset is comprised of an ever-changing blend of assets that don't have an absolute value. The total

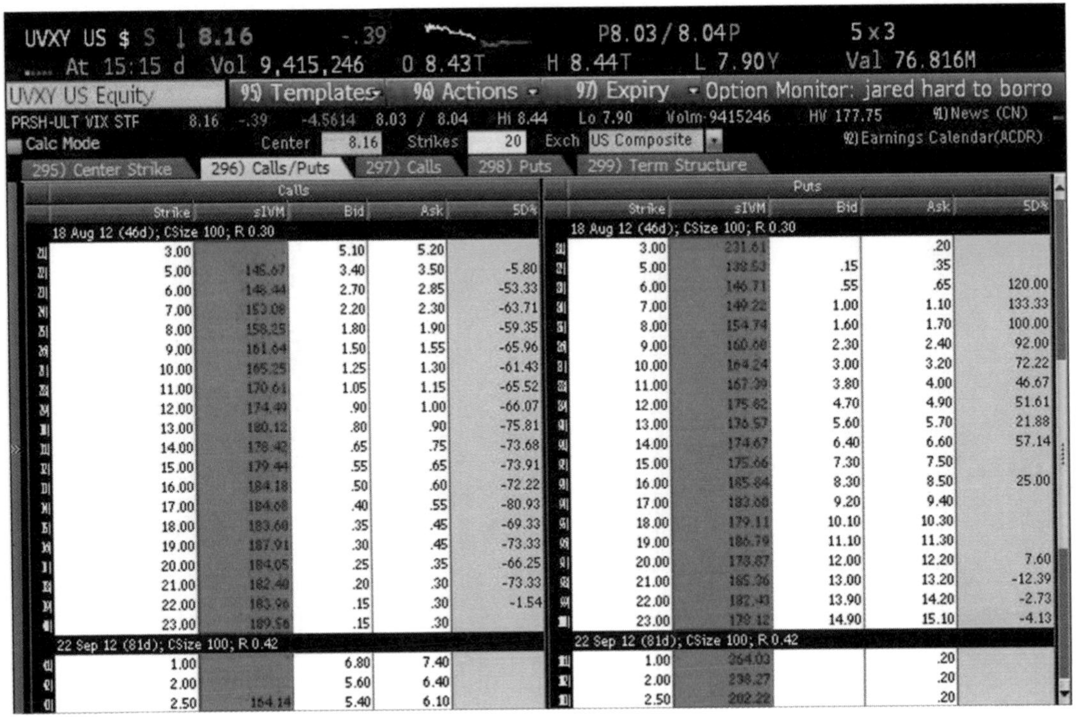

UVXY US $ S ↓ 8.16 -.39 P8.03/8.04P 5x3
At 15:15 d Vol 9,415,246 O 8.43T H 8.44T L 7.90Y Val 76.816M
UVXY US Equity 95) Templates 96) Actions 97) Expiry Option Monitor: jared hard to borro
PRSH-ULT VIX STF 8.16 -.39 -4.5614 8.03 / 8.04 Hi 8.44 Lo 7.90 Volm 9415246 HV 177.75 91) News (CN)
Calc Mode Center 8.16 Strikes 20 Exch US Composite 92) Earnings Calendar(ACDR)
295) Center Strike 296) Calls/Puts 297) Calls 298) Puts 299) Term Structure

Calls					Puts				
Strike	sIVM	Bid	Ask	SD%	Strike	sIVM	Bid	Ask	SD%
18 Aug 12 (46d); CSize 100; R 0.30					18 Aug 12 (46d); CSize 100; R 0.30				
3.00		5.10	5.20		3.00	231.61		.20	
5.00	145.67	3.40	3.50	-5.80	5.00	138.53	.15	.35	
6.00	148.44	2.70	2.85	-53.33	6.00	146.71	.55	.65	120.00
7.00	153.08	2.20	2.30	-63.71	7.00	149.22	1.00	1.10	133.33
8.00	158.25	1.80	1.90	-59.35	8.00	154.74	1.60	1.70	100.00
9.00	161.64	1.50	1.55	-65.96	9.00	160.68	2.30	2.40	92.00
10.00	165.25	1.25	1.30	-61.43	10.00	164.24	3.00	3.20	72.22
11.00	170.61	1.05	1.15	-65.52	11.00	167.39	3.80	4.00	46.67
12.00	174.49	.90	1.00	-66.07	12.00	175.62	4.70	4.90	51.61
13.00	180.12	.80	.90	-75.81	13.00	176.57	5.60	5.70	21.88
14.00	178.42	.65	.75	-73.68	14.00	174.67	6.40	6.60	57.14
15.00	179.44	.55	.65	-73.91	15.00	175.66	7.30	7.50	
16.00	184.18	.50	.60	-72.22	16.00	185.84	8.30	8.50	25.00
17.00	184.68	.40	.55	-80.93	17.00	183.08	9.20	9.40	
18.00	183.60	.35	.45	-69.33	18.00	179.11	10.10	10.30	
19.00	187.91	.30	.45	-73.33	19.00	186.79	11.10	11.30	
20.00	184.05	.25	.35	-66.25	20.00	173.67	12.00	12.20	7.60
21.00	182.40	.20	.30	-73.33	21.00	165.36	13.00	13.20	-12.39
22.00	183.96	.15	.30	-1.54	22.00	182.43	13.90	14.20	-2.73
23.00	189.56	.15	.30		23.00	179.12	14.90	15.10	-4.13
22 Sep 12 (81d); CSize 100; R 0.42					22 Sep 12 (81d); CSize 100; R 0.42				
1.00		6.80	7.40		1.00	264.03		.20	
2.00		5.60	6.40		2.00	238.27		.20	
2.50	164.14	5.40	6.10		2.50	202.22		.20	

Exhibit 2.30

return swaps that are used exaggerate these effects and make effective hedging and volatility risk a living hell for market makers.

It is also a product where investors tend to pile in during extreme scenarios; so when the VIX is very low, everybody and their mother is buying calls (usually out of the money). When the VIX is through the roof, the skew to the downside goes ballistic and the puts not only get expensive in general, but they may have extreme gaps in Ivol between them.

So because it's such a conundrum for the market makers, they pass the risk onto you in the form of extreme skew in both directions and major manipulation when the UVXY moves.

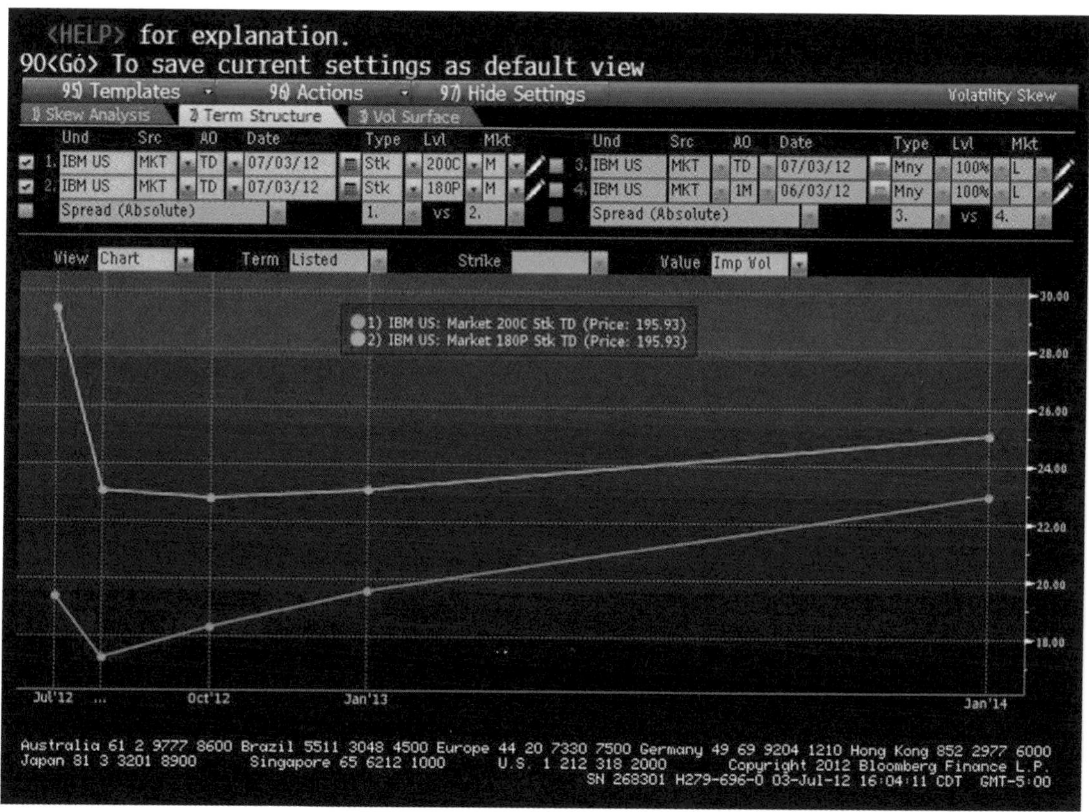

Exhibit 2.31

Horizontal Skew

Just as option prices can be skewed vertically (same month throughout strikes) they can be just as effectively, and usefully, skewed horizontally (same strike, different months). See Exhibit 2.31.

Horizontal skew measures the difference between varying months of the same class of options on a particular stock. If you are executing calendar spreads, diagonals, or just looking for a month that seems cheap or expensive in which to place

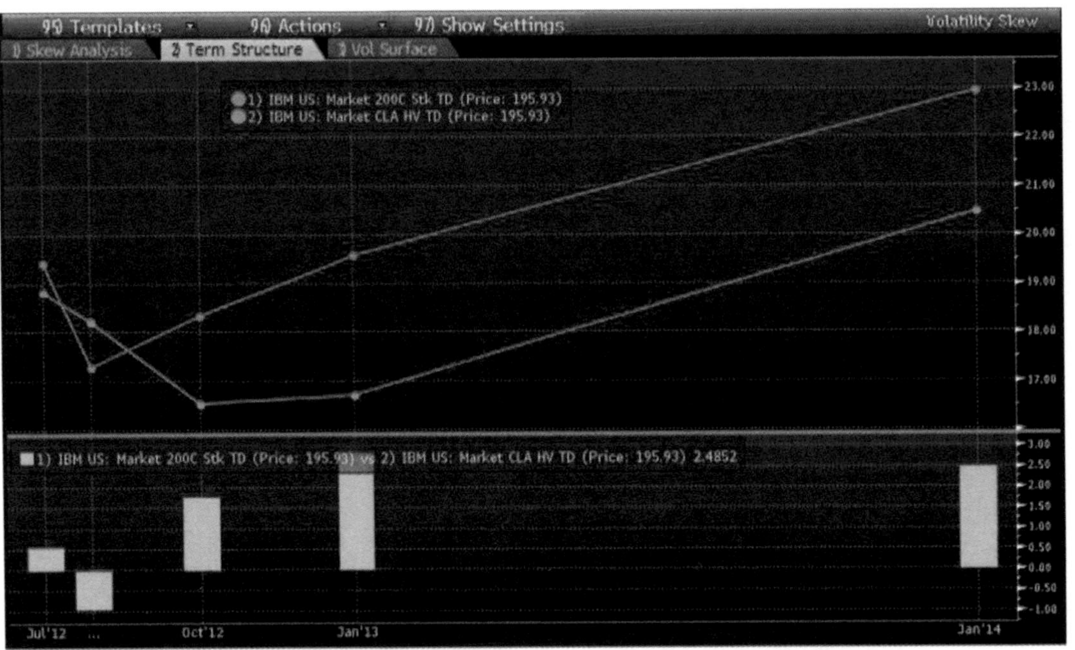

Exhibit 2.32

another spread, horizontal skew analysis is extremely helpful.

In the Bloomberg platform you can visualize horizontal skew the same way you did vertical in the SKEW screen, Option 1. This type of chart allows you to get a general sense for what months are cheap and which are expensive relative to one another. I generally layer on several months using the ATM strike and then view the absolute spread between them, which is shown in Exhibit 2.32.

If you are really fancy pants and perhaps a bit more artistic, use the Vol Surface function in the SKEW screen. It displays all months and strikes on a 3-D plane that you can manipulate to identify areas of interest and opportunity.

In Exhibit 2.33 you can see the SKEW screen surface function in action. The horizontal planes represent expiration and "Moneyness" (strike prices). The vertical elevation is the level of relative volatility with green representing lows and highs in red. You can pan, rotate,

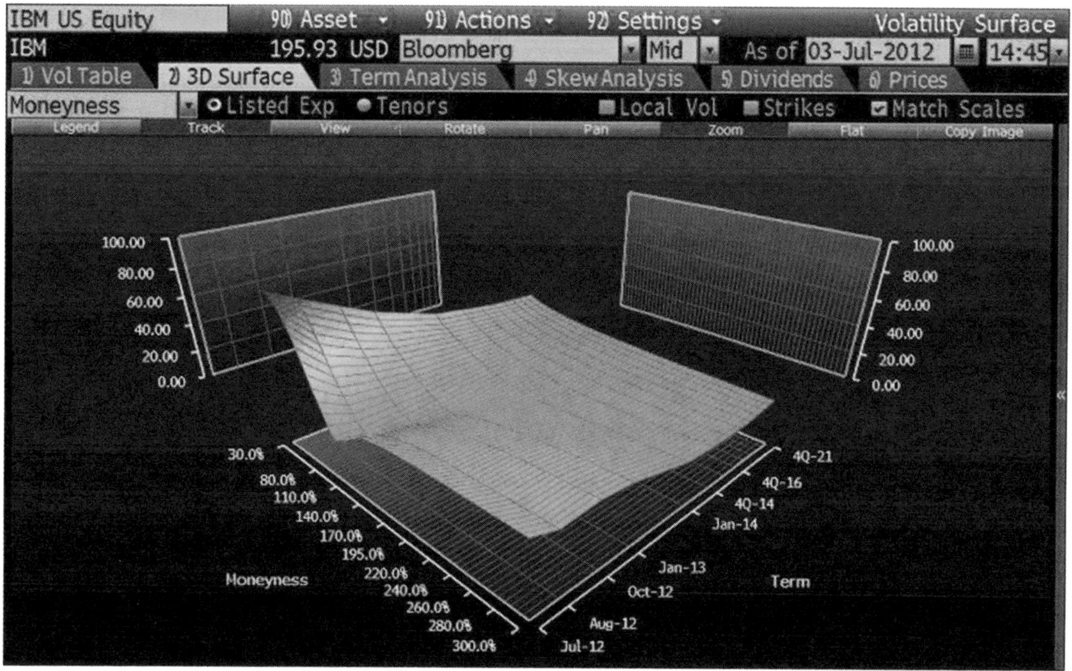

Exhibit 2.33

and zoom this image to pinpoint high and low spots on the plane and move your mouse over that particular strike and month to see the Ivol, Moneyness, and term of that specific point. The graphs in the back display the vertical and horizontal skew in chart form.

As a visual learner, this function helps me to look over an entire option class and spot the areas I want to be long or short. The key here is speed and accuracy, as the coloration and height allow you to quickly hone your target areas.

It may take a little getting used to, but it makes life easy when you want to scan quickly. As you can see here, the November out-of-the-money put options are pretty darn expensive. The upside calls, which have the higher "Moneyness," are also elevated.

P.S. Moneyness = (Strike Price/Spot Price) * 100

Horizontal skew is most used when you are trading a calendar or diagonal spread. It is typical that the front month options have the most amount of volatility, but you will also find volatility in months with earnings releases or corporate events.

When you are selecting your calendar or diagonal spread months, use horizontal skew along with price levels in the stock to buy and sell the best months. Most traders will buy the back month and sell the front month to get advantageous Ivol pricing, and also because of certain risks and Greek characteristics, which I discuss next.

In sum, don't get too caught up in skew; it should only be a minor, quick tweak to most of your trades, but it can come in handy if you are trying to identify how market participants feel about a stock. If a stock is abnormally skewed higher to the upside in a certain month (maybe an earnings month) there could be a fair reason to believe that investors may be leaning bullish; but be sure you have some other data to back that up.

CHAPTER 3

Visualizing the Greeks

Now it starts to get fun. After you've got the functionality and relationship basics down, it's time to learn how to quantify it all in real time.

The risk measurements we call the *Greeks* are the gauges for your high-performance fighter jet; without their assistance, you will be flying in the dark and may not notice a catastrophe looming around the corner. Whether you are trading one specific strategy or a fund with hundreds of different stock and option positions, you must use the Greeks to quantify your portfolio's sensitivity to changes in time and certain market conditions.

I detail each measurement and give you some practical methods for using each one as well as what to watch out for and how they may affect one another.

The most important thing that you should do besides looking at your current portfolio's risk measurements is to move your scenario forward in time and move the prices of the securities up and down. This is paramount because all Greeks are dynamic and can move erratically. If none of the Greeks are static you shouldn't be either.

A position that looks good today may look horrible a couple of days down the road and with just a small move in either direction. Don't forget that volatility will have an effect on nearly all your option positions. Know where it is and have an opinion of where it is going. Keep in mind that things can get hairy as you approach expiration. At that stage the Greeks may be changing quickly and doing things that seem abnormal. Watch your P&L and the price levels that you need to hold in the stock.

Even though I don't recommend it, there are ways to reduce your need to understand the Greeks. I outline these in detail in my book *Your Options Handbook* if you want to work around them. For now, let's explore their traits.

KEY POINT:

Greek values are generated by various pricing models.

Option Pricing Models

The majority of traders will never have to worry about selecting a certain pricing model on which to base their trades. Professional traders use mathematical models to price an option at a certain moment in time given certain parameters. Models like Black-Scholes, Cox-Ross, Binomial, and the like (you don't have to know these models to trade options) offer professional traders a theoretical value that they can buy and sell around.

You must remember that market makers are *not* generally taking bets on where the stock is headed, nor do they typically trade something unhedged (naked). Rather, for every action market makers take, they typically do something else (another trade in stock or options) to try and lock in a small amount of profit. This is very different from the way that you and I trade in the retail world. Frankly, for most of you, having a dynamic theoretical pricing model will do you little good because a simple change in a stock's price will completely change an option's value from being a good deal to a very bad one. Stick to the basics and follow my guidelines in the strategy section. Don't get suckered into paying high dollars for a model that tells you what an option is worth right now, because I can almost guarantee that the value you see will change from minute to minute when the market is open.

If you are a professional looking for price arbitrage in the options markets, Bloomberg certainly has pricing tools and models that can help you, but for this book, we assume that the basic option models are correct and the markets are determining the best price at the time you are about to trade it.

This means that the Greeks you see displayed in your option chain are good enough to base your trades on. Bloomberg does offer the ability for you to view an options theoretical value live while you trade. Although you shouldn't get too attached to that value, don't think that a wide bid-ask spread forces you to buy at the ask or sell at the bid. You can use the theoretical price calculator that's built into the OMON screen to find the real value of an option and trade around that. I go into details in the last chapter of this book.

Option Pricing Fact

Stocks that are more expensive also typically have more expensive options, even if they are similar in their volatility. For example, if you want to buy a $50 delta call with 40 days until expiration in a stock like GOOG (Google), which is trading at $530 per share and has been moving at roughly a 26 percent annualized volatility, you are going to pay $20.

YHOO (Yahoo!) on the other hand, which has been slightly more volatile than GOOG (it's moving at about a 28 percent volatility), has much cheaper options. The $50 delta call with 40 days until expiration will only cost you about 82 cents because YHOO's stock is about 1/50 the price of GOOG's stock.

This is perfectly normal, so don't freak out if your option prices seem cheap or expensive. It's all relative. Pay close attention to the implied volatility—that will tell the real story of relative value, not the option's price per se.

Delta

Delta is probably the most important Greek to understand because of its close correlation to your P&L. The other Greeks have influence, but the effects of delta can usually be felt the quickest as the underlying security moves around. It's also the Greek that effects your options the way a stock position would, making it almost second nature for the newbie to comprehend.

Delta is the first derivative and the Greek that options traders use to measure the change in the price of an option for every $1 change in the price of the underlying security (among other things that I get to shortly). Delta is scalable and compounding, meaning that the more options you buy on the same security, the more delta you will accumulate collectively and the more exposure your portfolio will have to movements in the underlying security.

Every option has its own unique delta that is constantly changing.

Delta will always have a value between 0.0 and 1.0 for a long call (and/or short put) and 0.0 and –1.0 for a long put (and/or short call).

Calls have a positive delta because of their positive correlation to the underlying stock. In other words, when stock prices go up, call prices should be rising, and when stocks drop, call prices should be decreasing. Because of this, the call option is assigned a positive delta.

If a call option has a delta of 0.60 and the option is worth $1 when the stock is trading $20, then that means that if the stock goes up $1 to $21, the option should be worth about $1.60 at this higher stock price. We got this price by adding the delta to the original option price, $1 plus 60 cents. This also means that if the stock were to instead drop by a dollar to $19, we would *subtract* the delta from the option price to determine the expected new price, $1 dollar minus 60 cents, which is 40 cents.

Calls profit from upward movements in stock, so it makes sense that they have a positive delta, but how about puts? Puts, on the other hand, will lose value when stocks rise because of the negative or opposite correlation they have with the underlying stock. Since puts increase in value as stock *drops*, they have a negative delta. In other words you subtract the delta amount from the put price as stock goes *up* and *add* it as stock goes *down*.

Can you see the relationship here? If you traded the same stock and observed both the 0.50 delta call option and the 0.50 delta put option while the stock moved $1, they both would change prices by the same amount, but in the opposite direction depending on which way the stock moved.

There is that relationship again between calls and puts. This is why you can tell what the put should be worth if you know what price of the call (and stock) is and vice versa. This is put-call parity in action!

KEY POINT:

The delta position of your portfolio shows your bias for the direction you want the market to move in. If you are long delta, then you desire a bullish move and will profit from it. A negative delta position means that you will profit from a bearish move in the stock.

Smart Investor Tip!

If you sell a call option, you will be short delta. Remember that a short delta position means that you want the asset to go lower.

Smart Investor Tip!

If you sell a put option, you will be long delta. Remember that a long delta position means that you want the asset to go higher.

Smart Investor Tip!

Big Delta, Small Delta

Everything is relative. A 300 delta position to some people may be very risky ($300 dollars in change for every $1 move in the stock), while to others it's menial. When you determine risk, delta should be a primary concern and you should find a number that is commensurate with your risk tolerance and thesis.

Delta's Other Functions

Delta has several functions. Primarily it is used to indicate how much an option's value will change for every one dollar move in the stock. But it has several other equally important uses.

Exposure to the Underlying Stock

Professional traders use delta to find their total exposure to a stock's movement and how their P&L will change as the stock's price changes. Remember that 100 shares of long stock will have a delta of 100. One hundred shares of short stock will have a delta of –100. Being entirely long or short stock is the most bullish or bearish you can be. If you were to buy a call with a delta of 0.75, for example, you would only be exposed to 75 cents of profit or loss for every dollar that stock moved. So if the stock jumped $1, you would make 75 cents and vice versa to the downside.

Because options contracts are bundles of 100, I might say that I was long 75 deltas, because I would make roughly $75 if the stock went up $1 and $75 if it dropped a $1.

If I bought another nine of those calls, I have now increased my net delta to 750 and will experience a $750 change in my P&L for every $1 the stock moves. This is where the element of compounding comes in and where you have to be careful.

Smart Investor Tip!

When an option has a delta of 1 (100) it is moving 1 to 1 with the underlying stock.

Another characteristic of delta is that it is *not* static. When you purchase a call with a delta of 0.70 and the stock drops $1, your new delta might drop as well—to 0.60 (for example). This effect slows down how much money you might lose if the stock goes against you. This works in the other direction, too. If you bought a call with a delta of 0.70 and the stock rallied $1 your call may then have a delta of 0.80, accelerating your profits. This rate of change is called *gamma*, the Greek I explore next. See Exhibit 3.1.

When you are initially constructing a position, be sure to move the price slider up and down to simulate how much will your P&L will change with different movements in the stock. This is especially important if you are selling options because you may not realize just how much risk you have if the stock were to move 5, 10, or 15 percent, which can and will happen from time to time.

Let's examine what happens to a "position" if you sold 30 out-of-the-money call options with a delta of 0.10 for 50 cents for a total delta of –300. See Exhibit 3.2.

At first, your P&L is not extremely sensitive, only 300 deltas short. But watch what happens if we simulate a realistic jump in the stock on an unexpected news story. See Exhibit 3.3.

What started as a position with minimal effect on your portfolio, now is causing a $1,500 move for every point change in your P&L on a stock that moves about $4 a day.

Because delta can and will fall if this stock were to continue to rise (remember, you sold calls and will have an upside-down delta to stock relationship), your position's delta could continue to plummet eventually to –3,000, which would mean the delta of the calls you bought had sunk to –100 and your P&L is now moving $3,000 for every one point move or $12,000 a day on this stock!

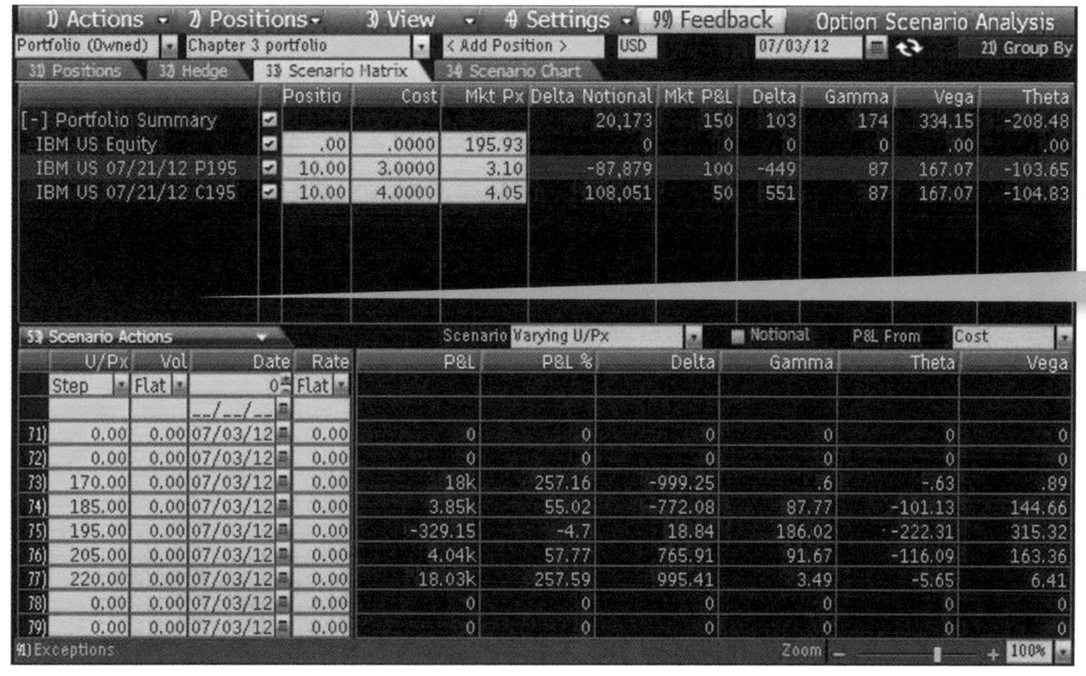

	Positio	Cost	Mkt Px	Delta Notional	Mkt P&L	Delta	Gamma	Vega	Theta
[-] Portfolio Summary				20,173	150	103	174	334.15	-208.48
IBM US Equity	.00	.0000	195.93	0	0	0	0	.00	.00
IBM US 07/21/12 P195	10.00	3.0000	3.10	-87,879	100	-449	87	167.07	-103.65
IBM US 07/21/12 C195	10.00	4.0000	4.05	108,051	50	551	87	167.07	-104.83

	U/Px	Vol	Date	Rate	P&L	P&L %	Delta	Gamma	Theta	Vega
	Step	Flat	0	Flat						
			--/--/--							
71)	0.00	0.00	07/03/12	0.00	0	0	0	0	0	0
72)	0.00	0.00	07/03/12	0.00	0	0	0	0	0	0
73)	170.00	0.00	07/03/12	0.00	18k	257.16	-999.25	.6	-.63	.89
74)	185.00	0.00	07/03/12	0.00	3.85k	55.02	-772.08	87.77	-101.13	144.66
75)	195.00	0.00	07/03/12	0.00	-329.15	-4.7	18.84	186.02	-222.31	315.32
76)	205.00	0.00	07/03/12	0.00	4.04k	57.77	765.91	91.67	-116.09	163.36
77)	220.00	0.00	07/03/12	0.00	18.03k	257.59	995.41	3.49	-5.65	6.41
78)	0.00	0.00	07/03/12	0.00	0	0	0	0	0	0
79)	0.00	0.00	07/03/12	0.00	0	0	0	0	0	0

Notice how the delta changes in the lower part of the OSA screen as the stock is simulated up and down.

Exhibit 3.1

In addition to your daily stress, you still have to figure out if the stock can still stay below the call strike that you sold, which was your ultimate goal. The most interesting part of this entire thing is that you could be losing $12,000 one Thursday and if the stock expires below the strike you sold, you could be profitable the very next day.

The question is whether that stress was too much or you and your now-empty bottle of Maalox to handle.

Moneyness and Delta

You may hear some traders, usually the math nuts, using the term **Moneyness**.

> DEFINITION:
> **Moneyness**
> Moneyness is a way to express an option's position in relation to the stock in a risk-neutral world. In other words, it's the likelihood of an option having positive value upon expiration and is actually different for calls and puts.

Cheap short options can get very pricey very quickly and devastate your P&L if the stock makes a sharp move against you.

	Positio	Cost	Mkt Px	Delta	Mkt P&L	Gamma	Vega	Theta	Delta Notional
[-] Portfolio Summary				-1534	-22,500	-128	-1,426.46	119.13	-300,638
IBM US Equity	.00	.0000	220.00	0	0	0	.00	.00	0
IBM US 10/20/12 C220	-30.00	.5000	8.00	-1534	-22,500	-128	-1,426.46	119.13	-300,638

	PxShift %	Vol	Date	Rate	P&L	P&L %	Delta	Gamma	Theta	Vega
	Step	Flat	3	Flat						
			--/--/--							
71)	-12.00%	0.00	07/06/12	0.00	-464.16	-30.94	-254.12	-50.53	40.59	-472.06
72)	-6.00%	0.00	07/06/12	0.00	-6.81k	-453.94	-770.75	-105.42	91.14	-1.05k
73)	-4.00%	0.00	07/06/12	0.00	-10.69k	-712.7	-1.01k	-119.54	105.84	-1.22k
74)	-2.00%	0.00	07/06/12	0.00	-15.66k	-1.04k	-1.27k	-128.43	116.58	-1.33k
75)	0.00%	0.00	07/06/12	0.00	-21.79k	-1.45k	-1.53k	-131.93	122.36	-1.39k
76)	2.00%	0.00	07/06/12	0.00	-29.07k	-1.94k	-1.79k	-129.48	122.92	-1.37k
77)	4.00%	0.00	07/06/12	0.00	-37.46k	-2.5k	-2.03k	-122.01	118.62	-1.3k
78)	6.00%	0.00	07/06/12	0.00	-46.89k	-3.13k	-2.26k	-110.52	110.14	-1.16k
79)	12.00%	0.00	07/06/12	0.00	-80.11k	-5.34k	-2.74k	-62.64	68.19	-609.09

Exhibit 3.2

Moneyness can be defined in several ways by using several methods. There are complex ways that Moneyness can be used to determine the probability of an option having positive monetary value on expiration. See Exhibit 3.4.

Using Moneyness as a percentage, a trader can determine an option's position relative to the ATM strike. The scale of Moneyness ranges from 0 percent to 200 percent, with 100 being at the money (spot price) and any Moneyness readings above 100 percent being the higher strikes. Readings below 100 percent are the lower strikes.

- A Moneyness of 100 percent is considered at the money.
- A Moneyness of 50 percent generally represents in-the-money calls and out-of-the money puts with a strike price that is below the stock price.

	Positio	Cost	Mkt Px	Delta	Mkt P&L	Gamma	Vega	Theta	Delta Notional
[-] Portfolio Summary				-2,045	165	-108	-1,227.60	143.37	-394,689
IBM US Equity	.00	.0000	230.00	0	0	0	.00	.00	0
IBM US 10/20/12 C220	-30.00	.5000	0.44	-2,045	165	-108	-1,227.60	143.37	-394,689

	U/Px	Vol	Date	Rate	P&L	P&L %	Delta	Gamma	Theta	Vega
	Step	Flat	0	Flat						
			--/--/--							
71)	210.00	0.00	07/20/12	0.00	-11.24k	-749.58	-987.99	-109.08	130.66	-1.11k
72)	215.00	0.00	07/20/12	0.00	-16.82k	-1.12k	-1.26k	-117.93	144.92	-1.23k
73)	220.00	0.00	07/20/12	0.00	-23.76k	-1.58k	-1.53k	-120.64	152.04	-1.29k
74)	225.00	0.00	07/20/12	0.00	-32.07k	-2.14k	-1.8k	-117.45	151.74	-1.28k
75)	230.00	0.00	07/20/12	0.00	-41.68k	-2.78k	-2.05k	-109.63	145.14	-1.2k
76)	235.00	0.00	07/20/12	0.00	-52.48k	-3.5k	-2.27k	-98.78	134.13	-1.08k
77)	240.00	0.00	07/20/12	0.00	-64.33k	-4.29k	-2.47k	-86.21	120.16	-912.64
78)	245.00	0.00	07/20/12	0.00	-77.07k	-5.14k	-2.63k	-72.24	103.57	-723.93
79)	250.00	0.00	07/20/12	0.00	-90.55k	-6.04k	-2.76k	-57.01	84.26	-530.96

Here is that same analysis using price change; note the danger to the upside.

Exhibit 3.3

- A Moneyness of 125 percent generally represents out-of-the-money calls and in-the-money puts with strike prices higher than the stock.

Probability of Being in the Money

Because I touched on the concept of Moneyness, I thought it would be an appropriate segue to talk about how delta can also tell us the probability of a single option being in the money.

Delta (to an extent) allows us to gauge the percentage chance that the option will be worth *anything* at expiration (that it will expire in the money). You can also think about delta as the probability of that option being worth more than 0 at expiry. It does *not* tell you

KEY POINT:

To find an option's Moneyness expressed in percentage terms use the following formula: (Strike Price ÷ Spot Price) × 100.

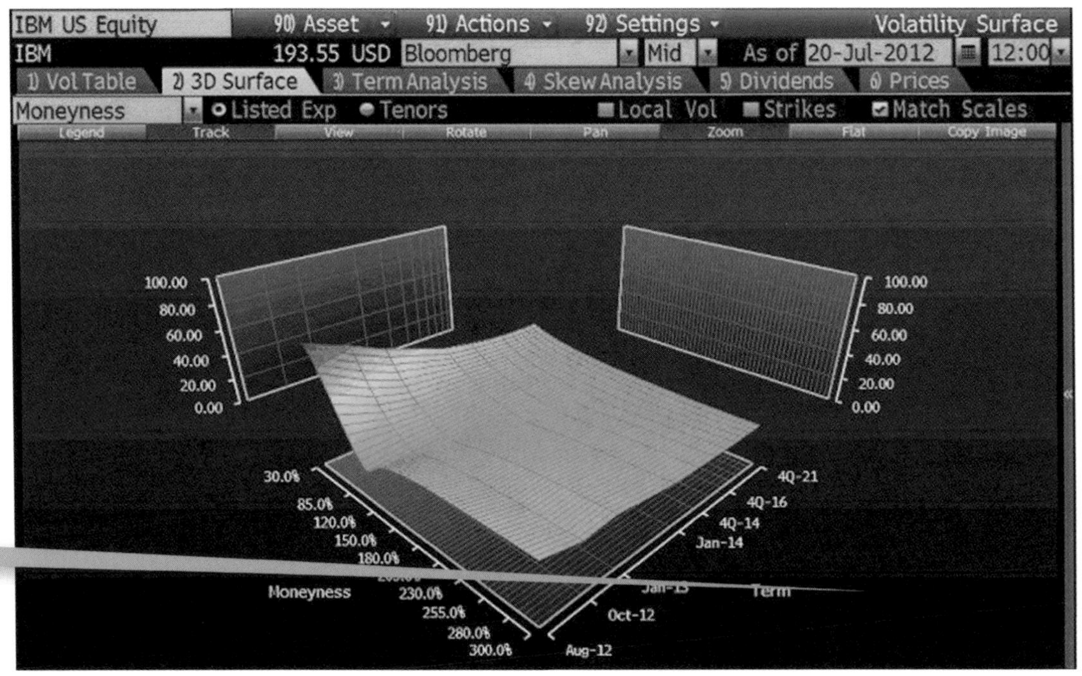

Using a visual reference like what you see here may help you to understand the concept of Moneyness and how it relates to delta.

Exhibit 3.4

the percentage chance that you will be profitable. The models that are used to figure delta would assume that 0.0001 is still positive value, but isn't much money, especially if you paid $10 for that option, so keep that in mind. See Exhibit 3.5.

Here's how it works: Assume that a call has a 0.20 delta. This means, given the current inputs of stock price, volatility, days until expiration, and so on, that option has a 20 percent chance of being in the money (by any amount) at expiration. Options that have a low delta are cheaper than the ones with a higher delta and are analogous to a long-shot horse that is paying 30 to 1. You likely wouldn't bet the farm on that horse, but you might place a little bet—because if he wins, the payoff may be substantial.

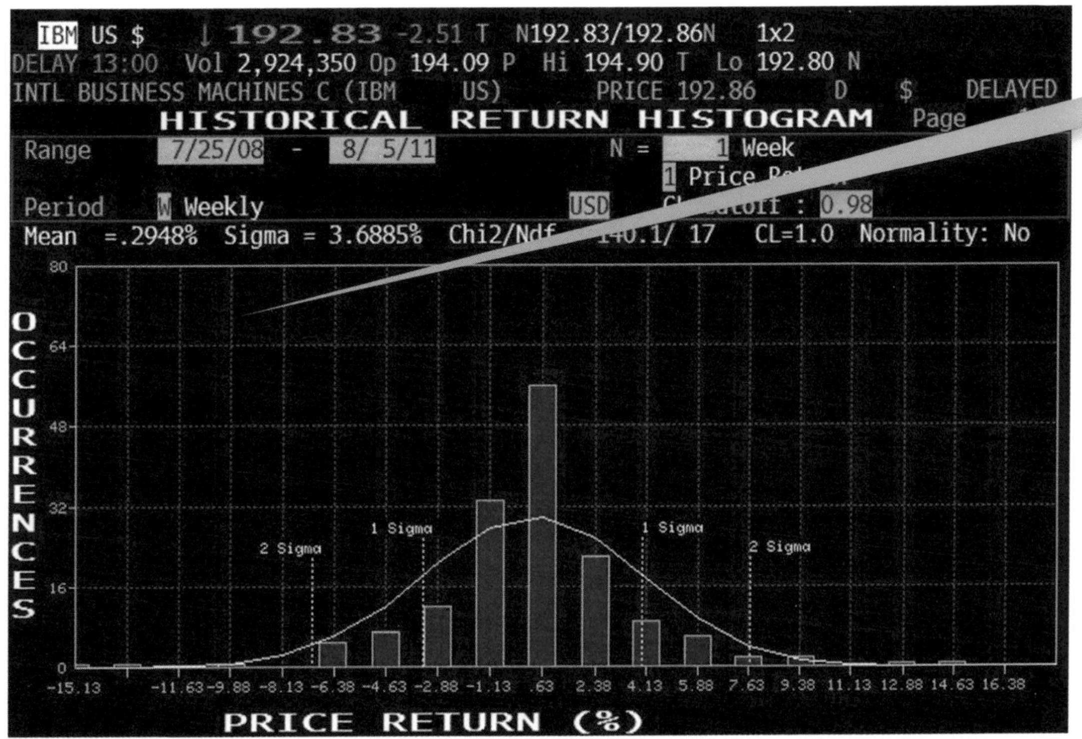

Exhibit 3.5

Bell curves offer realistic visualizations of movement over a given period of time. Use the sigma (standard deviation) to create realistic probability scenarios of an option expiring in the money.

Those call options and put options with low deltas are cheap for a reason—the odds are against you and the probability of that option "winning" or even being in the money on expiration is low. That doesn't mean that the option price can't jump in value beforehand and I often say that if you buy a cheap call or put and it's not being used for protection, sell it when you first get profitable.

Even though put deltas are expressed as negative numbers, the probability concept still applies the exact same way. A put with a delta of –0.15 would have 15 percent of expiring in the money.

KEY POINT:

Another characteristic of delta is that the more that an option is in the money, the higher the delta is. This makes intuitive sense because the more in the money an option is, the more likely it is to be exercised and, therefore, change in value exactly as the stock does. As an example, if stock XYZ trades for $54 per share, then the June 55 calls will have a higher delta than the June 60 calls because the June 55 calls are more in the money or, in this case, less out of the money and more likely to eventually be an exercise. For the puts this would be reversed—the June 60 puts would have a higher delta than the June 55 puts because the 60 puts are more in the money and, therefore, more likely to be an exercise.

KEY POINT:

The Black-Scholes model actually produces two deltas N(d1) and N(d2). The common delta that most of us use to measure P&L and change in an option price is N(d1). N(d2) is the risk-adjusted probability that the option will be exercised and is usually not displayed.

Dollar Delta

Dollar delta is another way to look at risk, rather than just looking at net deltas long or short, dollar delta factors in the price of the underlying security and can be used with stock positions as well.

To find the dollar delta of a stock position:

Number of shares long or short × the stock price

- If you were long 1,000 shares of IBM at $200, you would have $200,000 in dollar delta, which in this case is simply total funds as risk.

To find the dollar delta of an option position, the math is a bit different:

Dollar Delta = Current Price of Underlying × (Option's Delta × # of Option Contracts)

Enter delta as a whole number (e.g., 0.06 = 6)

- If you were long 10 contracts of the at-the-money IBM 200 calls that had a delta of 50, you would have $100,000 in dollar delta.

This may seem high, but if you think about it, 10 contracts of the 200 calls would cost you $200,000 if you wanted to exercise all of them. Dollar delta gets you thinking ahead and makes you aware of the type of risk you are fooling around with.

When I was a trader, we used dollar delta to keep our accounts in check and prevent catastrophe. Because we were frequently assigned on options during expiration, it was important to be aware of the fiscal ramifications.

My friends over at Options House took it a step further and came up with a great measurement for risk. They developed a "Leverage Risk" system that sets a value between 0 and 10 in increments of 2 and allows you to gauge just how much leverage risk you have in your account.

They gave the following example as an instance where leverage could get the best of you:

> If a customer were to buy a large quantity of out-of-the-money calls, and the markets were to trade up, and those calls were to be exercised, they would have a stock position yielding a dollar delta that is significantly greater than what their account can handle. An extremely large dollar delta position relative to account value can leave disproportionate risk.

The formula is simple: You merely find the percentage of total dollar delta to your entire portfolio's value. The scale of the different levels of risk has 10 being high risk and 0 being low. Options House went a step further and added beta weighting to their calculations.

Although technically delta is measured in cents because it is change per dollar and, therefore, can take any value from zero to a dollar, the convention for traders is to speak of deltas as whole numbers from zero to 100. It wouldn't be referred to as a 50-cent delta call, but rather a 50 delta call. Also, even though puts have negative delta, we wouldn't say, "that's a minus 30 delta put" or a "negative 30 delta put," it would just be a 30 delta put and it's implicitly understood that puts have negative delta and calls have positive delta.

How I Use Delta

The importance of delta varies depending on the strategy. In the case of long calls and puts, I tend to focus on delta much more and buy deep in the money options if I am trading them unhedged. I use delta first to select the options, then to gauge just how bullish or bearish I want to be in total.

For other strategies, I am less concerned with using delta to target the strikes because the trade might be focused more on the underlying getting to a certain price level, staying above or below a certain price level, or even on volatility moving in a certain direction. That doesn't mean that I ignore the delta all together, I just shift the delta importance to the allocation and exposure (beta) portion of the trade.

Regardless of the emphasis you place on each individual strategy's delta within your portfolio, it's helpful to look at the net dollar delta and the correlations of any stock in your portfolio (using portfolio beta) as a whole to manage risk. When I test a strategy, I move my forward date close to expiration to see how dramatic delta will become. If there are several trades in my portfolio that will gain delta close to expiration, I will generally adjust the strategy, hedge, or scale the number of contracts back.

I can also use delta to find out just how many shares of stock I need to buy or sell if I want to remain delta (direction) neutral or if I want to scale back or increase risk. Buying and selling stock around a position is called *gamma scalping* and I address that next.

As we examine each individual strategy, I discuss the importance and use of delta for each as well as offer guidelines for each.

Gamma

There are many books that skip over gamma or just mention it briefly. I feel like gamma is the red-headed stepchild of the Greeks, who maybe gets only a smidge more attention than its poor brother rho, which we get to shortly. See Exhibit 3.6.

Maybe this is because gamma is the only "second-order Greek" that most traders follow. I like to think of gamma as the "delta of the delta," as gamma measures the rate of change of the delta. Gamma, like the other Greeks, can and will change during the option's life. It is the only Greek that directly influences another Greek.

Pros may use different terms to describe the Greeks; delta is often called the *slope* of an option and gamma is sometimes described as the *curvature* of the option because as the underlying price changes, the option delta changes, too, in a nonlinear way. Gamma is used to describe this nonlinear change.

Most directional traders are more concerned with the ultimate outlook they have for the underlying instrument and how it relates to their strategy. In other words, you may know that you want IBM to get above $210 by October expiration and all you care about is the breakeven of your option.

For IBM to get to $210 by October expiration there needs to be some movement involved, being that the

Smart Investor Tip!

If you are buying a long call or long put as a proxy for being long or short stock, you want that option to behave as much like the stock as possible. To get that exposure, choose an option that is in the money with a delta of 0.70 to 0.90. Leverage will be on your side and you will be paying for minimal time value.

KEY POINT:

Gamma specifically measures the rate of change in an option's delta for every one-point move in the underlying stock.

Gamma will always appear as a bell curve; this is true if you plot one option with the *x*-axis as the underlying *price* or if you plot an entire option series with the *x*-axis being the strike *price* (ATM options have the highest gamma).

Exhibit 3.6

stock is currently at $190. Gamma will quantify just how fast the delta and your P&L will change given certain movements and time frames. See Exhibit 3.7.

Gamma is greatest in the at-the-money options and decreases as you go farther away from the ATM strike price. Gamma also tends to decrease the further out in time you go. This effect can be likened to whipping a long rope. At the end you are holding (current expiration or front month), the speed and volatility of that rope is extreme; at the far end of that 20-foot rope, the movement will be muted compared to the front. You'll find that this characteristic is common to other Greeks as well.

That means that you would theoretically have the most amount of Gamma in an option that was at the money and was just about to expire. This makes sense

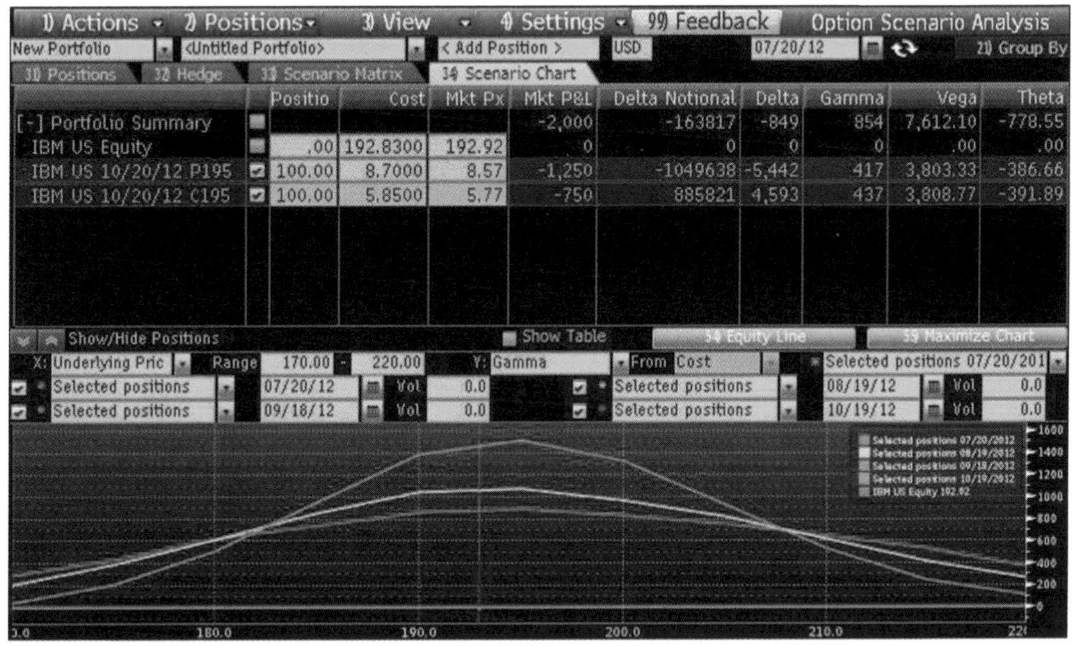

Exhibit 3.7

because on expiration that option will either have a delta of 0 or 1. If a stock was just about to expire and either going to be worth 1 or 0, you might guess that gamma would be near 1, which is the top of its range. Gamma is sort of like a free look into what delta will become as the stock moves around.

Understanding Gamma

For the retail trader, your relationship with gamma will most likely be similar to the relationship you share with a fifth cousin who lives in Greenland—distant. But gamma can be one of the most important risk management tools for options trading because it can act as a speedometer. The truth is, though, it's seldom used outside of the professional delta-neutral trading world.

For those of you who want to or do trade delta-neutral positions, gamma is your life! If you want to make the theoretical pricing models work as intended, you need to be delta-neutral, which means buying or selling shares constantly.

I have some great scalping tips and tricks I'll get to shortly, but first let's look at the some of the gamma relationships that matter to all.

Long Options = Long Gamma

When you purchase an option, you are getting long gamma, which means that delta is changing the way you would desire for the type of option you bought. That sounds a little odd I know, but think about it like this. . . .

When you purchase a call with a delta of 0.50 and a gamma of 0.15 and the stock moves up a dollar, your new delta might be something like 0.65, which means that essentially you are getting "more bullish" (making more money) as the stock rises, which is a good thing. I discussed this phenomena a bit earlier.

If that same stock were to drop $1, the new delta might be something like 0.45, making your bullish option position less bullish (making and also losing less money) and thus having less relation to the stock's movement. Trust me, these effects are only temporary, will change, and are not always desirable. Even though the stock moved down and your delta dropped a little, if the option is out of the money, it will continue to drop; in effect making it harder for you to make your money back! Again, never look at any one Greek in a vacuum.

In the professional market-making world, one of our objectives was to remain relatively delta-neutral. This meant have little risk associated with the stock movement itself. To accomplish this, we had to buy or sell stock (or other options) against our trades to mitigate our exposure.

If I were forced (as a market maker) to buy 10 puts with a –0.50 delta, I might buy 500 shares of stock to delta-neutralize my portfolio. If that stock dropped, I would be inclined to buy stock, because my put delta was accumulating (getting shorter deltas) and if it continued to do so, I could be in a world of hurt. If I did buy those shares and the stock then rallied I could sell those shares I bought as a hedge and capture a profit. Gamma is telling me how quickly I may have to hedge or how quickly my delta will get me into a situation where I am uncomfortable.

This was done to offset the theta (time decay) I was paying each day. You'll learn that for every positive in the options world, there is, to some extent, a negative. There truly is no such thing as a free lunch!

Given the ability to profit from any movement, it's common in volatile markets for most traders to have a position that has a net positive gamma. There is a tradeoff for this; you would prefer that the volatility of the options you are buying justifies the gamma position you want.

For example, what if a stock was moving at a 30 percent observed volatility, but you were buying options with an Ivol of 50—is it worth it? Are you scalping your long gamma/short theta position? Or are your options just too pricey and decaying faster than you are able to capture profits. If you are trading a more directional strategy, is the stock moving in your direction far enough and fast enough to profit?

Smart Investor Tip!

When you buy *any* option, you may be long gamma, but you are also typically paying theta, which means that it costs you money each day to be in that position. Theta is coming up next.

If you thought the Ivols were going to rise further, this would be okay and just like long options mean long gamma, long options also mean long vega and benefiting from the rise in Ivol. (Don't worry, we'll get to vega, too. For now, the simple definition of vega is that it measures an option's sensitivity to changes in implied volatility.)

There is no way to answer all these questions without looking at all the Greeks of your entire position and making a more informed decision.

Short Options = Short Gamma

When you are a net seller of options, you are generally short gamma, which means basically that the delta of the options or spread that you are positioned in will move *opposite of the stock.*

In a short gamma position your deltas will get closer to zero when the stock rises, and your deltas will get farther from zero when the stock falls. This can be big headache if you have a stock that's moving all over the place.

A good example of this is if you were to sell a 50 put with a delta of 0.50 and gamma of 0.10 with the stock at $50. (In this case you are long delta, because you sold the put.) If the stock rises to $51, your delta will *decrease* by 0.10 and you would in this case see an increase in your P&L. Be careful not to get gamma and delta mixed up. All gamma is measuring is the rate of change of the delta value, so if you are long delta and short gamma, you will still make money if the stock rises (you will just make less and less money as the stock goes higher).

In the case of this single put, gamma would diminish if the stock continued to move higher, but you would continue to profit all the way until the delta and the option price got closer zero. See Exhibit 3.8.

Some facts:

- When you sell an individual option, such as a call or a put, your position will always be short gamma—it will be greatest when the option is at the money and will diminish as the stock moves away from that point.
- Different spreads can go from being long gamma to short gamma and vice versa, depending on time and stock price.

Short gamma combined with zero or near zero delta means that you want that stock to stay perfectly still if at all possible. Most short gamma positions also want to see a decrease in implied volatility once the position is put on.

This is logical, because if buying options makes you long gamma and long vega, selling options makes you short gamma and short vega. A position that is short gamma can really behave oddly if you are not used to it. This is mainly because your delta (and often your P&L) is moving opposite to the stock.

Short gamma means that your position deltas are moving opposite to what the underlying stock is doing, so if you are short a call and the stock begins to move higher (not a good thing), you get shorter and shorter, which would mean you would have to buy

Smart Investor Tip!

If traders are long gamma, they may have the ability to scalp stock (for a profit) against their position to help offset theta they are paying. Being long gamma is warranted in some situations, typically if a stock is expected to be very volatile and hard to analyze.

DEFINITION:
Gamma scalping my stock
Gamma scalping my stock is the action of buying stock as a hedge and selling it for profit.

Smart Investor Tip!
If you decide to scalp short gamma, try to make sure that those losses from your negative scalping are less than the theta you are collecting and the vega profits you made.

stock to remain delta-neutral. Then, if the stock drops you get positive delta, which means that you may have to sell stock to neutralize, locking in a loss on your hedge (if you are hedging).

You might be thinking: What kind of a hedge is this? That logic makes no sense; buy high, sell low, how do I make money?

There's that trade-off again. When you are short options you are collecting theta; time benefits your position.

This is true for both calls and puts. You will also be short vega, so be sure to try and sell options when they are relatively expensive to give yourself that edge!

To do this, it might be advisable to hedge a little less often and look for normal oscillations. In other words, if the stock tends to rally sharply an hour before the close then come back down, it might not be a good idea to buy your hedge on that rally, just wait it out. Short gamma is actually worse on a stock that is trending against your delta position.

As you begin to understand more and more about position behavior, think about what gamma situation you would like to find yourself in. There is no right answer, because there is a time to buy and a time to sell options. But I encourage you to do this: The next time you make a trade—whether it is a single option or a spread—take a look at your gamma and watch how it behaves as you progress toward expiration.

Also remember that gamma is greatest in the at-the-money options, which means that you will see your biggest change in delta the closer the option is to the stock price. Gamma is also greatest in those options right before expiration (expiration Friday at 3:59 p.m. EST or whenever your options cease trading), because remember that an option will either have a delta of one or zero after expiring and the gamma will help dictate how fast it will change.

Gamma Trading Examples

There are right and wrong ways to trade gamma. At the end of the day, it really boils down to how well you know the stock and what other factors are involved in the trade (such as Greeks, premiums).

Often stocks will make dramatic moves over earnings reports and they can be fun times to be long gamma, but again there is a trade-off. Earlier I talked about using the value of the straddle to get a gauge of how much movement market participants were anticipating. If you are going to trade an event like earnings, the first determination you must make is whether you are more inclined to buy or sell the straddle. Do this by examining three things: the relative value of Ivol to Hvol; the historical percentage reactions the stock price has had to earnings (both positive and negative); and looking at the health of the company and its perceived ability to beat or miss estimates.

Your research should give you an idea of how far you think the stock will move on the report and in the days after. Once you have gathered that data, it's time to select your strategy and deal with your gamma.

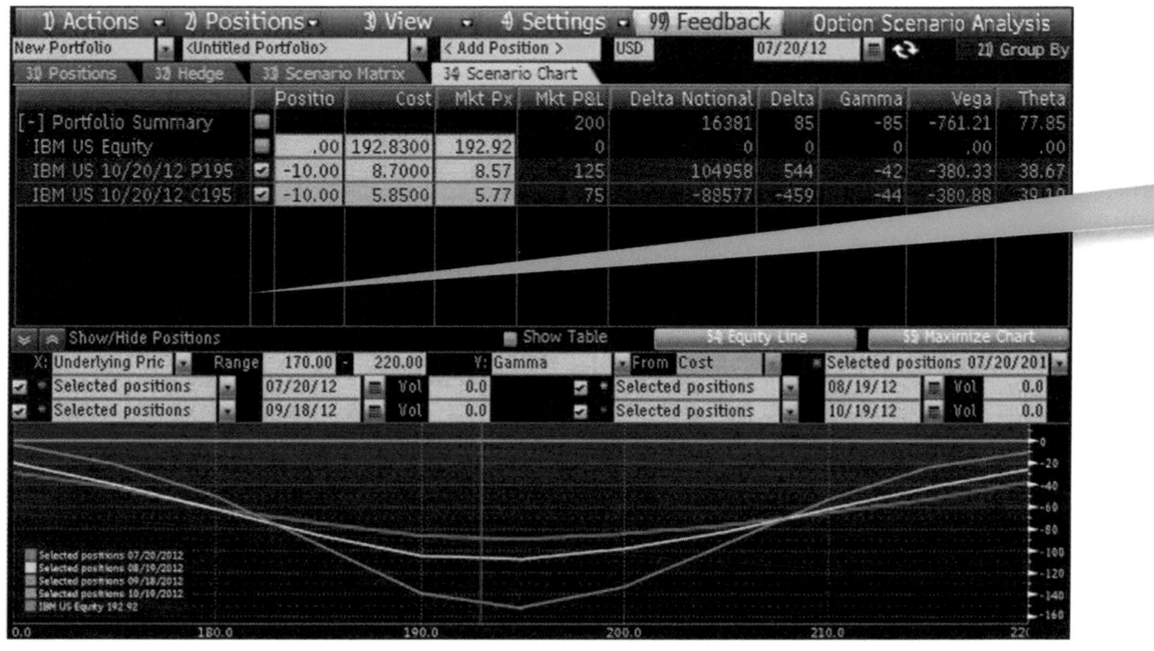

Exhibit 3.8

One thing to keep in mind when you are trading earnings is to account for the "Ivol crush" that happens most of the time. If you are planning on coming into the report with a long gamma strategy, chances are that you will be long vega as well. Be sure to get an idea of the average earnings Ivol crush and multiply that number by the vega of your strategy.

That's how much money you are almost guaranteed to lose in vega. After doing the math do you still think a long gamma trade is best? Is there a way to augment the trade with another spread or option that will reduce your vega, but maintain the gamma you want? Do you see the compounding effect?

Scalping for Dollars

One day you might have to answer this question: Do I get long a neutral strategy like a straddle or strangle and pray for a big move in the stock so that I can gamma scalp my stock out to overcome my theta and any reduction in implied volatility or do I sell the straddle, strangle, and so on, and pray that the stock stays within a range until expiration?

Herein lies the dichotomy of gamma as it relates to certain strategies. For example, one camp might be sellers of that straddle, thinking that there is no way that the stock moves greater than what the straddle sells for and their belief is that volatility is certain to come in.

The other camp may believe the exact opposite—that either volatility will expand or that they will be able to positively scalp their gamma or maybe that the eventual parity of their neutral will lead them to victory in the trade. For those traders who believe that volatility will actually increase, the appropriate strategy should be long, not short vega.

There is no right answer, but here are the basics of scalping long and short gamma and how you can profit (and lose) from them.

Long Gamma Scalping

If you bought the straddle earlier, you could make money several ways (see Exhibit 3.9):

- Simple direction asset movement would make you profitable—the stock moving away from the strike (in either direction) more than the amount you paid for the total straddle by expiration, $79.45 to the upside or $60.55 below would be your breakevens and any moves beyond that are gravy.
- Straddles can also make money from a jump in Ivol, which needs to be greater than the amount of theta that you are paying each day.
- You can also generate profits by scalping your gamma. The stock has to move around for you to do this, *and* you must also time your entries and exits and be extremely proactive in monitoring and trading the stock position.

Gamma scalping involves selling the amount of shares equal to your net delta. So if you bought 10 of the straddles above and the stock rose $3, you would have a net delta of roughly 239. If you thought the stock was going to drop from that point, you would maybe sell 240 shares, hoping to buy them back at a lower price. The same is true if the stock drops and deltas go negative; at this point you buy stock to hedge (right before you think the stock will rally) and sell them when the stock moves higher.

The profits generated are used to pay for the theta of being in the trade.

Short Gamma

Many pro traders will take the other side of the coin and get short gamma (short options) if there is high implied volatility that they believe will drop. Short gamma traders will pick a level or area the stock will get to, stay away from, or stay within. The variables all lie within what trade and strategy they choose. See Exhibit 3.10.

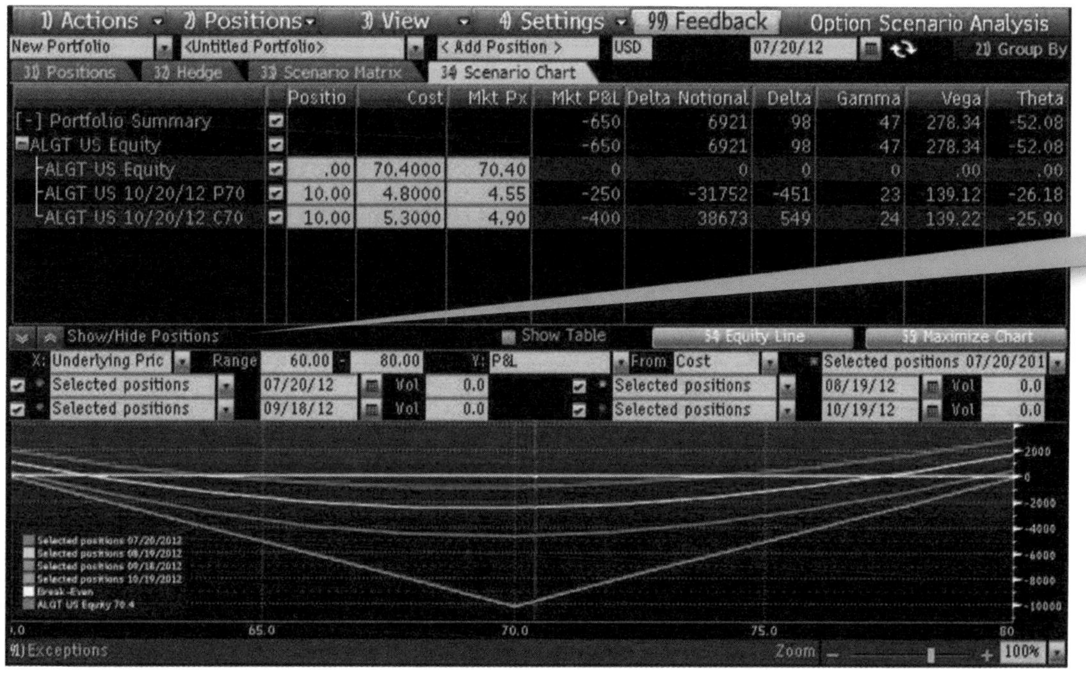

Exhibit 3.9

Long 10 ALGT 70 strike straddles with a total gamma of $47 and starting delta of 98.

Earnings

Because it is quite common for implied volatility to drop after an earnings report, some traders will get short gamma ahead of the announcement. This also means they will most likely be short vega and profit from the Ivol crush.

It's quite common to see the options markets pricing in a bigger move for earnings than what actually occurs. This can be a devastating blow for long gamma (long vega) traders. Many amateur traders get long a straddle or strangle going into a report and after the announcement end up with a loss, even with movement in the asset.

Don't be afraid of short gamma/short vega trades ahead of a report. If the breakevens of the strategy are outside where the stock ends up, you could have

DEFINITION:

Ivol crush:

Ivol crush: After an earnings event or similar unknown announcement that has potential for volatility, Ivol will rise ahead of the occasion. Once the announcement has been made (good or bad) there is a tendency for Ivol to come crashing down. This is called the *Ivol crush* and can be a detriment to long vega strategies.

IBM Ivol (in white) showing earnings Ivol crush.

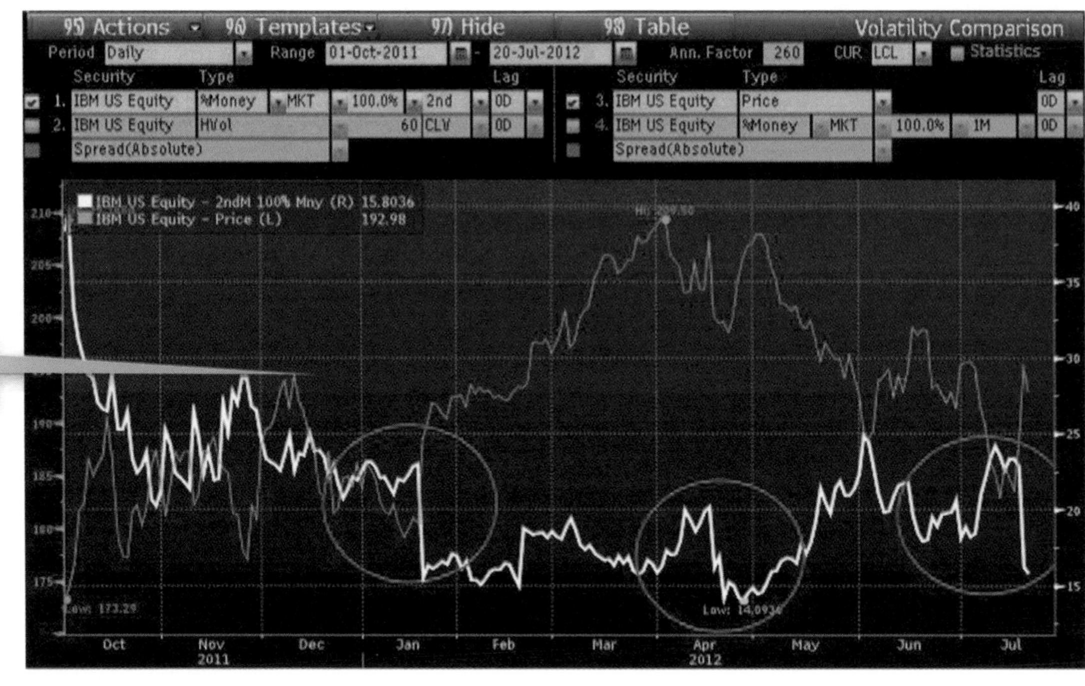

Exhibit 3.10

KEY POINT:

If you have a directional bias going into an earnings report or other type of potentially volatile announcement, position your strikes so that you are long or short the amount of delta that's suitable. You can test your position in the OSA screen.

a profit on your hands. In this case, you're not "trading" gamma, you're making your money from vega and theta and maybe delta if you position your strategy on the right side of the trade.

Because you are not hedged with a stock position, you will have greater risk exposure than a trader who does a full or partial hedge. As long as you are okay with the risk, then the trade is certainly viable if you've done your homework. Strategies like iron condors and butterflies are limited in risk and will carry less gamma and delta risk than a short straddle or strangle.

More advanced traders who want to capture the Ivol crush, but do not want to have as much risk, may opt to sell a straddle or strangle, and buy or sell shares of stock to offset their risk (get neutral).

Negative Gamma Scalping

Short-gamma scalpers have their work cut out for them. If your intention is to sell premium, but keep yourself hedged, you want to trade those hedges as *infrequently* as possible.

Selling an at-the-money straddle is an example of a short gamma position that may require hedging. It is a high-risk proposition with high margin costs when left unhedged—this is why most professionals look to buy or sell stock against that trade to even out their deltas and mitigate risk.

If the stock falls below your straddle strike, the short put delta gets you longer and longer and it may eventually force you to sell shares at a lower price to neutralize. In essence, the further your stock moves below strike, the longer your position delta gets—the hedge then forces you to sell stock when its spot price is low, which is never a good thing.

If the stock rallies above your straddle strike then your short call delta starts to kick in, making your position short more and more deltas the higher the stock goes (you will be losing money by the way), which means that you would have to buy stock to hedge. The eventual sum of sell low and buy high = a losing hedge trade, but there is a reason that some traders are okay with this.

Sell low and buy high? Something doesn't sound right! This is a struggle that dynamic hedgers have to face every day. Unlike the long straddle that is costing you theta as each day passes, the short straddle is **paying** you theta every day, assuming nothing else changes (like volatility or the stock price).

The goal is to collect that theta (cash) every day and hopefully it is more than what you are losing with your negative gamma scalping. Because delta changes every time a stock moves, option traders who want to remain neutral are forced to continuously adjust the hedges on their positions, which can really hurt if you overtrade. In a relatively stable market, with no surprises like a big change in volatility, collecting theta and having short gamma can be a profitable addition to a portfolio. In volatile, unpredictable environments, it can be a nightmare.

Approaching expiration, gamma can get even harder to manage and even downright stressful. You have to change your mind-set from a hedger to figuring out where the stock will end up after expiration and where your ultimate risk will lie if you want to hold the trade.

Theta

Of all the Greeks, I believe theta is one of the easiest to understand. It's something that is occurring all the time and tends to be semi-orderly until you get within a couple of weeks of expiration. Theta is also one of the most important Greeks because it truly is the core difference between the underlying asset and the derivative that trades on it—the expiration date. See Exhibit 3.11.

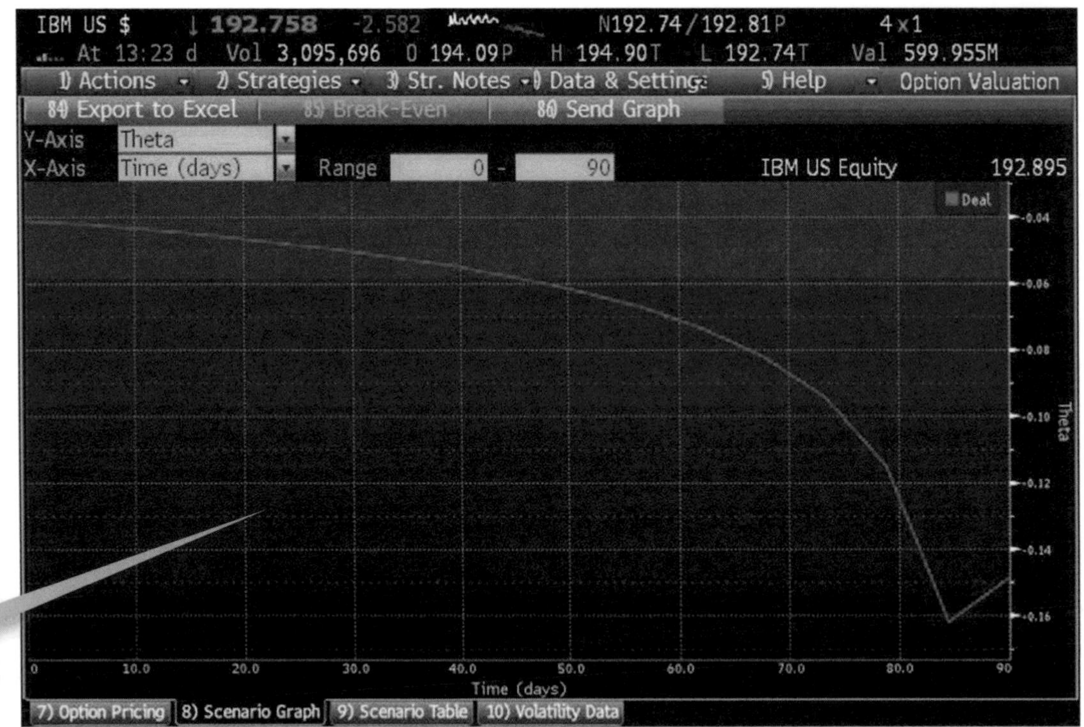

Time value (theta) decays over the life of an IBM option. The little burst at the end is an anomaly you will sometimes see near expiration when the option is near the money.

Exhibit 3.11

DEFINITION:
Theta
is the dollar amount that your option (or portfolio if you're looking at net theta) will lose each day.

All options are essentially decaying assets; just about all of them are losing some amount of money each and every day, including weekends, as they march toward expiration.

Depending on the strategy that you are employing, theta can act as your ally or enemy, and sometimes both depending on where the stock is in relation to some spreads. The amount of theta in a spread can (and usually will) change over time, and go from positive to negative. It may seem like you are collecting theta one day, and paying it out the next. Your analysis should run through different time and price scenarios to see the effects of theta on your position. This flip-flopping of theta from positive to negative only occurs with certain spread trades, not with individual options. But individual options can see dramatic changes in the amount of daily theta.

Expressed in Dollars

When examining the theta column in an option chain the values displayed there are in "dollars per day." So an option with a theta of 0.15 means that the option will decrease in value approximately 0.15 or $15 each and every day and that number will be ever changing. See Exhibit 3.12.

Generally speaking, if you sell options (or trade a spread with positive theta), your portfolio P&L will benefit from the passage of time.

When you purchase options or trade a spread with negative theta, time is costing you money. If you are paying theta, you can overcome that loss either by a major change in implied volatility (vega) or a favorable change in delta when the stock moves in your desired direction. See Exhibit 3.13.

Gamma, Theta, and Vega All Working Together

All Greeks are somewhat related, but there are a couple of rules that will help you make strategy selections.

If you are net long options—Your position will generally be *long gamma* and you will generally be *paying theta* and *long vega*. This type of position will be costing you some amount of money each day to keep on.

You can overcome this cost by: scalping gamma profitably (if you're a gamma hedger); profiting from your delta (preferred movement in the stock); or by an increase in Ivol.

If you are net short options—Your position will generally be *short gamma* and you will generally be *collecting theta* and *short vega*. This type of position will be generating some amount of money each day it is left in force.

Unlike the long position in this scenario you would want to keep the negative gamma scalping to a minimum (so it doesn't dig into the theta you're collecting). You can still profit from your delta (the preferred movement in the stock) and you can profit from a decrease in Ivol.

There's that tit-for-tat, trade-off thing again and it's logical when you think about it. Because markets are constantly moving randomly, it would make sense that a short gamma position gets more profitable over time because as a short gamma trader, you want the markets to stay still or within a range, which is basically the opposite of the market's natural way.

On the other hand, long gamma traders have the logical odds in their favor. If you make the assumption that the markets are going to move, which they do all the time, you are going to have to pay for the ability to profit from that.

It's sort of a rudimentary way to think about it, but it helps with your rationalization of risk later on. The reality is that your choice to be short gamma, long

As you can see in the chain, theta ("TM" column) varies from option to option and month to month; it is also dynamic as time progresses.

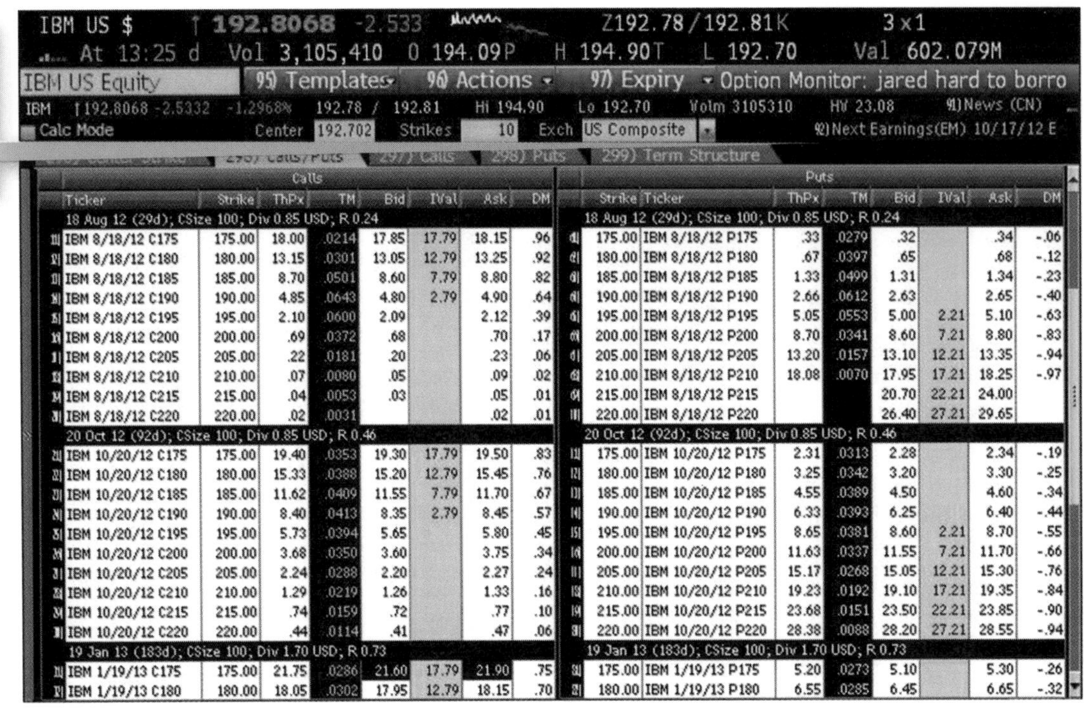

IBM US $ 192.8068 -2.533 Z192.78/192.81K 3x1

At 13:25 d Vol 3,105,410 O 194.09P H 194.90T L 192.70 Val 602.079M

IBM US Equity 95) Templates 96) Actions 97) Expiry Option Monitor: jared hard to borro

IBM 192.8068 -2.5332 -1.2968% 192.78 / 192.81 Hi 194.90 Lo 192.70 Volm 3105310 HV 23.08 91) News (CN)

Calc Mode Center 192.702 Strikes 10 Exch US Composite 92) Next Earnings(EM) 10/17/12 E

296) Calls/Puts 297) Calls 298) Puts 299) Term Structure

Calls								Puts							
Ticker	Strike	ThPx	TM	Bid	IVal	Ask	DM	Strike	Ticker	ThPx	TM	Bid	IVal	Ask	DM
18 Aug 12 (29d); CSize 100; Div 0.85 USD; R 0.24								18 Aug 12 (29d); CSize 100; Div 0.85 USD; R 0.24							
IBM 8/18/12 C175	175.00	18.00	.0214	17.85	17.79	18.15	.96	175.00	IBM 8/18/12 P175	.33	.0279	.32		.34	-.06
IBM 8/18/12 C180	180.00	13.15	.0301	13.05	12.79	13.25	.92	180.00	IBM 8/18/12 P180	.67	.0397	.65		.68	-.12
IBM 8/18/12 C185	185.00	8.70	.0501	8.60	7.79	8.80	.82	185.00	IBM 8/18/12 P185	1.33	.0499	1.31		1.34	-.23
IBM 8/18/12 C190	190.00	4.85	.0643	4.80	2.79	4.90	.64	190.00	IBM 8/18/12 P190	2.66	.0612	2.63		2.65	-.40
IBM 8/18/12 C195	195.00	2.10	.0600	2.09		2.12	.39	195.00	IBM 8/18/12 P195	5.05	.0553	5.00	2.21	5.10	-.63
IBM 8/18/12 C200	200.00	.69	.0372	.68		.70	.17	200.00	IBM 8/18/12 P200	8.70	.0341	8.60	7.21	8.80	-.83
IBM 8/18/12 C205	205.00	.22	.0181	.20		.23	.06	205.00	IBM 8/18/12 P205	13.20	.0157	13.10	12.21	13.35	-.94
IBM 8/18/12 C210	210.00	.07	.0080	.05		.09	.02	210.00	IBM 8/18/12 P210	18.08	.0070	17.95	17.21	18.25	-.97
IBM 8/18/12 C215	215.00	.04	.0053	.03		.05	.01	215.00	IBM 8/18/12 P215			20.70	22.21	24.00	
IBM 8/18/12 C220	220.00	.02	.0031			.02	.01	220.00	IBM 8/18/12 P220			26.40	27.21	29.65	
20 Oct 12 (92d); CSize 100; Div 0.85 USD; R 0.46								20 Oct 12 (92d); CSize 100; Div 0.85 USD; R 0.46							
IBM 10/20/12 C175	175.00	19.40	.0353	19.30	17.79	19.50	.83	175.00	IBM 10/20/12 P175	2.31	.0313	2.28		2.34	-.19
IBM 10/20/12 C180	180.00	15.33	.0388	15.20	12.79	15.45	.76	180.00	IBM 10/20/12 P180	3.25	.0342	3.20		3.30	-.25
IBM 10/20/12 C185	185.00	11.62	.0409	11.55	7.79	11.70	.67	185.00	IBM 10/20/12 P185	4.55	.0389	4.50		4.60	-.34
IBM 10/20/12 C190	190.00	8.40	.0413	8.35	2.79	8.45	.57	190.00	IBM 10/20/12 P190	6.33	.0393	6.25		6.40	-.44
IBM 10/20/12 C195	195.00	5.73	.0394	5.65		5.80	.45	195.00	IBM 10/20/12 P195	8.65	.0381	8.60	2.21	8.70	-.55
IBM 10/20/12 C200	200.00	3.68	.0350	3.60		3.75	.34	200.00	IBM 10/20/12 P200	11.63	.0337	11.55	7.21	11.70	-.66
IBM 10/20/12 C205	205.00	2.24	.0288	2.20		2.27	.24	205.00	IBM 10/20/12 P205	15.17	.0268	15.05	12.21	15.30	-.76
IBM 10/20/12 C210	210.00	1.29	.0219	1.26		1.33	.16	210.00	IBM 10/20/12 P210	19.23	.0192	19.10	17.21	19.35	-.84
IBM 10/20/12 C215	215.00	.74	.0159	.72		.77	.10	215.00	IBM 10/20/12 P215	23.68	.0151	23.50	22.21	23.85	-.90
IBM 10/20/12 C220	220.00	.44	.0114	.41		.47	.06	220.00	IBM 10/20/12 P220	28.38	.0088	28.20	27.21	28.55	-.94
19 Jan 13 (183d); CSize 100; Div 1.70 USD; R 0.73								19 Jan 13 (183d); CSize 100; Div 1.70 USD; R 0.73							
IBM 1/19/13 C175	175.00	21.75	.0286	21.60	17.79	21.90	.75	175.00	IBM 1/19/13 P175	5.20	.0273	5.10		5.30	-.26
IBM 1/19/13 C180	180.00	18.05	.0302	17.95	12.79	18.15	.70	180.00	IBM 1/19/13 P180	6.55	.0285	6.45		6.65	-.32

Exhibit 3.12

(collecting) theta or long gamma, short (paying) theta has everything to do with the relative value and risk of the strategy you are employing in conjunction with any directional biases your thesis may have given you.

This all assumes that you're not hedging your positions with stock. You should simply use gamma as a means to measure acceleration of your delta and use theta as a means to know just how many dollars your position will be generating or losing each day until you exit.

Nuances of Theta

There are exceptions to being net long options and long gamma as well as net short options and short gamma.

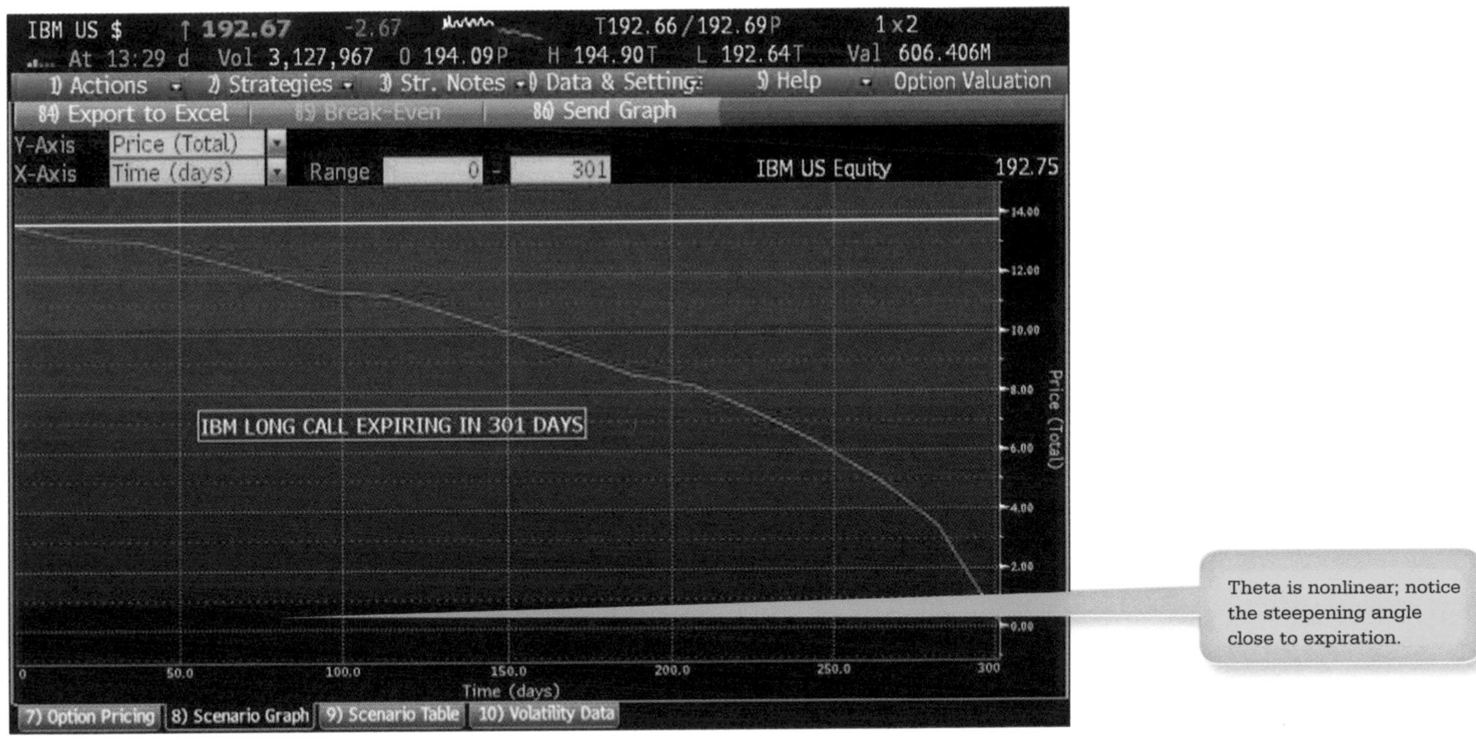

Exhibit 3.13

Take a look at the position displayed in the OSA screen in Exhibit 3.14. In this scenario, you are net short options, but long gamma and paying theta. This is because you are long the ATM calls and short 50 percent more OTM calls that have much less gamma.

Time spreads and ratios can make the gamma and theta relationship hard to correlate. You can never look at either of these in a vacuum, nor should you discount the other Greeks and how they influence one another and change with the passage of time and price. What is today will generally not be tomorrow when it comes to options and the stock market in general.

There are other exceptions and “morphing scenarios” where theta might go from positive to negative

KEY POINT:

Gamma and theta rules for any vertical spread:

When the stock is where it needs to be in relation to your strikes for you to make max profit at expiration, gamma will be negative and theta will be positive.

If the stock moves to a price that would cause you to lose money on expiration, gamma now turns positive and you will be short (paying) theta.

over time or depending on where the stock price is. A simple example would be the vertical spread, which we detail shortly.

Theta, I believe, should hold a bit more precedence than it usually gets in the typical pretrade analysis. The reality is that theta affects different strategies in different ways and with different levels of severity. Because the curve of time decay (which is the only thing theta affects) is nonlinear, you should run scenarios close to expiration to see just how aggressive time decay becomes and think about how you are going to trade it.

Your analysis might be pointing to a specific level or area in the stock and as long as the stock is in that range, you might have little or no worry about theta and some of the other Greeks. But did you ever have a stock moving in your favor but you weren't getting the reward you thought you would from the option strategy you choose?

I am sure you have if you have traded before.

This disappointment was most likely caused by overlooking how theta and some of the other Greeks change as you get closer to expiration, not some magical gremlin hiding your profits from you.

One of those strategies where you might see this is the long iron condor. It's a strategy that profits from a large move in the stock beyond the outer strikes. What most novice traders fail to realize is that it may not get profitable until very close to or just at expiration. See Exhibit 3.15.

Take a look at this iron condor in the SPX. The amount of theta in the 10-lot trade is $78.00 (debit) per day. Now might be a time when you wished you did your homework (hopefully you did): you may want to take the trade-off now for a small profit if you were worried about a pullback in the stock that would put it back between your long strikes. The question is *if* you will because you didn't achieve the profits you wanted!

There are some strategies where theta really doesn't have much effect and you may only need to deal with it minimally if at all. Deep-in-the-money options have minimal time value compared to their price. You may have an $8 option with an 85 delta that has only 30 cents of time value. In this case, if you are buying that call because you think the stock is going to jump by $10, should you really be concerned about the 30 cents? Probably not, but these exceptions are far and few between.

If the time value of the option or spread that you are trading is so minuscule compared to the intrinsic value or just in general, theta might be the least of your concerns.

Don't forget that theta, like the other Greeks, is compounding and if you buy 300 contracts of a 10 delta option that costs 15 cents and has a theta of 0.01, you might not think to look at theta because of the price. But when you put it into perspective and use the real cash value, that little theta is actually $300 a day of your money and growing!

Remember that theta may simply be the dollar amount the option will decay each day, but it can have compounding effects on your portfolio. It's not a bad

<HELP> for explanation. P110 EquityOSA

1) Actions · 2) Positions · 3) View · 4) Settings · 99) Feedback Option Scenario Analysis

Portfolio (Owned) Jared Big Portfolio < Add Position > USD 08/11/12 21) Group By

31) Positions 32) Hedge 33) Scenario Matrix 34) Scenario Chart

	Position	Mkt Px	M	Cost	Total Cost	Mkt Value	P&L	Delta	Delta Notional	Gamma	Theta	Vega	Rho	IVol	Beta
[-] Portfolio Summary					161,057	165,567	4,509		223,323		166.14	-273.54	91.00		
AAPL US Equity					30,685	30,660	-25	12	7,542	-1	10.90	78.24	39.28		
AAPL US Equity	50.00	621.70	l	615.7000	30,785	31,085	300	50	31,085	0	.00	.00	.00		1.00
AAPL US 11/17/12 C650	5.00	20.85	m	21.3000	10,650	10,425	-225	198	122,892	19	-81.92	615.69	295.30	25.20	1.00
AAPL US 10/20/12 C630	-5.00	21.70	m	21.5000	-10,750	-10,850	-100	-236	-146,435	-20	92.83	-537.46	-256.01	23.47	1.00
ATVI US Equity					824	1,478	654	929	10,814	-23	.55	-4.39	8.23		
ATVI US Equity	200.00	11.64	l	11.1200	2,224	2,328	104	200	2,328	0	.00	.00	.00		.64
ATVI US 09/22/12 P12	-20.00	.605	m	1.0000	-2,000	-1,210	790	1246	14,500	-91	9.20	-29.59	15.38	25.46	.64
ATVI US 09/22/12 P11	20.00	.18	m	.3000	600	360	-240	-517	-6,014	68	-8.65	25.20	-7.15	28.24	.64
CHK US Equity					-460	-380	80	-133	-2,627	-15	8.42	-15.23	-2.52		
CHK US Equity	.00	19.68	l	17.8900	0	0	0	0	0	0	.00	.00	.00		1.45
CHK US 09/22/12 C23	20.00	.18	m	.1000	200	360	160	281	5,521	33	-14.58	29.37	5.79	40.51	1.45
CHK US 09/22/12 C22	-20.00	.33	m	.2000	-400	-660	-260	-454	-8,937	-44	19.79	-39.73	-9.28	40.64	1.45
CHK US 09/22/12 P13	-20.00	.10	m	.3200	-640	-200	440	86	1,694	-7	11.50	-12.05	2.12	78.16	1.45
CHK US 09/22/12 P11	20.00	.06	m	.1900	380	120	-260	-46	-905	3	-8.29	7.18	-1.15	94.62	1.45
GLD US Equity					13,555	14,693	1,138	314	49,365	-56	29.31	-153.36	38.87		
GLD US Equity	100.00	157.18	l	155.5500	15,555	15,718	163	100	15,718	0	.00	.00	.00		.22
GLD US 09/22/12 P151	-10.00	1.025	m	2.0000	-2,000	-1,025	975	214	33,647	-56	29.31	-153.36	38.87	15.58	.22
GOOG US Equity					62,750	63,950	1,200	131	84,308	-11	91.08	-50.67	3.24		
GOOG US Equity	100.00	642.00	l	640.0000	64,000	64,200	200	100	64,200	0	.00	.00	.00		.99
GOOG US 08/18/12 P600	-50.00	.225	m	1.3000	-6,500	-1,125	5,375	130	83,203	-81	566.35	-246.17	13.58	27.59	.99
GOOG US 08/18/12 P595	50.00	.175	m	1.0500	5,250	875	-4,375	-98	-63,095	70	-475.26	195.51	-10.34	29.25	.99
HEP US Equity					-1,150	-1,088	63	-300	-19,783	-30	10.08	-42.62	-20.96		
HEP US Equity	.00	65.91	l	65.1600	0	0	0	0	0	0	.00	.00	.00		.49
HEP US 09/22/12 C65	-5.00	2.175	m	2.3000	-1,150	-1,088	63	-300	-19,783	-30	10.08	-42.62	-20.96	19.10	.49
IBM US Equity					38,404	38,873	469	332	66,117	-22	6.65	-57.31	30.54		
IBM US Equity	200.00	199.29	l	198.5200	39,704	39,858	154	200	39,858	0	.00	.00	.00		.84
IBM US 09/22/12 P195	-10.00	2.235	m	3.5500	-3,550	-2,235	1,315	325	64,694	-70	44.55	-240.05	75.03	15.36	.84
IBM US 09/22/12 P190	10.00	1.25	m	2.2500	2,250	1,250	-1,000	-193	-38,434	48	-37.90	182.74	-44.49	17.11	.84
QQQ US Equity					13,120	13,372	252	200	13,372	0	.00	.00	.00		
QQQ US Equity	200.00	66.86	l	65.6000	13,120	13,372	252	200	13,372	0	.00	.00	.00		1.04

Exhibit 3.14

idea to keep your eye on how much you are paying (or collecting) in your trade. Think of theta as rent—you'll either be paying or collecting it.

Vega

As I stated earlier, understanding historical and implied volatility should be the number one priority in your option education. It would make sense that vega, which measures an option's sensitivity to changes in implied volatility, should be equally as important. You'll find that grasping the concept of vega is much easier! See Exhibit 3.16.

Vega values are shown on your broker's platform usually in the option chain. Just like the other Greeks, vega will be unique to each and every option in the universe. Vega is measured in dollars, so if you are examining an option with a vega of 0.20, this means that the value of the option will increase roughly 0.20 (or $20 because options contracts are bundles

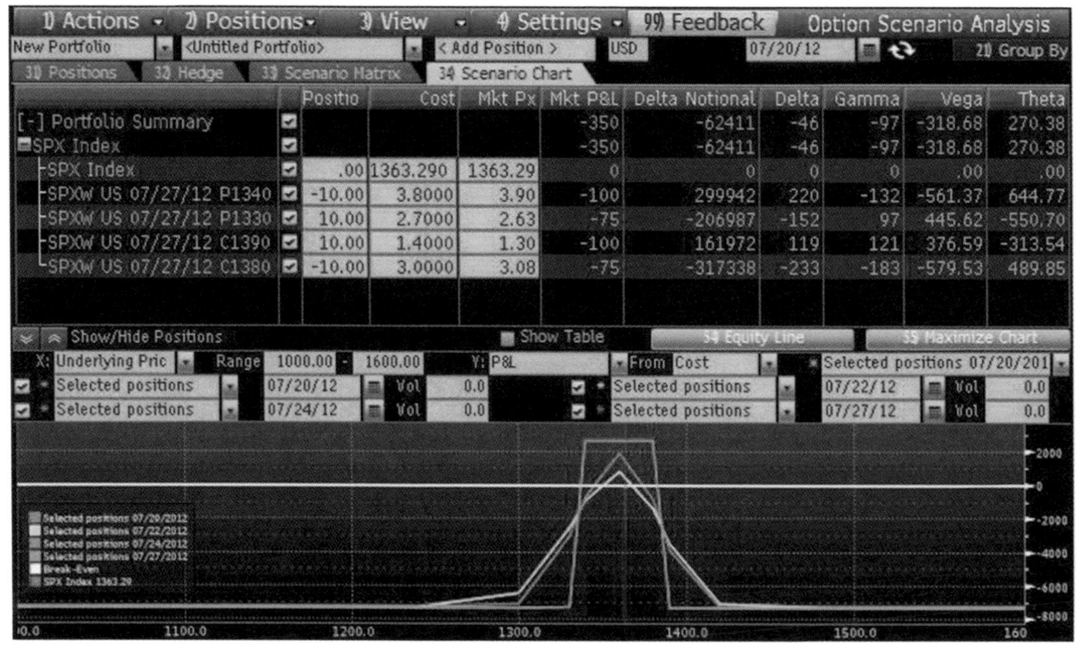

Exhibit 3.15

> **KEY POINT:**
> Volatility going from 10 percent to 11 percent is a 1 percent absolute change as is volatility going from 99 percent to 100 percent. Absolute can be thought of as actual change, not percentage change. Traders often refer to *absolute* changes as *handles*.

of 100) with a 1 percent *absolute* rise in volatility and will lose 0.20 with a 1 percent absolute decrease in volatility.

Vega is *a dynamic* measurement and will change throughout an option's life. Generally speaking, the more time an option has until expiration, the greater the vega when compared to the same strike in a nearer month. This is because there is more time value assigned to an option the further out in time you go. The more time value, the more vega (on a dollar basis) the option will have.

(There is a possibility that an option with a longer dated expiration has less vega as a percentage of its total premium.)

Remember that the implied volatility of an option is generally figured backward from its price. The price of the option is determined by a pricing model that uses several "objective" input values along with one "subjective" input value (implied volatility). But option prices are also determined by supply and demand and the only way to adjust option prices is by adjusting the implied volatility input! Tail wagging the dog?

Vega value, on the other hand, is determined solely by the option pricing model. You don't have to worry about all that Ivol and Hvol stuff if you are just trying to figure out how sensitive your option or spread will be to changes in Ivol. Just be aware of the forces that are tugging on the markets so you can be informed.

Vega is straightforward and will work as stated without too many nuances. If the security you are trading starts to become more volatile and implied volatility rises, the options with the greater vega will have the most change in price (based on vega alone; remember they will also be influenced by delta, theta, etc.). If Ivol is decreasing, an option price will also fall by the amount of vega × the change in Ivol.

The most amount of vega on a dollar basis will be found in the at-the-money option with the longest expiration date. It will slowly decay, along with theta, as the option approaches expiration. Vega also decreases as you move farther into the money or out of the money.

In many spreads you buy one option and sell another against it. This action will naturally reduce the amount of vega sensitivity in your position.

Nominal Vega

Because at-the-money options have the most amount of time value, they will have the most amount of vega. This is not always the greatest percentage change. When you are calculating vega and your risk, especially ahead of an event that could have a big influence on Ivol, be sure that you not only check nominal vega, but also vega as a percentage of price. It may cause you to rethink your strike selection or allocation to the trade.

Out-of-the-money options, both calls and puts, have the highest percentage sensitivity to changes in volatility. In other words, even though the vega looks the highest in the ATM options, the out-of-the-money options will be affected much more in terms of percentage change than the at- or in-the-money option. See Exhibit 3.17.

I will outline the vega sensitivity and risk for each strategy in this guide. As long as you grasp the basic concept, vega is a fairly simple Greek to manage. Because it decreases as you move closer to expiration, its effects are gradually lessened over time. If you want to place a higher emphasis on vega risk, trade longer dated options.

Rho

Rho is like the Pluto of the options world—it's sort of this far-off thing that most people don't know much about and don't pay attention to. When interest rates were much higher, rho, interest rates themselves, and the strategies and tactics used to trade them took a much more prominent role. Kind of like when Pluto was still considered a planet. But when you have rates

KEY POINT:

Just as with other Greeks, there are ways to mitigate your vega risk. Deep in-the-money options will have the least amount of vega in relation to their total price, and therefore will be the least susceptible to changes in volatility in percentage terms.

Certain vertical spreads will also neutralize your vega risk.

Smart Investor Tip!

Volatility affects the time-value portion of an option, and will cause the overall premium of that option to rise or fall. The vega of your option represents the change in value of the option for a 1 percent absolute change in Ivol.

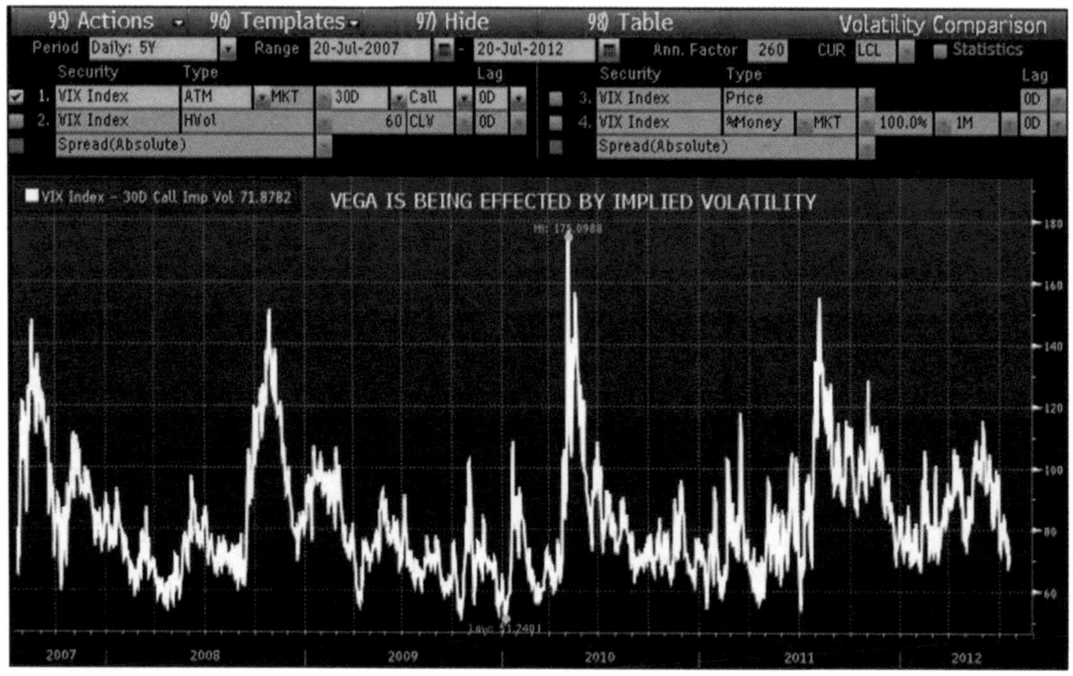

Exhibit 3.16

near zero, and little or no expectations for change, rho takes a bit of a sideline.

As you probably figured, rho is an option's sensitivity to changes in interest rates. Rho is the least important for most traders, especially those trading shorter dated options. This is because rho is greatest for *in-the-money, high-strike* options with the furthest expiration date. All calls have positive rho and all puts have negative rho.

Like delta, vega, and theta, rho is expressed in dollar terms and represents the change in the theoretical value of the option for a one percentage point (absolute) movement in interest rates. If you see an option with a rho of 00, it's perfectly normal. In fact, I tend to

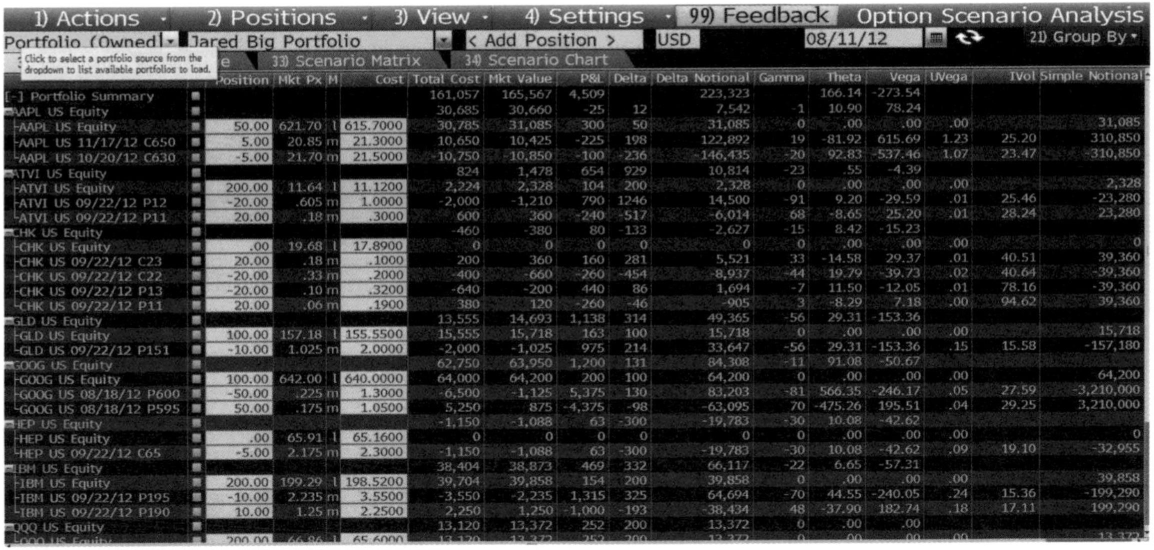

1) Actions 2) Positions 3) View 4) Settings 99) Feedback Option Scenario Analysis

Portfolio (Owned) Jared Big Portfolio < Add Position > USD 08/11/12 21) Group By

Click to select a portfolio source from the dropdown to list available portfolios to load. 33) Scenario Matrix 34) Scenario Chart

	Position	Mkt Px	M	Cost	Total Cost	Mkt Value	P&L	Delta	Delta Notional	Gamma	Theta	Vega	UVega	IVol	Simple Notional
[-] Portfolio Summary					161,057	165,567	4,509		223,323		166.14	-273.54			
AAPL US Equity					30,685	30,660	-25	12	7,542	-1	10.90	78.24			
AAPL US Equity	50.00	621.70	l	615.7000	30,785	31,085	300	50	31,085	0	.00	.00	.00		31,085
AAPL US 11/17/12 C650	5.00	20.85	m	21.3000	10,650	10,425	-225	198	122,892	19	-81.92	615.69	1.23	25.20	310,850
AAPL US 10/20/12 C630	-5.00	21.70	m	21.5000	-10,750	-10,850	-100	-236	-146,435	-20	92.83	-537.46	1.07	23.47	-310,850
ATVI US Equity					824	1,478	654	929	10,814	-23	.55	-4.39			
ATVI US Equity	200.00	11.64	l	11.1200	2,224	2,328	104	200	2,328	0	.00	.00	.00		2,328
ATVI US 09/22/12 P12	-20.00	.605	m	1.0000	-2,000	-1,210	790	1246	14,500	-91	9.20	-29.59	.01	25.46	-23,280
ATVI US 09/22/12 P11	20.00	.18	m	.3000	600	360	-240	-517	-6,014	68	-8.65	25.20	.01	28.24	23,280
CHK US Equity					-460	-380	80	-133	-2,627	-15	8.42	-15.23			
CHK US Equity	.00	19.68	l	17.8900	0	0	0	0	0	0	.00	.00	.00		0
CHK US 09/22/12 C23	20.00	.18	m	.1000	200	360	160	281	5,521	33	-14.58	29.37	.01	40.51	39,360
CHK US 09/22/12 C22	-20.00	.33	m	.2000	-400	-660	-260	-454	-8,937	-44	19.79	-39.73	.02	40.64	-39,360
CHK US 09/22/12 P13	-20.00	.10	m	.3200	-640	-200	440	86	1,694	-7	11.50	-12.05	.01	78.16	-39,360
CHK US 09/22/12 P11	20.00	.06	m	.1900	380	120	-260	-46	-905	3	-8.29	7.18	.00	94.62	39,360
GLD US Equity					13,555	14,693	1,138	314	49,365	-56	29.31	-153.36			
GLD US Equity	100.00	157.18	l	155.5500	15,555	15,718	163	100	15,718	0	.00	.00	.00		15,718
GLD US 09/22/12 P151	-10.00	1.025	m	2.0000	-2,000	-1,025	975	214	33,647	-56	29.31	-153.36	.15	15.58	-157,180
GOOG US Equity					62,750	63,950	1,200	131	84,308	-11	91.08	-50.67			
GOOG US Equity	100.00	642.00	l	640.0000	64,000	64,200	200	100	64,200	0	.00	.00	.00		64,200
GOOG US 08/18/12 P600	-50.00	.225	m	1.3000	-6,500	-1,125	5,375	130	83,203	-81	566.35	-246.17	.05	27.59	-3,210,000
GOOG US 08/18/12 P595	50.00	.175	m	1.0500	5,250	875	-4,375	-98	-63,095	70	-475.26	195.51	.04	29.25	3,210,000
HEP US Equity					-1,150	-1,088	63	-300	-19,783	-30	10.08	-42.62			
HEP US Equity	.00	65.91	l	65.1600	0	0	0	0	0	0	.00	.00	.00		0
HEP US 09/22/12 C65	-5.00	2.175	m	2.3000	-1,150	-1,088	63	-300	-19,783	-30	10.08	-42.62	.09	19.10	-32,955
IBM US Equity					38,404	38,873	469	332	66,117	-22	6.65	-57.31			
IBM US Equity	200.00	199.29	l	198.5200	39,704	39,858	154	200	39,858	0	.00	.00	.00		39,858
IBM US 09/22/12 P195	-10.00	2.235	m	3.5500	-3,550	-2,235	1,315	325	64,694	-70	44.55	-240.05	.24	15.36	-199,290
IBM US 09/22/12 P190	10.00	1.25	m	2.2500	2,250	1,250	-1,000	-193	-38,434	48	-37.90	182.74	.18	17.11	199,290
QQQ US Equity					13,120	13,372	252	200	13,372	0	.00	.00			
QQQ US Equity	200.00	66.86	l	65.6000	13,120	13,372	252	200	13,372	0	.00	.00	.00		13,372

Exhibit 3.17

keep rho off my normal option chain just to maximize space.

Rho helps us to understand the effects that interest rates have on the "forward price" of an underlying asset. As interest rates increase, forward prices rise, causing an increase in call values and a decrease in put values. Rho measures that amount of change.

Assume that you have a call with a theoretical value of $10, with a rho value of 0.30. If the current interest rate of 3 percent increases to 4 percent, you should expect the value of the call to increase 30 cents to $10.30 (roughly).

In that same example, if it were a put with a rho of −0.30 and a value of $10 (puts have negative rho), that same change in interest rates would cause the put to drop 30 cents to $9.70.

Rho is generally the Greek you are going to be least concerned with if you are a retail investor/trader, but shouldn't be ignored. At the time this was written, the GOOG January 2014 700 puts have a rho of more than $7, which would mean that a 1 percent change in rates would have a $700 effect per contract! See Exhibit 3.18.

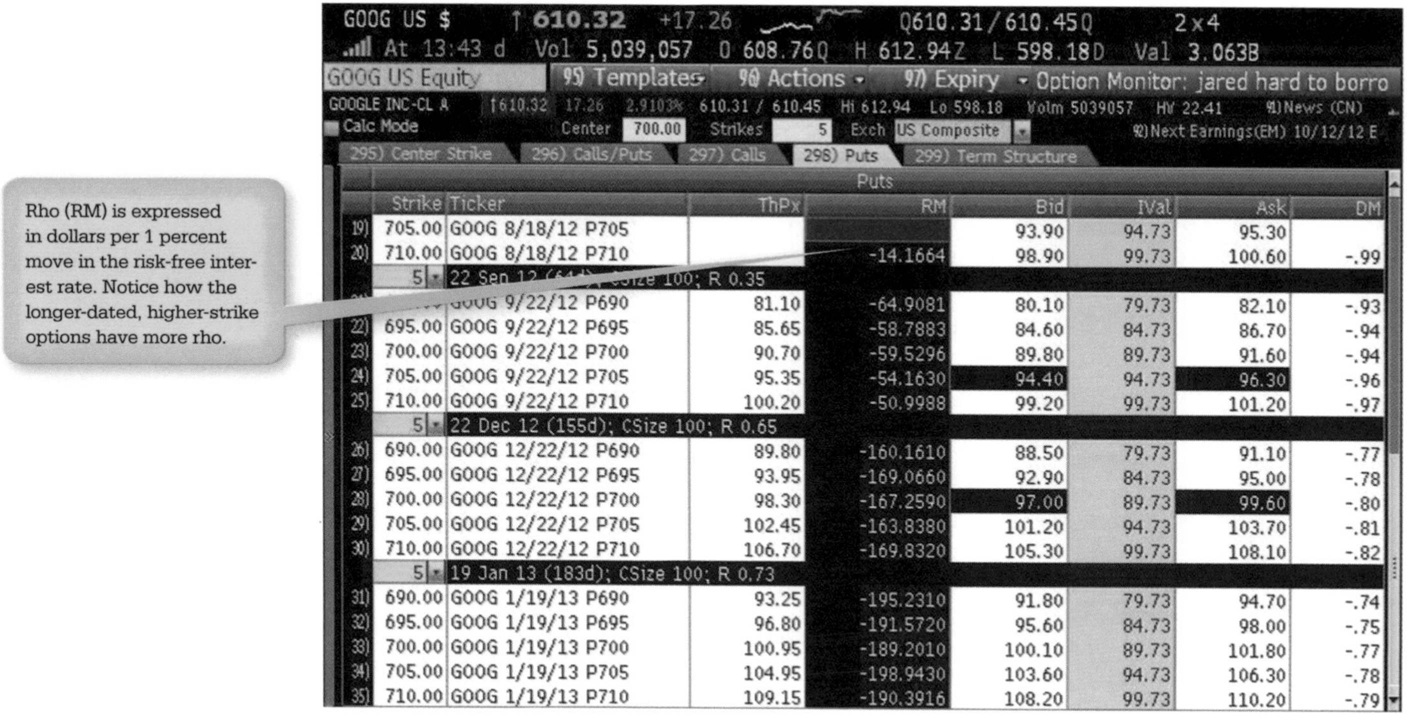

GOOG US $ ↑ 610.32 +17.26 Q610.31/610.45Q 2x4
At 13:43 d Vol 5,039,057 O 608.76Q H 612.94Z L 598.18D Val 3.063B
GOOG US Equity 95) Templates 96) Actions 97) Expiry Option Monitor: jared hard to borro
GOOGLE INC-CL A ↑610.32 17.26 2.9103% 610.31 / 610.45 Hi 612.94 Lo 598.18 Volm 5039057 HV 22.41 91) News (CN)
Calc Mode Center 700.00 Strikes 5 Exch US Composite 92) Next Earnings(EM) 10/12/12 E
295) Center Strike 296) Calls/Puts 297) Calls 298) Puts 299) Term Structure

	Puts							
	Strike	Ticker	ThPx	RM	Bid	IVal	Ask	DM
19)	705.00	GOOG 8/18/12 P705			93.90	94.73	95.30	
20)	710.00	GOOG 8/18/12 P710		-14.1664	98.90	99.73	100.60	-.99
	5	22 Sep 12 [illegible] CSize 100; R 0.35						
[illegible]	[illegible]	GOOG 9/22/12 P690	81.10	-64.9081	80.10	79.73	82.10	-.93
22)	695.00	GOOG 9/22/12 P695	85.65	-58.7883	84.60	84.73	86.70	-.94
23)	700.00	GOOG 9/22/12 P700	90.70	-59.5296	89.80	89.73	91.60	-.94
24)	705.00	GOOG 9/22/12 P705	95.35	-54.1630	94.40	94.73	96.30	-.96
25)	710.00	GOOG 9/22/12 P710	100.20	-50.9988	99.20	99.73	101.20	-.97
	5	22 Dec 12 (155d); CSize 100; R 0.65						
26)	690.00	GOOG 12/22/12 P690	89.80	-160.1610	88.50	79.73	91.10	-.77
27)	695.00	GOOG 12/22/12 P695	93.95	-169.0660	92.90	84.73	95.00	-.78
28)	700.00	GOOG 12/22/12 P700	98.30	-167.2590	97.00	89.73	99.60	-.80
29)	705.00	GOOG 12/22/12 P705	102.45	-163.8380	101.20	94.73	103.70	-.81
30)	710.00	GOOG 12/22/12 P710	106.70	-169.8320	105.30	99.73	108.10	-.82
	5	19 Jan 13 (183d); CSize 100; R 0.73						
31)	690.00	GOOG 1/19/13 P690	93.25	-195.2310	91.80	79.73	94.70	-.74
32)	695.00	GOOG 1/19/13 P695	96.80	-191.5720	95.60	84.73	98.00	-.75
33)	700.00	GOOG 1/19/13 P700	100.95	-189.2010	100.10	89.73	101.80	-.77
34)	705.00	GOOG 1/19/13 P705	104.95	-198.9430	103.60	94.73	106.30	-.78
35)	710.00	GOOG 1/19/13 P710	109.15	-190.3916	108.20	99.73	110.20	-.79

Rho (RM) is expressed in dollars per 1 percent move in the risk-free interest rate. Notice how the longer-dated, higher-strike options have more rho.

Exhibit 3.18

Changing Rates and Rho

Interest rates of all sorts have made headlines for the past five years—everything from the U.S. Fed making an unprecedented prediction to keep the Fed funds rate low to the wild sovereign debt rate swings in parts of Europe.

When economies around the world including ours in the United States were struggling to stay afloat and just about every country in the world was looking to devalue their currency, it seemed next to impossible that the United States was going to begin raising their rates.

In early 2012, the markets sensed a shift when the Fed seemed to put the kibosh on QE3. This was the first step toward tightening the belt, but still a ways away from raising rates. Even though low rates should be here for the time being, those of you reading this years from now may be in a different environment.

There have certainly been times in the past when rate changes came fast and furious, and there will be situations like those again in the future.

Here is how changing rates may affect options prices and what you need to know as a retail trader.

What is the correct rate to use when you are looking to trade long-dated options? The simple answer is to use the current risk-free rate for that time frame. But what if interest rates are in increasing mode? Or decreasing? How do you know which rate to use? How can rho help you with this risk?

For the call owners out there, an interest-rate hike will make your calls more expensive, which obviously is a good thing for you as an owner. Put owners will experience the opposite effect; they may see values drop as interest rates rise. When you are projecting what interest rates will be at some point in the future, you have to do a little more homework and there is no way to know for certain.

The reality is that market participants have probably done the same research, which means that there is a small chance of a surprise. That's not to say that an economic catastrophe couldn't send rates lower or unexpected growth and inflation couldn't spark an unexpected rate increase. Either of these scenarios would influence some option prices, perhaps in a negative way. You can use rho to see just how much of a dollar effect that would have on your portfolio and if you are okay with that risk.

If you want to bet with rho or take interest-rate-only risk, strategies such as the "jelly roll" can be used. Mastering interest-rate risk and techniques will not normally be your focus, although you can certainly choose to assume that risk, if it is indeed your focus. There are many more intricacies to finding rho and forward prices, which you can choose to explore in further reading.

Video:
How the Greeks are related

www.wiley.com/go/BloombergVisualGuidetoFinancialMarketsVideo1.html

Smart Investor Tip!

Deep out-of-the-money options have lower rho, while at-the-money and in-the-money options have a relatively higher rho; the higher the strike, the greater the rho will be.

More expensive stocks will have higher rho relative to cheaper stocks because higher dollar amounts invested would have greater interest rate returns.

Smart Investor Tip!

The rho for a call and put with the same strike price and the same expiration month are *not* equal.

CHAPTER 4

Visualizing Basic Strategies

Trading Calls and Puts

You notice that every strategy in this guide has a checklist of sorts. The goal here is to get into a consistent pattern of preparation, execution, and exit strategy. You might argue that consistency is hard to come by in the stock market. I believe that superior research and methods, and a sharp, knowledgeable execution of strategy can help you find rhythm and perhaps even harmony in a chaotic, noisy environment.

In Chapter 1 I laid out a checklist for you to go through and build your broad thesis. Once you've gathered your macro data, formed your thesis, narrowed down your stock, and plotted an expected trajectory for the asset, you then select your strategy and execute the trade. Remember that as you go through that list and conduct your subsequent research, each data point will have different weightings depending on both the strategy itself and your expected time horizon in the trade.

An example would be an impending earnings report that might have dramatic potential effects on a deep in-the-money call, but much less on a butterfly or condor. In other words, know the strengths, weaknesses, objectives, and nuances of each strategy and *test them first!* You *must* recognize what the key elements and characteristics are for each strategy, home in on them, and find the research/reasoning that satisfies them.

The boundaries of the checklists are flexible, but try to keep major deviations to a minimum.

Before you trade any strategy, you have to make decisions based on the appropriate tactic and the allocation within your portfolio. This allocation should be determined by an objective system that is easy to execute. Allocation and the strategies themselves should be examined collectively within your portfolio. Software makes it easy to simulate how an additional position will affect your global risk and eventually you won't even need the software.

Strategy Guide for Market Conditions

I want to share with you my strategy guide to help you quickly locate the best tactic for your initial thesis. From there you can apply the simple grading system that I outlined in Chapter 2. It will help you gauge the amount of your portfolio you have at risk in any one trade. Once you have come up with a strategy and allocation, you will need to execute your plan with the tactics, tips, and tricks you have learned for each unique strategy.

You can either back into this checklist with a strategy already in mind or use the checklist to determine what strategy you utilize. I think the latter is more appropriate, but everyone's mind works in its own way.

Once you determine the best strategy, you can quickly test it (either in a scenario screen or with a paper trade) and analyze its potential risk by using the strategy selection matrix on screen OV. See Exhibit 4.1.

Smart Investor Tip!

Don't forget to mind the correlation of all your trades to each other and to the market by finding the beta of your entire portfolio. Details in Chapter 7.

The Quick and Dirty Strategy Guide

- Market oversold, looking for broad market rebound in short term with quick profits with no specific target
  - *Long call*
  - *Bull-call spread (wide with near term expiration)*
  - *Bull-put spread (wide with near term expiration)*
- Market overbought, looking for broad market sell-off in near term with quick profits and no specific target
  - *Long put*
  - *Bear-call spread (wide with near term expiration)*
  - *Bear-put spread (wide with near term expiration)*
- Market neutral, looking for range-bound market movements over a certain time frame (less than 45 days)
  - *Short straddle*
  - *Short strangle*
  - *Short iron condor*
  - *Short iron butterfly*
  - *Long call or put butterfly*
- Expecting market (stock) to move higher quickly, volatility to climb
  - *Long call*
  - *Split strike risk reversal (buy call, sell put)*
- Expecting market (stock) to move higher slowly, volatility to fall
  - *Bull-call spread (tighter strikes, in or at the money)*
  - *Bull-put spread (tighter strikes, in or out of the money)*
  - *Broken wing butterfly (if you have a target)*
- Expecting market to move lower quickly, volatility to climb
  - *Long put*

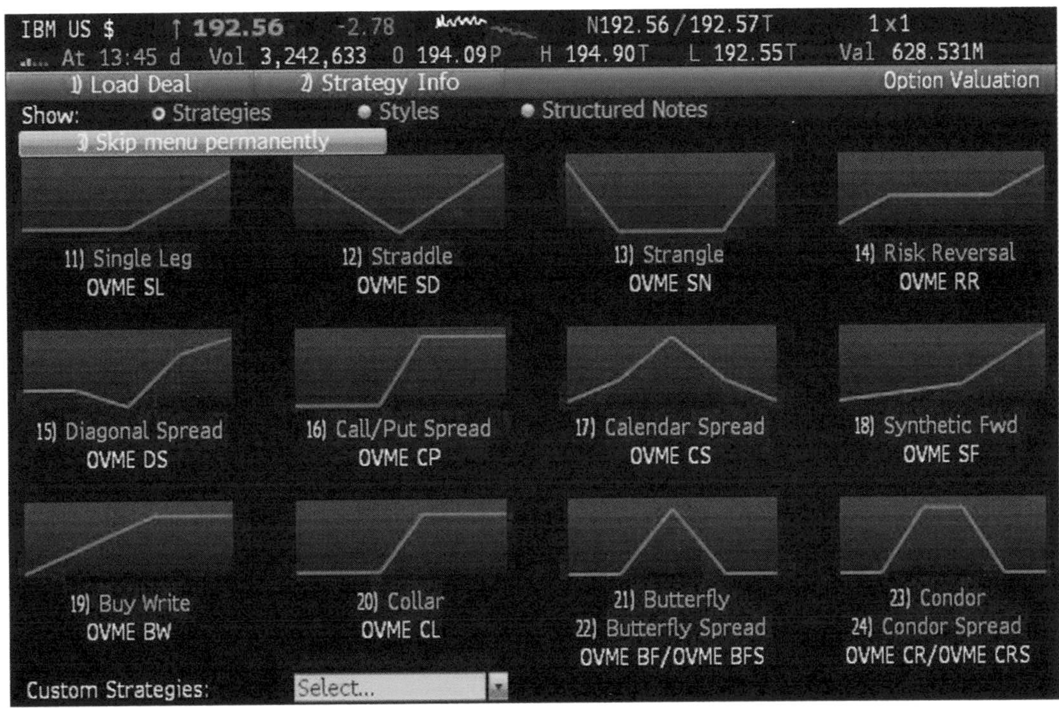

Exhibit 4.1

- Expecting market to drift lower, volatility to remain stagnant or drop
    - *Bear-put spread (in or at the money)*
    - *Bear-call spread (at or out of the money)*
    - *Long butterfly (if you know where the stock may end up)*
    - *Broken wing butterfly (better return than the butterfly, but you also need to have an idea where the asset will end up)*
    - *Ratio put spread (buy 1 higher strike, sell 1 lower strike all out of the money. The two short strikes should be your absolute support in the stock)*

- Asset going to be a big move in either direction, not sure which way, neutral to bullish on volatility
  - *Long straddle*
  - *Long strangle*
  - *Long iron condor or butterfly*
  - *Short call or put regular butterfly*
- Takeover rumor
  - Rumor mill chatter
    - *Bull-call spread for slow drift higher*
    - *Long regular butterfly with center strike positioned at expected takeover price*
  - Not publicly known (speculating)
    - *Bull-call spread to reduce cost, but placed above stock price*
    - *Out-of-the-money call*
  - Takeover already announced?
    - Cash
      - *Make sure breakeven of bullish strategy is a fair amount below takeover price.*
    - Stock
      - *Target company will have a tendency to move with the acquiring company. In this case, use the acquiring company as a barometer and a less aggressive bullish strategy, like an out-of-the-money (OTM) bull-put spread.*
    - Combination
      - *Target company will be partially correlated to the acquiring company. Be cautious and statistically advantaged in your strategy choice, but slightly more aggressive than an all stock deal.*
  - Long-term value stock play
    - *Set expected price rise and time frame.*
    - *Buy deep ITM call.*
  - Buy a stock with a large dividend that you want to capture along with moderate appreciation
    - *Own a dividend-paying stock that you expect to remain stagnant for a period, sell covered calls.*
- Earnings
  - Upcoming earnings—Neutral directional bias, bearish volatility bias
    - *Sell straddle or strangle with breakevens outside expected dollar move after report.*
    - *Sell iron butterfly (or buy long regular butterfly) with center strike near expected price after earnings.*
    - *Sell iron condor (or buy long regular condor) with inner strikes placed outside expected range after report.*
  - Upcoming earnings—Neutral directional bias, bullish volatility bias
    - *Buy straddle or strangle with breakevens inside expected dollar move after report.*
  - Upcoming earnings—Bullish bias

- *Initiate a bullish vertical spread where both strikes are lower than the spot price.*
- Upcoming earnings—Bearish bias
  - *Initiate a bearish vertical spread where both strikes are higher than the spot price*
- Upcoming earnings—Protecting long or short existing stock position
  - *Covered call (least protection)*
  - *Married put*
  - *Collar (most protection)*

The Call

The purchase of a call is a bullish act, in which the investor can choose a range of strike prices and deltas. Depending on the level of bullishness, the call delta and time frame can be adjusted accordingly. Deeper in-the-money calls mean more relation to the stock and higher strike prices. Out-of-the-money calls mean less correlation to the stock. See Exhibit 4.2.

One for one, the long call is about the most bullish bet you can place other than buying the stock itself. The advantage is that much of the analysis and methods you use to find an in-the-money call candidate would be the same as in the stock.

Delta is a huge factor in determining the call strike. Higher delta calls (0.70 and higher) tend to behave more like the underlying security, whereas calls with less of a delta will be more susceptible to other market forces such as volatility.

Optimal Scenario

In a perfect world, you want to be extremely bullish on the underlying security, expecting an explosion to the upside or a substantial price appreciation over the term of the option, preferably above the expiration break-even price (strike + premium paid). For the best-case scenario, implied volatility will be relatively low compared to observed volatility. The majority of indicators in your analysis should be decidedly bullish and pointing to growth from the macro view all the way down to the company level.

The charts should be leading up to a breakout, oversold in the near term and poised for a reversion to the mean (rally), or the stock should be underperforming its peers or the market when it should be rallying for longer term plays. Any other extremely bullish or breakout technical indicators will also be acceptable.

Advantages

Leverage—A key attribute is the long call's ability to offer immense amounts of leverage. Even a call that is purchased deep in the money (delta of 0.75 or more) will generally cost a fraction of the stock price and will still have the unlimited profit potential that long stock has.

When it comes to leverage, be careful to look at the breakeven of your call in combination with the delta. Sometimes the at- or out-of-the-money calls may not give you the big jump in dollar-based profits when the stock moves favorably. Remember that the cheaper the option, the lower your absolute profit target should

Smart Investor Tip!

Pay attention to earnings history (surprise!) and a stock's movement after the event if you are planning on holding your position through one or more earnings reports.

KEY POINT:

Long calls are also optimal in a market that is extremely oversold and you are expecting a quick rebound at which time you would take profits on the rally.

Using the search feature, you can input the optimal fundamental, technical, and option-related data to return only the candidates you want to see. Here is an example of a long call scan I created.

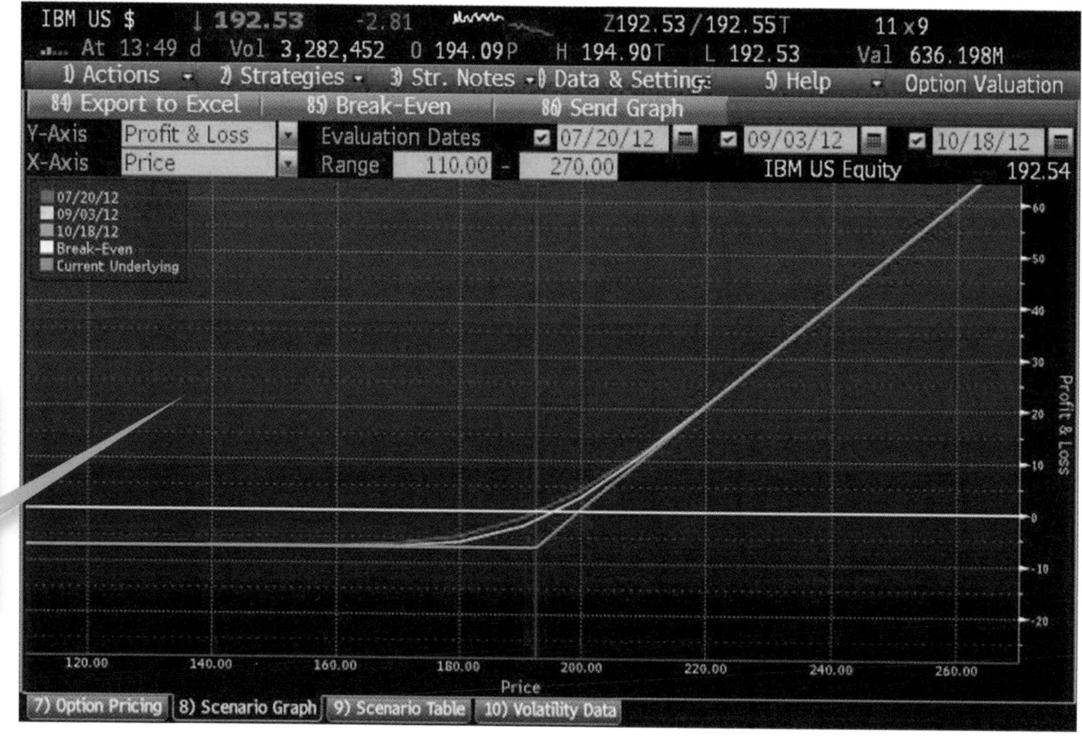

Exhibit 4.2

be—a 25 cent option that goes to 50 cents just doubled in value, but only returned you 25 cents per option!

Protection—For holders of short stock or a short delta options position, a call can be purchased ahead of a possible rally, reducing your upside price exposure. Long calls can also be used as part of a vertical or horizontal spread to increase the risk/reward ratio in a favorable way.

Risk reduction—Because of the lower cost of the call compared to the 100-share equivalent of stock, dollar risk will always be lower in comparison. Use caution not to purchase excessive contracts because of their price. Time decay and other factors may disadvantage your long call position. Furthermore, because of the higher breakeven of calls, you will be adding a type of statistical risk to your trade.

A technique that you can employ would be to purchase the same amount of call contracts that you would be willing to lose in the stock. This means that if you thought about buying 500 shares of a $100 stock and your stop loss was going to be placed at $90, perhaps you might purchase $5,000 worth of the appropriate call options, because that was how much you were willing to lose in the first place. Strike consideration is obviously a major factor.

Buying 100 options for 0.50 could be a foolish choice in this case. Use the call breakeven combined with the delta to select the appropriate option; don't just rely on easy math.

If you think that the stock is going to move about $5 before expiration, make sure that the call options you are buying have a breakeven below that level!

Flexibility—Because call options are trading all the time, you have the ability to trade in and out of a position as well as scale into and out of your position depending on what the stock does. You can also purchase several different strikes with your allocated funds to gain mixed exposure to a stock.

So for our earlier example where we had $5,000 to spend on a $100 stock that we thought was going to move at least $5, I might buy the 85, 90, 95, and 100 as opposed to only purchasing two 85 strike calls.

Disadvantages

Breakeven always higher than underlier—The long call is a statistically disadvantaged strategy because the breakeven will always be higher than the stock price at the time of entry. This means that if the stock stays flat up to expiration, you will gradually lose your time value and retain only your intrinsic value. If the option didn't have any time value to begin with, then your long call could be unprofitable.

Short theta—Time is generally not on your side when you purchase a call. As time passes by, the call is losing time value. This creates a sense of urgency in your thesis. Be sure to buy more than enough time for your trade to work out. Remember that at expiration you will always be left with any intrinsic value in that call.

Probability—Because breakeven is always going to be higher than the underlier, the underlier must generally rise in value. Because stocks can move up, down, or sideways, a long call bet is only profitable in 33 percent of the probable scenarios. This results in a statistical disadvantage, the only exception being a sudden jump in implied volatility. Arguably, this risk is offset by the reduced cost in the call.

Risk/Reward

The OSA screen below displays the Greeks for March 185 Call in IBM. Note the delta risk/cost of the option compared to the equivalent stock.

Long Call Greek Attributes

Delta

Positive—Delta can range from 0.01 to +1.00.
The higher the delta purchased (> 0.65), the more the call will behave like the stock. A lower-delta call (< 0.30) will react minimally when the stock moves and will be extremely sensitive to changes in volatility on a percentage basis.

Gamma

Positive—Gamma is greatest at the money. Long call deltas will increase in upward moves in the stock and decrease with downward moves; the gamma dictates just how much. Gamma is going to be your ally when the call is moving toward the money from an out-of-the-money position. As the call continues to move into the money, you start to lose gamma. You should hopefully be making money from delta when this happens. This might be a good time to sell the expensive call and use a portion of the profit buy a cheaper call if you feel the stock is going higher.

Theta

Short—You are paying theta. At-the-money options will have the highest theta. Theta can be overridden by looking at breakeven. Even though you may be giving up money in theta, you may be making it back with your delta. Be careful holding calls during the last three weeks before expiration; this is where theta starts to increase. This is especially true for at- and out-of-the-money options.

Vega

Long—You are always long vega, which means that you want implied volatility to increase, which will benefit your trade. A decrease in implied volatility will hurt your position. Don't forget to use the implied volatility charts before making your trade. If Ivol seems super high compared to past Ivol and Hvol, you might want to change your strike selection or use a spread.

Rho

Long—You want interest rates to rise as a general rule, but they will have minimal impact on your position. This is the least worry you have in the trade.

Shorter-term traders with a time horizon of an hour to a couple of days will most likely focus on higher delta calls so they can have more of a correlation to the underlying security's movement. The high delta of an in-the-money call mitigates the other Greek risks because time value is such a small portion of the option's total price.

If you anticipate being in the trade for more than a couple of days or will be holding over an event, you should place more emphasis on the other Greeks, so you can forecast how your calls will behave with changes during various market conditions.

Long call breakevens will *always* be higher than the current stock price, meaning that the stock must move higher by expiration for the call to be profitable. That is not to say that a call option cannot become profitable with no change in the stock price.

Smart Investor Tip!

Sellers of naked calls would have the opposite Greek characteristics. Naked short calls are *not* covered in depth in this guide as I believe traders should always offset their risk in a spread, unless they are used to establishing an advantageous short position in the stock.

Call Dynamics

Let's go through the thought process and steps needed before trading the call.

Step 1: Identifying the Target

Once you locate a stock, be sure to perform your due diligence. With a long call you *need* the stock to move higher, preferably quickly, during the trade. Consider other options strategies that can also be potentially profitable if you foresee a more moderate upside move or other risks in the trade.

Many traders tend to focus on a group of stocks. This is acceptable, just be sure that you don't pigeonhole yourself into just one group that may not be performing well. See Exhibit 4.3.

I typically trade the same group of 15 stocks over and over. As a market maker, I became accustomed to trading the same names all the time. I am extremely familiar with their earnings reports, trading patterns, volatility, and so on.

Often I will set both high- and low-price alerts that remind me to review the underlying stock, future, index, or whatever. Low-price alerts may be a trigger that a stock or index may be becoming a good "value." High-price alerts may be an indicator of a breakout or momentum.

Long call candidates are typically not stagnant stocks. Try to find a catalyst in upcoming news or in the marketplace. It is also never a bad thing to buy a call on weakness in your stock; however, use caution if a stock has dropped sharply because there may be a dramatic increase in implied volatility.

Catalysts: News, Technical, Fundamentals

Because you can use the long call for a myriad of bullish situations, your research can vary depending on what you are trying to accomplish. If you are specifically focused on oversold stocks that you expect to rebound, you're going to follow a different research path than someone who is looking to follow bullish analyst momentum for a longer-term trade.

The risk profile of the call is fairly simple and straightforward, which means the call trade could be appropriate in just about any bullish scenario. It just works better for some than others.

Motivations

- **News**—If your broad macro thesis is neutral to bullish, the long call can be used to trade bullish news on a particular security. If there is bullish sales news coming out or a build up into a product launch, such as a new iPhone, the long call can work because it's a straight bullish play with no limit to what you can make.
- **Earnings**—The long call is certainly not the optimal strategy for playing earnings, but it can be better than the stock if you spend way less money. Because of the Ivol earnings crush, the long call will suffer after the report is out. Look at the vega of the option you choose and do the math first. If you believe that the delta can overcome the vega drop, then proceed. For me, I'd use a vertical spread if I wanted to get directional. That minimizes my vega

KEY POINT:

To create a true long stock synthetic position, you must buy a call and sell a put at the same strike in the same month. Some very deep in-the-money calls will have a delta close to 1, which is *almost* the same thing, but lower in risk.

KEY POINT:

Because the vega of a call option is positive it is possible that if implied volatility rises, a call option could increase in value without a change in the stock price.

Here are a couple of filters to find potential candidates if you don't already have one stock or a group in mind. These scans can also produce ideas for other bullish strategies.

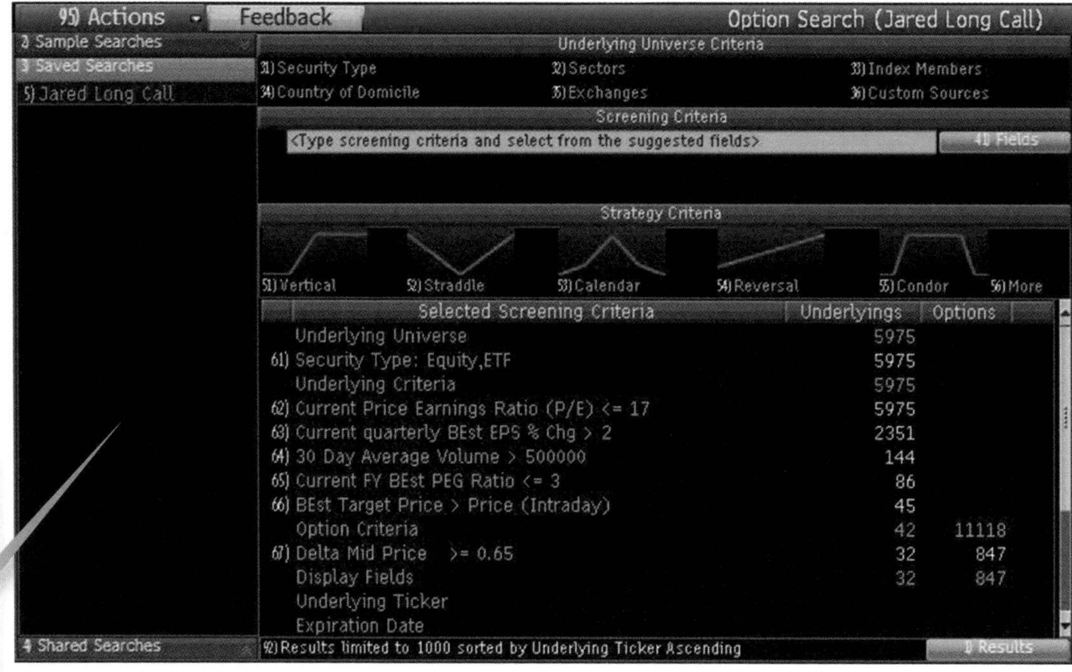

Exhibit 4.3

risk and, if positioned right, gives me a statistical edge!

- **Economic data to be released**—Just as in the earnings motivation, buying a call ahead of what you think will be good economic data might be better if you are only risking 10 percent of what you would have if you were buying the stock. With economic data, the Ivol crush usually isn't as severe as with earnings, which helps the call. I would still select a bullish vertical spread over just the long call.
- **Analyst upgrades and targets**—I have sort of a love/hate relationship with analysts. These men and women have to get as intimate as possible with the companies that they follow and make recommendations based on their findings and models. They probably have the

best sense of a company's health next to the executives themselves. The issue I have with analysts who work for the big firms like Morgan Stanley, Goldman Sachs, and JP Morgan is that they are sometimes slow (and less dramatic) to adjust their readings. My theory is that these companies have seas of brokers, funds, and financial planners that move their clients' money around based in large part on what analysts are recommending, making the analysts perhaps more pressured to prevent extreme variances in their trajectories.

That said, I do think that longer-term traders can use analyst targets, upgrades, and trends in general to buy calls on a particular stock. The added benefit of following analysts is that they will consider macro trends in their reports and recommendations, which makes your life a little easier.

- **Charts to identify patterns of support and other bullish technical indicators**—The long call can be the perfect vehicle for playing bullish technical trends, just make sure that the expected outcome of these patterns will overcome all the negatives of the call.

  An example might be a breakout above the 50-day moving average, which typically results in a 2 percent run over a week's time. If the theta of your call is greater than the expected 2 percent (times the delta of your option) the call may not be your best bet or you may need to select a different strike, month, and so on. This is where it helps to run a scenario analysis.

Step 2: Fundamental Analysis

If you are a longer-term investor, you obviously want to invest in a company that will not only be around in a couple of years, but will thrive. For day traders, fundamental analysis becomes less of an issue. In fact, there are some active traders who may trade a stock they know nothing about.

Just how bullish are you? The longer-term trader (more than a couple of weeks) should probably spend more time focusing on the fundamental areas of a stock. I tend to examine several screens before moving forward with a long call or any trade for that matter.

The following analysis techniques can be used to trade any strategy. The level of bullishness or bearishness will determine what strategy is best to apply to your findings.

At the end of the day, analysts spend their entire careers researching, modeling, and commenting on a handful of stocks. The analysts may not always be right, but it's never a bad thing to get an idea of their general sentiment, trends, and forward-looking opinions. You can also take their data and interpret it in your own way. In other words, let them do the legwork, and you can form your own opinion.

Analyst recommendations will give you an idea of their general thoughts and where the stock is in relation to their price targets. If you notice that the target price for stock is at least 15 percent higher than the current price and that the consensus recommendation is "buy" to "strong buy" and several analysts (pref-

Smart Investor Tip!

For a good call candidate, look for an underperforming stock with strong, stable earnings growth in the past as well as prospects for future growth, with a healthy balance sheet, and a product or service that is in demand.

erably the ones with a bigger following or higher past accuracy) are moving their estimates higher in the last 1 to 20 days, there may be impetus for the stock to move higher still. Analysts may have an axe to grind, but if they are taking action and sticking their head out, especially ahead of an earnings report, the security should gain support. This trick is quick and dirty but it's just another step to stack odds in your favor. See Exhibit 4.4.

Use the ANR screen to get more details on a stock that may be getting a little rich (or cheap) in price. I sometimes look at several of the analysts' past performance and accuracy with the stock, especially if one just made a brazen call (like Morgan Stanley did in March 2011 when it slapped a $1,000 target on Apple). This extra level of research will help with gauging the accuracy of their data and just how realistic their targets have been in the past. I place more credence in the analyst(s) who have been more accurate and whose price targets are usually met as opposed to the analyst just looking to get attention with an absurd call.

In the historical recommendations screen in Exhibit 4.5, you can see that this analyst from Janney Montgomery has been fairly on point and stable with his buy ratings. In fact, just a month or so after this shot was taken, IBM hit almost $208 per share.

Smart Investor Tip!

You can mouse over any broker's name in the ANR screen to get specifics on recommendations made at that time and view their past history.

The ANRP allows you to view the analyst's report card so to speak. Here you will be able to gauge just how accurate a particular analyst has been. I use this to assign a level of accuracy to each and every analyst's recommendations.

Multiples and valuation—Earnings multiples in relation to stock price and free cash flow can be plotted in the GF screen. I find this screen to be an excellent way to examine the relationships between these and other fundamental data sets. I look back several years to find high and low points and identify where the stock is in relation to its past and how the current economic and sector environments relate to different points in the past. See Exhibit 4.6.

The GF screen also helps me identify trajectories and find correlations between a stock's price movements and its relative valuations. This is a great place to look for warnings signals. If the stock's P/E multiple is getting into relatively high territory and the past has shown this to be a resistance level, I may pass on a long call and choose a more moderately bullish strategy with less risk.

Also, if the forward expectations for P/E growth are lofty, I may be deterred from using an aggressively bullish strategy because that may be setting the stock up for failure in its earnings report. See Exhibit 4.7.

In that case, it might be more prudent to take a little less delta and maybe collect some theta. It's also helpful to examine guidance in the last report and note how the stock performed after.

In the CF screen, I start with the quarterly view and then drill down to the monthly time frame, examining data for the past four years. I note the changes in P/E over each earnings report and look for patterns overall and seasonally and make sure that they are in line with my thesis.

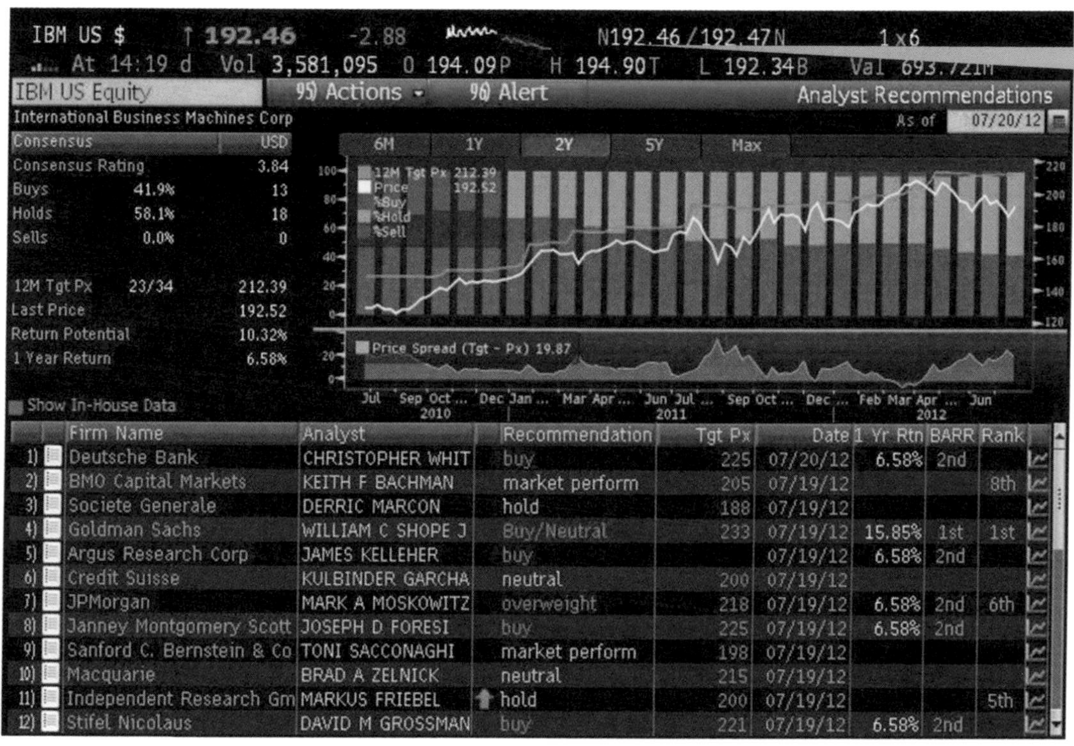

The ANR screen allows you to take a snapshot of analyst opinions, targets, and more.

Exhibit 4.4

If the stock's price is 10 percent higher than it was two quarters ago, but the trailing P/E is lower now than it was then, I would obviously feel more confident taking on a long delta in an earnings report.

Cross-reference the individual stock's basic fundamental measurements against other peers in its sector to help identify relative value.

While examining fundamentals, I will glance at the CF and DES screens for general data and company

If a very accurate and timely analyst is upgrading or downgrading a stock just ahead of an earnings report or in general, you should be more inclined to act on that data as opposed to someone with a history of inaccuracy or exaggerated (incorrect) targets.

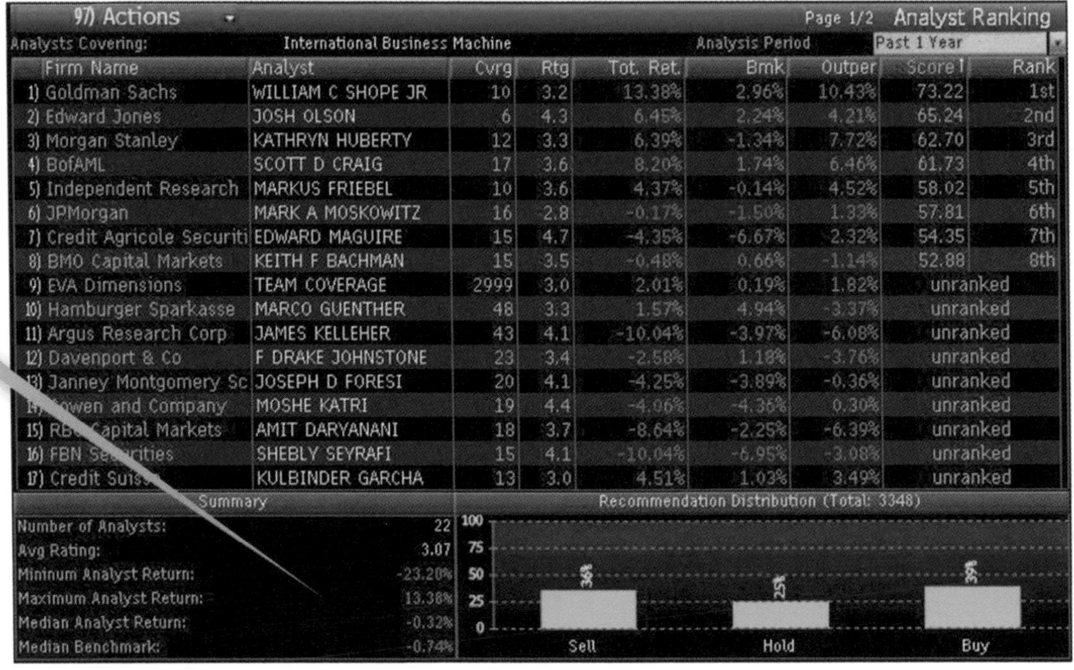

97) Actions | Page 1/2 | Analyst Ranking

Analysts Covering: International Business Machine | Analysis Period: Past 1 Year

Firm Name	Analyst	Cvrg	Rtg	Tot. Ret.	Bmk	Outper	Score	Rank
1) Goldman Sachs	WILLIAM C SHOPE JR	10	3.2	13.38%	2.96%	10.43%	73.22	1st
2) Edward Jones	JOSH OLSON	6	4.3	6.45%	2.24%	4.21%	65.24	2nd
3) Morgan Stanley	KATHRYN HUBERTY	12	3.3	6.39%	-1.34%	7.72%	62.70	3rd
4) BofAML	SCOTT D CRAIG	17	3.6	8.20%	1.74%	6.46%	61.73	4th
5) Independent Research	MARKUS FRIEBEL	10	3.6	4.37%	-0.14%	4.52%	58.02	5th
6) JPMorgan	MARK A MOSKOWITZ	16	2.8	-0.17%	-1.50%	1.33%	57.81	6th
7) Credit Agricole Securiti	EDWARD MAGUIRE	15	4.7	-4.35%	-6.67%	2.32%	54.35	7th
8) BMO Capital Markets	KEITH F BACHMAN	15	3.5	-0.48%	0.66%	-1.14%	52.88	8th
9) EVA Dimensions	TEAM COVERAGE	2999	3.0	2.01%	0.19%	1.82%	unranked	
10) Hamburger Sparkasse	MARCO GUENTHER	48	3.3	1.57%	4.94%	-3.37%	unranked	
11) Argus Research Corp	JAMES KELLEHER	43	4.1	-10.04%	-3.97%	-6.08%	unranked	
12) Davenport & Co	F DRAKE JOHNSTONE	23	3.4	-2.58%	1.18%	-3.76%	unranked	
13) Janney Montgomery Sc	JOSEPH D FORESI	20	4.1	-4.25%	-3.89%	-0.36%	unranked	
14) owen and Company	MOSHE KATRI	19	4.4	-4.06%	-4.36%	0.30%	unranked	
15) RB Capital Markets	AMIT DARYANANI	18	3.7	-8.64%	-2.25%	-6.39%	unranked	
16) FBN Se rities	SHEBLY SEYRAFI	15	4.1	-10.04%	-6.95%	-3.08%	unranked	
17) Credit Suis	KULBINDER GARCHA	13	3.0	4.51%	1.03%	3.49%	unranked	

Summary	
Number of Analysts:	22
Avg Rating:	3.07
Minimum Analyst Return:	-23.20%
Maximum Analyst Return:	13.38%
Median Analyst Return:	-0.32%
Median Benchmark:	-0.74%

Exhibit 4.5

filings. I do this for several reasons. First, I want to see if there has been any abnormal insider buying or selling. If I see that a current board member or executive is selling or buying large amounts of shares, it could influence my decision.

Performance vs. peers—The RV screen allows you to take a quick glance at a stock's key fundamentals versus its peers. With this screen I focus on companies based in the same country and allow Bloomberg to group them using the "Bloomberg Peers" selection. The goal here is to identify an outlier or abnormality in your comparison that might change how you feel about a trade.

You can compare and contrast just about any data point, but I am mostly concerned with price,

P/E, revenue growth, cash flow, PEG ratio, and price movements.

$$\textbf{PEG Ratio} = \frac{\textbf{Price/Annual Earnings}}{\textbf{Annual EPS Growth}}$$

If you look at IBM compared to its peers, it looks fairly decent by most measurements, but there are some points that make IBM look less attractive than it is. In Exhibit 4.8, if you look down at the Year/Year EPS growth, IBM looks much worse than the average. You can see the standard deviation is *huge*.

But look a little deeper and we find that this difference is due to a couple of stocks like QCOM, JNPR, and ALTR (that were experiencing recent meteoric growth) skewing the numbers. See Exhibit 4.9.

If something looks funky, make sure that you can easily justify it like we did here; otherwise, if you smell smoke, fire may not be far away.

Use the following steps to increase probability in your call choices and make the trade.

I generally focus on free cash generating stocks with low P/E's in a market and economic climate that will continue to be beneficial to the stock.

Fundies are tough because it's not always just about the numbers. I like stocks that have the potential to come into favor. These companies may have been out of the spotlight, but are in a position to benefit in the future. They are also the companies that generally have low expectations and therefore low earnings hurdles to clear.

Find momentum—If you are buying a call or looking for a strong bullish candidate, seek out companies that have a favorable wind blowing from several sources. Look for a company that is not only growing earnings (and has a history of doing so), but also popularity, not only from investors but analysts as well. Find a company whose products and services are not only in demand, but in a space that's desirable. Seek out stocks with strong technical trends that are getting stronger.

When you combine all those attributes, you are more likely to have a stock that rallies with strength and gives you the returns desired when utilizing a long call.

Step 3: Technical Analysis

I use technical analysis to confirm my bullish thinking and trigger my entry and exit. The key to any market trading system is simplicity. You should have your stock, strategy, and money management plan in place before making any trade! The reason for the plan is to try and mitigate any surprises. However, even with the best planning, you can still be wrong in a trade. Planning is also important in the mental preparation for your trade and to establish realistic expectations.

Technical analysis and "preset" entry and exit points really help take the emotional weight of the trade off your shoulders. It gives a bit more clarity and specificity to your investment thesis.

That said, all technical trading systems are flawed—none will offer you perfect results. In fact, some don't

KEY POINT:

A stock that has been bid up into earnings can have a "sell on good news" effect. This was the case with Cintas Corporation (CTAS: Nasdaq) in late March 2012 when the stock reported a phenomenal quarter, but ended down 3 percent on the day.

Smart Investor Tip!

You should review the overall climate for a stock's sector to support or contradict your thesis. An example would be the "cloud" stocks that were all rising despite high multiples during 2010 to 2011.

If the GF screen is revealing a rich relative valuation (high price), then adjust your strategy to be more neutral or bearish unless there is good objective bullish data that supports the stock's price levels.

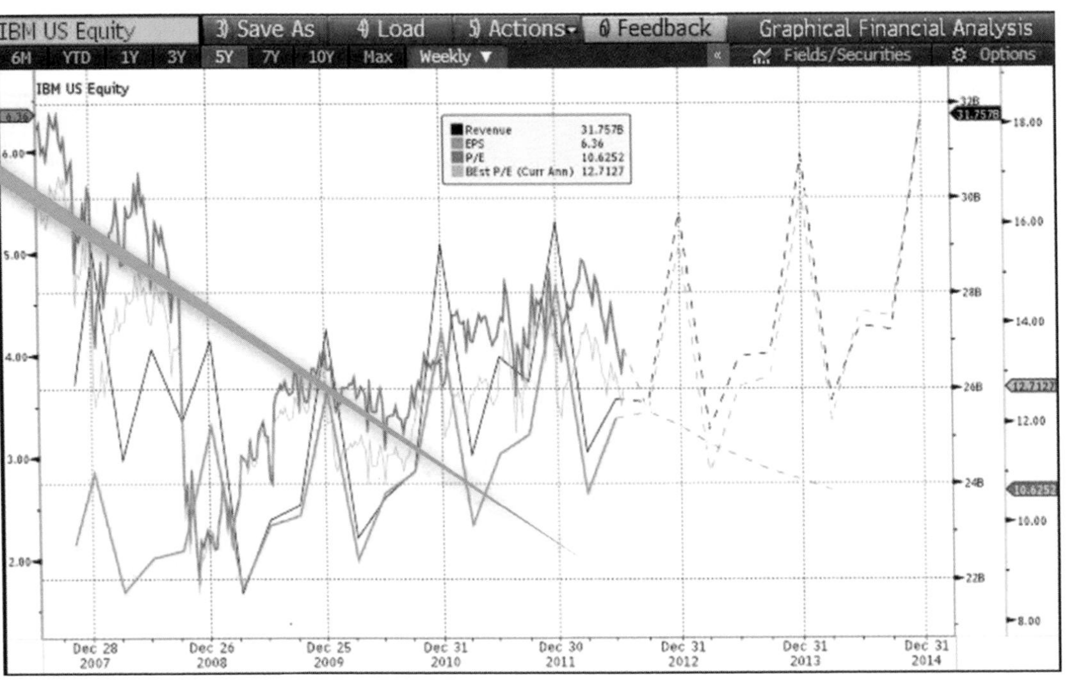

Exhibit 4.6

Smart Investor Tip!

Use the PEG ratio as a quick valuation metric to help you justify or disprove a high P/E. It allows you to determine the relative tradeoff among the price of a stock, the EPS, and the company's expected growth.

Stocks with lower PEG ratios (0 to 2) are going to be lower in risk even if their P/Es are elevated because of their earnings growth rate. But be warned that low PEG stocks with high P/E multiples will generally have an elevated chance for disappointment as expectations will be higher.

PEGs below .75 are generally stable earners with slower growth; negative P/E multiples will negate the effectiveness of the ratio.

offer any results at all. Your system should offer you an edge, just a slight advantage when it comes to timing your entries and exits into and out of positions. The more complicated and longer trades take to analyze, the more difficult it will be for you to execute and be successful. I use a proprietary system that is easy for me to read and to understand.

For trades that I hold for less than a month, I look at 20-, 50-, and 200-day moving averages and look for where a stock is in relation to all of them; they help

CTAS sell-off is highlighted in the circle. Notice how the P/E multiple is much lower at the right of the chart, but the stock price is the same as it was during the March dip.

Exhibit 4.7

me identify support and resistance points as well as determine trend.

A good rule of thumb is to look at the 200-day simple moving average (SMA) and look for your stock to be above it for a good long-term overall bullish trend. The 20 and 50 can offer you an inside look at short-term trend changes.

I also take a look at "standard 20," two standard deviation Bollinger bands, and look for oversold (prices below the bottom band) or overbought (prices above the top band) conditions. (This is an advanced technique that will require study; it is not intended for every trader.) But basically, I like to be a contrarian as a short-term trader. If a stock has breached the lower

Smart Investor Tip!

Remember that my trading patterns and habits may not be the same as your habits or patterns. What's important is that you remain consistent with your analysis points and know what analysts are projecting in the future for the company that you are trading.

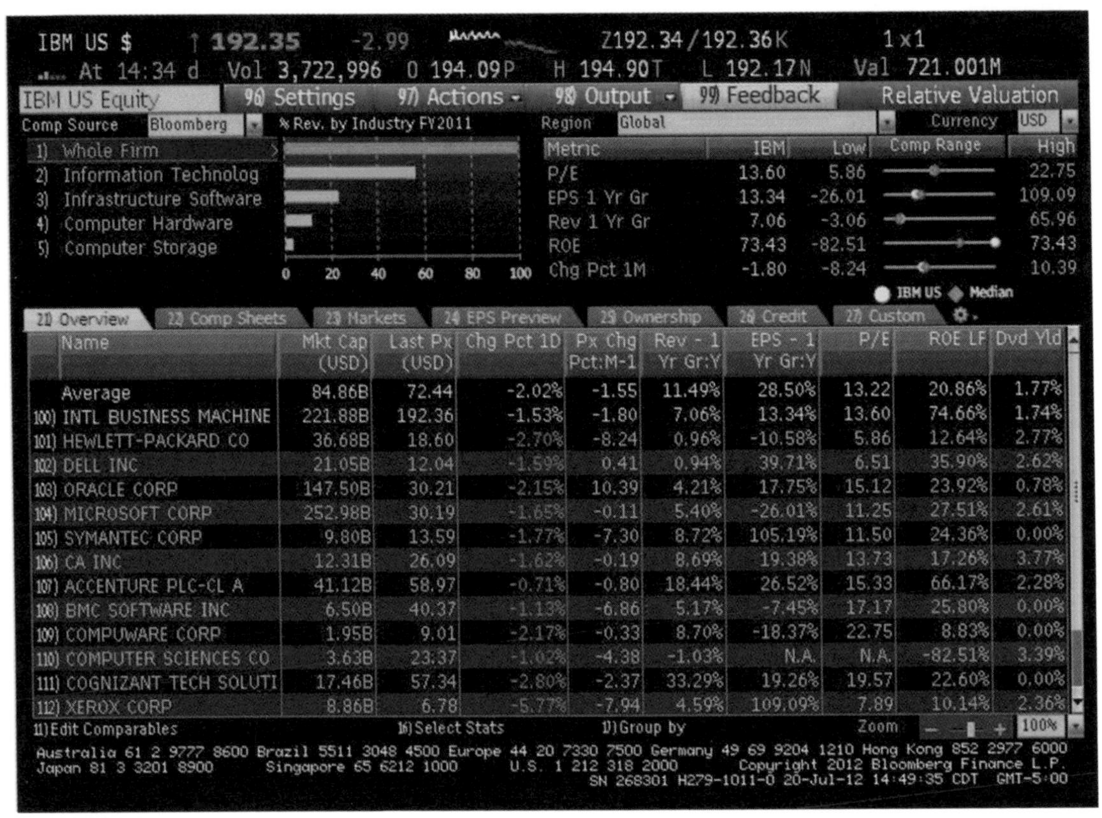

Name	Mkt Cap (USD)	Last Px (USD)	Chg Pct 1D	Px Chg Pct:M-1	Rev - 1 Yr Gr:Y	EPS - 1 Yr Gr:Y	P/E	ROE LF	Dvd Yld
Average	84.86B	72.44	-2.02%	-1.55	11.49%	28.50%	13.22	20.86%	1.77%
100) INTL BUSINESS MACHINE	221.88B	192.36	-1.53%	-1.80	7.06%	13.34%	13.60	74.66%	1.74%
101) HEWLETT-PACKARD CO	36.68B	18.60	-2.70%	-8.24	0.96%	-10.58%	5.86	12.64%	2.77%
102) DELL INC	21.05B	12.04	-1.59%	0.41	0.94%	39.71%	6.51	35.90%	2.62%
103) ORACLE CORP	147.50B	30.21	-2.15%	10.39	4.21%	17.75%	15.12	23.92%	0.78%
104) MICROSOFT CORP	252.98B	30.19	-1.65%	-0.11	5.40%	-26.01%	11.25	27.51%	2.61%
105) SYMANTEC CORP	9.80B	13.59	-1.77%	-7.30	8.72%	105.19%	11.50	24.36%	0.00%
106) CA INC	12.31B	26.09	-1.62%	-0.19	8.69%	19.38%	13.73	17.26%	3.77%
107) ACCENTURE PLC-CL A	41.12B	58.97	-0.71%	-0.80	18.44%	26.52%	15.33	66.17%	2.28%
108) BMC SOFTWARE INC	6.50B	40.37	-1.13%	-6.86	5.17%	-7.45%	17.17	25.80%	0.00%
109) COMPUWARE CORP	1.95B	9.01	-2.17%	-0.33	8.70%	-18.37%	22.75	8.83%	0.00%
110) COMPUTER SCIENCES CO	3.63B	23.37	-1.02%	-4.38	-1.03%	N.A.	N.A.	-82.51%	3.39%
111) COGNIZANT TECH SOLUTI	17.46B	57.34	-2.80%	-2.37	33.29%	19.26%	19.57	22.60%	0.00%
112) XEROX CORP	8.86B	6.78	-5.77%	-7.94	4.59%	109.09%	7.89	10.14%	2.36%

Exhibit 4.8

Bollinger band, but remains above its 200-day SMA and either its 20- or 50-day SMA, I would be a buyer on weakness.

Step 4: Selecting the Best Call

When you are contemplating a trade—there are a myriad of call strikes to select—your choice should be based on several factors:

Implied Volatility—If implied volatility is extremely high, but you are still expecting the stock to rally with strength there are two tactics you can use:

1. Buy a deep in-the-money call with a delta of 0.70 to 0.90 that has a minimal amount of time value in comparison to intrinsic. This will ensure that when the stock moves higher, your call value will increase as well. It will also diminish the amount of time value in your call, which in turn reduces the negative effects of high Ivol.
   a. The downside to this is the higher cost of the option, which implies more capital risk. A remedy is to reduce the number of contracts.
2. Look at the break-even levels for each call and if you can find an OTM call strike that offers you a breakeven that is fairly below where you think the stock will be before expiration, then choose that one. Try to stay away from at-the-money strikes because they contain so much time value.
   a. The downside to this is that the higher strike price means that the stock *must* rise above the strike before it expires. The call will be much cheaper, but again, the probability of significant profits is reduced because of breakeven. Don't forget percentages here. If you buy a call for $0.35 and can sell it for $0.70, you have made 100 percent!

Time Horizon—Long calls will always have breakevens higher than the underlying spot price. Always give yourself a cushion when you are buying a long call and never be afraid to buy an extra month or two, especially in markets that are *not* trending. I detail these methods in *Your Options Handbook*.

Cost (breakeven)—I always say that cost is relative. Price shouldn't be your biggest hurdle: if the delta is right and the implied volatility is right, then price is just price. More important than both for the average retail trader is breakeven. If your breakeven at expiration is simply unattainable, unrealistic, or not in line with your expectations, then you should find another call option. Don't focus so much on the nominal value of the call . . . instead, use the implied volatility and breakevens to guide you.

That said, if you have the choice between two in-the-money calls, one with delta of 0.75 that costs $5 and another with a delta of 0.80 that costs $8, does the extra 0.05 delta as a percentage of price warrant the option cost? Might be better in that case to go with the cheaper one.

Price target in the underlying security—Because you have an elevated breakeven, your price target should preferably exceed your break-even expiration. In other

Smart Investor Tip!

I always do my trade monitoring in the daily chart. It is the first stable warning of a change in trend for all strategies. It will have absolute control over my entries and exits for a short-term trade and slightly less impact on my monitoring of longer term trades as long as my charts are stable in the week and month.

Smart Investor Tip!

For those of you who are simply looking for stock replacement with leverage and minimal exposure to other market forces, a call option with a delta of 0.75 to 0.95 may be your best choice.

Smart Investor Tip!

If you are still getting acquainted with the Greeks, a deep in-the-money call may be the best solution if you are just looking for leverage on your trades.

IBM US Equity | 95) Customize | 96) Output | 97) Actions | Relative Valuation

Peers Bloomberg Peers | Region Country of Domicile | Closest | 50 By Mkt Cap

Show - Bloomberg Themes - | Add Column | 93) Fields

Name	Last Px	Chg Pct 1D	Ret YTD Pct	Mkt Cap	Rev - 1 Yr Gr:Y	EPS - 1 Yr Gr:Y	P/E	ROE LF	Dvd Ind Yld	P/E
Average	33.90	-1.68%	-10.81%	37.17B	20.59%	102.93%	17.49	20.66%	0.73%	17.49
Std. Deviation	59.88	5.44%	22.32%	71.84B	18.19%	262.85%	11.71	20.77%	1.08%	11.71
INTL BUSINESS MACHINES...	185.24	-0.26%	28.36%	218.33B	4.29%	15.51%	14.29	70.17%	1.62%	14.29
2) APPLE INC	374.94	-0.65%	16.24%	348.47B	65.96%	82.02%	13.55	41.67%	0.00%	13.55
3) MICROSOFT CORP	25.30	-0.94%	-6.95%	212.83B	11.94%	28.17%	9.37	44.16%	3.16%	9.37
4) ORACLE CORP	30.60	-0.71%	-1.53%	154.36B	32.82%	38.52%	16.54	24.75%	0.78%	16.54
5) INTEL CORP	24.29	-0.21%	19.53%	123.68B	24.19%	160.76%	10.29	27.21%	3.46%	10.29
6) CISCO SYSTEMS INC	18.42	-0.32%	-7.93%	99.15B	7.94%	-13.97%	14.17	13.79%	1.30%	14.17
7) QUALCOMM INC	55.67	-1.26%	14.24%	93.58B	36.20%	28.37%	19.47	17.80%	1.54%	19.47
8) HEWLETT-PACKARD CO	27.99	2.57%	-32.80%	55.62B	10.02%	17.76%	6.25	23.04%	1.71%	6.25
9) EMC CORP/MASS	23.07	-1.28%	-0.74%	47.06B	21.31%	70.37%	21.17	13.00%	0.00%	21.17
10) TEXAS INSTRUMENTS INC	30.05	-1.12%	-5.95%	34.34B	33.94%	129.31%	12.17	27.24%	2.26%	12.17
11) DELL INC	14.90	-0.13%	-9.96%	27.18B	16.24%	86.30%	7.34	47.23%	0.00%	7.34
12) COGNIZANT TECH SOLUTI...	66.23	-1.36%	-9.63%	20.01B	40.07%	34.07%	24.26	23.26%	0.00%	24.26
13) BROADCOM CORP-CL A	32.77	-0.49%	-24.19%	17.66B	51.84%	1538.46%	17.62	16.88%	0.00%	17.62
14) MOTOROLA SOLUTIONS INC	45.57	-1.09%	23.33%	14.83B	6.25%	N.A.	19.73	15.32%	1.93%	19.73
15) NETAPP INC	34.74	-2.77%	-36.79%	12.80B	30.30%	58.47%	14.72	18.21%	0.00%	14.72
16) SYMANTEC CORP	16.19	0.12%	-3.29%	11.93B	3.43%	-12.50%	16.69	14.86%	0.00%	16.69
17) JUNIPER NETWORKS INC	22.56	-0.75%	-38.89%	11.87B	23.44%	436.36%	22.56	7.83%	0.00%	22.56
18) ALTERA CORP	35.21	-0.41%	-0.35%	11.30B	63.49%	200.00%	13.44	35.96%	0.91%	13.44

Compare | Stats: Min | Max | Avg | Std Dev | More... | Grouping None | Zoom 100%

Exhibit 4.9

words, you should be able to overcome the time value portion of your option in the trade.

Use technicals to help rationalize this level. If your charts and/or analysis are telling you that the stock has a low probability of climbing to your breakeven, select another strike or select another strategy, such as a vertical spread.

Buying a lower delta is not necessarily a bad thing. Just understand that the relationship between stock and option will be more dependent on other factors, meaning that the stock may have to move further faster for you to potentially profit. When placing a directional trade, in other words, if you are just buying a call because you feel the stock will increase in value, the delta that may *not* be desirable to purchase would be the 0.40 to 0.60 range. At-the-money options have the most amount of time value, relative to the other options. Remember, time value is the decaying part of the option (more time value means you must lose more per day to get to zero by expiration). Having the most amount of time value means the option is also the most sensitive to volatility changes.

Choosing the right delta—Delta selection should be based on how you want an individual option to be related to the stock, the current Ivol to Hvol relationship, your time frame, and of course how far you believe the stock will go. See Exhibit 4.10.

The second part of choosing the best delta really is doing a bit of backward math. Once you've answered the above questions and found the right option specifically, you will now have to determine how many options to buy. Remember, delta is cumulative. Buying more options will increase your net delta in your portfolio.

Find a number that feels comfortable and remember that deltas are essentially the dollars that your portfolio will fluctuate with movements in the stock, so choose your contract size carefully.

Refer back to the allocation grading system in Chapter 2.

Choosing expiration—Having enough time for your trade to work is a risk many options traders have to contend with. One of the ways to determine how much time to buy is to look back on your past trading history. If you have a history of being in trades for an average of a month, then maybe you should buy a minimum of 60 days to expiration (DTE). If you have never traded live before, you should practice your trading methods with paper trades. Take a look at your practice trades in your virtual account and use those as a guide for how long you tend to be in trades. Before you begin to trade real money, be sure you understand all risks involved.

As a general rule, you should place at least 25 or more trades in your virtual account and have a written trade plan before using real money.

I am typically an active-to-swing trader, meaning that I usually stay in my positions anywhere from a couple of minutes to about three days, maximum. Your time horizon is important to determine *before* you place your trade. It not only helps determine

KEY POINT:

Stop Loss = Option Price Tactic:

You can subtract your (stock) stop-loss amount from the stock price and that's the strike that you buy.

Using this formula, if GOOG is $600 and I subtract $55 (stop loss amount) from it, I may purchase the 540 or 550 strike call.

KEY POINT:

Not sure how to objectively estimate realistic volatility? Use average true range (ATR).

ATR is the rolling 14-period average of a stock's greatest movement in a given time frame and can be measured in minutes, days, weeks, months, and so on.

I use ATR as a gauge for estimating realistic movements over a given period of time to place my targets and stop losses.

Multiply the ATR of the time frame. I think I will be in the trade by the delta to find the option's expected price variations.

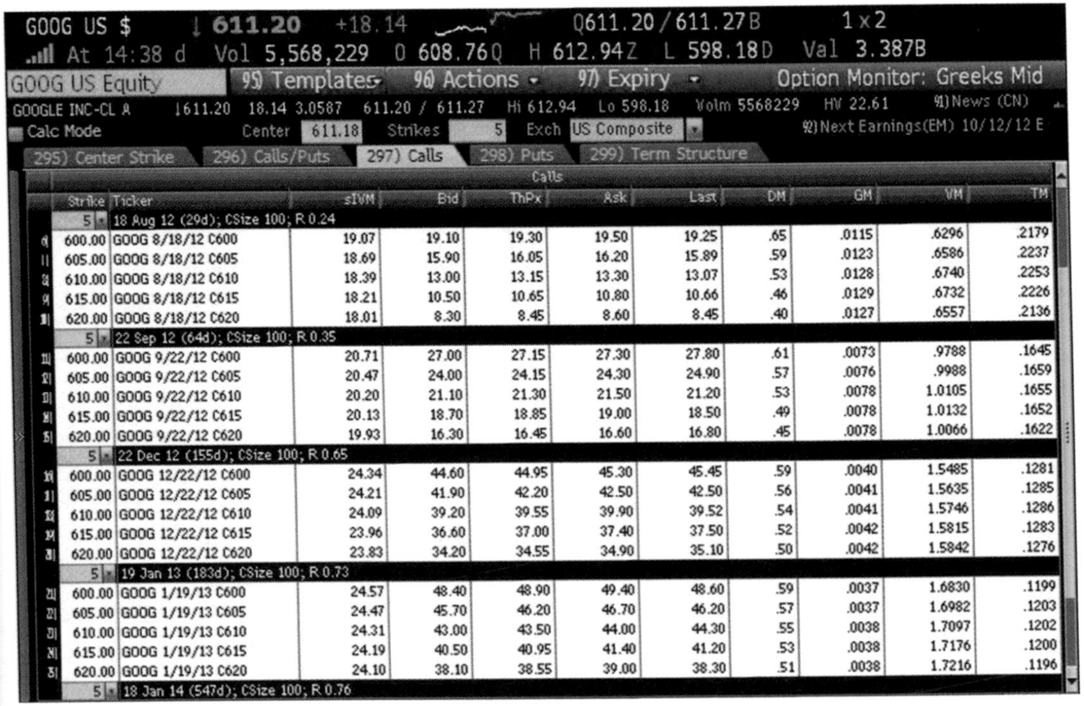

GOOG US $ ↓ 611.20 +18.14 Q611.20 / 611.27B 1 x 2
At 14:38 d Vol 5,568,229 O 608.76Q H 612.94Z L 598.18D Val 3.387B
GOOG US Equity 95) Templates 96) Actions 97) Expiry Option Monitor: Greeks Mid
GOOGLE INC-CL A ↓611.20 18.14 3.0587 611.20 / 611.27 Hi 612.94 Lo 598.18 Volm 5568229 HV 22.61 91) News (CN)
Calc Mode Center 611.18 Strikes 5 Exch US Composite 92) Next Earnings(EM) 10/12/12 E
295) Center Strike 296) Calls/Puts 297) Calls 298) Puts 299) Term Structure

Strike	Ticker	sIVM	Bid	ThPx	Ask	Last	DM	GM	VM	TM
5	18 Aug 12 (29d); CSize 100; R 0.24									
600.00	GOOG 8/18/12 C600	19.07	19.10	19.30	19.50	19.25	.65	.0115	.6296	.2179
605.00	GOOG 8/18/12 C605	18.69	15.90	16.05	16.20	15.89	.59	.0123	.6586	.2237
610.00	GOOG 8/18/12 C610	18.39	13.00	13.15	13.30	13.07	.53	.0128	.6740	.2253
615.00	GOOG 8/18/12 C615	18.21	10.50	10.65	10.80	10.66	.46	.0129	.6732	.2226
620.00	GOOG 8/18/12 C620	18.01	8.30	8.45	8.60	8.45	.40	.0127	.6557	.2136
5	22 Sep 12 (64d); CSize 100; R 0.35									
600.00	GOOG 9/22/12 C600	20.71	27.00	27.15	27.30	27.80	.61	.0073	.9788	.1645
605.00	GOOG 9/22/12 C605	20.47	24.00	24.15	24.30	24.90	.57	.0076	.9988	.1659
610.00	GOOG 9/22/12 C610	20.20	21.10	21.30	21.50	21.20	.53	.0078	1.0105	.1655
615.00	GOOG 9/22/12 C615	20.13	18.70	18.85	19.00	18.50	.49	.0078	1.0132	.1652
620.00	GOOG 9/22/12 C620	19.93	16.30	16.45	16.60	16.80	.45	.0078	1.0066	.1622
5	22 Dec 12 (155d); CSize 100; R 0.65									
600.00	GOOG 12/22/12 C600	24.34	44.60	44.95	45.30	45.45	.59	.0040	1.5485	.1281
605.00	GOOG 12/22/12 C605	24.21	41.90	42.20	42.50	42.50	.56	.0041	1.5635	.1285
610.00	GOOG 12/22/12 C610	24.09	39.20	39.55	39.90	39.52	.54	.0041	1.5746	.1286
615.00	GOOG 12/22/12 C615	23.96	36.60	37.00	37.40	37.50	.52	.0042	1.5815	.1283
620.00	GOOG 12/22/12 C620	23.83	34.20	34.55	34.90	35.10	.50	.0042	1.5842	.1276
5	19 Jan 13 (183d); CSize 100; R 0.73									
600.00	GOOG 1/19/13 C600	24.57	48.40	48.90	49.40	48.60	.59	.0037	1.6830	.1199
605.00	GOOG 1/19/13 C605	24.47	45.70	46.20	46.70	46.20	.57	.0037	1.6982	.1203
610.00	GOOG 1/19/13 C610	24.31	43.00	43.50	44.00	44.30	.55	.0038	1.7097	.1202
615.00	GOOG 1/19/13 C615	24.19	40.50	40.95	41.40	41.20	.53	.0038	1.7176	.1200
620.00	GOOG 1/19/13 C620	24.10	38.10	38.55	39.00	38.30	.51	.0038	1.7216	.1196
5	18 Jan 14 (547d); CSize 100; R 0.76									

Exhibit 4.10

DO IT YOURSELF

Look back at your past two years of trading (or your total history if less than two years). Find the average time you were in a trade. Then take your longest trade and average those two numbers (the average and the longest trade)—whatever number you come up with, add 30. The result is a good minimum days until expiration (DTE) to purchase when you are making trades.

Smart Investor Tip!

Some traders will find a dollar amount that they were willing to lose in a comparable stock investment then only use that loss amount as the total they are willing to spend on all their option contracts.

what strategy you employ, but also how much time you buy.

I developed the formula in the Do It Yourself box myself. It does not guarantee that you will always buy the right option, but it is a guideline to start with. I use this guideline because many traders that I have taught over the years have experienced a trade where they felt they needed to hold an option longer than expected. This situation is why I choose to add 30 (or more) days to my average trade length.

Obviously, purchasing more time for what you deem to be a more long-term investment is generally not a bad thing, although I would be careful buying less time, as we all know that sometimes things don't go exactly as planned in the market. Having more time in your trade may open some other choices that you may not have had available to you if you were out of time. Most traders do not want to be long an option with 20 DTE or less because time value begins to erode more exponentially the closer you get to expiry. Experienced traders who understand the more advanced behaviors of options may choose to trade front-month options.

Setting stops—My stops are usually based on the price of the underlying asset, not the call option. I do this because my thesis is built around its movement, not my option's. A good option trader will know what the proper option is to trade, so the rest should lie in the performance of the underlier, not in the option, because I know how that will react.

For the long call, it's all about good bullish strength, fundamental momentum, and technical levels being maintained. If any of those data change, you might consider taking the trade off the table and finding a better candidate. See Exhibit 4.11.

The most common occurrence that prematurely boots traders out of their call positions (and others as well) is the normal price variation that occurs in any stock. Stocks don't generally go straight up; they oscillate. When the broad market has a bad day it can drag perfectly good stocks with it. What you need to do is first identify what a "normal" oscillation is for the stock and then note how correlated to the stock market it is.

To quantify these measurements I use both ATR and beta.

To find out what a "normal" movement is, just look at the ATR of a given time frame. So if you are wondering what the average movement is over a week, check out the weekly ATR; if it's $10, then you should be able to tolerate a $10 move per week in either direction.

If you want to set a stop based on the stock making an abnormal move, you can use the ATR, stock price, and your delta to find a level to get out.

Moving up your stops—Once in the trade you should have an understanding of the stock's ATR, normal volatility, support and resistance points, earnings, news, and so on.

Depending on the amount of time you plan on being in the trade, adjusting your stop losses higher may have a higher or lower priority; the shorter the duration of the trade, the more aggressive you may have to be in adjusting your stops. Once I am in a profitable trade, I try to move my stop to at least breakeven, as long as it's not too close to the stock's normal movements (check ATR for this).

For me, I seldom put physical stops in the market, because they are seen by the market makers and in some cases, especially volatile stocks with wide bid-ask markets, my stop could get triggered, with my stop getting filled at even a lower level because of the spread.

I set price alerts on both the underlying asset and the option that send me emails and pop-ups on my

DO IT YOURSELF

Use this method for the option stop loss: Take the stock's ATR for the time frame that you want to be in the trade (monthly max) then multiply it by 1.2 [a risk factor I came up with], then multiply by the delta.

Then, whatever number you come up with, subtract that from the option's price.

If the ATR is $20 and your $40 option has a 0.70 delta, the math looks like this:

$40 – [($20 ATR × 1.2) × 0.70 *DELTA*]
= Stop Loss placed at $23.20

The stop-loss order would be placed at $23.20 in this case. That means you would have to tolerate a $16.80 draw down. This loss may seem steep, but remember that you may have been willing to originally tolerate a much bigger loss in the stock, all the while having much more cash tied up in the trade.

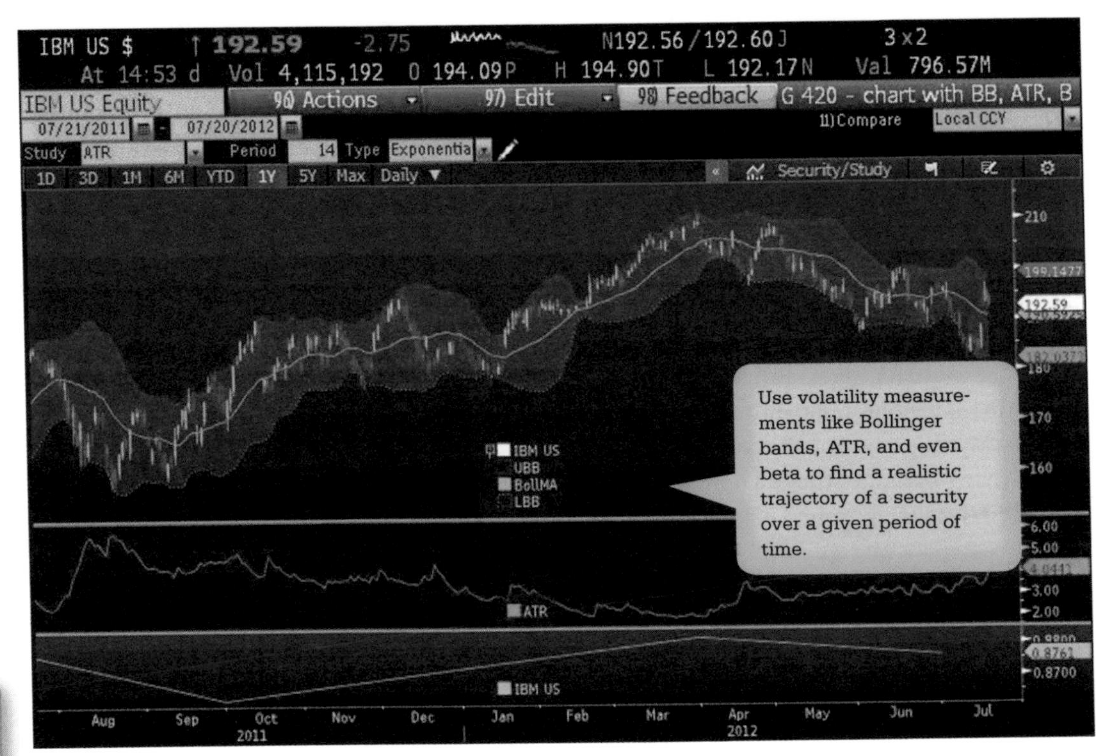

Exhibit 4.11

Smart Investor Tip!

If you use "trigger" orders from your brokers, those are generally housed on the broker's servers and don't hit the live market until their criteria are met. This keeps the market makers from leaning or prematurely filling my stop loss orders. If you like having physical stops in place, try to use the broker's trigger orders, not orders with the word "stop" in it.

screen. I do this for profit targets and stop losses. There are times when I will swap out my regular stop loss for a trailing stop that ratchets higher as the stock climbs, but will lock in place preventing it from moving lower. See Exhibit 4.12.

Step 5: Monitoring/Closing the Trade

Because calls can get pricey and are generally more price sensitive than many spreads, they are one of the strategies that you might monitor more closely than normal.

Exhibit 4.12

Price alerts can and should be set for targets and stops to keep track of your trades along with your initial thesis. Monitoring multiple positions manually 24/7 can be tedious.

If the trade is going in your favor, you should be proactive in protecting your profits. In the beginning stages of the trade, you should have already either entered your stop loss or at least had a psychological stop level where you were going to exit the trade. As the stock moves higher, don't be afraid to move your stop loss higher as well. Trailing stops can also be used to lock in and protect your existing profits. Do *not* be greedy. Stick to your plan and execute it.

If I begin to see cracks in the foundation of my trade, I will usually take profits on calls that I am long. This skittishness is more for shorter duration trades. For the longer trades, I will tolerate a bit more of a breakdown, but I never want to have a substantially positive trade go negative on me.

Items to Check When Monitoring

- Changes in macro data, news, and so on
- Changes in chart patterns
- Changes in sentiment
- Earnings
- Stop loss
- Target profits
- Techniques for protection

Repair versus exit—Deciding to repair or completely abandon a trade has many determining factors. Long calls can be added to on the fly to create all kinds of spreads, but generally there isn't a ton of repair that can be done if things are going really bad.

Some points to consider are:

- Has the fundamental picture changed in the stock?
  - Might be better to simply exit if things are getting nasty.
  - For more neutral changes, you can sell a call against your long call and turn it into a bull call

KEY POINT:

For the shorter term "swing"-type trader who wants to try a different strategy, look for stocks that have made dramatic, abnormal moves in either direction in a day's time and look for a reversion or reversal in the other direction the following day. A stock that has far exceeded its ATR and Bollinger Band on high volume with no major news might be a candidate for a reversion to the mean trade. It's a great way to capture some quick profits. Use screen MOST to look for stocks making big moves.

spread. Be sure that premiums and breakevens make sense.

- Have the charts broken down?
  - A minor blip in the charts might not be too bad and could just mean that you sell some of your contracts and let the others ride. A drop below a major trend line (50- or 200-day MA) might be a reason to simply bail out.
- Was there an earnings occurrence?
  - If earnings were just okay and the stock is up, flat, or slightly down, I will almost always sell a call. No reason to stick around if your bullish target delivered just decent results.
  - If the report was a complete blowout and the stock is up 10 percent, you have to ask a couple of questions: Did you hit your original profit target? If so, exit. Would you buy a call in the stock at these levels? If you wouldn't, then sell.
- Have you gone beyond your original stop loss point?
  - If the trade has exceeded your stop loss level, why are you in the trade? If you have a rational, objective, data-supported reason, then maybe you can stay for a little longer. If not, *sell!*
- Is the trade consuming you?
  - If a bad trade is consuming your psychological capital, its compounding effects may drain more than your bank account. You obviously took on too much risk or lied to yourself about it being a good trade. Take the hit and move on. You will feel better afterward, I promise.
- Do you really have enough time in your long call position to turn it into a spread?
  - Some traders seem to think that an at- or out-of-the-money call that is near expiration is still okay to spread off. There are so many variables here, it's hard to say, but unless the call is deep in the money and you can get a good amount of premium for an at- or out-of-the-money call to sell against it you might as well just sell or roll it to the next month if you think the stock just needs more time.
  - Rolling a trade should allow you to get slightly better pricing than selling the one and buying the other separately.
- Will your repair not only be feasible, but dramatically improve the trade?
  - Some positions are beyond repair and for some reason traders try to get creative and end up with a bigger mess on their hands. If you were bullish in a trade with a call, but you've taken such a loss that you are now trying to sell a call against it to turn it bearish, you might want to go back to the drawing board and rethink a new trade.
- If you extend the life of the trade, will the extra time for minimal loss recovery justify the capital committed to the trade?

Smart Investor Tip!

If you have a profit, don't be afraid to take it or at least protect it with a trailing stop. Because of the nature of the call and its negative theta and sometimes close correlation with the stock, you are paying to be in the trade every day and if the stock moves drastically against you, your call may move drastically against you as well. Focus on percentage returns in the option, not the dollar amount.

- Don't roll a trade that you are feeling bad about. If you are going to prolong pain, have a damn good reason for doing it. I rolled a bear call spread in Apple twice in 2012 and lost $30,000 because I wanted to be right and my ego got the best of me.
- I made the trade despite every bone in my body telling me not to. I fought a stock that was up 45 percent in a couple months, not because data pointed to it going down, but because I was cocky. That emotion cost me the value of a car.

Covered Call (Buy-Write)

The covered call, also called the buy-write, requires the trader to be long stock and short a call (1 for every 100 shares) against it. Covered calls are considered moderately bullish and can even be considered neutral because at the end of the day you want the stock to move upward only to the strike price of the call or at least remain stable. The one thing you do not want the stock to do is move lower. See Exhibit 4.13.

The goal of the trade is to capture time value and profit from the time decay of the short call while the long stock position maintains stability or slight appreciation.

Max profit in a covered call or buy-write is:

(Strike Price of Short Call + Premium Received) – Cost Basis in the Stock

Max risk in a covered call or buy-write is:

Long Stock Cost Basis – Short Call Premium

Breakeven in a covered call is:

Long Stock Cost Basis – Short Call Premium

The sale of the call limits the stock's upside potential to the difference between the purchase price of the stock and the strike price plus the premium you receive for the call. This sacrifice to the upside allows traders to reduce their cost basis and partially hedge against a pullback in the stock.

Optimal Scenario

You want to be predominantly bullish on the underlying security, but it should be reaching a temporary resistance point or entering into a seasonal slowdown in movement. The covered call can also be used for a stock that is in a channel. You sell the call at the top of the channel and buy it back at the bottom, all the while maintaining your long stock and capturing small profits with the option. For the best-case scenario, implied volatility will be relatively high compared to observed volatility when you go to sell the call. The majority of indicators in your analysis should be decidedly bullish and pointing to moderate growth from the macro level all the way down to the company level. See Exhibit 4.14.

The optimal expiration situation would be for the stock to move to the call strike price and expire just a penny below (so you are not assigned). Because of the multitude of call strikes that you can sell and your

KEY POINT:

The covered call/buy-write is similar in risk and reward to a naked short put (remember the synthetics). Your broker only requires a portion of the total risk of the short put as margin, which may be more cost-effective.

When you sell put, you want the stock to just stay above the strike that you sold, at which point you retain the credit you sold it for. If the stock falls below the put strike you sold, you may be forced to purchase the stock at the strike price of the put. You will still retain the credit you sold it for, thus reducing your cost basis in the stock.

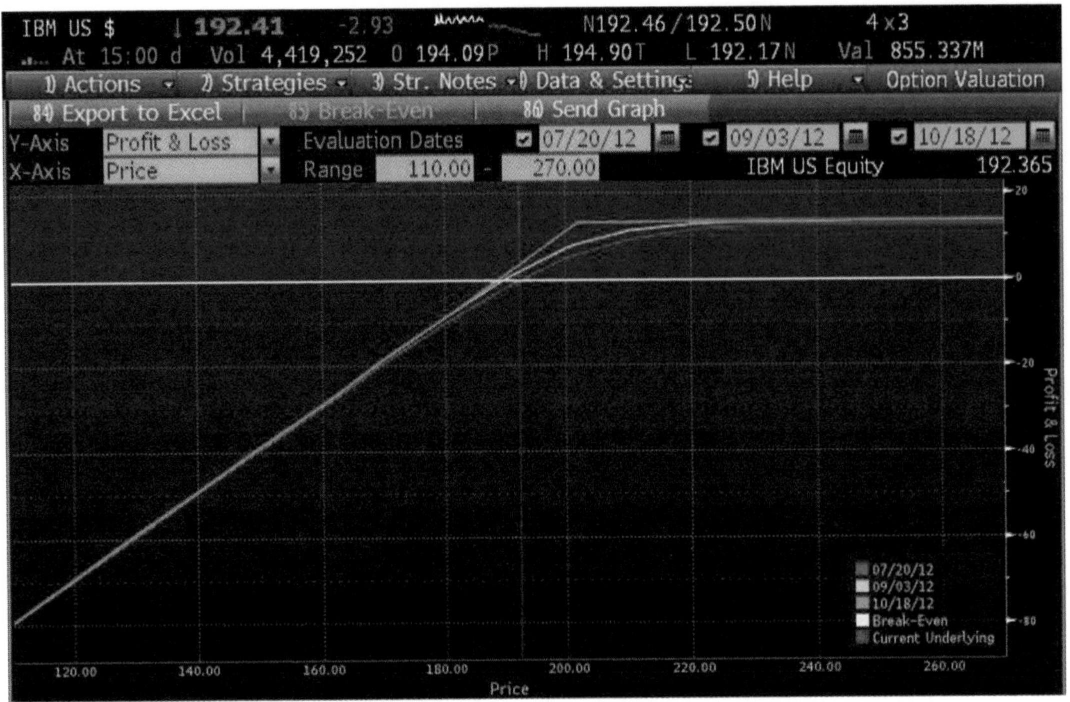

Exhibit 4.13

original cost basis in the stock, the probability of profit in this trade varies.

The charts should be bullish but leading up to a resistance point—perhaps slightly overbought in the near term.

Covered calls are also optimal in a market that is moving sideways or in transition. Keep in mind that the overall sentiment and fundamentals of the stock should still be bullish. See Exhibit 4.15.

Buy-Write Variance

The buy-write will be similar, but will be timed differently. Instead of waiting for the stock to peak like you would for the covered call, enter the buy-write in a

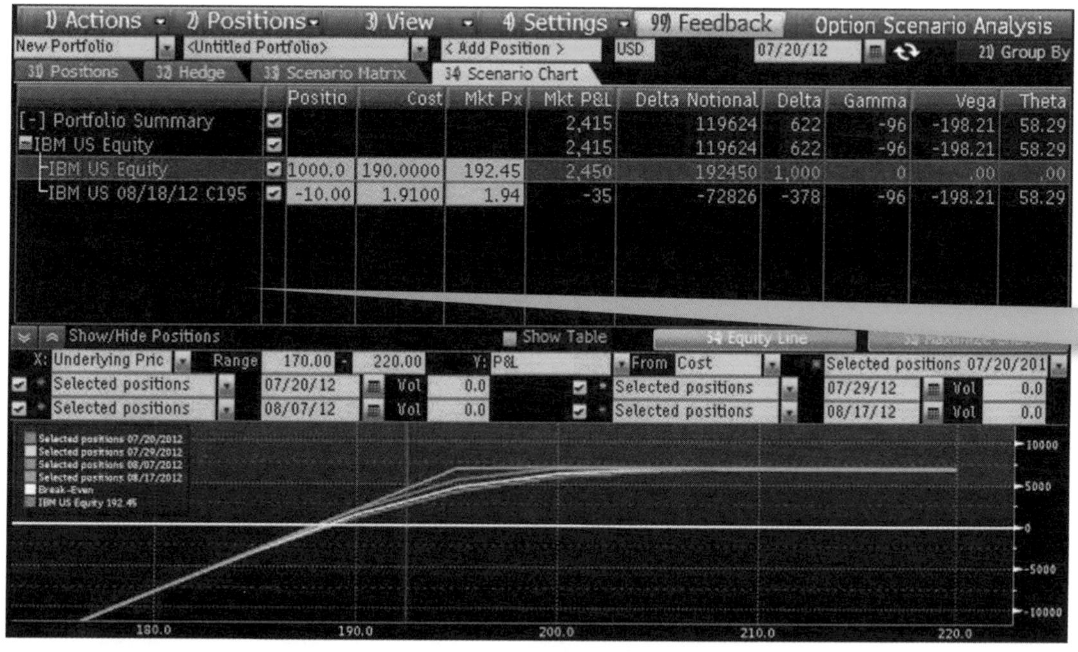

As you can see by the structure of the covered call/buy-write, you have increased capital at risk and more downside exposure than with a call option.

Exhibit 4.14

stable trend or before a moderate upside move. Everything else essentially remains the same in terms of thesis. Strike selection may vary slightly. See Exhibit 4.16.

Advantages

Covered calls can offer a moderately bullish trader a way to partially protect a long stock position from a momentary pullback. Covered calls can also be used to increase returns over flat (sideways) periods in the market.

Time decay—The main benefit the covered call offers is the ability for the trader to gain profits from the passage of time.

Protection—For holders of long stock, a covered call can be used as a *partial* hedge against a minor pullback. Because the protection level

Covered calls can be bought and sold while you still remain long the shares; use technical analysis to assist in timing those trades.

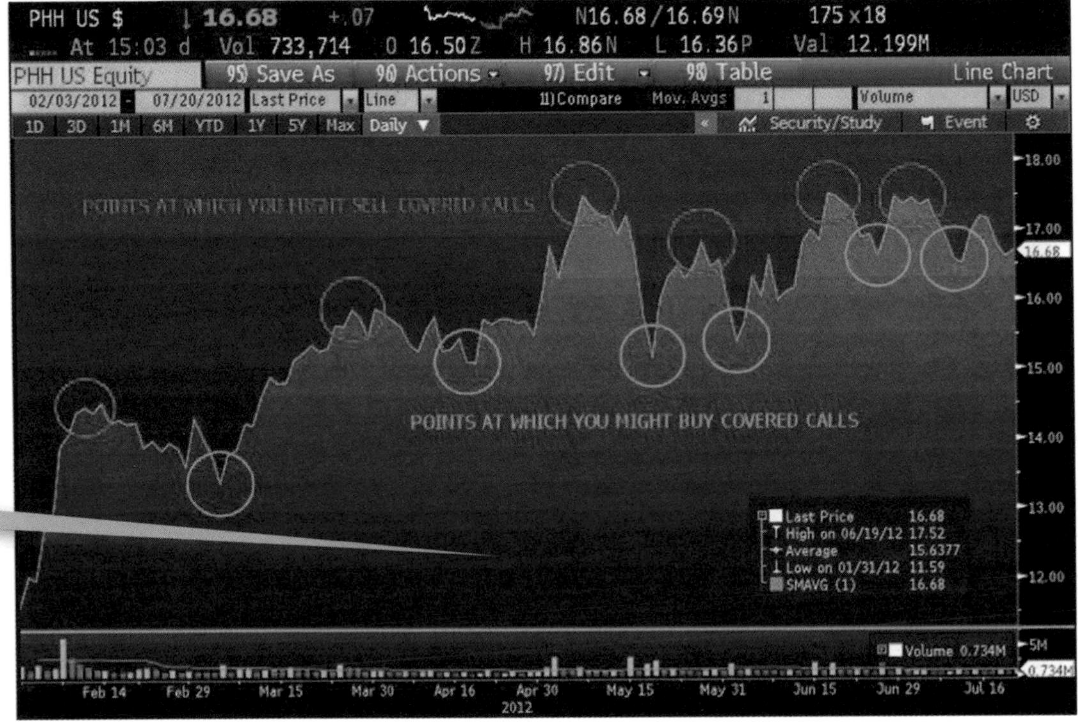

Exhibit 4.15

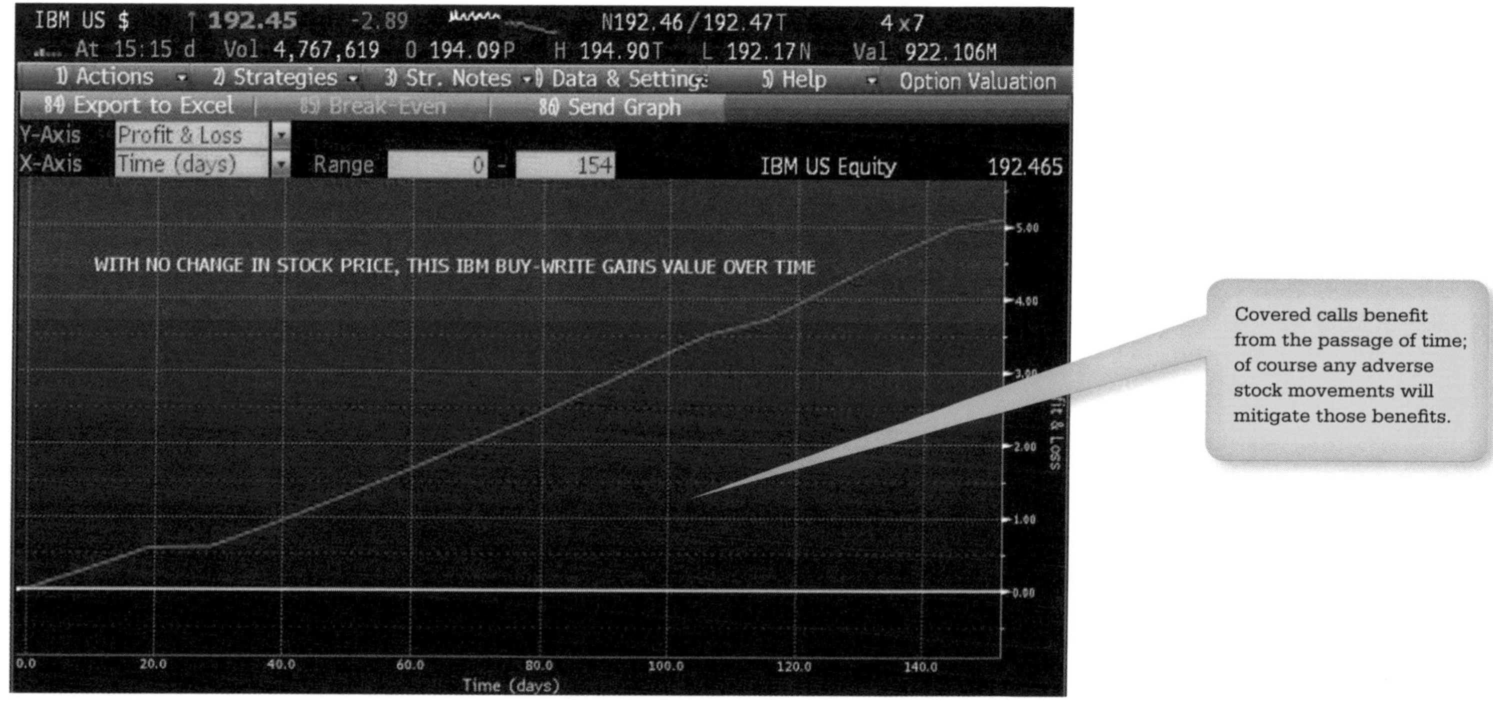
IBM US $ ↑192.45 -2.89 N192.46 / 192.47T 4 x 7
At 15:15 d Vol 4,767,619 O 194.09P H 194.90T L 192.17N Val 922.106M
1) Actions 2) Strategies 3) Str. Notes 4) Data & Settings 5) Help Option Valuation
84) Export to Excel 85) Break-Even 86) Send Graph
Y-Axis Profit & Loss
X-Axis Time (days) Range 0 - 154
IBM US Equity 192.465
WITH NO CHANGE IN STOCK PRICE, THIS IBM BUY-WRITE GAINS VALUE OVER TIME
5.00
4.00
3.00
2.00
1.00
0.00
Profit & Loss
0.0 20.0 40.0 60.0 80.0 100.0 120.0 140.0
Time (days)
Covered calls benefit from the passage of time; of course any adverse stock movements will mitigate those benefits.

Exhibit 4.16

Smart Investor Tip!

Covered calls can cap potential profits. As the stock moves above the short call, its delta moves closer to 1 and will completely negate further profitability unless it is bought back. If you think a stock is going to make a bullish run, buy back the call unless your goal is to have the stock called away from you.

Smart Investor Tip!

Covered call writers sometimes use the term *renting* their stock out. This term is used because for both the buy-write and covered call the stock is used as "collateral" for the short call. The long stock is a hedge or an offset for the upside risk of a short call.

is somewhat limited, some traders add a long put and create a collar. The call can be sold and bought back at will, which enables you to "trade the volatility" with less risk and tax consequences than buying and selling your entire stock position.

Adjusting the strike of the call will determine the amount of "protection" or bullishness you want. I will discuss this in detail shortly.

Risk reduction—Because the sale of the call generates a premium, your theoretical risk is less than just having owned the stock outright. A covered call that is executed properly should have a break-even that is lower than the stock.

Risk can also be reduced by the short call's delta, which will offset the 100 delta of the stock.

Flexibility—There are no restrictions to the strike and month at which you can sell a covered call. This allows for quite a bit of flexibility to choose the best call for your thesis and level of bullishness or bearishness. Although your time horizons are flexible, I prefer to sell shorter dated call options and continuously roll them to the next month as needed.

It may seem like a better deal (and maybe easier) to simply sell an option with three or more months until expiration, but the speed at which those options decay will be slower than the near month options. Furthermore, longer dated options will have more vega, which could hurt you if Ivol rises.

Disadvantages

Limited upside—The strike price of the call you sell should be a level at which you would feel comfortable selling the stock. Not that it will automatically happen, but it's a good way to rationalize the selection. Think about it this way. When you sell that call, you have essentially obligated yourself to deliver shares at the strike, the premium that you receive from that sale is considered payment for that risk. You do have the option of buying back the call at any time. See Exhibit 4.17.

Minimal protection—You may sell a call for $1, but the stock may drop $10. In that case, you only partially offset your risk. Because of this partial protection, you should always have an underlying bullish sentiment on the stock. If you sentiments are bearish, collar it or sell your stock!

Assignment risk—Assignment risk can be addressed in two ways. You can choose a strike at which you would be okay with selling the stock or you can buy back the call if the stock is moving higher, even if you have to pay what you sold it for or more.

Don't forget that the profit from the stock will generally overcome the loss in the call and time decay should also be helping out!

Timing—Timing a covered call can be a little tricky because it's hard to know when a stock is going to stop its upward momentum. I use technical

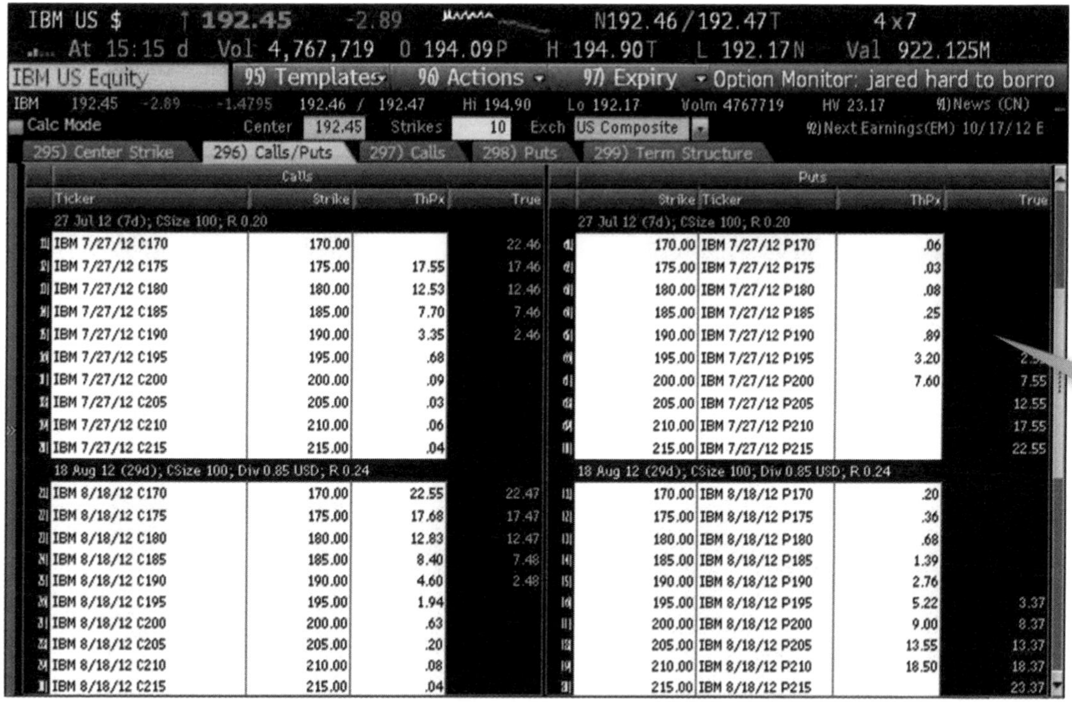

IBM US $ 192.45 -2.89 N192.46/192.47T 4x7
At 15:15 d Vol 4,767,719 O 194.09P H 194.90T L 192.17N Val 922.125M
IBM US Equity 95) Templates 96) Actions 97) Expiry Option Monitor: jared hard to borro
IBM 192.45 -2.89 -1.4795 192.46 / 192.47 Hi 194.90 Lo 192.17 Volm 4767719 HV 23.17 91) News (CN)
Calc Mode Center 192.45 Strikes 10 Exch US Composite 92) Next Earnings(EM) 10/17/12 E
295) Center Strike 296) Calls/Puts 297) Calls 298) Puts 299) Term Structure

Calls				Puts			
Ticker	Strike	ThPx	True	Strike	Ticker	ThPx	True
27 Jul 12 (7d); CSize 100; R 0.20				27 Jul 12 (7d); CSize 100; R 0.20			
IBM 7/27/12 C170	170.00		22.46	170.00	IBM 7/27/12 P170	.06	
IBM 7/27/12 C175	175.00	17.55	17.46	175.00	IBM 7/27/12 P175	.03	
IBM 7/27/12 C180	180.00	12.53	12.46	180.00	IBM 7/27/12 P180	.08	
IBM 7/27/12 C185	185.00	7.70	7.46	185.00	IBM 7/27/12 P185	.25	
IBM 7/27/12 C190	190.00	3.35	2.46	190.00	IBM 7/27/12 P190	.89	
IBM 7/27/12 C195	195.00	.68		195.00	IBM 7/27/12 P195	3.20	[illegible]
IBM 7/27/12 C200	200.00	.09		200.00	IBM 7/27/12 P200	7.60	7.55
IBM 7/27/12 C205	205.00	.03		205.00	IBM 7/27/12 P205		12.55
IBM 7/27/12 C210	210.00	.06		210.00	IBM 7/27/12 P210		17.55
IBM 7/27/12 C215	215.00	.04		215.00	IBM 7/27/12 P215		22.55
18 Aug 12 (29d); CSize 100; Div 0.85 USD; R 0.24				18 Aug 12 (29d); CSize 100; Div 0.85 USD; R 0.24			
IBM 8/18/12 C170	170.00	22.55	22.47	170.00	IBM 8/18/12 P170	.20	
IBM 8/18/12 C175	175.00	17.68	17.47	175.00	IBM 8/18/12 P175	.36	
IBM 8/18/12 C180	180.00	12.83	12.47	180.00	IBM 8/18/12 P180	.68	
IBM 8/18/12 C185	185.00	8.40	7.48	185.00	IBM 8/18/12 P185	1.39	
IBM 8/18/12 C190	190.00	4.60	2.48	190.00	IBM 8/18/12 P190	2.76	
IBM 8/18/12 C195	195.00	1.94		195.00	IBM 8/18/12 P195	5.22	3.37
IBM 8/18/12 C200	200.00	.63		200.00	IBM 8/18/12 P200	9.00	8.37
IBM 8/18/12 C205	205.00	.20		205.00	IBM 8/18/12 P205	13.55	13.37
IBM 8/18/12 C210	210.00	.08		210.00	IBM 8/18/12 P210	18.50	18.37
IBM 8/18/12 C215	215.00	.04		215.00	IBM 8/18/12 P215		23.37

Here I have isolated the intrinsic value as a column, so you can observe just how much time value the covered call and its corresponding puts have.

Exhibit 4.17

indicators to help me target overbought scenarios. Some indicators might be the Bollinger band in the daily chart, combined with ATR (look for a stock that has moved beyond its daily ATR). I'll also look for an abnormal run in the stock and then sell my call when it looks overextended. See Exhibit 4.18.

Buy-write timing is essentially the opposite. Because you will be establishing a new stock position, I like to enter the buy-write on a sharp, preferably abnormal pullback. So for the buy-write, you use technicals to find an oversold condition. The added bonus in a sell-off is that the calls may be inflated with the increase in Ivol.

Smart Investor Tip!

If your short call is deep in the money and has little or no time value, you are running a high risk of assignment. Another way to check your risk of assignment is to look at the put with the corresponding strike. If the put has little or no value (0 bid – 0.05 ask) then your call is trading at parity and risk for assignment is high.

CMG US $ S 316.98 -86.88 T317.14/317.17P 1x1
At 15:15 d Vol 9,789,861 O 328.45T H 335.80T L 307.20N Val 3.114B
CMG US Equity
95) Save As
96) Actions
97) Edit
98) Table
Line Chart
Period 240 Range 180 08:30 - 15:00 Line
11) Compare
Mov. Avgs 1
No Lower Chart
1D 3D 1M 6M YTD 1Y 5Y Max 240 Min
Security/Study
Event
CLEAR OVEREXTENTION
440
420
400
380
360
340
317.17
300
Nov
2011
Dec
Jan
Feb
Mar
Apr
2012
May
Jun
Jul

Exhibit 4.18

Covered Call Greek Attributes

Delta

Positive—Even though you are short a call, the net delta will always be positive (might be 0 if stock goes high enough). Delta can range from 0.01 to 0.99. You will always remain net long unless the stock moves up so high that the short call delta rises to 1. If this is the case, you should expect to be assigned. See Exhibit 4.19.

The higher the strike sold the more of a positive net delta you will have and vice versa. If you are more bullish, sell your call out of the money. Less bullish, sell closer to the money (call delta of 0.40 – 0.60).

Gamma

Negative—You will have the most short gamma when the stock is right at the strike. Don't be misled by the gamma; even though it is short, your risk is higher to the downside as dictated by your delta. Delta can only go to zero when the stock rises, and to 1 when it falls.

Theta

Long—You are collecting theta. At-the-money options will pay the most theta, and have the most time value; the goal in the covered call is to sell a call option with a high amount of time value at a strike that you believe the stock will stay **below** by the expiration date.

Theta can also be misleading when you are selecting expiration. You might see a higher nominal theta in an option with more time, but the shorter duration option will usually see a sharper increase in that theta the closer you are to expiration. Theta is one of the main keys of this trade.

Vega

Short—You are short vega, which means that you want implied volatility to decrease. Preferably you should target an option with high relative Ivol.

Use the implied volatility charts before making your trade. If Ivol seems extremely low compared to past Ivol and Hvol, you might want to change your strike/month selection or justify that vol should be moving lower in general.

Rho

Short—You want interest rates to fall as a general rule, but they will have minimal impact on your position as you will be trading a short dated option.

How Is a Buy-Write Different?

When a trader executes a buy-write (or a covered call) she should receive a premium for that call (not counting the cost of the stock). This premium, which can vary greatly depending on the stock price, its volatility, and which option is chosen, will be the total premium received in the trade (you can profit more than the premium received if the strike price is higher than the stock price).

Smart Investor Tip!

Stocks tend to have a normal pattern. They may rally for three to five days and then pull back. If you have a stock that's up for six or more days straight and you are profitable, consider selling an at- or out-of-the-money call as a precaution.

Smart Investor Tip!

Deep in-the-money options can provide more of a hedge, but their minimal time value diminishes the theta they will allow you to collect.

KEY POINT:

Covered calls can be effective if you want to get long shares. But if you are unsure about timing, you can execute a buy-write.

If the shares rally, you may be limited to the return of the call premium. If the stock drops, you can buy the call back and the profit made from the call will lower your breakeven in the stock.

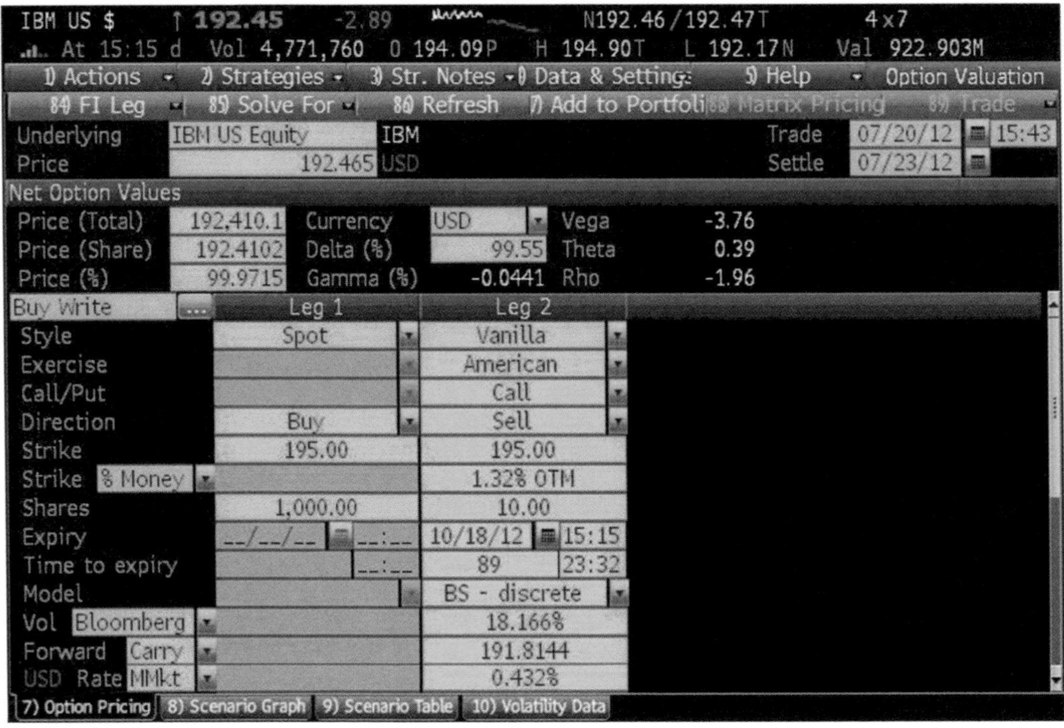

Exhibit 4.19

If you were to purchase ABC stock for $50 and sell the 55 call for $1, the most you could make on this trade is $6, no matter how high the stock goes. Keep this in mind when choosing your call strike to sell.

Let's explore typical reasoning and application of the buy-write first. We discuss the differences between it and the covered call shortly after.

Selling a call is a bearish act, and it obligates the seller to deliver the stock at the strike price if assigned. In a buy-write, bearishness is offset by the purchase of the stock. Buy-write traders want to be long the stock, but may be concerned about a short-term pullback or they have a neutral view on the stock's direction and feel the yield they are collecting from the sale of the call is acceptable in the time they are in the trade.

Buying stock outright is one of the most bullish opinions and greatest downside risks you can have when compared to buying call option because call options are lower in cost and thus lower in dollar risk.

The short call benefits from the passage of time (positive theta), meaning that the trader will collect time decay (theta) each day.

Selling a call against stock you own can limit your upside potential. Buy-write traders tend to sell at-the-money options that have the most amount of time value so they can capture the highest yield.

Covered Call Dynamics

Let's run through the steps of the covered call and buy-write strategies.

Step 1: Identifying the Target

A covered call candidate is going to have similarities to the long call candidate in terms of the bullish sentiment you want to look for. The bullish conditions for the covered call don't have to be as strong as the long call itself. Unlike the call, the covered call will either be executed on an existing stock you own for some temporary protection or to bring in some additional income while it's moving sideways.

A buy-write candidate on the other hand should be a stock *not in your portfolio* that you feel is either stable or bullish that you wouldn't be opposed to owning. The short call yield should be sufficient enough to justify the downside risk in buying the stock. See Exhibit 4.20.

Typically covered calls should be sold with less than 60 DTE (30 or less even better). They can be employed with more or less time, but are generally held until the desired outcome is achieved or the stock begins to plummet, in which case you may want to re-evaluate the entire position and close it.

You can target buy-write candidates through a scan where you search for overall bullish fundamentals and technicals on a stock that has very high relative implied volatility.

Exhibit 4.21 shows a couple of filters that you can find in screen OS (Option Search) to find potential covered call candidates if you don't already have one in mind. These scans can also produce ideas for other bullish strategies.

Covered calls should be similar to long call candidates, but with less short-term bullish catalysts. Unlike long calls, you are going to focus heavily on Ivol being more expensive when compared to historical or Hvol.

Catalysts—Follow the same research path as you would for a long call in terms of the underlying market tone and healthy fundamentals, but watch out for near term events that could catapult the stock much

Smart Investor Tip!

A more advanced technique would be to buy back the call—potentially at a loss—if the stock began to rally, which would uncap the potential return.

KEY POINT:

The basic premise for both strategies is the same, however the buy-write candidate should be sideways to bullish and the covered call candidate should be sideways to temporarily bearish. This is because of the timing of execution. Perhaps it makes sense to think of the covered call as a repair or modification to an existing (preferably profitable or breakeven) position, whereas the buy-write is a completely new trade.

Smart Investor Tip!

In some cases, covered calls are executed to purposely have the stock called away. If you are in a stock that is going sideways and want to sell, but not in a hurry, sell an at- or slightly in-the-money call to get a better deal on your exit.

IBM US Equity | Calls | 96) Export to Excel | 97) Expiry | Covered Option Write Calculator

Price 189.27 | Margin 100.0 % | Interest 0.88 %

Commissions: Per Share 0 | Per Contract 0

Trade 07/24/12 | Settle 07/27/12 | Expiration 10/19/12 | Settle 10/24/12 | 89 Days between Settlements

Use Simple Interest | Use Compound Interest | Dividend: Reinvest .44 % | Tot @ Exp 0.85

Expiring 19 Oct 2012 | Standstill: Exp Prc 189.27 | Breakeven: 0.0 % Max | Exercised: 10/19/12

	Strike	Bid	Ask	Price	T Val	Standstill Simple	Standstill Annual	Breakeven Target	Breakeven Annual	Exercised Simple	Exercised Annual
12)	155.00	34.45	36.80	34.45	0.18	0.67%	2.76% *	153.97	2.76%	0.67%	2.76%
13)	160.00	29.80	30.05	29.80	0.53	0.87%	3.6% *	158.62	3.6%	0.87%	3.6%
14)	165.00	25.20	25.45	25.20	0.93	1.08%	4.52% *	163.22	4.52%	[illegible]	4.52%
15)	170.00	20.80	21.05	20.80	1.53	1.41%	5.92% *	[illegible]	5.92%	1.41%	5.92%
16)	175.00	16.70	16.90	16.70	2.43	[illegible]	8.03% *	171.72	8.03%	1.9%	8.03%
17)	180.00	12.85	[illegible]	[illegible]	3.58	2.51%	10.71% *	175.57	10.71%	2.51%	10.71%
[illegible]	[illegible]	9.50	9.65	9.50	5.23	3.38%	14.62% *	178.92	14.62%	3.38%	14.62%
19)	190.00	6.65	6.75	6.65	6.65	4.11%	17.95%	181.77	19.82%	4.51%	19.82%
20)	195.00	4.35	4.45	4.35	4.35	2.81%	12.05%	184.07	26.56%	5.91%	26.56%
21)	200.00	2.70	2.75	2.70	2.70	1.9%	8.04%	185.72	35.32%	7.65%	35.32%
22)	205.00	1.59	1.64	1.59	1.59	1.3%	5.44%	186.83	46.08%	9.68%	46.08%
23)	210.00	0.90	0.95	0.90	0.90	0.93%	3.87%	187.52	58.78%	11.93%	58.78%
24)	215.00	0.51	0.55	0.51	0.51	0.72%	2.99%	187.91	73.32%	14.35%	73.32%
25)	220.00	0.28	0.36	0.28	0.28	0.6%	2.47%	188.14	89.44%	16.86%	89.44%
26)	225.00	0.15	0.18	0.15	0.15	0.53%	2.19%	188.27	107.07%	19.42%	107.07%
27)	230.00	0.00	0.18	0.18	0.18	0.54%	2.25%	188.24	126.68%	22.08%	126.68%
28)	235.00	0.00	0.15	0.15	0.15	0.53%	2.19%	188.27	147.34%	24.71%	147.34%

Ex-Date	Amt
08/10/12	.85
__/__/__	.00

Use the Covered Option Write Calculator to quickly find the best return out of an option chain given your expectations in the stock. Use the "Standstill," "Breakeven," and "Exercised" columns together to find balance in return/risk.

Exhibit 4.20

Smart Investor Tip!

The buy-write can be used in place of a long call if you found that Ivols were extremely high. Make sure that the high volatility isn't due to an event like earnings or an FDA announcement; in that case another strategy may be more appropriate.

higher. (This isn't a deal-breaker, but these events might make it better to just buy the call.)

The covered call may be a stock stuck in a rut or losing favor or momentum. Sell your call when it looks like the stock might be rolling over in price. Do this ahead of the drop to mitigate the loss in the stock and capture the most premium.

For the buy-write, focus on good stocks outside of your portfolio. You would be entering into a new trade with a positive delta, so get into these trades ahead of similar bullish catalysts you would find for the long call. There may even be instances where you were looking at a long call but saw that Ivol was elevated. This may be an opportune time to utilize a buy-write.

- **Earnings**—The covered call is not the optimal strategy for playing earnings, but it can reduce risk if you are holding a long stock position through an earnings report. Because of the Ivol earnings crush, the covered call will benefit from short vega after the report is out.
  - As long as the stock stays stable or doesn't drop too far beyond the value of the call you sold, then the trade was effective.
  - If the stock jumps way above the short call strike you will miss out on a good part of that upside, but with the call moving in the money the time value will diminish and you will be able to capture it.
  - If you feel that the stock will continue its run after earnings, don't be afraid to buy it back and get long delta.
  - Like the call, look at the vega of the option you choose and do the math first, this time thinking opposite. If you believe that the potential profits from vega (and theta) can overcome the potential missed delta, then proceed.
- **Economic data to be released**—Sell a covered call against a stock position to provide a partial hedge.
- **Charts to identify patterns of support and other bullish technical indicators**—The covered call can be the perfect vehicle for playing moderate bullish technical trends and channels or for stocks with more volatility.

Step 2: Fundamental Analysis

Fundamental analysis should match what you want for a long call. For a covered call or buy-write, you can have a stock that is slightly "less than perfect," but still strong. Don't forget that you will still have a long stock position that can be risky and expensive.

The deciding factors for covered call/buy-write versus long call will be that covered call candidates don't need the super bullish momentum like long call stocks. In fact, covered call candidates can be stocks that maybe aren't in the favored sector(s) because the short call premium is generating return for your account in lieu of actual stock price appreciation.

Step 3: Technical Analysis

You want to sell calls with a strike price at or near resistance levels in the chart of the stock you are trading. Time the sale of the covered call for when you notice momentum slowing down or a capitulation buy, which precedes a reversal. You will want to sell your call before the stock begins to sell off. Use overbought indicators as well as trend indicators such as MACD and stochastics to spot a slowing trend. The overall long-term trend of the stock should still be bullish.

With the covered call you are going to have to look at the charts with two sets of eyes so to speak; you will have a longer-term view with a focus on the longer duration charts and pattern that support your long stock. The long-term technicals should be bullish. Find major support levels and bullish patterns in the

KEY POINT:

Covered call writers may also have a tendency to want to keep their stock, meaning they may be slightly less aggressive in selling their calls opting to sell an out-of-the-money call versus at the money.

This decision may be for sentimental value (stock has been gifted to them, etc.) or a desire to hold the stock in the belief that it will continue to rise in value or for favorable tax reasons.

Smart Investor Tip!

For quick conformation of a long-term bullish trend, I look for the stock to be above the 200-day simple moving average (SMA) and preferably the 50-day average to be above it as well.

When the 50-day crosses below the 200-day and remains there for two days, that may be a cue that the bullish trend is ending.

Exhibit 4.21

monthly or weekly charts to support your investment in the stock itself. See Exhibit 4.22.

Your other analysis will be for the short call portion of the trade; here you will be focusing your eyes on the daily chart, using its levels to trade in and out of the short call. Remember that the shorter time frame charts (like the daily) may have completely different patterns. See Exhibit 4.23.

For extra cues to trade the short call take a look at standard 20, two standard deviation daily Bollinger bands, and look for oversold or overbought conditions. If a stock has breached the lower Bollinger band, but remains above its 200 SMA and, let's say, its 20, or 50 SMA, I will buy back the short call.

This works the same to the upside as well, at which point I may sell the covered call. See Exhibit 4.24.

Smart Investor Tip!

For the short call, I look at 10-, 20-, and 50-day moving averages and the stock's relative position to all of them to identify support and resistance points as well as determine trend.

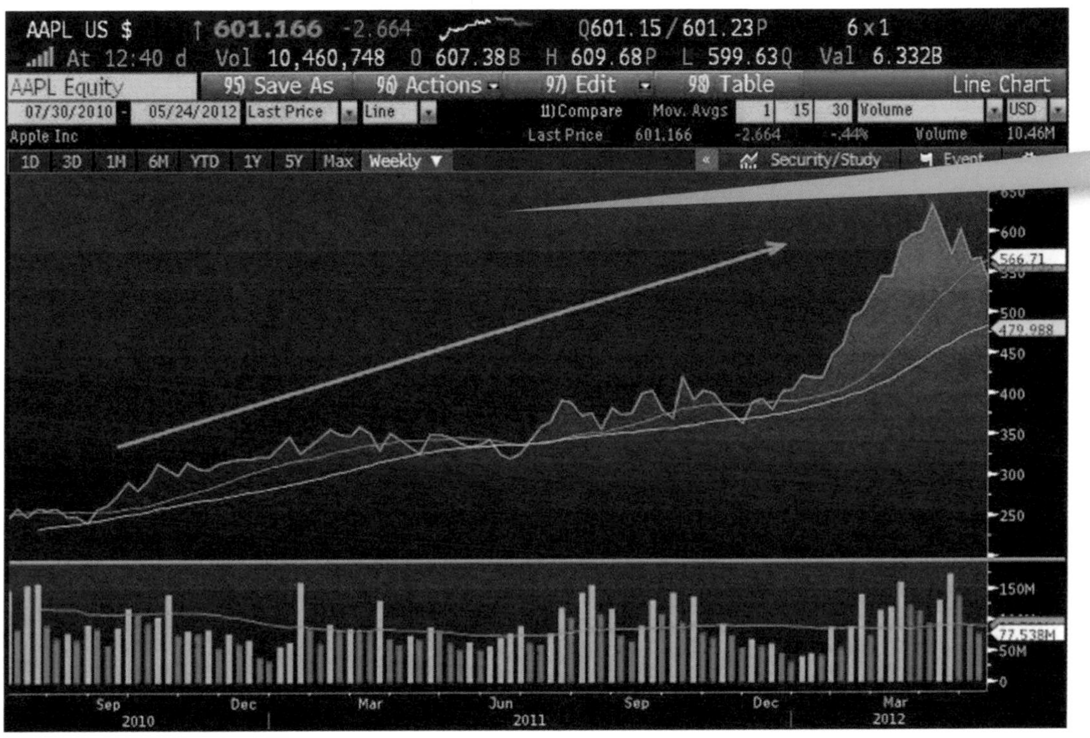

Exhibit 4.22

Resistance—Find a resistance point that you think the stock will have trouble getting through. This could be a 52-week high, a moving average, a price level that it struggled at before, or even a price target that analysts set. That is where you may consider selling the call.

Support—If the stock were to drop, how far do you think it will go? This may be the level that you buy back your call (massaging the trade) or it may be the amount of hedge or protection you want to sell the call for. This is a balancing act, because if you are super

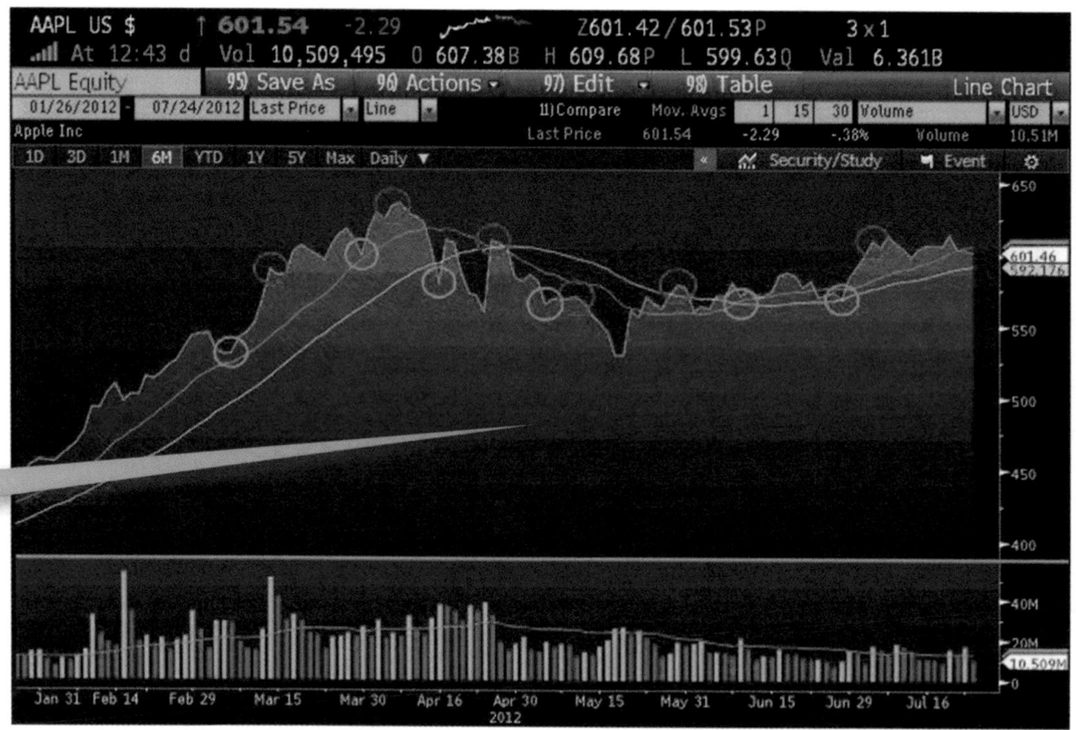

Drill down into a shorter-duration chart using support and resistance levels to time the sales and subsequent repurchases of your covered call trades.

Exhibit 4.23

bullish on the stock, you may move your strike price higher to allow appreciation in the stock and receive less premium, whereas if you think the stock could drop a large amount, you may reduce your short-call strike and get more premium as a hedge.

Step 4: Selecting the Best Covered Call

Although the timing of the buy-write and covered call may vary, the characteristics and focal points of the call to sell are similar. Here are the most important aspects for an optimal trade.

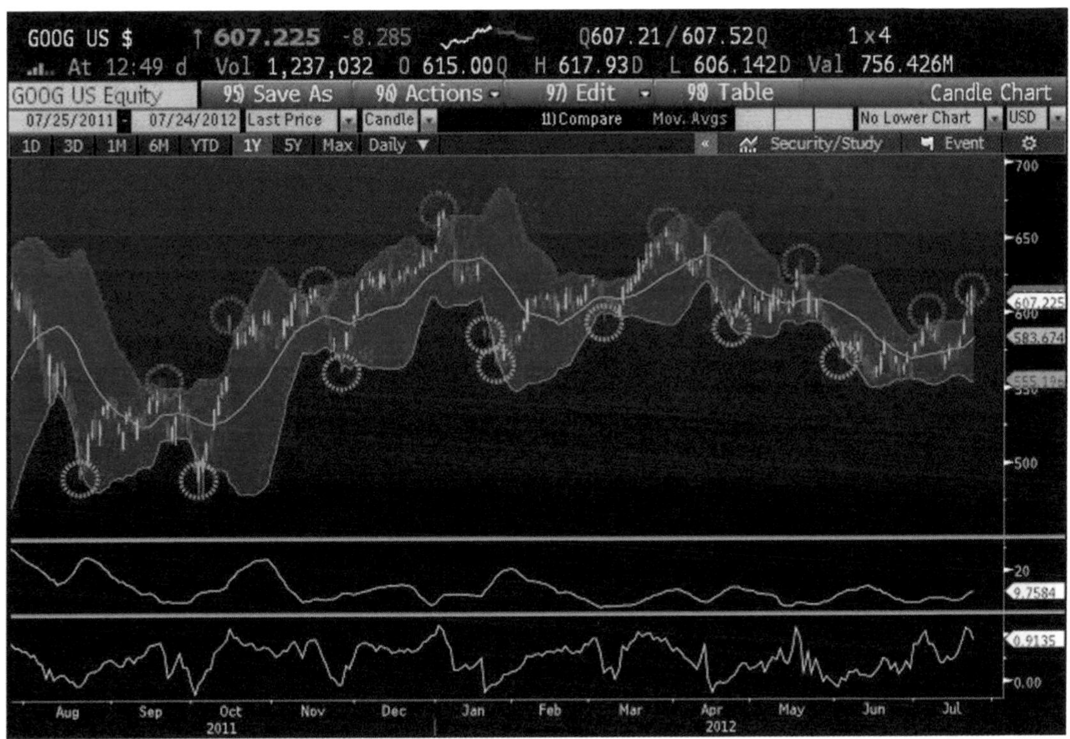

Exhibit 4.24

Implied volatility—*Find expensive options!* The more implied volatility the better! This doesn't mean blindly selling every expensive option on every stock, but you should be looking at selling the calls with the highest premium to strike value. This should be done with your cost basis in the stock in mind. See Exhibit 4.25.

For a buy-write on a stock that you don't already own, you might scan the markets for $20 to $60 (remember that you have to buy in blocks of 100) stocks in the technology sector that meet certain fundamental requirements. Once the stock passes your fundie (fundamental criteria) test, the very next step should be to sift through those stocks and use

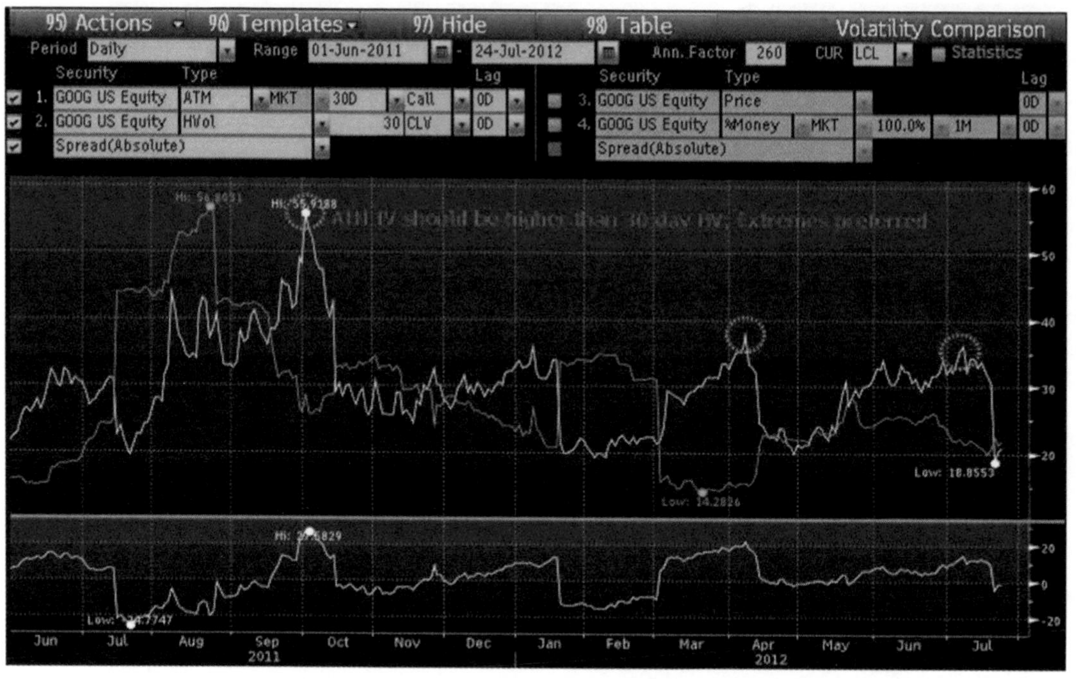

Exhibit 4.25

a scan to target call options with a delta of 0.30 to 0.60 that have the highest premium/strike ratio. See Exhibit 4.26.

Narrow down the top stocks in the results of that scan to find the one or two that you like the best based on your knowledge/comfort in the stock, its technicals, news, and so on.

When executing a covered call, find the call with the most time value, but that has a strike + premium that you would be okay with should you have to sell the stock and that is preferably higher than your cost basis in the stock.

For example: If you own a stock at $21 and the $22.50 call can be sold for $1.20, your max profit would

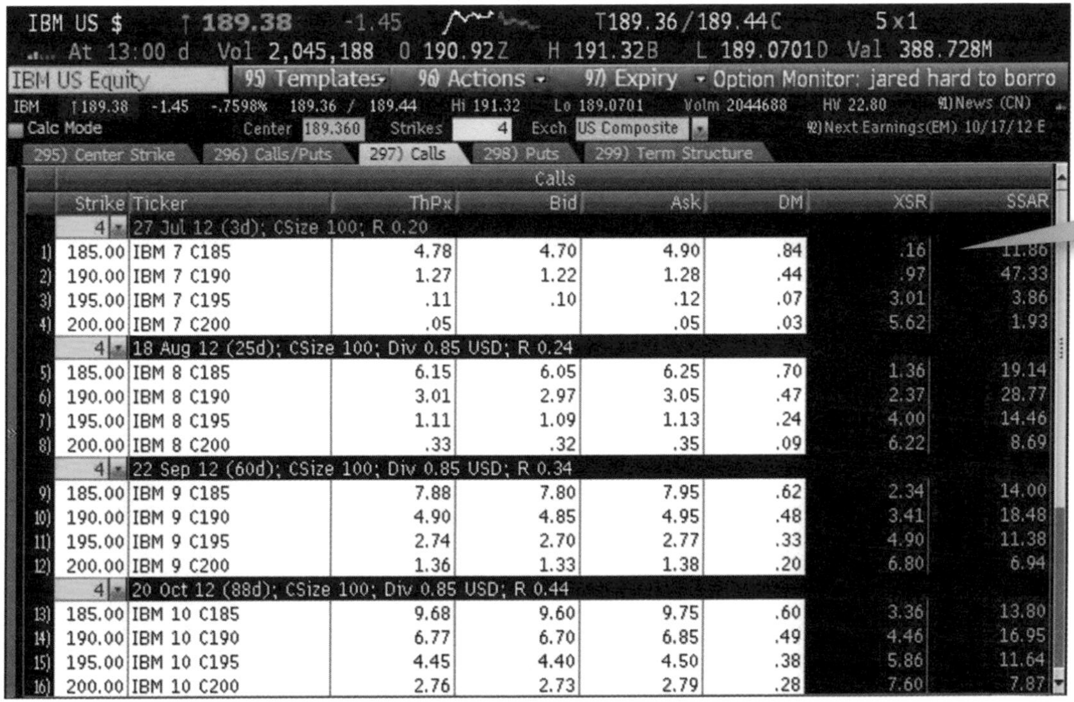

IBM US $ ↑189.38 -1.45 T189.36/189.44C 5x1
At 13:00 d Vol 2,045,188 O 190.92Z H 191.32B L 189.0701D Val 388.728M
IBM US Equity 95) Templates 96) Actions 97) Expiry Option Monitor: jared hard to borro
IBM ↑189.38 -1.45 -.7598% 189.36 / 189.44 Hi 191.32 Lo 189.0701 Volm 2044688 HV 22.80 91) News (CN)
Calc Mode Center 189.360 Strikes 4 Exch US Composite 92) Next Earnings(EM) 10/17/12 E
295) Center Strike 296) Calls/Puts 297) Calls 298) Puts 299) Term Structure

	Calls							
	Strike	Ticker	ThPx	Bid	Ask	DM	XSR	SSAR
	4	27 Jul 12 (3d); CSize 100; R 0.20						
1)	185.00	IBM 7 C185	4.78	4.70	4.90	.84	.16	11.86
2)	190.00	IBM 7 C190	1.27	1.22	1.28	.44	.97	47.33
3)	195.00	IBM 7 C195	.11	.10	.12	.07	3.01	3.86
4)	200.00	IBM 7 C200	.05		.05	.03	5.62	1.93
	4	18 Aug 12 (25d); CSize 100; Div 0.85 USD; R 0.24						
5)	185.00	IBM 8 C185	6.15	6.05	6.25	.70	1.36	19.14
6)	190.00	IBM 8 C190	3.01	2.97	3.05	.47	2.37	28.77
7)	195.00	IBM 8 C195	1.11	1.09	1.13	.24	4.00	14.46
8)	200.00	IBM 8 C200	.33	.32	.35	.09	6.22	8.69
	4	22 Sep 12 (60d); CSize 100; Div 0.85 USD; R 0.34						
9)	185.00	IBM 9 C185	7.88	7.80	7.95	.62	2.34	14.00
10)	190.00	IBM 9 C190	4.90	4.85	4.95	.48	3.41	18.48
11)	195.00	IBM 9 C195	2.74	2.70	2.77	.33	4.90	11.38
12)	200.00	IBM 9 C200	1.36	1.33	1.38	.20	6.80	6.94
	4	20 Oct 12 (88d); CSize 100; Div 0.85 USD; R 0.44						
13)	185.00	IBM 10 C185	9.68	9.60	9.75	.60	3.36	13.80
14)	190.00	IBM 10 C190	6.77	6.70	6.85	.49	4.46	16.95
15)	195.00	IBM 10 C195	4.45	4.40	4.50	.38	5.86	11.64
16)	200.00	IBM 10 C200	2.76	2.73	2.79	.28	7.60	7.87

I sometimes add the percentage returns (actual) and annualized returns (XSR and SSAR columns) to my OMON screen to quickly target the most profitable candidates.

Exhibit 4.26

be $2.70 until expiration with the stock at $22.50 or higher.

If you have a greater fear of the stock dropping, then choose a strike closer to (or even lower than) the stock price.

Look at the breakeven/yield and profit potential levels for several calls to find the one you feel most comfortable with. Maybe the $25 call for $0.75 is a better fit for you because you believe the stock has more upside. The 25 call will have a lower yield and higher breakeven than the 22.50 call, but it will allow for more upside potential.

Use the "time value" column to quickly scan the chains and find the juiciest options. See Exhibit 4.27.

Smart Investor Tip!

Think about expiration and assignment. If you had to deliver the stock at the strike and only keep the premium, do you think that the potential return is acceptable?

You can take it a step further and isolate time value as well as standstill and exercised returns (actual and annualized) to your OMON option chain for quicker calculations.

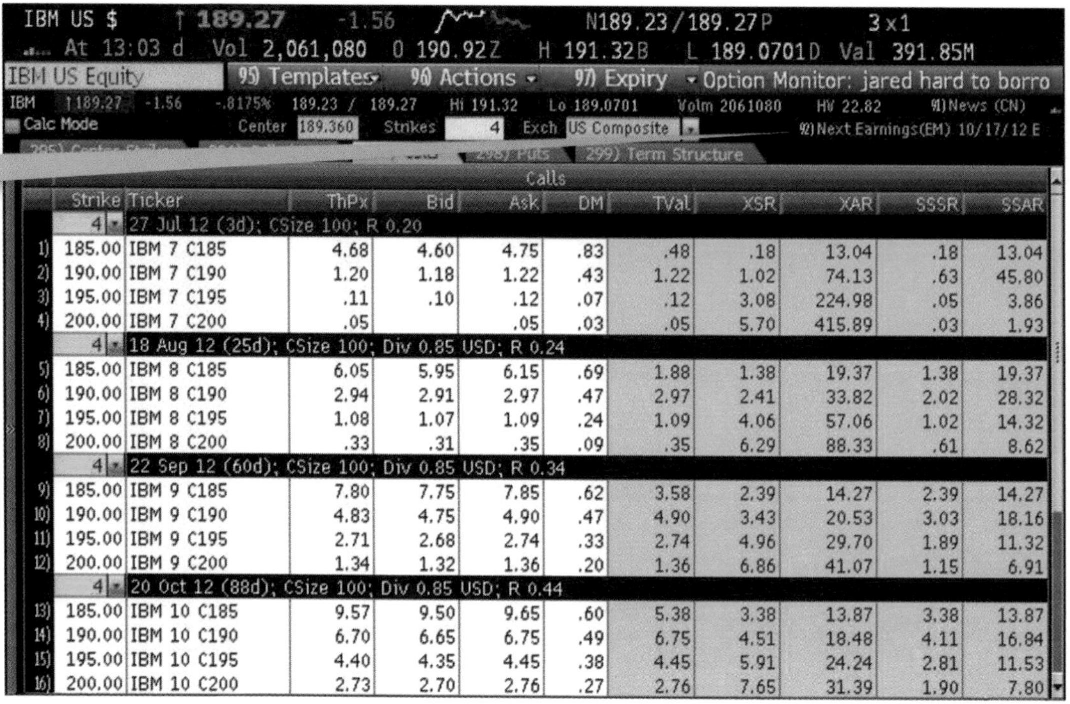

IBM US $ ↑ 189.27 -1.56 N189.23/189.27P 3x1
At 13:03 d Vol 2,061,080 O 190.92Z H 191.32B L 189.0701D Val 391.85M
IBM US Equity 95) Templates 96) Actions 97) Expiry Option Monitor: jared hard to borro
IBM ↑189.27 -1.56 -.8175% 189.23 / 189.27 Hi 191.32 Lo 189.0701 Volm 2061080 HV 22.82 91) News (CN)
Calc Mode Center 189.360 Strikes 4 Exch US Composite 92) Next Earnings(EM) 10/17/12 E
298) Puts 299) Term Structure

Calls

	Strike	Ticker	ThPx	Bid	Ask	DM	TVal	XSR	XAR	SSSR	SSAR
	4	27 Jul 12 (3d); CSize 100; R 0.20									
1)	185.00	IBM 7 C185	4.68	4.60	4.75	.83	.48	.18	13.04	.18	13.04
2)	190.00	IBM 7 C190	1.20	1.18	1.22	.43	1.22	1.02	74.13	.63	45.80
3)	195.00	IBM 7 C195	.11	.10	.12	.07	.12	3.08	224.98	.05	3.86
4)	200.00	IBM 7 C200	.05		.05	.03	.05	5.70	415.89	.03	1.93
	4	18 Aug 12 (25d); CSize 100; Div 0.85 USD; R 0.24									
5)	185.00	IBM 8 C185	6.05	5.95	6.15	.69	1.88	1.38	19.37	1.38	19.37
6)	190.00	IBM 8 C190	2.94	2.91	2.97	.47	2.97	2.41	33.82	2.02	28.32
7)	195.00	IBM 8 C195	1.08	1.07	1.09	.24	1.09	4.06	57.06	1.02	14.32
8)	200.00	IBM 8 C200	.33	.31	.35	.09	.35	6.29	88.33	.61	8.62
	4	22 Sep 12 (60d); CSize 100; Div 0.85 USD; R 0.34									
9)	185.00	IBM 9 C185	7.80	7.75	7.85	.62	3.58	2.39	14.27	2.39	14.27
10)	190.00	IBM 9 C190	4.83	4.75	4.90	.47	4.90	3.43	20.53	3.03	18.16
11)	195.00	IBM 9 C195	2.71	2.68	2.74	.33	2.74	4.96	29.70	1.89	11.32
12)	200.00	IBM 9 C200	1.34	1.32	1.36	.20	1.36	6.86	41.07	1.15	6.91
	4	20 Oct 12 (88d); CSize 100; Div 0.85 USD; R 0.44									
13)	185.00	IBM 10 C185	9.57	9.50	9.65	.60	5.38	3.38	13.87	3.38	13.87
14)	190.00	IBM 10 C190	6.70	6.65	6.75	.49	6.75	4.51	18.48	4.11	16.84
15)	195.00	IBM 10 C195	4.40	4.35	4.45	.38	4.45	5.91	24.24	2.81	11.53
16)	200.00	IBM 10 C200	2.73	2.70	2.76	.27	2.76	7.65	31.39	1.90	7.80

Exhibit 4.27

Time horizon—Covered call and buy-writes alike should try to target options with shorter expirations. If you remember our Greek discussions, theta tends to accelerate dramatically in the last 30 days of an option's life. With that said, covered calls and buy-writes, because they involve selling an option, should typically be done with less than 60 days until expiration. I find that this time frame allows you to get a decent amount of premium, good theta, and not tie yourself to the trade for too long. Remember that you can always sell another call if you choose. Also, in the last 30 days of an option's life, if the stock dips sharply, you may see that call drop to 5 or 10 cents, and you can then buy it back and resell another call if the stock rallies.

Total cost (breakeven)—Actual cost is not what's important. Breakeven, potential yield (premium), and potential upside are all considerations. Think about expiration and assignment. If you had to deliver the stock at the strike and only keep the premium, do you think that the potential return is acceptable?

If you are in a loss in your stock and are selling calls to make back some of your losses, then your thought process may be different. In that case, you may not want to be assigned and may have to run a couple theoretical scenarios in the calculator to see how you could potentially massage the position into a profitable one.

Premium—The amount of premium you receive for your short call has a direct influence on your total cost and risk. Selling a call for 20 cents or less may not be worth it (unless the stock is below $15).

Don't sell a covered call for peanuts. If you have a $50 stock and you can only sell the $55 call for 0.25, is it worth it? If you think the stock is just going to rocket to $54.99 and stay there, then maybe, but if you think the stock could easily drop $2 or $3 dollars, maybe you need to lower your strike (giving you a higher premium) or even find another stock.

The premium is predicated on time and volatility. The more time you have in your option, the more credit you should receive. This is again another balancing act, finding the perfect balance between time and premium received and what the stock could *realistically* do in the time until expiration. Use your charts and ATR!

Delta and the Greeks—The covered call and buy-write both involve long stock and one simple option, so the Greeks are not a huge factor in determining the strike to choose, but they are helpful in running hypothetical scenarios.

For example, you can use delta to see just how bullish you want to be. But I believe that most covered call and buy-write traders are more concerned about yield and their relative cost in the stock and the spread itself. This means that you will probably not use delta to dictate what strike you choose. I generally don't either.

What you can use is the vega of an option along with theta to see how sensitive your position will be to changes in Ivol (that hopefully will drop) and to the progression of time. See Exhibit 4.28.

When you run your theoretical model, be sure that the time decay, vega, and delta all feel good as the trade moves closer to expiration. If the stock has a habit of fluctuating 5 percent in a month's time, then you should use those assumptions when testing your trade in the position simulator. Move the stock up and down 5 percent and see how your portfolio's P&L behaves. Don't like it? Change your strike selection.

The theta can also help determine the best strike to choose. The theta will be highest at the money, so choose your strikes as close as possible to at the money if the other factors allow you to.

Smart Investor Tip!

If you are thinking about a covered call or buy-write, don't be afraid to test out different strikes and expirations in the scenario calculator. Use the calculator (OV or OSA) to move the stock along the expected path you think it will take and see which option has the best effect on your P&L.

Smart Investor Tip!

Double-check your covered call orders and make sure that they line up with both the stock and option markets as most brokers ask you only to enter a single price.

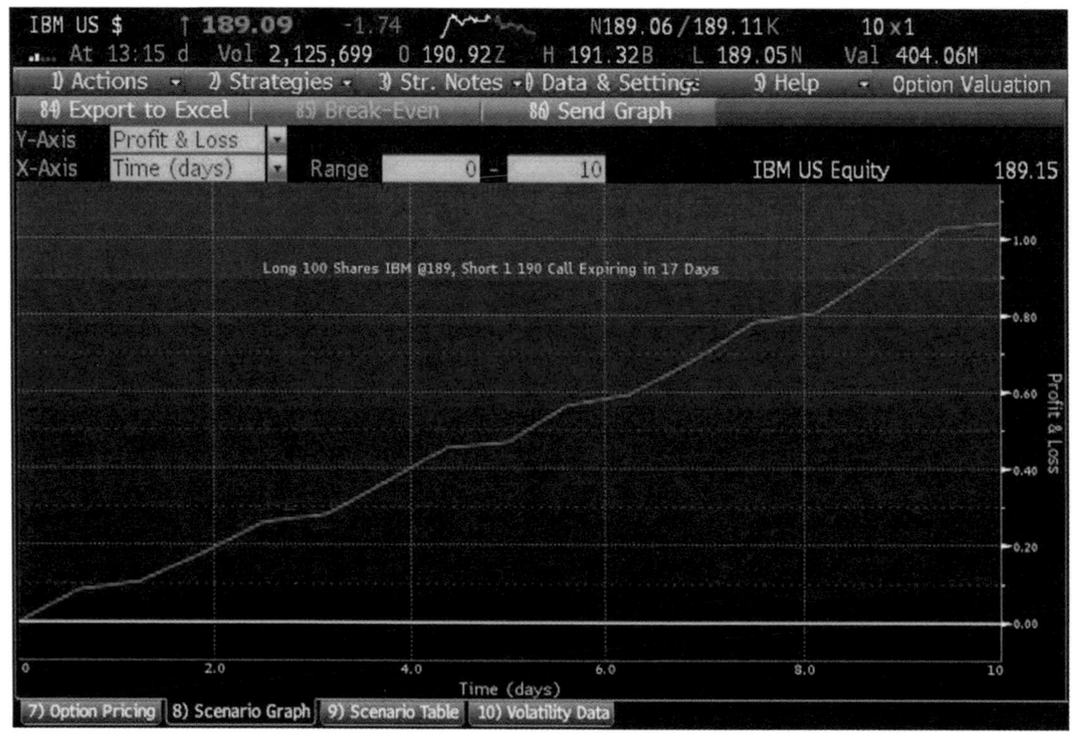

Exhibit 4.28

Smart Investor Tip!

Buy-writes are usually done with either the intention of being called out and capturing the yield of the call or they are a way to acquire stock for a lower cost basis.

Gamma and rho shouldn't be major considerations for the covered call, although gamma will be higher in the front months and will change the delta faster, which could hurt or help your trade.

The expiration that you choose will determine which Greeks will have more influence on your position.

Choosing expiration: Covered calls and buy-writes can be executed by using just about any expiration you desire. There are a couple of rules that you need to know when it comes to choosing expiration.

35 days or less—These options will have less sensitivity to vega and more focus on theta as a percentage of the option price. They will also have more gamma and the deltas will move faster. For most traders of covered calls and buy-writes, this is going to be the range to focus on because you are not tied to the position for too long and are benefiting from the acceleration of time decay while still getting a little vega benefit.

45 to 90 days—These options will be decaying much more slowly, but will be higher in price, which may be a choice if you want to sell a higher strike call because you think the stock will slowly drift up to that strike. These calls will also have more vega giving you more potential profit if Ivol is extremely high and it drops; conversely, more vega could hinder you if Ivol continues to rise. If you don't have the ability to trade your portfolio as much and want to capture slow appreciation in a stock with a better yield, these expirations might be an alternative.

90 days plus—These options will have the most vega relative to the others, which will be the main Greek that you are betting on. Deltas will move more slowly and there will be the least gamma. Time decay will occur, but at a slower pace. If you have a stock that is extremely beaten up and has extremely high volatility that you expect to come in sharply while the stock just inches higher, then these calls can be an option.

Covered call, buy-write variations: The buy-write is just that: the simultaneous purchase of long stock and sale of a call. Buy-write traders tend to enter a position after a recent retracement in the stock, or at a time they deem appropriate for a bullish entry—meaning that they would want the stock to rally from that point because their main goal is to collect the premium from the short call and have the stock called away.

Traders sell the call that fits their yield/breakeven/risk profile the best (usually at-the-money strike) with the intention to have the stock called away from them, meaning that if traders bought stock at $100 and sold the 100 call, they would be forced to sell it at $50.

That doesn't sound so great at first glance, but what if traders were able to sell the call for $10? Even though traders do not make anything on the stock, they retain the $10—and in this case would realize a 10 percent return less commissions. The issue here is that you have to be comfortable with only making $10; limited profit can in itself be a risk to some traders.

Order ticket nuance: When trading a buy-write the trader typically enters one price for the entire trade; in other words, if the trader wanted to buy IBM stock at $198.00 and sell the January 200 call for $8.10 (stock ask $200 – option bid $8.20 = $189.80), the buy-write trade may be entered as seen in Exhibit 4.29 (this may vary from broker to broker).

Note how the limit price is just one price; it does *not* specify the call or stock amounts individually. The good news is that this price is your new cost basis in the stock; so if it's above $200 and you are forced to sell at $200, you make $15 or 8.18 percent

Smart Investor Tip!

If you are basing your stop loss on a dollar amount, don't forget to factor in the call premium that you receive.

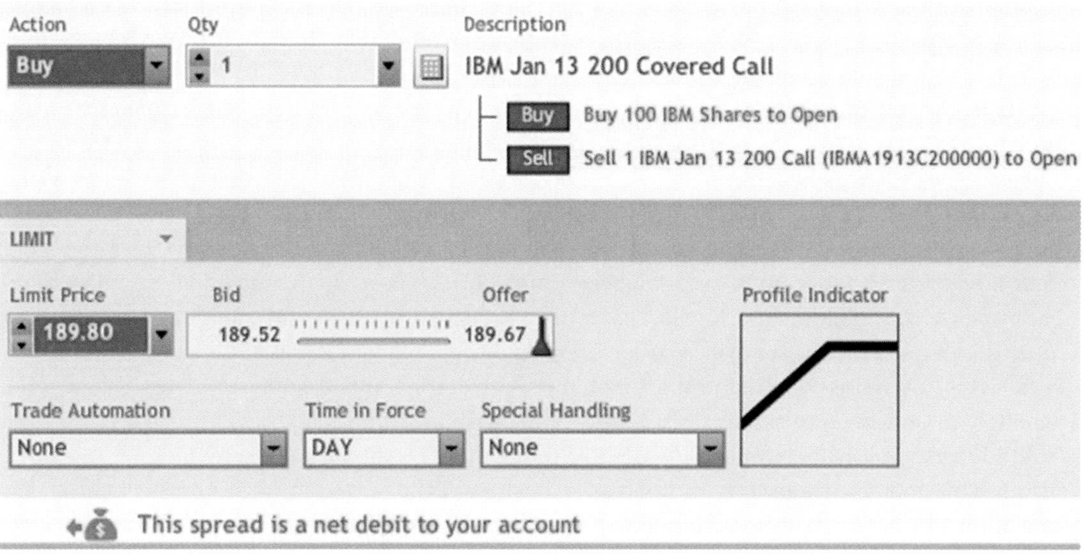

Exhibit 4.29

in 30 days' time, which is 158.19 percent annualized. Not too shabby.

Volatility considerations: Vega, Hvol, and Ivol must be considered. But it's not that easy; if Ivol is elevated it may seem like a good sale, but that Ivol may be high for good reason.

Remember how I said earlier that options get more expensive in volatile markets? Well, yes, that means that you may be able to sell your covered call for more money, but that also means that stock may have a higher probability of moving lower or up through your short call, limiting your upside.

When you sell a call against long stock, your max profit is your strike + premium – cost basis in the stock. The key to this strategy is finding a stock that may have more expensive options due to things happening around it.

For covered call traders who own stock longer term, elevated volatility (high relative VIX) environments are a benefit, but at the same time can be a curse. When Ivol is spiking higher than what you observe in Hvol, you may be happy you got to sell the call for an extra $1, but if the stock is going to fluctuate an extra $5 or more during the period you're in the trade is it really worth it?

Ivol trends and their subsequent influences on option prices can be a trigger for a trade, but do your homework (Google search, check the news, earnings, buyouts, bankruptcies, etc.) before selling your call.

Another nuance of volatility in the covered call is that you typically want to time the sale of a covered call when a stock is up but not selling off. Calls are more expensive when stocks are higher and you will be able to potentially collect a higher premium when a stock is up but beginning to weaken as opposed to it already falling off a cliff. When stocks are rallying, Ivol is usually dropping, so in actuality, the covered call trader may not need to place as much importance on high Ivol because chances are that some of it will be sucked out in the days that the stock has been rallying.

At the end of the day, if you are happy with the amount of premium that you are receiving, and you have set up the trade the way that you want with a plan in place, volatility may not be a huge concern. Just be aware of the effects it will have on your position and how you can maximize profit and limit loss using it.

Setting stops: Just like call options, my stops are usually based on the price of the underlying asset, not the spread value itself. In the case of the covered call, this is even more appropriate because you are long actual stock and will typically have much more risk than the long call.

The decision to stay in a covered call is still all about good bullish strength, fundamental momentum, and technical levels being maintained. If any of that changes, you might consider taking the trade off the table and finding a better candidate.

The difference here is that the long stock does *not* have an expiration date and if you are tolerant and not at your maximum pain threshold, you can stay in the long stock trade and continue to sell calls month after month and even choose an option that is lower to get more premium or protection. See Exhibit 4.30.

Use the same ATR techniques to determine what "normal" expected movements are for the stock. If the stock is exceeding those levels and it's not being caused by a broad market force, the trend or sentiments may be changing. Don't forget to check volume as well.

Moving up your stops: Your stops for the trade can be looked at in one of two ways:

1. You can view the trade as a whole and move your stops based on the entire buy-write price. If this is the case, you will monitor the net price of the

Smart Investor Tip!

If you originally sold an *out-of-the-money* call for $1 and the stock rallies past it, it's okay! If the time value is less than $1 when you buy it back you are still making a profit no matter what! You can close that call and resell a call that is at or out of the money to capture more time value.

KEY POINT:

You can sell fewer calls than shares that you own. This position would be appropriate if you thought the stock had the potential to really move higher. The extra deltas will allow you to participate in more upside than you would if you sold one call for every 100 shares you owned.

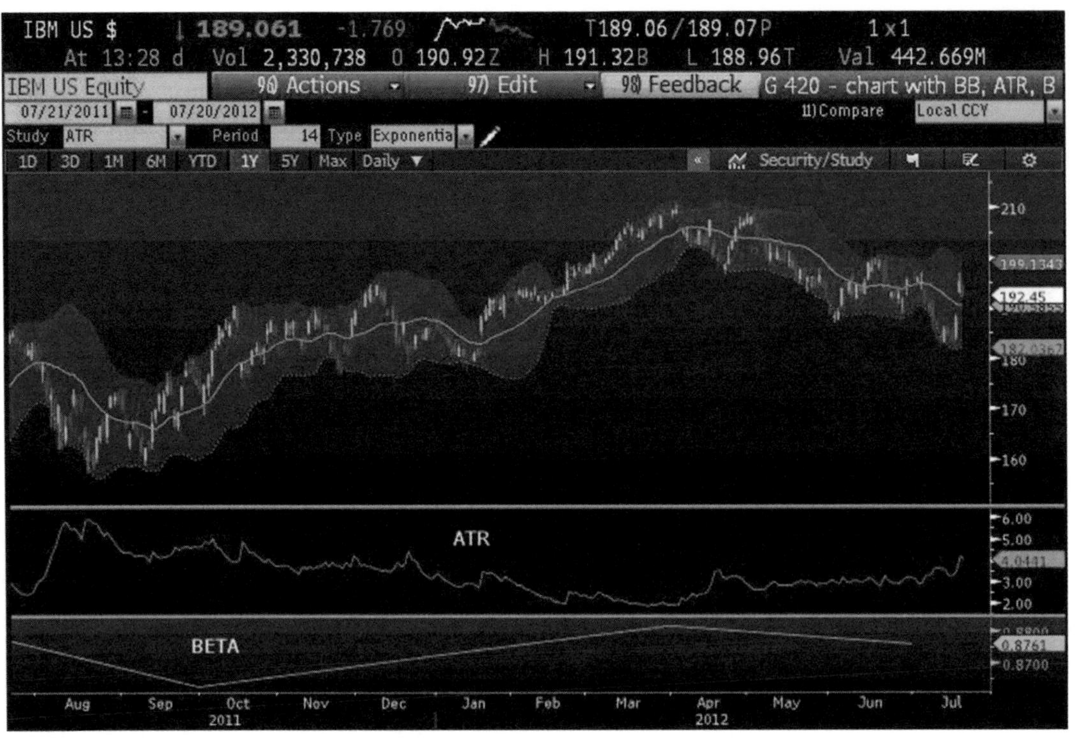

Exhibit 4.30

STEP-BY-STEP

Has the fundamental picture changed in the stock?

- It might be better to simply exit if things are getting nasty.
- For more neutral to temporary changes, you add a long out-of-the-money put to the covered call and create a collar.
- You can sell the long put and buy back the short call after the stock has dropped and you think it will rally.

Have the charts broken down?

- A minor blip could just mean that you sell some of your contracts.
- A drop below a major trend line (50- or 200-day MA) might be a reason to simply bail out.

spread and set your absolute level of loss (based on objective levels and data) and simply pull the plug if things go wrong.

If the trade is working and you are in a buy-write that you intended on having called away, there may not be much you have to do in the way of adjusting your profit. What you can do, once the stock moves in a favorable direction, is place a stop on the net trade to prevent it from falling below breakeven. Stops like this

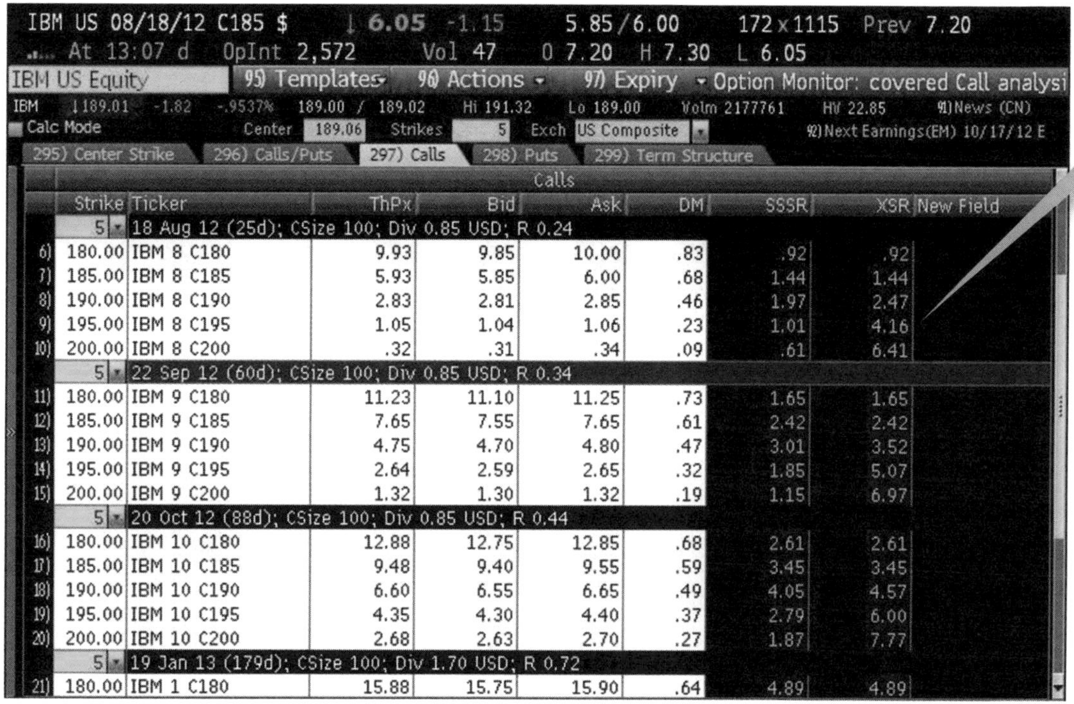

IBM US 08/18/12 C185 $ ↓6.05 -1.15 5.85/6.00 172x1115 Prev 7.20
At 13:07 d OpInt 2,572 Vol 47 O 7.20 H 7.30 L 6.05
IBM US Equity 95) Templates 96) Actions 97) Expiry Option Monitor: covered Call analysi
IBM ↓189.01 -1.82 -.9537% 189.00 / 189.02 Hi 191.32 Lo 189.00 Volm 2177761 HV 22.85 91) News (CN)
Calc Mode Center 189.06 Strikes 5 Exch US Composite 92) Next Earnings(EM) 10/17/12 E
295) Center Strike 296) Calls/Puts 297) Calls 298) Puts 299) Term Structure

Calls

	Strike	Ticker	ThPx	Bid	Ask	DM	SSSR	XSR	New Field
	5	18 Aug 12 (25d); CSize 100; Div 0.85 USD; R 0.24							
6)	180.00	IBM 8 C180	9.93	9.85	10.00	.83	.92	.92	
7)	185.00	IBM 8 C185	5.93	5.85	6.00	.68	1.44	1.44	
8)	190.00	IBM 8 C190	2.83	2.81	2.85	.46	1.97	2.47	
9)	195.00	IBM 8 C195	1.05	1.04	1.06	.23	1.01	4.16	
10)	200.00	IBM 8 C200	.32	.31	.34	.09	.61	6.41	
	5	22 Sep 12 (60d); CSize 100; Div 0.85 USD; R 0.34							
11)	180.00	IBM 9 C180	11.23	11.10	11.25	.73	1.65	1.65	
12)	185.00	IBM 9 C185	7.65	7.55	7.65	.61	2.42	2.42	
13)	190.00	IBM 9 C190	4.75	4.70	4.80	.47	3.01	3.52	
14)	195.00	IBM 9 C195	2.64	2.59	2.65	.32	1.85	5.07	
15)	200.00	IBM 9 C200	1.32	1.30	1.32	.19	1.15	6.97	
	5	20 Oct 12 (88d); CSize 100; Div 0.85 USD; R 0.44							
16)	180.00	IBM 10 C180	12.88	12.75	12.85	.68	2.61	2.61	
17)	185.00	IBM 10 C185	9.48	9.40	9.55	.59	3.45	3.45	
18)	190.00	IBM 10 C190	6.60	6.55	6.65	.49	4.05	4.57	
19)	195.00	IBM 10 C195	4.35	4.30	4.40	.37	2.79	6.00	
20)	200.00	IBM 10 C200	2.68	2.63	2.70	.27	1.87	7.77	
	5	19 Jan 13 (179d); CSize 100; Div 1.70 USD; R 0.72							
21)	180.00	IBM 1 C180	15.88	15.75	15.90	.64	4.89	4.89	

Exhibit 4.31

Again, use standstill and exercised return calculations to help reposition your trade and ensure that the returns are in line with your thesis and expectations.

won't protect you if the stock gaps down. If you feel there is a high chance of this happening, take your profit and maybe reposition the trade at a later date (after a pullback), take half or more of your position off and leave the balance to reduce risk, or substitute the trade for a vertical bull call spread.

2. If you are fairly certain that you are holding the stock long term, then your risk management will have everything to do with the short call itself. If this is the case you should have stop targets. If the stock rallies and the short call loses all its parity, you should take that call off and reposition as a short call with time value. See Exhibit 4.31.

STEP-BY-STEP

Was there an earnings occurrence?

- **If earnings were just okay and the stock is up, flat, or slightly down, consider holding, buy a put for protection to roll short call to a lower strike or next month.**
- **If you have profit in the trade, there is no reason to keep the trade on if the future looks iffy.**
- **If the report was a complete blowout and the stock is up 10 percent, maybe take profits?**
- **If you didn't hit your profit target, you can get more aggressive (defensive) by purchasing the short call back and reselling an at-the-money call (for the shorter term traders).**
- **For the longer term traders, buy your in-the-money call back and sell the next month at-the-money or lower strike.**

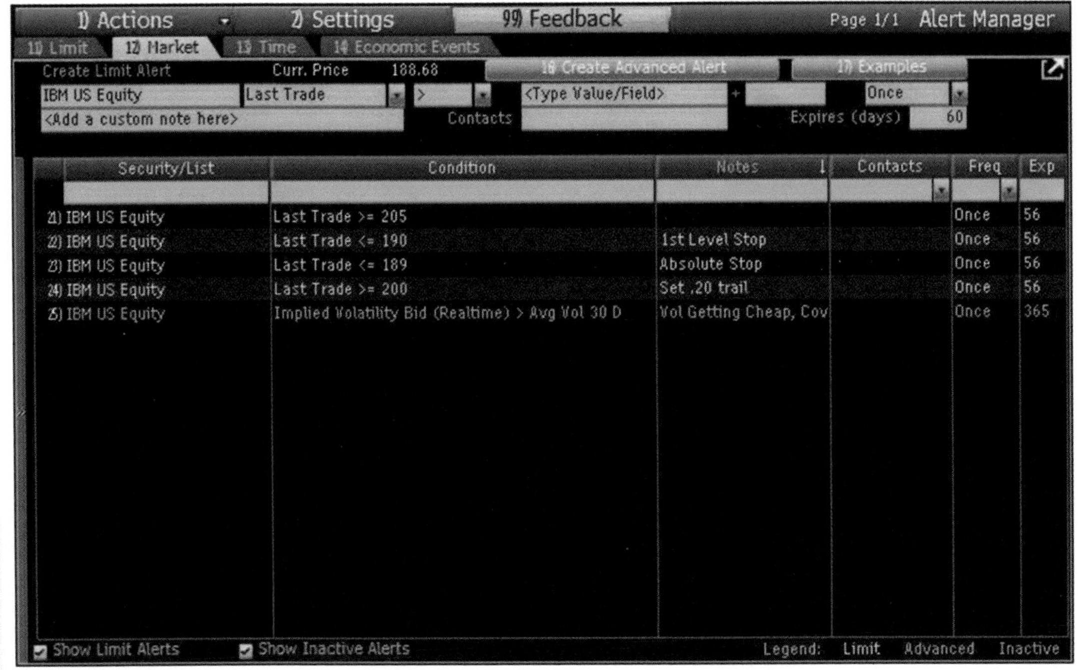

Exhibit 4.32

You should also have a stop point at which you buy the short call back. If a call that you sold for $1 drops to $0.05, it might be best to take it off and sell a lower strike or the next month out (if you think the stock will continue dropping). If the stock is stable, you can also sell the next month with maybe a higher strike, but if the stock seems like it wants to rally, wait on your next sale.

Set those price alerts on both the underlying asset and the option to remind you of levels that are being hit. Do this for profit targets and stop losses. See Exhibit 4.32.

Step 5: Monitoring/Closing the Trade

The covered call and buy-write starts hurting you when the stock drops more than the amount of the

STEP-BY-STEP

Have you gone beyond your original stop loss point?

- **If you extend the life of the trade, will the extra time for minimal loss recovery justify the capital committed to the trade?**
- **Don't roll a trade that you are feeling bad about. If you are going to prolong pain, have a damn good reason for doing it.**
- **If your reason for being in the stock is no longer valid, get out or switch into another strategy that has less cost, less risk, and maybe more probability.**

IBM US $ ↑ 188.8236 -2.006 P188.81/188.83N 2x5
At 13:36 d Vol 2,391,923 O 190.92Z H 191.32B L 188.56D Val 454.374M
1) Actions 2) Strategies 3) Str. Notes 4) Data & Settings 5) Help Option Valuation
84) Export to Excel 85) Break-Even 86) Send Graph
Y-Axis Profit & Loss Evaluation Dates 07/24/12 09/07/12 10/22/12
X-Axis Price Range 110.00 - 270.00 IBM US Equity 188.81
07/24/12
09/07/12
10/22/12
Break-Even
Current Underlying
50
40
30
20
10
0
-10
-20
Profit & Loss
120.00
140.00
160.00
180.00
200.00
220.00
240.00
260.00
Price
7) Option Pricing 8) Scenario Graph 9) Scenario Table 10) Volatility Data

Exhibit 4.33

Smart Investor Tip!

Since Ivol tends to increase as stocks fall, put options tend to get an extra boost when compared to the same delta call with the same move in the stock.

KEY POINT:

Long puts can be combined with covered calls to create a protective collar; the covered call helps finance the cost of the put.

call premium, which means that you are a net loser on the trade. In the early stages of the trade you might just want to relax and let theta do its job as long as you think the stock will recover.

If not, you can buy back the call for a profit and roll it to a lower strike or even another month as I just discussed. If the trade is going in your favor, you should be proactive in protecting your profits. In the beginning stages of the trade, you should have already entered your stop loss and had an idea of how high the stock would go.

If those levels are violated and you think that the stock will continue to move, you should be proactive and adjust your position to get longer or shorter deltas; this is done by adjusting the strike, month, and number of contracts you sold.

Trailing stops can also be used to lock in and protect your existing profits. Do *not* be greedy. Stick to your plan and execute it.

Like the call, if you begin to see cracks in the foundation of the trade, it might be best to take profits on the spread and reevaluate; this is especially true for buy-writes. For the longer trades, I tolerate a bit more of a breakdown, but I never want to have a substantially positive trade go negative on me.

Items to Check When Monitoring

- Changes in macro, company news, and so on
- Changes in chart patterns, levels
- Changes in sentiment
- Earnings
- Stop loss
- Target profits

Repair versus exit: Because of the relatively high risk involved with covered calls and buy-writes, you should be extra sensitive to changes in the bullish trajectory of your stock.

Long Put

Long puts can be a lower-risk way of expressing a short view in a security, when compared to taking a short position in that security itself. It's essentially an alternative to shorting a stock. In some stocks that you cannot short, a put may be your only method of expressing a bearish opinion.

Other than a short stock synthetic, the long put is the most bearish single option bet you can place other than shorting the stock itself.

Delta is a huge factor in determining the put strike. Higher delta puts (–0.70 and higher) tend to behave more like the underlying security, whereas puts with less of a delta will be more susceptible to other market forces such as volatility. The goal of the trade is to profit from the drop in price of the underlying security. Long puts like quick movements to the downside and are limited in profit with the stock going to zero.

Max profit in a long put is: Strike Price of Put – Premium Paid

Max risk in a long put is: Premium Paid

Expiration breakeven in a long put: Strike Price of Put – Premium Paid

Optimal Scenario

In a perfect world, you want to be extremely bearish on a stock that has not yet begun to fall. This is because Ivol tends to increase when stocks drop and the long put favors a low relative Ivol on entry.

When you purchase a put, you are looking for a very strong downside move, preferably below your expiration breakeven of the option that you choose.

The majority of your indicators (fundamental or technical) should be signaling caution or a severe deterioration in the stock's demand or business strength. This could also be caused by sector influences.

The charts should be leading up to a major resistance, overbought in the near term, or poised for a reversion to the mean (selloff, since the stock has been rallying). It could also be an overvalued stock that has been outperforming its peers or the market when there is little reason or fundamentals to back up its rally. Any other extremely bearish or breakdown technical indicators will also be acceptable. See Exhibit 4.34.

Advantages

Long puts can offer a bearish trader a reasonable facsimile to short stock or can be purchased out of the money to speculate on a large move lower.

Leverage—A key attribute is the long put's ability to offer immense amounts of leverage. Even a put that is purchased deep in the money (delta of –.75 of more) will generally cost a fraction of the stock price, but at the same time offer much of the same profit potential.

When it comes to leverage, be careful to look at the breakeven of your put in combination with the delta if you are looking for a move of a certain size. Sometimes the at- or out-of-the money puts may not give you the big jump in profits when the stock moves favorably. Remember that the cheaper the option, the lower your absolute profit target should be; a 25 cent option that goes to 50 cents just doubled in value!

Protection—For holders of long stock or a long delta options position, a put can be purchased ahead of a possible sell-off, reducing your downside price exposure. Long puts can also be used as part of a vertical or horizontal spread to increase the risk/reward ratio in a favorable way.

Risk reduction—Because of the lower cost of the put compared to the 100 share equivalent of short stock, dollar risk will always be lower in comparison. Compared to short stock, the put is more favorable by far because of its fixed cost/max risk.

Buying 100 options for .50 is probably a foolish choice in this case. Use the put breakeven combined with the delta to select the appropriate option. If the breakeven of the put you are buying is lower than where you think the stock will end up on expiration, you should choose a different put.

Flexibility—Because put options are trading when the stock is trading, you have the ability to trade in and out of a position as well as scale into and out of

KEY POINT:

A technique that you can employ would be to purchase the same amount of put contracts that you would be willing to lose in a comparable short stock position.

So if you thought about shorting 500 shares of a $100 stock and your stop loss was going to be placed at $110, perhaps you might purchase $5,000 worth of puts, because that was how much you were willing to lose in the first place.

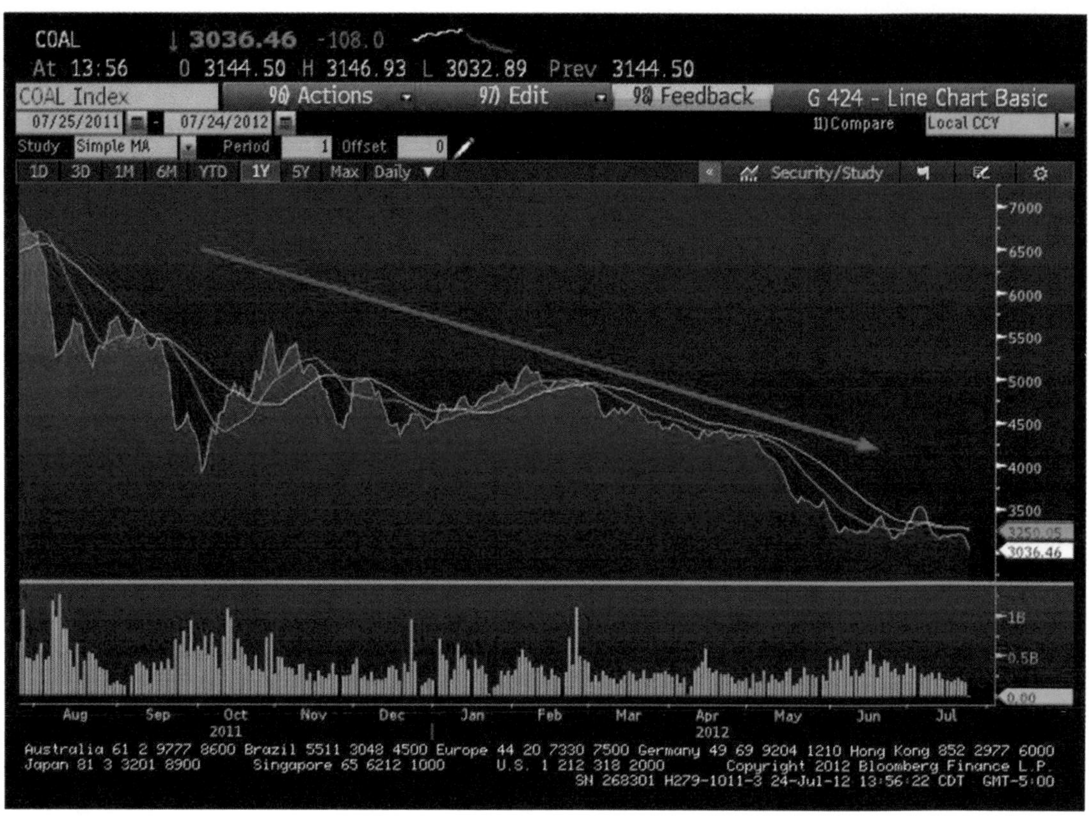
COAL
3036.46 -108.0
At 13:56 O 3144.50 H 3146.93 L 3032.89 Prev 3144.50
COAL Index
96) Actions
97) Edit
98) Feedback
G 424 - Line Chart Basic
07/25/2011 - 07/24/2012
11) Compare
Local CCY
Study Simple MA Period 1 Offset 0
1D 3D 1M 6M YTD 1Y 5Y Max Daily
Security/Study
7000
6500
6000
5500
5000
4500
4000
3500
3036.46
1B
0.5B
0.00
Aug Sep Oct Nov Dec Jan Feb Mar Apr May Jun Jul
2011
2012
Australia 61 2 9777 8600 Brazil 5511 3048 4500 Europe 44 20 7330 7500 Germany 49 69 9204 1210 Hong Kong 852 2977 6000
Japan 81 3 3201 8900 Singapore 65 6212 1000 U.S. 1 212 318 2000 Copyright 2012 Bloomberg Finance L.P.
SN 268301 H279-1011-3 24-Jul-12 13:56:22 CDT GMT-5:00

Exhibit 4.34

your position depending on what the stock does. You can also purchase several different strikes with your allocated funds to gain mixed exposure to a stock; but this tactic can add complexity and is not recommended if you are managing many positions or if you are a beginner.

Disadvantages

Breakeven is always lower than underlier—The long put is a statistically disadvantaged strategy because the breakeven of the put will always be lower than the stock price at the time of entry (because of time value). This means that if the stock stays flat up to expiration, you will gradually lose your time value and retain your intrinsic value (if you had any to begin with).

Short theta—Time is not on your side when you purchase a put. As time passes by, the put is losing time value. This creates a sense of urgency in your thesis. Be sure to buy more than enough time for your trade to work out. Remember that at expiration you will always be left with any intrinsic value in that put. See Exhibit 4.35.

Probability—Because breakeven is always going to be lower than the underlier, the underlier must generally fall in value for you to make money (or break even), resulting in a statistical disadvantage. (The only exception would be a sudden jump in implied volatility.) Arguably, this risk is offset by the reduced cost of the put. See Exhibit 4.36.

Risk/Reward

Long puts will have limited risk and limited reward, being that stocks can only fall to zero ($0). Make sure you account for this difference if you are transitioning from calls to puts. Keep in mind that it is more common for stocks to rise over time, so put trades may be shorter in duration—but not always.

Long Put Greek Attributes

Note the unique Greek characteristics detailed in Exhibit 4.37; these can and will change with time, price, volatility, and strike selection, just as in call options.

Delta

Negative—Delta can range from −0.01 to −1.00. The higher the delta purchased (> −0.65), the more the put will behave like the stock. A lower-delta put (< −0.30) will react minimally when the stock moves and will be extremely sensitive to changes in volatility on a percentage basis.

Gamma

Positive—Gamma is greatest at the money. Long put deltas will decrease in upward moves in the stock and increase with downward moves; the gamma dictates just how much. Gamma is going to be your ally when the put is moving toward the money from an out-of-the-money position. As it continues in the money and loses gamma, you should hopefully be making money from delta. This might be a good time to sell the expensive put and

Smart Investor Tip!

If you think that the stock is going to move about $5 before expiration, make sure that the put options you are buying have a breakeven below that level!

Smart Investor Tip!

Even though −0.70 is less than −0.65 mathematically, most traders would say that the delta of −0.70 is greater than −0.65.

Smart Investor Tip!

If Ivol seems extremely high compared to past Ivol and Hvol, consider adjusting your strike selection or use a spread.

Like calls, long puts decay over time and are nonlinear in that decay.

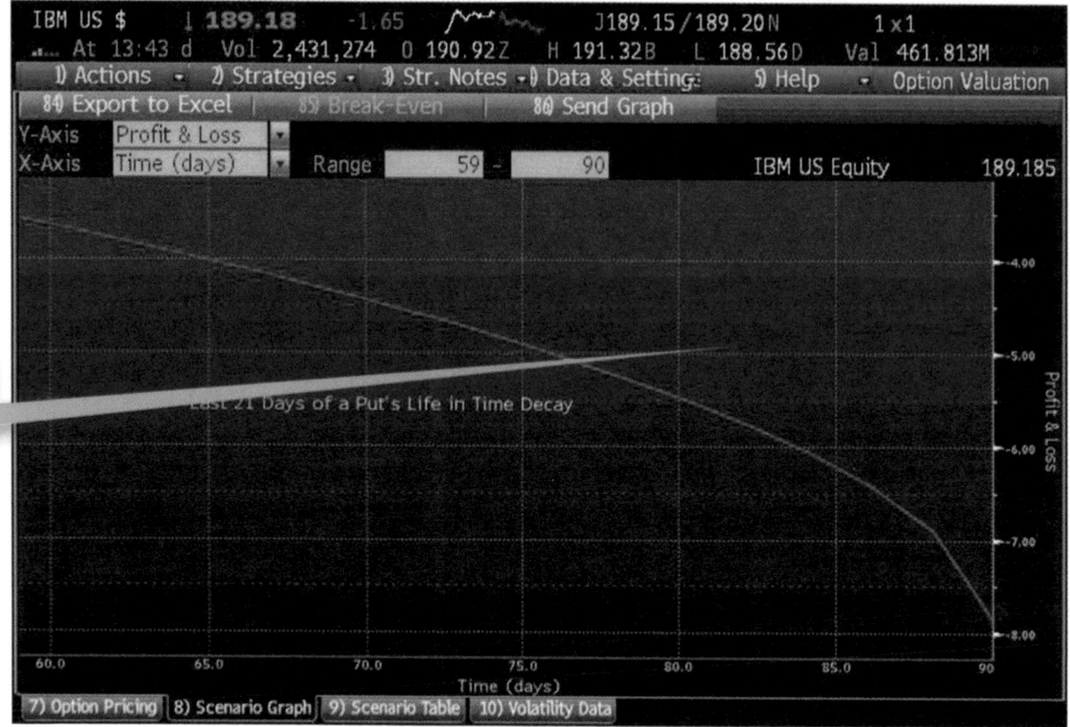

Exhibit 4.35

use a portion of the profit to buy a cheaper put if you feel the stock is going higher.

Theta

Short—You are paying theta; at-the-money options will pay the most theta. Theta can theoretically be overridden (at expiration) by looking at breakeven. Even though you may be giving up money in theta, you may be making it back with your delta.

Be careful holding puts the last three weeks before expiration; this is where theta starts to

Exhibit 4.36

increase. This is especially true for at- and out-of-the-money options.

Vega

Long—You are always long vega, which means you want implied volatility to increase, which will benefit your trade. A decrease in implied volatility will hurt your position.

Rho

Short—You want interest rates to fall as a general rule, but they will have minimal impact on your

Here is a typical put's risk profile expressed in Greek terms along with a visual graphic of risk.

Exhibit 4.37

position unless you are trading long dated, high strike options. This is generally the least worry you have in the trade. See Exhibit 4.38.

Shorter-term traders with a time horizon of an hour to a couple days will most likely focus on higher delta (negative) puts so they can have more of a correlation to the underlying security's movement. The high delta of an in-the-money put mitigates the other Greek risks because time value is such a small portion of the option's total price.

If you anticipate being in the trade for more than a couple of days or will be holding over an event, you should place more emphasis on the other Greeks, so you can forecast how your puts will behave with changes during various market conditions.

Long Put Dynamics

Let's examine the process for trading a long put.

Step 1: Identifying the Target

Be sure that once you have located a potential bearish stock candidate that you perform your due diligence. With a long put you *need* the stock to move lower, preferably quickly, during the trade. Consider other options strategies that can be potentially profitable if you see a more moderate downside move or other risks in the trade. Because markets tend to generally move higher over long periods of time and companies are in business to make, not lose money, targeting put candidates may be not only a bit more difficult, but may be shorter in duration than your typical call candidates. See Exhibit 4.39.

Those same stocks that you may have bought calls on at one point may become put candidates. Don't forget to get familiar with a stock's earnings reports, trading patterns, volatility, and so on. If a stock looks like it's getting a little rich in valuation and the market is looking tired overall, it might be time to strike with a long put for a short term retracement or protracted trend.

If a stock is getting overbought, I want to know because it might be a reason to jump in short. You can use an alert to trigger when a stock moves outside its daily ATR, above its Bollinger band, or when certain fundamental levels are hit (high P/E, negative growth in earnings, etc.).

Long put candidates are typically not stagnant stocks. Try to find a catalyst in upcoming news or in the marketplace. It is also never a bad thing to buy a call on weakness in your stock; however, use caution if a stock has dropped sharply because there may be a dramatic increase in implied volatility, so be cautious.

Catalysts—News, Technical, Fundamentals

Long puts are versatile and can be used for different levels and durations of bearishness; your research can vary depending on what you are trying to accomplish. If you are specifically focused on overbought stocks that you are looking to revert to mean, you're going to follow a different research path than someone who is looking to follow bullish analyst momentum for a longer term trade.

Motivations

- **News**—If your broad macro thesis is cautious to bearish, the long put can be used to trade bearish news on a particular security. Taking a bearish position can be tricky because the world and markets are generally bearish. If news is extremely poor on a stock and it has already moved lower, think about the longer term consequences before jumping in, as it may bounce from buyers looking for a discount.
- Look for news that seems like it could be the start of a bigger and more damaging or lasting problem.
- **Earnings**—The long put is certainly not the optimal strategy for playing earnings, but it can be less risky than short stock if you reduce your

Smart Investor Tip!

To create a true short stock synthetic position, you must buy a put and sell a call at the same strike in the same month. Some very deep in-the-money puts will have a delta close to –1, which is *almost* the same thing, but limited in risk.

KEY POINT:

Because the vega of a put option is positive it is possible that if implied volatility rises, a put option could increase in value without a change in the stock.

Smart Investor Tip!

Increasing "short interest" in a stock may be a sign that more and more investors are beginning to express a negative sentiment in the stock, which is another way to sniff out potential upcoming weakness.

Note the difference in Greeks between the in-the-money and out-of-the-money puts detailed here. If you are looking for a short stock substitute, utilize higher-delta puts.

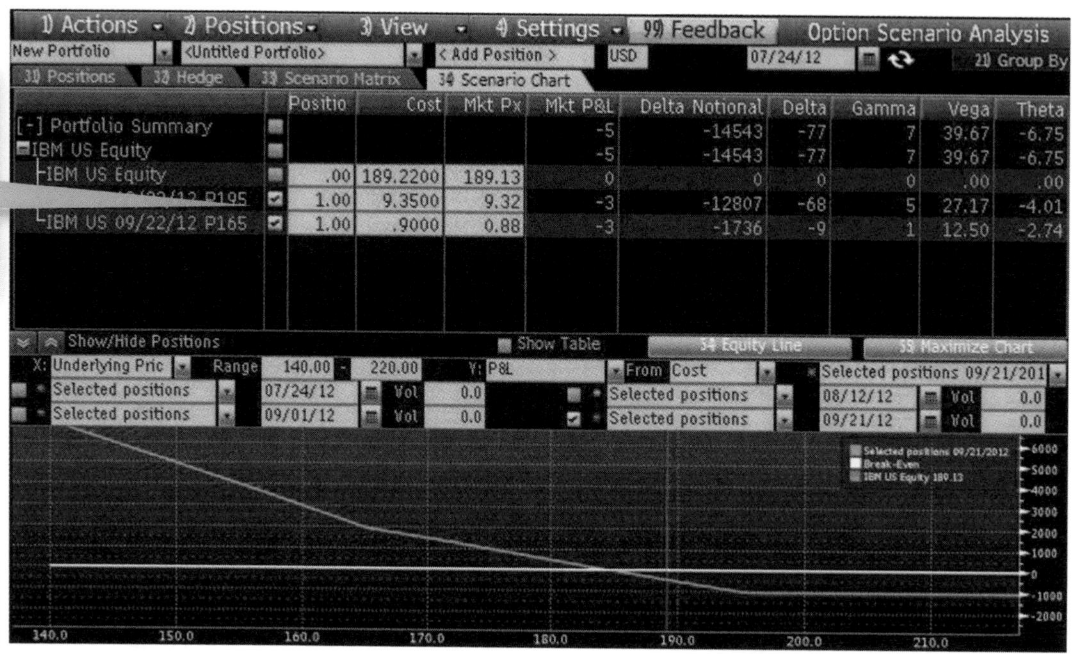

Exhibit 4.38

Smart Investor Tip!

Shorter duration trades may depend more heavily on technical patterns, whereas longer duration trades will need to see deterioration in fundamentals.

Smart Investor Tip!

If you truly believe that a stock has a high risk of dropping over earnings and you're long stock, don't be afraid to place a collar on it. We discuss that strategy shortly.

cost comparatively. Because of the Ivol earnings crush, the long put may suffer after the report is out. Look at the vega of the option you choose and do the math first; if you believe that the delta can overcome the vega drop, then proceed. For me, I'd use a vertical spread if I wanted to get directional. They will minimize vega risk and if positioned right will give you a statistical edge!

- **Economic data to be released**—Just as in the earnings motivation, buying a put ahead of what you think will be bad economic data might be better if you are only risking a smaller percentage of what you would have if you were shorting the stock. With economic data, the Ivol crush usually isn't as severe, which helps the deterioration in the put. I would still select a

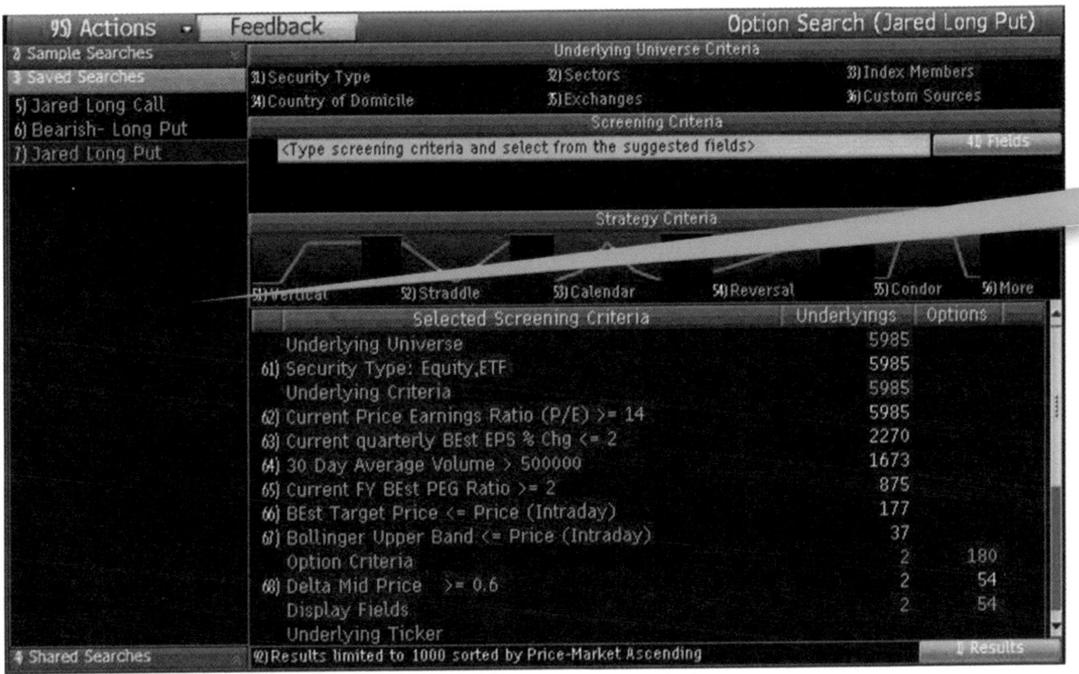

Here are a couple of bearish filters to find potential candidates if you don't already have one in mind. These scans can also produce ideas for other bearish strategies.

Exhibit 4.39

bearish vertical spread over the put for this type of event.

- **Analyst downgrades and targets**—Just as analysts make bullish calls and targets, sometimes they move expectations lower. (Read my comments in the long call section.)

I actually feel more comfortable following an analyst's sell recommendations than buys. If an analyst issues a strong sell and slaps a price target on a stock that's 20 percent or lower, I generally pay attention as long as my research confirms.

Longer-term traders can use analyst targets, downgrades, and trends in general to buy puts on a particular stock. The added benefit of following analysts is that they will consider macro trends in

Smart Investor Tip!

The fundamental techniques that I spell out for the long put transcend all bearish strategies. The level of bearishness that you discover, along with the relative strength in the charts, volatility trends, and upcoming events or the lack thereof will determine what bearish strategy you use.

Smart Investor Tip!

You should feel uneasy when you are reviewing their balance sheet.

There are myriad technical tools and methods; choose one that is proven, effective, and completely understandable. The more complex it is, the more hesitation and potential for a misread and bad trade.

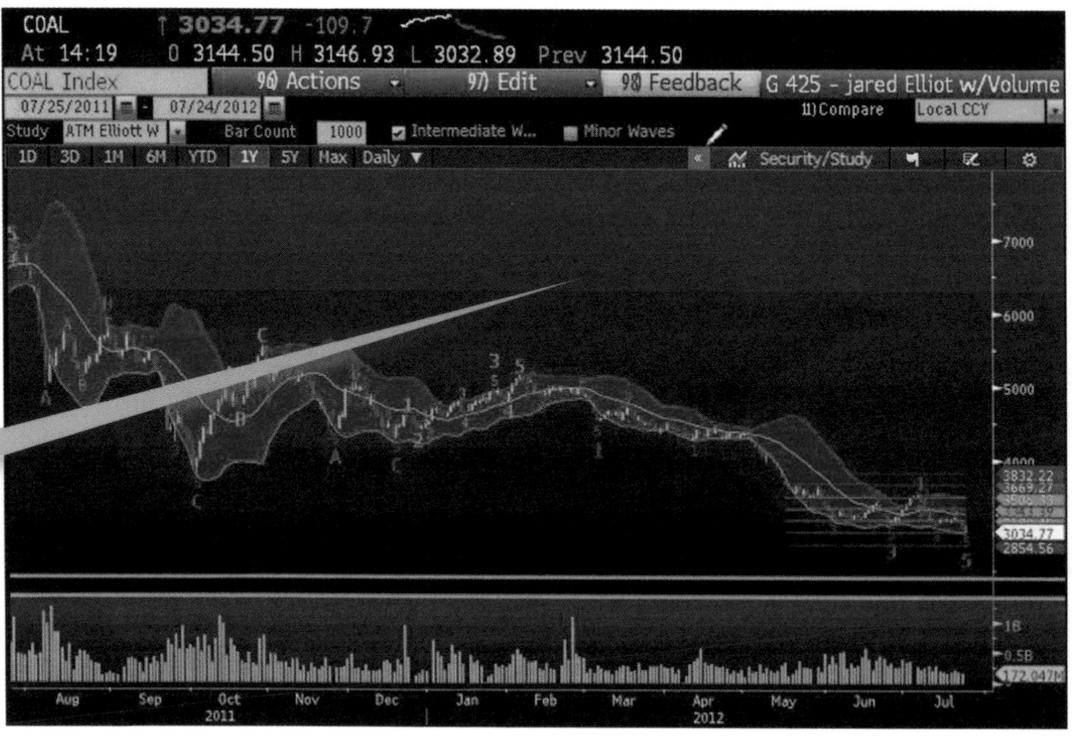

Exhibit 4.40

their reports and recommendations, which makes your life a little easier.

- **Charts to identify patterns of resistance and other bearish technical indicators**—The long put can be the perfect vehicle for playing bearish technical trends; just make sure that the expected outcome of these patterns will overcome all the negatives of the put. See Exhibit 4.40.

Step 2: Fundamental Analysis

Fundamental analysis should be the polar opposite of what you want for a long call. For a long put, you should seek out stocks that are overbought, expensive relative to peers and the market.

Candidates could have poor growth readings in the near term and little prospect for a complete turnaround. They could be companies that are "rising with the tide"; stocks that people are buying because the market is going up. There should be considerable risks to their business or they may have a plethora of competitors that are squeezing them out (think RIMM in 2011). High debt, elevated short interest relative to the market or peers, and so on.

Another optimal bearish fundamental situation is a stock that has actually been delivering earnings growth, but the expectations are so high for the stock that everything they do seems to be met with sellers.

There were periods in 2011 where AMZN (Amazon) was growing and looking strong, but there were doubts about their margin and ability to deliver and sell the Kindle against the iPad. If you have skill and experience, you can find these "darlings" that might be getting a cold shoulder on news releases or around earnings.

You can visualize fundamentals to look for abnormal trends in certain measurements that could be leading to a selloff in the stock in the CE screen shown in Exhibit 4.41.

Step 3: Technical Analysis

Long puts are best used when the stock is expensive and traders are complacent. This is because the sock has more room to drop, investors are more likely to take profits quicker at higher levels, and Ivol of the put is low.

In the charts, I time my entry by using a daily chart where I have identified resistance levels. Those levels, which can be the top of a channel, a 52-week high, or just an area that the stock is having difficulty, can be great areas to buy the put. Timing of the purchase is an art where you want to preferably get into the put while the stock is still moving up. Even though the stock may rise a little bit higher after your entry, I feel this is more advantageous than trying to jump in when a stock is dropping and Ivol is spiking.

I have found that over the years, if I have weak volume, weakening charts, a resistance level, and no real strong bullish catalysts, buying a put on an up day, near the top is almost always better for my shorter-term trade style. See Exhibit 4.42.

Like the covered call technical analysis, I use the daily chart to trigger and time my trade and use the week and/or month charts to confirm trend.

Unlike the covered call, the long put chart should preferably be flat to weak in the 20-, 50-, and 200-day moving averages. Look for where a stock is in relation to all of them; they help me to identify support and resistance points as well as determine trend.

A good rule of thumb is to look at the 200-day simple moving average (SMA) and look for your stock to be below it for a confirmation of a bearish trend.

Smart Investor Tip!

If you plan on being in the trade for two weeks or less, use your week chart to determine weakness and identify bearish trends, then time with your day chart.

If you plan on being in the trade for three weeks or more, look to your month chart for a sideways or bearsh trend and time the entry of the put with your day chart.

KEY POINT:

Active or swing traders who are in a trade for a couple hours to a couple days can keep their eyes focused on the daily chart only; just be more disciplined with your stops.

Just as we did with the calls, look for value anomalies—but this time on the high side. Target securities with fundamentals that are unsustainably high (for a retracement) or overall weakening fundamental trends.

Exhibit 4.41

You can also utilize the overbought techniques I outlined in the technical section of the covered call strategy to time your entry into the put. See Exhibit 4.43.

Step 4: Selecting the Best Put

There are a myriad of put strikes to select. Your choice should be a based on several factors:

Implied volatility—If implied volatility is extremely high, but you are still expecting the stock to drop sharply, there are two tactics you can use:

1. Buy a deep in the money put –0.70 to –0.90 that has a minimal amount of time value in comparison to intrinsic. This will ensure that when the stock moves lower, your put value will increase

Exhibit 4.42

as well. It will also diminish the amount of time value in your put, which in turn reduces the negative vega effects of high Ivol.

a. The downside to this is the higher cost of the option, which implies more risk. A remedy is to reduce the number of contracts.

2. Look at the break-even levels for each put in the chain and if you can find an OTM put strike that offers you a breakeven that is **above** where you think the stock will be before expiration, then choose that one. Try to stay away from at-the-money strikes because they contain so much time value

Smart Investor Tip!

For those of you who are simply looking for short stock replacement with leverage and minimal exposure to other market forces, then a put option with a delta of −0.75 to −0.95 may be your best choice.

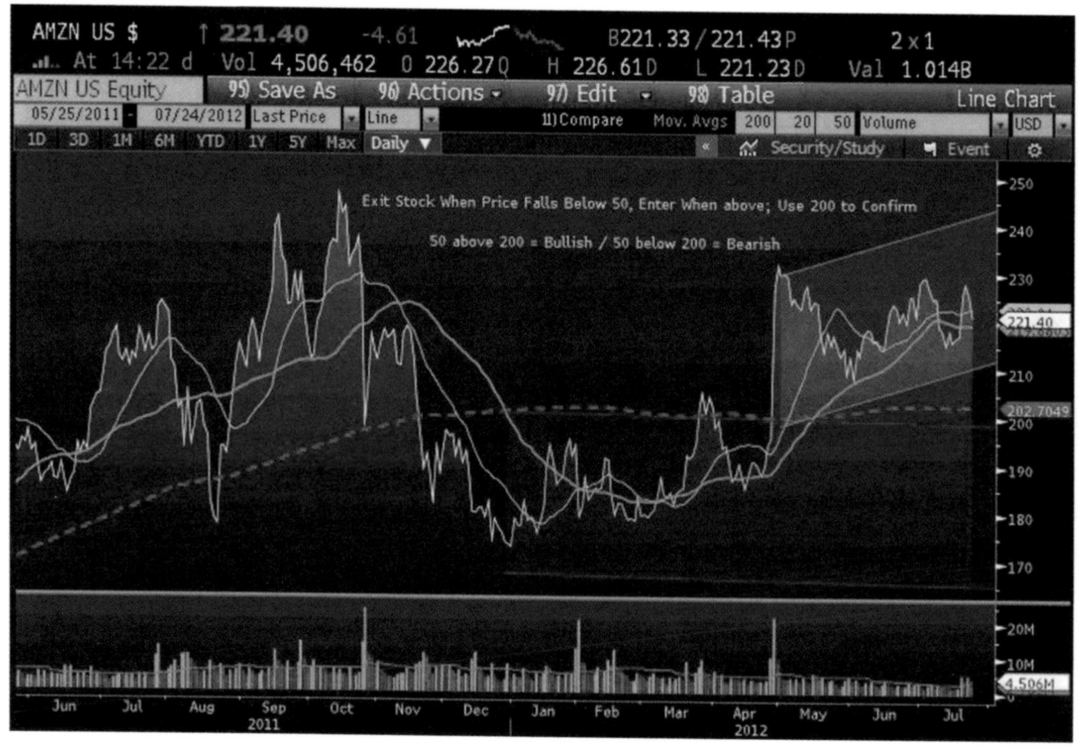

Exhibit 4.43

a. The downside to this is that the lower strike price means that the stock *must* fall below the strike (and breakeven) before it expires. These puts will be cheaper, but again, the probability of significant profits is reduced because of breakeven. Don't forget percentages here. If you buy a put for .35 and can sell it for .70, you have made 100 percent!

Time horizon—Long puts will always have breakevens lower than the underlying spot price. Always give yourself a cushion when you are buying a long put and never be afraid to buy an extra month or two, especially in markets that are *not* trending.

Cost (breakeven)—I always say that cost is relative. Price shouldn't be your biggest hurdle. If the delta is right and the implied volatility is right, then price is just price. More important than both for the average retail trader is breakeven. If your breakeven at expiration is simply unattainable, unrealistic, or not in line with your expectations, then you should find another put option or use a different strategy altogether. Don't focus so much on the nominal value of the put; instead, use the implied volatility and breakevens to guide you.

That said, if you have the choice between two in-the-money puts, one with delta of –.75 that costs $5 and another with a delta of –.80 that costs $8, does the extra .05 delta as a percentage of price warrant the additional cost? Might be better in that case to go with the cheaper one.

Price target in the underlying security—Because you have a reduced breakeven (which is not good in a short trade), your price target should exceed your breakeven expiration. In other words, you should be able to overcome the time value portion of your option in the trade. This isn't the only way you can make money, but it helps with rationalizing and selecting a put versus another trade.

Use technicals to help rationalize this level. If your charts and/or analysis is telling you that the stock has a low probability of falling below the breakeven of the put, select another strike or select another strategy, such as a vertical spread.

Choosing the Right Delta

The first priority (step) in delta selection should be related to how you want an individual option to be related to the stock, the current Ivol to Hvol relationship, your time frame, and of course how far you believe the stock will go.

In-the-Money Put to Synthesize a Short Stock Position

In the money means that the put option has intrinsic or real value. In-the-money options have a strike price that is higher than the current stock price. Deeper in-the-money puts (those with a delta of –0.65 to –1) tend to behave more like the stock, mimicking its moves with greater accuracy. Don't forget that puts will have an *inverse* relationship to the stock.

These options will provide you with less leverage and will cost more than cheaper, lower delta options, but will tend to behave more like a stock. They are a good choice if you believe the stock will move lower, but are not thinking there will be a large fast move in the stock. They also will be the least sensitive to changes in time and implied volatility on a percentage basis compared to at-the-money and out-of-the-money options. In-the-money puts will be more expensive than at- or out-of-the-money options.

Smart Investor Tip!

Do you want high a correlation to stock? Notice high relative Ivol to Hvol? Expect moderate stock movement in a shorter period of time? Choose a higher delta.

Want slightly lower correlation to stock, notice low relative Ivol to Hvol? Expect more volatile stock movement over a greater period of time? Choose a lower delta.

KEY POINT:

Delta and ATR: ATR can be used to the downside as well to select delta and set stops and targets.

All the tips I discuss for the long call can be used for a long put as well.

At-the-Money Put to Get More Vega Sensitivity for Quicker Downward Moves —Delta of –0.65 to –0.35

At- or near-the-money options have the highest amount of time value and thus the most sensitivity to changes in volatility as well as the greatest theta, on a dollar basis, than any other option. Unless you are making your bets on volatility, at-the-money options can be the worst choice, in that they may have more volatile profit and loss swings with changes in delta, volatility, and time all having great potential influence on the price of these options.

Out-of-the-Money Put for a Dramatic Move, Protection or a "Flier" on a High-Risk Trade —Delta of –0.35 to –0.01

These are the lottery tickets, as I like to call them. Out-of-the-money options are cheap for a reason. When you purchase an out-of-the-money put, be sure to examine its breakeven (put strike-premium) and make sure that level is where you think the stock can be below by expiration. Out-of-the-money options may require the stock to move fast and far down for you to be profitable. If you believe a stock is going to fall off a cliff and do so in a volatile manner, an out-of-the-money option can be used. These may also be used as inexpensive, protective "insurance policies" against long stock positions, if you want to protect against a catastrophic loss. See Exhibit 4.44.

The second part of choosing the best delta really is doing a bit of backward math. Once you've answered the earlier questions and found the right option specifically, you will have to now determine how many options to buy, which will increase your net delta in your portfolio.

Find a number that feels comfortable with your risk tolerance and remember that deltas are essentially the dollars that your portfolio will fluctuate with movements in the stock, so choose your contract size carefully.

Refer back to the allocation grading system in Chapter 2.

Choosing Expiration

Having enough time for your trade to work is a risk many options traders have to contend with. One of the ways to determine how much time to buy is to look back on your past trading history. If you have a history of being in trades for an average of a month, then maybe you should buy a minimum of 60 days to expiration (DTE). If you have never traded live before, you should practice trading your methods. Take a look at your practice trades in your virtual account and use those as a guide to how long you tend to be in trades. Before you begin to trade real money, be sure that you understand all risks involved; as a general rule, you should place at least 25 or more trades in your virtual account and have a written trade plan before using real money.

Classify your trade style (active, swing, mid-term, long-term investor) ahead of time and add an extra month to however long you think the max time in the trade will be.

Exhibit 4.44

Your time horizon is important to determine *before* you place your trade. It not only helps determine what strategy you employ, but also how much time you buy and how far you think the stock will drop. The longer the trade, the more possibility for movement.

See the Do It Yourself box here for a formula that I developed myself; it does not guarantee that you will always buy the right option, but it is a guideline to start with.

Purchasing more time for what you deem to be a more long-term investment is generally not a bad thing, although I would be careful buying less time, as we all know that sometimes things don't go exactly as planned in the market. Having more time in your

DO IT YOURSELF

Look back at your past two years of trading (or your total history if less than two years), then take all the trades you made and take the time you were in them and average them all. Then take your longest trade and average those two numbers (the average and the longest trade)—whatever number you come up with, add 30. The result is a good minimum days to expiration (DTE) to purchase when you are making trades.

Smart Investor Tip!

Some traders will find a dollar amount that they were willing to lose in a comparable stock investment then only use that loss amount as the total they are willing to spend on all their option contracts.

Smart Investor Tip!

Remember that by buying puts, you are fighting the inherent nature of the marketplace. Statistically speaking, stocks tend to rise over time. Because of this, I am generally quicker to take profits (or losses) on a put.

trade may open some other "options" that you may not have had available to you if you were out of time.

Open Interest

As a general rule, it is good to see open interest of 100 or more, and to utilize caution when placing a trade that makes you more than 25 percent of the total open interest. Remember, when months are added the Monday after expiration day, you may see zero open interest in that strike, while there may be a great deal of open interest in that same strike in the prior (or next) expiration month. If that is the case, take the lower of the two months and cut it in half, which may be a good estimate of where the additional month's open interest may end up. This again is one of my quick formulas and it is *not* an assurance of open interest, just a best guess.

Check Your Average Stock Volume

Don't forget to look for stocks that trade more than 600,000 shares average daily volume—1 million is preferred; the more the better!

Setting Stops

Like I do in the calls, my long put stops are usually based on the price of the underlying asset, not the put option itself. I do this because my thesis is built around the asset's movement, not my option's.

Your stops should obviously be placed at a level that is psychologically and monetarily acceptable to you, but at the same time need to be placed with the stock's volatility and technical levels in mind. Just because a stock moves against you when you first get in, it doesn't mean that you are wrong. But if it moves in a manner that is outside of its "normal" volatility, maybe you picked the wrong stock or maybe the market is just too strong in this case.

For the long put, it's all about bearish momentum, a breakdown of fundamentals and technical levels being compromised. If any of that changes, you might consider taking the trade off the table and finding a better candidate altogether.

Like I described with the call, familiarize yourself with the normal price variations that occur in any stock you are trading in. When the broad market has a good day it can lift bad stocks with it. If you notice this trend, you can use these days for entry as well. First identify what a "normal" oscillation is for the stock and then note how correlated to the stock market it is. (More on correlations in Chapter 7.) See Exhibit 4.45.

To quantify these measurements I use both ATR and beta.

To find out what a "normal" movement is, just look at the ATR of a given time frame. So if you are wondering what the average movement is over a week, check out the weekly ATR; if it's $10, then you should be able to tolerate a $10 move per week in either direction (consider your net deltas in these calculations).

If you want to set a stop based on stock making an abnormal move, you can use the ATR, stock price, and your delta to find a level to get out.

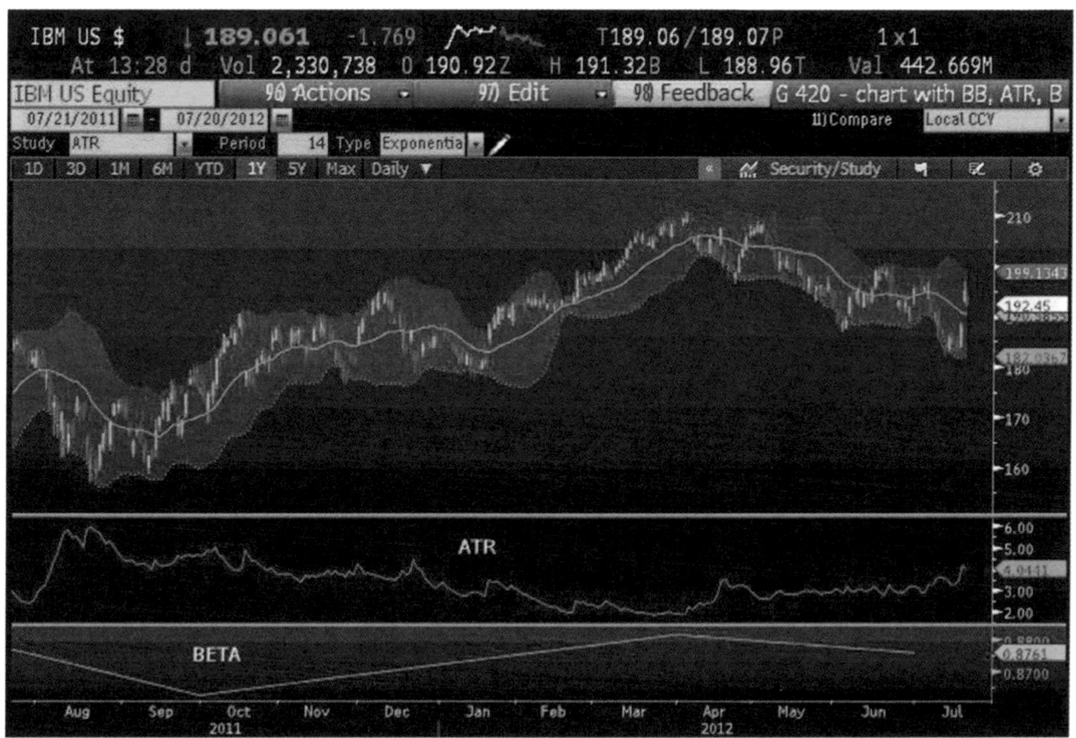

Exhibit 4.45

STEP-BY-STEP

Long put option stop loss

- **Take the stock's ATR for the time frame that I want to be in the trade (monthly max) then I multiply it by 1.2 [a risk factor I came up with] then multiply by the delta.**
- **Then, whatever number you come up with, subtract that from the option's price.**
- **If the ATR is $20 and my option has a 0.70 delta the math looks like this:**

Option Price $40 – [($20 *ATR* × 1.2) × 0.70 *DELTA*] = Stop Loss placed at $23.20

- **My stop-loss order would be placed at $26.20 in this case. In this case you would have to tolerate a $16.80 draw down. (This loss may seem steep, but remember that you may have been willing to originally tolerate a much bigger loss in the stock, all the while having much more cash share tied up in the trade.)**

Moving Up Your Stops

Once in the trade you should have an understanding of the stock's ATR, normal volatility, support and resistance points, earnings, news, and so on.

Depending on the amount of time you plan on being in the trade, adjusting your stop losses up or down may have a higher or lower priority. The shorter the duration of the trade, the more aggressive you may have to be in adjusting your stops to proactively protect profit; longer duration trades may see adjustments of stops lower to account for temporary rallies. Once I am in a profitable trade, I try to move my stop to at least breakeven, as long as it's not too close to the stock's normal movements (check ATR for this).

For me, I seldom put physical stops in the market, because they are seen by the market makers and in some cases, especially volatile stocks with wide bid-ask markets, my stop could get triggered, with my stop getting filled at even a lower level because of the spread.

Just as in calls, I set price alerts on both the underlying asset and the option to send me email and pop-ups on my screen. I do this for profit targets and stop losses. There are times when I swap out my regular stop loss (on the option) for a trailing stop that ratchets higher as the stock drops, but locks in place preventing it from moving lower. See Exhibit 4.45. Because stocks generally fall faster than they rise, you may have to take profits quicker (and be less strict) in your long put trades. Use alerts to keep you on top of your positions as shown in Exhibit 4.46.

Smart Investor Tip!

Stops on puts can be a little confusing because if you are basing your stop or trigger on the stock, it will be set at a price higher than where you got in, whereas the put option stops will be placed at a price below.

Smart Investor Tip!

If you use "trigger" orders from your brokers, those are generally housed on the broker's servers and don't hit the live market until their criteria are met; this keeps the market makers from leaning or prematurely filling my stop loss orders. If you like having physical stops in place, try to use the broker's trigger orders, not orders with the word "stop" in it.

Step 5: Monitoring/Closing the Trade

Depending on whether your thesis is that the stock should have a quick sharp drop or a slow meltdown over time, your level monitoring and tolerance will vary. I always do my trade monitoring in the daily chart; it is the first stable warning of a change in trend for all strategies. It will have absolute control over my entries and exits for a short-term trade and have slightly less impact on my monitoring of longer-term trades as long as my charts are stable in the week and month.

If a longer-term trade is going in your favor, you should be proactive in protecting your profits. In the beginning stages of the trade, you should have already either entered your stop loss or had an idea of how high the stock would go and determined levels that you deemed acceptable and not. See Exhibit 4.47.

If you held on for another week—or worse, three weeks—you would be in a world of pain as a swing trader.

For the longer-term trader, the hold may have been worth the wait because the stock got all the way down to $11! The monthly ATR at the time was more than $2.20, so the longer-term trader was within his or her tolerance even on the rally in May.

When you are using ATR or another method to set stop and target levels in a stock you must act if those levels are violated and you think that the stock will continue to move.

If the stock is moving against you, has hit your mental stop, and it looks like it might keep rallying, either close the trade or see if you can morph it into a vertical.

If the stock is dropping and your profit target is hit, I generally take it unless there are *extremely* compelling, objective reasons that I think the stock will move further.

Trailing stops can also be used to lock in and protect your existing profits. Do *not* be greedy. Stick to your plan and execute it.

Exhibit 4.46

If you begin to see cracks in the foundation of the trade, it might be best to take profits on the put and reevaluate. For the longer trades, I will tolerate a bit more of a rally, but I never want to have a substantially positive trade go negative on me—puts especially because of their "antimarket" sentiments.

Items to Check When Monitoring

- Changes in macro, company news, and so on
- Changes in chart patterns, levels
- Changes in sentiment
- Earnings
- Stop loss
- Target profits

Smart Investor Tip!

If a swing trader can capture one to three times the ATR on the profit side, that is a win!

Assume you entered a put on March 9, 2011, when the stock was at $17.50, and it quickly went to $15.81. Would you have exited? If you were a swing trader, this was probably a huge win, and at the time, the daily ATR was 50 cents. Don't be greedy!

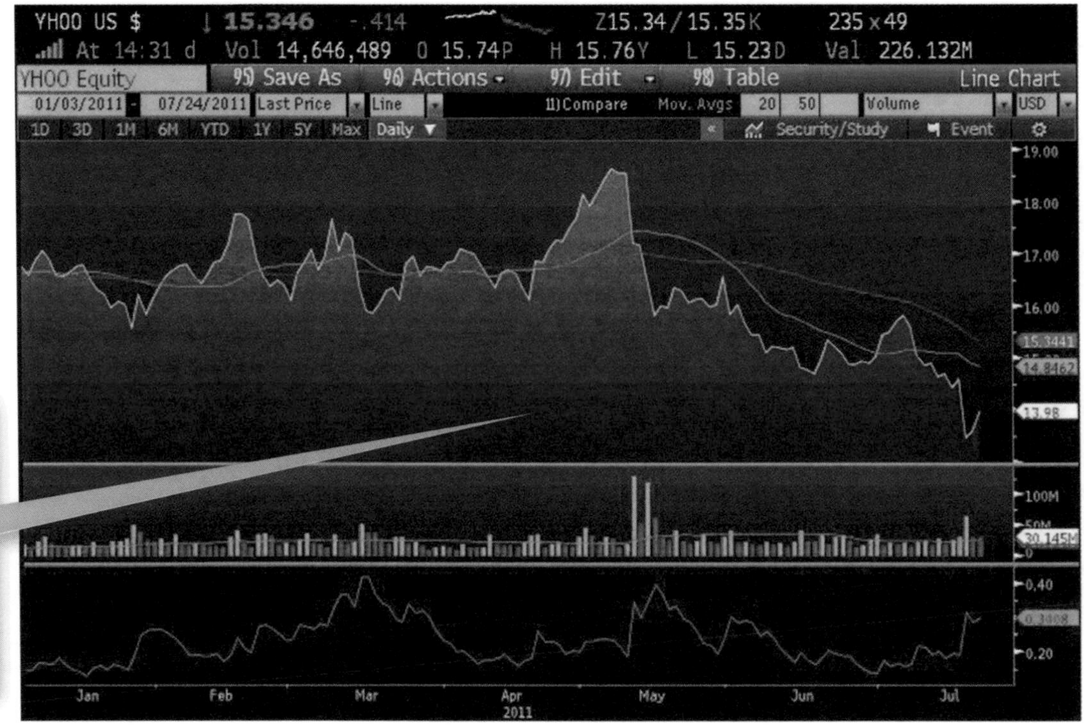

Exhibit 4.47

Repair versus Exit

Straight long puts can be repaired by selling a put against them (vertical spread morph) or even buying stock against them to participate in a rally.

When you sell a put against a long put to turn it into a bear-put spread, you should already be profitable or at least at breakeven in the put that you bought. This is because a losing put trade may require you to sell a put that not only doesn't help the trade much because of low premium, but caps your profit. Often a bad losing trade cannot be easily repaired.

You would also want to sell a put that brings in at least 30 cents of value and has a breakeven that is attainable. If you bought an in-the-money put to begin with you might be able to sell another in- or at-the-money put and give yourself some breathing room and still make money.

The reason for turning a put into a bear put spread (or bearish diagonal spread) would be that you "very bearish" thesis turned "a little less bearish."

The short put does *not* have to be the same month as your long put, in which case you would be creating a diagonal bear spread.

Bad Repair

See Exhibit 4.48.

Good Repair

See Exhibit 4.49.

Can you see the differences and the risks?

Some points to consider are:

- Has the fundamental picture changed in the stock?
  - Might be better to simply exit if things are getting very positive (news, economy, sentiment, etc.).
  - For more neutral to temporary changes, you add a short put and turn into a spread (if strikes and premiums allow you to). Your delta will be lower and P&L less volatile. The credit of the short put will raise your breakeven, but your profit will be capped.
  - You can buy back the short put if the stock temporarily rallies and you believe that it will fall again quickly.
- Have the charts gotten stronger?
  - A minor bullish blip in the charts might not be too bad and could just mean that you sell some of your contracts and let the others ride. A rally above a major trend line (50- or 200-day MA) might be a reason to simply bail out. Daily chart patterns will be more important to the shorter term long put traders.
- Was there an earnings occurrence? See Exhibit 4.50.
- If earnings were flat and the stock is flat or slightly lower, I will always reevaluate the trade and see if I want to continue holding, sell a put for protection, or just bail out. If you have profit in the trade, no reason to keep the trade on if the future looks iffy. Remove the trade all together or sell a large portion of the contracts/shares.
  - Read the commentary! If the company expressed concerns over the next quarter and the market is still shaky, the next leg will probably be lower. If the company said that the worst is behind it and things are starting to look up, it might be time to get out!
  - If the report was a complete miss and the stock is down 10 percent, you have to now ask a couple of questions: Did you hit your original profit target? If so, exit. Dead cat bounces are always possible.

If you didn't attain your profit target, you can get more aggressive (defensive) by selling a put and increasing your chance of success statistically. If the

> **KEY POINT:**
>
> **If you want to repair or morph a long put into a put spread, you must be able to sell a put that has a strike that is *lower* than the original put's breakeven (strike-premium). This will ensure that you can profit in the trade. If you don't do this, you may be locking in a loss.**

If you are attempting to repair a trade, pay close attention to your break-evens and risk graphs. This is where it helps to be visual. Can you see the issue with this scenario?

Exhibit 4.48

Smart Investor Tip!

Remember that every trade is a new one; every day you are in an existing position, ask yourself if you still would enter this trade as a completely brand new trade at the price at that moment. If not, you should consider an exit.

stock just dropped sharply, there might be a rally coming; if the rally doesn't come, the premium collected from the short put can reduce your cost even further.

- Have you gone beyond your original stop loss point?
  - If things are going against you and the trade has exceeded your stop loss level, why are you in the trade?
- Is the trade consuming you?

  Take the hit and move on.
- Will your repair not only be feasible, but dramatically improve the trade?
  - Some positions are beyond repair and for some reason traders try to get creative and end up with a nightmare on their hands. If you were bearing on a stock in a long put, but you've

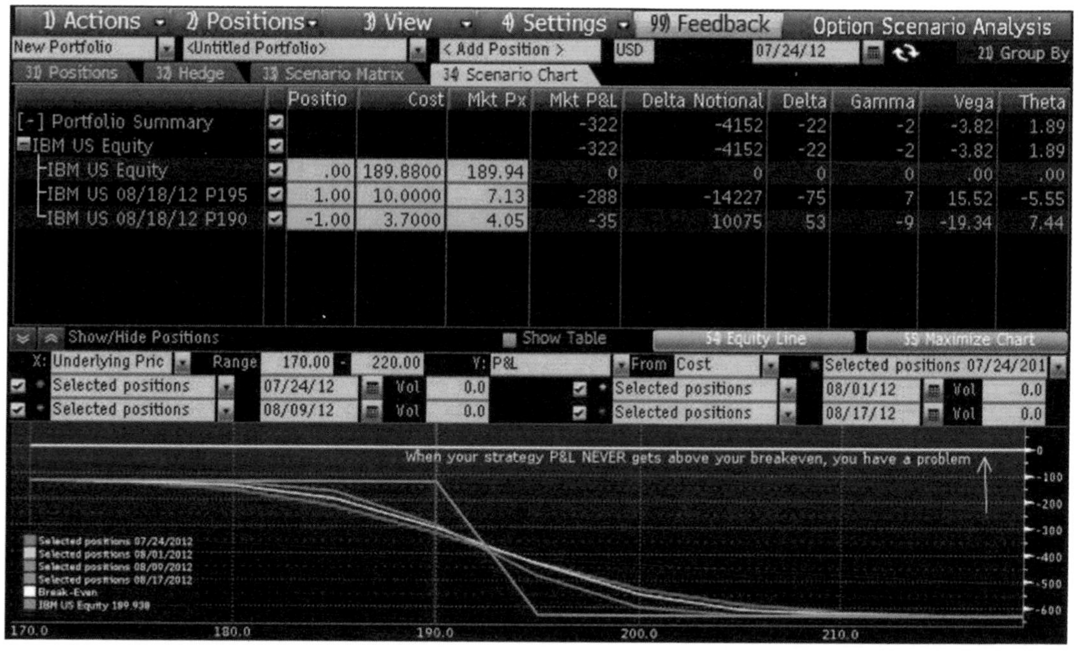

Exhibit 4.49

taken such a loss that you are now trying to sell a put against it to actually turn it bullish, you might want to go back to the drawing board and rethink a new trade. You obviously got it wrong in this one; reevaluate your finds and see where the error occurred. Then gather your wits and do it right. Not many traders will continuously win being wrong but lucky frequently.

- If you extend the life of the trade, will the extra time for minimal loss recovery justify the capital committed to the trade?
  - Don't roll a trade that you are feeling bad about. If you are going to prolong pain, have a damn good reason for doing it.
  - If your reason for being in the put is no longer valid, get out or switch into another strategy

KEY POINT:

The long put has a negative correlation with the underlying stock. The put rises in value as the underlying stock drops and falls in value when the stock rises. You do *not* have to have the cash or margin required to short stock when you purchase a put.

STEP-BY-STEP

- **Considering the above requirements, let's compare an IBM buy-write to the same short put and look at risk/return. At the end of the day, you'll find that because long stock plus short call = short put, synthetically they are both the same. There are, however, some cost and execution nuances to keep in mind.**

Use volatility to help guide you; there are often occurrences in the option markets that are not reflected in the stock price. Use the Hvol/Ivol spread as a visual reference to create a more effective barometer for anomalies.

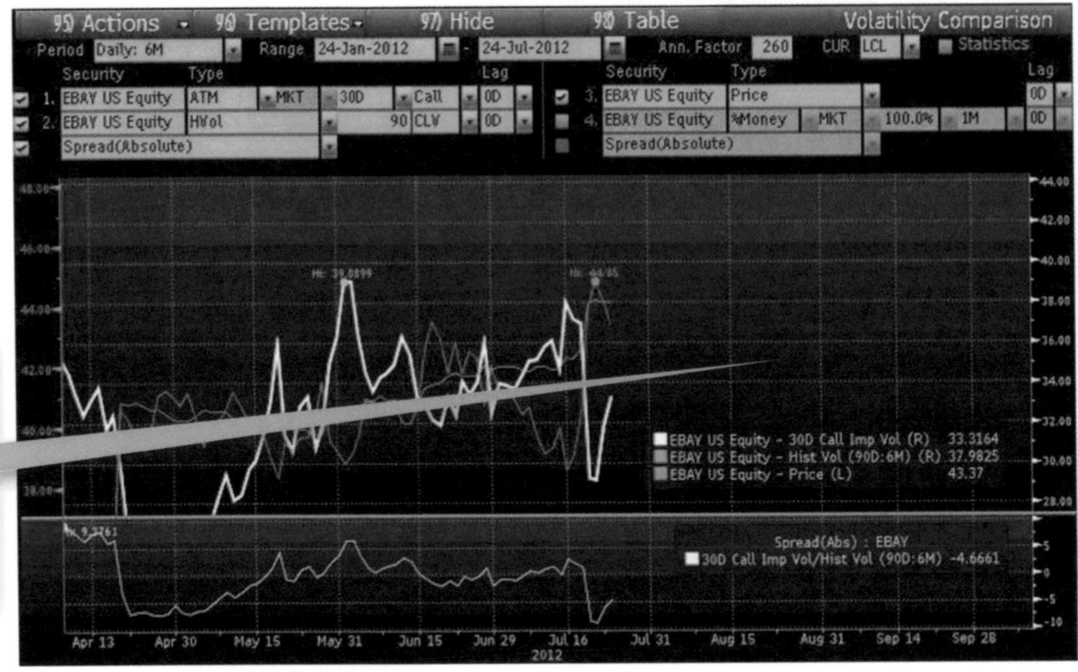

Exhibit 4.50

that has less cost, less risk, and maybe more probability.

Selling Puts

From an execution, psychological, and risk standpoint, short puts are identical to buy-writes, just without the cost of the stock. Your broker will require that you put up the following margins (which can and will vary).

- Twenty percent of the underlying stock price minus any out-of-the-money amount *plus* option premium, *or* 10 percent of the strike price plus option premium, whichever is greater.
- Short option requirements for 3X Leveraged ETFs use 60 percent and 30 percent.
- Short option requirements for 2X Leveraged ETFs use 40 percent and 20 percent.

IBM US $ ↓189.88 -.95 N189.84/189.89N 3x2
At 14:46 d Vol 2,981,788 O 190.92Z H 191.32B L 188.56D Val 566.207M
IBM US Equity 95) Templates 96) Actions 97) Expiry Option Monitor: covered Call analysi
IBM ↓189.88 -.95 -.4978% 189.84 / 189.89 Hi 191.32 Lo 188.56 Volm 2981788 HV 22.74 91) News (CN)
Calc Mode Center 189.98 Strikes 8 Exch US Composite 92) Next Earnings(EM) 10/17/12 E
295) Center Strike 296) Calls/Puts 297) Calls 298) Puts 299) Term Structure

	Calls							Puts					
	Ticker	Strike	ThPx	Bid	Ask	DM		Strike	Ticker	ThPx	Bid	Ask	DM
	18 Aug 12 (25d); CSize 100; Div 0.85 USD; R 0.24							18 Aug 12 (25d); CSize 100; Div 0.85 USD; R 0.24					
9)	IBM 8 C175	175.00	15.25	15.10	15.40	.93	57)	175.00	IBM 8 P175	.58	.56	.60	-.10
10)	IBM 8 C180	180.00	10.63	10.50	10.75	.86	58)	180.00	IBM 8 P180	1.10	1.07	1.12	-.18
11)	IBM 8 C185	185.00	6.48	6.40	6.55	.72	59)	185.00	IBM 8 P185	2.13	2.11	2.16	-.33
12)	IBM 8 C190	190.00	3.25	3.20	3.30	.50	60)	190.00	IBM 8 P190	4.03	3.95	4.10	-.53
13)	IBM 8 C195	195.00	1.24	1.21	1.26	.26	61)	195.00	IBM 8 P195	7.10	7.00	7.20	-.75
14)	IBM 8 C200	200.00	.38	.37	.40	.10	62)	200.00	IBM 8 P200	11.25	11.15	11.35	-.90
15)	IBM 8 C205	205.00	.13	.11	.15	.04	63)	205.00	IBM 8 P205	16.02	15.85	16.20	-.96
16)	IBM 8 C210	210.00	.06	.04	.08	.02	64)	210.00	IBM 8 P210	20.93	20.75	21.10	-.99
	22 Sep 12 (60d); CSize 100; Div 0.85 USD; R 0.34							22 Sep 12 (60d); CSize 100; Div 0.85 USD; R 0.34					
17)	IBM 9 C175	175.00	16.02	15.90	16.15	.84	65)	175.00	IBM 9 P175	1.77	1.74	1.79	-.18
18)	IBM 9 C180	180.00	11.88	11.80	11.95	.75	66)	180.00	IBM 9 P180	2.66	2.63	2.69	-.27
19)	IBM 9 C185	185.00	8.20	8.15	8.25	.63	67)	185.00	IBM 9 P185	4.00	3.95	4.05	-.37
20)	IBM 9 C190	190.00	5.20	5.10	5.20	.49	68)	190.00	IBM 9 P190	6.00	5.95	6.05	-.51
21)	IBM 9 C195	195.00	2.93	2.89	2.96	.35	69)	195.00	IBM 9 P195	8.80	8.75	8.85	-.65
22)	IBM 9 C200	200.00	1.48	1.45	1.50	.21	70)	200.00	IBM 9 P200	12.33	12.20	12.45	-.79
23)	IBM 9 C205	205.00	.68	.65	.71	.12	71)	205.00	IBM 9 P205	16.65	16.10	17.20	-.87
24)	IBM 9 C210	210.00	.29	.27	.30	.06	72)	210.00	IBM 9 P210	21.55	20.00	23.10	-.90
	20 Oct 12 (88d); CSize 100; Div 0.85 USD; R 0.44							20 Oct 12 (88d); CSize 100; Div 0.85 USD; R 0.44					
25)	IBM 10 C175	175.00	17.35	17.20	17.50	.77	73)	175.00	IBM 10 P175	3.13	3.05	3.20	-.23

Exhibit 4.51

In the buy-write scenario with the purchase of 100 shares @ $190 and the sale of the 185 call for $8.15; your margin cost in the trade would be roughly $9,100 (50% of total risk). Max risk is $18,185.00 per buy-write. See Exhibit 4.51.

The IBM Sept 185 put can be sold for $4.00. Based on the rules, 20 percent of the underlying stock ($37.98) – the out-of-the-money amount ($4.88) + option premium $4.00 is $37.10 × 100 (option controls 100 shares) would be $3,710 (this was the greater of the two calculations).

The short put would cost you **$3,710 in margin**; the **max risk is $18,100** (185 strike price – $4.00 put premium × 100).

Smart Investor Tip!

I tend to favor this trade in an IRA, conservative account, or a situation where you want to protect a certain level of profit attained in an existing position. It's a great strategy to employ temporarily when bullish stocks move into a channel or get dragged down with political or economic news.

Although the max risk is similar to the 185 covered call, the margin requirements are much lower (these requirements may vary from broker to broker).

Look at the delta of the two . . . notice something interesting??

Nuances

Inability to "trade" in and out of the short put—When you are in a buy-write, you can buy and sell the call as the stock moves up and down. In the short put, you may not have the P&L deviation you want because the delta will generally be low if the put is out of the money. On the flip side, this can also be an advantage, because if the stock drops sharply you will have less sensitivity (unless you sell extra puts just before the stock drops) and thus fewer losses. This all has to do with the position of the short put (and covered call) in relation to the stock.

If you initially sold a call that was way out of the money and the stock rallied up to it slowly, chances are that the delta of the stock gave your P&L a nice boost. If you sold that same put (which would be in the money) you should see a similar effect, but there may be more variables that could affect your trade.

Because of put/call parity, the returns should be similar, but it really is more of a psychological effect on the trader.

Timing—Because you are not already long the stock, if you thought the stock was going to take off, but your put is way out of the money, you are not going to benefit from its rally unless you buy some stock or buy a call with some serious delta. This is where some prefer to have the buy-write on, so they can just cover the call quickly and let the shares ride. Again, if you thought the stock was going to run, you could just come in with a bid delta call and sell it when the stock is higher, capturing profit.

At the end of the day it really boils down to a personal preference. The key with the short put is that you have to be prepared (at least psychologically) to own the stock at your break-even level.

The Collar

The *collar* is simply a hybrid of a covered call and a long put, usually at or below the stock price. The trade is often executed to protect, collar, or "fence" a stock within a range. It's best used when stocks have been running for a bit, you're profitable, and are concerned about a pullback. See Exhibit 4.52.

From a risk/behavioral perspective, it generally looks and behaves similar to a bullish vertical spread, hence the similar P&L graph.

Max profit in a collar is:

Short Call Strike – Net Cost Basis in Collar (Long Stock Price + Short Call Premium – Long Put Premium)

Max risk in a collar is:

Net Cost Basis in Collar – Put Strike Price

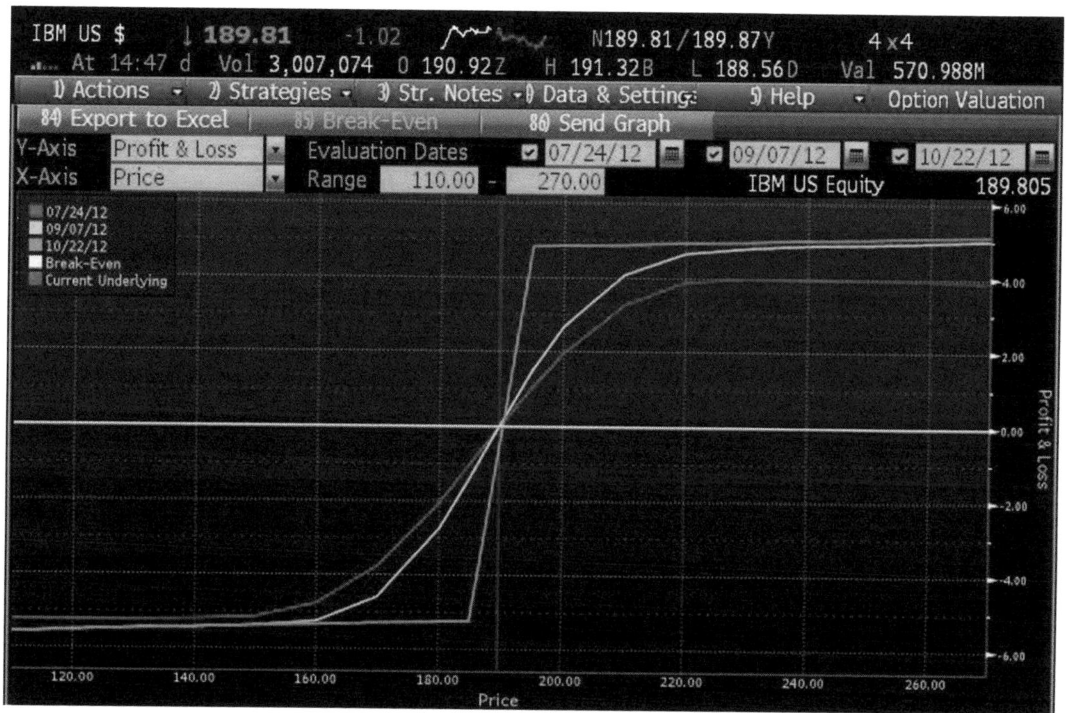

Exhibit 4.52

Expiration breakeven in a collar is:

Net Cost Basis in Collar (Long Stock Price + Short Call Premium – Long Put Premium)

Optimal Scenario

In a perfect world, you want to be neutral on a stock, with little directional bias or a range-bound forward thesis.

When you purchase a collar, you are preparing for a downside move and looking to protect your existing asset. The majority of your indicators (fundamental or technical) should be bullish but signaling caution or deterioration in the stock's demand or business strength in the short term, caused by sector influences.

The charts should be leading up to a major resistance, overbought in the near term or poised for a

Smart Investor Tip!

If you were to buy a stock then sell a call and buy a put with the same strike, you have synthetically sold stock. That means that your net position will have a zero delta and no relation to the stock. Your only risk at that point would be if interest rates change.

Smart Investor Tip!

A short call and a long put with the same strike are equivalent to being short stock at that strike price; if you did that trade and bought stock at the same time, that would be called a conversion and is a directionless, generally riskless strategy.

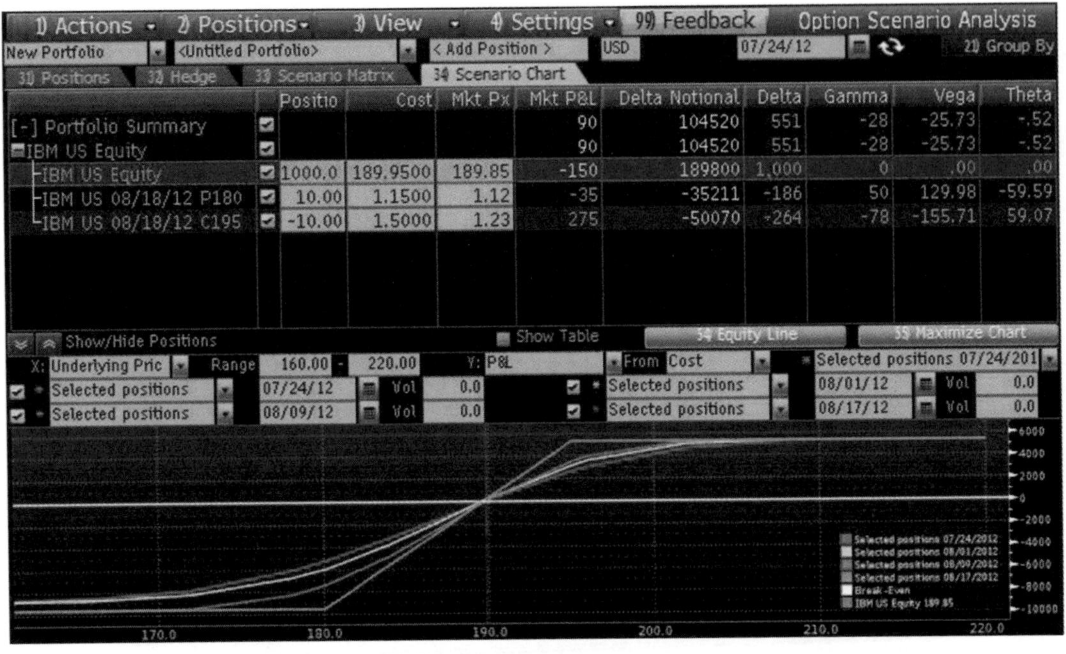

Exhibit 4.53

reversion to the mean (sell-off, because the stock has been rallying). It could also be an overvalued stock that has been outperforming its peers or the market when there is little reason or fundamentals to back up its rally. Any other extremely bearish or breakdown technical indicators will also be acceptable. See Exhibit 4.53.

- *Sentiment.* Neutral in a sense, but can be bullish, bearish, or neutral depending on your selection of strikes and cost basis in the stock with a bias for protection to the downside and the potential for limited upside. This sentiment can vary with the choice of strikes and premium paid and/or received in the trade.

- *Risk.* Varies, but limited to cost basis in stock (pretrade stock cost ± debit or credit for spread) minus put strike.
- *Potential reward.* Limited to upside call strike–cost basis.
- *Passage of time.* Varies.
- *Probability characteristics.* Protective strategy, sets absolute loss limits, while limiting upside, probability of profitability in trade depends on price at which the stock is owned and what strikes are chosen to sell call-buy put.
- *Time in trade.* Typically short term, generally used to protect over a known event; however, collars (credit collars preferably) can be used to protect a stock against a sharp downturn in a longer-term trade. Months of strikes can be staggered and adjusted with time.
- *When to apply this strategy.* You have a moderate to extremely aggressive bearish opinion of the stock.
- *How you will win.* If done for a credit, stock should stay between strikes above where you own the stock.

If done for a debit, and the stock drops, you can trade out of the collar to offset your loss in the stock. If the stock tanks way below your strike, you still retain the right to sell it back up at your put strike. Typically, the goal of the collar is to offer short-term absolute protection.

If you own the stock much lower, and just want to lock in a bottom price, collars can be done for even money (minus commission). This could be used in a retirement account where you need to maintain a minimum value of a large amount of stock, perhaps employing the strategy before an event or after the stock has had a strong rally.

Breakeven at Expiration = Stock Cost Basis ± Premium Paid or Received

How you will get hurt:

- *Stock stays flat up to expiration.* You will gradually lose your time value and retain your intrinsic value if you had any to begin with. If the trade was done for a credit, this outcome will be desired. If the trade is done for a debit, this will cost you money if both option strikes are out of the money, because they will both expire worthless.
- *Stock rises.* You will typically make more from your stock than you will lose in the options. If the trade is done for a credit and the short call strike is at or above the stock price at the time of initiating the spread, you will be profitable. Remember, if the stock is above the short-call strike on expiration, you will be forced to sell your shares and limit your profit.
- *Stock falls.* The put value will increase and the call value will decrease if the stock falls, creating a potentially profitable situation in those two options. However, you will be losing on your long stock position. If you still want to retain the stock

position because you think the stock will recover, the collar can be removed for a profit. If your sentiment has changed and you are no longer bullish on the stock, the collar can be closed out (hopefully for a profit) and the stock sold.

The Collar Dissected

Covered Call + a Long Put = Relatively Cheap Protection for Long Stock

One collar is 100 shares of long stock, one at- or out-of-the-money short call, and one at- or out-of-the-money long put, with the call strike and put strike being different.

The cost of the long put is partially, fully, and sometimes in excess offset by the credit from the sale of the short call.

Applying this strategy is easier said than done, and there is certainly a technique and reasoning that you need to apply to the collar. In reality, the more profitable in the stock you are, the more "wiggle room" you have to select the best strikes without costing you.

Application of the Collar

The Collar = (Long stock + short call + long put [with different strikes])

The call strike is always greater than the put strike and usually both are out of the money, but not always.

Collar Greek attributes are:

- Delta

  Generally *net* positive when both the call and put are out of the money. Your stock delta will override the two smaller negative deltas of the (out-of-the-money) short call and long put. The closer the options strikes are to the stock, the lower the net delta position will be.

  Delta can be negative if you buy an in-the-money put and sell an in-the-money call. Remember assignment risks.

- Gamma

  Gamma will vary but is generally minimized because the short call and long put will tend to neutralize each other. The goal is to have the collar expire with the stock just below the short call strike. Gamma will get more positive if the stock drops toward the long put strike and more negative as the stock moves to and above the short call strike.

  This is a trade where you will remain heavily focused on delta and breakevens.

- Theta

  Varies. If the collar is done for a credit and the stock is in between the long put strike and short call strike, you will collect theta. If you do the trade for a debit and the stock falls below the long put strike, you begin to get short theta and the position is costing you money each day.

  With the stock above your short call, you will still be collecting theta if you did the trade for a credit, but you will also be limited in how much you can make because the short call obligates you to sell your stock at that strike.

If you think the stock is going to rise above your short call, close the collar beforehand to get long delta! You can always reenter.

- Vega

  Varies. Typically with the stock near your short call strike you will have a minimal short vega bias; however, as the stock approaches the long put strike, your bias will actually change to become long vega because the put is gaining delta and is becoming the dominant option. Again, making a bet on volatility is not the objective in this strategy; focus on your cost basis in the stock and how much protection you want versus the amount of premium paid or collected in the trade.

- Rho

  Minimal risk.

The short call strike is always greater than the long put strike.

So when would a trader use a collar? Suppose you had shares of stock in a company that you want to keep long term and would like the stock to stay within a certain range, perhaps because they are shares held in your IRA. For instance, let's assume that you have 1,000 shares of IBM, which, hypothetically is currently trading at $100 per share. This stock position is a large part of your retirement nest egg and the market is beginning to look a bit turbulent, possibly after rallying for some time. A collar can be a low-cost or costless way to protect your investment over time.

Collars can also be used ahead of an earnings report or other event that you suspect may be volatile. The collar will help offer you relatively cheap or costless insurance on your stock position. Depending on how you structure the collar (which strikes you choose) you may even get a credit, which would actually reduce your cost basis in the stock.

You can also use an in-the-money call and an in-the-money put, which would then give you a net negative delta when done one to one with the stock. You might use this variation if you wanted to remain long the shares, but take a very bearish temporary trade on the stock. See Exhibit 4.54.

IBM Collar Example

The year is 2008: The market is performing well, everything seems great. When everything is looking rosy we generally forget about the need for a hedge (or downside protection) and tend to relax some of our trading rules because the irrational exuberance has taken hold not only of us, but of the masses, so any doubt you may have is diminished by the predominance of data that is flowing through the media and the net. Let's assume that back then IBM was trading at $100 per share and looked fairly strong from a technical and even fundamental perspective.

Smart Investor Tip!

Collars can be traded all at once, buying puts and selling calls at the same time. You can also "leg in" to the trade; sell the calls first, then buy the puts or vice versa.

But since the short call and long put are both bearish, there is generally no advantage to using a legging in technique.

Smart Investor Tip!

By selling a higher strike call you allow the stock more room to rally, but lessen the amount of premium received to offset the price of the put.

The closer the put is to the stock price the more bearish you are on the stock and the more that put will cost.

So if you are more bullish, widen the space between the call and the put and move the call strike further from the stock and vice versa if you are more bearish by tightening the space between strikes around the spot price.

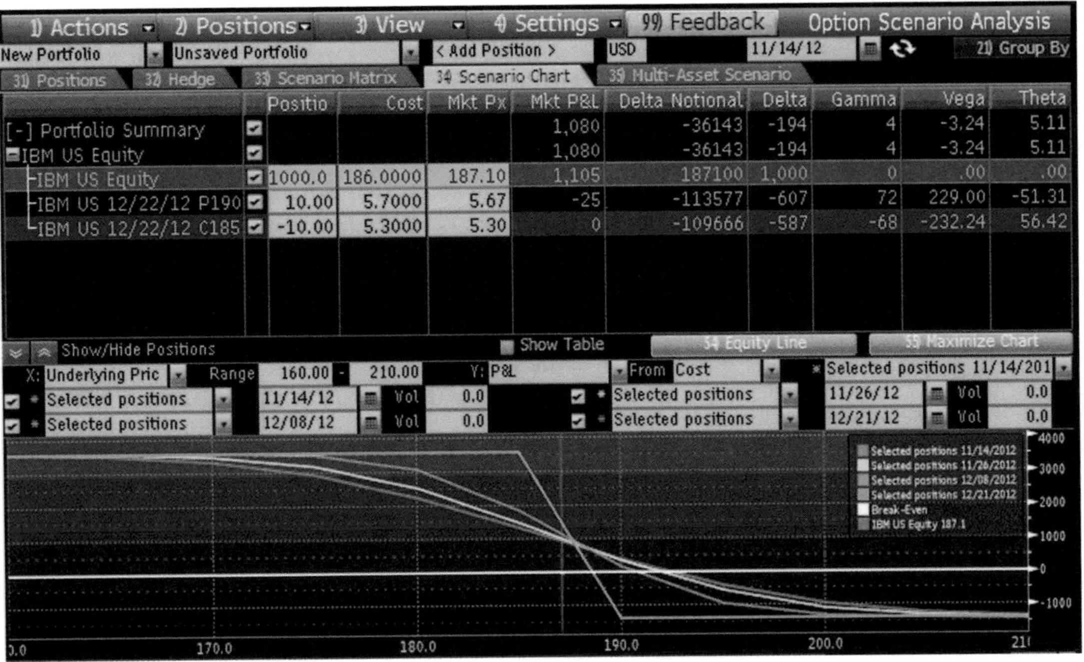

Exhibit 4.54

You would be devastated if IBM were to fall a large amount. You have owned IBM for some time with an average cost basis of $70 per share.

In this example we are long 1,000 shares of stock, which means that we can sell 10 July 110 calls and buy 10 July 90 puts for a credit of 10 cents.

This trade limits the upside of IBM to $110, but "stops you out" at $90. The $0.10 credit goes toward reducing your cost basis.

You would obviously want to buy enough time that you feel you need the protection for.

Strike Selection

Choosing the strikes for the call and the put really comes down to personal choice on costs and credit of the trade, as well as the amount of downside protection, and the opinion you have on the stock.

My personal preference is to also include the implied volatility of the options and the historical volatility of the stock when calculating the possible moves that a stock could make in the time frame that you have the collar in place.

Be sure to also account for any earnings or corporate events that could be a catalyst for volatility. Earnings often bring abnormal movements along with them; the collar can be a way to minimize that increased volatility effect on your portfolio.

Here is how you can use volatility to find the expected range of a stock.

Volatility in Your Calculations

If you are a bit more advanced, you can use volatility to select your strikes. In other words, if IBM had an average Hvol of 30 percent and it was $100 per share, this means that in the simplest terms, it's reasonable for IBM to vary 30 percent up or 30 percent down in a year about 70 percent of the time (one standard deviation). This does not mean that IBM cannot move beyond those levels; it just means there is a much lower probability of that occurring.

Remember, historical is just that—it is what has happened in the past—so pay attention if the Ivol is extremely elevated or depressed.

Implied volatility: If the Ivol of the options are, let's say 40 percent hypothetically, then the market is pricing in some bigger potential moves for IBM. This could be due to perceived events in the stock itself, the sector, or even the market as a whole. Once you become more comfortable with the concept of volatility, you may be able to use this to your advantage; however, being knowledgeable about volatility doesn't mean that you'll be profitable. I generally will default to the higher volatility for a quick way of finding the probability of movement in a stock moving forward in the near term. So simply: if the implied volatility is greater, use it. If the historical volatility is great, then it might be my choice.

Exhibit 4.55 helps me get a gauge of IBM's "expected movement" so I can better select strikes. Buying a May 170 put may be way too far out of the money if there is only a 1 percent chance that it could get down there. Make sure you buy a put that offers realistic protection! At this point ($100), I am fairly happy with my return on the stock, and as long as it stayed above $90 per share I would be okay with that.

Let's also assume that for my account, if the stock went to $110 I would sell it. (Remember that the short call may obligate you to deliver the stock at the strike price you sell.) Based on this rationale, I have found my maximum loss amount of $10 ($100 share price minus $90 strike for put), and I am acceptable with the $110 on the high side. By now you are probably thinking, "How did you come up with the 110 call to sell?" Well, I did say earlier that it comes down to the cost and credit of the trade and the amount of downside protection that you want? So, hypothetically, looking at the 90 put with 160 days until expiration and the 110 call with 160 days to expiration, I can buy the put for $5.10 and sell the call for $5.10.

These prices allow me to put the collar on for free, minus commissions, which will hedge me if the stock

Smart Investor Tip!

While in the trade, you will still collect and retain any dividends paid. Be sure that you understand the potential tax implications if you are called away in your position or if you choose to exercise your long put. In addition, this strategy is complex and not suitable for all investors.

Here you see the histogram that enables you to view the observed dollar and percentage movements of a security. This can be used to more accurately predict future price distribution over a given time frame.

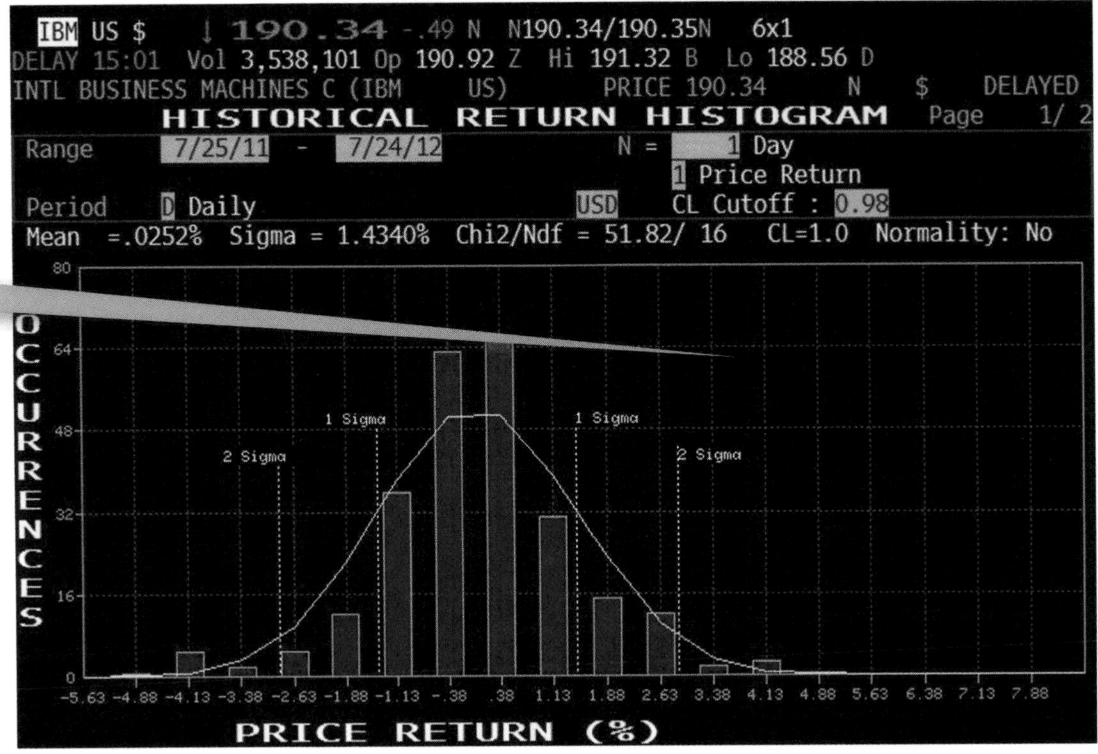

Exhibit 4.55

drops below $90 and may force me to sell my stock if it goes to $110.

My maximum risk in this particular trade from this point until options expiration is $10 (the stock is currently at $100).

No matter how low the stock goes, I will lock in a gain of $20 on the stock ($90 strike on put minus the $70 cost basis)—as long as my position is in effect. (This is what Bernard Madoff stated that he was doing, but indeed he did not actually place the trades.)

In trading, as well as in many parts of our lives, there is no such thing as a free lunch and in this case, because we sold the 110 call, I have limited my upside, so my maximum profit in this trade is $40. My cost basis is $70. The short call obligates me to sell the stock at $110 if it is trading above that number on expiration $110 – $70 = $40.

Some traders prefer to buy the put for as long as they intend on being in the trade and either selling a call in the same time frame or selling a call with 30 to 40 days to expiration (DTE) so they can take advantage of accelerated time decay in the last month. When using this method, expect the trade to be a debit if the strikes are spaced evenly apart. Remember that you can continue to sell a call the next month and potentially increase or decrease your strike price according to where the stock is at that point.

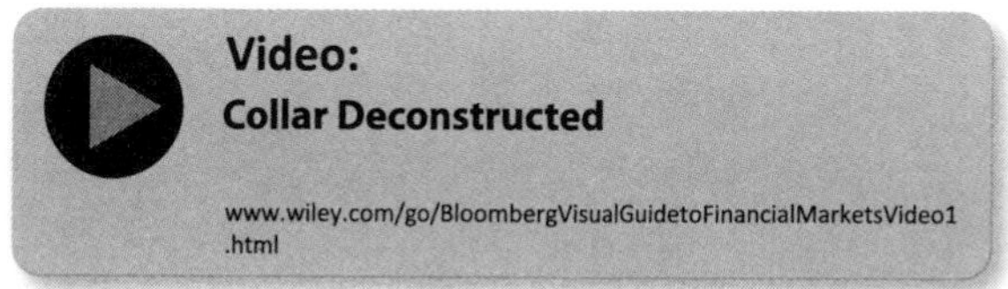

If the stock rallies with strength to the upside, a more advanced technique would be to buy back the call (potentially at a loss), which would uncap the potential return. Some traders may choose to resell the call and perhaps repurchase a put, both of them with higher strikes.

CHAPTER 5

Visualizing and Trading Vertical Spreads

Basic vertical spreads provide several advantages or unique trade characteristics and are a simple alternative for most beginning to intermediate option traders. For the advanced folks, they are great simple tools that can be quickly executed and augmented into many of the more complex strategies that are used. Most of the more complex strategies are comprised of two or more verticals either working in concert or opposition. All verticals have extremely concrete rules and behavioral characteristics native to only them. See Exhibit 5.1a and Exhibit 5.1b.

Verticals are my favorite option strategies because they are simple to employ and are also the building blocks of many other more complex strategies.

Vertical Spread Relationships and Risk

It doesn't matter what vertical spread (call or put) you use—they are all essentially the same; just look for the best ROR (return on risk) you can find and choose that one.

There is a difference when it comes to bullish or bearish verticals. I review the risk/reward and nuances of each. I also detail the methods, tactics, and tricks you can use to make the most of them.

DEFINITION:
Vertical
means that both call options expire in the same month. Nonratio means that for every one option (call or put) you buy, you only sell one option against it.

All bullish vertical spread risk graphs will have this shape: limited risk, limited reward, with the right side higher than the breakeven level.

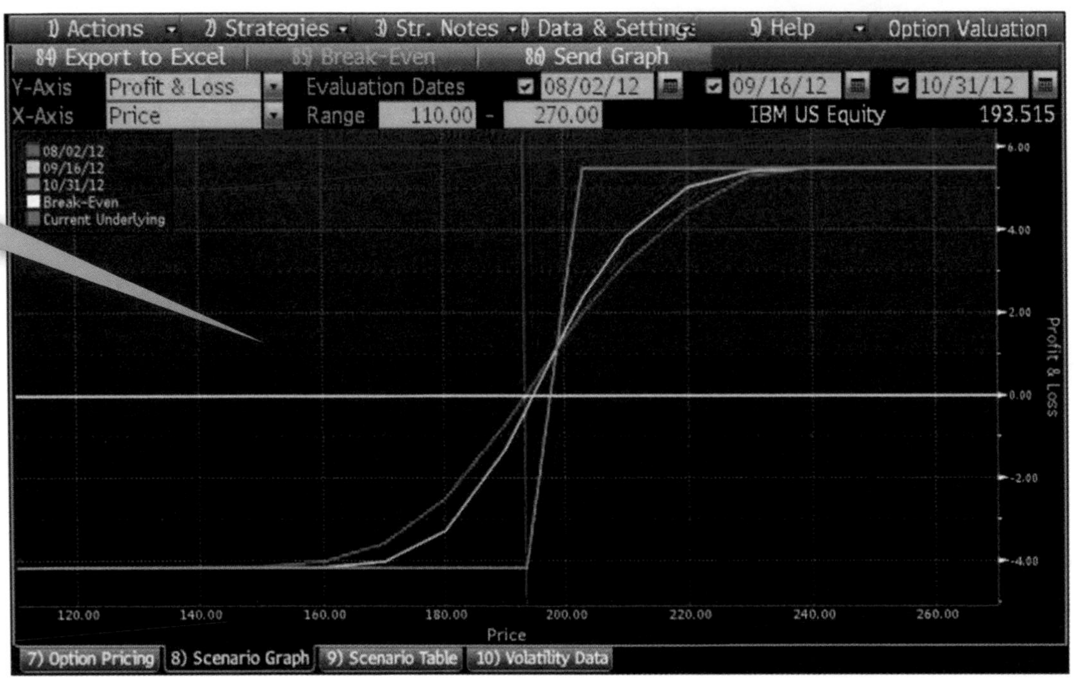

Exhibit 5.1a

KEY POINT:

Ratio vertical spreads or backspreads (I know backspreads as long gamma spreads) will buy or sell more of one option versus the other. For example, selling one 50 call and buying two 55 calls; these spreads will add elements of risk that are atypical of the risk/reward and behavioral traits of straight verticals. Margin effects will also differ. I discuss margin throughout this book, but it's best to consult your broker or cboe.com for specifics.

Here is an example of their similarities:

In-the-money *debit call* spread = Out-of-the-money *credit put* spread with same strikes and action (buy/sell)

In-the-money *debit put* spread = Out-of-the-money *credit call* spread with same strikes and action (buy/sell)

Credit Spreads versus Debit Spreads

So which do you choose? Selecting which spread to employ depends on several factors:

- Bullish or bearish
- Probability preference
- Credit or debit (comfort level, risk tolerance)

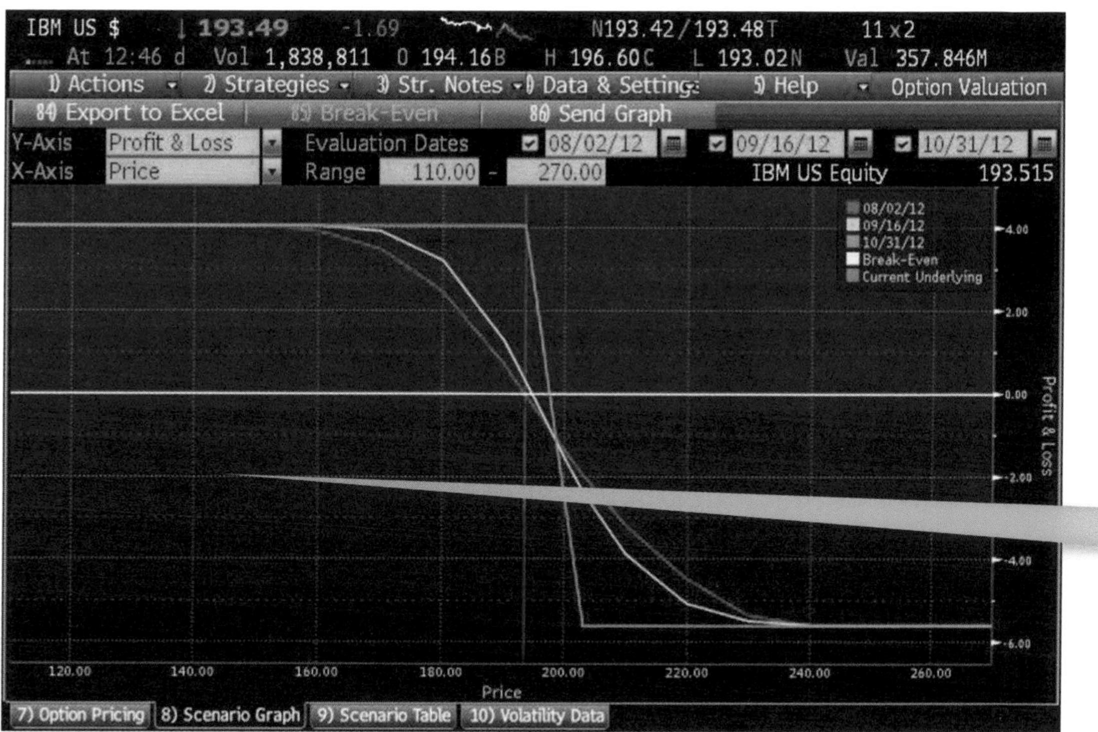

Bearish vertical spread risk graphs will be exactly the opposite, with profit as the stock moves below the breakeven level.

Exhibit 5.1b

- Price target in stock
- Cost or margin requirement

Whichever type you choose, just know that profit and loss (P&L) characteristics and the Greeks are the same when comparing puts to calls/debit to credit, but behavior can appear different in a credit/debit comparison (it's really not).

Whether you buy or sell a call spread or put spread, you have to get yourself familiar with the demeanor of that spread as well as the credit or debit nuances discussed previously. The ultimate factor when comparing a credit or debit spread should be which will you make the most money on and thus have the lowest risk.

Here are some of the characteristics of *all* vertical spreads:

- Negate certain Greek risks

  Because an option is bought while the other is sold. This is useful in a situation where you want to be directionally one-sided, but volatility is a bit rich or the skew is not favorable.

Visual example—UVXY

If you thought SPX volatility was going to rise and wanted to use option on the UVXY but didn't like the skew or the way Ivols were manipulated, you could use a vertical spread to neutralize your vega risk, lower your overall delta/cost risk, and increase probability in the trade compared to just buying the call or UVXY itself. See Exhibits 5.2, 5.3, and 5.4.

- Reduce cost of your debit trades.
  - Because a nonratio vertical spread will always contain one long and one short option, costs will always be less expensive than simply buying the one leg by itself. Stocks don't rise to infinity and it's very likely that you would be happy with a 20, 40, or even 70 percent return on your investment with a breakeven that's more favorable than buying a straight call or put.
  - Many vertical spreads can be structured to achieve this return.
- Limit your risk by adding a long option to your naked short (credit) trades.
  - Selling a naked option can not only expose you to a large amount of risk, but it can eat up your margin, prohibiting you from placing other trades. By purchasing a long option against your short to create a vertical spread, you are limiting your risk and capping your margin requirements to the width of your spread!
  - You can do this on the fly if you want to free up capital or have concerns about a volatile short-term move in the stock.
    - In this case you would be legging into the trade and you could theoretically trade out of one side or the other to morph the trade back to its original form or completely reverse the trade altogether.
- Increased probability.
  - By purchasing long vertical spreads that are in the money, or selling verticals out of the money,

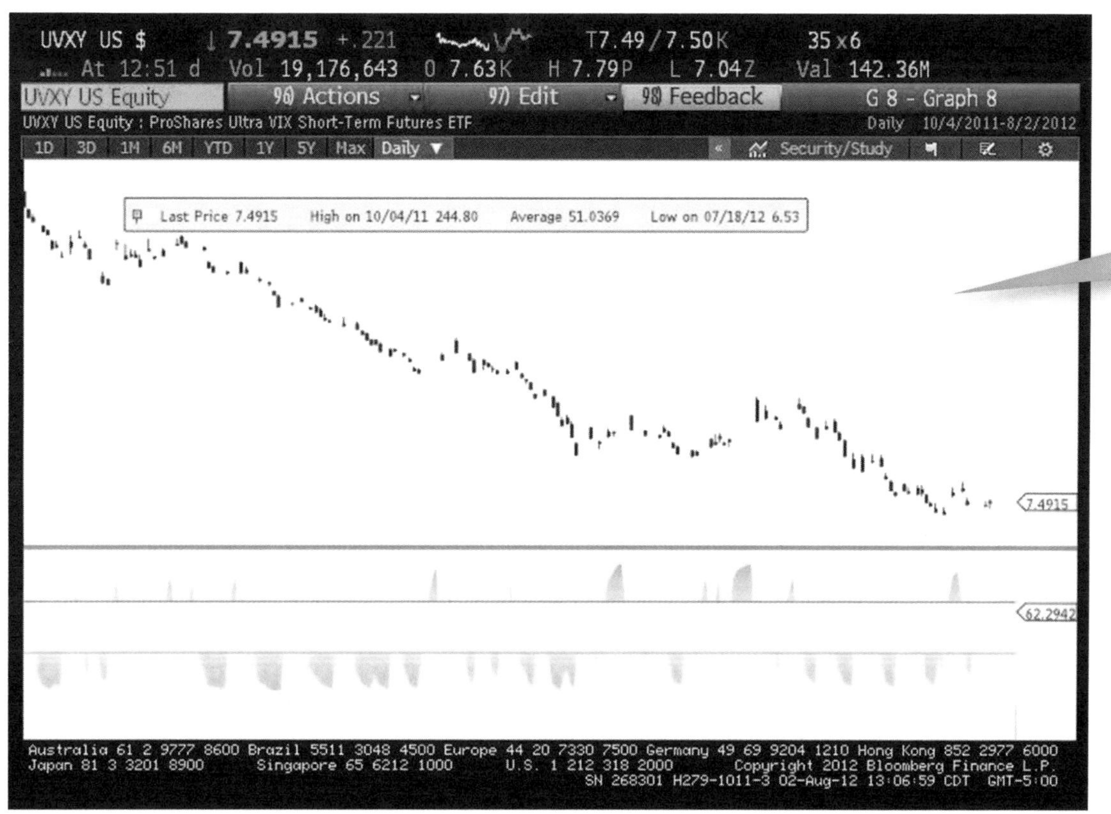

Here you can see that UVXY is trading at an all-time low; contrarians might be looking for a rally from these levels.

Exhibit 5.2

Ivol is just slightly higher than Hvol, but the issue here is more about the SKEW and manipulation/variation of Ivol, which could have detrimental effects on the purchase of a long call even if UVXY rallies.

Exhibit 5.3

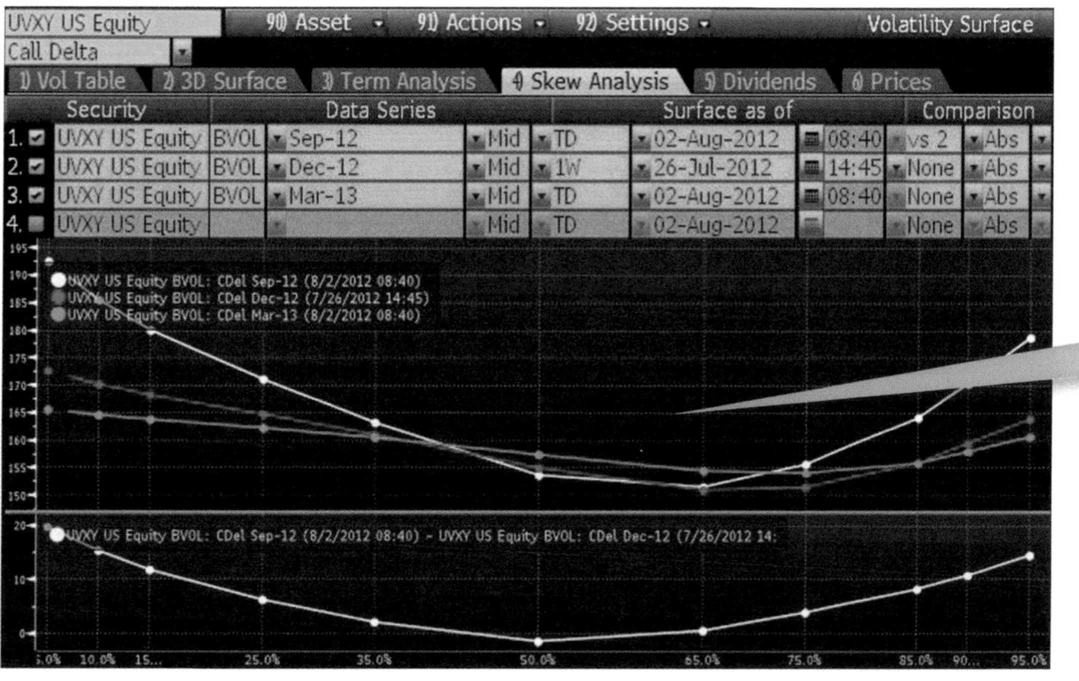

The SKEW screen tells the story here and shows us the dramatic difference in Ivol between the ATM and OTM options. This might be the perfect scenario for a vertical spread to neutralize the vega of the position.

Exhibit 5.4

Instead of buying just a long ITM call in a volatile stock like GOOG, consider the purchase of a vertical call spread, which will reduce your breakeven and increase probability (GOOG was trading at $624).

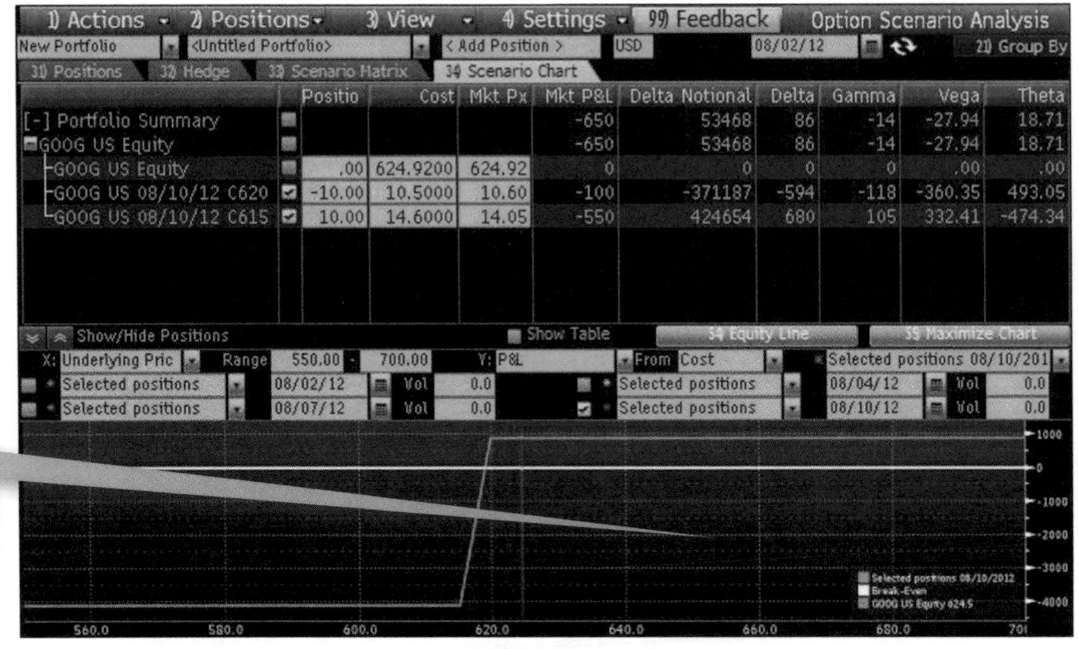

	Positio	Cost	Mkt Px	Mkt P&L	Delta Notional	Delta	Gamma	Vega	Theta
[-] Portfolio Summary				-650	53468	86	-14	-27.94	18.71
GOOG US Equity				-650	53468	86	-14	-27.94	18.71
GOOG US Equity	.00	624.9200	624.92	0	0	0	0	.00	.00
GOOG US 08/10/12 C620	-10.00	10.5000	10.60	-100	-371187	-594	-118	-360.35	493.05
GOOG US 08/10/12 C615	10.00	14.6000	14.05	-550	424654	680	105	332.41	-474.34

Exhibit 5.5

you are inherently increasing the statistical probability of success of your trade. The trade-off is that your profit is limited, but for some scenarios this strategy will make the most sense, especially in sideways transitional markets that are lacking strong directional trends. See Exhibit 5.5.

Put Credit Spread/Call Debit Spread—Bullish Verticals

For this book, I group the spreads slightly differently for better comprehension. Because both the bull-call and bull-put spreads have the same exact behaviors when it comes to the relation to the stock price, they are

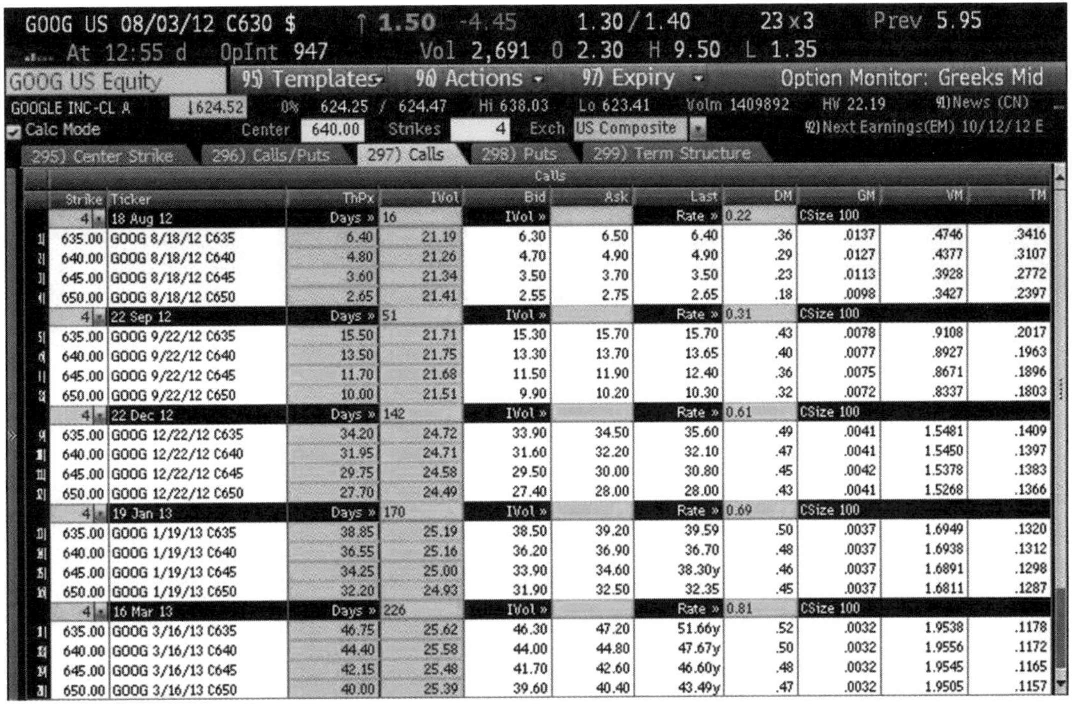

GOOG US 08/03/12 C630 $ ↑ 1.50 -4.45 1.30 / 1.40 23 x 3 Prev 5.95
At 12:55 d OpInt 947 Vol 2,691 O 2.30 H 9.50 L 1.35
GOOG US Equity 95) Templates 96) Actions 97) Expiry Option Monitor: Greeks Mid
GOOGLE INC-CL A ↓624.52 0% 624.25 / 624.47 Hi 638.03 Lo 623.41 Volm 1409892 HV 22.19 91) News (CN)
Calc Mode Center 640.00 Strikes 4 Exch US Composite 92) Next Earnings(EM) 10/12/12 E
295) Center Strike 296) Calls/Puts 297) Calls 298) Puts 299) Term Structure

Calls

Strike	Ticker	ThPx	IVol	Bid	Ask	Last	DM	GM	VM	TM
4	18 Aug 12	Days »	16	IVol »		Rate »	0.22	CSize 100		
635.00	GOOG 8/18/12 C635	6.40	21.19	6.30	6.50	6.40	.36	.0137	.4746	.3416
640.00	GOOG 8/18/12 C640	4.80	21.26	4.70	4.90	4.90	.29	.0127	.4377	.3107
645.00	GOOG 8/18/12 C645	3.60	21.34	3.50	3.70	3.50	.23	.0113	.3928	.2772
650.00	GOOG 8/18/12 C650	2.65	21.41	2.55	2.75	2.65	.18	.0098	.3427	.2397
4	22 Sep 12	Days »	51	IVol »		Rate »	0.31	CSize 100		
635.00	GOOG 9/22/12 C635	15.50	21.71	15.30	15.70	15.70	.43	.0078	.9108	.2017
640.00	GOOG 9/22/12 C640	13.50	21.75	13.30	13.70	13.65	.40	.0077	.8927	.1963
645.00	GOOG 9/22/12 C645	11.70	21.68	11.50	11.90	12.40	.36	.0075	.8671	.1896
650.00	GOOG 9/22/12 C650	10.00	21.51	9.90	10.20	10.30	.32	.0072	.8337	.1803
4	22 Dec 12	Days »	142	IVol »		Rate »	0.61	CSize 100		
635.00	GOOG 12/22/12 C635	34.20	24.72	33.90	34.50	35.60	.49	.0041	1.5481	.1409
640.00	GOOG 12/22/12 C640	31.95	24.71	31.60	32.20	32.10	.47	.0041	1.5450	.1397
645.00	GOOG 12/22/12 C645	29.75	24.58	29.50	30.00	30.80	.45	.0042	1.5378	.1383
650.00	GOOG 12/22/12 C650	27.70	24.49	27.40	28.00	28.00	.43	.0041	1.5268	.1366
4	19 Jan 13	Days »	170	IVol »		Rate »	0.69	CSize 100		
635.00	GOOG 1/19/13 C635	38.85	25.19	38.50	39.20	39.59	.50	.0037	1.6949	.1320
640.00	GOOG 1/19/13 C640	36.55	25.16	36.20	36.90	36.70	.48	.0037	1.6938	.1312
645.00	GOOG 1/19/13 C645	34.25	25.00	33.90	34.60	38.30y	.46	.0037	1.6891	.1298
650.00	GOOG 1/19/13 C650	32.20	24.93	31.90	32.50	32.35	.45	.0037	1.6811	.1287
4	16 Mar 13	Days »	226	IVol »		Rate »	0.81	CSize 100		
635.00	GOOG 3/16/13 C635	46.75	25.62	46.30	47.20	51.66y	.52	.0032	1.9538	.1178
640.00	GOOG 3/16/13 C640	44.40	25.58	44.00	44.80	47.67y	.50	.0032	1.9556	.1172
645.00	GOOG 3/16/13 C645	42.15	25.48	41.70	42.60	46.60y	.48	.0032	1.9545	.1165
650.00	GOOG 3/16/13 C650	40.00	25.39	39.60	40.40	43.49y	.47	.0032	1.9505	.1157

Exhibit 5.6

completely interchangeable and essentially the same, except that the bull put gives you your max profit up front and the bull call costs your max risk up front.

Now, if you vary the strike selection, width of the strikes, and the premium paid or received then you will have variances in comparative behavior and P&L. But if you select the same strikes and month of a put spread to sell, the call spread you buy will behave the same.

You should get your mind accustomed to the fact that calls and puts are essentially one in the same and call and put spreads are also relatively identical.

There are some situations where one is preferred over the other, but the only deciding factor is that there is the price paid or premium collected in one versus the other. The exceptions generally are on stocks that are either hard to borrow or in assets where put-call parity doesn't hold. VIX options are one of the exceptions, as are assets that have extremely wide bid-ask spreads. In that case, it is usually advisable to choose the spread that is more out of the money. So if you are bullish, you sell an out-of-the-money put spread (if you are choosing probability over return) and vice versa if you are bearish.

Bullish Vertical Spreads

Bullish vertical spreads can be used to express many different levels of bullishness, time durations, and probabilities. Here are the three basic formats that the trade may take. These general plans should contain much more specific criteria to get the risk/reward and cost right where you want them. Everything revolves around how high and how fast you think an asset can rise in value over a period of time.

Extremely bullish over the long term, but want to reduce cost (see Exhibit 5.6):

- Two-month to two-year expiration bull vertical spreads that are placed far above the stock price can be used to express a **low-probability, low-cost, high-return outlook** if you believe that the stock is going to explode above a certain level by a given period of time.

  These bullish verticals will usually be call spreads, because they will be out of the money and generally have tighter bid-ask spreads. They are great to use when Ivol skew is elevated to the upside because the vertical spread negates the vega risk in the trade to an extent. The short call (or put) should be placed at a level that you feel the stock will be above come expiration.

  Break-even and max profit levels will always be higher than the current stock price, but it will be cheaper than just buying a call outright.

Moderately bullish over the long term (see Exhibit 5.7):

- Six-month to two-year expiration bull vertical spreads that are placed just at or above the stock price can be used to express a more balanced probability and return scenario with low cost where you think the stock will gradually rise in value over the short strike over a given period of time.

  Breakeven will be at or slightly above the current stock price, but max profit will be above the current stock price.

Neutral to moderately bullish in the short term (see Exhibit 5.8):

- Ten-day to two-month expiration bull vertical spreads that are placed right at or below the stock price can be used to express a high probability, slightly lower return with moderate cost where you think the stock can simply stay above a certain level.

  This strike positioning will allow you to better use the bull put spread, because the puts will now start to be equal price or cheaper than the calls and have a propensity for tighter bid-ask spreads.

  Breakeven will generally be lower than the current stock price, allowing the stock a little more bearish leeway. You can also position strikes so

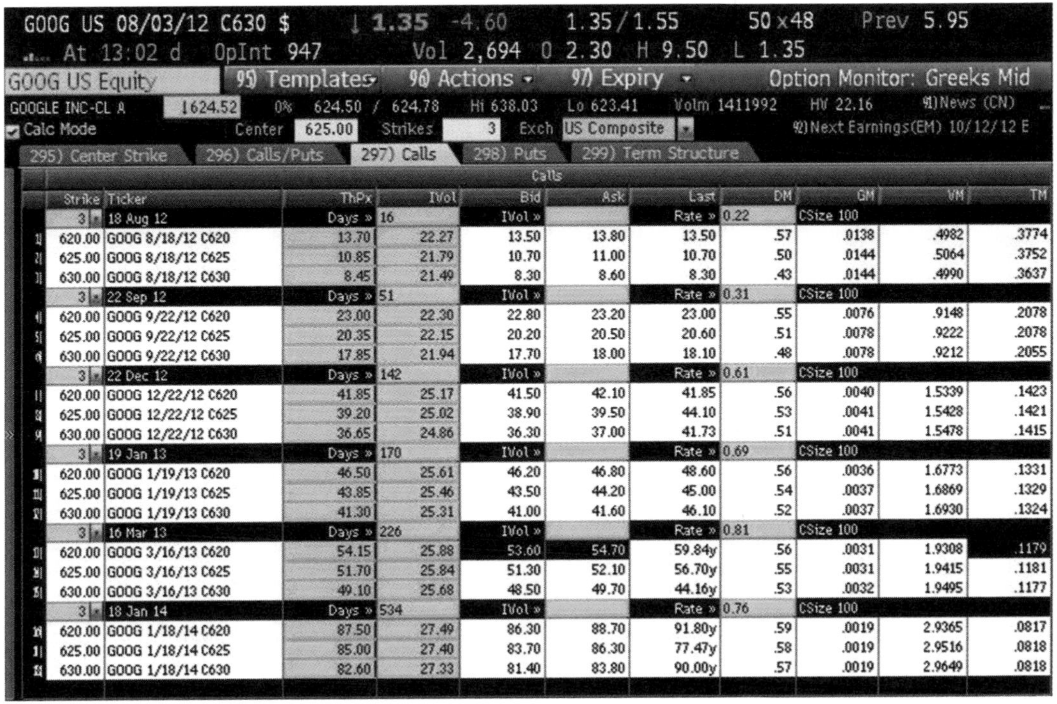

GOOG US 08/03/12 C630 $ ↓1.35 -4.60 1.35/1.55 50x48 Prev 5.95
At 13:02 d OpInt 947 Vol 2,694 O 2.30 H 9.50 L 1.35
GOOG US Equity 95) Templates 96) Actions 97) Expiry Option Monitor: Greeks Mid
GOOGLE INC-CL A ↓624.52 0% 624.50 / 624.78 Hi 638.03 Lo 623.41 Volm 1411992 HV 22.16 91) News (CN)
Calc Mode Center 625.00 Strikes 3 Exch US Composite 92) Next Earnings(EM) 10/12/12 E
295) Center Strike 296) Calls/Puts 297) Calls 298) Puts 299) Term Structure

Calls

Strike	Ticker	ThPx	IVol	Bid	Ask	Last	DM	GM	VM	TM
3	18 Aug 12	Days »	16	IVol »		Rate »	0.22	CSize 100		
620.00	GOOG 8/18/12 C620	13.70	22.27	13.50	13.80	13.50	.57	.0138	.4982	.3774
625.00	GOOG 8/18/12 C625	10.85	21.79	10.70	11.00	10.70	.50	.0144	.5064	.3752
630.00	GOOG 8/18/12 C630	8.45	21.49	8.30	8.60	8.30	.43	.0144	.4990	.3637
3	22 Sep 12	Days »	51	IVol »		Rate »	0.31	CSize 100		
620.00	GOOG 9/22/12 C620	23.00	22.30	22.80	23.20	23.00	.55	.0076	.9148	.2078
625.00	GOOG 9/22/12 C625	20.35	22.15	20.20	20.50	20.60	.51	.0078	.9222	.2078
630.00	GOOG 9/22/12 C630	17.85	21.94	17.70	18.00	18.10	.48	.0078	.9212	.2055
3	22 Dec 12	Days »	142	IVol »		Rate »	0.61	CSize 100		
620.00	GOOG 12/22/12 C620	41.85	25.17	41.50	42.10	41.85	.56	.0040	1.5339	.1423
625.00	GOOG 12/22/12 C625	39.20	25.02	38.90	39.50	44.10	.53	.0041	1.5428	.1421
630.00	GOOG 12/22/12 C630	36.65	24.86	36.30	37.00	41.73	.51	.0041	1.5478	.1415
3	19 Jan 13	Days »	170	IVol »		Rate »	0.69	CSize 100		
620.00	GOOG 1/19/13 C620	46.50	25.61	46.20	46.80	48.60	.56	.0036	1.6773	.1331
625.00	GOOG 1/19/13 C625	43.85	25.46	43.50	44.20	45.00	.54	.0037	1.6869	.1329
630.00	GOOG 1/19/13 C630	41.30	25.31	41.00	41.60	46.10	.52	.0037	1.6930	.1324
3	16 Mar 13	Days »	226	IVol »		Rate »	0.81	CSize 100		
620.00	GOOG 3/16/13 C620	54.15	25.88	53.60	54.70	59.84y	.56	.0031	1.9308	.1179
625.00	GOOG 3/16/13 C625	51.70	25.84	51.30	52.10	56.70y	.55	.0031	1.9415	.1181
630.00	GOOG 3/16/13 C630	49.10	25.68	48.50	49.70	44.16y	.53	.0032	1.9495	.1177
3	18 Jan 14	Days »	534	IVol »		Rate »	0.76	CSize 100		
620.00	GOOG 1/18/14 C620	87.50	27.49	86.30	88.70	91.80y	.59	.0019	2.9365	.0817
625.00	GOOG 1/18/14 C625	85.00	27.40	83.70	86.30	77.47y	.58	.0019	2.9516	.0818
630.00	GOOG 1/18/14 C630	82.60	27.33	81.40	83.80	90.00y	.57	.0019	2.9649	.0818

Exhibit 5.7

the break-even and max profit levels are *below* the stock, like the chain you see in Exhibit 5.5.

With either of these scenarios, they will each have the following general behaviors:

How you will win everything:

Stock stays above your short strike by expiration (call or put spread).

How you can get hurt:

Stock stays flat up to expiration. If you positioned your vertical spread *below* the stock price when the trade was initiated, a stock that stays flat can actually allow you to attain maximum profit in the trade as long as it's above strike upon expiry.

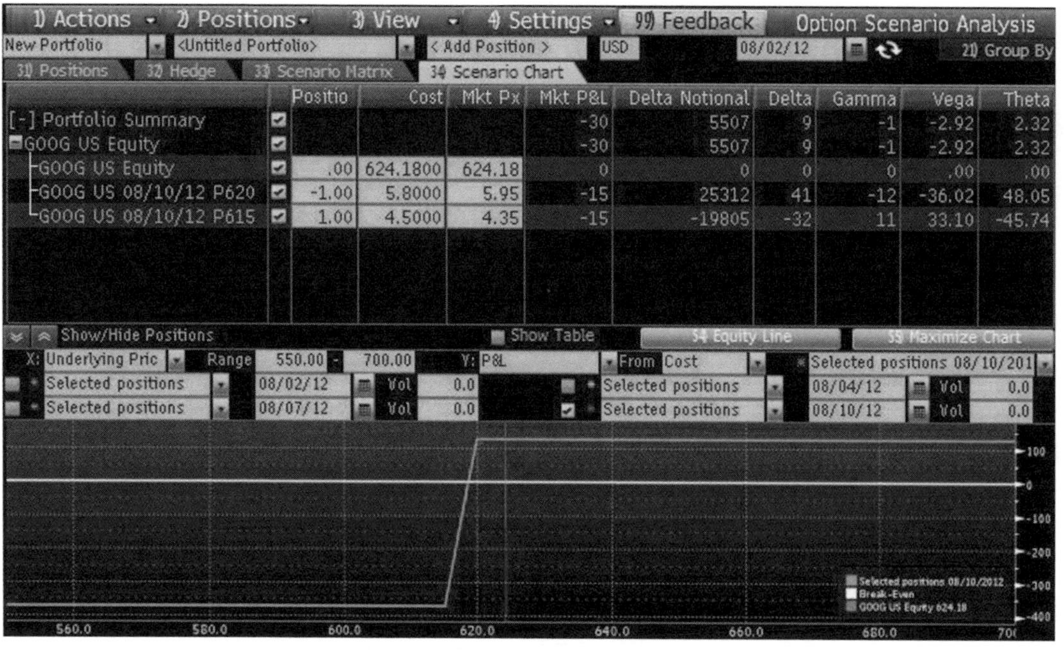

Exhibit 5.8

If you positioned your bullish vertical strikes above the stock price on entering, then this will hurt you.

Stock drops. Depending on where your strikes are positioned, the level of pain you feel will vary. There are cases where the bullish vertical is so far below the stock price that a modest drop can still turn out to be good for the spread.

If the spread is at or above the stock price when you put the trade on, you will feel more pain. The most volatility will be felt when the spread is at the money.

Bullish Vertical Spread Greek Attributes

Exhibit 5.9 shows examples of bullish put and call spreads. Apples to apples, they are the same; however,

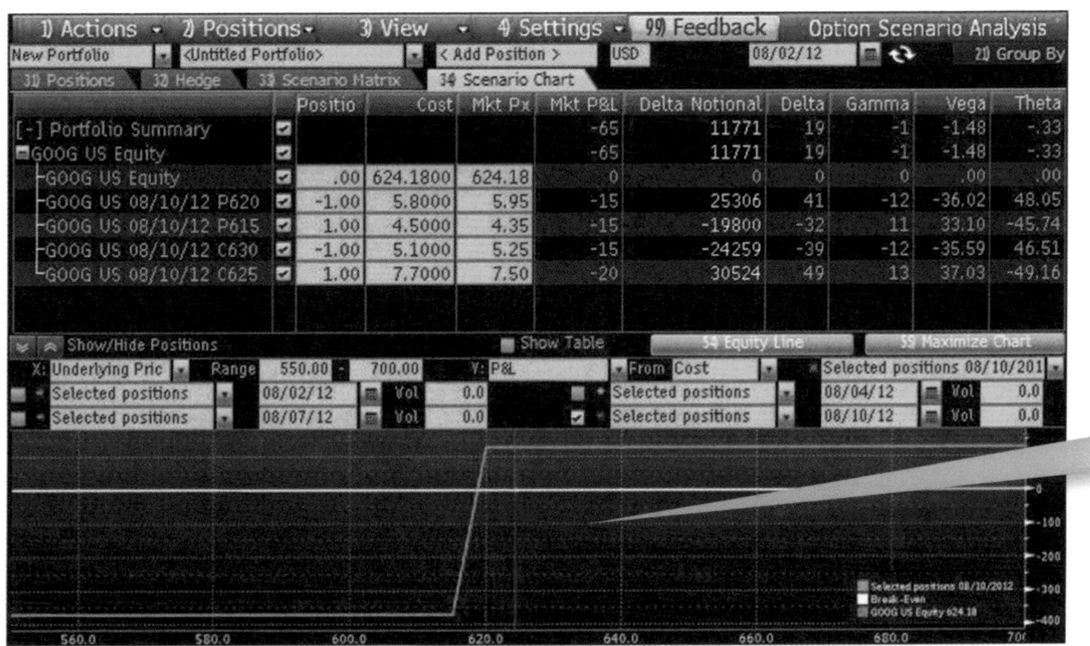

	Positio	Cost	Mkt Px	Mkt P&L	Delta Notional	Delta	Gamma	Vega	Theta
[-] Portfolio Summary				-65	11771	19	-1	-1.48	-.33
GOOG US Equity				-65	11771	19	-1	-1.48	-.33
GOOG US Equity	.00	624.1800	624.18	0	0	0	0	.00	.00
GOOG US 08/10/12 P620	-1.00	5.8000	5.95	-15	25306	41	-12	-36.02	48.05
GOOG US 08/10/12 P615	1.00	4.5000	4.35	-15	-19800	-32	11	33.10	-45.74
GOOG US 08/10/12 C630	-1.00	5.1000	5.25	-15	-24259	-39	-12	-35.59	46.51
GOOG US 08/10/12 C625	1.00	7.7000	7.50	-20	30524	49	13	37.03	-49.16

Look at the risk graph; even though I have a bull call and a bull put spread in the scenario graph, the line is unchanged. This is because they are identical in risk!

Exhibit 5.9

their relation to the stock (in, at, out of the money will be opposite). As you go through the Greeks, remember that both the long call spread and the short put spread want the stock to move higher. When the stock is moving up and down, the Greeks for both spreads will change almost identically. Again, the only difference is that out-of-the-money puts will be the same as in-the-money calls and vice versa.

Delta

Always positive—Delta can range from 0.02 to 0.98.

Call spread—The call spread delta is highest when it's just ATM (in between strikes selected). As the stock moves higher, the call spread will lose delta because both calls are moving to 0 deltas. If the call spread continues to move very deep in the money, the delta will eventually decline to zero.

Put spread—Like the calls, the most delta will be when the spread is just at the money or in between strikes. It will decrease as the stock moves up or down outside either strike.

Gamma

Varies—Can range from positive to negative depending on position of stock in relation to strikes.

Call spread—Gamma will be positive if the stock is generally in the middle or *below* the midpoint between the strikes, generally peaking just below the long strike. It will start to get negative as the stock moves above the center point of the strikes. When this is happening, you are moving into your profitable zone. Once the stock eclipses the short strike to the upside, it begins to move to zero. At that point the calls will both be in the money.

Put spread—Gamma will be positive if the stock is generally in the middle or *below* the midpoint between the strikes, generally peaking when the stock moves just below the long strike. It will start to get negative as the stock moves above the center point of the strikes. When this is happening, you are moving into your profitable zone. Once the stock eclipses the short strike to the upside, it begins to move to zero. At that point the puts will both be out of the money.

The closer the short option is to the stock price, the more variance you will have in your P&L.

Theta

Varies—Can range from positive to negative depending on position of stock in relation to strikes.

The simple rule to remember for the theta, as it pertains to your profitability, is to know that if the stock is *above* your breakeven, then time decay is generally helping you (positive).

- If the stock is *below* your breakeven, that time decay is hurting you.
- If both strikes of a call spread are *in the money*, then theta will always be positive.
- If both strikes of a put spread are *out of the money*, then theta will always be positive.

The contrary is also true for both.

Vega

Varies—Can range from positive to negative depending on position of stock in relation to strikes.

Call and put spread—Vega will be positive if the stock is generally in the middle or *below* the midpoint between the strikes, generally peaking just at or below the long strike. It will start to get negative as the stock moves above the center point of the strikes. When this is happening, you are moving into your profitable zone. Once the stock eclipses the short strike to the upside, it will peak and then begin to move to zero.

Rho

Minimal risk—Because one strike negates the other.

However, if you have a very expensive stock and your strikes are extremely wide, with a year or more until expiration, you could have exposure, especially if you are trading a large amount of contracts.

If you are trading these types of spreads, check the rho in your calculator.

Advantages

Both bullish vertical choices have their pros and cons. Depending on the positioning of strikes in relation to the stock and how wide they are, those pros and cons may not only ebb and flow, but completely reverse each other. Wherever you see an asterisk (*), there may be two sides to that attribute. Let me explain:

Time decay—When the stock is *above* the short strike of a bull put or bull call, time decay is absolutely on your side. As the stock drops below your break-even point between strikes, theta turns negative and starts hurting you. The further out of the money you sell the put spread or deeper in the money you buy the call spread can help to ensure that time will work for you in the trade.

Protection—Protection can come in many forms in the bullish vertical spread. When you think about it one way, the long side of the spread is protection against disaster with the short side of the spread.

Because verticals tend to mitigate the effects of most Greeks, they can also protect you against overexposure to any one Greek. The tighter the strikes in the spread are to one another, the less exposure you will have to each Greek. I talk more about this when we discuss strike positioning.

You can use the spread itself to hedge a long or short stock or option position.

Risk reduction—Risk can be reduced in several ways using verticals. The most apparent is the reduced cost of a vertical spread versus the purchase of the option alone.

Risk reduction also occurs because of the coverage that the long option provides against the short.

Finally, as discussed earlier, you can use techniques to reduce exposure to certain Greeks.

Flexibility—Depending on just how bullish you are or what you find to be the advantages in the trade, you have an extraordinarily wide selection of spreads to choose from. Don't feel limited by some of the theoretical constraints of the vertical spread. If you fiddle around enough with the months, strikes, and widths between spreads, you are bound to find something that interests you.

Disadvantages

Limited upside—In the case of a debit vertical spread, the most you can make is the difference between strikes minus the debit paid. The farther out of the money you buy that vertical, the higher the upside potential, but the probability obviously goes down. The opposite is true for spreads that are positioned at or in the money (already in their profitable area).

Although these seem like detriments, you can still buy a statistically advantaged spread (one where the stock can move against you and you can still make a profit) and make 90 percent on your trade. Is that so bad?

> **Smart Investor Tip!**
>
> If you are long 1,000 shares of SPY for a long-term trade, you might want to employ a collar if you believe the market could experience a short-term pullback. But let's say you find the levels and strikes you want to use but you would have to pay for the collar; you should actually use a *bear*-put vertical instead of the put and maybe get a credit to do the trade. Just make sure that you place your short put strike at the lowest level you feel the market can go.

KEY POINT:

Use the calculator in the OSA screen to advance your time and price to a realistic target for the underlying asset. If your $5 spread will be worth about $4.50 at that point, then either accept that as your profit target or trying widening or narrowing strikes until you find a profit/loss trajectory that agrees with your thesis.

KEY POINT:

Assume you find a fairly bullish candidate (XYZ) through a fundamental scan. In your technical and news analysis you find that markets are overbought and news is mixed. XYZ is trading at $52.20 and you notice that there is a ton of support around the $50 level.

If XYZ lacks the near-term catalysts needed to propel this stock higher, you might consider selling the 50/45 put spread for $1.70.

In this case, you have a strong bullish foundation with support that may be lacking further bullish motivation.

You can also make 52 percent on your risk, even if the stock slides $2.20. Not bad.

In credit spreads, the only profit you can make is the credit you brought in at the onset of the trade. There are cases where you can lose more than you make. This is also true of debit spreads if you have a statistical advantage in the trade.

The reality is that stocks don't rise to infinity nor do they generally fall to zero from $100 in a matter of a couple months. If you use what you have learned in your fundamental and technical analysis, you should be able to form a realistic best-and worst-case scenario for a stock. Use those levels to guide your strike selection.

Max profit nuances—With all vertical spreads there are some differences if you are coming from the long call/long put world. An example of the most common frustration is if you were to buy a 50/55 call spread and the stock goes to $55.25 about a month before the spread is set to expire. You were right in your thesis, but instead of the spread being worth $5 (like it would be on expiration) it is trading for $4.

The reason for this is the time value that is left in the short strike. That time value prevents the spread from getting to its max value. For more volatile stocks, that spread would be worth even less because the Ivol of that short option would be higher.

There are two ways to mitigate this behavior:

1. If you are bullish, place your vertical spread way below the stock price. The farther away from the short strike it is, the more profit you will see from your spread.

   If you are bearish, then place your vertical spread above the stock price. You may sacrifice a little profit because of positioning, but those options that are farther from the stock will lose time value before those at the money options do. It generally doesn't matter whether you use calls or puts; it's all about position.
2. If you buy or sell a spread, try to use the shortest expiration possible that still allows the stock to get above or below the point you want it to. In other words, be precise. If you believe that the stock can get to $55 in two months, don't buy six months of time. If you buy more time, the stock will have to move farther for the spread to reach max value.

Targeting a Bullish Vertical

Like all strategies, you should complete a series of consistent steps to arrive at the most probable trade.

Step 1: Identifying the Target

The target for a bullish vertical can be as bullish as a high delta call candidate or less bullish than a buy-write.

Although the conditions can vary, it is still preferred to have an overall bullish thesis from the macro down to the stock.

If you have come this far in the guide, you obviously know how to identify bullish candidates. From there, depending on what the charts and fundamentals are doing, you can fine-tune your trade by using the vertical.

Step 2: Fundamental Analysis

Start with the same analysis you would do for a long call or long stock and as you go through the grading system and are finding several flaws in the trade or perhaps a chance that the level of bullishness in the stock or broad market is not worthy of a big delta trade like a call or stock, then start looking for strong support levels and trends in the charts that may make the trade more suited for a bullish vertical spread.

The optimal fundamental scenario for a bullish vertical can vary. The data to focus on are:

Ivol/Hvol— If Ivol is too high for a single call, use the vertical to offset risk.

Stagnant sector—If the stock's sector doesn't seem to have many catalysts for explosive upside growth than consider a bullish vertical at or below the stock price to lower your breakeven below the stock price.

Earnings or important economic data—If there is an earnings report in the near term or a major economic event or decision like interest rates on the horizon, you can add both a statistical advantage and risk reduction by using a vertical. In this case, you can adjust the width and position of the spread to find a delta and breakeven that suits your opinion.

Step 3: Technical Analysis

Again, most of the bullish spreads are going to want the same technical trends that long call or long stock players want to see. The caveat is that the formations don't necessarily have to be "as bullish." You can lean more on support levels with a bullish vertical that is at or below the stock price as opposed to "needing" a bullish catalyst as you would with a long call. In other words, if you have stable fundamentals and a strong support level you feel the stock won't go below (as opposed to indicators pointing to a strong move higher), the bull vertical would be a potential candidate.

If you trade a bullish vertical that is **above** the stock price, you will be looking for the same bullish catalysts you would want with a long call or long stock, but the vertical could be used to reduce risk.

Step 4: Selecting the Bullish Vertical Spread

This section is large because I detail the nuances of strike selection, time, risk, and other variables in both the call and put verticals.

Strike Price Width Considerations

Determining the width of your spread and which strikes to buy and sell is really a matter of personal risk tolerance, behavioral preference, and sentiment on the stock. Depending on the relationship of the strikes themselves to the stock and whether you are bullish or bearish, there are an infinite number of width configurations to constructing a vertical spread.

Here are some quick basic relationships and positioning guidelines to help guide you into the right spread. Before you trade anything, be sure to run the

Smart Investor Tip!

Just because the vertical spread will generally have a lower delta and lower cost than the comparable long call, it doesn't mean that you should buy more of the verticals to get to the delta of the long call, unless you are extremely bullish and/or feel the breakeven in the bull call spread justifies the delta.

KEY POINT:

For all bullish verticals, you will have a bullish market sentiment, which will vary depending on where you place the spread.

The higher the spread strikes are in relation to the stock, the more bullish you are. The wider the spread is, the greater the reward and the risk as well.

Smart Investor Tip!

If you are only selling the short portion of your vertical spread for less than 20 cents, just make sure it's worth it. For a $1 spread where you capture 20 cents, that may not be bad, but if you trade a spread $5 wide or more, it may not be worth it to cap your profits (call spread) for 20 cents. Just be aware of your risk/reward and the values of your options.

Smart Investor Tip!

For stocks priced from $20 to $100 I generally choose spreads that are $5 wide; for stocks over $100, I may increase that to $10. For lower-price stocks and some ETFs, I may reduce my spread width to $2 or even a dollar if there are strikes at every dollar. Because I like odds in favor of and not against me, I tend to position bull vertical spreads at or below the stock price.

Greeks in the calculator screen. This is because just about all your Greeks will change as you widen and narrow your spread.

Let's compare two call spreads that both share the same long strike, but one has a short strike $5 away (we say $5 wide) and the other is $10 wide. Notice the differences in risk and Greek exposure! It's not that one is better than the other, but what risk do you want to have, given the research you have done on the stock?

- Are you more bullish? Then widen out the spread.
- Less bullish, tighten the spread up.
- Concerned that Ivol is way too high, then narrow the spread (notice the vega in the comparison).
- Wider spreads will have *greater* sensitivity to all the Greeks. See Exhibit 5.10.

The more you test strike-width scenarios and how they behave, the easier and quicker the selection process will be.

Spread Positioning

The spread width and actual positioning of the spread in relation to the underlying spot price should be a harmonious process. Adjust both until you find the breakeven, risk, and Greek characteristics that you are comfortable with.

The further your spread is above the stock price, the cheaper it will be, in turn offering you the potential for an increased return. Because there is no such thing as a free lunch, those spreads placed above the spot price are less likely to be profitable on expiration.

If you are less bullish, move your short strike lower. If markets are shaky you might want to put both options below the stock price; just be prepared to pay more (margin on puts) and get less return.

Bullish vertical spread behavior will vary greatly depending on the positioning and width of strikes. Remember that bullish spreads placed above the spot price will be costing you theta each day and will be looking for volatility to increase. See Exhibit 5.11.

Bull vertical spreads placed below the spot price will allow you to collect theta. Think about what you are trying to accomplish and be *realistic!*

If you find a stock that has a high probability of exploding to the upside, position yourself in a bullish vertical spread that is wide and above the spot price to get the most bang for your buck.

At the end of the day your thought process should revolve around rationalizing the short option strike with past stock movements, technical levels, volatility, or you can even use forward earnings projections combined with your short-call strike price to see if the P/E ratio at that price at some finite point in the future is feasible.

Setting Realistic Goals (Advanced)

You can use technical levels, sentiment and analysts' price targets to rationalize a realistic return (and risk) on a bullish vertical spread.

Think in terms of the risk/reward of the spread itself and combine those elements with realistic price movements that have been observed in a stock. Let's

1) Actions 2) Positions 3) View 4) Settings 99) Feedback Option Scenario Analysis

New Portfolio <Untitled Portfolio> < Add Position > USD 08/02/12 21) Group By

31) Positions 32) Hedge 33) Scenario Matrix 34) Scenario Chart

	Positio	Cost	Mkt Px	Mkt P&L	Delta Notional	Delta	Gamma	Vega	Theta
[-] Portfolio Summary				-18	7486	39	1	11.94	-2.24
IBM US Equity				-18	7486	39	1	11.94	-2.24
IBM US Equity	.00	193.4900	193.49	0	0	0	0	.00	.00
IBM US 09/22/12 C200	-1.00	1.9400	1.98	-4	-5471	-28	-6	-24.03	4.02
IBM US 09/22/12 C195	1.00	3.9500	3.90	-5	8540	44	6	28.13	-5.00
IBM US 10/20/12 C205	-1.00	2.0900	2.11	-2	-4639	-24	-4	-27.58	3.17
IBM US 10/20/12 C195	1.00	5.8500	5.77	-8	9056	47	5	35.42	-4.43

53) Scenario Actions Scenario Varying U/Px Notional P&L From Cost

	U/Px	Vol	Date	Rate	P&L	P&L %	Delta	Gamma	Theta	Vega
	Step	Flat	0	Flat						
			--/--/--							
71)	175.00	0.00	08/02/12	0.00	-499.04	-86.49	11.41	2.28	-2.01	13.9
72)	180.00	0.00	08/02/12	0.00	-424.42	-73.56	19.04	3.05	-2.85	18.81
73)	185.00	0.00	08/02/12	0.00	-308.13	-53.4	27.84	3.22	-3.3	20.72
74)	190.00	0.00	08/02/12	0.00	-149.36	-25.89	35.56	2.43	-2.99	17.43
75)	195.00	0.00	08/02/12	0.00	40.46	7.01	39.79	.78	-1.87	9.01
76)	200.00	0.00	08/02/12	0.00	240.23	41.63	39.36	-.98	-.43	-1.81
77)	205.00	0.00	08/02/12	0.00	428.99	74.35	35.71	-1.77	.32	-12.16
78)	210.00	0.00	08/02/12	0.00	595.64	103.23	30.23	-3.05	1.55	-20.3
79)	215.00	0.00	08/02/12	0.00	726.22	125.86	21.31	-3.91	2.72	-20.98

At the top part of the screen you can compare the deltas and other Greeks of the two different spreads. Don't forget to factor in breakeven levels if you are calculating risk/return.

Exhibit 5.10

use S&P 500 ETF (SPY) as an example, because it is a common reference for the performance of the market and the SPY is one of the most heavily traded ETFs. See Exhibit 5.12.

In the SPY bull-call spread risk profile in Exhibit 5.13 the spread is similar to buying the stock in terms of its statistical success, in that the breakeven is close to the stock price (136.60 for spread versus 135.86 for the stock). If I am placing my breakeven right around the current stock price, I want to be sure that my return potential on the spread is commensurate with the statistical returns of the asset that I am trading (SPY) in a given period of time (in this case, two months).

There are essentially two easy methods I use to calculate realistic return over a given period: *Hvol* and *ATR*. Analyzing either the stock's ATR or standard

Smart Investor Tip!

Positioning your spread around the stock price is a whole different variable and requires skill and thought. I discuss positioning in each specific vertical. The combination of width and position determines risk, probability, rate of return, and cost/credit.

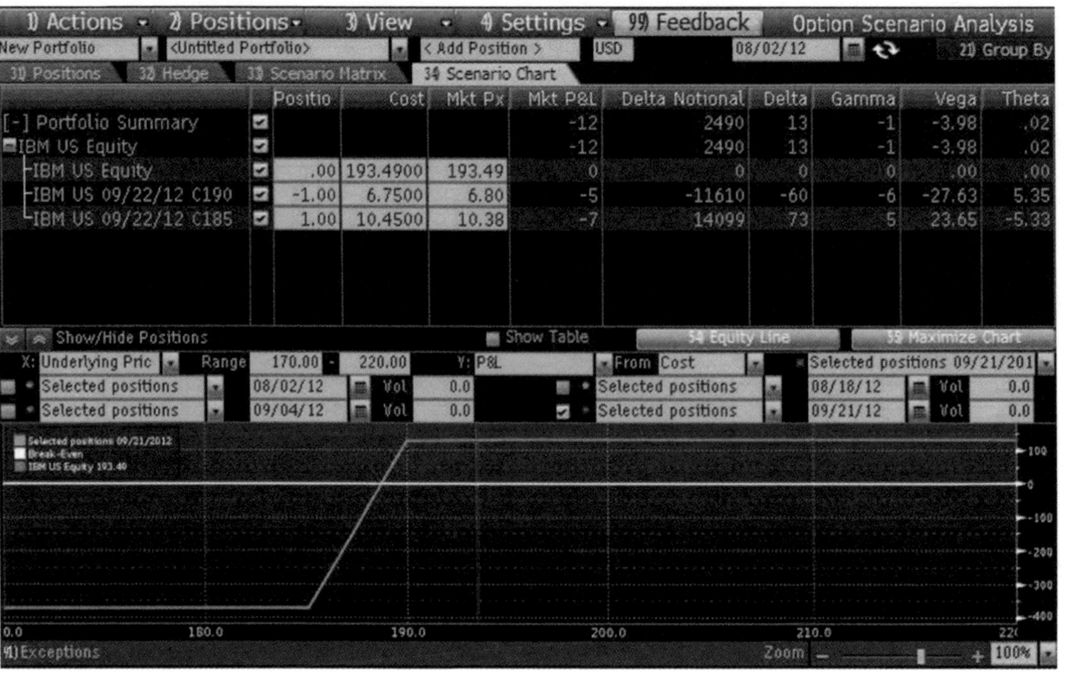

Exhibit 5.11

> **Smart Investor Tip!**
>
> If the breakeven was much higher, the statistical probability of success is lower, but the potential return should be greater.
>
> If the breakeven was below the current stock price, the stock is already where it needs to be for me to make max profit in the trade, so the odds of success (statistically) are higher.

> **Smart Investor Tip!**
>
> You should *first* choose the short call strike that's a level where you feel very *confident* that the stock will be above on or just before expiration day. Then select the strike below it based on how confident you are and how much risk you want to take.

deviation (volatility) for that time period will enable you to deduce a reasonable forward estimate of movement; you can also use an amalgam of both by averaging them out.

ATR: ATR is expressed in dollars, so it is very easy to calculate, just use your charts or GV screen and determine your trade length. The difficulty with ATR is calculating its forward value to the exact day with precision. ATR finds the largest move that a stock makes, so you will often have a higher result being that volatility calculations generally only take settlement to settlement prices into account.

ATR time frame usage:

- One to six days, use the daily ATR.
- One to three weeks, use the weekly ATR.

Exhibit 5.12

Using Volatility Comparison, you can not only look for volatility anomalies or favorable conditions, but also analyze the standard deviations and average price of any time period you choose! This right side visual is perfect for finding sticky price areas.

- One to three months, use the monthly ATR.
- Three to six months, use the quarterly ATR.

ATR is more of a "quick and dirty" way to find anticipated movement.

Hvol: By analyzing Hvol, you should be able to get more specific with your predictions and smooth out some of the noise. Hvol will give you the percentage chance a stock will touch or move through a certain price in your selected time frame. Because historical volatility uses close-to-close prices (not intraday oscillations) it may often be lower when compared to ATR.

The nice thing is that you don't have to do all the math in your head, just enter in the stock and the expiration date along with a volatility input and the Volatility Comparison screens will show you what a

Smart Investor Tip!

Volatility (Ivol and Hvol) is always expressed as an annualized percentage, so you may have to figure backward if you are staying in for shorter time frames. Also keep in mind that Hvol and Ivol percentages represent one annualized standard deviation, which occurs 78 percent of the time.

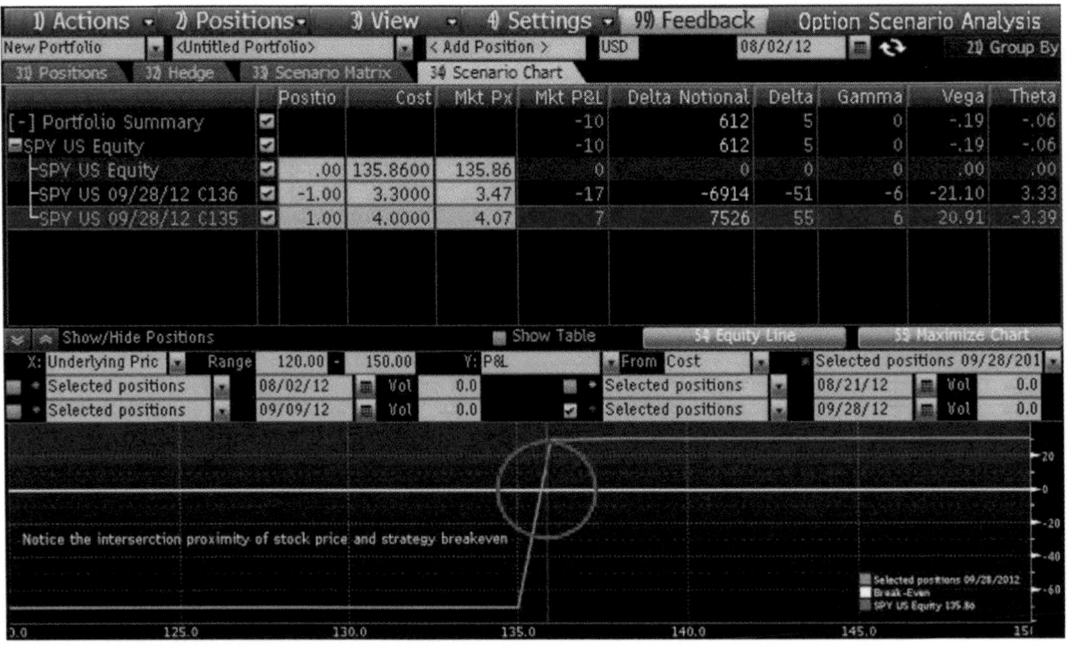

Exhibit 5.13

1-, 2-, and 3-standard deviation move will be in the stock along with the percentage chance the stock has of getting to those levels or a specific price level you choose. See Exhibit 5.14.

Exhibit 5.15 shows SPY at **$136** and the implied volatility of the at-the-money options with **60 days away** (not shown here) at **17.30** percent (IVol). This data implies that one standard deviation in the SPY 60 days out would be $131.05 to the downside and $150.79 to the upside.

So there is roughly a 70 percent chance the index will stay within those levels if volatility stays around 17.30 percent.

The VC screen shown in Exhibit 5.15 tells us that the observed volatility over the past 60 days is

16.75 percent with a standard deviation of 2.62 percent. We can also see that we are closer to a relative high point in volatility based on the mean and the position of the current value in the bell curve.

There are a couple ways to look at the above statistical probabilities:

- This is a realistic, probable range for the SPY over the next 70 days.
- Placing your short strike of a bullish spread at $149 or lower is a realistic expectation, but not highly probable. In fact there is a 36.5 percent chance SPY will touch $149, but only a 17.5 percent chance it will finish above.
- Move your short strike down until you at least have a 50 percent statistical probability of the asset at least touching your short strike.
    - The $146 level has a 52 percent chance of being touched; that is the first strike I would probably sell.
- Because you are *not* adding any statistical edge in the trade, your profit targets should be reasonable when it comes to the movement of the asset.
    - If you are trading a bullish spread that has a breakeven that is higher than the stock (statistically disadvantaged), then you should quantify just how probable (or improbable) your target is by using this method.

If you bought the 137/147 call spread for 2.50, you will probably have made more than 50 percent on your spread risk if SPY went up to $146 in a month, so do you even need it to travel up to $149? Think smart; use these tactics to rationalize your profit and stop loss selections.

Also consider real market conditions in conjunction with statistics: Can the S&P really get up to 1,490 (rough conversion, SPY is one-tenth of SPX) within that time frame? Even though it's less than one standard deviation, the market climate may negate such a move or level. Statistics are one thing; market sentiment, news, earnings, technicals, and the myriad of real market forces are another.

Furthermore, to achieve a 50 percent return on a stock trade, SPY itself would have to go to almost $209, which would mean the S&P 500 would have to rally to roughly 2,090 or more; a level never seen in the index. Don't compare percentage returns of the stock to that of a spread or option.

Setting Stops

To the downside, there is about a 30 percent statistical chance that SPY would touch $128. When you are dealing with verticals, your loss will generally be much less than the stock and with SPY at $128, you may be close to your max loss point. The good news is that max loss point may only be a couple of dollars as opposed to $11 in the stock. If the stock were to make a big move, you might decide that the trade has gone wrong and it's just time to go.

SPY is just an example; you can obviously adjust your risk to your comfort level, but placing your stop

Smart Investor Tip!

Ivol will often be higher than Hvol, but not always. Use a combination of the two, but pay attention to what the Ivol is telling you. If it's more than 15 percent higher than Hvol, what's the reason or justification? It might be a clue to increase your volatility estimations and adjust your stops and targets.

Smart Investor Tip!

Think About This: Your profit targets should be well within the realm of possibility and your stop losses should be closer to the edge of what's possible.

KEY POINT:

These techniques and analyses are all based on the stock price, but they are levels that should result in your taking action in your spread. Because of all the variables (Greeks) in a spread, I wouldn't set a trigger order in the stock to take me out of the option unless I couldn't be there to watch my position for a prolonged period.

Exhibit 5.14

loss too close may prematurely exit you from the trade—too far and you may be risking too much.

This method, along with technical analysis, can be used to figure not only stop losses and targets, but also to recognize normal movement versus periods of irrational behavior. "Normal" can change in the blink of an eye, but if the market is screaming higher or selling off for no apparent reason, you at least have a gauge on what the normal range may be.

If you are a contrarian, you can use these "abnormal" events to buy or sell into for a reversion to the mean. You can even use these events to trade against a losing position that you have, to help recoup losses.

Before any trade takes place, you should establish an exit strategy and set stop loss levels, even if not entered as an order. Because bull vertical spreads are limited in risk and sometimes can have a high probability of statistical success, your stop loss may be your total risk in the trade. Use common sense; if you were a longer-term trader who intended on holding SPY for several months, your stop loss may be upward of $15, which is the monthly ATR (average true range) of SPY. If you position your spread correctly, even at the money so the breakeven is the same as the underlying, no matter what happened to SPY, your max risk might be $1 to $4. So for your risk management in this trade, you may allow the trade to go to max loss.

If the $10 wide call spread we just reviewed was in the money, it would cost more, but have a higher probability of success because the stock is already where it needs to be on expiration for you to make money. The increased cost will increase risk, because it costs more, but the higher probability should justify that cost.

With many debit vertical spreads, because of their nature (risk/cost is commensurate with probability), stop losses and money management may be done on the front end, in that you limit the amount of spreads you buy to an acceptable level assuming the worst-case scenario.

In other words, make sure that you understand the probability characteristic of your trade; you don't have to lose your entire investment, but if that is the way you want to trade (risking the entire spread), just use the number of spreads to meter your risk.

You can use technicals to assist you in setting stops and targets; moving averages and support/resistance levels like those in Exhibit 5.15 can be trigger points for entry and exit.

Finding "Risk Harmony" takes a ton of practice.

Smart Investor Tip!

If you are utilizing leverage and buying the same amount of spreads as you would have spent in the stock (which I don't think is prudent) then you should get in the habit of having tighter spreads because if that spread goes to zero, so does all your investment.

Bullish Credit Vertical—Using Puts

The entire process I just detailed is the same for bullish vertical put or call spreads alike. There are some very slight differences in the construction of the two and their "personalities." Think of them as fraternal twins who *think* and *act* exactly alike, but it's their looks that differ. See Exhibit 5.16.

Construction: To create a bull-put spread, you must sell a put with a *higher* strike than the one that you bought on a one-to-one ratio. The goal of the bull-put spread is to have the underlying asset finish above the *short* strike on expiration.

To qualify as a plain vertical spread, strikes *must* be in the same month, both will be puts; the one with the higher strike must be sold and one with the lower strike must be bought, period.

It doesn't matter what strikes are selected. See Exhibit 5.17.

Max profit in a credit put vertical spread is:

The Net Credit Received

Max risk in a credit put vertical spread is:

Distance Between Strikes – the Credit Received

Sometimes all you need is a clean, definable channel and some major moving averages to find support and resistance levels in a stock. Use those levels to guide your strike selection in vertical spreads.

Exhibit 5.15

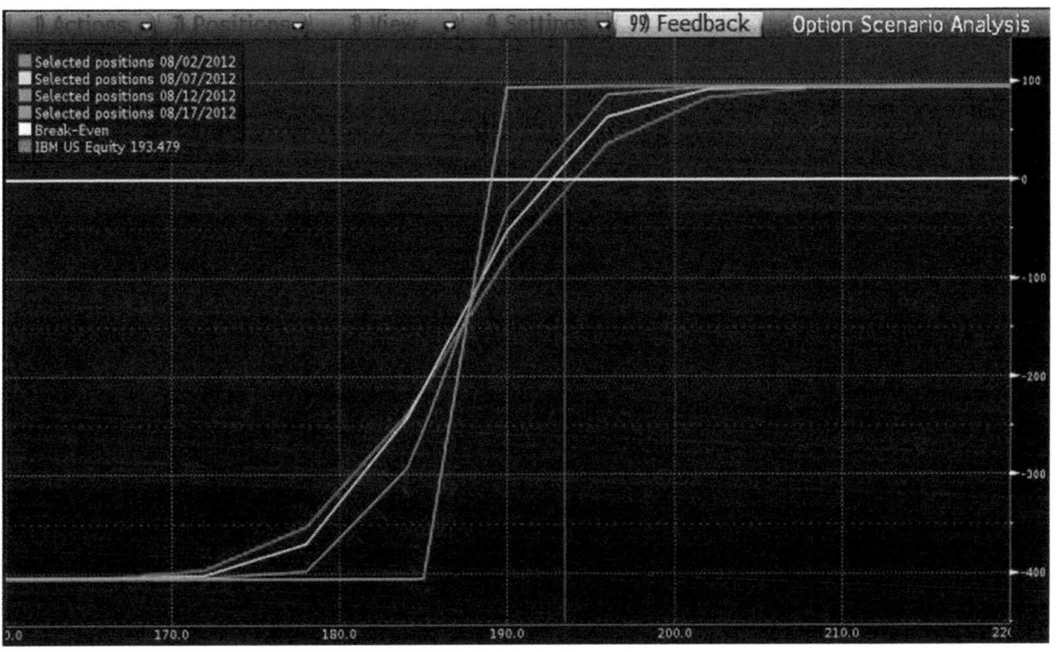

Exhibit 5.16

KEY POINT:

Bull-put vertical spreads are always done for a credit. The credit received is dependent on the volatility of the stock, its position, the selection (expiration and strike) along with the distance of the strikes from one another.

The credit is the most you will ever make in the trade.

Remember that for a put vertical spread to be bullish, the higher strike must be sold and the lower strike purchased.

Exhibit 5.17

Breakeven in a credit put vertical spread is:

Short Put Strike – Credit Received

Let's assume that IBM was trading at $198. If you were to sell the IBM November 195/190 put spread for a credit of $1.61 (which means selling the 195 put and buying the 190 put), you are limiting your risk to the width of the strikes ($5), minus the credit received ($1.61), which gives you a total downside risk in this example of $3.39. $3.39 is all you could ever lose. See Exhibit 5.18.

The advantage of this trade is that IBM could drop to $195 by June expiration and you would still retain the $1.61 credit, which is a 47 percent return on your risk.

The disadvantage is that the $1.61 credit you receive is the maximum profit you can potentially make

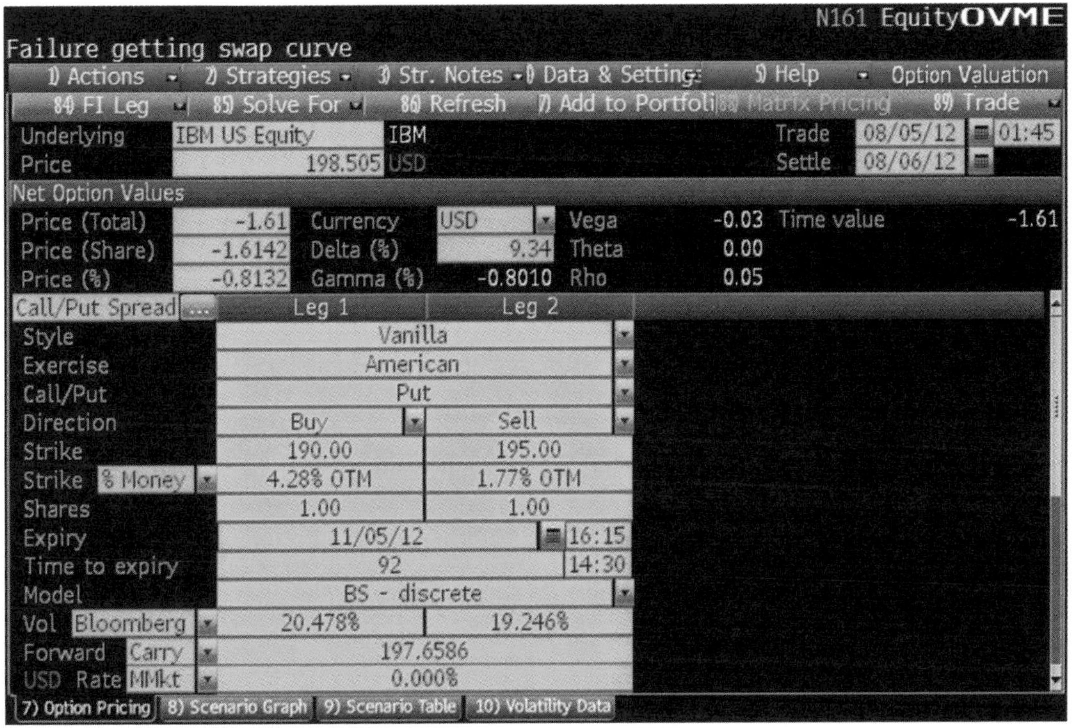

Exhibit 5.18

in the trade—not a penny more. For some stock traders, this factor may be hard to deal with. Greed, for many of us, is a tough emotion to control. For others, like me, the fact that IBM could go down and my *bullish* strategy can still make 47 percent, makes me feel pretty damn good.

Buy low and sell high still applies! In the bull-put spread, you sell first in the hopes of that spread becoming cheaper later on so you can buy it back for less or let it expire worthless. Selling a spread for the most you could ever possibly make is an odd feeling for some people. Let's rationalize this trade another way: Imagine I paid that $3.39 (my max risk) for that spread and then determine what a good return is from that aspect.

If you bought a stock for $3.39 and it went to $5 in a month, would you be happy? I think so.

The problem is that this theoretical stock would never get above $5. If you knew that little fact, you would probably feel better about selling it for $5. Do you see what I am getting at? It's all in the way you frame it in your mind.

Here are some examples of gain/loss:

Remember this adage: *The wider the width (of the spread), the greater the gain and potential pain.*

Sell the 55 put and buy the 50 put for a 1.00 credit = $4 max loss

Sell the 55 put and buy the 45 put for a 2.00 credit = $8 max loss

Sell the 55 put and buy the 40 put for a 3.00 credit = $12 max loss

KEY POINT:

The bull-call vertical spread will have the same rules as the bull-put spread, only calls will be used and the trade will be done for a debit versus a credit.

If you are executing the trade correctly, the ROR should be very close for the same strike spread using calls or puts.

Risk will also be identical and so will cost (margin) in most cases.

Determining how wide you want to make your spread should be dictated by both the amount of the credit you take in and how far you think the stock could fall if things went wrong. The less likely you think it is that the stock will drop, widen your spread. The more likely you think it is that the stock will drop, narrow your spread.

Here's what it looks like hypothetically. Let's say that you were moderately bullish on XYZ Corporation and thought it could at least stay above $100 for the next 20 days; it's hypothetically trading at $110.

The June 100 puts, which expire in 21 days and have a delta of 0.23, are trading for $1. The 95 put can be bought for $0.25; it has a delta of 0.06, so if you were to sell the January 100 put for $1 and buy the January 95 put for $0.25 at the same time, you would be selling the January 100/95 put spread for a limit price of $0.75.

Since the spread is $5 wide, your maximum profit potential in the trade would be $0.75 or 15 percent on your risk of $4.25 (spread width [$5] minus the credit received [$0.75]). Maximum loss occurs when the stock is *below* the long strike at expiration. Your breakeven, at expiration, is your short strike minus the credit you received for the total spread.

Meaning that in our example, your breakeven (excluding commissions) would be the stock at $99.25 at expiration. (100 [short strike] – $0.75 [credit received] = $99.25).

- **Margin:** The margin requirement for a bull-put spread usually is the width of the strikes minus the credit. So in the above case the margin requirement would be $4.25 (100 – 95) – $0.75. I bet that the call spread with the same strikes would probably cost $4.25 as well.
- **Breakeven:** Breakeven is the strike price of the short put minus the credit. Below this level, the spread begins to lose money on expiration. In the above example the breakeven was $189.79. See Exhibit 5.19.

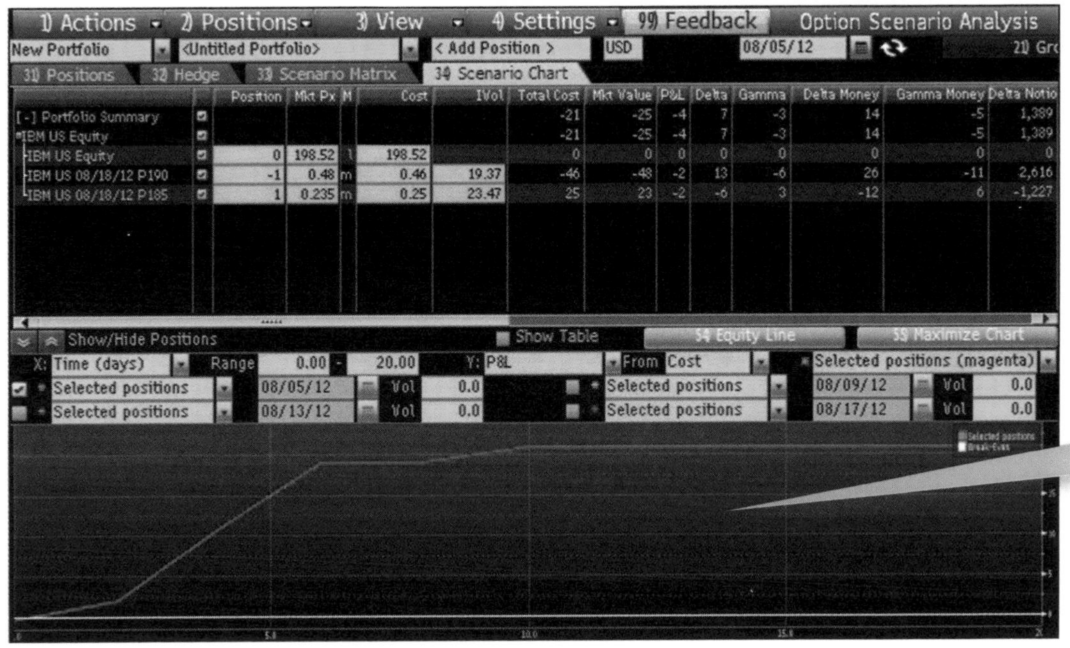

This bull put spread was put on for a 21-cent credit; when you subtract the credit from the short put strike of 190, you have your breakeven of $189.79. IBM stock was at $198.52.

Exhibit 5.19

Bullish Debit Vertical—Using Calls

In a debit trade, you pay the full amount up front and this is the most you can lose (it's exactly the same "net cost" of the put credit spread because you have to put up margin). You might also think of it as putting your maximum loss up front, with the goal to sell the spread for more than you paid. This is where the name "debit vertical" comes from.

All the risk and Greek characteristics remain the same as do the parameters for spread width and positioning.

To create a bull-call spread, you must sell a call with a *higher* strike than the one that you bought on a one-to-one ratio. The goal of the bull-call spread is to have the underlying asset finish above the *short* strike on expiration.

Smart Investor Tip!

If you are wanting to buy a call vertical as a substitute for a put vertical, but the calls have huge bid-ask spreads, a quick and dirty way to see what the call spread can be bought for is to take the amount you can sell the put spread for and subtract it from the difference in strikes.

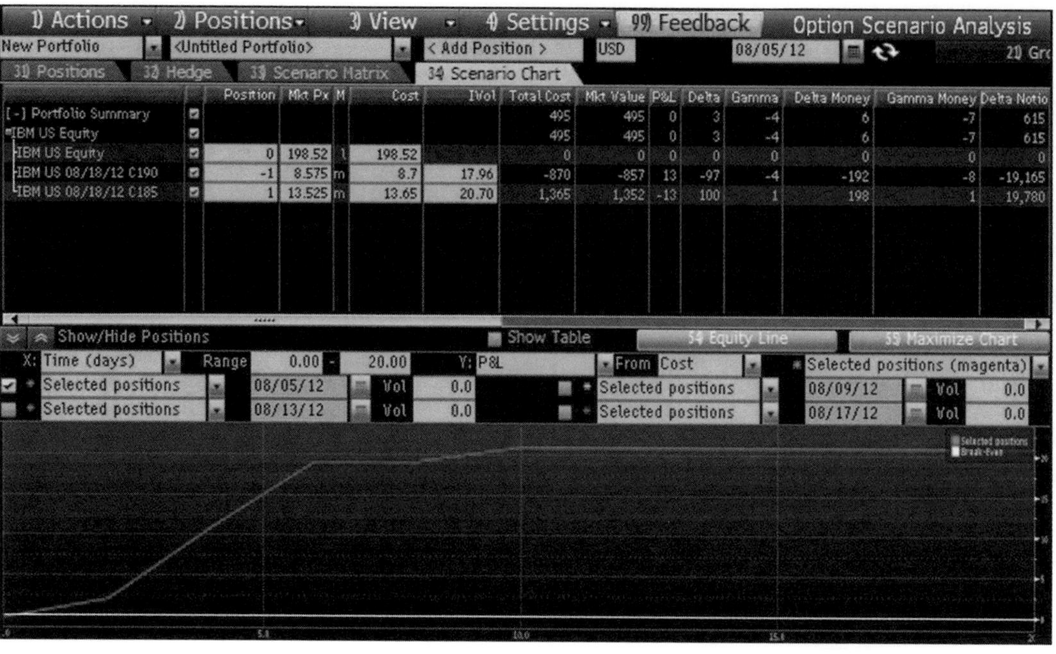

Exhibit 5.20

To qualify as a plain vertical spread, strikes *must* be in the same month, both must be calls; the one with the higher strike must be sold and one with the lower strike must be bought, period.

It doesn't matter what strikes are selected. See Exhibit 5.20.

Using the same scenario and strikes that we did in the first put vertical example, there is a good chance that you would be able to *buy* the 185 call and sell the 190 call for $3.95, which would be an in-the-money bull-call spread.

The spread, even though you are now using calls, would behave *exactly* like the bull-put spread. If IBM was anywhere above $190 on expiration, the call spread would leave you with a profit potential of $1.05, which is the same as the short put spread.

Max profit in a debit call vertical spread is:

Distance Between Strikes – Debit Paid

Max risk in a debit call vertical spread is:

The Net Debit Paid

Breakeven in a debit call vertical spread is:

Long Call Strike + Net Debit Paid

Debit/credit nuances: Call spreads like all vertical spreads are limited in both risk and reward. They involve the purchase of one call and the sale of another call against it.

When a call spread is bought, it is bullish because you are buying a call with a larger delta and selling a smaller delta call against it. Buying a larger delta will inherently cost more and will have a lower strike than the one you are selling, therefore you will be "buying" (or *long*) the spread. Delta is the rate of change in an options price for every $1 move in the stock. The higher the delta, the more expensive the option costs in the same expiration month.

In a debit vertical spread, you can*not* lose more than what you pay. This doesn't mean that you can't lose money, but it does let you know right at the onset of the trade your amount of "risk." If you buy a call spread, you typically have a moderately bullish outlook on the stock, meaning that you want it to rise in value. There is another rule you must know when buying a vertical call spread—the spread will not be worth more than the difference in strikes. This means that if you buy a 90 call and sell a 100 call you have a 10-point spread and that spread isn't worth more than $10. If you pay $5 for that spread, your maximum profit potential is $5 or 100 percent in that case.

At expiration, the bull-call spread will be at its maximum value if the stock is above the call you sold. In basic terms, you want the stock to rise above the short strike before the spread's expiration date. This does not mean that you cannot be profitable if the stock does not reach above the short strike by expiry, but as a general rule (if you are just getting started) the basic goal is to have the stock get above the short strike. So we have established that buying a vertical call spread is a bullish event. Now, the question is: What strikes do we buy and sell and what month do we purchase the spread in?

Bull-call spread nuances: In the call spread, you must pay your maximum loss up front; the goal is to sell them for more than you paid, netting a profit. No margin in this trade.

The concept of buying a vertical spread may be easier for new traders to grasp because it falls back in line with what most of stock and beginner options traders are used to—paying for something up front then selling it for more later.

Because the debit vertical shares a similar mindset that most traders already employ, the mechanics of the trade are familiar and therefore the behavior and money/risk management of the trader is generally easier than credit spreads.

Which to choose? We know the goal of selling a vertical put spread is to have the stock finish *above* the option you sold at expiration. We have also established that bullish vertical put and call spreads are essentially the same, so why choose one over the other?

Smart Investor Tip!

If you are not yet comfortable with the concepts of credit spreads, remember that you can substitute an in-the-money debit spread for an out-of-the-money credit spread and vice versa.

Rules of the vertical still apply, except that when you are buying a vertical you always *buy* the deeper in-the-money call or put.

Smart Investor Tip!

I generally choose to utilize puts for bullish vertical spreads that I want to place below the stock price. This is because the bid-ask spreads will be cheaper and allow for easier execution as opposed to expensive in-the-money calls.

Remember the goals: We want the stock to get to and stay above the short strike up until expiration and we want to get the best ROR (return on risk).

Typically, when I sell put spreads, I sell them out of the money at the onset of the trade (below the stock price), this way the stock is already where I want it to be. Unlike buying a put spread, I will usually sell the put spread with 40 days or less until expiration, because time passing by benefits my position. As long as my spread is out of the money, time decay will be working in my favor because both options will be getting cheaper and—because I collected a credit if the spread is worth zero at expiration—that is a good thing for me.

This trade may have an upside-down risk/reward ratio, because the trade should have a higher statistical probability of being successful. Let me explain.

If you have a stock that you feel is going to rise in value and let's say that stock is trading at $46, if you were to sell the 40 put for $1.50 and simultaneously purchase the 35 put for $0.50, you now have a 40/35 bear-put spread on for a credit of $1. Let's also assume that these options expire in 20 days, meaning that as long as the stock stays above $40 for the next 20 days you will retain your $1.

Now keep in mind that if the stock falls below $39 you will incur a loss. Your maximum loss potential in this trade is $4, because it is a $5 spread and you bought in $1. (Spread width minus credit equals risk.)

If we take the analysis a step further and use the volatility logic discussed earlier, we can look back at the historical volatility of a stock as well as the implied volatility to determine a realistic movement in a stock over a given period of time and then look at the potential reward and potential risk in a trade before selecting strikes and pulling the trigger.

Assume the 30-day Hvol is 18 percent, with the stock trading at $46—that's $9 higher or lower during a year's time or roughly $3 (use GVscreen to find this) in a month's time. If we have sold our spread $6 away from the current stock price, we have a major statistical edge. In our example, we sold the 40 put and bought the 35 and our max profit can be attained even with a two standard deviation move, which occurs less than 10 percent of the time!

Step 5: Monitoring/Closing the Trade

Monitoring and exiting both bullish vertical spreads are very similar. The only difference will be whether you "buy to close" in the put spread or "sell to close" in the call spread.

Your monitoring priorities will vary depending on your spread position, width, and expiration.

For tighter spreads well below the spot price:

Spreads that are at least one-half of a standard deviation below the stock price and are less than $5 wide.

Because these spreads are already positioned to make max profit and are less sensitive to market and other influences (volatility, etc.) they require less general maintenance. As long as the stock is maintaining a neutral to moderately bullish pattern, all is good. Just let time value work its magic.

Usually the only reason to jump ship on a spread like this is if there is a major material change in stock or market fundamentals or sentiment or if the stock breaches a key technical level. Earnings may also be a reason to exit with your profit in hand.

For wider spreads well below the spot price:

Spreads that are at least one-half of a standard deviation below the stock price and are greater than $5 wide.

For tighter spreads near the spot price:

These spreads will fluctuate with movements in the stock price, but will be less susceptible to changes in the Greeks relative to wider spreads. Because the spread was placed near the money, its breakeven will be close to the underlying stock price.

This means that I will generally exit a little faster than I would with spreads that are below the stock price. A problem you will find is that if there is still a good amount of time left until expiration or if Ivol is relatively high, these spreads may not see as much of a profit because the short option is still holding a great deal of value. Because it's close to the long strike, that value will offset the net profit of the spread.

If you are looking for a quick move in the stock, widen your spreads so you can get out quickly if the stock moves.

For wider spreads near the spot price:

Wide spreads that are near (at) the stock price tend to have the highest correlation with the asset. This correlation usually peaks when the spot price is between the strikes and you are close to expiration.

These spreads are generally used when you are looking to get the most of minor stock moves in the short term, so I tend to exit these spreads the quickest. Because these spreads are highly correlated and more expensive relative to spreads that are above the spot price, use very realistic targets and exit or adjust the trade when you have profit.

Wide, at-the-money spreads are the most sensitive and generally require the most monitoring. Use GTC limit orders to set your profit target.

For tighter spreads well above the spot price:

These spreads are generally executed if you have a bullish outlook, but for some reason you wanted to reduce risk to Greeks or if your analysis found that lower risk was warranted.

Tight spreads that are above the stock price shouldn't be very volatile in price changes compared to wider spreads or spread near the money. Good for traders who can't monitor as often or who want less volatility in their portfolio.

The tight spreads want to have the stock clear above the short strike and need to be close to expiration if you expect to get the max profit from them. Because the strikes are so tight, you may not get the increase in value that you would with a wider spread

KEY POINT:

With any vertical, you can always roll up in strikes or roll out in time (or both). If you bought a wide ($10) bull spread for $3 that is at the money and is now very profitable ($7), you can sell that spread, capture the $4 profit and buy a spread that is higher in strikes for a portion of the profits. Only do this if you think the stock will continue to rise. This way you have a guaranteed profit in the whole trade and can still make additional profit if the stock continues. It's a proactive method to manage risk.

KEY POINT:

When you sell a put vertical where both strikes are below the spot price, the stock can do one of three things and you can still have a successful trade. In the example above, the stock can rally from here, it can stay flat, or it can fall to $40 and you would still be profitable.

and therefore you must be more conservative in your profit goals. Think in percentage terms! If you buy a vertical spread that is $10 above the current spot price for $1 and it goes to $1.40, you just bagged at 40 percent profit; don't be afraid to take it and adjust strikes if you think the stock will go higher.

For wider spreads well above the spot price:

Wide spreads that are above the spot price can gain good delta acceleration as the stock moves to and above the long strike. Wider spreads cost more, but you have the ability to make more money than tighter ones. You also see your P&L ramp up or down quicker.

I like to use the wider spreads if I think a stock has the potential to really explode to the upside. Your confidence in a quick rally should be the determining factor in selecting a wider spread versus a tighter one.

Because volatility is greater and you have more risk in a wider spread, you should be able to monitor the position closer than you would a tight spread. Hopefully the Ivol crush that generally occurs when a stock rallies will help your P&L.

I generally lock in profit quickly and roll up or out if I think the stock will continue to move higher, like the at-the-money spreads.

Vertical Spread Example

It's June 1, 2010, and the market has been recently corrected, but is having an extremely tough time building momentum. The S&P and Dow Jones have given back all their gains for the year. Price-to-earnings multiples on the S&P 500 are at historic low levels and for the most part, companies seem to be growing. Unemployment is high, but looks to be improving. Europe is still shaky and the euro has been weakening against the dollar, causing dollar-denominated commodities and oil to slide lower. U.S. multinational companies may experience weakness due to the strong dollar. Many short-term technicals have broken down on the major indices and on many of the stocks that are contained within. Some select stocks and longer-term technical indicators seem to be intact, suggesting a continuation of the bull market, with this being a momentary pullback. Although the bulk of the news is moderately positive, there are still risks and consequently, volatility, and the VIX remain elevated.

What Are the Key Characteristics of the Thesis?

- Moderately bullish sentiment.
- High volatility.
- Long-term support levels.
- Underlying concern for systematic sovereign risk.
- Limited growth potential.

Rationale: A bull-call spread may provide a solution in this instance, as it offers limited risk, lower vega exposure, and the ability to set the maximum risk by adjusting spread width—a lower upfront cost than just purchasing a call outright, but still an excellent return on risk given the limited upside anticipation.

The SPY would be the most common way to express this view; however, there are other specialized ETFs and even individual stocks that you may think will fit your thesis best and satisfy your desired outcome. For me, there are three ways I would approach this situation.

First, I could find a quality, low beta stock that is more defensive in nature and has been beat up pretty bad with a low earnings multiple, looking for a pop in that individual stock.

Second, I could target a sector with an ETF that has underperformed in the rallies, but bore all the brunt of the sell-offs, looking for value there.

Third, I could just buy the SPY or DIA looking for a broad market recovery. This method has pros and cons: A pro would be the fact that I am hedged in the SPY with 500 different stocks and 30 in the DIA, but at the same time; the con is that those indices could flounder over the next couple months as sectors within them rotate and the losers cancel out the winners making for a flat trade.

The benefit here is that if I choose the SPY, I could structure the strikes in a way that doesn't require much upside in the index for me to attain a decent return.

Spread selection: For this trade, looking at the chart and forward P/E of the S&P 500, which was about 13.11 times earnings on June 1, 2010, I felt that there was a large amount of value and a viable trade for the intermediate term (one to three months) in the SPY.

I chose a spread that expired in September 2010, which was 112 days away; it was six points wide and was partially in the money, for several reasons.

A $6 wide spread that cost me $3.55 to buy allows me to potentially make another $2.45 on the trade in about four months if SPY is above $112 on September expiration. This is almost a 70 percent return on my risk capital or about 230 percent annualized return.

With the uncertain prospects, I wanted a statistical edge. The breakeven in this trade is $109.55 (long strike + premium paid), SPY was trading at $109.37, which means that if the index just moves up 0.18, I will be at a point where I won't make or lose any money, all while having only $3.55 at risk at all times.

Trade management: If your original thesis and/or the stock's technical breaks down, reevaluate your commitment to the trade and possibly exit or adjust to avoid catastrophe. The shorter the duration of the trade, the greater the urgency to act. Often I take the profits on a trade and wait if I don't have the time to research what is going on.

On the flip side, if things are looking strong, it does not hurt to sell into a little strength. You can exit altogether, or roll up or out, or combine the two with a portion of your profits. Remember that if you traded 10 contracts initially, you could always reduce that number to 5.

Smart Investor Tip!

When you sell a put spread out of the money, time is working for you, meaning that the spread gets cheaper as you move closer to expiration.

When the short put spread is in the money, time starts working against you, meaning that if both options strike, and are higher than the current stock price, the spread hurts you because it gets more expensive as you move closer to expiration.

Your new spread is going to cost you the same amount of money and doesn't give you a statistical advantage.

Get in the habit of booking profits and constantly reducing risk as a stock moves in your favor.

Video:
Selecting Strikes in a Bullish Vertical Spread
www.wiley.com/go/BloombergVisualGuidetoFinancialMarketsVideo1.html

Put Debit Spread/Call Credit Spread—Bearish Verticals

Take everything you just learned and reverse it. That is how bearish verticals will behave and be constructed. The only difference is that the call spread now is a credit and the put spread now is a debit.

Targeting a Bullish Vertical

Like all strategies, you should complete a series of consistent steps to arrive at the most probable trade.

Bearish vertical spreads can be used to express many different levels of bearishness, time durations, and probabilities. Here are the three basic formats that the trade may take. These general plans should contain much more specific criteria to get the risk/reward and cost right where you want them. Everything revolves around how high and how fast you think an asset can fall in value over a period of time. See Exhibit 5.21.

Extremely bearish over the longer term, but want to reduce cost:

- Two-month to two-year expiration bear vertical spreads that are placed far below the stock price can be used to express a low-probability, low-cost, high-return scenario where you think the stock is going to severely correct below a certain area by a given period of time.

  These bullish verticals will usually be put spreads, because they will be out of the money and generally have tighter bid-ask spreads. They are great to use when Ivol skew is elevated to the downside because the vertical spread negates the vega risk in the trade to an extent. The short call (or put) should be placed at a level that you feel the stock will be below come expiration.

  Break-even and max profit levels in these types of spreads will always be lower than the current stock price, but it will be cheaper than just buying a put of the same strike outright. See Exhibit 5.22.

Moderately bearish over the short to long term:

- One-month to two-year expiration bear vertical spreads that are placed just at or below the stock price can be used to express a more balanced probability and return scenario with low cost where you think the stock will gradually decline in value below the short strike over a given period of time.

IBM US $ C 198.52 +4.07 N 198.51/198.50 1x5 EquityOMON
As of Aug3 DELAYED Vol 3,278,231 Op 196.48 T Hi 198.95 D Lo 196.16 B
IBM US Equity 95) Templates 96) Actions 97) Expiry Option Monitor: jared basic white
IBM 198.52 0% 198.51 / 198.50 Hi 198.95 Lo 196.16 Volm 3278231 HV 21.68 91) News (CN)
Calc Mode 94) Fields Center 175.00 Strikes 5 Exch US Composite 92) Next Earnings(EM) 10/17/12 E
295) Center Strike 296) Calls/Puts 297) Calls 298) Puts 299) Term Structure

Puts

Strike	Ticker	ThPx	IVol	Bid	Theo	Ask	IVal	DM	TM	Volm
5	22 Sep 12	Days »	48	IVol »		Rate »	0.30	CSize 100; Div 0.85 USD		
165.00	IBM 9/22/12 P165	.25	27.80	.23	.02	.27		-.03	.0146	
170.00	IBM 9/22/12 P170	.39	26.05	.35	.07	.42		-.05	.0186	37
175.00	IBM 9/22/12 P175	.56	24.01	.54	.22	.59		-.07	.0225	28
180.00	IBM 9/22/12 P180	.87	22.07	.85	.56	.89		-.11	.0326	97
185.00	IBM 9/22/12 P185	1.39	20.40	1.36	1.24	1.41		-.17	.0392	73
5	20 Oct 12	Days »	76	IVol »		Rate »	0.39	CSize 100; Div 0.85 USD		
165.00	IBM 10/20/12 P165	.72	27.36	.69	.09	.74		-.06	.0193	151
170.00	IBM 10/20/12 P170	.99	25.86	.97	.23	1.02		-.09	.0234	2206
175.00	IBM 10/20/12 P175	1.40	24.47	1.37	.53	1.43		-.12	.0276	82
180.00	IBM 10/20/12 P180	1.98	23.08	1.94	1.09	2.02		-.17	.0367	139
185.00	IBM 10/20/12 P185	2.77	21.62	2.73	2.01	2.81		-.23	.0395	129
5	19 Jan 13	Days »	167	IVol »		Rate »	0.68	CSize 100; Div 1.70 USD		
165.00	IBM 1/19/13 P165	2.56	25.99	2.49	.81	2.62		-.13	.0226	12
170.00	IBM 1/19/13 P170	3.20	24.97	3.10	1.36	3.30		-.16	.0255	73
175.00	IBM 1/19/13 P175	4.00	23.98	3.90	2.16	4.10		-.20	.0281	73
180.00	IBM 1/19/13 P180	4.97	22.96	4.90	3.27	5.05		-.25	.0272	92
185.00	IBM 1/19/13 P185	6.20	21.99	6.10	4.71	6.30		-.30	.0289	116
5	18 Jan 14	Days »	531	IVol »		Rate »	0.77	CSize 100; Div 5.40 USD		
165.00	IBM 1/18/14 P165	10.88	26.34	10.55	5.36	11.20		-.25	.0175	
170.00	IBM 1/18/14 P170	12.35	25.89	12.05	6.79	12.65		-.28	.0185	
175.00	IBM 1/18/14 P175	13.88	25.26	13.60	8.44	14.15		-.31	.0181	
180.00	IBM 1/18/14 P180	15.55	24.68	15.25	10.33	15.85		-.34	.0186	10

Exhibit 5.21

Breakeven will be at or slightly below the current stock price, but max profit will be below the current stock price. See Exhibit 5.23.

Neutral to moderately bearish in the short term:

- Ten-day to two-month expiration bear vertical spreads that are placed right at or *above* the stock price can be used to express a high probability, slightly lower return with moderate cost where you think the stock can simply stay below a certain level.

This strike positioning favors the use of the bear-call spread, because the calls, which are out of or near the money, will generally be cheaper than

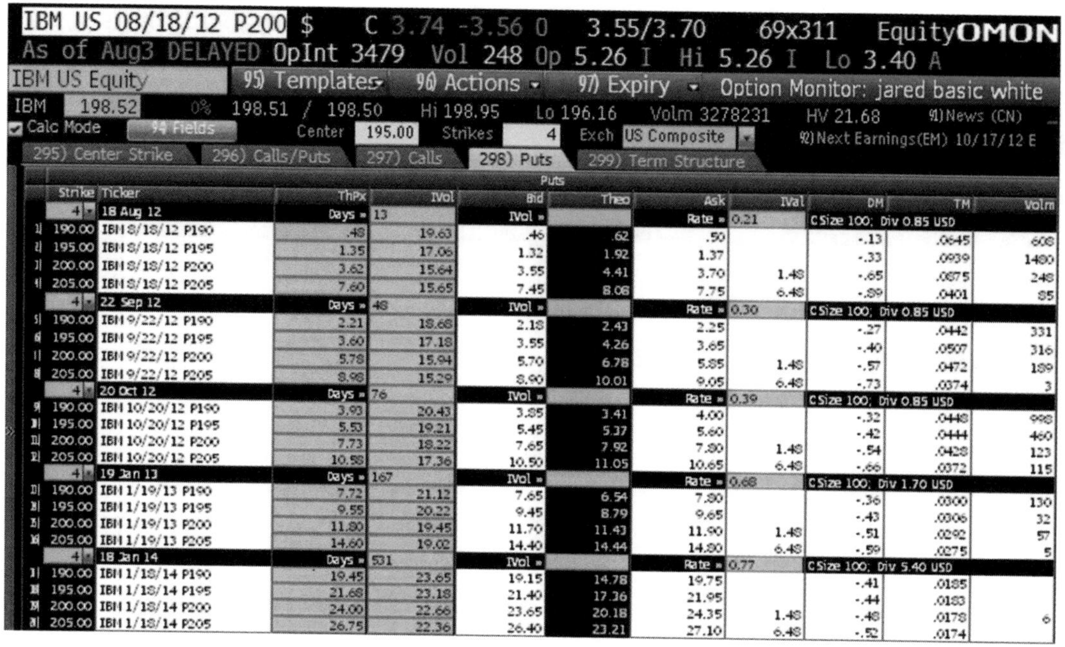

IBM US 08/18/12 P200 $ C 3.74 -3.56 0 3.55/3.70 69x311 EquityOMON
As of Aug3 DELAYED OpInt 3479 Vol 248 Op 5.26 I Hi 5.26 I Lo 3.40 A
IBM US Equity 95) Templates 96) Actions 97) Expiry Option Monitor: jared basic white
IBM 198.52 0% 198.51 / 198.50 Hi 198.95 Lo 196.16 Volm 3278231 HV 21.68 91) News (CN)
Calc Mode 94 Fields Center 195.00 Strikes 4 Exch US Composite 92) Next Earnings(EM) 10/17/12 E
295) Center Strike 296) Calls/Puts 297) Calls 298) Puts 299) Term Structure

Puts

Strike	Ticker	ThPx	IVol	Bid	Theo	Ask	IVal	DM	TM	Volm
4	18 Aug 12	Days =	13	IVol =		Rate =	0.21	CSize 100; Div 0.85 USD		
190.00	IBM 8/18/12 P190	.48	19.63	.46	.62	.50		-.13	.0645	608
195.00	IBM 8/18/12 P195	1.35	17.06	1.32	1.92	1.37		-.33	.0939	1400
200.00	IBM 8/18/12 P200	3.62	15.64	3.55	4.41	3.70	1.48	-.65	.0875	248
205.00	IBM 8/18/12 P205	7.60	15.65	7.45	8.06	7.75	6.48	-.89	.0401	85
4	22 Sep 12	Days =	48	IVol =		Rate =	0.30	CSize 100; Div 0.85 USD		
190.00	IBM 9/22/12 P190	2.21	18.68	2.18	2.43	2.25		-.27	.0442	331
195.00	IBM 9/22/12 P195	3.60	17.18	3.55	4.26	3.65		-.40	.0507	316
200.00	IBM 9/22/12 P200	5.78	15.94	5.70	6.78	5.85	1.48	-.57	.0472	189
205.00	IBM 9/22/12 P205	8.98	15.29	8.90	10.01	9.05	6.48	-.73	.0374	3
4	20 Oct 12	Days =	76	IVol =		Rate =	0.39	CSize 100; Div 0.85 USD		
190.00	IBM 10/20/12 P190	3.93	20.43	3.85	3.41	4.00		-.32	.0448	998
195.00	IBM 10/20/12 P195	5.53	19.21	5.45	5.37	5.60		-.42	.0444	460
200.00	IBM 10/20/12 P200	7.73	18.22	7.65	7.92	7.80	1.48	-.54	.0428	123
205.00	IBM 10/20/12 P205	10.58	17.36	10.50	11.05	10.65	6.48	-.66	.0372	115
4	19 Jan 13	Days =	167	IVol =		Rate =	0.68	CSize 100; Div 1.70 USD		
190.00	IBM 1/19/13 P190	7.72	21.12	7.65	6.54	7.80		-.36	.0300	130
195.00	IBM 1/19/13 P195	9.55	20.22	9.45	8.79	9.65		-.43	.0306	32
200.00	IBM 1/19/13 P200	11.80	19.45	11.70	11.43	11.90	1.48	-.51	.0292	57
205.00	IBM 1/19/13 P205	14.60	19.02	14.40	14.44	14.80	6.48	-.59	.0275	5
4	18 Jan 14	Days =	531	IVol =		Rate =	0.77	CSize 100; Div 5.40 USD		
190.00	IBM 1/18/14 P190	19.45	23.65	19.15	14.78	19.75		-.41	.0185	
195.00	IBM 1/18/14 P195	21.68	23.18	21.40	17.36	21.95		-.44	.0183	
200.00	IBM 1/18/14 P200	24.00	22.66	23.65	20.18	24.35	1.48	-.48	.0178	6
205.00	IBM 1/18/14 P205	26.75	22.36	26.40	23.21	27.10	6.48	-.52	.0174	

Exhibit 5.22

Smart Investor Tip!

Because stocks have a propensity to increase in value over time and tend to correct quickly, I find that bearish trades tend to be shorter in duration and may warrant more conservative profit targets.

the puts and have a propensity for tighter bid-ask spreads.

Breakeven will generally be higher than the current stock price, allowing the stock a little more upside leeway. You can also position strikes so the break-even and max profit levels are *above* the stock, like the chain you see above.

How you will win everything:

Stock stays below your short strike by expiration (call or put spread).

How you can get hurt:

Stock stays flat up to expiration. If you positioned both strikes of your vertical spread *above* the stock price when the trade was initiated, a stock that stays flat can actually allow you to attain maximum profit in the trade as long as it's below the short strike on expiry. If you positioned the bearish vertical strikes *below* the stock price on entering, then the above scenario will hurt you.

Stock rallies. Depending on where your strikes are positioned, the level of pain you will feel will vary. There are cases where the bearish vertical is so far above the stock price that a modest rally can still turn out to be good for the spread.

If the spread is at or below the stock price when you put the trade on, you will feel more pain. The most volatility will be felt when the spread is at the money.

Bearish Vertical Spread Greek Attributes

Exhibit 5.24 shows examples of bearish put and call spreads. Apples to apples, they are the same; however, their relation to the stock (in, at, out of the money) will be opposite. As you go through the Greeks, remember that both the short-call spread and the long-put spread want the stock to move lower (below the short strike). When the stock is moving up and down, the Greeks for both spreads will change almost identically. Again, the only different is that out-of-the-money calls will be the same as in-the-money puts and vice versa.

Delta

Always negative—Delta can range from –0.02 to –0.98.

Call spread—Generally the call spread delta is highest when it's just ATM (in-between strikes selected). As the stock moves lower, the call spread will lose delta (and value) because both calls are moving to 0 deltas. If the stock moves against you and the call spread continues to move in the money, the P&L variation will reduce as both call deltas offset one another as they both move toward a one delta. At that point you will be reaching your max loss point.

Put spread—Like the calls, the most delta will be when the spread is just at the money or in-between strikes. Delta will decrease as the stock moves up or down outside either strike. When you are close to expiration, the spread would have more deltas

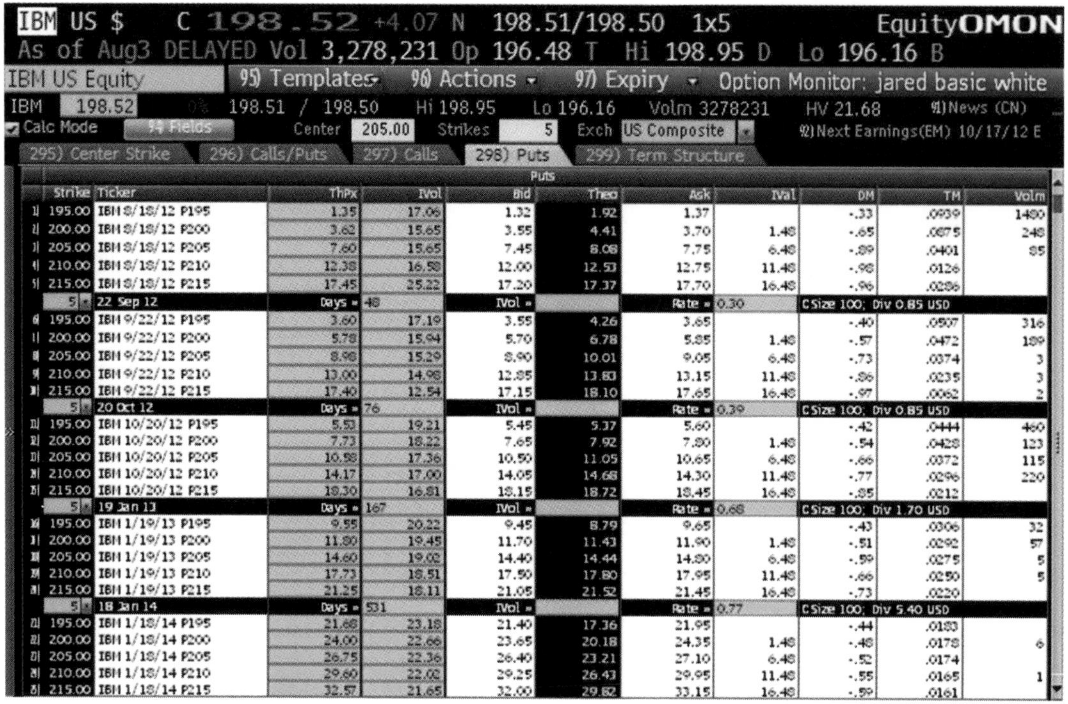

IBM US $ C 198.52 +4.07 N 198.51/198.50 1x5 EquityOMON
As of Aug3 DELAYED Vol 3,278,231 Op 196.48 T Hi 198.95 D Lo 196.16 B
IBM US Equity 95) Templates 96) Actions 97) Expiry Option Monitor: jared basic white
IBM 198.52 0% 198.51 / 198.50 Hi 198.95 Lo 196.16 Volm 3278231 HV 21.68 91) News (CN)
Calc Mode 94) Fields Center 205.00 Strikes 5 Exch US Composite 92) Next Earnings(EM) 10/17/12 E
295) Center Strike 296) Calls/Puts 297) Calls 298) Puts 299) Term Structure

Puts

Strike	Ticker	ThPx	IVol	Bid	Theo	Ask	IVal	DM	TM	Volm
195.00	IBM 8/18/12 P195	1.35	17.06	1.32	1.92	1.37		-.33	.0939	1480
200.00	IBM 8/18/12 P200	3.62	15.65	3.55	4.41	3.70	1.48	-.65	.0875	248
205.00	IBM 8/18/12 P205	7.60	15.65	7.45	8.08	7.75	6.48	-.89	.0401	85
210.00	IBM 8/18/12 P210	12.38	16.58	12.00	12.53	12.75	11.48	-.98	.0126	
215.00	IBM 8/18/12 P215	17.45	25.22	17.20	17.37	17.70	16.48	-.96	.0286	
5	22 Sep 12	Days =	48	IVol =		Rate =	0.30	CSize 100; Div 0.85 USD		
195.00	IBM 9/22/12 P195	3.60	17.19	3.55	4.26	3.65		-.40	.0507	316
200.00	IBM 9/22/12 P200	5.78	15.94	5.70	6.78	5.85	1.48	-.57	.0472	189
205.00	IBM 9/22/12 P205	8.98	15.29	8.90	10.01	9.05	6.48	-.73	.0374	3
210.00	IBM 9/22/12 P210	13.00	14.98	12.85	13.83	13.15	11.48	-.86	.0235	3
215.00	IBM 9/22/12 P215	17.40	12.54	17.15	18.10	17.65	16.48	-.97	.0062	2
5	20 Oct 12	Days =	76	IVol =		Rate =	0.39	CSize 100; Div 0.85 USD		
195.00	IBM 10/20/12 P195	5.53	19.21	5.45	5.37	5.60		-.42	.0444	460
200.00	IBM 10/20/12 P200	7.73	18.22	7.65	7.92	7.80	1.48	-.54	.0428	123
205.00	IBM 10/20/12 P205	10.58	17.36	10.50	11.05	10.65	6.48	-.66	.0372	115
210.00	IBM 10/20/12 P210	14.17	17.00	14.05	14.68	14.30	11.48	-.77	.0296	220
215.00	IBM 10/20/12 P215	18.30	16.81	18.15	18.72	18.45	16.48	-.85	.0212	
5	19 Jan 13	Days =	167	IVol =		Rate =	0.68	CSize 100; Div 1.70 USD		
195.00	IBM 1/19/13 P195	9.55	20.22	9.45	8.79	9.65		-.43	.0306	32
200.00	IBM 1/19/13 P200	11.80	19.45	11.70	11.43	11.90	1.48	-.51	.0292	57
205.00	IBM 1/19/13 P205	14.60	19.02	14.40	14.44	14.80	6.48	-.59	.0275	5
210.00	IBM 1/19/13 P210	17.73	18.51	17.50	17.80	17.95	11.48	-.66	.0250	5
215.00	IBM 1/19/13 P215	21.25	18.11	21.05	21.52	21.45	16.48	-.73	.0220	
5	18 Jan 14	Days =	531	IVol =		Rate =	0.77	CSize 100; Div 5.40 USD		
195.00	IBM 1/18/14 P195	21.68	23.18	21.40	17.36	21.95		-.44	.0183	
200.00	IBM 1/18/14 P200	24.00	22.66	23.65	20.18	24.35	1.48	-.48	.0178	6
205.00	IBM 1/18/14 P205	26.75	22.36	26.40	23.21	27.10	6.48	-.52	.0174	
210.00	IBM 1/18/14 P210	29.60	22.02	29.25	26.43	29.95	11.48	-.55	.0165	1
215.00	IBM 1/18/14 P215	32.57	21.65	32.00	29.82	33.15	16.48	-.59	.0161	

Exhibit 5.23

if it were near the short put as opposed to the long one for obvious reasons.

Gamma

Varies—Can range from positive to negative depending on position of stock in relation to strikes.

Call spread—Gamma will be positive if the stock is generally in the middle or *below* the midpoint between the strikes, generally peaking when the stock is just above the long strike. It will start to get negative as the stock moves below the center point of the strikes. When this is happening, you are moving into your profitable zone. Once the stock breaches the short strike to the downside, it begins to move to zero. At that point the calls will both be out of the money and where you want them to be.

Put spread—Gamma will be positive if the stock is generally in the middle or *above* the midpoint between the strikes, generally peaking when the stock moves just above the long strike. It will start to get negative as the stock moves below the center point of the strikes. When this is happening, you are moving into your profitable zone. Once the stock breaches the short strike to the downside, gamma begins to move to zero. At that point the puts will both be in the money.

The closer the short option is to the stock price, the more variance you will have in your P&L.

Theta

Varies—Can range from positive to negative depending on position of stock in relation to strikes.

The simple rule to remember for the theta, as it pertains to your profitability is to know that if the stock is *below* your breakeven, then time decay is generally helping you (positive).

- If the stock is *above* your breakeven that time decay is hurting you.
- If both strikes of a call spread are *out of the money*, then theta will always be positive (good).
- If both strikes of a put spread are *in the money*, then theta will always be positive.

The contrary is also true for both.

Vega

Varies—Can range from positive to negative depending on position of stock in relation to strikes.

Call and put spread—Vega will be positive if the stock is generally in the middle or *below* the midpoint between the strikes, generally peaking just at or above the long strike. It will start to get negative as the stock moves below the center point of the strikes. When this is happening, you are moving into your profitable zone. Once the stock eclipses the short strike to the downside, it will peak and then begin to move to zero as the stock continues to move in the direction you want it to.

Rho

Minimal risk—Because one strike negates the other.

However, if you have a very expensive stock and your strikes are extremely wide with a year or more until expiration, you could have exposure, especially if you are trading a large amount of contracts.

If you are trading these types of spreads, check the rho in your calculator.

All the advantages and disadvantages for bearish verticals are identical to that of bullish verticals. Another major advantage to using a bearish vertical compared to short stock is that you will not have the risk or margin requirements. Because stocks naturally go higher and tend to have shorter term corrections

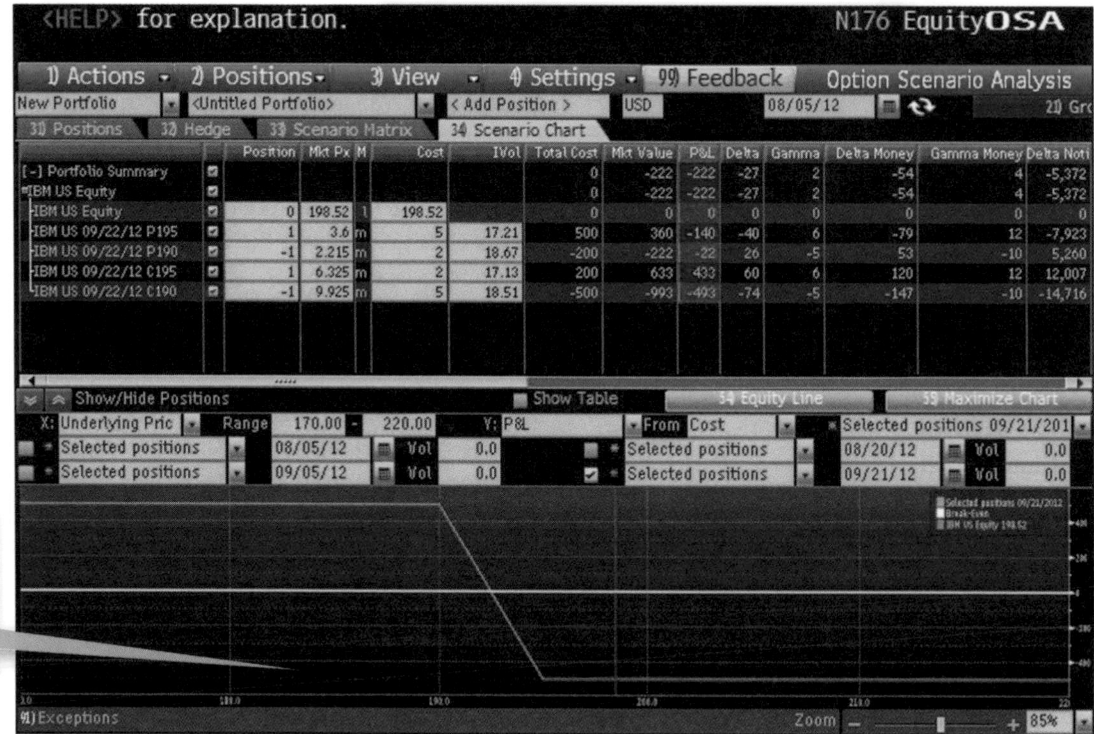

Bear vertical spreads (calls and puts) will always have a risk graph shaped like a Z; profit and loss are both limited.

Exhibit 5.24

along the way, it's advisable to use the statistical advantage that verticals can give you to stack the odds in your favor as much as possible.

A disadvantage to bearish vertical spreads is that Ivol and skew both tend to increase when a stock drops. This will inflate the far out-of-the-money options more than would occur with the same move to the upside. This added Ivol in your short option could take away a bit of your profit.

Step 1: Identifying the Target

The target for a bearish vertical can be as bearish as a high delta long put candidate or less bearish than an out-of-the-money put with a low delta.

Although the conditions can vary, it is still preferred to have an overall bearish thesis from the macro down to the stock. It could also be a frothy market and/or stock that you are expecting a short-term correction from.

If you have come this far in the guide, you obviously know how to identify bearish candidates. From there, depending on what the charts and fundamentals are doing, you can fine-tune your trade by using the vertical.

I scan the markets for stocks that have high P/E PEG ratios and not so great growth in the past couple months. I also run scans for bearish verticals with the best yields on overbought stocks by going to the OSCN/WSRC screens.

Step 2: Fundamental Analysis

Start with the same analysis you would do for a long put or short stock. As you go through the grading system and are finding several flaws in the trade or perhaps a chance that the level of bearish sentiment in the stock or broad market is not worthy of a big delta trade like a put or short stock, then start looking for strong resistance levels and trends in the charts that may make the trade more suited for a bearish vertical spread.

You can also try to identify levels that the market or stock just can't seem to eclipse and place your bearish vertical just above that level the next time the stock rallies toward it. Those levels don't just have to be technical; if a sector's P/E range is about 15 to 25 and you have a stock that is losing a little steam but is still trading at 33 times earnings, it might be worth a deeper look.

Be sure that there are minimal bullish catalysts that might justify the elevated valuation. See Exhibit 5.25.

If you are anticipating a slow meltdown of a stock over time, bearish verticals that are placed below the stock price may be the perfect medicine:

Ivol/Hvol—If Ivol looks elevated use the vertical to offset risk.

Strong sector, bad stock—If the stock's sector is artificially supporting a stock that has underlying issues, consider a bearish vertical at or above the stock price to raise your breakeven above the stock price and let time decay work in your favor as the stock tops out then moves lower.

Earnings or important economic data—Verticals can mitigate risk of a major economic event or decision like interest rates on the horizon. It may be best to tighten the spread and position it above the spot price.

Smart Investor Tip!

Use the calculator in the OSA screen and advance your time and price to where you believe it will be according to your thesis. If you see that your $5 spread will be worth about $4.50 at that point, then either accept that as your profit target or try widening or narrowing strikes until you find a profit/loss trajectory that agrees with your thought process.

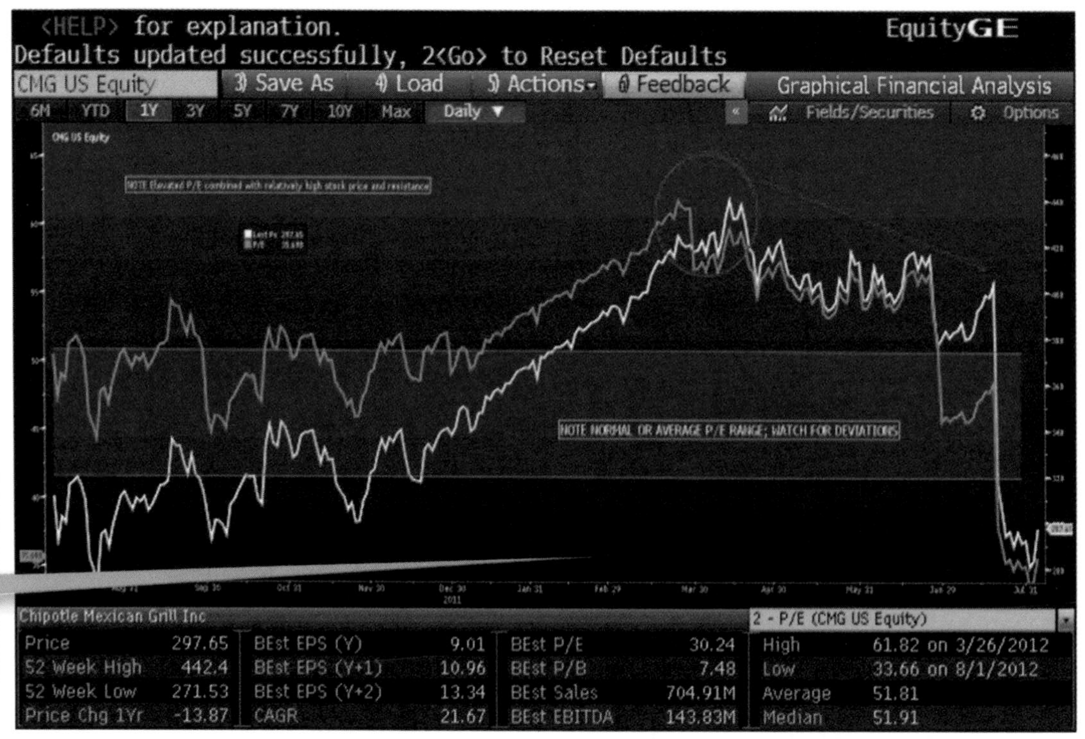

If P/E and price seem relatively rich but you are in a market that is stubbornly bullish, it might be best to utilize a bearish vertical spread as opposed to a long put.

Exhibit 5.25

Step 3: Technical Analysis

Again, most of the bearish spreads are going to want the same technical trends that long-put or short-stock traders want to see. The caveat is that the formations don't necessarily have to be "as bearish." Depending on strike positioning, you can lean more on resistance levels with a bullish vertical that is at or above the stock price as opposed to "needing" a bearish catalyst as you would with a long put or if the spread were placed below the spot price. In other words, if

Overall bearish trends are favored for a bearish vertical spread.

Exhibit 5.26

you have shaky fundamentals and a strong resistance level you feel the stock won't go above, but perhaps a neutral overall market, the bear vertical would be a potential candidate.

If you trade a bear vertical that is **below** the stock price, you will be looking for the same bearish catalysts you would want with a long put or short stock, but the vertical could be used to reduce risk. Be sure that your target for the stock is *below* the short strike of the spread you choose. See Exhibit 5.26.

Step 4: Selecting the Bearish Vertical Spread

The nuances of strike selection, time, risk, and other variables in both the call and put bear verticals are identical to bull verticals.

Smart Investor Tip!

Just because the vertical spread will generally have a lower negative delta and lower cost than the comparable long put, it doesn't mean that you should buy more of the verticals to get to the delta of the long put, unless you are extremely bearish and/or feel the breakeven in the bear vertical spread justifies the delta.

- **Strike price width considerations**
  - Every rule and behavior is the same with bearish verticals as with bull verticals. The wider the spread, the higher the risk and greater variations and exposure to Greeks compared with tight spreads.
- **Spread positioning**
  - When positioning your spread, use the same logic that was detailed for the bull verticals, just in reverse. Remember that bear spreads placed above the spot price will have a statistical advantage and spreads placed below will allow for more profit, but with lower probability.
- **Setting realistic goals**
  - Use the same tools and analysis techniques as the bullish verticals, except now the downside will be your profit goal and the upside will be where you place your stop. Hvol and ATR calculations remain the same; remember that volatility does *not* determine direction, just speed of movement.
  - Stocks tend to go higher over the long term and make quick sharp corrections, so I generally will take my profits quickly on a bear vertical—more so than in my bullish trades.
- **Setting stops**
  - Like the bull verticals, you can use several techniques to find "Risk Harmony" in a trade. Find that acceptable loss point that is comfortable mentally and is in line with the asset's volatility combined with a profit target that is realistic and in line with your probability in the trade.
  - It's strange because there are times when you buy a bear-put spread that is below the stock price for little money; the stock moves and although you make 50 percent, it still doesn't seem like enough, so you hold and end up losing. This is why it's imperative to run synthetic scenarios so that you can see what the real potential value of your spread would be if the stock dropped to a certain level by a specific time.

Bearish Credit Vertical—Using Calls

Behaviorally, this spread is identical to the bear-put vertical. But like the *bull*-put vertical, it's done for a credit, which is the max profit you can attain in the spread. When it comes to positioning, width, risk, and so on, simply use the techniques outlined for bearish spreads: thesis, Greeks, same strike positioning and target, and stop loss rules. See Exhibit 5.27.

When using calls to express a bearish sentiment you will always receive a credit to do the trade and be required to post margin that is equal to your risk (which will be the same risk that you would have in a bear put spread). See Exhibit 5.28.

Max profit in a credit call vertical spread is:

The Net Credit Received

Max risk in a credit call vertical spread is:

Distance Between Strikes – the Credit Received

Breakeven in a credit call vertical spread is:

Short Call Strike + Credit Received

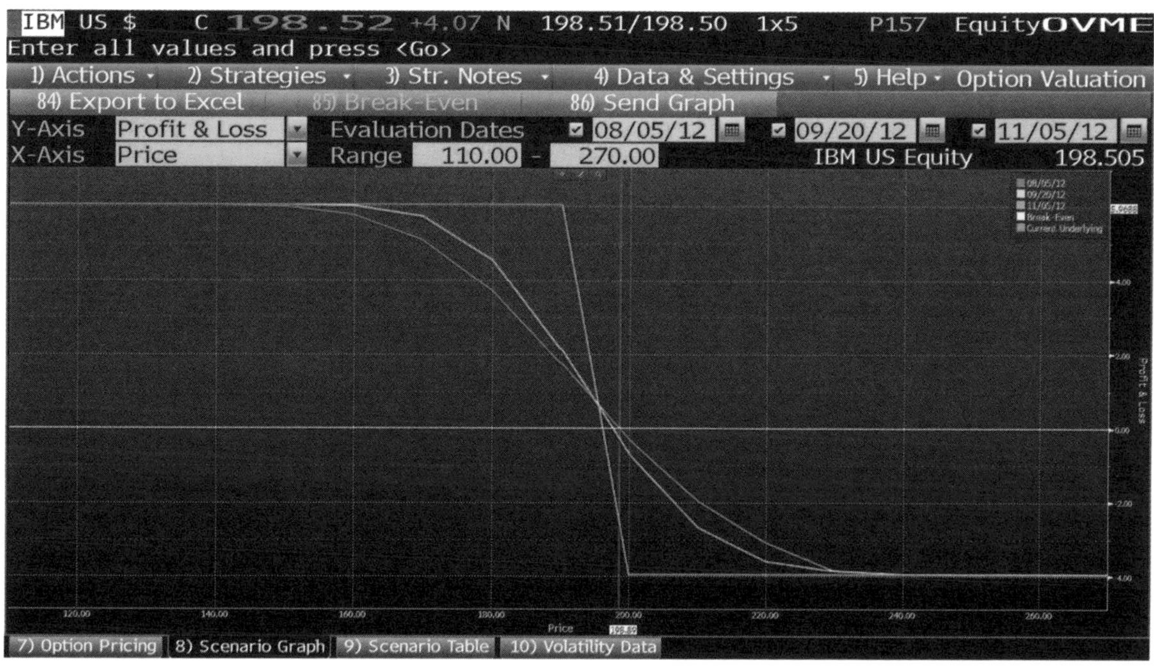

Exhibit 5.27

To create a bear-call spread, you must *sell* a call with a *lower* strike than the one that you bought on a one-to-one ratio. The goal of the bear-call spread is to have the underlying asset finish below the *short* call strike on expiration.

To qualify as a plain bearish call vertical spread, strikes *must* be in the same month, both must be calls; the one with the higher strike must be bought and the one with the lower strike must be sold, period.

It doesn't matter what strikes are selected in relation to the spot price.

Example: Bear call in action: A bearish example would be selling the Goldman Sachs (GS) July 155/165 call spread for $2.10 (which means selling the 155 call

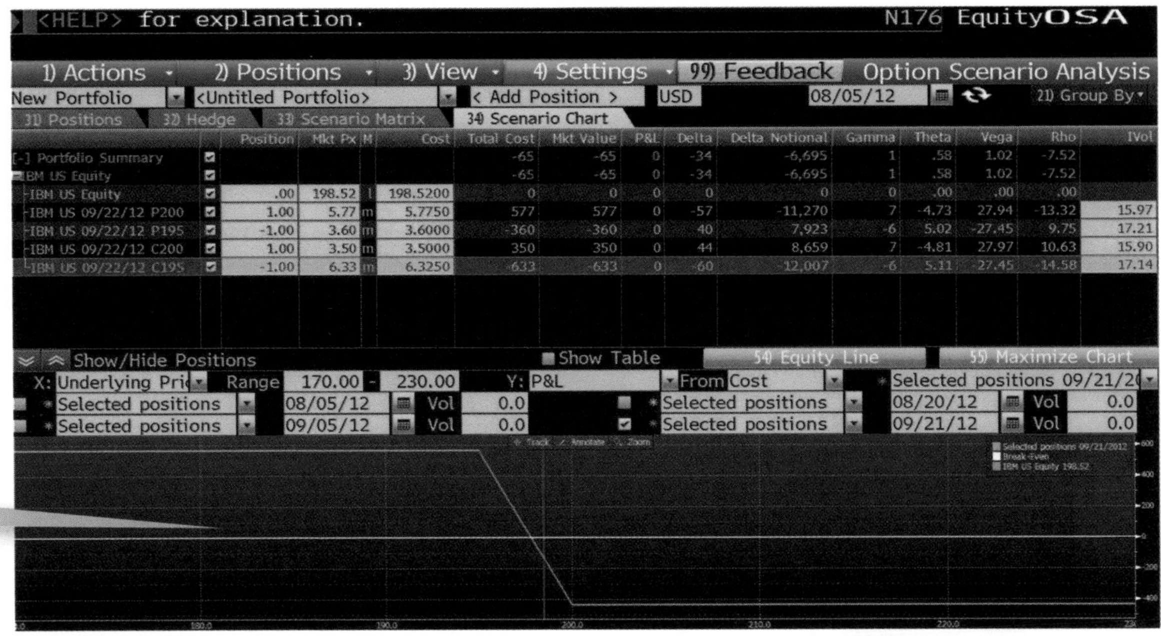

As I demonstrated earlier with the bullish spreads, calls and puts are the same in these spreads. Here we have similar bear call and put vertical spreads together and the risk graph is unchanged.

Exhibit 5.28

and buying the 165 call). Here you are limiting your risk to the width of the strikes ($10) minus the credit received ($2.10), giving total *upside* risk in this example of $7.90.

The breakeven, or the point at which you will not make or lose money, at expiration is $157.10. This means that GS could hypothetically rise to that level and when the options expire, you would break even in the trade (excluding commissions). Because of this characteristic, you have a statistical success advantage because the stock can be trading anywhere from $157.10 down to zero and you can potentially profit. This doesn't mean that if GS were to rally you couldn't lose money ahead of expiration.

Another advantage of this trade is that GS could actually rally to $155 by July expiration and you would still retain the $2.10 credit, which is a 27 percent return on your risk. The disadvantage is that the $2.10 credit you receive is the maximum you can potentially make in the trade.

Bear-Call Nuances

Selling a larger delta call means that it will inherently have a lower strike, higher delta, and a higher value than the one you are buying; therefore, you will be "selling" the spread—or collecting a credit for the spread. You are also said to be *short* the spread.

When you sell a call spread, you are collecting money into your account; this is also called a *credit* trade. Short-call spreads will behave entirely differently from long call spreads.

Remember that no matter how far the stock drops, you can*not* make more than what you initially sold the spread for.

If you sell a call spread for $1 and the stock plummets, that $1 is all you will make. Unlike the long-call spread, if you sell a call spread, typically you have a moderately bearish outlook on the stock—meaning that you want it to drop in value.

The second rule you must know when selling a vertical call spread is that you can sometimes lose more than the credit you brought in, meaning that if you sold the spread for a dollar and the stock goes up, you could potentially lose more than the dollar you brought in.

The third rule is that when you sell a vertical call spread, you cannot lose more than the difference in strikes, minus the credit you brought in. Meaning that if you sell a 95 call and buy a 100 call for a net credit of $1, you have a five-point spread that you collected $1 for, making your max loss $4. This is an example of an upside-down risk and reward ratio. You can make a dollar, but you have $4 of potential risk. Like selling a put spread, this may sound like a bad deal if you just look at that part of the trade. But there is a reason why a trader may select this strategy, which is typically because there is a higher probability of success in the trade and limited loss potential when compared to short stock.

Risk Examples

Consider risk/return when you are selecting the width and position of your spread. It's natural to chase the higher returns, but make sure that the short strike is in a place you believe the stock will be below and that the total risk if things go horribly wrong is acceptable to both your wallet and your psyche.

- Sell the 50 call and buy the 55 call for a 1.00 credit = $4 max loss.
- Sell the 50 call and buy the 60 call for a 2.00 credit = $8 max loss.
- Sell the 50 call and buy the 65 call for a 3.00 credit = $12 max loss.

Determining how wide you want to make your spread should be determined by both the amount of the credit you are taking in and how far you think the stock could rally if things went wrong. The less likely

KEY POINT:

Bear-call vertical spreads will always be done for a credit. The credit received will be dependent on the volatility of the stock, its position, the selection (expiration and strike) along with the distance of the strikes from one another.

The credit is the most you will ever make in the trade.

Smart Investor Tip!

A short-call spread is similar in behavior to an in-the-money bear-put spread, but it is a credit trade.

KEY POINT:

I tend to favor bear calls over bear puts if I am positioning my strikes *above* the spot price. This again is because the calls will be out of the money and therefore cheaper with tighter bid-ask spreads allowing better pricing and fills.

Exhibit 5.29

you think it is that the stock will rally, widen your spread. The more likely you think it is that the stock will rally, narrow your spread.

Bearish Debit Vertical—Using Puts

Behaviorally, this spread is identical in every risk and behavioral characteristic to the *bear-call* vertical. But like the *bull-call* vertical, it's done for a debit, which is the max loss you can incur in the trade. When it comes to positioning, width, risk, and so on, simply use the techniques outlined for bearish spreads; same strikes, same buying and selling action; only now you will use puts, pay a debit, and *not* be required to post margin. See Exhibit 5.29.

To qualify as a plain vertical spread, strikes *must* be in the same month, both will be puts; the *lower* strike

Smart Investor Tip!

The goal of selling a vertical call spread is to have the stock finish *below* the call you sold at expiration.

will be sold and the *higher* strike will be bought, period. The strikes can be anywhere in relation to the spot price.

Max profit in a debit put vertical spread is:

Distance Between Strikes – the Premium Paid

Max risk in a debit put vertical spread is:

The Premium Paid

Breakeven in a debit put vertical spread is:

Long Put Strike – Premium Paid

To create a bear put spread, you must *sell* a put with a *lower* strike than the one that you bought on a one-to-one ratio. The goal of the bear-put spread is to have the underlying asset finish below the *short*-put strike on expiration.

To qualify as a plain bearish put vertical spread, strikes *must* be in the same month, both must be puts; the one with the higher strike must be bought and the one with the lower strike must be sold, period.

It doesn't matter what strikes are selected in relation to the spot price.

The spread, even though you are now using puts would behave almost *exactly* like the bear-call spread.

By tightening your spreads, you will reduce your potential return, but lower your risk, generally speaking. If you are selling wider spreads, you are most likely more confident in your thesis on direction.

In a debit trade you will pay the full amount up front and this is the most you can lose (it's exactly the same "net cost" of a credit spread because you have to put up margin).

Using the same scenario and strikes as the bear-call spread example, there is a good chance that you would be able to buy the 165 put and sell the 155 put for a net debit of $7.90, leaving you with a potential profit of $2.10, which is the same potential profit as the call spread.

When to Use Put Spreads

If bear-call and put spreads are identical in risk, then why use one over the other? I will generally select put spreads if I am placing my spread *below* the stock. This is because the puts are out of the money and therefore cheaper, with tighter bid-ask spreads. That characteristic makes it easier to get into and out of the position, whereas the same strike calls might have a bid-ask spread that's $1 wide!

When it comes to selecting a spread with strikes that are *at* the money, I focus on return on risk. Which spread will allow me to make the most? If the $5 wide call spread can be sold for $1, but the same put spread can be bought for $3.90, than I will select the puts.

Consider risk/return when you are selecting the width and position of your debit put spread. It's natural to chase the higher returns, but make sure that the short strike is in a place you believe the stock will be below and that the total risk if things go horribly wrong is acceptable to both your wallet and your psyche.

1. Sell the 50 put and buy the 55 call for a $4 debit = $4 max loss ~ $1 max profit
   25 percent return

KEY POINT:

Bear-put vertical spreads will always be done for a debit. The debit (price) paid will be dependent on the volatility of the stock, its position, the selection (expiration and strike) along with the distance of the strikes from one another.

***Never* buy a spread for the same or more than the spread width!**

If you have a $5-wide spread (e.g., 50/55) and you pay $5.05, you are *guaranteed* a loss!

Smart Investor Tip!

Because the calls are in the money, they are going to be more expensive than the out-of-the-money puts on the same lines; they will also have a higher delta. Because of these two things, those calls will tend to have higher bid-ask spreads than the puts. If you choose to trade the call spread in place of the put spread, use caution and use limit orders.

2. Sell the 50 put and buy the 60 call for a $7 debit =
   $7 max loss ~ $3 max profit
   43 percent return
3. Sell the 50 put and buy the 65 call for a $10 debit =
   $10 max loss ~ $5 max profit
   50 percent return

In all the above cases the $50 strike was the level you believed the stock would stay below. Selection number three was the most bearish (and risky) of the three. The percentage return will vary depending on volatility skew. In this case the widest spread gave the best return, but that is not always the case.

Always Check the Percent Return When Comparing Vertical Spreads!

Determining how wide you want to make your spread should be determined by both the amount of the credit you are taking in and how far you think the stock could rally if things went wrong. The less likely you think it is that the stock will rally, widen your spread. The more likely you think it is that the stock will rally, narrow your spread.

A Walk through a Basic Vertical Put Spread Purchase

We will assume it's January 1, 2009. Let's say that you thought ABC Corporation was going to go from $105, which is its current trading price, to $90 or lower over the next three months.

You start looking at the options and find the June 2009 puts, the 115 put will cost you $17 to buy; it currently has a delta of –0.68; the 90 put can be sold for $6.50, it has a delta of –0.37. If you were to buy the June 115 put for $17 and sell the June 90 put for $6.50 at the same time, you would actually be buying the June 115/90 put spread for a limit price of $10.50. The spread is $25 wide, so your maximum profit potential in the trade would be $12.50 or 119 percent. Your maximum risk in the trade is your original investment of $10.50 or $1,150 per spread. Maximum loss occurs when the stock is *above* the long strike at expiration. Your breakeven at expiration is your long strike minus what you paid for the total spread. Meaning that in our example, you would not make or lose money (excluding commissions) if the stock was 104.50 at expiration (115 [strike] – 10.50 [cost of spread] = $103.50) 104.50.

When the put spread is out of the money, time is working against you, meaning that the spread gets cheaper as you move closer to expiration—which is obviously not beneficial because you are long. When the spread is in the money, time is actually working for you, meaning that if both put options are in the money or have strikes that are higher than the current stock price, the spread benefits or gets more expensive as you move closer to expiration.

CHAPTER 6

Visualizing and Trading Butterflies, Condors, and Complex Spreads

Butterflies, condors, and other complex spreads can be appropriate measures when standard options just don't offer the risk/reward and dynamics that complement the thesis that you have determined.

They can fill trade strategy voids or be utilized as an inexpensive means of protecting another position or an entire portfolio. The nuances and nonlinear behavioral characteristics of certain spreads can make them difficult for the beginner to understand, serving as a barrier to entry. I suggest paper trading all of them to get a better feel for how their values change with different occurrences in the market.

When you are managing a portfolio of multiple positions, it can become quite a task just to be able to track the interrelationships of all of your strategies not just on one stock, but as a whole. Keep these relationships in mind when you are constructing more complicated trades on top of one another.

Ratios and Backspreads

Ratios or backspreads can be employed in several scenarios and with a multitude of mind-sets. Generally the ratio is 2:1 (short versus long or long versus short), but you can adjust that ratio as much as you want depending on your thought process and risk tolerance in the trade. They are actually quite simple to execute and understand. You can think about them either as a long or short vertical where you buy extra options (calls or puts) because you want to participate in the possibility of an unexpected move in the asset in the direction you choose.

DEFINITION:
A ratio
is simply a vertical in which you buy or sell more than one option against another.

Smart Investor Tip!

Backspreads and ratio spreads can have some odd behavior and P&L tendencies, especially if you are using ratios other than 2:1 or have a decent amount of time left until expiration. For example, if you trade a 50/60 call backspread (short one 50, long two 60) for a $1 credit, you will have a "loss area" in between the short call and above the two long calls on expiration. Make sure that you believe the stock will either stay below the short call or explode beyond the long call enough to offset this risk.

Smart Investor Tip!

A "quick and dirty" way to find probability of a certain price level is to use the delta of the out-of-the-money option. So if the asset is trading for $100 and the $80 put has a 30 delta, than there is roughly a 30 percent chance that stock will finish below $80. You could take it a step further and use OV to display Nd2 (the second delta) to find the real probability measurement.

Or you sell an extra option because you firmly believe that the stock will not go beyond a certain price by the expiration date of your spread. That level is your short strike price.

If you are long more options than you are short you have a backspread position. Backspreads can be done with calls or puts. See Exhibit 6.1.

Ratios combine volatility opinions with directional opinions. It comes to ratio-ing individual options or spreads against each other or against a stock position; sometimes we get so lost in "the box" that we fail to rationalize the benefit of just a couple of minor deviations from what comes naturally.

Increasing Odds

Long calls and puts are statistically disadvantaged from a P&L break-even standpoint, meaning that the underlying asset must move for you to profit on expiration. Your breakeven will always be worse than if you had just bought or shorted the underlying outright.

So theoretically speaking, barring changes in volatility or anomalies, your odds of success when buying a call or put are less than 50/50 when it comes to the movement of the underlying.

The advantage or trade-off for this statistical break-even disadvantage is that the single option offers leverage, lower cost, and so on. In the options world, everything is a compromise. In a sense, there is no such thing as a free lunch. Just about every positive aspect of an option strategy has a negative. It prioritizes the attributes of the strategy.

There is a time and place for single options, but most professionals seldom use single options for the bulk of their trading. By introducing both simple and complex spreads into your repertoire, you can gain more leverage, reduce costs and other benefits, in addition to gaining a statistical edge against the price movement of the stock.

When you work with more complex spreads you may have to determine more precise price ranges or movement speed (volatility) for an asset over a given period of time, so it becomes even more important to learn standard deviation, read charts, and have the capability to plot a realistic trajectory for an asset until your trade is complete.

Don't just rely on models—Apple's 50 percent rise in a couple of months in 2012 was not predicted by its implied volatility alone!

As you consider each strategy, you have to think in terms of benefits and detriments. What are you giving up (in odds) and what exactly will you be gaining (in potential profits) by putting this trade on?

This question should be asked of every strategy you are thinking of executing.

Butterflies, Iron Butterflies, Condors, and Iron Condors

All four of these can be used when you want to get more precise or more vague with your future expectations

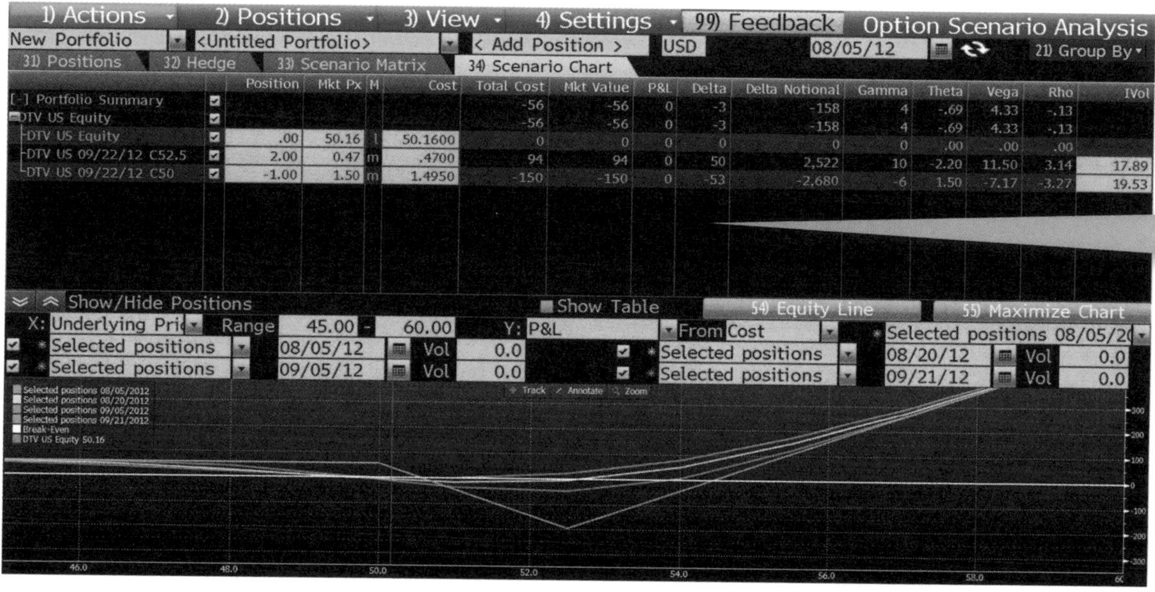

Backspreads can seem to behave oddly if you are not familiar with them; they also can quickly change in profitability as they approach expiration, depending on where the stock is in relation to your strikes. Pictured is a call backspread.

Exhibit 6.1

of a stock. They can also be used to take advantage of high or low Ivol/Hvol and their expected relationship to one another.

These four strategies are similar in structure, risk, and preferred outcome as they relate to one another and whether you are buying or selling. This is because all four are simple combinations of two vertical spreads that can be comprised of call spreads, put spreads, or one of each. Butterflies are also called *flies* for short.

The main difference among all of them is going to be how wide your "profit zone" will be and where you believe that profit zone should be placed.

This means that if you thought a stock was going to end up somewhere between \$52 and \$55 by June expiration, you might employ one of these tactics; if you

Smart Investor Tip!

Regular (not iron) butterflies and condors can be confusing when it comes to being long or short. If you are short a fly or condor you are always paying for the spread and when you are long a fly or condor, you are always collecting a credit.

DEFINITION:

A butterfly

is simply the combination of two vertical call spreads that are of equal width (long and short strike) that share a strike price in the middle.

KEY POINT:

Just like vertical spreads, it doesn't matter whether you use puts or calls; they both behave the same. It is more important whether you bought or sold the fly when it comes to risk.

thought it might be in the $60 to $65 range, you might simply adjust strike selection and width to get you the best risk/reward for your money.

Butterflies

Butterflies are great for a target price or no target at all. Butterflies can be used to anticipate a stock gravitating to a specific price or area or to speculate on a move away from a certain area without having a directional bias. They are extremely versatile.

Both spreads expire in the same month. You can think of the butterfly as a one-to-one combination of strikes equidistance apart. There are *always* three strikes in a butterfly spread.

Butterflies can either be bought or sold. It's all about what you do to the "wings," which are the outer strikes. If you bought the wings, you are long the butterfly; sell the wings and you are short the fly. The options must both be calls or puts, but not mixed to be classified as a regular fly. It doesn't matter which you use in terms of the ultimate goal and Greek sensitivities of the spread itself, it's all about getting the best price and lowest risk!

Buy one, sell two, buy one = Long fly
or
Sell one, buy two, sell one = Short fly

Long fly examples are shown in Exhibits 6.2 and 6.3 of long call and long put for IBM.

Short fly examples are shown in Exhibits 6.4 and 6.5 of short call and short put for IBM.

Long Butterfly

A long butterfly wants the stock to expire right at the center strike. This is where you would realize the most profit, so this is really a range-bound or target sort of strategy. I sometimes use a butterfly if I think the stock is going to end up as a certain price on or near expiration and I park my center strike right at that level. Even though a butterfly may be cheaper than buying a call or put to speculate on the move, be sure that you consider commissions in the trade as some brokers will charge per leg and even if they don't, each butterfly is a four-contract transaction.

The strike positions and 1–2–1 (long-short-long) formation remains the same for both. Whether you use calls or puts, the max profit would occur if the stock was at the center strike when the butterfly was expiring.

Wider butterflies will be more expensive, but may have a wider profit zone; narrower flies will cost less and have a tighter profit zone. See Exhibit 6.6.

Below are the P&L scenarios for a long butterfly:

Max profit in a long butterfly is:

Distance Between Strikes – the Premium Paid

Max profit occurs when:

The Stock Is at the Center Strike on Expiration

Profit zone in a long butterfly is between:

Lower Strike + Premium Paid and Upper Strike – Premium Paid

Max risk in a long butterfly is:

The Premium Paid

Max loss in a long butterfly occurs when:

The Stock Is Above or Below the Outer Strikes

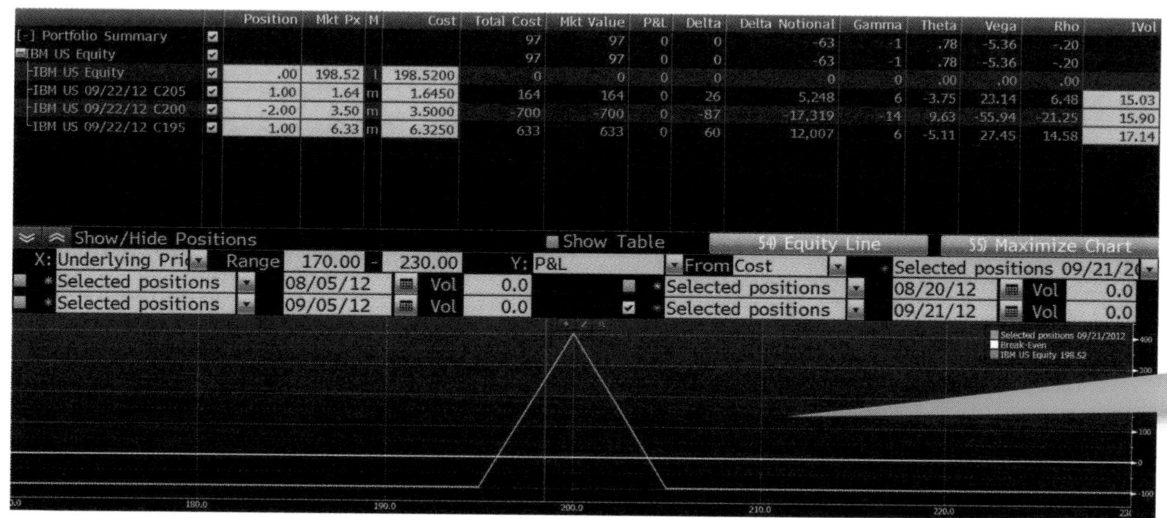

	Position	Mkt Px	M	Cost	Total Cost	Mkt Value	P&L	Delta	Delta Notional	Gamma	Theta	Vega	Rho	IVol
[-] Portfolio Summary					97	97	0	0	-63	-1	.78	-5.36	-.20	
IBM US Equity					97	97	0	0	-63	-1	.78	-5.36	-.20	
IBM US Equity	.00	198.52	l	198.5200	0	0	0	0	0	0	.00	.00	.00	
IBM US 09/22/12 C205	1.00	1.64	m	1.6450	164	164	0	26	5,248	6	-3.75	23.14	6.48	15.03
IBM US 09/22/12 C200	-2.00	3.50	m	3.5000	-700	-700	0	-87	-17,319	-14	9.63	-55.94	-21.25	15.90
IBM US 09/22/12 C195	1.00	6.33	m	6.3250	633	633	0	60	12,007	6	-5.11	27.45	14.58	17.14

Long call fly: Maximum profit is at center strike, and the risk graph looks like a witch's hat.

Exhibit 6.2

Breakevens

If the max profit is made when the stock is right in the middle of the fly, it would also make sense that you make less money the farther away the stock is from the center strike. You will lose your entire premium if you hold the fly until expiration and the stock is outside your outer strikes.

Profitable zone is between lower strike + net debit and higher strike – net debit. So if you paid $1 for the above fly, you will be profitable on expiration anywhere between 46 and 54.

Generally you will have a neutral or semi-range-bound sentiment with a bias toward decreasing volatility and uncertainty. Because you will want the spread to expire with the stock right at center strike, you may place your center strike at a "sticky" area around support or resistance.

If you place the fly ATM at the onset of the trade, then you believe that the stock will not experience a drastic change in price over the duration of the spread. Optimally, it is a stock that tends to be range bound with minimal corporate events scheduled up until expiry.

KEY POINT:

Long butterfly = debit. You will always pay to be long a butterfly and you can never lose more than what you pay; however, you could leg into a long butterfly for a credit, which means that you are guaranteed a profit of whatever credit you received. You would also have the potential to make more if the position expired with the stock right at the center strike price.

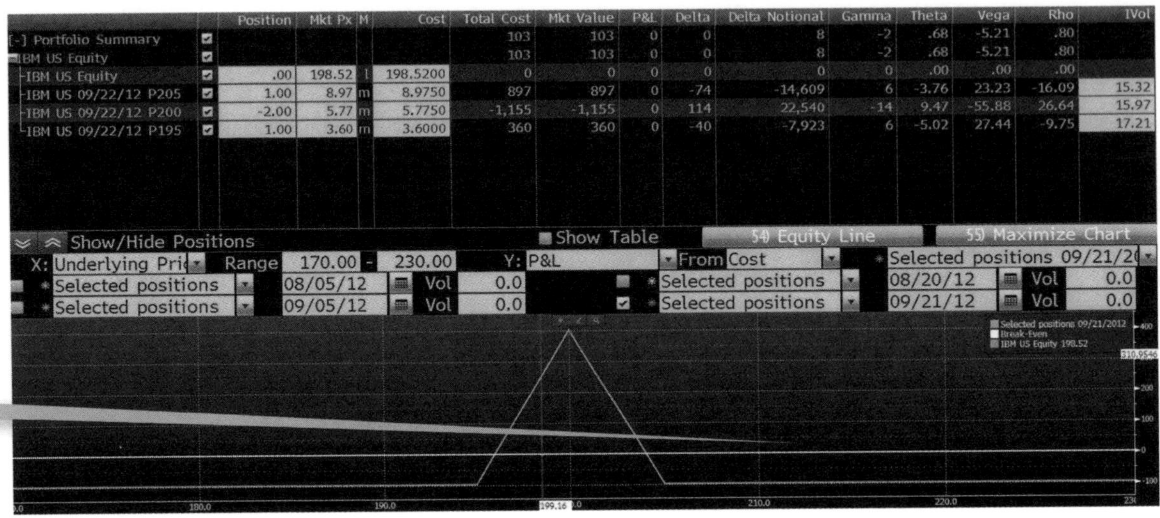

	Position	Mkt Px	M	Cost	Total Cost	Mkt Value	P&L	Delta	Delta Notional	Gamma	Theta	Vega	Rho	IVol
[-] Portfolio Summary					103	103	0	0	8	-2	.68	-5.21	.80	
IBM US Equity					103	103	0	0	8	-2	.68	-5.21	.80	
IBM US Equity	.00	198.52	l	198.5200	0	0	0	0	0	0	.00	.00	.00	
IBM US 09/22/12 P205	1.00	8.97	m	8.9750	897	897	0	-74	-14,609	6	-3.76	23.23	-16.09	15.32
IBM US 09/22/12 P200	-2.00	5.77	m	5.7750	-1,155	-1,155	0	114	22,540	-14	9.47	-55.88	26.64	15.97
IBM US 09/22/12 P195	1.00	3.60	m	3.6000	360	360	0	-40	-7,923	6	-5.02	27.44	-9.75	17.21

Long put fly: Maximum profit is at center strike, identical to a long call fly.

Exhibit 6.3

Smart Investor Tip!

Buy out-of-the-money wide butterflies on a stock that you think will drift lower or higher toward a certain level and stay there. Cheap butterflies can be used as a way to protect against a slow meltdown or melt up. Keep in mind that if a stock quickly falls or rallies to your short strike way before expiration, you may not see a profit because the time value of your short center options will increase.

You will also be looking for Ivol to drop if the fly is in your profit zone.

Long (Call or Put) Fly Greek Attributes

Delta

Varies. Delta is zero when the stock is at the center strike because the delta of the opposing spreads cancel each other out. As the stock rises, the delta gets shorter (because you want the stock to be right at the center strike at expiration) and reaches its apex around the upper long strike at which point it begins to move back to zero the higher the stock goes.

As the stock drops, the delta gets longer (because you want the stock to be right at the center strike at expiration) and reaches its apex around the lower long strike at which point it begins to move back to zero the lower the stock goes.

Your delta will always be pointing toward a move to the center strike.

Gamma

Varies. Gamma is generally negative with the long fly, and is greatest when the stock is right at the cen-

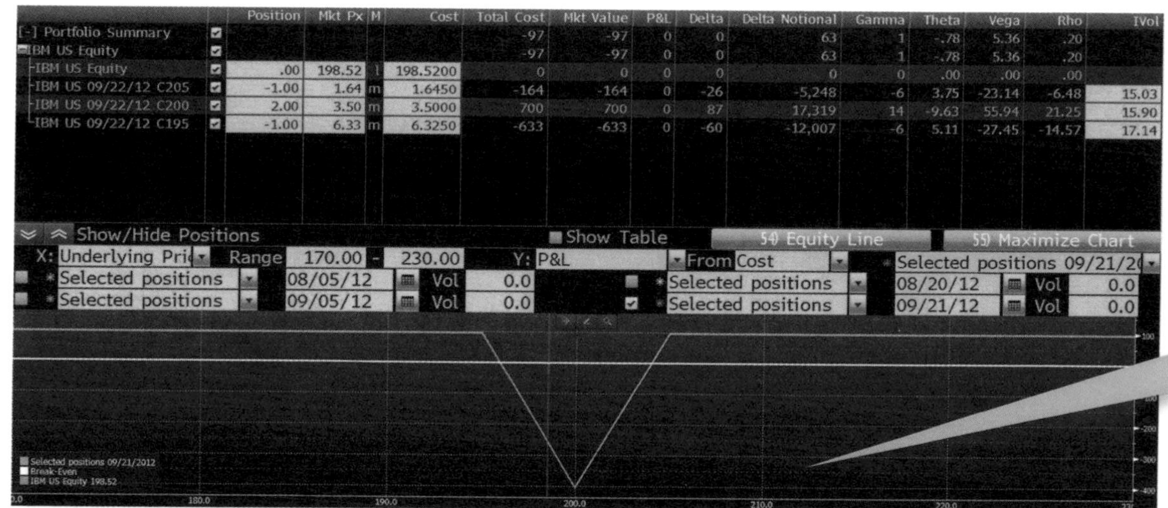

Short call fly: Maximum profit is above or below the outer strikes; the risk graph looks like a crater or V. You do not want the stock near the center strike on expiration.

Exhibit 6.4

ter strike. If the stock moves away from the outer strikes, gamma will turn positive as you will want the stock to move back into the profitable zone.

Theta

Varies. If the stock is within break-even levels, time decay will be beneficial to the position. If the stock is outside of the spread's break-even levels or outside the outer strikes, time decay is generally a detriment to the position.

Vega

Varies. When the stock is between the long strike prices, the position is short vega (you want volatility to drop); if the stock is outside of the long strikes, the position becomes long vega.

Remember that a long butterfly is constructed of two opposing vertical call spreads *or* two opposing vertical put spreads. It does not matter whether calls or spreads are used; the strike prices determine risk, cost, and Greeks sensitivity.

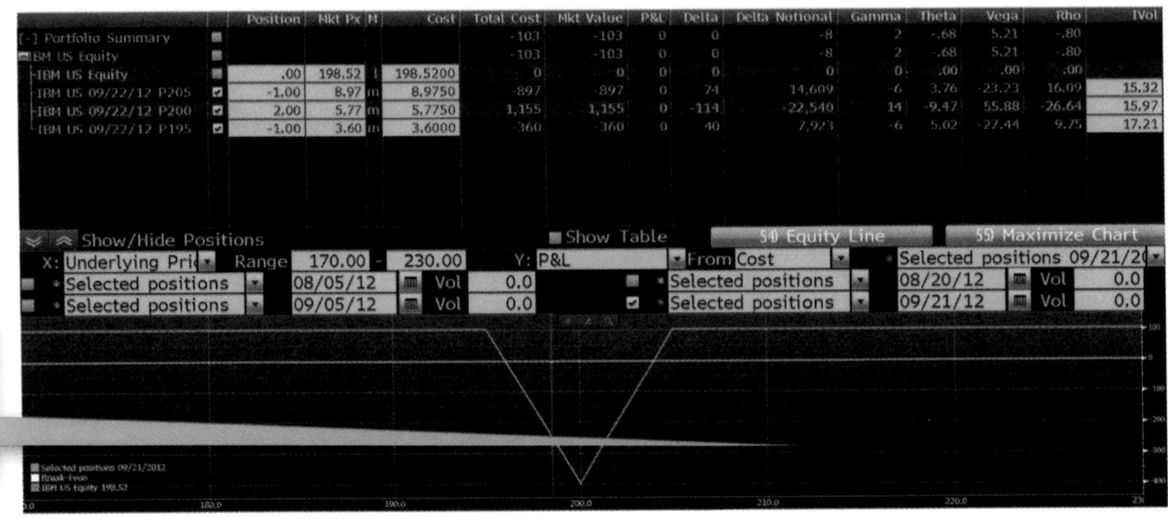

Short put fly: Maximum profit is above or below the outer strikes; risk and reward are identical to a short call fly.

Exhibit 6.5

Selecting Strikes and Expiration

The most you can make is the width of the spreads minus what you paid for the spread. So the selection of the strike prices has everything to do with where you think the stock will end up on expiration.

I can tell you that there is *not* a perfect guideline to strike selection, just do your best to find a probable area where the stock will end up. You can use a butterfly placed above or below the stock ahead of an earnings report if you think the stock will rally or fall to a certain area and stay there. Sometimes I will place these little cheap flies ahead of an earnings report for a small amount of money hoping to capture the Ivol crush and have the stock move to my profit zone.

The probability characteristics of a long fly will vary, but if the spread is placed with the short strike at the current stock price, probability of success rises because the stock can potentially move up or down (slightly) with you still resulting in a profit.

Typically butterflies are bought with less than 45 DTE and sometimes much less. Although exceptions can be made, trading long-term butterflies is

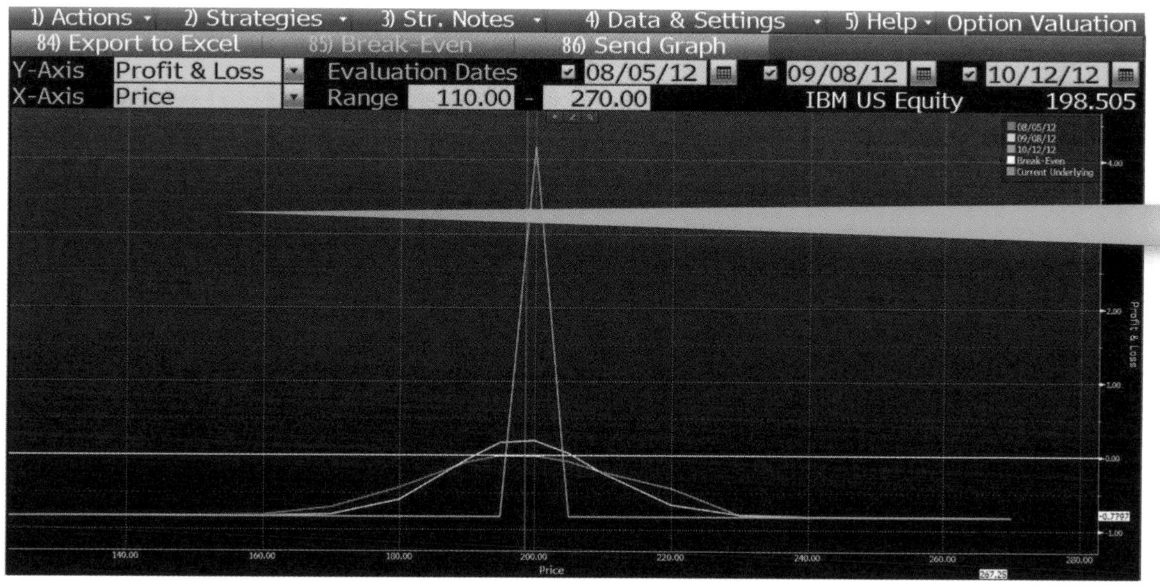

A long butterfly can use either calls or puts, but does not use both. Maximum profitability (or loss) is realized when at or close to expiration.

Exhibit 6.6

not going to bring you much profit unless the strikes are very far apart ($10-plus) and the stock's volatility moves dramatically.

Short Butterfly

The short butterfly wants the stock to move as far away from the outer strikes as possible. It can be thought of as a long straddle with a short strangle around it. A short butterfly, like the long, can either use calls or puts, but does not use both. The strike positions and 1–2–1 (short-long-short) formation remains the same, but here you are short the "wings." In the short fly, whether you use calls or puts, the max profit would occur if the stock was above or below your outer or short strikes when the butterfly was expiring.

You will always collect a credit to be short a butterfly and remember that the credit you receive is the most you can make in the trade. You can leg into the spread to try and maximize the credit you receive.

Smart Investor Tip!

If the profit zone of the long butterfly does not suit your needs, then try to substitute a long condor or short iron condor to get a more appropriate (wider) profit zone. Don't rule out the butterfly though; if Ivol in the short strike is high enough, the butterfly may have the same profit zone as a condor!

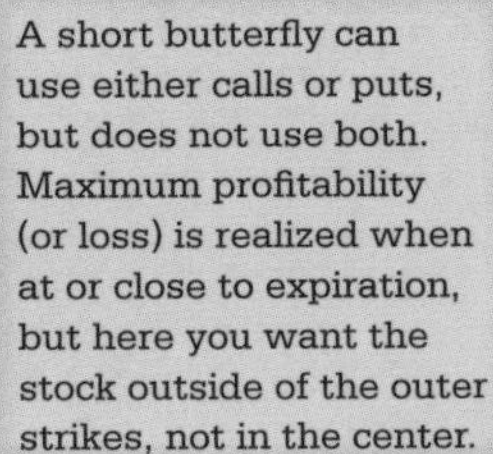

A short butterfly can use either calls or puts, but does not use both. Maximum profitability (or loss) is realized when at or close to expiration, but here you want the stock outside of the outer strikes, not in the center.

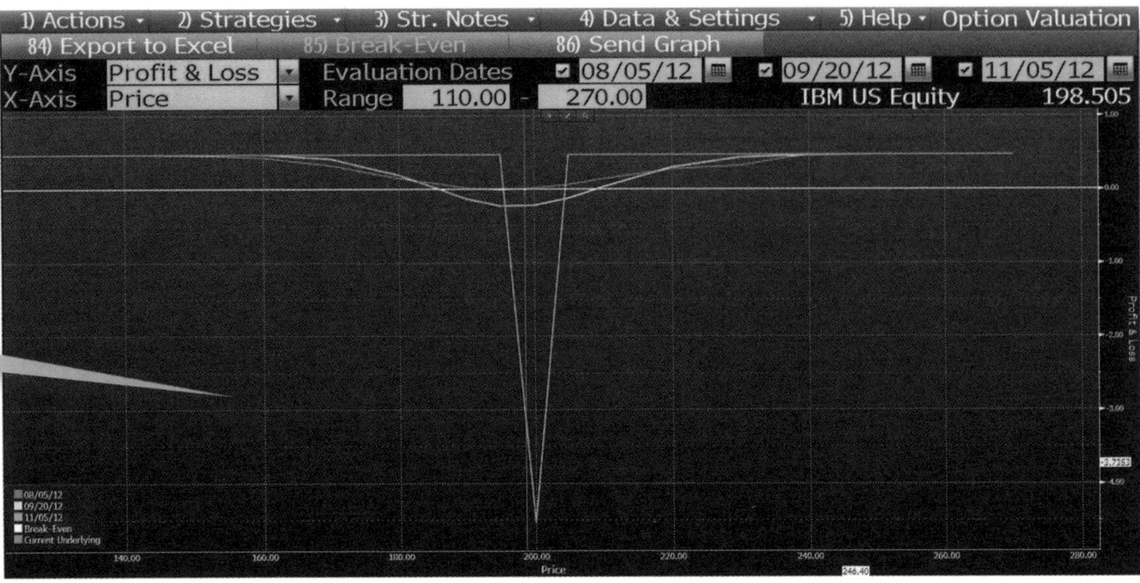

Exhibit 6.7

KEY POINT:

Check and compare your break-even levels (profit zone) before execution. Short butterflies are also limited in reward and in risk, but you can lose more than the credit you receive for the trade, especially if the fly is already away from the stock price. The closer the fly is to the stock price, the greater the credit received. The wider the fly is, the greater the credit will be, but so will the potential risk.

Like the long fly, it does not matter whether calls or puts are used, just use the options with the highest credit as that's all you'll ever make in the trade. Because you would realize the most profit when the stock is outside the outer strikes, the short fly tends to be more of a volatility strategy or one that is used when you think the stock is about to make a large move and *not* revert back to where it was trading.

If could be also used if you think that the stock is going to end either above or below a certain level by expiration. Some traders will sell a fly when they know a stock will move, but the markets are really shaky and unpredictable.

Even though a butterfly may be cheaper than buying a straddle or strangle to speculate on the move, be sure that you consider the limited profit potential and

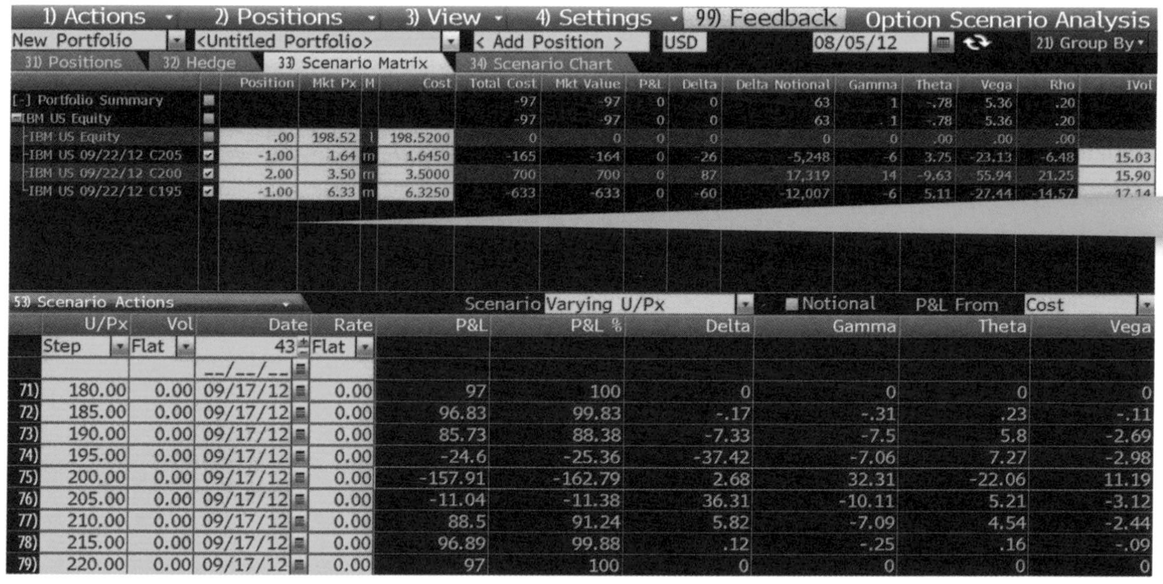

	Position	Mkt Px	M	Cost	Total Cost	Mkt Value	P&L	Delta	Delta Notional	Gamma	Theta	Vega	Rho	IVol
[-] Portfolio Summary					-97	-97	0	0	63	1	-.78	5.36	.20	
IBM US Equity					-97	-97	0	0	63	1	-.78	5.36	.20	
IBM US Equity	.00	198.52	l	198.5200	0	0	0	0	0	0	.00	.00	.00	
IBM US 09/22/12 C205	-1.00	1.64	m	1.6450	-165	-164	0	-26	-5,248	-6	3.75	-23.13	-6.48	15.03
IBM US 09/22/12 C200	2.00	3.50	m	3.5000	700	700	0	87	17,319	14	-9.63	55.94	21.25	15.90
IBM US 09/22/12 C195	-1.00	6.33	m	6.3250	-633	-633	0	-60	-12,007	-6	5.11	-27.44	-14.57	17.14

	U/Px	Vol	Date	Rate	P&L	P&L %	Delta	Gamma	Theta	Vega
71)	180.00	0.00	09/17/12	0.00	97	100	0	0	0	0
72)	185.00	0.00	09/17/12	0.00	96.83	99.83	-.17	-.31	.23	-.11
73)	190.00	0.00	09/17/12	0.00	85.73	88.38	-7.33	-7.5	5.8	-2.69
74)	195.00	0.00	09/17/12	0.00	-24.6	-25.36	-37.42	-7.06	7.27	-2.98
75)	200.00	0.00	09/17/12	0.00	-157.91	-162.79	2.68	32.31	-22.06	11.19
76)	205.00	0.00	09/17/12	0.00	-11.04	-11.38	36.31	-10.11	5.21	-3.12
77)	210.00	0.00	09/17/12	0.00	88.5	91.24	5.82	-7.09	4.54	-2.44
78)	215.00	0.00	09/17/12	0.00	96.89	99.88	.12	-.25	.16	-.09
79)	220.00	0.00	09/17/12	0.00	97	100	0	0	0	0

With IBM at $198.52, this short call fly is not in its profit zone (the trade was done for a $0.97 credit); note the Greeks and potential P&L on the bottom of the chart.

Exhibit 6.8

even the commissions in the trade as some brokers will charge per leg and even if they don't, each butterfly is a four contract transaction. See Exhibit 6.7.

Below are the P&L scenarios for a short butterfly:

Max profit in a short butterfly is:

The Credit Received

Max profit occurs when:

The Stock Is Above or Below the Outer Strikes on Expiration

Profit zone in a short butterfly is between:

Outside of the Following: Lower Strike + Credit Received and Upper Strike – Credit Received

Max risk in a short butterfly is:

Distance between Strikes – the Credit Received

Max loss in a short butterfly occurs when:

The Stock Is Pinned at the Center Strike on Expiration

Generally you will have a neutral or volatile sentiment with a bias toward increasing volatility and

KEY POINT:

The probability characteristics of the short fly vary with placement and strike width, but if the spread is placed with one of the short strikes above or below (not in between) the current stock price, probability of success rises because the stock can potentially move up or down with you still resulting in a profit.

Think about this: You have a $100 stock with an Hvol of 40 percent (a one-standard deviation move over 30 days is roughly $12). If you were to sell the 95/100/105 fly for $3, your breakevens would be $98 and $102. According to this model, there is only a 13.83 percent chance your stock will finish inside your breakevens. There is a much smaller chance that you will lose everything if the stock pins at $100 on expiration.

Would you risk $2 to make $3 if you had an 86 percent chance of making something? Perhaps . . .

In this analysis, we weren't looking for how far away the stock could go, just the odds of it staying in our loss area. It's advisable to combine this analysis with some fundamental or technical data that supports movement.

This thought process can also be applied to long straddles and strangles and long iron condors.

uncertainty. Because you want the spread to expire with the stock above or below the outer strikes of the fly, you want to place at least one of the outer strikes at a level that you feel confident the stock can move through. You should use volatility analysis to help rationalize your selection.

If you place the fly ATM at the onset of the trade, then you will be able to receive the most premium, but you must believe that the stock will experience a drastic change in price over the duration of the spread. Optimally, it is a stock that tends to be semi-unpredictable, perhaps with corporate events scheduled before expiry to act as catalysts. Try to time the trade so that the expiration date is just after the expected move in the stock so that time decay works in your favor.

You will also be looking for Ivol to drop if the fly is in your profit zone (if the stock is already outside the outer strikes, you will want it to rise if you sell the fly and the stock is at your center strike). See Exhibit 6.8.

Breakevens and Profitability

Before you enter into a short call or put butterfly, you need to find where your "profit zone" will be. Unlike the long fly, when you sell a fly, you want the stock as far as possible from the center strike. The max profit is made when the stock is above or below your outer short strikes.

- Your upper breakeven will be above your higher short strike minus your credit received.
- The lower breakeven level will be the low short strike plus the credit you receive.
- With the stock in between those levels you will lose *more* money than the credit you received. Above or below those levels you will retain a portion of your credit until the stock is outside of the highest and lowest strikes at which time you will retain your entire credit.

For example, if you collected $1 for the 55/50/45 fly, you will be profitable on expiration with the stock above 54 or below 46, which would also be your "profitable zone." The more you collect, the lower the chance you have of losing money because your breakevens are closer to one another. You would lose the most money with the stock at 50.

Short (Call or Put) Fly Greek Attributes

Delta

Varies. With time to go to expiration, delta is lowest when the stock is at the center strike; however, as the stock moves above the center strike, delta will increase as you want the stock to move higher. It will peak around the upper short strike and then begin to decrease as profit potential is limited. Delta will be 0 with the stock above the upper short strike.

As the stock moves below the center strike, delta will get shorter as you want the stock to move lower. It will peak around the lower short strike and then begin to decrease as profit potential is limited to the downside as well. Delta will be 0 with the stock below the lower short strike.

The delta will become one if the stock expires anywhere between your middle and outer strikes.

Gamma

Gamma is generally positive with the short fly, and is greatest when the stock is right at the center strike. Once the stock begins to move outside of the outer strikes of the butterfly, gamma will turn negative as you are now in your profit zone.

Theta

If the stock is outside its break-even levels (in profit zone), time decay is generally beneficial to the position. If the stock is inside of the spread's break-even levels (ultimately inside the outer strikes), time decay is generally a detriment to the position. The bottom line is that you want the stock to be outside the outer strikes if you want to collect time decay.

Vega

When the stock is between the short strike prices (not in your profit zone), the position is long vega (you want volatility to rise); if the stock moves outside of the short outer strikes, the position becomes short vega.

Selecting Strikes and Expiration

The most you can make is the credit you receive. So the selection of the strike prices has everything to do with where you think the stock will end up on expiration. In this case, you want to select outer strikes that the stock will be *away* from.

Just as in the long fly, there is *not* a perfect guideline to strike selection, just do your best to find the least probable area where the stock will end up and put your **loss** zone there. If the stock tends to be less volatile and tends to trend well or channel, you may want to tighten up your strikes, so your loss area is smaller. You can use a butterfly placed at the stock price ahead of an earnings report if you think the stock will rally or fall to a certain area and stay there or go further in one direction. An ATM short fly would be appropriate for a stock that is about to release earnings; just look back at the average percentage move of the stock over the past couple earnings reports and place your short strikes *inside* that amount.

The probability characteristics of a short fly will vary, but if the spread is placed with one of the short strikes away from the current stock price, the probability of success rises because the stock can potentially move up or down (slightly) with you still resulting in a profit. This positioning will bring in less credit and allow for less profit of course.

Time in trade (duration of trade). Typically, butterflies are sold with less than 45 DTE (time to expiration) and sometimes much less. Although, exceptions can be made, it's best to keep the time frames short unless your spread is very wide ($10-plus) and you expect an extraordinary move to occur over a long period of time.

Smart Investor Tip!

If the profit zone (or credit) of the short butterfly does not suit your needs, then try to substitute a short condor or *long* iron condor to get a more appropriate (wider) profit zone. Don't rule out the butterfly though; if Ivol in the long strike is high enough, the butterfly may have the same profit zone as a condor!

Condors

From thesis to behavior, butterflies and condors are a lot alike. They are both combinations of two call or put vertical spreads. The difference is the "dead spot" in the center, which equates to less gamma and different behavior in the condor compared to the fly. See Exhibit 6.9.

If you look at their P&L charts you can see the similarity and the difference at the same time. Both are limited in risk, both will have similar characteristics whether they are long or short, but their breakeven, cost, Greeks, and therefore risk will vary slightly.

Butterflies and condors are similar in that they are constructed by either the sale or purchase of two call spreads *or* two put spreads. The Greek attributes are also similar; however, condors differ in that they *do not* share a center strike like a butterfly. A condor always has space in between the two spreads and uses *four* strikes.

- Butterflies are spread among three strike prices.
- Condors are spread among four strike prices.

Option patterns can be all calls or all puts.

Buy one, sell one, sell one, buy one = Long condor

or

Sell one, buy one, buy one, sell one = Short condor

Some long and short condor examples are illustrated in Exhibit 6.10.

A short condor example is shown in Exhibit 6.11.

Because of this, condors are generally wider in strike width and thus have wider breakevens (both positive and negative). There are scenarios where the butterfly and condor may be close in risk and breakevens, especially if their outer strikes are evenly spaced apart and the center strikes are near each other.

Condor/Fly Comparison

SPY at $140.80

SPY 136/141/146 fly for $2.30

versus

136/141/142/146 condor for $2.80

Which is the better deal?

The fly makes **$2.70** potential profit if SPY expires right at $141, you risk **$2.30,** and the breakevens are $138.30 and $143.70 ($5.40 wide).

The condor makes **$2.20** with SPY anywhere between 141 and 142 on expiration, you risk **$2.80** and the breakevens are $138.80 and $144.20 ($5.40 wide).

Tough choice? Both breakevens are $5.40, which means that your profit zone is the same. You make a little less on the condor, but have a wider area where you don't have to worry about it.

Here you have to think about the chances of SPY expiring more than 50 cents away from $141, because that is the advantage the fly would give you. If you think that there is a good shot that SPY will finish close to $141, but probably more than 50 cents away, choose the condor; if you think it's going to pin $141, choose the fly. See comparisons in Exhibits 6.12a and 6.12b.

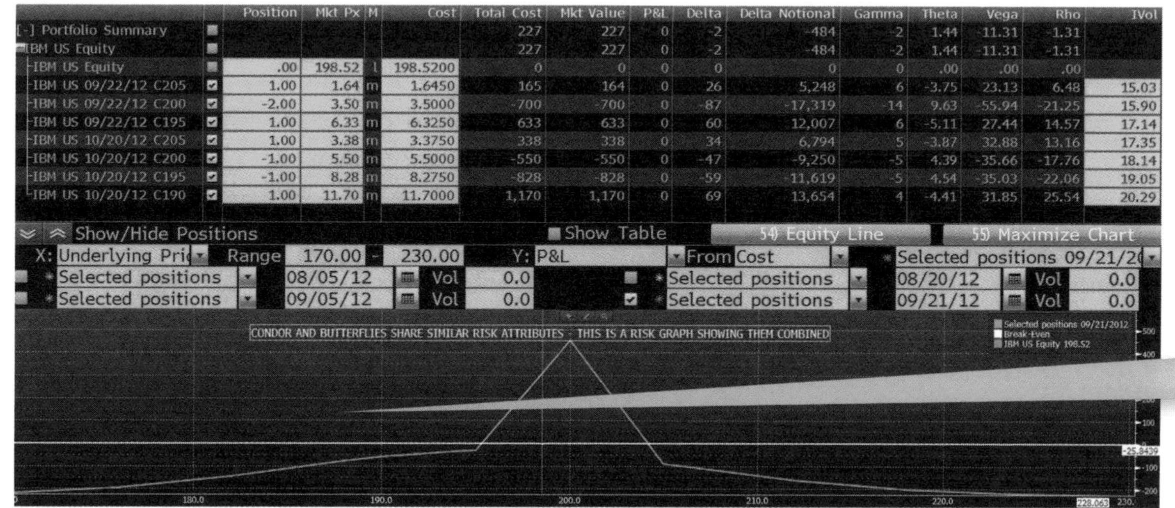

Not much changes (in basic risk terms) when you add a condor to a fly, but if the fly were omitted, the top of the risk graph would flatten out.

Exhibit 6.9

Long Condor

The long condor is identical to the long fly in the ultimate goal, but now you have a wider center area as opposed to a single stock price. The condor will use two call spreads *or* two put spreads combined just like the butterfly. See Exhibit 6.13.

The strike positions and 1–1–1–1 (long-short-short-long) formation is the same for puts or calls. Whether you use calls or puts, the max profit would occur if the stock was between the two short center strikes when the condor was expiring.

For a condor to be *long*, you will be short the inner strikes and long the outer strikes, as in Exhibit 6.14.

In the long condor, the characteristics and risks are very similar to a long butterfly, but there are some subtle differences:

Four strikes—The condor will *always* use four strikes. The distance between the *inner* strikes is called the *width*. The distance between the *inner* strikes to each of the outer strikes is called the *wingspan*.

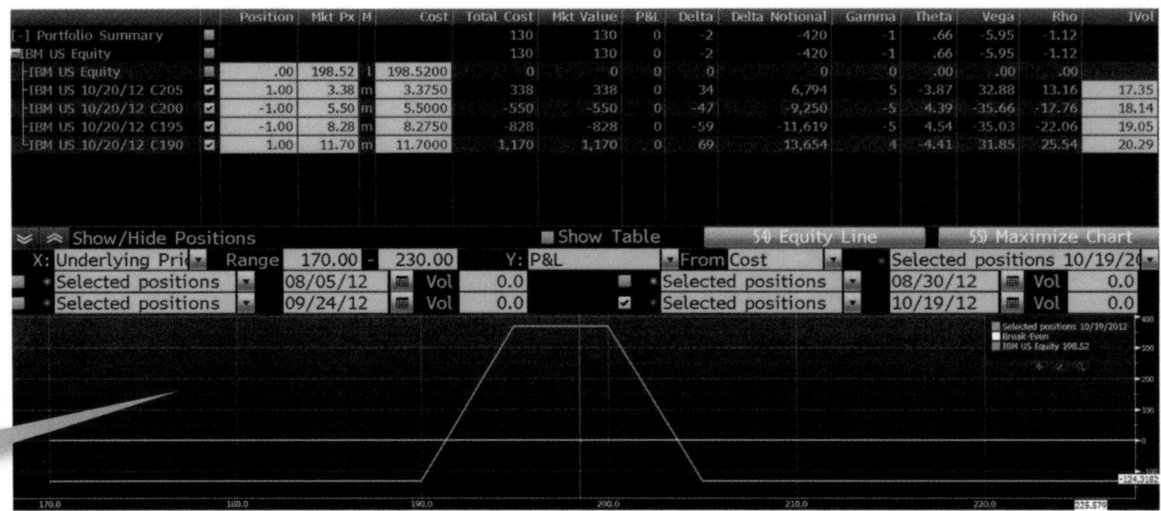

	Position	Mkt Px	M	Cost	Total Cost	Mkt Value	P&L	Delta	Delta Notional	Gamma	Theta	Vega	Rho	IVol
[-] Portfolio Summary					130	130	0	-2	-420	-1	.66	-5.95	-1.12	
IBM US Equity					130	130	0	-2	-420	-1	.66	-5.95	-1.12	
IBM US Equity	.00	198.52	l	198.5200	0	0	0	0	0	0	.00	.00	.00	
IBM US 10/20/12 C205	1.00	3.38	m	3.3750	338	338	0	34	6,794	5	-3.87	32.88	13.16	17.35
IBM US 10/20/12 C200	-1.00	5.50	m	5.5000	-550	-550	0	-47	-9,250	-5	4.39	-35.66	-17.76	18.14
IBM US 10/20/12 C195	-1.00	8.28	m	8.2750	-828	-828	0	-59	-11,619	-5	4.54	-35.03	-22.06	19.05
IBM US 10/20/12 C190	1.00	11.70	m	11.7000	1,170	1,170	0	69	13,654	4	-4.41	31.85	25.54	20.29

Exhibit 6.10

Smart Investor Tip!

The condor may give you more flexibility if you have a wider potential outcome for the stock, but again don't count out the butterfly. Depending on Ivol, the butterfly may offer the same breakevens and save you commission. You will not only consider how much you pay for the condor versus the fly, but also the fact that you will now have an area of max profitability versus a point of max profitability. ***Condors will usually cost more than the corresponding fly with similar spaced strikes.***

- For the condor to be balanced in risk and to be a true condor, the *width* can be any distance apart, but the *wingspan must* be the same on both sides!

More variables—With the additional strikes come additional variables to consider. Now, instead of choosing one distance between all strikes, you need to strike a harmony between the width and wingspan to find the breakevens and behavior that you desire.

Adjusting the width to \$10 and only having \$5 wingspan is fine, but your strike selections should also be predicated on selling the most expensive Ivol and buying the cheapest, in addition to your thesis of course.

You will also notice that your P&L and Greeks tend to slow down when the stock is between strikes, so if you are long that might be a good thing; if you are short, it may become frustrating. *Test, test, text!* See Exhibit 6.15.

Below are the P&L scenarios for a long condor:

Max profit in a long condor is:

Wingspan – the Premium Paid

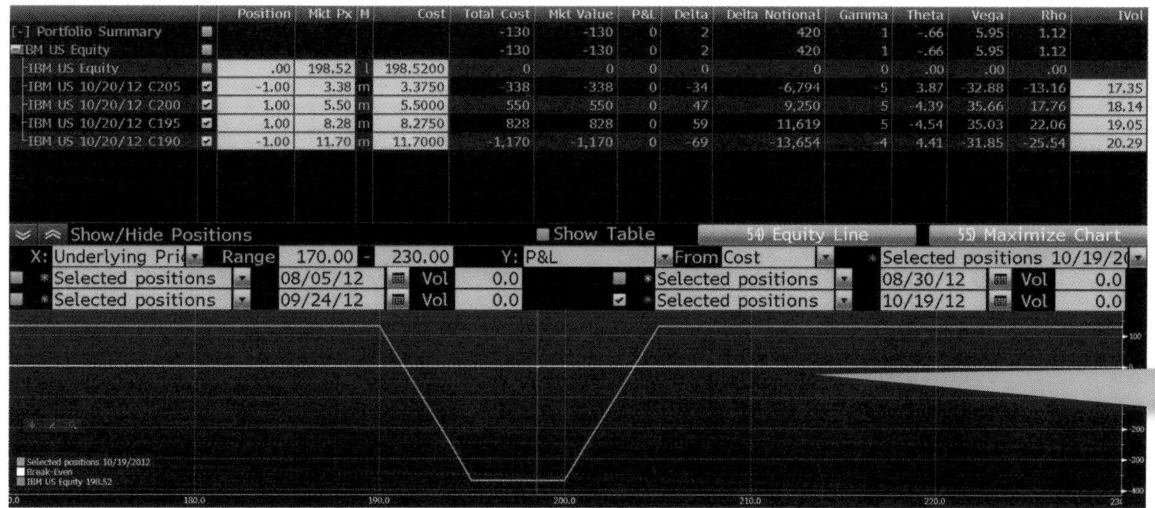

	Position	Mkt Px	M	Cost	Total Cost	Mkt Value	P&L	Delta	Delta Notional	Gamma	Theta	Vega	Rho	IVol
[-] Portfolio Summary					-130	-130	0	2	420	1	-.66	5.95	1.12	
IBM US Equity					-130	-130	0	2	420	1	-.66	5.95	1.12	
IBM US Equity	.00	198.52	l	198.5200	0	0	0	0	0	0	.00	.00	.00	
IBM US 10/20/12 C205	-1.00	3.38	m	3.3750	-338	-338	0	-34	-6,794	-5	3.87	-32.88	-13.16	17.35
IBM US 10/20/12 C200	1.00	5.50	m	5.5000	550	550	0	47	9,250	5	-4.39	35.66	17.76	18.14
IBM US 10/20/12 C195	1.00	8.28	m	8.2750	828	828	0	59	11,619	5	-4.54	35.03	22.06	19.05
IBM US 10/20/12 C190	-1.00	11.70	m	11.7000	-1,170	-1,170	0	-69	-13,654	-4	4.41	-31.85	-25.54	20.29

The short condor, like the short fly, wants the stock to be above or below the outer strikes on expiration.

Exhibit 6.11

Max profit occurs when:

The Stock Is between Inner Strikes on Expiration

Profit zone in a long condor is between:

Lower Wing Strike + Premium Paid and Upper Wing Strike – Premium Paid

Max risk in a long condor is:

The Premium Paid

Max loss in a long condor occurs when:

The Stock Is Above or Below the Outer Strikes

Scenario and usage should mimic what you would want in the long butterfly. The long condor would be used if you found that the risk/reward characteristics of the long fly didn't suit you.

The wingspan is your profit focus, its width, minus what you pay is how much potential profit you can make—it has nothing to do with the inner width!

Behavior

In the long butterfly (call or put) the max profit would only be with the strategy expiring with the stock right at the center strike; any deviation from that point would take away from profitability.

		Position	Mkt Px	M	Cost	Total Cost	Mkt Value	P&L	Delta	Delta Notional	Gamma	Theta	Vega	Rho	IVol
[-] Portfolio Summary	■					180	201	21	5	646	-4	.89	-8.31	.58	
SPY US Equity	■					180	201	21	5	646	-4	.89	-8.31	.58	
SPY US Equity	■	.00	139.35	l	139.3490	0	0	0	0	0	0	.00	.00	.00	
SPY US 09/22/12 C146	☑	1.00	0.48	m	.5000	50	48	-2	15	2,136	5	-1.57	11.83	2.68	12.41
SPY US 09/22/12 C142	☑	-1.00	1.61	m	1.6000	-160	-161	-1	-36	-5,011	-8	2.72	-18.67	-6.22	13.54
SPY US 09/22/12 C141	☑	-1.00	2.07	m	2.1000	-210	-207	3	-42	-5,842	-8	2.95	-19.51	-7.22	14.03
SPY US 09/22/12 C136	☑	1.00	5.21	m	5.0000	500	521	21	67	9,363	6	-3.21	18.04	11.33	16.51

53) Scenario Actions — Scenario: Varying U/Px — ■ Notional — P&L From: Cost

	U/Px	Vol	Date	Rate	P&L	P&L %	Delta	Gamma	Theta	Vega
	Step	Flat	47	Flat						
			__/__/__							
71)	136.00	0.00	09/21/12	0.00	-180	-100	0	0	0	0
72)	137.00	0.00	09/21/12	0.00	-80	-44.44	0	0	0	0
73)	138.00	0.00	09/21/12	0.00	20	11.11	0	0	0	0
74)	139.00	0.00	09/21/12	0.00	120	66.67	0	0	0	0
75)	141.00	0.00	09/21/12	[illegible]	[illegible]	177.78	0	0	0	0
[illegible]	[illegible]	0.00	09/21/12	0.00	220	122.22	0	0	0	0
77)	144.00	0.00	09/21/12	0.00	120	66.67	0	0	0	0
78)	145.00	0.00	09/21/12	0.00	20	11.11	0	0	0	0
79)	146.00	0.00	09/21/12	0.00	-80	-44.44	0	0	0	0

SPY short condor strike selection and risk; note the potential P&L on the bottom.

Exhibit 6.12a

In the long condor, the strikes are spread out, which means that as long as the stock stays *anywhere* between the two short center strikes (which are also called the *body*), the spread will be worth its max value. This higher probability of full profitability comes at a cost—less potential profit. In a long condor the credit that you receive for the spread will be less than if you traded a similarly spaced and positioned long butterfly. Call and put condors both have similar behaviors.

Long condors will begin to lose money if the stock moves above or below your break-even points, but because the condor is spread out, the stock has to move further for the maximum loss to occur when compared to a similar width butterfly.

Long (Call or Put) Condor Greek Attributes/Sentiment

Condor Greeks are similar to long (call or put) butterflies, just with wider space between spreads, lessening the speed at which the Greeks change when the stock is in between the inner strikes.

This means the gamma will be less short in the center than it would in a butterfly and vega will also be less when the stock is in between the inner strikes.

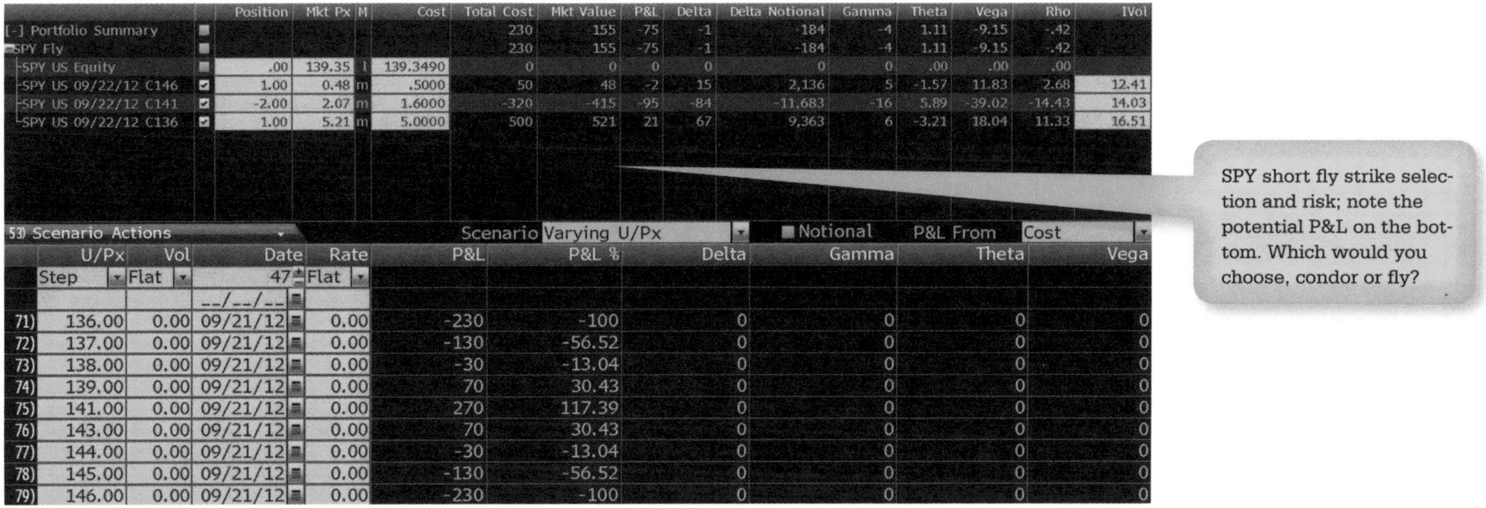

		Position	Mkt Px	M	Cost	Total Cost	Mkt Value	P&L	Delta	Delta Notional	Gamma	Theta	Vega	Rho	IVol
[-] Portfolio Summary						230	155	-75	-1	-184	-4	1.11	-9.15	-.42	
SPY Fly						230	155	-75	-1	-184	-4	1.11	-9.15	-.42	
SPY US Equity		.00	139.35	l	139.3490	0	0	0	0	0	0	.00	.00	.00	
SPY US 09/22/12 C146		1.00	0.48	m	.5000	50	48	-2	15	2,136	5	-1.57	11.83	2.68	12.41
SPY US 09/22/12 C141		-2.00	2.07	m	1.6000	-320	-415	-95	-84	-11,683	-16	5.89	-39.02	-14.43	14.03
SPY US 09/22/12 C136		1.00	5.21	m	5.0000	500	521	21	67	9,363	6	-3.21	18.04	11.33	16.51

53) Scenario Actions — Scenario Varying U/Px — Notional — P&L From Cost

	U/Px	Vol	Date	Rate	P&L	P&L %	Delta	Gamma	Theta	Vega
	Step	Flat	47	Flat						
			--/--/--							
71)	136.00	0.00	09/21/12	0.00	-230	-100	0	0	0	0
72)	137.00	0.00	09/21/12	0.00	-130	-56.52	0	0	0	0
73)	138.00	0.00	09/21/12	0.00	-30	-13.04	0	0	0	0
74)	139.00	0.00	09/21/12	0.00	70	30.43	0	0	0	0
75)	141.00	0.00	09/21/12	0.00	270	117.39	0	0	0	0
76)	143.00	0.00	09/21/12	0.00	70	30.43	0	0	0	0
77)	144.00	0.00	09/21/12	0.00	-30	-13.04	0	0	0	0
78)	145.00	0.00	09/21/12	0.00	-130	-56.52	0	0	0	0
79)	146.00	0.00	09/21/12	0.00	-230	-100	0	0	0	0

SPY short fly strike selection and risk; note the potential P&L on the bottom. Which would you choose, condor or fly?

Exhibit 6.12b

Short Condor

The short condor is identical to the short fly in the ultimate goal, but now you have a wider center area as opposed to a single stock price. The center area is where you will lose the most money in your short condor. The short condor will also use two call spreads *or* two put spreads combined just like the butterfly. See Exhibit 6.16.

You will always collect a credit to do the trade. The closer the strikes are to the money, the greater the credit received will be.

The most you can make in a short condor is the credit you collect; be sure to compare the risk/reward of your condor. If you are only collecting 20 cents on a $5 wide condor, the stock better be *far* away from one of the *outer* strikes.

Below are the P&L scenarios for a short condor:

Max profit in a short condor is:

The Credit Received

Max profit occurs when:

The Stock Is Above or Below Outer Strikes on Expiration

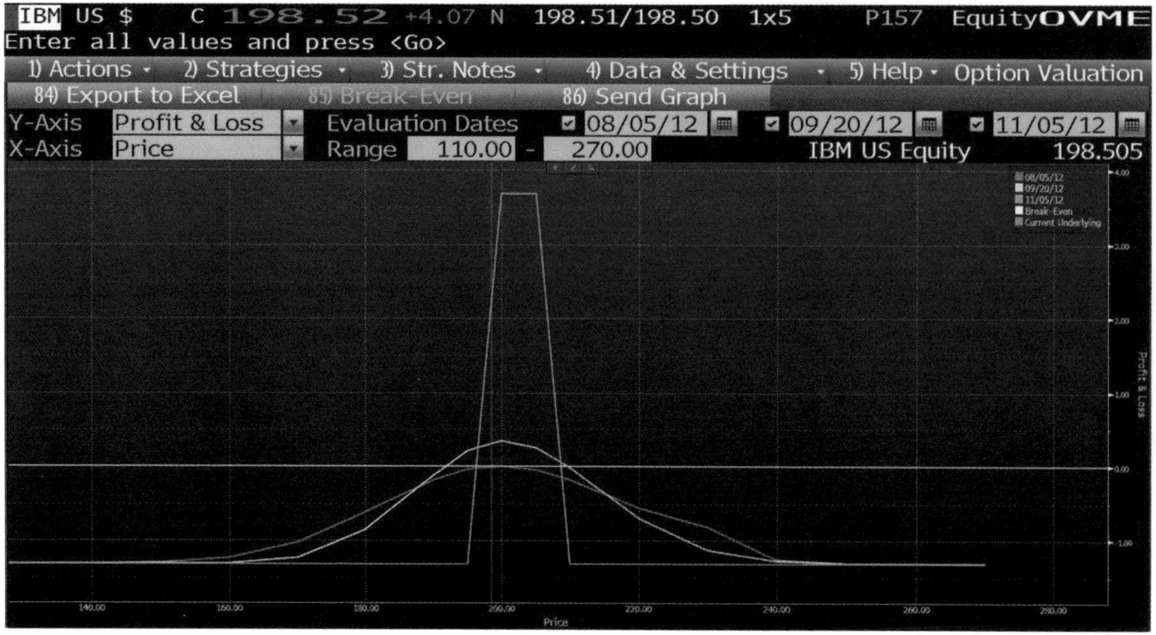

Exhibit 6.13

Profit zone in a short condor is between:

Lower Inner Strike – Credit Received and Upper Inner Strike + Credit Received

Max risk in a short condor is:

The Wingspan Distance – the Credit Received

Max loss in a short condor occurs when:

The Stock Is Between the Inner Strikes

The strike positioning rules and 1–1–1–1 (short-long-long-short) formation is the same for put or call condors. Whether you use calls or puts, the max profit would occur if the stock was *above* or *below* the two long *outer* strikes when the condor was expiring. The worst-case scenario is the stock stalling between your inner strikes on expiration.

The separation and distance between the center strikes in a condor is what makes it different from the shared strike in a butterfly.

Exhibit 6.14

For a condor to be *short*, you will be long the inner strikes and short the outer strikes (remember it's about the wings), as illustrated in Exhibit 6.17.

Profitability

In a short fly (call or put) the max profit would be the fly expiring with the stock outside of the outer strikes; the same is true for the short condor, except here it's all about the wingspan and outer strikes.

The condor's other behaviors are similar as well, but in the condor, the strikes are spread out, which means as long as the stock stays *anywhere* above or below the two short strikes, the spread will be worth its max value.

The wider the spread, the harder it will statistically be to achieve this, so the condor may yield more. But if you are looking at the same spread width, the condor will yield less than the comparable fly. It depends

Notice how profits increase if the stock stays between the inner strikes as you move closer to expiration. The graph on the bottom is displaying P&L over time, not stock price.

Exhibit 6.15

on the width, wingspan, and Ivol of the options involved.

IBM Short Condor versus Short Fly

With IBM at $199.60 (real market prices)

The July (90 DTE) 200/210/220 short fly can be sold for $2.25.

versus

The July 200/205/215/220 condor can be sold for $1.70

Is the condor really yielding less?

Remember that the risk lies in the wingspan, which in this case is $5 in the condor and $10 in the fly's span.

In the above case, you get a better return on risk in the condor ($1.70 on $5 risk = **37 percent**) versus ($2.25 on $10 = **22.5 percent)** in the fly. The trade-off here is the extra 55 cents you get in breakeven advantage in the fly. Is it worth it?

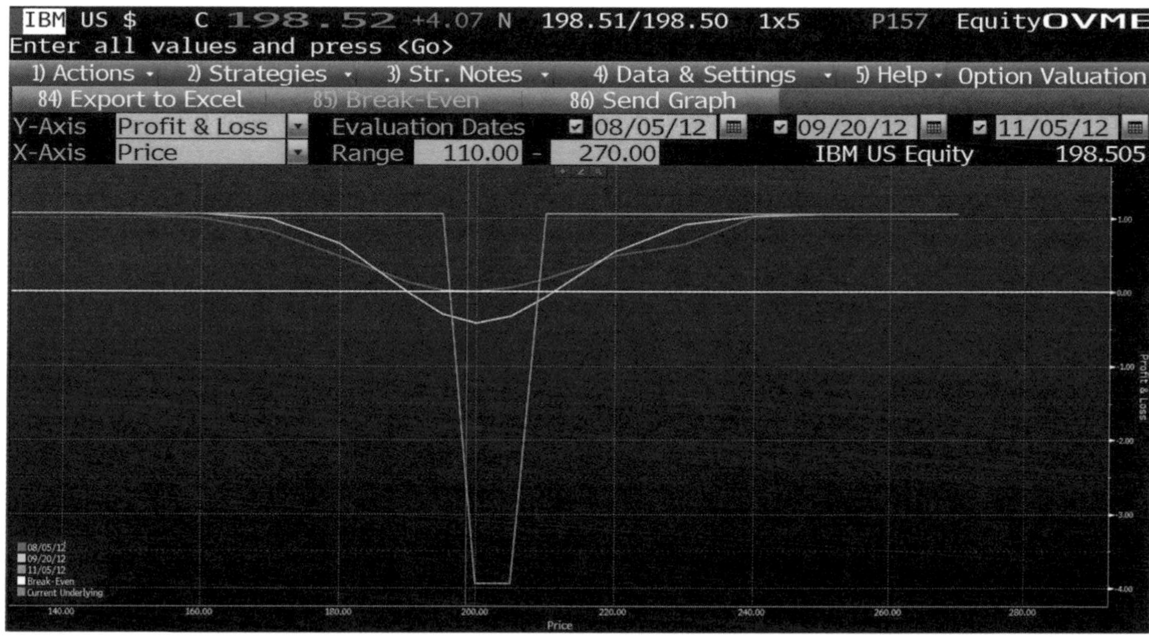

Exhibit 6.16

Again these are all things for you to consider. Call and put condors both have similar behaviors, so don't forget to compare them all.

Behavior

If there is a large amount of time left before expiration, your short condor may only experience a small profit if any at all. Condors, like flies, can be a bit finicky when there is either a large amount of time left or when the vertical skew and Ivol in general is changing.

Run tests in your scenario using the OSA screen to simulate the moves that you think could take place in the stock and see what happens to your P&L. If you are unsatisfied with the profits you would make if the move were to happen quickly, you can try and widen out your wingspan (and tighten your width if you need to).

Short condor strike positioning is important and goes hand in hand with creating the perfect risk/reward scenario given your thesis on the stock.

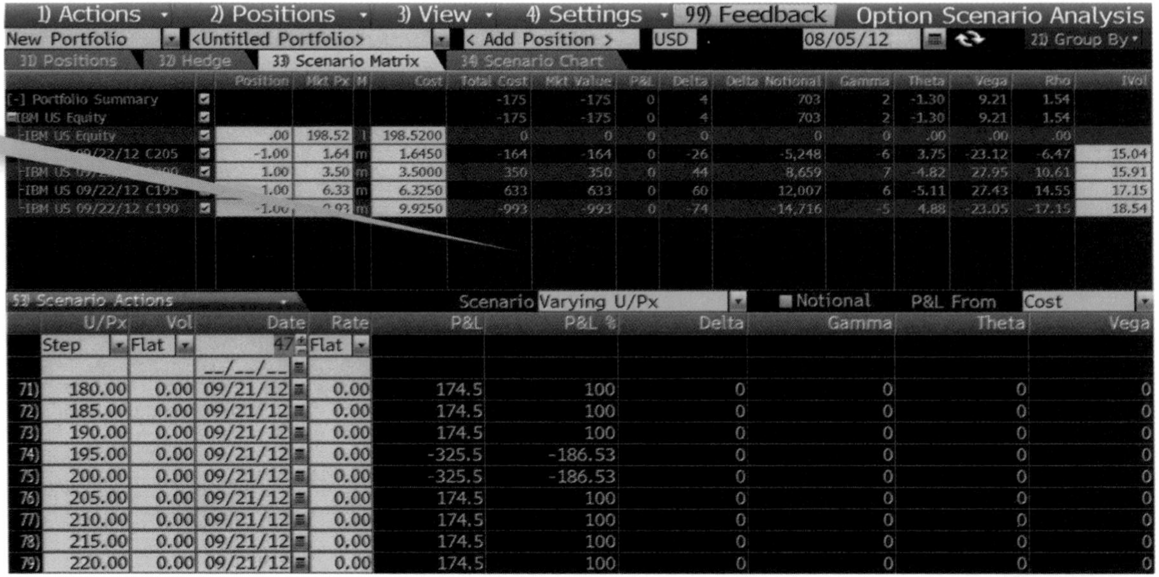

1) Actions ▾ 2) Positions ▾ 3) View ▾ 4) Settings ▾ 99) Feedback Option Scenario Analysis

New Portfolio ▾ <Untitled Portfolio> ▾ < Add Position > USD 08/05/12 21) Group By ▾

31) Positions 32) Hedge 33) Scenario Matrix 34) Scenario Chart

		Position	Mkt Px	M	Cost	Total Cost	Mkt Value	P&L	Delta	Delta Notional	Gamma	Theta	Vega	Rho	IVol
[-] Portfolio Summary	☑					-175	-175	0	4	703	2	-1.30	9.21	1.54	
IBM US Equity	☑					-175	-175	0	4	703	2	-1.30	9.21	1.54	
IBM US Equity	☑	.00	198.52	l	198.5200	0	0	0	0	0	0	.00	.00	.00	
[illegible]/22/12 C205	☑	-1.00	1.64	m	1.6450	-164	-164	0	-26	-5,248	-6	3.75	-23.12	-6.47	15.04
IBM US [illegible]	☑	1.00	3.50	m	3.5000	350	350	0	44	8,659	7	-4.82	27.95	10.61	15.91
IBM US 09/22/12 C195	[illegible]	1.00	6.33	m	6.3250	633	633	0	60	12,007	6	-5.11	27.43	14.55	17.15
IBM US 09/22/12 C190	☑	-1.00	[illegible]	m	9.9250	-993	-993	0	-74	-14,716	-5	4.88	-23.05	-17.15	18.54

53) Scenario Actions ▾ Scenario Varying U/Px ▾ ■ Notional P&L From Cost ▾

	U/Px	Vol	Date	Rate	P&L	P&L %	Delta	Gamma	Theta	Vega
	Step ▾	Flat ▾	47	Flat ▾						
			--/--/--							
71)	180.00	0.00	09/21/12	0.00	174.5	100	0	0	0	0
72)	185.00	0.00	09/21/12	0.00	174.5	100	0	0	0	0
73)	190.00	0.00	09/21/12	0.00	174.5	100	0	0	0	0
74)	195.00	0.00	09/21/12	0.00	-325.5	-186.53	0	0	0	0
75)	200.00	0.00	09/21/12	0.00	-325.5	-186.53	0	0	0	0
76)	205.00	0.00	09/21/12	0.00	174.5	100	0	0	0	0
77)	210.00	0.00	09/21/12	0.00	174.5	100	0	0	0	0
78)	215.00	0.00	09/21/12	0.00	174.5	100	0	0	0	0
79)	220.00	0.00	09/21/12	0.00	174.5	100	0	0	0	0

Exhibit 6.17

KEY POINT:

When you are setting your profit targets or in a profitable position, don't be greedy! Use percentages and logic to guide you. If the stock has made a dramatic move in your favor, ask yourself if there is a chance it will revert to the mean and take your profit away. If you think it will continue to move in your favor, don't be afraid to scale out of the position.

KEY POINT:

Iron butterflies and iron condors can use the *same exact* strikes as a regular fly or condor. Just remember the rules: iron condors encompass four different strike prices and iron butterflies, like regular butterflies, encompass only three strike prices.

Testing scenarios are the best way to get a feel for behavior, but even then, Ivol fluctuations can get a bit squirrely when approaching expiration. I prefer to use short condors ahead of an event that should provide movement along with a major Ivol crush to get my spreads' outer strikes as far away as possible and for all my options to move to total parity, which is the point I make the most!

Short condors begin to lose money if the stock stays between your inner strikes or breakeven points. If the stock is stuck in between the inner strikes and it's getting close to expiration (< 10 days), you may want to evaluate the trade and salvage it by purchasing the condor back (closing it).

Short (Call or Put) Condor Greek Attributes/Sentiment

Short condor Greeks are similar to the short (call or put) butterfly, just with wider space between spreads, lessening the speed at which the Greeks change when the stock is in between the inner strikes. Inside those inner strikes you will have less gamma and thus a slower P&L change if the stock starts to move. You will also have a wider area where you will be paying theta in between those inner strikes. All else remains the same.

Iron Spreads

If you preface a butterfly or condor with the word *iron* you are denoting that the spread is a **combination** of a call spread *and* a put spread in which both types are used; **both** spreads will be sold or bought.

All the rules of regular butterflies and condors apply, but iron spreads use a vertical call spread **and** a vertical put spread instead of two of the same type of verticals that construct regular condors or butterflies.

Iron spreads are used to maximize profit potential and target the cheaper options with tighter bid-ask spreads as opposed to a regular butterfly or condor that may have one side out of the money, but the other closer to or in the money, making the options pricier. Traders also like iron spreads because they are easier to intuitively understand. See Exhibit 6.18.

Typically, but not all the time, both spreads are placed out of the money and you are making the bet that the stock will either stay between your closest strikes (selling an iron) or that the stock will explode beyond the long strikes (buying an iron).

Iron spreads have the same Greek behavior as their regular condor brethren. The only difference here is that you are using a call spread *and* a put spread. Also note the change in nomenclature: *a long* iron spread (butterfly or condor) wants the stock to move away from the outer strikes and the *short* iron spread wants the stock to either stay between the inner strikes (iron condor) or pin the center strike (iron butterfly).

Short Iron Butterfly

The short iron butterfly is a bit different than a regular fly. Here you combine a bear-call vertical and a bull-put vertical that share a center strike price (the short strike). The maximum profit occurs if the short iron butterfly expires right at the short strike.

Below are the P&L scenarios for a short iron butterfly:

Max profit in a short iron butterfly is:
Credit Collected
Max profit occurs when:
The Stock Is at the Center Strike on Expiration
Profit zone in a short iron butterfly is between:
Center Strike Plus (and) Minus Credit Received
Max risk in a short iron butterfly is:
Credit Collected – Distance Between Strikes
Max loss in a short iron butterfly occurs when:
The Stock Is Above or Below the Outer Strikes

See Exhibit 6.19 for a structure example using IBM.

In Exhibit 6.19, the stock would have to be right at $200 on expiration for you to make the most money! The max profit in this iron butterfly would only be

Smart Investor Tip!

When trading an iron spread (butterfly or condor) you are short the spread when you collect money to do the trade and long the spread when you pay money to do the trade. This differs from regular butterflies and condors where you are long if you "buy the wings" of those spreads, which would mean that you actually collect a credit, and short if you are "short the wings," which means that you actually pay for the spread. I didn't make this up; you can thank our options founding fathers for the confusion.

Smart Investor Tip!

Even though the behavior and goal of the short iron butterfly is the same as the long butterfly, the iron condor is a credit trade where you get the *max* you can ever make up front and then hope that the stock pins the center strike so that you can keep all your profit. You will have to *buy* back the short iron butterfly when you close it.

Notice how the call spread and the put spread are out of the money and therefore less expensive, with lower bid-ask spreads. Long iron condors are identical to short regular condors.

Exhibit 6.18

attained if the stock expired right at $200. But let's assume for this example that you collected $4.03 (shown above) between both vertical spreads in the fly. Because you collected money, this means that you have two break-even points, one to the upside and one to the downside of the center strike by the amount of the credit. The more money you collect, the wider the profit zone on expiration.

Smart Investor Tip!

The further away the iron fly is from the stock price at the onset, the more credit you will receive.

Breakevens (Profit Zone)

Notice how the P&L graph shows the same witches hat formation that we see in the long butterfly. Where the short iron butterfly gets tricky is that it is a credit trade first that deteriorates (gets more expensive) the further the stock travels from the center. Because you have to "buy to close" it, there is potential for you to lose more than the credit received. See Exhibit 6.20.

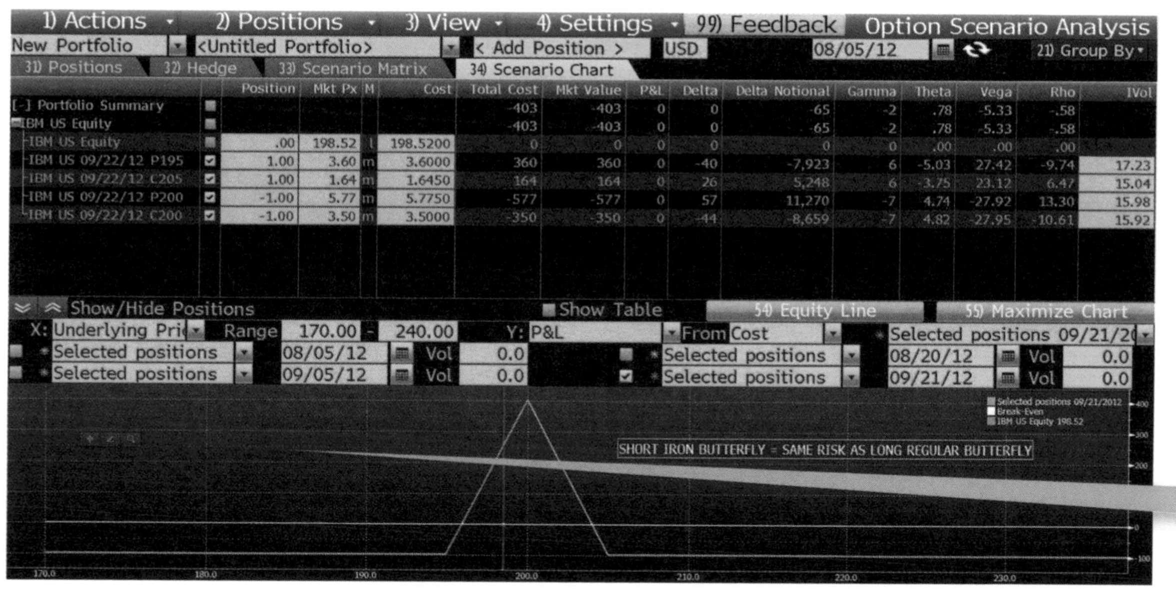

	Position	Mkt Px	M	Cost	Total Cost	Mkt Value	P&L	Delta	Delta Notional	Gamma	Theta	Vega	Rho	IVol
[-] Portfolio Summary					-403	-403	0	0	-65	-2	.78	-5.33	-.58	
IBM US Equity					-403	-403	0	0	-65	-2	.78	-5.33	-.58	
IBM US Equity	.00	198.52	l	198.5200	0	0	0	0	0	0	.00	.00	.00	
IBM US 09/22/12 P195	1.00	3.60	m	3.6000	360	360	0	-40	-7,923	6	-5.03	27.42	-9.74	17.23
IBM US 09/22/12 C205	1.00	1.64	m	1.6450	164	164	0	26	5,248	6	-3.75	23.12	6.47	15.04
IBM US 09/22/12 P200	-1.00	5.77	m	5.7750	-577	-577	0	57	11,270	-7	4.74	-27.92	13.30	15.98
IBM US 09/22/12 C200	-1.00	3.50	m	3.5000	-350	-350	0	-44	-8,659	-7	4.82	-27.95	-10.61	15.92

In this example, you are short the 195/200 put spread for which you're bullish (you want the stock at $200 or higher on expiration), and you're also short the 200/205 call spread for which you're bearish (you want the stock at $200 or lower on expiration). Obviously the best place for the stock in this case is $200.

Exhibit 6.19

This trade is similar in practical reasoning to the long standard butterfly. The reason you might choose one over the other would be the ability to attain more premium or if you better grasp using two short verticals, rather than a long short combined.

There are several reasons that a trader may employ a short iron butterfly, but the basic one is that you have a stock that is going to stay within a very tight range by expiration. Iron butterflies can potentially become profitable before expiration and can be exited at anytime if you are profitable or to avoid losses. Use the same logic that you would if you were thinking of employing the long fly, but check the short iron fly to see if there is better profit potential. The Greeks are identical to a regular **long call or put** butterfly.

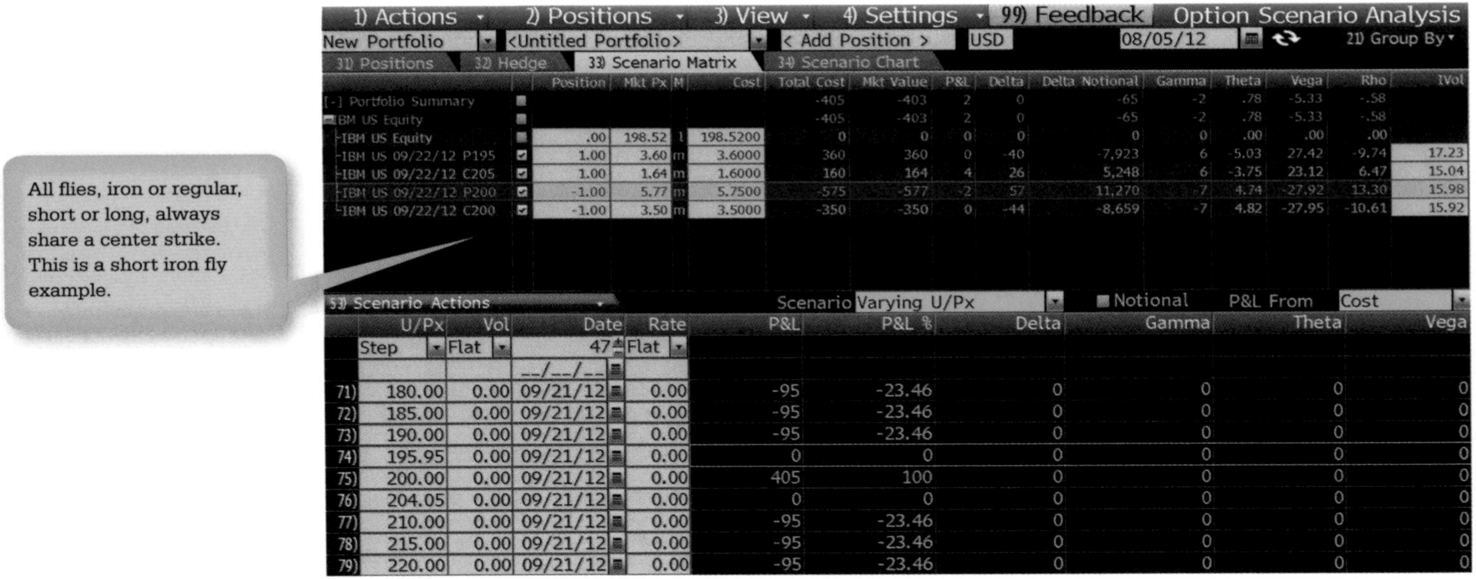

All flies, iron or regular, short or long, always share a center strike. This is a short iron fly example.

1) Actions · 2) Positions · 3) View · 4) Settings · 99) Feedback · Option Scenario Analysis

New Portfolio · <Untitled Portfolio> · < Add Position > · USD · 08/05/12 · 21) Group By

31) Positions · 32) Hedge · 33) Scenario Matrix · 34) Scenario Chart

	Position	Mkt Px	M	Cost	Total Cost	Mkt Value	P&L	Delta	Delta Notional	Gamma	Theta	Vega	Rho	IVol
[-] Portfolio Summary					-405	-403	2	0	-65	-2	.78	-5.33	-.58	
IBM US Equity					-405	-403	2	0	-65	-2	.78	-5.33	-.58	
IBM US Equity	.00	198.52	l	198.5200	0	0	0	0	0	0	.00	.00	.00	
IBM US 09/22/12 P195	1.00	3.60	m	3.6000	360	360	0	-40	-7,923	6	-5.03	27.42	-9.74	17.23
IBM US 09/22/12 C205	1.00	1.64	m	1.6000	160	164	4	26	5,248	6	-3.75	23.12	6.47	15.04
IBM US 09/22/12 P200	-1.00	5.77	m	5.7500	-575	-577	-2	57	11,270	-7	4.74	-27.92	13.30	15.98
IBM US 09/22/12 C200	-1.00	3.50	m	3.5000	-350	-350	0	-44	-8,659	-7	4.82	-27.95	-10.61	15.92

53) Scenario Actions · Scenario Varying U/Px · Notional · P&L From Cost

	U/Px	Vol	Date	Rate	P&L	P&L %	Delta	Gamma	Theta	Vega
	Step	Flat	47	Flat						
			__/__/__							
71)	180.00	0.00	09/21/12	0.00	-95	-23.46	0	0	0	0
72)	185.00	0.00	09/21/12	0.00	-95	-23.46	0	0	0	0
73)	190.00	0.00	09/21/12	0.00	-95	-23.46	0	0	0	0
74)	195.95	0.00	09/21/12	0.00	0	0	0	0	0	0
75)	200.00	0.00	09/21/12	0.00	405	100	0	0	0	0
76)	204.05	0.00	09/21/12	0.00	0	0	0	0	0	0
77)	210.00	0.00	09/21/12	0.00	-95	-23.46	0	0	0	0
78)	215.00	0.00	09/21/12	0.00	-95	-23.46	0	0	0	0
79)	220.00	0.00	09/21/12	0.00	-95	-23.46	0	0	0	0

Exhibit 6.20

Greek/Sentiment Considerations

The Greeks and behavior of the spread are identical to the long butterfly; the major differences are the credit versus debit nuances.

Long Iron Butterfly

The long iron butterfly combines a bull-call vertical and a bear-put vertical that share a center strike price (the long strike). The max profit would occur if the stock was above or below the outer short strikes. It is almost identical in behavior to the short butterfly.

Below are the P&L scenarios for a long iron butterfly:

Max profit in a long iron butterfly is:

Distance Between Strikes – Premium Paid

Max profit occurs when:

The Stock Is Above or Below the Outer Strikes on Expiration

Profit zone in a long iron butterfly is between:

Outside of the Following: Center Strike + Premium Paid and Center Strike – Premium Paid

Max risk in a long iron butterfly is:

The Premium Paid

Max loss in a long iron butterfly occurs when:

The Stock Is Pinned at the Center Strike on Expiration

The reason here is obviously because you have a feeling the stock will move in a big way, you just don't know where. See Exhibit 6.21.

The optimal situation is the same as the short butterfly. The long iron butterfly can be used to trade earnings or another potentially volatile event. Just make sure that your break-even levels are *inside* where you think the stock can realistically go by the time the trade expires.

Profitability

The max profit in long iron butterfly would be attained if the stock expired either below the short put or above the short-call strikes on expiration. But the profit is limited. Profit is limited to the distance between strikes minus what you paid. Let's assume for this example that you paid $2 for the iron butterfly. The strikes are spaced $5 apart, and because you paid $2 for the entire spread, the most you could ever make would be $3.

Breakevens

(Similar to put butterfly.) To find your break-even levels in the long iron butterfly, you simply add and subtract what you paid for the spread from the center strike—those two numbers are the levels the stock must be at for you to make or lose nothing on the trade.

Losses

Like the short butterfly, maximum loss will occur if the stock pins at the center strike on expiration. Although this may be highly unlikely, if you trade a stock that has a history of gravitating toward strikes, you may want to evaluate an exit before getting too close (< 7 days) to expiration. You will be losing money in the trade if the stock expires within the break-even levels. If there are no more potential catalysts in the trade, it may be best to walk away or roll the trade to the next month.

If you roll, just make sure you *add* all the debits you paid to find your cost basis.

Greek Considerations/Sentiment

The Greeks are identical to a regular *short* call or put butterfly with the same strikes.

There are several reasons that a trader may employ a long iron butterfly, but the basic one is that you have a stock that is going to experience a huge move outside of your outer short strikes. Iron butterflies can potentially become profitable before expiration and can be exited at any time if you are profitable or to avoid losses. See Exhibit 6.22.

Iron Condors

There are two types of iron condors, just like the iron butterfly. Like regular condors, iron condors

KEY POINT:

The long iron butterfly is an alternative to the short butterfly. It acts the same exact way and has the same risk/reward characteristics, only you *pay* your *max* risk up front!

Smart Investor Tip!

Even if you buy an iron butterfly and the stock makes a dramatic move outside of either of your short strikes, the spread may not trade at its maximum value before expiration because of time value, which may be left in the options that you are short. Don't get frustrated. Remember your return on risk: if you bought the spread for $2 and you can sell it for $3—that is a 50 percent return!

1) Actions ▾ 2) Positions ▾ 3) View ▾ 4) Settings ▾ 99) Feedback Option Scenario Analysis

New Portfolio ▾ <Untitled Portfolio> ▾ < Add Position > USD 08/05/12 21) Group By ▾

31) Positions 32) Hedge 33) Scenario Matrix 34) Scenario Chart

	Position	Mkt Px	M	Cost	Total Cost	Mkt Value	P&L	Delta	Delta Notional	Gamma	Theta	Vega	Rho	IVol
[-] Portfolio Summary					405	403	-2	0	65	2	-.78	5.33	.58	
IBM SHORT IRON FLY					405	403	-2	0	65	2	-.78	5.33	.58	
IBM US Equity	.00	198.52	l	198.5200	0	0	0	0	0	0	.00	.00	.00	
IBM US 09/22/12 C205	-1.00	1.64	m	1.6000	-160	-164	-4	-26	-5,248	-6	3.75	-23.12	-6.47	15.04
IBM US 09/22/12 C200	1.00	3.50	m	3.5000	350	350	0	44	8,659	7	-4.82	27.95	10.61	15.92
IBM US 09/22/12 P200	1.00	5.77	m	5.7500	575	577	2	-57	-11,270	7	-4.74	27.92	-13.30	15.99
IBM US 09/22/12 P195	-1.00	3.60	m	3.6000	-360	-360	0	40	7,923	-6	5.03	-27.42	9.73	17.23

Scenario Actions ▾ Scenario Varying U/Px ▾ Notional P&L From Cost ▾

	U/Px	Vol	Date	Rate	P&L	P&L %	Delta	Gamma	Theta	Vega
	Step	Flat	47	Flat						
			--/--/--							
71)	180.00	0.00	09/21/12	0.00	95	23.46	0	0	0	0
72)	185.00	0.00	09/21/12	0.00	95	23.46	0	0	0	0
73)	190.00	0.00	09/21/12	0.00	95	23.46	0	0	0	0
74)	195.95	0.00	09/21/12	0.00	0	0	0	0	0	0
75)	200.00	0.00	09/21/12	0.00	-405	-100	0	0	0	0
76)	204.05	0.00	09/21/12	0.00	0	0	0	0	0	0
77)	210.00	0.00	09/21/12	0.00	95	23.46	0	0	0	0
78)	215.00	0.00	09/21/12	0.00	95	23.46	0	0	0	0
79)	220.00	0.00	09/21/12	0.00	95	23.46	0	0	0	0

Here, you are long the 200/195 put spread for which you're bearish (you want the stock at or below $195 by expiration), and you are also long the 200/205 call spread (you want the stock at or above $205 on expiration). You pay a debit for both spreads, which means you want that stock to get as far away from those outer strikes as possible.

Exhibit 6.21

encompass four strikes and combine a vertical call spread *and* a vertical put spread.

The same Greek sensitivities apply to iron condors as they do with regular condors. Iron condors can be alternatives to regular condors as both spreads will tend to be out of the money and have tighter bid-ask spreads and potentially better pricing and more liquidity.

The iron condor, both long and short, involves a long- or short-call spread combined with a long- or short-put spread. Both spreads are typically out of the money and if you bought the call spread, you would also be a buyer of the put spread (long iron condor). This spread wants movement outside of outer strikes.

If you sell the call spread you would also sell the put spread (short iron condor). This spread wants the stock to expire between the inner strikes, similar to the long regular condor.

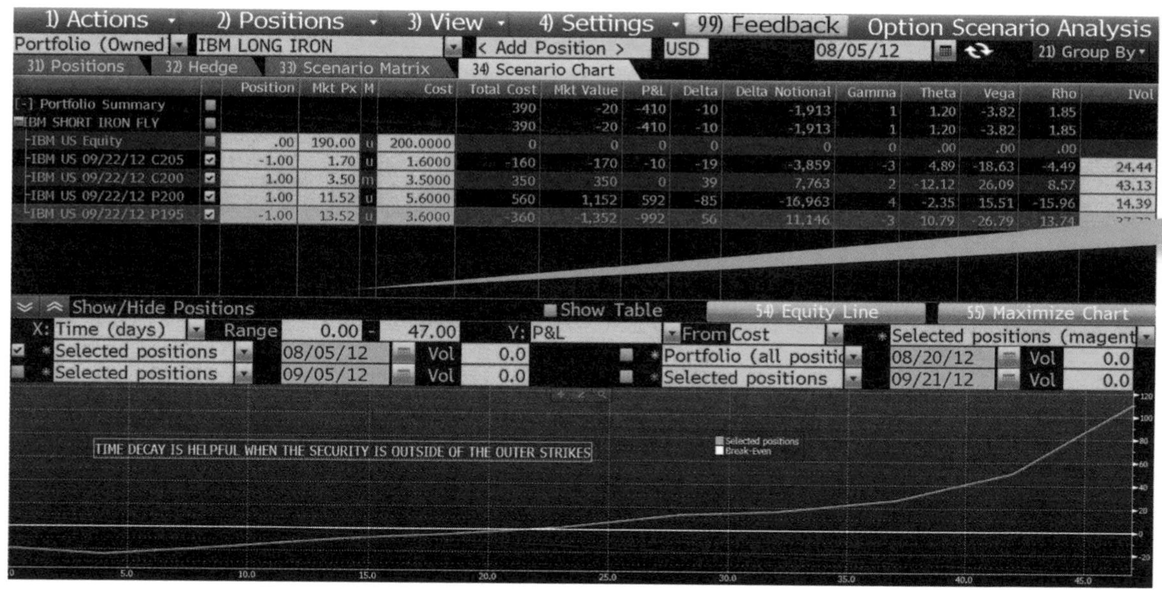

Notice how time can help your P&L if you are already profitable, but will really hurt if you're stuck in the middle of the strikes.

Exhibit 6.22

Smart Investor Tip!

The words "long" or "short" when used in relation to iron condor refer to whether you pay (long) or collect (short) premium.

Smart Investor Tip!

So if the call spread was $5 wide, the put spread should also be $5 wide. The difference between the two spreads can be $5, $10, $15, or whatever you deem appropriate. The spreads *cannot* share a strike price for the trade to be considered an iron condor. Remember to keep the outer strikes the same distance apart on both sides and adjust the strikes in and out to find your desired break-even/profit area.

Broken Wing Condors

Like regular condors, the inner strikes (width of spread) do not have to be equidistant from where the stock is trading or a specific distance from each other. However, for a traditional iron condor that has a balanced risk profile, the strikes of the outer strikes should be equidistance from the inner strikes. See Exhibits 6.23 and 6.24.

Spread Spacing and Composition

The width in between the call spread and the put spread can be as wide or as narrow as you wish. The

STEP-BY-STEP

Strike selection is probably the most crucial part of any multileg strategy and especially for the iron condor. Also important is the amount of premium you are paying and/or collecting. Don't forget, you have a total of four strikes to decide on, the results of which can be either rewarding or devastating. Let me walk you through my rationale.

Inner Strike Selection (Width)

Choosing what inner strikes to use is a balance between the range you think the stock or index can stay within (or outside of) combined with the amount of premium you can receive (or pay) in the spread once you determine what your outer strikes will be. In addition to choosing how wide your inner strikes are going to be, you may need to skew the strikes higher or lower if you think that the stock is at the upper or lower end of its expected range, or if you think it's right in the middle of the expected range, you can choose to place the strikes equidistance from the current price of the stock.

Outer Strike Selection (Wingspan)

Selecting the outer strikes also takes some practice and coordination with the spacing of the inners. The distance from the inner strikes that you sell to the outer strikes that you will be buying determines two things:

1. The amount of total premium received, which influences your breakevens.
The further the outer strikes are from the inner strikes, the cheaper they will be because they will be further out of the money. The less you pay for those strikes will mean that you will retain more of the credit you brought in for the short strikes if you are selling an iron condor. The further the outer strikes are from the inner strikes the wider the breakevens; if you are buying the iron condor, the further the distance between breakevens the harder it is to make money.

2. The amount to total risk you are willing to take.
The further the outer strikes are from the inner strikes the more you can potentially lose in the trade if you are selling the spread. In the short iron condor, those outer strikes are like your stop loss; the most you can lose in a short iron condor is the difference between one inner strike and one outer strike minus the premium you received for the spread.

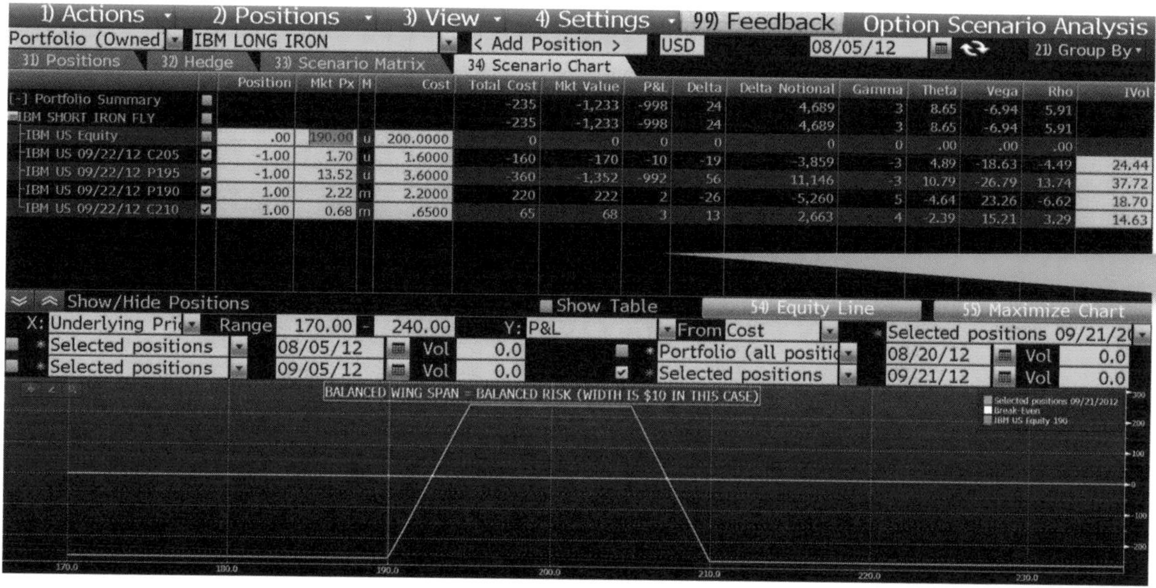

If you fail to space the outer strikes evenly on both sides from the inner strikes, you will now have a broken wing iron condor, which will affect margin requirements, risk, behavior, and reward potential.

Exhibit 6.23

narrower the distance between the spreads (width), the more expensive the iron condor will be.

Long Iron Condor

For the buyer of the spread, this higher cost means higher risk (because of the greater cash outlay), but also means a higher statistical probability of success because a narrower spread means that the stock doesn't have to travel as far for the spread to move to its maximum value. If the buyer of an iron condor chooses to buy a call spread and a put spread that are far apart from one another, they will be cheaper, but the statistical probability of that stock moving further by expiration becomes less and less. Remember, the buyer of a condor wants the stock to move outside the outer short strikes.

Below are the P&L scenarios for a long iron condor:

Max profit in a long iron condor is:

The Wingspan Distance – the Debit Paid

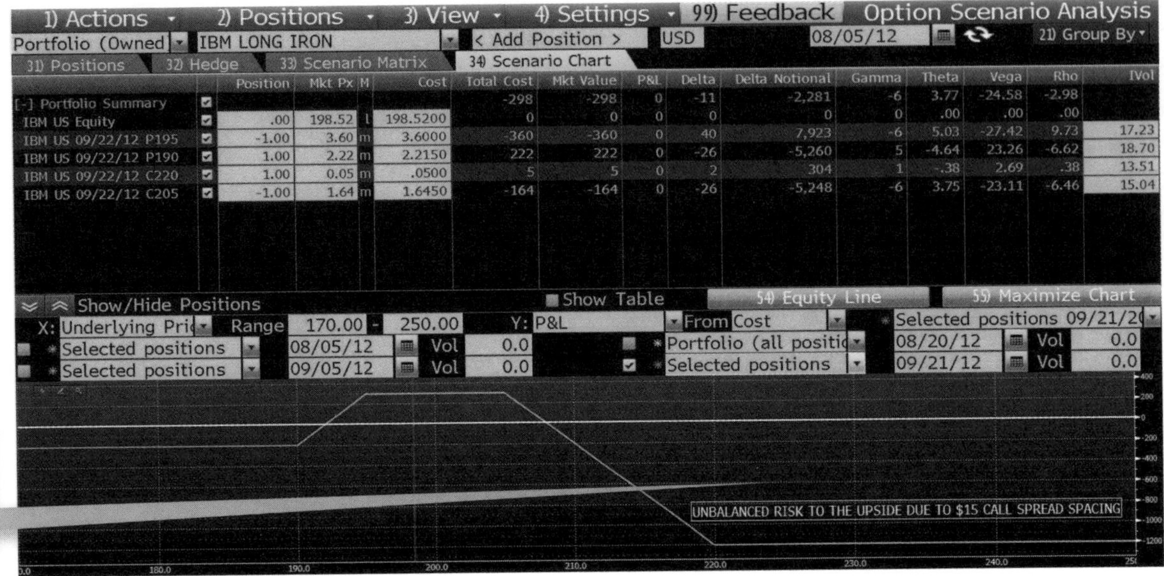

Here we broke the upper wing of the iron condor by spacing out the call spread more than the puts.

Exhibit 6.24

Max profit occurs when:

The Stock Above or Below Outer Strikes on Expiration

Profit zone in a short condor is between:

Lower Inner Strike – Debit Paid and Upper Inner Strike + Debit Paid

Max risk in a short condor is:

The Debit Paid

Max loss in a short condor occurs when:

The Stock Is Between Inner Strikes on Expiration

In a long iron condor the risk is always limited to whatever is paid for the entire spread. Even though you are theoretically buying a call and put vertical spread, you would only enter one price to buy them both. Finding the potential reward is also simple. On expiration, you can only profit fully on one of the spreads, not both, so to find the max profit potential, take the total premium paid for the iron condor and subtract it from the width of one of the spreads (they should both be equal). If the call and put spreads are

$5 wide and you paid $2 for the condor, the most you can make is $3.

When you buy an iron condor, you are making the bet that the stock will make a large move, up or down, preferably past one of the outer (short) strikes in the spread by expiration, or at least move past your break-even point. These strategies are great ahead of an earnings report when you are able to set your breakevens within levels that the stock has realistically reached. Because the Ivol crush will only help you if the stock is outside the outer strikes, I often position the long iron condor's strikes a little tighter than normal. Specifically, I try and get the width as tight as possible and the wingspan as wide as I can so that I get more gamma and delta exposure as the stock moves.

Short Iron Condors Can Also Be Used to Strategize around Earnings

The probability characteristics of the long iron condor will vary based on how far the inner and outer strikes are spaced apart and how much is paid for the entire condor. The closer the long strikes are to the current stock price, the higher the probability of the stock moving through the strikes (and thus your P&L responding positively); however, the closer the long strikes are to the stock, the more the condor will cost, thus increasing risk. There's that trade-off again. For me, I would err on the side of probability when I am buying or selling an iron condor.

Typically iron condors are bought with a suitable amount of time for the stock to move outside of the short strikes; the time in the trade may encompass a corporate or economic event that is a potential catalyst for movement. Generally, they are bought with 25 to 90 DTE, but can sometimes be placed with less time, if you think the stock will make a quick move to a certain level. If you choose a shorter duration, you will have more gamma (movement exposure), but you may also experience accelerated time decay if the stock doesn't move in the last two weeks of the spread's life.

You better have a strong conviction that the stock will move if you play it close to earnings.

Strike Selection and Risk Nuances

In some cases, because the strikes of a condor are spread further out, it will take a larger move in the stock for you to reach your profitable zones, which lie at some point above and below your inner long strikes.

To find your upside breakeven at expiration, take the net amount you paid for the iron condor and add it to the long-call strike, the sum of those numbers will be your upside break-even point at which you *begin* to *make* money. You will continue to profit until the stock rises to the short-call strike, at which time your profit will be capped out.

For example, if you bought a condor for $1 and your call spread strikes are long the 50, short the 55, your profitable zone is from $51 to $55 (above 55 you would still profit, only that profit is capped at $4,

Smart Investor Tip!

The closer the call and put spreads are to one another, the greater the premium collected will be—however, the greater the statistical risk for the trader to lose because the break-even levels will be closer. Try to get the most premium possible, while still structuring your breakevens *outside* where you think the stock can end up on expiration.

which is the distance between the call spread strikes minus the net premium paid).

To the downside, you will subtract the amount you paid for the condor from the long put strike; that remainder is your downside breakeven at which point you would begin to make money on expiration. You will continue to profit until the stock falls to the short put strike, at which time your profit will be capped out.

For example, if you bought that same condor for $1 and your put spread strikes are long the 40, short the 35, your profitable zone is from $39 to $35 (below $35 you would still profit, only that profit is capped at $4, which is the distance between the put spread strikes minus the net premium paid).

If you are within 80 percent of your potential max profit in the trade and you still have more than four days until expiration, it might be best to take profit and move on to your next trade unless you are extremely confident the stock will not revert to the center of your iron condor.

Long Iron Condor Greek Attributes

Greeks will be identical to a short regular condor with the same strikes. The only major difference will be the credit/debit trade nuances, but P&L will be net affected the same way.

Short Iron Condor

Short iron condors are the same as regular long condors in that they want the stock to expire between the inner strikes to make max profit on expiration. The only difference is that you will collect a credit in a short iron condor that will be the most you will ever make. You can (but not always) lose more than you bring in. See Exhibit 6.25.

Below are the P&L scenarios for a short iron condor:

Max profit in a short iron condor is:

The Credit Received

Max profit occurs when:

The Stock Is Between Inner Strikes on Expiration

Profit zone in a long condor is between:

Lower Inner Strike – Credit Collected and Upper Inner Strike + Credit Collected

Max risk in a long condor is:

Wingspan Distance – Credit Collected

Max loss in a long condor occurs when:

The Stock Is Above or Below the Outer Strikes

Many iron condor sellers will space the call and put spreads as far away from one another where they can still get an acceptable premium, usually at levels outside of support and resistance for the stock or at levels of low statistical probability. Many times this will result in an upside-down reward/risk ratio, but the high probability of the trade justifies the poor return.

Similar to the long condor, when you sell an iron condor, you are making the bet that the stock will remain within the inner (short) strikes of the spread (rangebound) by expiration. Ivol should preferably be relatively elevated with the expectation that it will

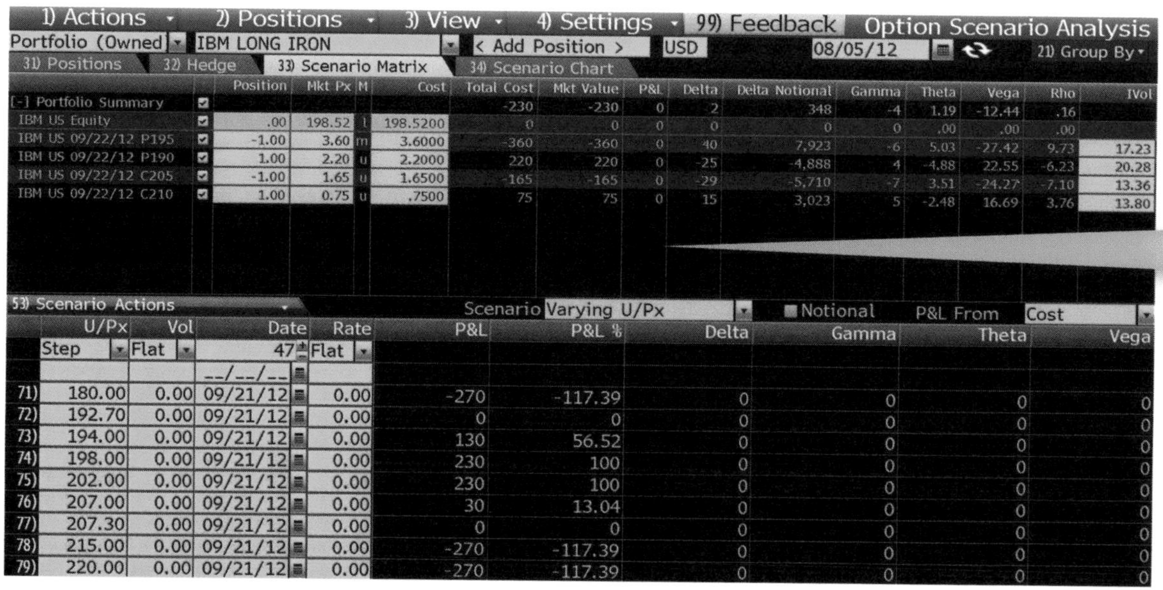

	Position	Mkt Px	M	Cost	Total Cost	Mkt Value	P&L	Delta	Delta Notional	Gamma	Theta	Vega	Rho	IVol
[-] Portfolio Summary					-230	-230	0	2	348	-4	1.19	-12.44	.16	
IBM US Equity	.00	198.52	l	198.5200	0	0	0	0	0	0	.00	.00	.00	
IBM US 09/22/12 P195	-1.00	3.60	m	3.6000	-360	-360	0	40	7,923	-6	5.03	-27.42	9.73	17.23
IBM US 09/22/12 P190	1.00	2.20	u	2.2000	220	220	0	-25	-4,888	4	-4.88	22.55	-6.23	20.28
IBM US 09/22/12 C205	-1.00	1.65	u	1.6500	-165	-165	0	-29	-5,710	-7	3.51	-24.27	-7.10	13.36
IBM US 09/22/12 C210	1.00	0.75	u	.7500	75	75	0	15	3,023	5	-2.48	16.69	3.76	13.80

	U/Px	Vol	Date	Rate	P&L	P&L %	Delta	Gamma	Theta	Vega
	Step	Flat	47	Flat						
			--/--/--							
71)	180.00	0.00	09/21/12	0.00	-270	-117.39	0	0	0	0
72)	192.70	0.00	09/21/12	0.00	0	0	0	0	0	0
73)	194.00	0.00	09/21/12	0.00	130	56.52	0	0	0	0
74)	198.00	0.00	09/21/12	0.00	230	100	0	0	0	0
75)	202.00	0.00	09/21/12	0.00	230	100	0	0	0	0
76)	207.00	0.00	09/21/12	0.00	30	13.04	0	0	0	0
77)	207.30	0.00	09/21/12	0.00	0	0	0	0	0	0
78)	215.00	0.00	09/21/12	0.00	-270	-117.39	0	0	0	0
79)	220.00	0.00	09/21/12	0.00	-270	-117.39	0	0	0	0

Short iron condors, as shown here, want the stock to remain between the short inner strikes.

Exhibit 6.25

drop. Use your GV, HIVG, and HVG screens to check Ivol versus Hvol.

Just like selling an iron butterfly, you are expecting minimal movement in the stock, but unlike the butterfly, the condor, because of the strike spacing, will allow the stock a wider berth and allow you a greater chance of making the maximum profit in the trade. This increased width also means that your profitable zone will be wider than in a short iron butterfly.

Expiration date. Typically, iron condors are sold with shorter durations to take advantage of the accelerated time decay that occurs in the last month of an option's life. Also, remember that the longer you are in a strategy like this, the more you leave yourself and the position susceptible to events that may crate volatility in the stock, both corporate and economic. So you will want to account for those events when selecting your strikes before you enter. In fact, the short iron condor

Smart Investor Tip!

Although both the long and short iron condor can be a great strategy to employ with limited risk (and limited reward) there are four options (also called legs) involved in each condor (iron and regular) that is traded. Be sure to check with your broker to determine commission costs, as they may eat up a portion of your profits. Some brokers charge a single commission for a spread (up to four legs); others treat the legs of the spread as individual options.

Smart Investor Tip!

You can often lose more than the credit you receive when you sell an iron condor; don't be afraid to take risk off the table if you think that the stock is going to keep moving in one direction.

Also remember that you can become profitable before expiration and also lose money even if the stock doesn't get outside your expiration profitable zone. If you feel that the stock will remain within that zone, you can leave the spread on and it will eventually become profitable if the stock remains within that range.

KEY POINT:

Hopefully by now the relationships between regular and iron butterflies and regular condors and iron condors are becoming clearer. They are all basically interchangeable. The only reason to choose one over the other would be to find the one with the least risk and greatest return. In the figures see the strike price positioning for the short and long iron condors. Just like we took a long regular butterfly and turned it into a short iron butterfly by using a combination of calls and puts versus one or the other, condors become iron condors when you do the same.

is a great way to capture the Ivol crush after an earnings report. Just be sure that your breakevens (preferably inner strikes) are *outside* of typical movements over past earnings reports.

Irons can be sold with 15 to 50 days until expiration, but they can sometimes be placed with even more or less time. It's all about support and resistance for the stock and the strength of your belief that the stock will stay between your short strikes. If Ivol is extremely high and the skew is steep far out in time, you can sell an iron condor with six months until expiration. Just keep in mind that your bet here is more for vega than anything.

If you have a bias that the stock may move in one direction or the other, reduce the wingspan of the side that you think the stock may move toward. This will give you a broken wing condor, but it will reduce risk. If the stock does the opposite, than you may be in more pain than you originally thought, so be sure to test your theory and adjust your contract size and width accordingly.

Strike Selection

Determining the best strikes should be similar to the process you utilize in the long regular condor. Key in on those break-even levels and perhaps even "leg in" to the spread. This can be done by selling the call spread when the stock has been rallying and then letting the stock drop before executing the short put spread. This will help to improve your credit and reduce risk.

To find your profitable zone at expiration, take the net amount you received for the iron condor and add it to the long call strike. The sum of those numbers will be your upside break-even point at which you *begin* to *lose* money. You will continue to *lose* until the stock rises to the short call strike, at which time your *loss* will be capped out.

As an example of upside breakeven, consider that if you sold a condor for $1 and your call spread strikes are long the 50, short the 55, your profitable zone is from the current stock price up to $51 on expiration. Above 51 you would begin to lose money. That loss is capped at $4, which is the distance between the call spread strikes minus the net premium collected on the entire spread.

To the downside, you will subtract the net amount you collect for the condor from the short put strike. That remainder is your downside breakeven at which point you would begin to *lose* money on expiration. You will continue to lose money until the stock falls to the long put strike, at which time your losses will be capped out.

A downside break-even example would be if you sold that same condor for $1 and your put spread strikes are short the 40, long the 35. Your profitable zone is from the current stock price down to $39. Below 35 you would begin to lose money. That loss is capped at $4, which is the distance between the put spread strikes minus the net premium collected on the entire spread.

Risk Nuances

For the seller of an iron condor, the risk is always limited to the distance of the wingspan (or the wider of the wingspan spreads, if the spreads aren't equally spaced) minus the net credit received on entry. Even though you are theoretically selling a call and put vertical spread, you would only enter one price to sell them both. This is your net credit. You can also only lose on one spread or the other, not both, because the stock can only be at one price on expiration. This is why risk is only limited to one side. If the call and put spreads are $5 wide and you collect $2 for the condor, the most you can lose is $3, so you would be risking $3 to make $2.

Finding the potential reward is also simple. On expiration, with a short iron condor you can actually profit fully on both of the spreads. This only occurs when the entire spread expires with the stock between the short *inner* strikes (at which point all options expire worthless). At this point you would retain the net credit you received. Max profit in a short iron condor is *always* the net credit you bring in.

Short Iron Condor Greek Attributes

Greeks will be identical to a long regular condor with the same strikes. The only major difference will be the credit/debit trade nuances, but P&L will be net-affected the same way.

Implied Volatility Considerations

In a perfect world, when selling an iron condor you want to do so in a period of relatively high volatility, with the anticipation that it will drop. Looking at a comparison below, you will notice the implied vol is not only above the historical vol but the level of implied volatility is on the neutral to slightly elevated side when compared to the past six months of data.

Look ahead at corporate events so that you can rationalize any abnormal differences. If the catalyst and potential for movement is greater than the breakevens you are finding in the short iron condor, you might want to switch to a long iron condor and bring the breakevens closer.

There is no perfect guideline for where implied volatility should be in relation to historical; rather, it is better to see it in an elevated state and preferably on the way down, as this will help your net short vega in the short iron condor.

Technical Tips

Use support and resistance levels on the daily chart and identify overbought and oversold conditions to key in on ranges for a stock or index when selecting your strikes.

Draw **Fibonacci lines** on a one-year daily chart to help determine near-term support and resistance levels and find an envelope for your stock to travel in.

Fibonacci levels are used by technical analysts to locate support and resistance levels within a stock by using daily, weekly, or monthly charts, but for condors and butterflies, I stick to the daily chart because most of these trades are completed in less than 30 days.

DEFINITION:

Fibonacci lines

The Fibonacci number sequence is created by adding the last two numbers in the sequence to create the next number (i.e., 1,1,2,3,5,8,13,21,34,55,89,144Š ƒ). The first three numbers in the sequence are normally dropped for analysis purposes. The number sequence creates some interesting mathematical relationships.

The most commonly used are: the ratio of any number to its next higher number, which approaches a constant value of .618 (e.g., 34/55 = .618, 55/89 = .618); the ratios of alternate numbers which approach a constant .382 (e.g., 21/55 = .382, 34/89 = .382).

Traders use these patterns in many ways, but I use them as a horizontal (price) indicator connecting the highest point in a period to the lowest to establish support and resistance levels. Most important, I look to Fibonacci levels for retracement in a trend.

Smart Investor Tip!

If you buy an iron condor you will lose your entire premium paid if the spread expires with the stock between the inner long strikes. However, if the stock moves quickly, you can see profitability in the spread even if the stock doesn't reach your expiration profit zone; don't be afraid to take profits if you think the stock is going to stop moving or revert back to where it was before, at which time you may find yourself in a losing situation.

Smart Investor Tip!

In high-dollar stocks and indices like the SPX, GOOG, and so on, bid-ask spreads in the options tend to be wider than normal. To mitigate negative P&L effects, I highly suggest using limit orders and working your bids and offers just around the midvalue point of the spread.

Always start in the middle and adjust if you need to; pay a little more than the midprice if you are a buyer, sell for a little less than the midprice if you are selling the spread.

To draw the line, find the highest and lowest closing point of the past year and connect those points. The Fibonacci banks will form within that band.

If a certain Fibonacci level coincides with a moving average or other indicator, it only strengthens my support or resistance level hypothesis. To take it a step further, I will examine the standard deviation of the asset over the time period and try to position my inner strikes at least 1.2 SDs away.

My belief is that enough people use the most popular technical indicators to make them self-fulfilling prophecies to a point. It's like a free look into the heads of the masses.

Video:
Short Iron for Earnings

www.wiley.com/go/BloombergVisualGuidetoFinancialMarketsVideo1.html

Use a Probability Calculator

Use a probability calculator to find a realistic range in all your trades, but especially with butterflies, condors, straddles, and strangles, which are all dependent on specific movements to be profitable.

The HIVG, HVG, and HRH screens will help you to better anticipate the statistical probability of your trade winning and losing. Be careful when leaning solely on statistics; anything can happen in the real world and those anomalies that you think aren't possible are the ones that usually blow up your account. But by using a calculator you have an objective view that you can use in conjunction with your fundamental and technical thesis.

In the probability calculator, you will be asked to input an expiration date and a volatility factor along with dividends and interest rates. The good news is that Bloomberg does a good job at figuring the rate and dividends for you. For the volatility factor, I look to the at-the-money implied volatility and the 30-day historical volatility; I use whichever is greater in my forward calculation to be more conservative. Sometimes I look over the past 90 days and take an average of both, which helps to smooth any anomalies.

Use your break-even points to calculate statistical probability on expiration. See Exhibit 6.26.

Legging In versus All In

The short iron condor is basically the combination of a bull-put spread and a bear-call spread, so you can "leg in" or execute each spread separately. For example, if a stock has been selling off and you think it's ready for a mean reversion (bounce) you could sell the put spread first (which is the bullish portion) then once the stock rallies you could execute the call spread side (the bearish portion). Some advantages and disadvantages are:

- **The advantages** of this method may allow you to not only maximize the amount you get for each spread and in turn the entire condor, but you can also potentially widen the distance between the inner strikes because the stock's movement will

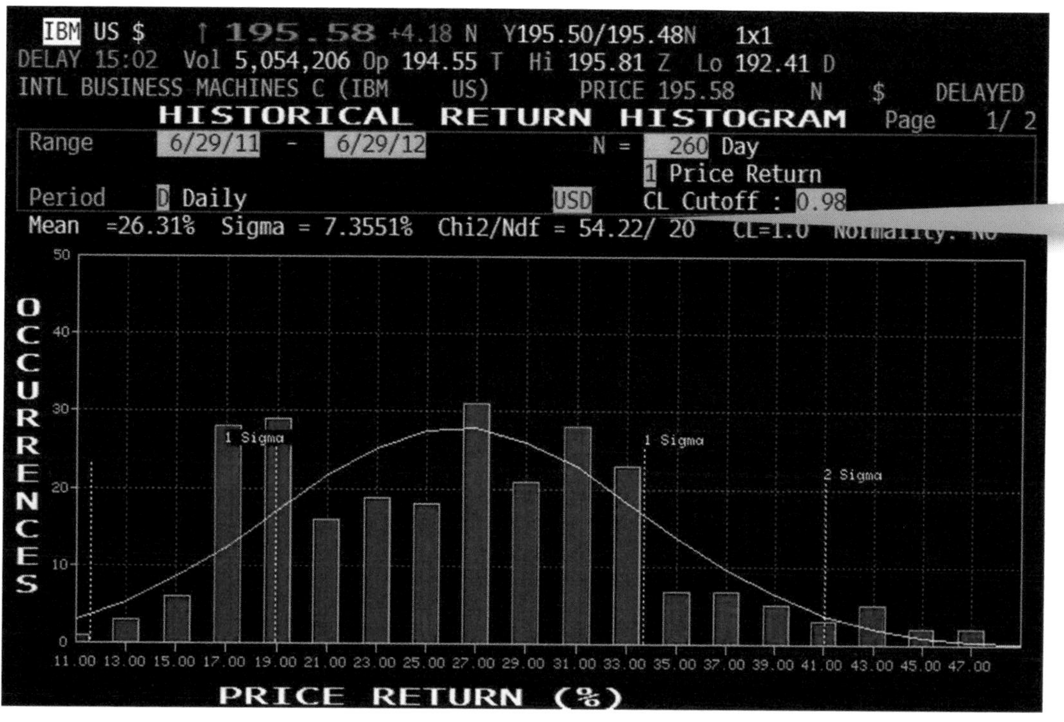

Exhibit 6.26

You can use observe volatility bell curves along with volatility charts to find probable price distributions. Although this can help with rationale, don't fall into the trap of putting all your faith in statistics. It's not a bad thing to overlay some fundamental levels as well!

allow you to gain value in both the call and put spreads. Use this method if you are really good at timing the market or for a particular stock and you are comfortable with the way an iron condor is constructed.

- **The disadvantage** of "legging in" could be that the stock never bounces and you have to sell the put spread for less or vice versa if you were selling the put spread first. Also, depending on your broker, commissions may be higher if you complete the spread in two parts. Again, depending on your broker, you may be required to put up margin in *both* the call and put spread. In most cases, when they are executed at the same time, you will only need to put up margin in one, because you can only lose on one side.

Smart Investor Tip!

If you are trading individual stocks around earnings, the more analysts that cover a stock, typically, the less chance you have for surprises, but this certainly doesn't mean that the stock cannot do something dramatic. Look at how it has traded over earnings in the past to gain insight into its typical behavior. Trading in indexes may also help to mitigate earnings surprises, but they will *not* eliminate them.

CHAPTER 7

Managing Your Risk

Tactics, Tips, and Volatility Tricks

This chapter explores specialized tactics and strategies that I use to trade and control risk as well as some of the tips and golden nuggets of the trading wisdom I have learned throughout the years.

Volatility is the end all, be all of professional options trading. Because every option strategy you employ will be related to it, try to incorporate it into *everything* you do as an option trader.

As you become more advanced, relaxed, and confident in trading options, you will naturally begin to manage more and more trades at once, possibly with several different strategies on multiple stocks, all of which will have an effect on one another at least to some extent.

Assuming that Exhibit 7.1 is a snapshot of your current portfolio:

- Do you think this many positions are too hard to manage?
- Are the strategies complementing each other or opposing?
- What effects do the trades have on one another?
- What happens to those positions if the market moves up or down 5 percent?
- Can this portfolio be sufficiently hedged?
- Do you even care about their relationship to one another or the market as a whole?

These are just some of the thoughts that should be running through your head when considering adding or subtracting trades from your portfolio or placing hedges to slow down or mitigate certain types of risk.

This is what a typical trading account might look like: multiple positions, each with unique risk characteristics and nuances.

1) Actions ▾ 2) Positions ▾ 3) View ▾ 4) Settings ▾ 99) Feedback Option Scenario Analysis

Portfolio (Owned) ▾ Jared Big Portfolio ▾ < Add Position > USD 08/05/12 21) Group By ▾

31) Positions 32) Hedge 33) Scenario Matrix 34) Scenario Chart

	Position	Mkt Px	M	Cost	Total Cost	Mkt Val	P&L	Delta	Delta Notional	Gamma	Theta	Vega	Rho	IVol
[-] Portfolio Totals					[illegible]	162,103	1,046		274,194		189.14	-382.06	149.82	
AAPL US Equity					30,685	30,535	-150	19	11,528	-3	12.60	68.19	38.20	
AAPL US Equity	[illegible]	615.70	l	615.7000	30,785	30,785	0	50	30,785	0	.00	.00	.00	
[illegible]	5.00	21.125	m	21.3000	10,650	10,563	-88	186	114,816	14	-83.78	614.50	288.93	27.36
[illegible]L US 10/20/12 C630	-5.00	21.625	m	21.5000	-10,750	-10,813	-63	-218	-134,073	-17	96.38	-546.31	-250.73	25.95
ATVI US Equity					824	964	140	859	9,554	16	-2.31	6.94	6.34	
ATVI US Equity	200.00	11.12	l	11.1200	2,224	2,224	0	200	2,224	0	.00	.00	.00	
ATVI US 09/22/12 P12	-20.00	1.02	m	1.0000	-2,000	-2,040	-40	1531	17,026	-62	7.13	-24.44	19.79	27.47
ATVI US 09/22/12 P11	20.00	.39	m	.3000	600	780	180	-872	-9,696	77	-9.44	31.38	-13.45	28.44
CHK US Equity					-460	-480	-20	2	41	-13	10.53	-17.51	.67	
CHK US Equity	.00	17.89	l	17.8900	0	0	0	0	0	0	.00	.00	.00	
CHK US 09/22/12 C23	20.00	.115	m	.1000	200	230	30	173	3,092	18	-10.43	20.20	3.67	48.30
CHK US 09/22/12 C22	-20.00	.205	m	.2000	-400	-410	-10	-277	-4,952	-25	14.84	-28.31	-5.83	49.02
CHK US 09/22/12 P13	-20.00	.33	m	.3200	-640	-660	-20	223	3,989	-13	21.63	-24.34	5.97	83.45
CHK US 09/22/12 P11	20.00	.18	m	.1900	380	360	-20	-117	-2,089	7	-15.52	14.95	-3.14	97.45
GLD US Equity					13,555	13,840	285	394	61,298	-60	33.10	-191.97	60.93	
GLD US Equity	100.00	155.55	l	155.5500	15,555	15,555	0	100	15,555	0	.00	.00	.00	
GLD US 09/22/12 P151	-10.00	1.715	m	2.0000	-2,000	-1,715	285	294	45,743	-60	33.10	-191.97	60.93	16.10
GOOG US Equity					62,750	63,008	258	178	114,204	-28	113.08	-130.27	16.64	
GOOG US Equity	100.00	641.33	l	640.0000	64,000	64,133	133	100	64,133	0	.00	.00	.00	
GOOG US 08/18/12 P600	-50.00	1.20	m	1.3000	-6,500	-6,000	500	412	264,166	-156	1,002.35	-878.57	87.79	27.10
GOOG US 08/18/12 P595	50.00	.975	m	1.0500	5,250	4,875	-375	-334	-214,095	127	-889.27	748.30	-71.15	28.23
HEP US Equity					-1,150	-1,013	137	-265	-17,269	-27	10.42	-46.44	-20.87	
HEP US Equity	.00	65.16	l	65.1600	0	0	0	0	0	0	.00	.00	.00	
HEP US 09/22/12 C65	-5.00	2.025	m	2.3000	-1,150	-1,013	137	-265	-17,269	-27	10.42	-46.44	-20.87	20.77
IBM US Equity					38,404	38,319	-85	334	66,337	-9	3.98	-41.42	30.93	
IBM US Equity	200.00	198.52	l	198.5200	39,704	39,704	0	200	39,704	0	.00	.00	.00	
IBM US 09/22/12 P195	-10.00	3.60	m	3.5500	-3,550	-3,600	-50	399	79,237	-61	50.62	-273.38	96.77	17.28
IBM US 09/22/12 P190	10.00	2.215	m	2.2500	2,250	2,215	-35	-265	-52,604	52	-46.65	231.95	-65.84	18.75
QQQ US Equity					13,120	13,120	0	200	13,120	0	.00	.00	.00	
QQQ US Equity	200.00	65.60	l	65.6000	13,120	13,120	0	200	13,120	0	.00	.00	.00	
USO US Equity					2,400	2,860	460	342	11,656	-20	7.26	-24.65	11.29	
USO US Equity	.00	34.07	l	34.0700	0	0	0	0	0	0	.00	.00	.00	
USO US 09/22/12 C32.5	-40.00	2.435	m	2.6000	-10,400	-9,740	660	-2715	-92,504	-124	59.48	-174.71	-106.26	32.16
USO US 09/22/12 C31.5	40.00	3.15	m	3.2000	12,800	12,600	-200	3057	104,160	104	-52.23	150.06	117.55	32.95
YHOO US Equity					929	949	20	233	3,725	-8	.49	-4.93	5.69	
YHOO US Equity	20.00	15.97	l	15.9700	319	319	0	20	319	0	.00	.00	.00	

Exhibit 7.1

Another issue is that you will most likely experiment with new strategies that may not be so "vanilla" in nature. As you layer more and more trades, a challenge becomes the constant, effective management of these trades in real time individually or as a global position. If you continue to layer more strategies at once, you must be aware at how they will dynamically influence and augment one another and how they will morph as time, price, volatility, and other factors change.

It is paramount that you have a method and set of rules/tools to help you understand the effects of the markets and of all our positions on each other as time, price, volatility, and interest rates change. See Exhibit 7.2.

Whether you allow Bloomberg to house your trades in real time or if you are entering them manually parallel to another broker, you should be constantly running different scenarios to test your response to different market conditions.

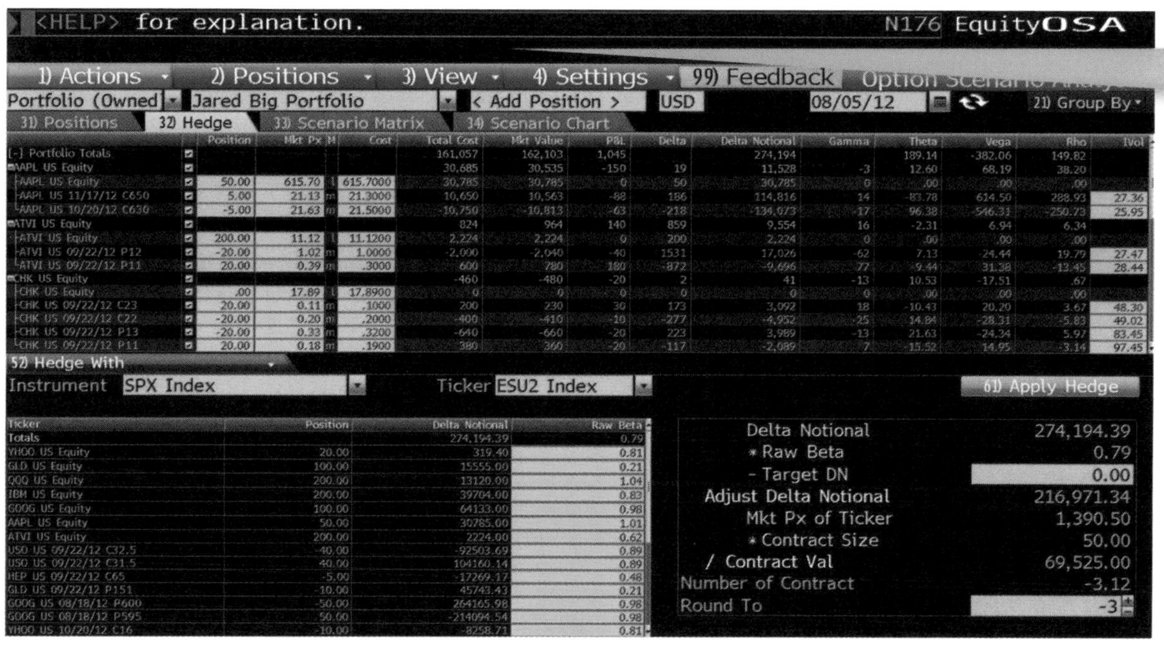

Here we can see that position's net delta and other Greeks, along with a basic hedge using three full SPX futures; but is that enough to truly hedge this portfolio against all risk?

Exhibit 7.2

Relax, You're (Hopefully) in Total Control

When I was a market maker on the floor, I generally only traded one security at a time, but would have hundreds, if not thousands of different positions on calls and puts spanning several expirations. It was next to impossible for me to just get long an IBM call butterfly and let it be. I would begin to take in other inventory that would change my original mind-set. Back then, my goal at that time was to remain constantly hedged (delta-neutral) and buy or sell options and/or stock to adjust my "Greek exposure" based on my sentiments and thesis.

Because I was forced into trades my risk management was on an ad hoc, global scale. If I found myself getting short deltas and short gamma, I may have acted by purchasing some long calls to offset this risk, if that was my goal. I had to trade defensively and often was put on the wrong side of trades.

As a retail trader or "market taker," you are initiating your own trades on your time based on your research and analysis, but that doesn't preclude you from executing several strategies in one stock at one time, nor should it. The ability to pick and choose your strategies gives you an edge and allows your account to be completely focused on your goal, not on what others force on you.

So assuming that you are controlling your own strategies there is no reason why you shouldn't be extremely methodical in your approach and relate your trades to one another as best you can.

Combining Positions

If you don't tend to be more directional in your trades or tend to take a neutral bias by using leveraged, statistically advantaged trades, you still want to look at just how much exposure your total account has in all the Greeks to find any hidden pockets of risk. One of the most basic concepts of risk management I watch is something called **dollar delta**.

DEFINITION:
Dollar delta
tells you how much real risk you have in actual dollars when compared to the underlying or option strike.

Dollar delta is helpful if you tend to trade large amounts of contracts and take on higher leverage risk. Calculate as follows:

Option dollar delta = Current Price of Underlying * Option Delta * number of Option Contracts * 100 (share size of each contract)

The option dollar delta is the key here. If you are trading 40 call contracts with a 100 strike price, you have control over 4,000 shares of stock, with $400,000 worth of value. This may not seem like much, but what if your total account value is $100k? What if you had to exercise? Are you trading too many contracts?

Stock Dollar Delta = the Number of Shares * Stock Price

Aggregate all positions together to find your portfolio dollar delta in each underlying/position. If the dollar deltas mitigate one another in stocks that *are* highly correlated, you may have risk somewhat under control or at least less of it. If you find that your dollar delta is greater than 300 percent of your account value, you may have some adjustments/hedges to make.

Why look at this measurement?

Dollar delta will give you a more realistic picture of absolute risk, not just delta at the moment of the trade.

In the screen shown in Exhibit 7.3 you can see that the net delta position here in IBM is only about 500, but the dollar delta risk is much higher. Are you comfortable with the dollars at play here? Can you afford to get long or short that much stock with or without margin?

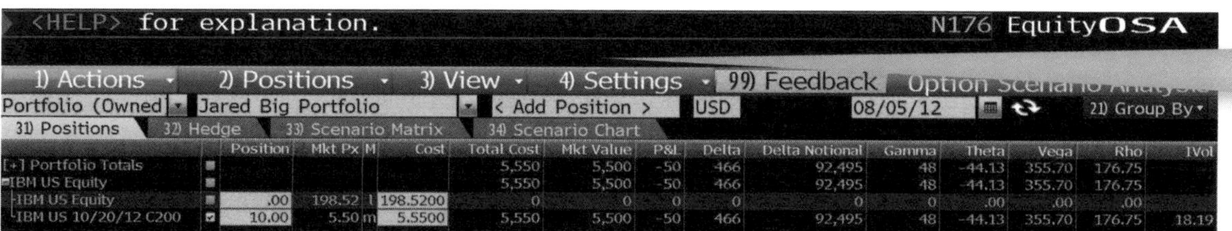

<HELP> for explanation. N176 EquityOSA

1) Actions 2) Positions 3) View 4) Settings 99) Feedback Option Scenario Analysis

Portfolio (Owned) Jared Big Portfolio < Add Position > USD 08/05/12 21) Group By

31) Positions 32) Hedge 33) Scenario Matrix 34) Scenario Chart

	Position	Mkt Px	M	Cost	Total Cost	Mkt Value	P&L	Delta	Delta Notional	Gamma	Theta	Vega	Rho	IVol
[+] Portfolio Totals					5,550	5,500	-50	466	92,495	48	-44.13	355.70	176.75	
IBM US Equity					5,550	5,500	-50	466	92,495	48	-44.13	355.70	176.75	
IBM US Equity	.00	198.52	l	198.5200	0	0	0	0	0	0	.00	.00	.00	
IBM US 10/20/12 C200	10.00	5.50	m	5.5500	5,550	5,500	-50	466	92,495	48	-44.13	355.70	176.75	18.19

Exhibit 7.3

If you took delivery of those 1,000 shares of IBM at $200, are you prepared to handle the margin requirements? Dollar delta can help you calculate if you are in over your head!

Global Correlations and Hedging

Strategy selection and individual risk control is essential; but even if you are making the right strategy choices, you need to examine your entire trading account as one dynamic entity in addition to the individual strategies contained within.

An Example Using Bull-Put Spreads

Assume you sold 10 OTM vertical bull-put spreads in the following stocks:

- GOOG
- AAPL

1) Actions 2) Positions 3) View 4) Settings 99) Feedback Option Scenario Analysis

Portfolio (Owned) Jared Chapter 7 Mock < Add Position > USD 08/05/12 21) Group By

31) Positions 32) Hedge 33) Scenario Matrix 34) Scenario Chart

	Position	Mkt Px	M	Cost	Total Cost	Mkt Value	P&L	Delta	Delta Notional	Gamma	Theta	Vega	Rho	IVol
[-] Portfolio Totals					-8,400	-9,180	-780		150,746		193.96	-321.99	142.86	
AAPL US Equity					-990	-1,060	-70	72	44,176	-23	74.04	-88.65	13.95	
AAPL US Equity	.00	615.70	l	615.7000	0	0	0	0	0	0	.00	.00	.00	
AAPL US 08/18/12 P	-10.00	2.31	m	2.2600	-2,260	-2,310	-50	169	104,087	-61	268.25	-279.11	33.37	22.70
AAPL US 08/18/12 P	10.00	1.25	m	1.2700	1,270	1,250	-20	-97	-59,911	37	-194.21	190.46	-19.42	24.13
GOOG US Equity					-3,000	-3,300	-300	74	47,687	-5	8.89	-64.59	65.45	
GOOG US Equity	.00	641.33	l	641.3300	0	0	0	0	0	0	.00	.00	.00	
GOOG US 09/22/12 P	-10.00	13.90	m	13.8000	-13,800	-13,900	-100	390	250,201	-51	196.03	-881.72	339.04	21.07
GOOG US 09/22/12 P	10.00	10.60	m	10.8000	10,800	10,600	-200	-316	-202,514	46	-187.14	817.14	-273.59	21.66
IBM US Equity					-810	-820	-10	100	19,872	-19	14.60	-83.37	24.94	
IBM US Equity	.00	198.52	l	198.5200	0	0	0	0	0	0	.00	.00	.00	
IBM US 09/22/12 P1	-10.00	1.385	m	1.3600	-1,360	-1,385	-25	172	34,148	-36	39.66	-180.55	43.40	20.46
IBM US 09/22/12 P1	10.00	.565	m	.5500	550	565	15	-72	-14,277	17	-25.05	97.18	-18.47	24.05
LNKD US Equity					-1,000	-1,100	-100	150	16,315	-17	75.66	-33.42	5.66	
LNKD US Equity	.00	108.51	l	108.5100	0	0	0	0	0	0	.00	.00	.00	
LNKD US 08/18/12 P	10.00	.35	m	.4000	400	350	-50	-58	-6,288	9	-65.69	22.67	-2.16	68.74
LNKD US 08/18/12 P	-10.00	1.45	m	1.4000	-1,400	-1,450	-50	208	22,604	-27	141.35	-56.09	7.81	59.80
PCLN US Equity					-2,600	-2,900	-300	34	22,696	-2	20.76	-51.96	32.86	
PCLN US Equity	.00	663.99	l	663.9900	0	0	0	0	0	0	.00	.00	.00	
PCLN US 09/22/12 P	-10.00	18.65	m	18.6000	-18,600	-18,650	-50	279	184,992	-22	356.50	-798.88	261.41	42.01
PCLN US 09/22/12 P	10.00	15.75	m	16.0000	16,000	15,750	-250	-244	-162,296	21	-335.74	746.92	-228.56	42.31

Exhibit 7.4

Here is what your account might look like with 10 bullish put spreads in these stocks.

- IBM
- PCLN
- LNKD

Obviously you have a bullish sentiment on each of these stocks individually. You are going to be long delta, short gamma, short vega and collecting theta at the onset of the trades. See Exhibit 7.4.

If all goes well and these stocks all move higher and stay well above their short strikes, you should have a gradual gain to overall P&L and light volatility in that P&L, not to mention make a killing in profits. But sometimes, particularly with short gamma positions like this, happy, comfortable situations can turn into a nasty condition quickly. The credits you received quickly disappear and you start to get shorter gamma, long delta, and you are losing money really fast. Now those dollars you were collecting each day turn into thousands in losses at the blink of an eye.

You could just blow out of some or all of your positions take the loss and regroup or . . . Bloomberg offers a hedging function that will hedge your delta with the appropriate stock index to neutralize or reduce price risk and/or volatility. This is a great function and technique to utilize if stocks have been rising for a while and may be due for a turn.

Maybe another simple solution here would be to *buy* a put spread in the SPX, NDX, QQQ, or SPY. These five stocks are all highly correlated to both the S&P 500 and the Nasdaq, the latter being more appropriate in this case.

You have a total of 50 spreads on in this account, for a total credit of $8,400. Depending on how fearful you are and obviously on the cost of the put spread, you could buy an OTM put spread to help buffer any sharp drop in the index.

If the index sold off and you thought it was going to bounce, you could sell the long put spread (hedge) and let your original positions ride.

Beta weighting your portfolio in addition to option scenario analysis is vital!

Don't forget to theorize different time and volatility scenarios to "stress test" your strategies.

Portfolio Margin (PM)

A major benefit for professional traders is their ability to trade large amounts of stock and options with the least amount of capital committed.

Portfolio margining looks at the relationships between stock and the underlying options that you have in your account and relates their risk globally, allowing for a real view of risk and costs, versus weighting each individual strategy's margin requirements.

Stock or short options by themselves can eat up a ton of available cash in your account. This cash can be used for other investments.

An example would be a trader who owns 1,000 shares of IBM at $170 and only wants to commit $5,000 in cash and risk to the trade. This risk would be possible if he or she were also long the 165 put for whatever month he or she chooses. PM would only

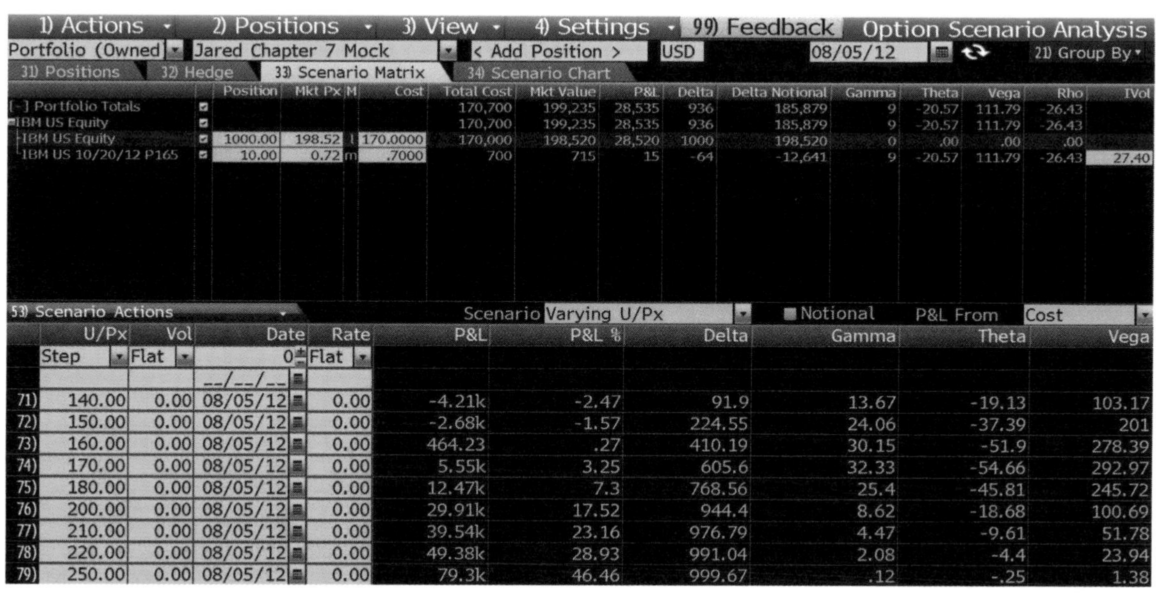

Exhibit 7.5

require him to commit his real risk in the trade. See Exhibit 7.5.

This is a far cry from the $85,000 that would be needed if the stock were bought in a regular margin account.

The cost of the put would be factored into the equation, but that cost could also be financed with the sale of an out-of-the money call or other option.

Another way to think about it is that PM allows you to create a synthetic position and only have the cost of the synthetic to cover. See Exhibit 7.6.

The bottom line is that portfolio margining dramatically reduces risk and capital commitments allowing you to trade freely. As you add positions into your account, margin requirements are dynamically updated.

PM can reduce risk, but it also changes risk and Greek behavior. What if I bought a January 180 straddle in IBM versus the long put? Does my global risk change? Use the P&L hypothetical models in the OSA chart feature to visualize these changes. In the OSA screen you can also adjust for volatility; in the earlier

Smart Investor Tip!

If you are equity heavy in your portfolio and want to free up some cash quickly without selling your long stock positions, you could either buy a put or create a collar. If you have portfolio margin, the free cash will be available in one trading day when the options settle.

Smart Investor Tip!

Only a select number of brokers offer portfolio margining and typically a minimum account size is required. PM requirements vary from broker to broker. Be sure you learn the specifics and understand the individual broker's margin policies, as they are all unique.

By executing a married put, I morphed long IBM stock and a long put into a long call, which is much less risky to own!

Exhibit 7.6

simulation I decided to add a little realistic boost to volatility if IBM drops.

Visualizing your global positions can be priceless when considering forward market events and your exposure. You'll sometimes be surprised at how dramatically the scenario chart changes when you add just a simple hedge.

A Case Study: PM in a Pickle

One of the most important aspects of having a PM account is your ability to quickly reduce your absolute risk in a trade or free up capital to make another trade. In a volatile marketplace, having this ability is priceless. It can also prevent major losses from an excessive assignment.

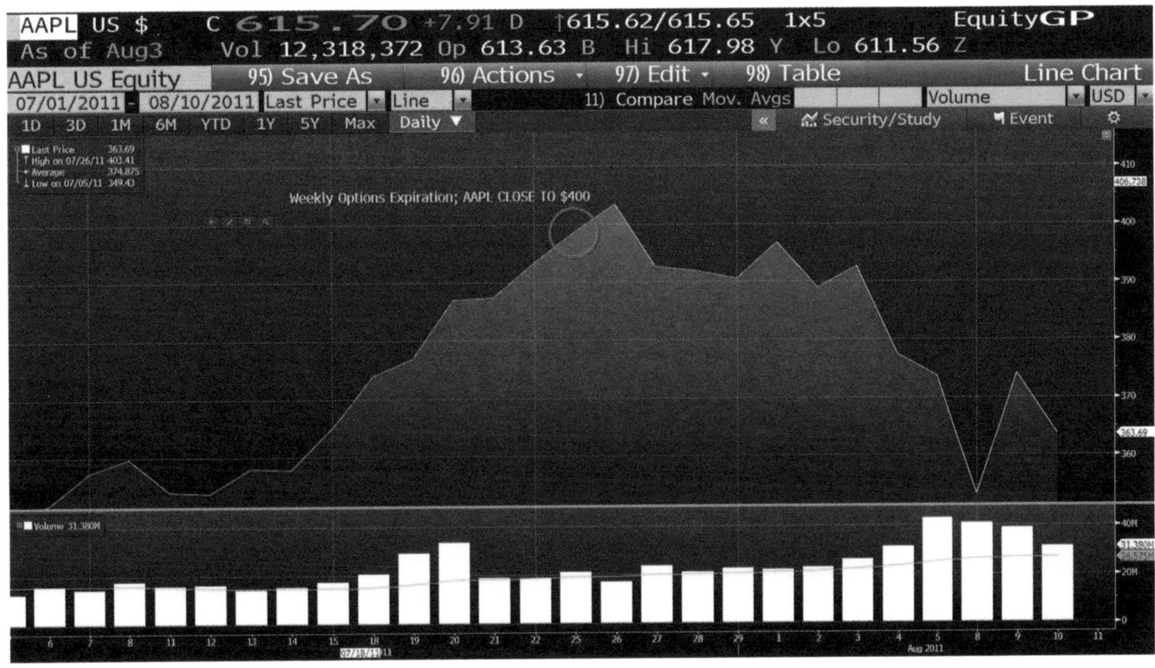

Exhibit 7.7

I am going to walk you through an actual situation that occurred in my fund with my partner in July 2011. See Exhibit 7.7.

We were short the July 400/410 call spread and we were profitable, so I entered an order to close the spread for .20 debit, as the stock was trading at $395 just before expiration. Little did I know that there was a standing Good Till Canceled (GTC) order to close the spread for a .05 debit. Sure enough, that GTC order was executed after we thought we were flat for the day and had run out for a meeting.

At the close on Friday, Apple was just above $400, which prompted our broker to exercise our long calls (40 of them), which we had no idea we had. Come

Smart Investor Tip!

Always check existing GTC and limit orders so you don't duplicate or reenter a trade in the opposite direction.

Monday, the stock was trading down to $396 and we were long 4,000 shares at $400, a $1.6 million trade!

This is not the position we wanted to have, but we did not want to take a loss. Immediately, I bought the $380 put and sold the 400 call for a credit of about $6.

This did two things: It dropped my margin requirement (and risk) to $80,000, which was much more digestible, and reduced our cost basis down to $394. After some luck and shuffling, we were able to successfully trade out of the collar for a profit of about 4 percent on our risk.

Without PM, we would have been forced to sell our Apple position at a loss or tie up an extraordinary amount of cash while waiting for the trade to work out.

More Hedging Techniques

By now you should have a firm grasp of how to manage risk in your individual strategies. But what do you do when you accumulate 3, 5, 10, 20 different positions that together create market exposure that you may not want?

I remember in early 2011 I was adding more and more semi-bearish positions in about 12 different stocks. Individually, they were modest in delta risk and just about all were statistically advantaged, meaning that the stocks could rise and I could still end up profitable.

When I stopped to examine the total deltas I was short. It amounted to more than 9,000 in all the positions and because I was short gamma, I got shorter delta as the stocks went higher. My dollar delta looked ugly. When I dug deeper, I realized that my positions had become *highly* correlated to the S&P 500 over the past three months.

So as the market marched higher, I started to feel the pain. The first thing I did was offset my longer term bearish trades with some bullish vertical spreads. Then I took a short position in the UVXY for a little while, which helped.

But what is the best way to gauge your portfolio's risk and hedge it off at least partially?

Index Weighting for Better Hedging

The WGT screen allows you to see the underlying security's weighting in all the indices that it belongs to. If you are focusing on a small amount of stocks, you can combine their weighting in an index, along with *beta* and volatility to determine the best hedge. See Exhibit 7.8.

This is helpful in several ways. First, identify the most efficient index to use as a hedge by locating the index(es) it is most heavily weighted in (you can combine several positions here). This is important because there could be several indices that your position(s) belong to. IBM for example is part of 97 different indices. You're not going to use all of them!

You can group stocks that are in similar sectors and indices together and hedge them separately if you really want to get specific or creative by using a

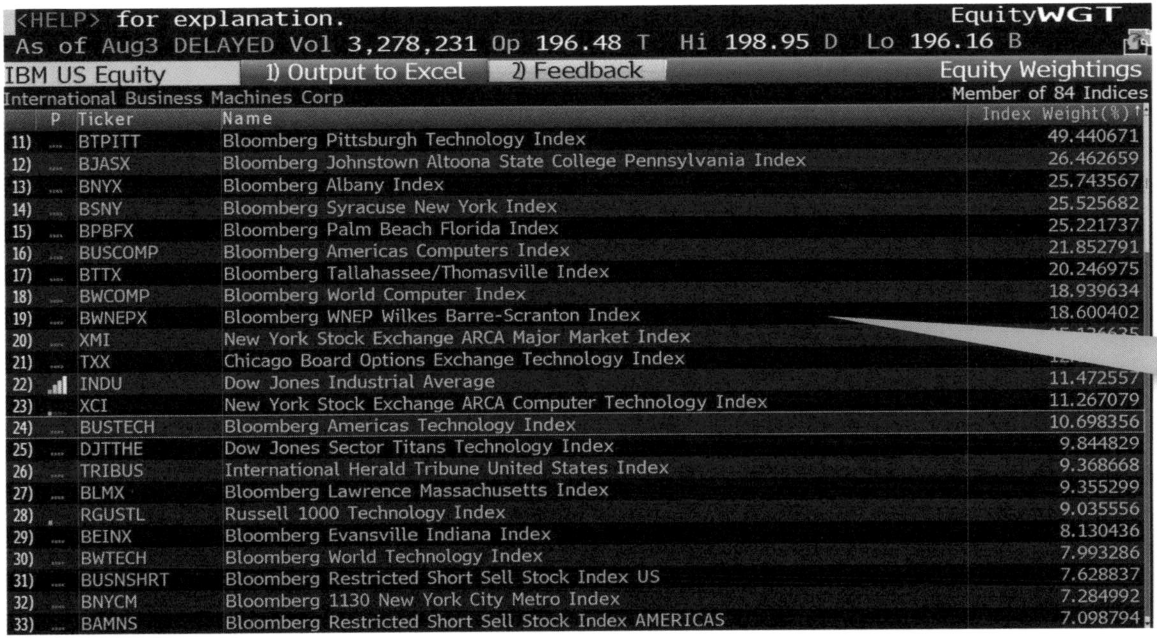
<HELP> for explanation. EquityWGT
As of Aug3 DELAYED Vol 3,278,231 Op 196.48 T Hi 198.95 D Lo 196.16 B
IBM US Equity 1) Output to Excel 2) Feedback Equity Weightings
International Business Machines Corp Member of 84 Indices

	P	Ticker	Name	Index Weight(%)
11)	...	BTPITT	Bloomberg Pittsburgh Technology Index	49.440671
12)	...	BJASX	Bloomberg Johnstown Altoona State College Pennsylvania Index	26.462659
13)	...	BNYX	Bloomberg Albany Index	25.743567
14)	...	BSNY	Bloomberg Syracuse New York Index	25.525682
15)	...	BPBFX	Bloomberg Palm Beach Florida Index	25.221737
16)	...	BUSCOMP	Bloomberg Americas Computers Index	21.852791
17)	...	BTTX	Bloomberg Tallahassee/Thomasville Index	20.246975
18)	...	BWCOMP	Bloomberg World Computer Index	18.939634
19)	...	BWNEPX	Bloomberg WNEP Wilkes Barre-Scranton Index	18.600402
20)	...	XMI	New York Stock Exchange ARCA Major Market Index	[illegible]
21)	...	TXX	Chicago Board Options Exchange Technology Index	[illegible]
22)		INDU	Dow Jones Industrial Average	11.472557
23)		XCI	New York Stock Exchange ARCA Computer Technology Index	11.267079
24)	...	BUSTECH	Bloomberg Americas Technology Index	10.698356
25)	...	DJTTHE	Dow Jones Sector Titans Technology Index	9.844829
26)	...	TRIBUS	International Herald Tribune United States Index	9.368668
27)	...	BLMX	Bloomberg Lawrence Massachusetts Index	9.355299
28)		RGUSTL	Russell 1000 Technology Index	9.035556
29)	...	BEINX	Bloomberg Evansville Indiana Index	8.130436
30)	...	BWTECH	Bloomberg World Technology Index	7.993286
31)	...	BUSNSHRT	Bloomberg Restricted Short Sell Stock Index US	7.628837
32)	...	BNYCM	Bloomberg 1130 New York City Metro Index	7.284992
33)	...	BAMNS	Bloomberg Restricted Short Sell Stock Index AMERICAS	7.098794

The WGT screen gives the exact weighting of a security within an index; it's fantastic for finding the best hedging vehicle.

Exhibit 7.8

statistically advantaged spread as a hedge in a highly correlated index on a ratio basis. Basically, you might be long 10 IBM 170/175 call spreads in your portfolio (with IBM at $185) at a cost of $3 and want to build a hedge in case markets move lower, but you don't want to put the hedge on in IBM because the option volatility or strikes may not be favorable, so you instead find an index or ETF that IBM is a large component of (+25 percent).

Now assume that the index is trading at $100 and has a lower volatility than IBM has, but you are able to sell the 105/100 call spread for $1 and do that trade four times. Not only are you statistically advantaged, but you have a low relative volatility hedge, reducing

Smart Investor Tip!

Identify if your stock or its peers are having a controlling influence on an index that may be out of line with broad market. Use the correlation/weight WGT screen to quantify the relationship between a particular index and the S&P 500 (or other broad diverse index) further.

DEFINITION:
Beta

is a stock's correlation and relative volatility when compared to an index.

Smart Investor Tip!

For easy math, just average the daily, weekly, and monthly beta going back one year.

your risk in the original spread trade by $4; your hedge was only 4 spreads against your original 10.

If IBM drops, you can use the profits to offset the risk. If IBM rises, the index should rise more slowly and thus you should make more than you are losing. At some point you may remove the hedge if IBM keeps rallying, or if IBM stays relatively flat, you will gain from both your original trade and your hedge!

This is just one of numerous ways you could hedge. If the *index* is very expensive ($500 plus) maybe a butterfly with a near-term expiration might be a good cheap alternative and allow some extra profit on a move against you.

It's all about your thesis and what you want your risk to be.

Beta versus Volatility

Just when you thought you had enough comparing and contrasting historical volatility with implied volatility, there is another measurement that I believe is crucial in risk management and strike and strategy selection as well as setting appropriate profit targets: beta. See Exhibit 7.9.

In a way, beta can directly play into the prices of options and may actually give you an edge. Check out the BETA screen to research further and visualize this indicator.

Beta in Option Pricing Models?

Beta is *not* figured into an option's price at all. *The option (price) doesn't necessarily care how volatile or correlated an asset is to the index it belongs to.* Options are simply assigned an implied volatility number and the model (along with other data) and a price is created. But that doesn't mean that beta can't be an indicator of where Ivol or Hvol may be headed. See Exhibit 7.10.

Try to examine beta in different time frames and over different events to spot patterns and to increase accuracy with patterns. Start four years back and work your way forward; try to correlate beta shifts with different periods in the market if you really want to get nuts.

If you have a stock (correlated to the S&P 500 index) that has a high beta (2-plus) that is moving at a 30 Hvol with options priced around the same 30 Ivol level, you might be more of a buyer if you notice the index is now moving at a 35 Hvol. If the stock goes back to its normal beta of 2 and the index stays volatile, you might be successful at buying a straddle and scalping gamma or just making money on movement. This isn't guaranteed, but it can be a neat little trick.

Portfolio Beta

To take things a step farther, portfolio beta is a simple measurement that allows you to view your correlation and exposure to overall market movement and control risk in addition to delta and volatility. This measurement of risk goes hand in hand with delta because of its ability to not just gauge how your positions will move with the market on a one-to-one basis (delta)

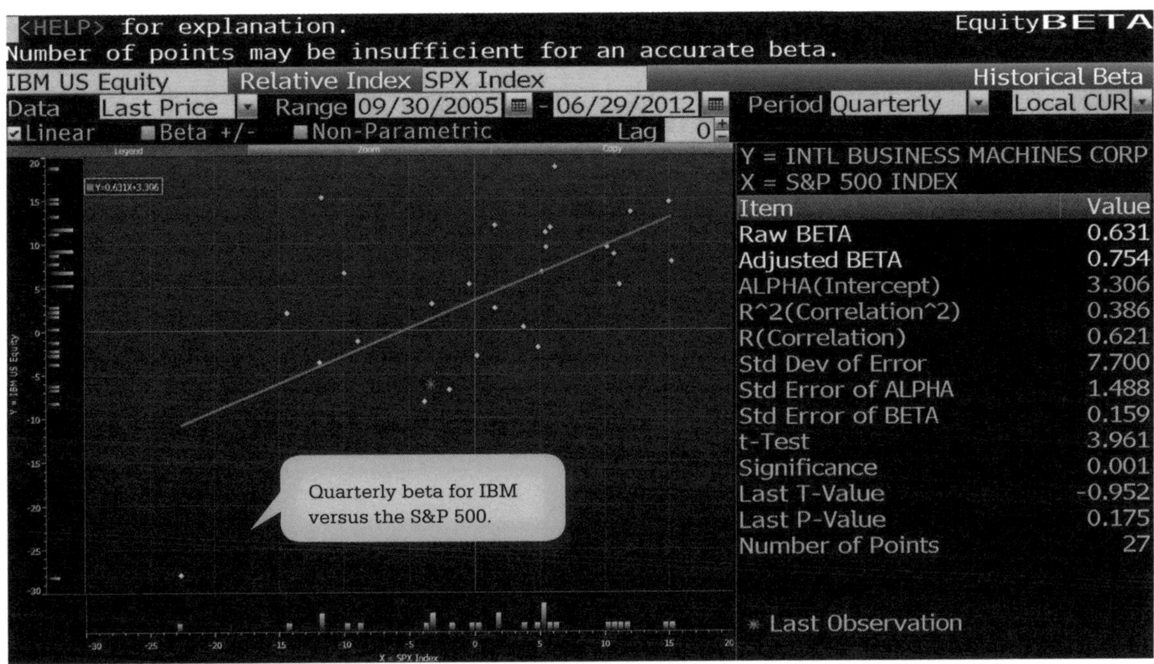

Exhibit 7.9

but it will allow you to better quantify the acceleration (or opposite) of your position when the broad market starts to move.

An asset whose returns vary more than the market's returns over time can have a beta with an absolute value greater than 1.0. If the asset is also closely correlated to the market, its beta will be greater than 1.0, but will generally be less than 1 if the asset is less correlated. A positive beta means that the asset's returns generally follow the market's returns, in the sense that they both tend to be above their respective averages together, or both tend to be below their respective averages together.

A stock whose returns vary less than the market's returns has a beta with an absolute value less than 1.0. An asset has a beta of zero if its returns change

Daily beta for IBM versus the S&P 500.

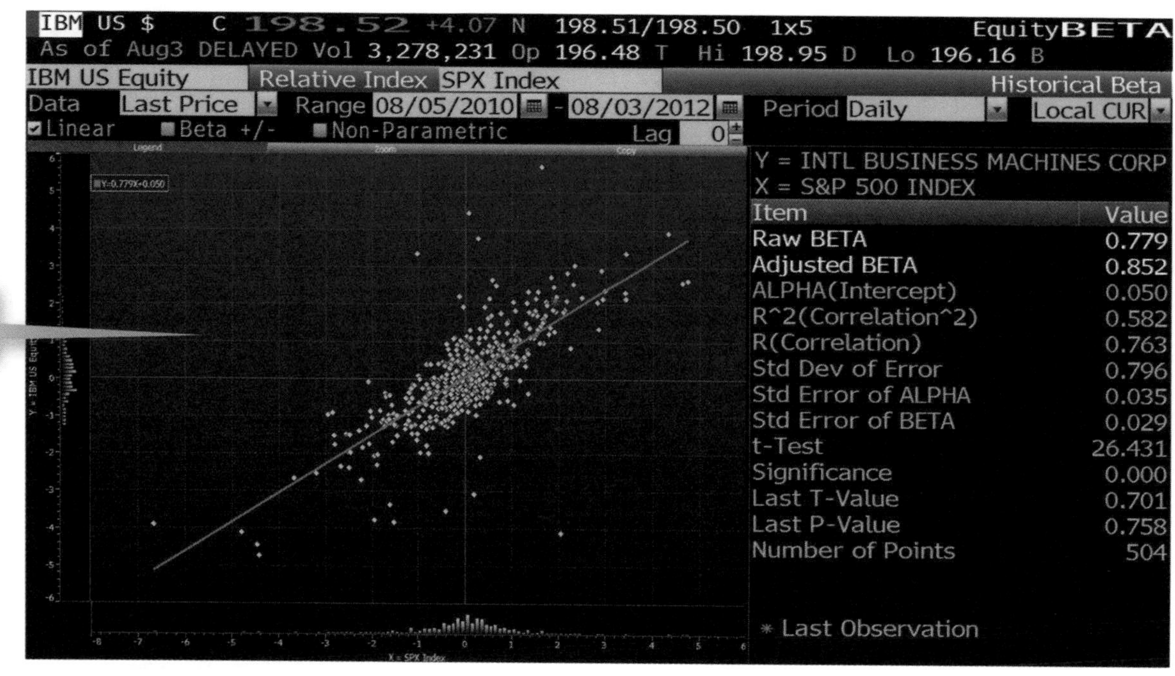

Exhibit 7.10

independently of changes in the market's returns (minimal correlation).

As beta turns negative, it means that the asset's returns generally move opposite the market's returns: one will tend to be above its average when the other is below its average. The more opposite the returns are to one another the more negative the beta.

You can layer your option exposure and risk along with the beta of the stock. Assume you wanted to be long 1,000 deltas by purchasing calls on a stock, but found the stock had a beta of 3. Unless you're okay with the added risk to the market, you might want to either scale back the risk (contract size) or change strategies in that particular stock as not to take on too much risk. You will know how volatile the stock

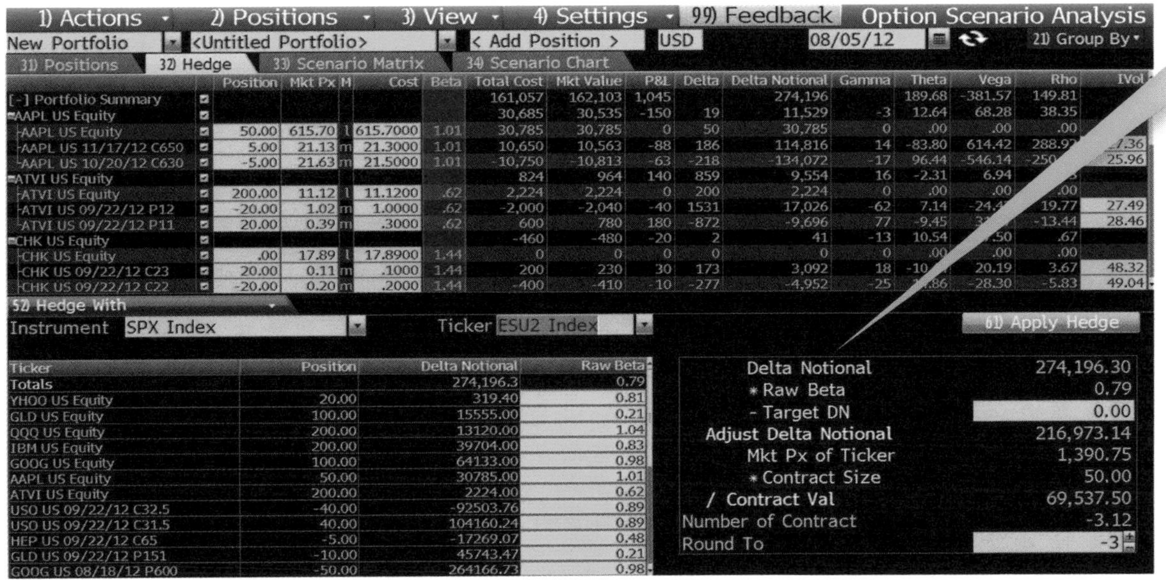

Exhibit 7.11

is on its own by looking at Hvol and Ivol. But what if the big economic picture starts to change and things shift negative? That stock may get really volatile really quick. See Exhibit 7.11

Think of portfolio beta as a "free look" at the gamma of your portfolio; gamma doesn't "know" how correlated the stock will be in relation to the markets, so using beta can be helpful.

I use portfolio beta in conjunction with my analysis of the Greeks and my selection of new trades in the portfolio. If I have a portfolio with an extremely high beta, I may select less correlated or lower volatility stocks or strategies until I reduce risk, unless of I am okay with that exposure.

Trading and Dealing with Options Expiration

An option would not be an option without an expiration date. The expiration date is crucial in determining

Raw beta is the portfolio's stock correlation to the market. Take that raw beta and multiply it times your net portfolio delta to get a more accurate read on your complete P&L!

Smart Investor Tip!

There is a function on Bloomberg that allows you to find portfolio beta quickly (screen OSA), but it never hurts to know how to manually figure this measurement out.

STEP-BY-STEP

To Figure Portfolio Beta:

1. **Find the betas for all your stocks.**
2. **Multiply each beta by the percentage of your total portfolio that stock represents.**
3. **Add all the weighted betas together to arrive at your portfolio's overall beta.**

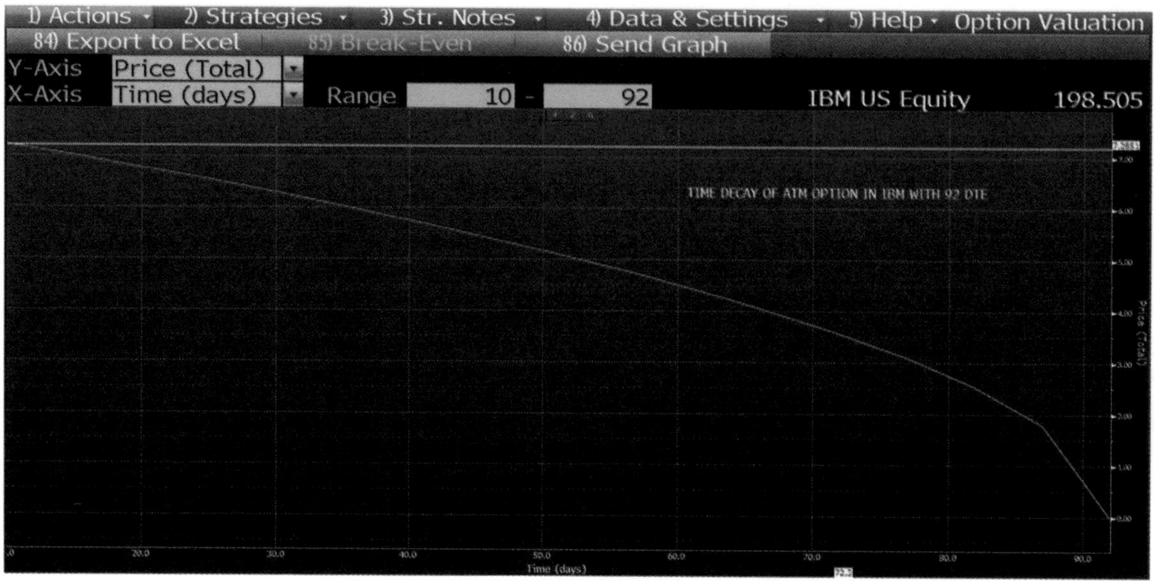

Exhibit 7.12

the theoretical value of an option. It is also one of the more difficult things for new options traders to deal with because stocks, unlike options, don't come with an expiration date, although some do go bankrupt from time to time.

Options are wasting assets, meaning that part of their value will naturally decay as expiration approaches, even if the underlying stock itself is performing according to plan. Time decay is nonlinear, so as expiration Friday draws closer, the amount of time value an option will lose with each passing day increases. See Exhibit 7.12.

Typically, option contracts expire according to a predetermined calendar. For instance, for U.S. exchange-listed equity option contracts, the expiration date is always on the Saturday that follows the third Friday of the month, unless that Friday is a market holiday, in which case the final day of trading is Thursday (and expiration is still on Saturday). The market is not open on Saturday, so that Friday is called *options expiration day* because it is the last day that you can trade out of that option and typically the day you are making the decision to exercise your long options or get prepared to be assigned on your short options.

There are two types of options expiration.

1. **American**—Can be exercised anytime up until expiration, most equity options that trade on U.S. exchanges are U.S. expiration.
2. **European**—Can only be exercised on expiration day (the last trading day); many cash-settled indexes are European expiration.

Equity Options

Most standard options that are traded on individual equities in the United States on U.S. exchanges are U.S. expiration, meaning that you can exercise them at any time up until expiration. (You can also be assigned if you are short.)

Index Options

Most cash index options (not ETFs) are European expiration, meaning that you can only exercise them on expiration day, which by the way may *not* be the third Friday. Some indexes actually cease trading the third Thursday of the month and are marked to the opening price of the stocks contained in that index on Friday. These options are usually settled in cash, not stock, so there is *no* assignment risk.

ETFs

Exchange-traded funds (ETFs) generally expire the same way U.S. equity options do, on the third Friday of their expiration month. Check the prospectus or website of the ETF for specifics.

Binary Options

Binary options will only be worth $1 or $0 at expiration. There are binary options listed on certain select stocks and indexes but they are not exercisable into stock or cash other than their final value on expiration. They generally expire with standard options; however, there are now OTC binary option brokers who have daily expirations. Make sure you research them thoroughly before committing one cent. Most binary options are not exercisable into stock and have very unique characteristics.

Expiration Cycles

Each and every set of options has its own expiration cycle. Essentially, the cycle sets the months that the stock will have options offered. This is in addition to every stock, index, and ETF having the first two months of options available to trade at all times. There are some exceptions to this cycle as some options have contracts in every month and some products have additional quarterly and even weekly options. Most equity options trade with expiration months in one of the following four expiration cycles:

1. **January cycle**: Expirations in January, April, July, October (the first month of each quarter).

DEFINITION:
Exercise
describes the action that the owner of a call or put takes to execute his or her right to convert that option into stock.

KEY POINT:
Remember that for every buyer there is a seller and vice versa.

DEFINITION:
Assignment
describes the condition of being short an option and forced to buy or sell shares of stock when the "owner" of that option chooses to exercise.

2. **February cycle**: Expirations in February, May, August, November (second month).
3. **March cycle**: Expirations in March, June, September, December (third month).
4. **Weeklies and quarterlies**: Weekly options begin trading the Thursday before the following expiration Friday, allowing about seven days to trade them before they expire. Quarterlies are listed for trading for four consecutive calendar quarters plus the last quarter of the next calendar year. Both of these expiration types are only listed on a handful of equities and indexes, check cboe.com for details.

LEAPS

LEAPS have a fancy name and there may be some subtle nuances to trading them, but in essence they are just longer dated options with one to four years out until expiration. They eventually turn into regular options and follow standard expiration rules.

Exercise and Assignment Risks

There are many option traders who have never been through an exercise or assignment where they were actually long or short an option after the close of trading on the third Friday of an options expiration month and had to manually do something. Typically, most traders close out their positions before expiration, which is not a bad thing. Expiration is an important time in which you reduce risk. How you handle it could have serious consequences on your portfolio and risk. For example, if you bought one call with a strike price of $50, you can exercise that call and you will be the proud owner of 100 shares of stock at $50 per share. Of course, you have to have the money to do so.

If you bought one put with a strike price of $50 and chose to exercise your option, you would end up short 100 shares at a price of $50.

Typically, most investors who are buying calls and puts do not hold their positions until expiration and therefore do *not* end up exercising them.

Assignment

Assignment works the opposite of exercise, in that a trader who is short one call with a strike price of $50 will be forced to *sell* 100 shares of stock at $50. Now those can be shares that you already may own, or you may have to assume a short position, the latter potentially having much more risk.

If you are short one put with a strike price of $50 and you are assigned, you will be forced to *buy* 100 shares of stock at $50. Again, depending on your investment objective and risk tolerance that may be good or bad.

It's important to know that the Options Clearing Corporation (OCC) specifies that any equity option that is $0.01 or more in the money will be automatically exercised, so that if you are long a call that is 0.01 or more in the money at 4 p.m. Eastern Standard Time on expiration Friday, you may end up with 100 shares of stock in your account come Monday. This works the same way if you are long a put, only you may end up with 100 shares short in your account on Monday.

There are instances where you do *not* want to exercise your option. You would most likely do this if your option is just at the money and you are not sure whether you will be automatically exercised. If your option is in the money and you don't have the money to take on the stock position or if you don't want to have a stock position, just *sell* the option before the market closes or let it expire!

If you are short, and that option is in the money by a cent or more, you will most likely have to either sell stock if you are short a call or buy stock if you are short a put, so be aware that automatic exercise will cause an automatic assignment as well.

Don't just think that because you have the money or margin in your account to cover the exercise or assignment transaction, you should let the automatic exercise happen.

Remember that if you are long or short, your delta position may be dramatically different come Monday, if the market makes a drastic move against you over the weekend. The option that may have cost you $5,000 now may have $50,000 or more at risk.

It is imperative to not only run position scenarios after expiration, but also that you talk to your brokers ahead of expiration to get specifics on how they treat exercise/assignment, or have a plan to exit or convert into stock, if that is what you choose to do.

Advanced Education on Early Exercise

Most traders do not exercise options early, unless there is a huge dividend (for a call) or they are a professional that gets a short stock rebate (for a put).

When an option is exercised, any remaining time value left in that option is forfeited. The exceptions to this rule are fairly simple and there are only certain instances where an early exercise is warranted.

For short positions in your account, which can be part of spreads, early assignment is something you need to be aware of and know how to deal with if and when it happens. If you are short an option (put or call) that is deep in the money, you run a much higher risk of being assigned early because these options may be devoid of any time value and, depending on the situation, may be candidates for early exercise as they would be better as a stock than stay an option.

Spreads that generally get hurt from early assignment are:

Short vertical spreads (bear call and bull put)
Short iron condors
Long condors
Long butterflies

In most of these cases, an early assignment on one or more of the options in your spread means that the stock is *not* where you want to be. Again, this will usually occur if the option (call or put) is deep in the money and there is either not much time until expiration (call) or there is a lot of time (put).

Smart Investor Tip!

To take on a stock position by exercise or assignment, purchase a cheap out-of-the money put or call to hedge your trade in volatile markets, or if there is a news event on expiration weekend. Find a strike that is just above your stop loss level and buy at least 30 days until expiration, so that the two days of weekend theta won't be too expensive and you can sell back your option on Monday if nothing happens.

Smart Investor Tip!

Be careful if you are in a spread and the stock is in between strikes as you may not be assigned on one, but automatically exercised on another causing you to come in with a long or stock position that you are unprepared for.

KEY POINT:

Lower the price of the call by the amount of the dividend and raise the price of the put by the amount of the dividend. Depending on the expiration date, the option will adjust automatically for the amount of the dividend.

Smart Investor Tip!

Getting assigned on one or more of your short positions in a spread can potentially throw a monkey wrench into your risk management, or change the dynamics of your entire trade and even force you to realize the maximum loss (or profit) in the trade.

DO IT YOURSELF

Assume that you have the 50/55 put spread and the 60/65 call spread and that you are long for a $3 debit. The stock is now at $75, it's two days before expiration, and you get an assignment notice on your 65 call. What happens now and what's the best way to handle it?

Smart Investor Tip!

If a trade has moved against you dramatically, you should have a point at which you exit the trade, roll the trade, or salvage it from total loss. If you are assigned in any of the above spreads, you will most likely assume the max loss by exercising the long option(s) against it. This will prevent further losses if the stock were to move against you.

The probability of this happening would be increased if a stock pays big dividends or if interest rates are high.

Spreads that generally benefit from early assignment are:

Long vertical spreads (bull call and bear put)
Long iron condors
Short condors
Short butterflies

In the above spreads, an early exercise may be a blessing and give the max profit if you were to exercise the long portion of your spread.

Early exercise could also occur in a short straddle that has gone wrong, where the stock has moved way beyond your short strikes and if there is a dividend on the way. At that point you are essentially short stock (your short call is in the money) and you should have a damn good reason to be holding on that long.

Another common occurrence is when you are long a time spread (horizontal/calendar) and the stock makes a sharp move and puts your short option (which is the one that is expiring first) deep in the money. This usually occurs with calls because of the time duration.

Early assignment is rare if you are handling your money management and risk properly.

When Should You Exercise an Option Early?

There are only two basic reasons to exercise an option early. If you own a call option that has *no* time value (deep in the money) and there is a large dividend coming up, you would want to exercise your call to capture the dividend. When you do this, you will have delta risk because you are now long the shares. See Exhibit 7.13.

Depending on whether you are a professional market maker, you may receive a credit for being short stock; if the credit you will receive for short stock is greater than the time value left in the put then that put should be exercised. Like the call, you will have short delta risk, but it should be the same as the long put because it will have close to a one delta anyway. See Exhibit 7.14.

Dividends (Call Exercise)

Call options should be exercised in advance of expiration if the dividend amount is greater than the time-value amount. Typically this is an option that is very deep in the money or close to expiring. In many cases, if an option has time value left, you should sell it in the open market, capture the time value, and then just purchase the stock to collect the dividend (remember that options do not pay dividends like stocks do).

Call Value Formula and Rationale

$$\text{Call value} = \text{Intrinsic value} + \text{Interest rate value} + \text{Volatility value} - \text{Dividend value}$$

If you have a deep in-the-money call that is trading close to parity and there is a dividend on the horizon,

HEP US $ C 65.16 -1.26 N 65.16/65.45 1x1 EquityOMON
As of Aug3 DELAYED Vol 29,117 Op 65.61 N Hi 65.61 N Lo 64.52 N
HEP US Equity 95) Templates 96) Actions 97) Expiry · Option Monitor: jared basi...
HOLLY ENERGY PAR 65.16 0% 65.16 / 65.45 Hi 65.61 Lo 64.52 Volm 29117 HV 21...
Calc Mode 94) Fields Center 60.00 Strikes 4 Exch US Composite 92) Next Earnings(EM) 10/26/12 E
295) Center Strike 296) Calls/Puts 297) Calls 298) Puts 299) Term Structure

Puts

	Strike	Ticker	ThPx	IVol	Bid	Theo	Ask	IVal	IVal	DM	TM	DvAm	DvDt
	4	22 Sep 12	Days »	48	IVol »		Rate »	0.30	CSize 100				
1)	55.00	HEP 9 P55	.13	28.66	.10	.01	.15		.15	-.04	.0066	.9250	11/7
2)	60.00	HEP 9 P60	.45	23.49	.40	.25	.50		.50	-.15	.0137	.9250	11/7
3)	65.00	HEP 9 P65	1.80	20.31	1.50	1.73	2.10		1.50	-.47	.0200	.9250	11/7
4)	70.00	HEP 9 P70	5.10	17.75	4.50	5.20	5.70	4.84		-.86	.0099	.9250	11/7
	4	17 Nov 12	Days »	104	IVol »		Rate »	0.49	CSize 100; Div 0.93 USD				
5)	55.00	HEP 11 P55	.57	26.37	.50	.14	.65		.65	-.12	.0089	.9250	11/7
6)	60.00	HEP 11 P60	1.32	22.53	1.20	.87	1.45		1.30	-.26	.0120	.9250	11/7
7)	65.00	HEP 11 P65	3.27	21.09	2.95	2.90	3.60		3.60	-.51	.0137	.9250	11/7
8)	70.00	HEP 11 P70	6.40	18.43	5.80	6.39	7.00	4.84	2.16	-.79	.0082	.9250	11/7
	4	16 Feb 13	Days »	195	IVol »		Rate »	0.75	CSize 100; Div 1.87 USD				
9)	55.00	HEP 2 P55	1.35	24.85	1.20	.59	1.50		1.50	-.19	.0090	.9250	11/7
10)	60.00	HEP 2 P60	2.70	23.20	2.45	1.86	2.95		2.95	-.34	.0099	.9250	11/7
11)	65.00	HEP 2 P65	4.85	21.50	4.40	4.23	5.30		4.70	-.53	.0090	.9250	11/7
12)	70.00	HEP 2 P70	7.95	19.94	7.30	7.69	8.60	4.84	3.76	-.72	.0054	.9250	11/7
	4	18 Aug 12	Days »	13	IVol »		Rate »	0.21	CSize 100				
13)	55.00	HEP 8 P55	.10	54.55			.10		.10	-.04	.0213	.9250	11/7
14)	60.00	HEP 8 P60	.20	36.30		.01	.20		.20	-.10	.0305	.9250	11/7
15)	65.00	HEP 8 P65	.93	21.48	.70	.85	1.15		1.15	-.47	.0432	.9250	11/7
16)	70.00	HEP 8 P70	4.85	18.56	2.70	4.86	7.00	4.84	2.16	-.98	.0032	.9250	11/7

HEP is a huge dividend payer (the DvAm column shows the next dividend amount); the calls will be adjusted for that dividend, and in-the-money calls may be exercised to capture it.

Exhibit 7.13

you may want to exercise that option (because you can't sell it for a premium over parity) and collect the dividend, rather than hold on to it.

If stock is trading at $50, and the market in the 45 call is $4.90 to $5.20 (99 delta) with five days until expiration, the stock goes ex-dividend 30 cents tomorrow.

You should exercise that call today (you can only sell it in this case for less than parity) to capture 30 cents in dividend. You may have risk in the stock moving, but you would have that regardless if you stayed in the call position.

Remember that because the call is so deep in the money, it has lost its "optionality" and is behaving much like the stock, so the trader is simply substituting the 100 delta call with 100 shares of stock.

Capturing dividends can also be done by using deep in-the-money call spreads; a trader might

Smart Investor Tip!

Don't just buy an in-the-money call to exercise and capture the dividend. You're better off trading the stock directly to reduce slippage between the bid-ask prices. Deep in-the-money options will have wide spreads!

Apple was just about to distribute a $2.65 dividend; these ITM calls might be susceptible to exercise. Keep in mind that if you exercise a call, you still have risk because you will now have long stock.

AAPL US $ C 615.70 +7.91 D ↑615.62/615.65 1x5 EquityOMON
As of Aug3 Vol 12,318,372 Op 613.63 B Hi 617.98 Y Lo 611.56 Z
AAPL US Equity 95) Templates 96) Actions 97) Expiry Option Monitor: DIV LOOK
APPLE INC 615.70 0% 615.62 / 615.65 Hi 617.98 Lo 611.56 Volm 12318372 HV 23.91 91) News (CN)
Calc Mode 94) Fields Center 560.00 Strikes 4 Exch US Composite 92) Next Earnings(EM) 10/18/12 E
295) Center Strike 296) Calls/Puts 297) Calls 298) Puts 299) Term Structure

	Strike	Ticker	ThPx	IVol	Bid	Ask	Theo	IVal	DM	TVal	DvAm	DvDt
	4	18 Aug 12	Days »	13	IVol »		Rate »	0.21	CSize 100; Div 2.65 USD			
1)	555.00	AAPL 8/18/12 C555	60.80	33.28	60.55y	61.05y	60.72	60.70	.99		2.6500	8/9
2)	560.00	AAPL 8/18/12 C560	55.78	30.01	55.55y	56.00y	55.72	55.70	.99		2.6500	8/9
3)	565.00	AAPL 8/18/12 C565	50.78	27.71	50.60y	50.95y	50.74	50.70	.99		2.6500	8/9
4)	[illegible]	[illegible]/12 C570	45.80	26.23	45.60y	46.00y	45.77	45.70	.99		2.6500	8/9
	4	22 Sep 12	Days »	48	IVol »		Rate »	0.30	CSize 100; Div 2.65 USD			
5)	555.00	AAPL 9/22/12 C555	62.55	26.48	62.30y	62.80y	62.21	60.70	.88	2.10	2.6500	8/9
6)	560.00	AAPL 9/22/12 C560	58.13	26.07	57.90y	58.35y	57.89	55.70	.86	2.20	2.6500	8/9

Exhibit 7.14

KEY POINT:

Calls are not an early exercise other than right before the stock goes ex-dividend!

Smart Investor Tip!

Professionals (market makers) who hold short stock in their accounts may receive a rebate, but retail traders (market takers) do not. Retail traders should never exercise a put option unless the puts are held inside of an estate or liquidation of an account where the controller of the account is not familiar with options and wants to convert the option into a short stock position.

buy 10,000 deep call spreads for parity or a little bit under hoping to capture a dividend by taking advantage of the random assignment methods of the OCC. This usually requires that the traders have low commissions and exercise costs, otherwise the trade would cost too much and carry too much risk.

Call Spread Dividend Exercise Example

A trader buys 10,000 of the 45/50 call spreads for $5 times with the stock at $55, with less than five days until expiration. The stock goes ex-dividend $0.30 tomorrow; traders then exercise all the long calls and hope that they do not get assigned on all of their short calls; therefore, they are able to capture the dividend. Those short call options that are left are covered by a long stock, reducing risk unless there is a catastrophe and the stock falls below the short call strike.

This trade can only be done by professionals with low commission rates and exercise costs in a stock that is very heavily traded.

Assuming that 100 of their short calls go unexercised, traders can potentially capture ([100 contracts * 100 shares] * 0.30) or $3,000 in dividends. Again, traders are susceptible to market risk if they are unhedged.

Interest (Put Exercise Reasoning)

Exercising a put may be slightly more complicated and even less common. In low interest rate environments, it is even rarer. Dividends are a positive for put values, because they lower the forward prices of the asset. Interest rates are obviously a negative for put values. As interest rates rise, put values will decrease because increasing interest rates increase the forward price of an asset. See Exhibit 7.15.

Professionals who own a deep in-the-money put may choose to exercise if the put is trading close to parity (U.S. put options will *never* trade for less than parity) as they may be able to get a short stock rebate that is greater than the time value of that put itself.

If you are considering the early exercise of a put, it is paramount to have an idea about not only the interest rate environment (rising or falling) but also the short interest in the stock that you are trading as both can have effects on your put exercise decision.

For most retail traders, early exercise is *not* a typical occurrence. Retail traders should focus on their risk going into and coming out of expiration day, particularly if they have a spread on and the stock is in between strikes or near its short or long strike, as there is uncertainty whether it will be assigned or they have to exercise their options. Sometimes it is best to just sell or buy your position back to the marketplace, rather than take a chance on expiration and run the risk of coming in Monday with long or short stock that is moving against you.

This also goes for a covered call that is close to where the stock is closing on Friday. If you want to keep the stock, just buy the call back to remove your risk of being assigned. Remember that the OCC will automatically exercise an option that is one cent in the money, unless the trader instructs otherwise, so your chances of being assigned are certainly high.

Binary Options as a Spread Substitute?

Binary options may not have taken off in the listed market, but they are really popular in the OTC (over the counter) marketplace.

Binary options are nothing new, but certainly have their share of pros, cons, and nuances. The biggest hurdle is their lack of selection and liquidity in the listed arena. Depending on when you read this, they are either growing in popularity or have completely gone away from the exchanges.

But their popularity is flourishing online.

KEY POINT:

That short stock rebate may be jeopardized if that stock becomes hard to borrow or interest rates drop. At that point the put exercise may have been a bad decision because the interest money that was supposed to be collected ceases to be paid or is reduced.

Smart Investor Tip!

Early exercise may be more common in lower volatility stocks versus higher ones because of the reduced risk of the stock blowing through the exercised call or put. Put exercise would also be more common in a rising interest rate environment and in options listed on a relatively stable stock that is liquid and has minimal risk of becoming hard to borrow.

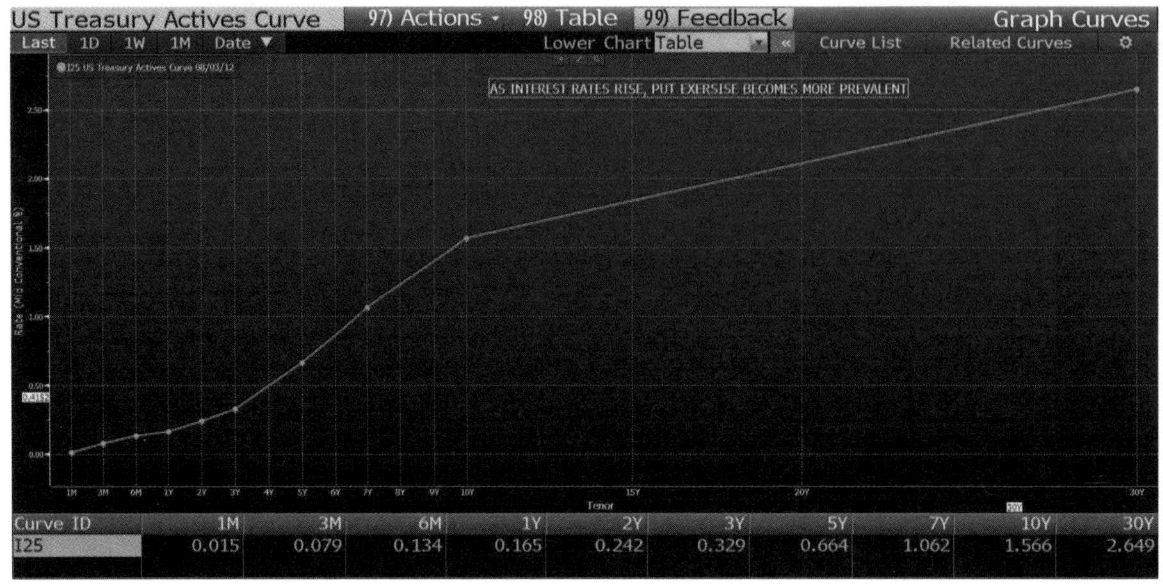

Curve ID	1M	3M	6M	1Y	2Y	3Y	5Y	7Y	10Y	30Y
I25	0.015	0.079	0.134	0.165	0.242	0.329	0.664	1.062	1.566	2.649

Exhibit 7.15

Return of the Bucket Shops?

One thing I did notice is that "brokerage" and other finance/technology companies are offering their own binary options that you can trade online. These trades are mostly over the counter (OTC) with minimal regulation and perhaps elevated counterparty risk. Buyer beware!

The online binary options also come with a myriad of different rules and variables depending on the site you go to. They are priced more like horse races as opposed to using real models, with supply and demand purely driving price. You can still use what you know about options to find the bad bets and you can run the binary prices through the Bloomberg pricing model to get a gauge of TheoVal and what sort of real chance you have. See Exhibit 7.16.

www.binary-options-brokers.com is a site that refers traders to different companies that trade OTC binaries. Keep in mind that most of these are *not* exchange traded and many of these companies are offshore, out of U.S. regulatory reach. Proceed with caution!

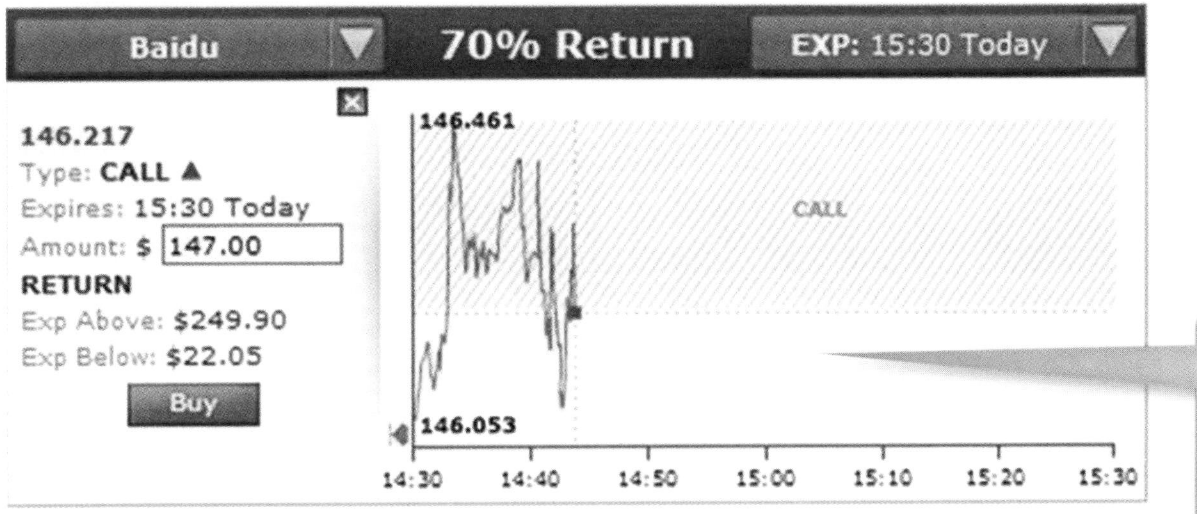

Here is an example of an online binary option quote that expires on BIDU in a couple of hours. There are several ways that online, unstandardized binaries trade; be sure you understand the specific nuances and use caution!

Exhibit 7.16

I don't care how attractive some of these bets look, you must understand the product and probability to trade it most effectively and safely. Don't make your bets on excitement and emotion.

Binary options, also called *all-or-nothing options*, *digital options*, or *fixed return options* (FROs), are offered and traded across many markets. Second, there is not much open interest and so the spreads are fairly wide. On the outside, when you examine the valuation of binary options, they really begin to look much like N(d2), the probability that the option finishes in the money (the other delta).

Using the Black-Scholes or other models, you can interpret the premium of the binary option in the risk-neutral world as the expected value = probability of being in-the-money * unit, discounted to the present value. Value can be determined for any period of time.

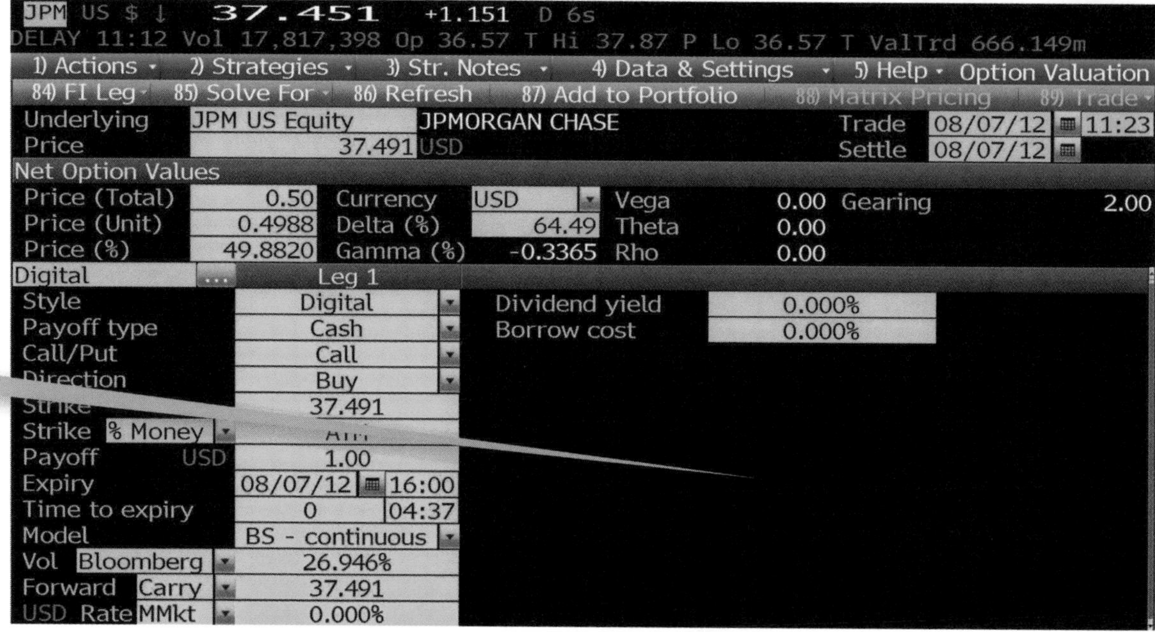

Here you pay $100 to make $78 or lose $90. There is $12 of "vig" in the trade for the house. But that vig is what makes this a bad trade, not to mention that the payout is not 1 to 1 and you cannot change the price of the binary; you can only make the bet that the stock will be above or below the current price.

Exhibit 7.17

Think about it as an absolute bet on delta, where you buy a 30 delta call for 30 cents and statistically have a 30 percent or so statistical shot of winning. The thing with traditional binaries is that they have a fixed payout of 0 or 1.

The problem is the absolute return where the option returns either one or nothing. It's a risk/reward question that you have to ask yourself.

When I want to find if a binary option is worth it, I might look at a $1 call spread with the short strike being the same as the binary option I am looking at. You can use Bloomberg's OV strike synthetic screen to find the theoretical value of a strike if one doesn't exist. See Exhibits 7.17 and 7.18.

I cannot recommend or deter you from any of these new binary option companies, because I just don't

By creating the binary synthetic in JPM, I can quantify the market in the binary option quote for accuracy. Usually the value/cost of a binary is somewhere between Nd1 and Nd2 delta; the payout here, along with the price of the option, is unique. Theoretically, we are paying $0.56 (maybe a little less given the downside $10) for this option if we factor the risk/reward from the previous chart.

Exhibit 7.18

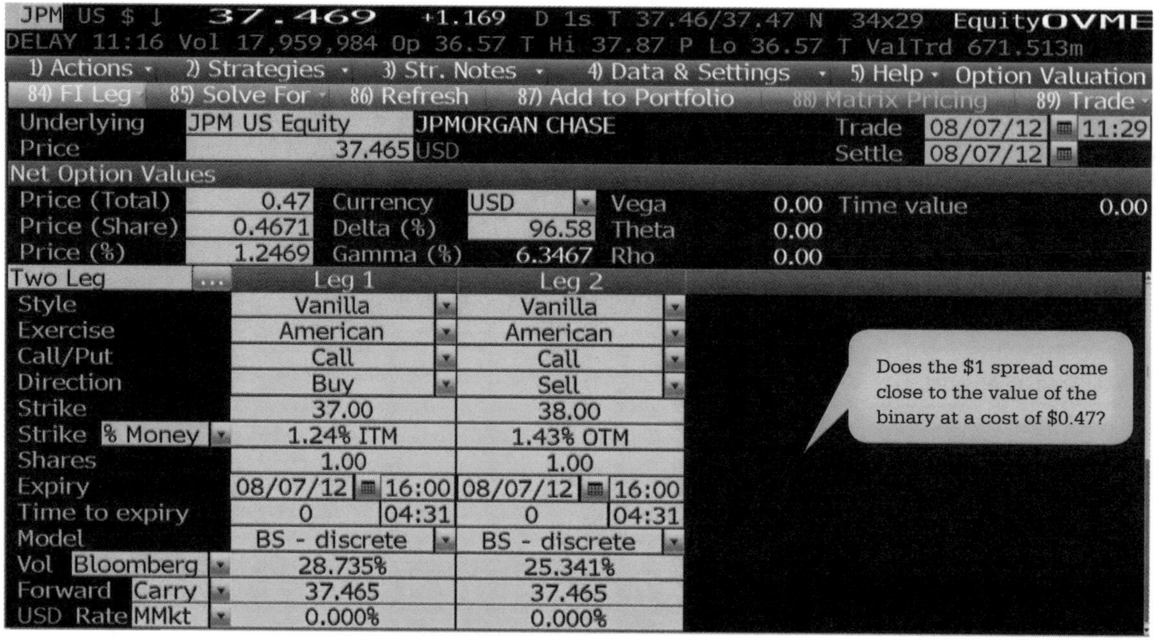

JPM US $ ↓ 37.469 +1.169 D 1s T 37.46/37.47 N 34x29 Equity OVME
DELAY 11:16 Vol 17,959,984 Op 36.57 T Hi 37.87 P Lo 36.57 T ValTrd 671.513m
1) Actions · 2) Strategies · 3) Str. Notes · 4) Data & Settings · 5) Help · Option Valuation
84) FI Leg · 85) Solve For · 86) Refresh 87) Add to Portfolio 88) Matrix Pricing 89) Trade ·

Underlying JPM US Equity JPMORGAN CHASE Trade 08/07/12 11:29
Price 37.465 USD Settle 08/07/12

Net Option Values

Price (Total)	0.47	Currency	USD	Vega	0.00	Time value	0.00
Price (Share)	0.4671	Delta (%)	96.58	Theta	0.00		
Price (%)	1.2469	Gamma (%)	6.3467	Rho	0.00		

Two Leg	Leg 1	Leg 2
Style	Vanilla	Vanilla
Exercise	American	American
Call/Put	Call	Call
Direction	Buy	Sell
Strike	37.00	38.00
Strike % Money	1.24% ITM	1.43% OTM
Shares	1.00	1.00
Expiry	08/07/12 16:00	08/07/12 16:00
Time to expiry	0 04:31	0 04:31
Model	BS - discrete	BS - discrete
Vol Bloomberg	28.735%	25.341%
Forward Carry	37.465	37.465
USD Rate MMkt	0.000%	0.000%

Does the $1 spread come close to the value of the binary at a cost of $0.47?

Exhibit 7.19

have enough information to offer a complete and honest review. You will have to compare these companies yourself and use caution. Some of these companies spell their risks out, others not so much. They even indicate that their markets might be completely different from the ones you see on the exchanges. Their expiration times are also different.

Is there a binary, vertical spread relationship? A binary call option is in many ways similar to a tight $1 vertical spread using two synthetic vanilla options with strike prices equidistance around the binary strike, except that the expiration outcome has no variance, only 1 or 0 (true binary options can be bought and sold up until expiration). One can model the value of a binary cash-or-nothing option using $1 vertical spreads as a comparison. See Exhibit 7.19.

There are obviously other ways you can trade and compare them. Assume the spot price is $50 and the 40/45 put spread is $0.50 bid with 30 days until expiration. In this trade, you have $4.50 at risk for a $0.50 credit, or an 11 percent return on risk (ROR). Even with that ROR, you can still lose much more money than you brought in—nine times as much.

Compare that to selling the 45 put binary for $0.15. That option will only be worth zero or one at expiry, so we risk $0.75 on a $0.15 credit, or 20 percent ROR. You still risk five times what you stand to make (like you did in the put spread). But also remember that there is no middle ground . . . this is either going to be one or zero.

The breakeven in the put spread is $44.50 and you gradually lose money as the stock drops. The *absolute* breakeven on the binary is $45 in the stock.

If you are thinking of trading an OTC binary, try to correlate its return to a similar trade in the real listed option markets. You might find a better deal.

Trading Earnings

Four times a year we get to take an in-depth, inside look at the health and well-being of major corporations. These four checkpoints can offer important signals on a stock's journey to glory or oblivion. They also serve as catalysts for volatility of asset value as well as major changes in the Ivol of the derivatives. If you know what to look for and how to exploit these events, they can also be extremely profitable occasions. See Exhibits 7.20 and 7.21.

There are several ways I like to trade earnings depending on what results I discover in my pretrade analysis. Again, there is no magic bullet or one perfect way to structure risk when trading around earnings. The variables surrounding the event are immense, which makes it difficult to form one strategy without looking at all of the variables collectively.

Depending on the final outcome of my analysis, I may have completely changed my initial thoughts on strategy simply based on one data point. You must be prepared to be flexible or even walk away from a trade because earnings are generally the most volatile events for a stock. Careful consideration must be taken for each part of your analysis. Make sure all the pieces fit.

Taking Delta

For directional trades where you are contemplating taking on more than fractional delta risk, the stock *must* have certain attributes and meet certain tests or I will move to a more neutral or volatility based strategy. If you are hell-bent on trading a stock over earnings with a large directional bias that doesn't meet all your fundamental and/or technical criteria (but that maybe you have a strong "feeling" about), you should at least reduce your contract size and weigh your dollar delta exposure.

If you were thinking of buying a single option or stock, maybe you could sell another option against your long one to mitigate cost and Ivol crush, or if you buy the stock, overlay a wide collar around it, just in case.

From my perspective, it is almost always advantageous to give myself some statistical advantage if I am trading over an earnings report because of the un-

Smart Investor Tip!

Just because you "think" the stock will move a certain way doesn't give real rationale for risk. Quantify it! At least with some subjective reasoning you'll have some hard data to help you manage the trade (psychologically and monetarily) if it goes against you.

	Ann Date	Per	Per End	C	Reported	Comp	Estimate	%Surp	Enhanced	%Enh Surp	%Px Chg	T12M	P/E
Average of Absolute Values								4.25%		2.58%	3.52%		
11)	07/17/2013	Q2 13	06/13						3.975			15.80	12.56
12)	04/17/2013	Q1 13	03/13						3.160			15.43	12.87
13)	01/17/2013	Q4 12	12/12						5.361			15.17	13.09
14)	10/17/2012	Q3 12	09/12				3.611		3.683			14.61	13.59
15)	07/18/2012	Q2 12	06/12		3.510	3.510	3.428	2.39%	3.476	0.98%	3.77%	14.28	13.70
16)	04/17/2012	Q1 12	03/12		2.780	2.780	2.651	4.87%	2.704	2.81%	-3.53%	13.86	15.05
17)	01/19/2012	Q4 11	12/11		4.710	4.710	4.621	1.93%	4.689	0.45%	4.43%	13.49	13.63
18)	10/17/2011	Q3 11	09/11		3.280	3.280	3.222	1.80%	3.277	0.09%	-4.12%	12.96	13.49
19)	07/18/2011	Q2 11	06/11		3.090	3.090	3.022	2.25%	3.090	0.00%	5.67%	12.50	13.72
20)	04/19/2011	Q1 11	03/11		2.410	2.410	2.296	4.97%	2.318	3.97%	-0.39%	12.04	13.54
21)	01/18/2011	Q4 10	12/10		4.180	4.180	4.080	2.45%	4.159	0.50%	3.35%	11.58	12.67
22)	10/18/2010	Q3 10	09/10		2.820	2.820	2.748	2.62%	2.789	1.11%	-3.36%	10.99	12.21
23)	07/19/2010	Q2 10	06/10		2.625	2.610	2.575	1.36%	2.636	-0.99%	-2.50%	10.57	11.68

Exhibit 7.20

known factor as well as to take advantage of inflated Ivol. In simple terms, I want my breakeven to be less if I have a long bias, or higher if I have a short bias on my strategy.

This directional, but statistically advantaged, trade can be accomplished through a myriad of strategies. My favorites are vertical spreads, broken wing butterflies, split strike risk reversals (bullish or bearish), and even double vertical spreads.

Give the stock some breathing room with these spreads; look at past movements over earnings and do your best to position your breakeven at least 50 percent of the distance away from where you think the stock could travel if it moved against you.

Exhibit 7.21

For example, if the stock is priced at $100 and has moved an average of 10 percent over the past earnings periods, then place your breakeven at $95 or lower if you are bullish or $105 or higher if you are bearish.

Checklist Before Entry

Use this list just like the grading system from Chapter 2. If certain criteria are not met, then reduce the grade of the potential trade (and subsequent level of bullishness or bearishness) accordingly. What is different about this grading system is that it is specific to an event and you can combine contract sizing risk control with strategy selection and augmentation.

- If all components are extremely strong and pointing in one direction (let's say bullish), then you might just go and buy a call spread that is at

Smart Investor Tip!

The more analysts cover a stock, typically, the less chance you have for major surprises and subsequent moves in the stock. It doesn't mean that the stock cannot do something dramatic, just less chance of the "unexpected."

I prefer to see at least four to five analysts minimum. With a bevy of analysts covering a stock you will be able to read deeper into some of the nuances surrounding the reports and key in on the major risks that are shared among analysts.

the money with a breakeven at or higher than the current stock.

- If most components are in line and things look bullish you might move that call spread deep in the money to allow the stock to move a bit.
- If signals are more mixed, but you think the stock might move 10 percent, then maybe you can sell a fly or buy an iron butterfly that has breakevens within a 10 percent range on either side.
- If you have a slight bias, you can always position that fly to favor the side you favor.

Ahead of an earnings report, there are numerous types of forces pulling on a stock's price and volatility and they usually won't all be going in one direction. The key is to bring together all the data points and hopefully create a high probability trade through detailed forensics and observations of current data. Let me go through some of the major data points and variables you need to be aware of.

To take a large directional bet, I want to see just about all of the following questions answered with a yes or favor the direction you are trading in. *Obviously, if you were looking at a bearish candidate you would use the following logic in reverse.*

- **Analyst conviction**—Are the majority (85 percent plus) of analysts bullish (in agreement) on the stock with higher price targets at least 5 percent to 10 percent higher than the current price?
- **Analyst upgrades one to two weeks ahead of report**—Have any analysts stuck their neck out and revised higher than the consensus average? If so, that should tell you that this analyst(s) really believes in the stock and chances are they are taking that risk for good reason. Analysts don't like to be wrong or look like fools and even though they sometimes can't help but end up that way, they are usually quite thorough in their analysis of a stock's industry and individual health.
- **Consensus price target and rating**—At least 10 percent higher than current price? Ratio of buys to sells? Buys should be at least 20 percent higher than sells, negate holds unless more than 30 percent of total at which time you should count holds as sells if target is lower than current stock price or as buys if target is higher than current stock price.
- **Industry/sector/product trends**—Are there headwinds, tailwinds in the sector?
  - Are big expectations already baked in? (If so, this is a bad thing.)
  - Is the stock the best in breed?
  - What was commentary on last earnings call? (If commentary was strong and the stock has not been overbought compared to peers and the general market, it may be a good indicator of a bullish move.)
  - If the majority of these trends are in your favor, then you can add some risk into the trade.

- **P/E multiple**—If the trailing P/E is more than 40 percent of sector or peer average there better be a damn good reason for it; if not, I wouldn't be a buyer. If the P/E is within ±30 percent of sector P/E average then I look to the forward to make sure it's less than 15 percent higher than sector average. (Where can you find data on sector P/E average?)
- **Recent stock price movements**—Outside Bollinger bands? Where is the stock in relation to its last report and what multiple was it trading at then? If the multiple is lower now and markets are neutral to favorable, it greatly increases changes for a rally.

- This means looking back two to five years in volatility and skew history to get a more complete range in addition to analyzing the past two to four months of data and past earnings patterns so you can form a complete thesis that has some objective data behind it. If you see that OTM calls are unusually bid up in an asset that doesn't usually see that type of skew, it may be worth the research—someone may know something.

Gauging Response and Movement

- **Average surprise (EM screen #2)**—Here you can see just how volatile the stock tends to be. This figure should be used in conjunction with the ATM straddle and other volatility measurements to select your strategy and set your breakevens, targets, and stop losses.
- **Surprise/Px Chg correlation (EM screen #2)**—If you believe that the stock is going to surprise based on its past surprise factors, analyst movements, and momentum as well as strong sector fundamentals, you need to know how this stock tends to respond to positive surprises. This can be a bit tricky and will vary from stock to stock. I generally look at how much a company surprised versus how much the stock moved.
- **HVol considerations**—Look at the volatility of the stock going into earnings. Has it increased? Has the volatility been increasing but in one direction (moving the stock abnormally higher or lower)? As stock climbs higher, it is my opinion that the chances and amount of a rally after the event become less and less.
- **Ivol considerations/straddle check**—Cross reference implied a one-day move (EM screen #2) with the at-the-money straddle (less than 10 days) as a percentage of the current stock price. If the options markets are more than 20 percent greater than the implied one-day movement you see on Bloomberg, you might want to complement your directional strategy with a short vega option strategy. You can also use the implied volatility of the front month ATM options to synthesize a two-day straddle in the options pricing calculator to get the real expected movement.

Once you have researched these data points, you can put them all together and form your thesis. You

Smart Investor Tip!

Ahead of the earnings report you may notice changes in the volatility skew or *smile* as we like to call it. The changes that are occurring in that skew can clue you in on what bets professionals are making in the option markets, allowing you to go beyond volatility and actually find directional bias through the option prices.

KEY POINT:

Take a quick look at the *Surprise/Px Chg Corr* number, which gives you a good idea of just how the two are linked. Looking at MNST (Exhibit 7.22), you can see that it has a positive average surprise of 2.42 percent and a 0.35 positive price correlation to that surprise.

should be able to obviously determine if you are bullish or bearish, but most important just how confident in your sentiment. When you combine that fundamental confidence with statistical and technical data you will then be able to make a specific determination of strategy, strike placement, contract size as well as an exit strategy.

Let's look at a real scenario with Monster Beverage Company and go through the rationale:

Case Study: MNST Earnings 2/23/12

Around February 20, 2012, I did a search for some upcoming earnings reports that I could use to trade. I targeted Monster Beverage roughly three days prior to its report. I tried to pick a stock that I don't normally follow so that I could go through my rationale and methods, and demonstrate how I analyze and trade earnings without bias or previous mental baggage.

If I am not at all familiar with a company, the first place I generally go is the company information screen to find out what company does, its sector, and check the last couple of months of news to get a better feel for where the company is at in relation to its peers and the market. I double-check to make sure it's not being acquired or in the midst of litigation, which would not only throw a monkey wrench into my trade, but also add an unusual skew to the options that has nothing to do with the earnings itself.

MNST was the random stock that was selected. I do like its energy drinks and so do most of my peers, so I guess the Peter Lynch "invest in what you know" factor was there. See Exhibit 7.22.

On the surface, the stock looks fairly strong with decent growth over the past few years, minus a rough year in 2010. The stock is up 85 percent over the past year and 15.5 percent year-to-date (YTD). The YTD looks good versus the peers; the yearly performance may be skewed because of the peers being compared or if the stock was dramatically sold off in the period.

The reality here is that MNST is an interesting case as it recently changed its investor brand and image from Super Hippie Hansen's Natural to Monster Beverage (which Wall Street seems to like more).

The company was certainly a leader in their space at the time and even though the big bottlers like Coke and Pepsi had their energy drinks in competition, Monster had momentum and some good-tasting product. Trading at 36 times earnings, the company had high expectations for growth, which along with the rally in the stock adds risk to the trade and automatically deters me trading any strategy with a breakeven equal to or greater than the stock. See Exhibit 7.23.

Analyst Conviction

The current target is \$57.25, \$4 or 7.5 percent above the current price, which is good but not stellar. Current estimates are for 37 cents and if you dig deeper into the range of individual estimates, you can see that most of the analysts are in a fairly tight range (0.35 to 0.39). When I see this I believe that there is less chance

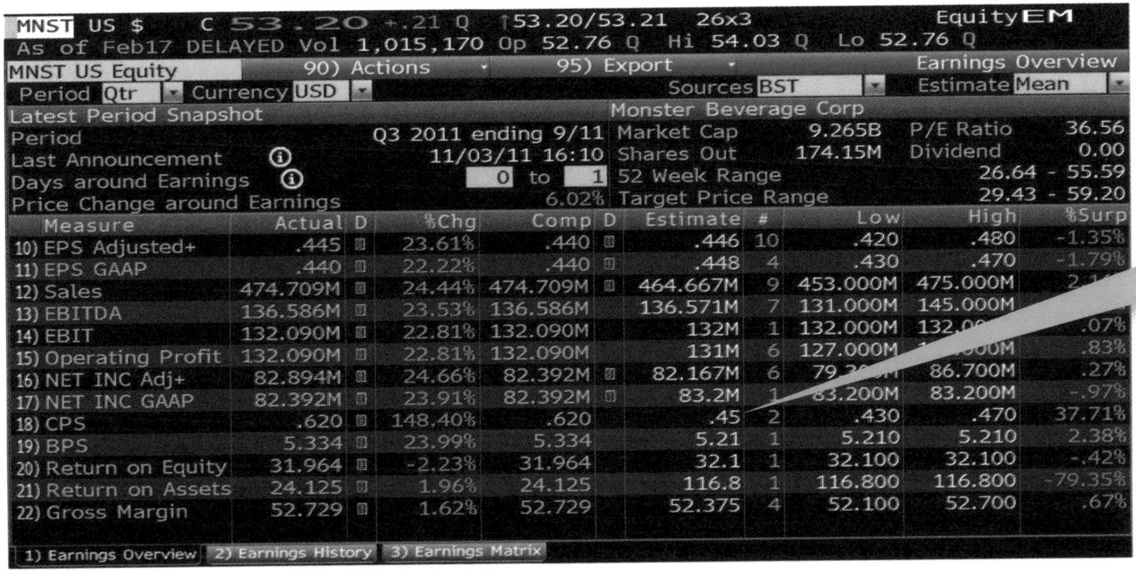

MNST US $ C 53.20 +.21 Q ↑53.20/53.21 26x3 Equity EM
As of Feb17 DELAYED Vol 1,015,170 Op 52.76 Q Hi 54.03 Q Lo 52.76 Q
MNST US Equity 90) Actions 95) Export Earnings Overview
Period Qtr Currency USD Sources BST Estimate Mean

Latest Period Snapshot		Monster Beverage Corp			
Period	Q3 2011 ending 9/11	Market Cap	9.265B	P/E Ratio	36.56
Last Announcement	11/03/11 16:10	Shares Out	174.15M	Dividend	0.00
Days around Earnings	0 to 1	52 Week Range			26.64 - 55.59
Price Change around Earnings	6.02%	Target Price Range			29.43 - 59.20

Measure	Actual	D	%Chg	Comp	D	Estimate	#	Low	High	%Surp
10) EPS Adjusted+	.445		23.61%	.440		.446	10	.420	.480	-1.35%
11) EPS GAAP	.440		22.22%	.440		.448	4	.430	.470	-1.79%
12) Sales	474.709M		24.44%	474.709M		464.667M	9	453.000M	475.000M	[illegible]
13) EBITDA	136.586M		23.53%	136.586M		136.571M	7	131.000M	145.000M	[illegible]
14) EBIT	132.090M		22.81%	132.090M		132M	1	132.000M	[illegible]	.07%
15) Operating Profit	132.090M		22.81%	132.090M		131M	6	127.000M	[illegible]	.83%
16) NET INC Adj+	82.894M		24.66%	82.392M		82.167M	6	[illegible]	86.700M	.27%
17) NET INC GAAP	82.392M		23.91%	82.392M		83.2M	1	83.200M	83.200M	-.97%
18) CPS	.620		148.40%	.620		.45	2	.430	.470	37.71%
19) BPS	5.334		23.99%	5.334		5.21	1	5.210	5.210	2.38%
20) Return on Equity	31.964		-2.23%	31.964		32.1	1	32.100	32.100	-.42%
21) Return on Assets	24.125		1.96%	24.125		116.8	1	116.800	116.800	-79.35%
22) Gross Margin	52.729		1.62%	52.729		52.375	4	52.100	52.700	.67%

1) Earnings Overview 2) Earnings History 3) Earnings Matrix

EM screen #1 is a quick snapshot and report card of the last earnings report. Always consider typical volatility movements over earnings reports, as they may have a major impact on your strategy.

Exhibit 7.22

for a complete anomaly in results and thus expect a lower volatility event compared to a stock that has analyst with more than a 15 percent range between them.

Analyst Upgrades

I do like the fact that the Stifel Nicolaus analyst took his estimate from the consensus number to the top of the range just days ahead of the report—this is a very bullish sign. The next step would be to take a look at his track record to determine just how much confidence I have in his opinion. There were a couple adjustments downward for next quarter, which are okay, but just make sure that they aren't too far off from consensus. Additionally, this might be a clue that future expectations are flattening out, which can actually be

MNST's EM screen #3 tells me that on balance the 11 analysts (good coverage) are somewhat neutral to bullish (six buy/five sell), which is a positive sign, and the consensus rating is 4.09, which indicates an overall buy rating.

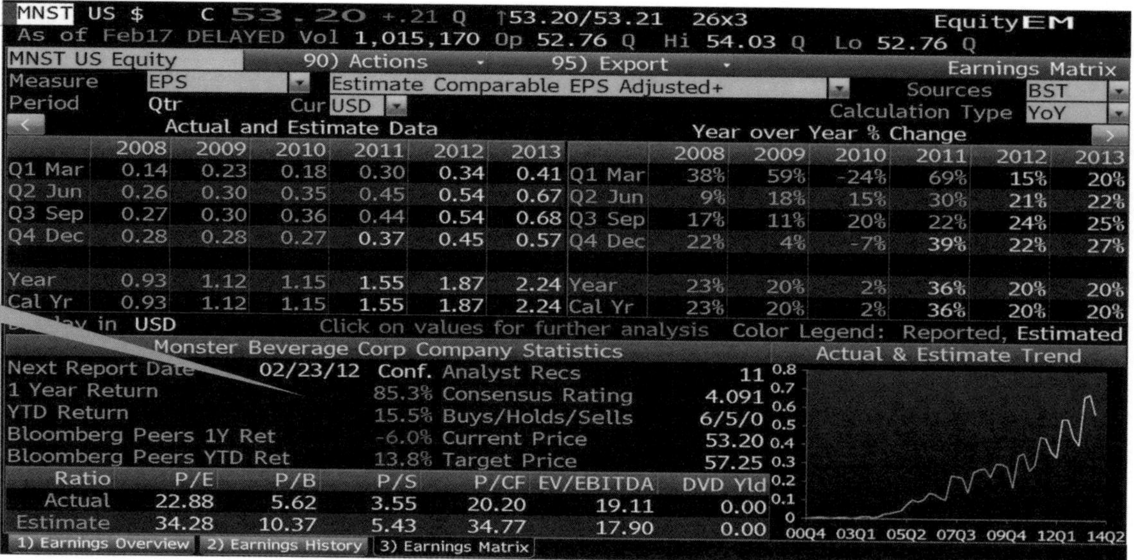
MNST US $ C 53.20 +.21 Q ↑53.20/53.21 26x3 EquityEM
As of Feb17 DELAYED Vol 1,015,170 Op 52.76 Q Hi 54.03 Q Lo 52.76 Q
MNST US Equity 90) Actions 95) Export Earnings Matrix
Measure EPS Estimate Comparable EPS Adjusted+ Sources BST
Period Qtr Cur USD Calculation Type YoY

Actual and Estimate Data

	2008	2009	2010	2011	2012	2013
Q1 Mar	0.14	0.23	0.18	0.30	0.34	0.41
Q2 Jun	0.26	0.30	0.35	0.45	0.54	0.67
Q3 Sep	0.27	0.30	0.36	0.44	0.54	0.68
Q4 Dec	0.28	0.28	0.27	0.37	0.45	0.57
Year	0.93	1.12	1.15	1.55	1.87	2.24
Cal Yr	0.93	1.12	1.15	1.55	1.87	2.24

Year over Year % Change

	2008	2009	2010	2011	2012	2013
Q1 Mar	38%	59%	-24%	69%	15%	20%
Q2 Jun	9%	18%	15%	30%	21%	22%
Q3 Sep	17%	11%	20%	22%	24%	25%
Q4 Dec	22%	4%	-7%	39%	22%	27%
Year	23%	20%	2%	36%	20%	20%
Cal Yr	23%	20%	2%	36%	20%	20%

Display in USD Click on values for further analysis Color Legend: Reported, Estimated

Monster Beverage Corp Company Statistics

Next Report Date	02/23/12 Conf.	Analyst Recs	11
1 Year Return	85.3%	Consensus Rating	4.091
YTD Return	15.5%	Buys/Holds/Sells	6/5/0
Bloomberg Peers 1Y Ret	-6.0%	Current Price	53.20
Bloomberg Peers YTD Ret	13.8%	Target Price	57.25

Ratio	P/E	P/B	P/S	P/CF	EV/EBITDA	DVD Yld
Actual	22.88	5.62	3.55	20.20	19.11	0.00
Estimate	34.28	10.37	5.43	34.77	17.90	0.00

Exhibit 7.23

a good thing. If analysts are just moderating their expectations, but the company delivers a decent report, it could make for a rally on the news. See Exhibit 7.24.

Industry/Sector/Product Trends

This is a tough one to call, but I would say that in early 2012 investors were optimistic that the jobs situation was improving and consumers were spending. I guess there was also some odd logic that I had about the need for increased productivity from the average worker and how energy drinks and overall health awareness was increasing in popularity, driving sales for Monster.

There were certainly more tailwinds than headwinds, which also gave me a bullish push overall.

Stock Price and Expected Movement

At the time, MNST was definitely close to its highs, although it had pulled back slightly. Looking back over time in the GP (Bloomberg Command GP) chart in Exhibit 7.25 shows that the stock has tended to sell off

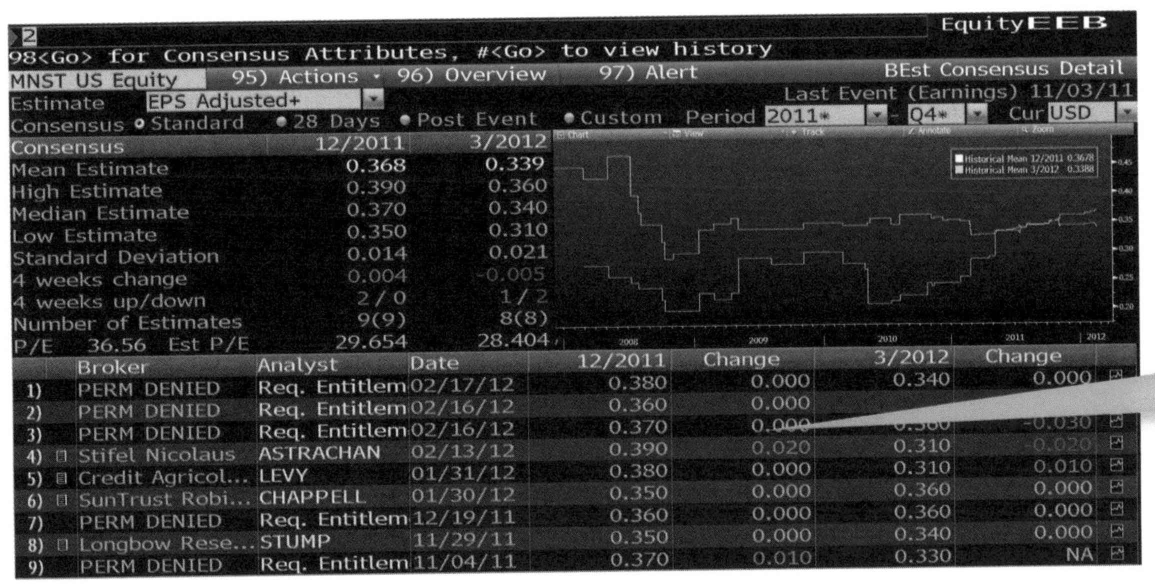

Here is the analyst tracking page, which allows me to see if analysts are getting more bullish or bearish ahead of the number.

Exhibit 7.24

ahead of earnings and move higher on good results. The company missed slightly last quarter and the stock still rallied.

There was support around the $48.75 level at the time and the 50-day moving average was way below that at roughly $42.

Average Surprises and Correlations

Q4 2010 was not a good one for MNST, but when you look at the reaction of the stock in the %Px Chg column, you can see this baby has moved up an average of +7 percent for the past six quarters. Last, I look at the P/E graph and see just how expensive the stock was going into each of the reports. If the multiple was just slightly lower than it is now, it's even more of a reason to buy.

The average move for MNST was about 7.84 percent over an earnings event (+–three days), so I needed to take that into consideration, in addition to the implied one-day move on the EM screen as well as

Exhibit 7.25

my synthetic straddle outcome. I will generally average all three of these to find an expected outcome. See Exhibit 7.26.

An elevated Ivol with Hvol less than 30 is typical when you are up against an earnings report and the past earnings reports will allow you to see just how dramatic the Ivol crush will be. It's a good idea to run a test with the Ivol crush and see how it affects your potential strategy. See Exhibits 7.27 and 7.28.

Here I built a straddle that expires just after earnings assuming the 50 vol that the real ATM straddle is trading at. The theoretical value of this straddle is $2.22 or 4.17 percent of strike (synthetic 52.20). The implied one-day move (on the EM screen matrix) is 7.75 percent. So the options markets are looking a little cheap perhaps.

In the real world March is the front month and the 52.50 straddle is trading for $5.55 (with .70 parity to

	Per End	Ann Date	Per	Actual	%Chg	Comp	Est	%Surp	%Px Chg	T12M	P/E
10)	09/12	11/23/12	Q3 12		22.19%		0.544			1.79	29.72
11)	06/12	08/23/12	Q2 12		20.83%		0.544			1.70	31.29
12)	03/12	05/23/12	Q1 12		14.83%		0.339			1.60	33.25
13)	12/11	02/23/12	Q4 11		38.78%		0.368			1.56	34.10
14)	09/11	11/03/11	Q3 11	0.445	23.61%	0.440	0.446	-1.35%	6.02%	1.46	29.89
15)	06/11	08/04/11	Q2 11	0.450	30.43%	0.450	0.421	6.89%	8.40%	1.37	29.54
16)	03/11	05/05/11	Q1 11	0.295	68.57%	0.295	0.247	19.43%	4.52%	1.27	23.71
17)	12/10	02/24/11	Q4 10	0.265	-7.02%	0.265	0.313	-15.34%	7.88%	1.15	22.73
18)	09/10	11/04/10	Q3 10	0.360	20.00%	0.360	0.359	0.28%	0.82%	1.17	19.92
19)	06/10	08/05/10	Q2 10	0.345	15.00%	0.345	0.331	4.23%	7.66%	1.11	17.62
20)	03/10	05/06/10	Q1 10	0.175	-23.91%	0.175	0.233	-24.89%	-12.20%	1.06	20.46
21)	12/09	02/25/10	Q4 09	0.285		0.285	0.264	7.95%	2.90%	1.12	17.14

The EM #2 screen is a great place to find earnings statistics. Here I can see that on average they have surprised to the upside 2.42 percent of the time. Check the past four or five reports and see how trends are shaping up and how the stock has responded to different reports.

Exhibit 7.26

the call). That means that the straddle is 10.5 percent of strike, which is more than the normal movement.

As I write this, I have no idea what MNST will report, but based on the fact that the implied move is $7.75 and the straddle is trading for 10.5 percent of strike, it might be more advantageous to sell volatility here if you are making a short term trade. See Exhibit 7.29.

I would love to have the ability to trade the synthetic straddle by using the current volatility and subsequent pricing, but you cannot trade an option that expires this Friday if it's not there (unless you know someone willing to take the other side of that FLEX option).

The reality is that Ivol is elevated and for good reason.

The Trade Selection

Based on my findings, I have a fairly strong bullish fundamental thesis that is backed by hard data and past results. Technically, the stock is a little overbought, but

In the GV screen you can see how front month Ivol is extremely elevated at almost 49 percent and Hvol is less than 30.

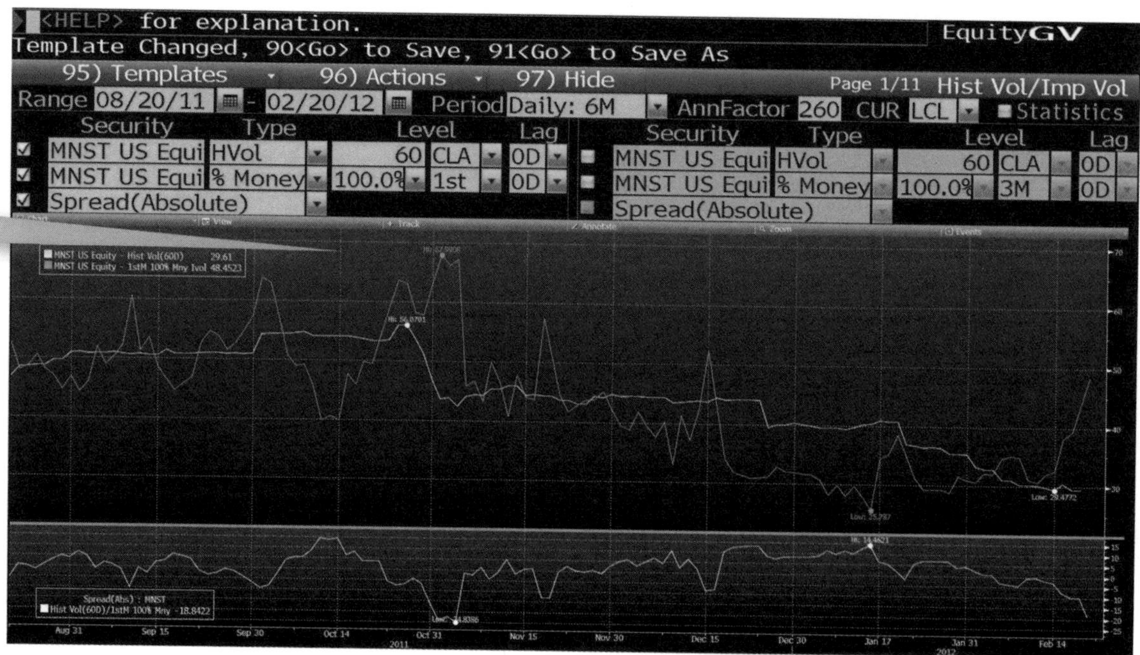

Exhibit 7.27

is not outside its Bollinger Bands or ATR at the time I am making the trade. MNST has support around just below the $49 level.

Analysts are looking bullish and an accurate analyst stuck his nose (2 cents or 5.4 percent) out ahead of the report, which adds to my confidence.

Volatility is extremely elevated and a 30 percent to 40 percent Ivol crush after the report is not out of the question. The stock has averaged a 7.75 percent move over earnings and the front month straddle is trading at 10.5 percent of the stock's value, which probably doesn't make it the best choice, especially because my synthetic straddle is only pricing in a 4 percent move for the report itself.

Based on my findings I am okay with taking some delta in a bullish direction, but I want to be short volatility and have limited risk with a breakeven that

MNST US $ C 53.20 +.21 Q ↑53.20/53.21 26x3 EquityOVME
As of Feb17 DELAYED Vol 1,015,170 Op 52.76 Q Hi 54.03 Q Lo 52.76 Q
1) Actions · 2) Strategies · 3) Str. Notes · 4) Data & Settings · 5) Help· Option Valuation
84) FI Leg· 85) Solve For· 86) Refresh 87) Add to Portfolio 88) Matrix Pricing 89) Trade·

Underlying MNST US Equity MONSTER BEVERAGE Trade 02/20/12 14:42
Price 53.205 USD Settle 02/20/12

Net Option Values

Price (Total)	2.22	Currency	USD	Vega	0.04	Time value	2.22
Price (Share)	2.2172	Delta (%)	2.12	Theta	-0.27		
Price (%)	4.1673	Gamma (%)	15.2709	Rho	0.00		

Two Leg ...	Leg 1		Leg 2	
Style	Vanilla		Vanilla	
Exercise	American		American	
Call/Put	Call		Put	
Direction	Buy		Buy	
Strike	53.205		53.205	
Strike % Money	ATM		ATM	
Shares	1.00		1.00	
Expiry	02/24/12	16:15	02/24/12	16:15
Time to expiry	4	01:33	4	01:33
Model	BS - discrete		BS - discrete	
Vol Bloomberg	50.000%		49.000%	
Forward Carry	53.2056		53.2056	
USD Rate MMkt	0.189%		0.189%	

7) Option Pricing 8) Scenario Graph 9) Scenario Table 10) Volatility Data

Example of a four-day synthetic straddle in MNST.

Exhibit 7.28

is roughly 3.87 percent away from the current stock price (7.75 percent expected move × 50 percent).

With the stock at $53.20, that puts my preferred breakeven at least $2.05 cents below at $51.15. The most straightforward directional strategy that comes to mind is a bull-put spread that is slightly wider than normal to get more vega and delta, perhaps a $10 wide spread.

Because support is around $48, which is also more than 10 percent away, I am comfortable that position my spread is around that level, with the long strike below it. The long strike will prevent catastrophe and the support level and distance in the stock will hopefully give me some breathing room and time to react.

Right now the March 50/40 put spread can be sold for $1.25, which is a 14 percent return on risk; I could

The OMON screen for MNST showing option values at the time of the trade.

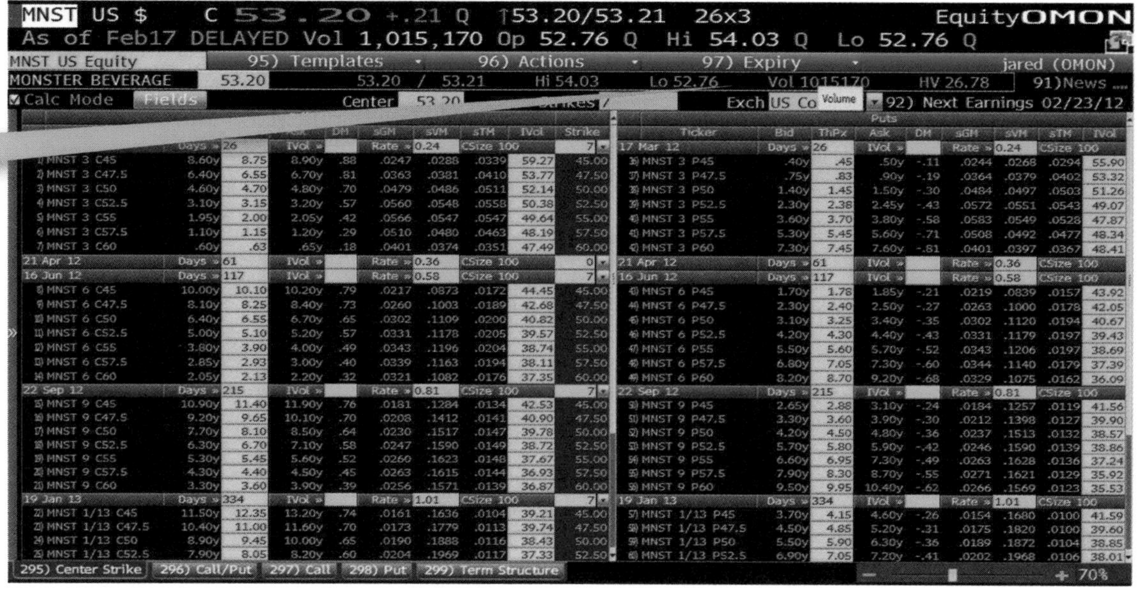

Exhibit 7.29

also sell the 50/45 for $1 or the 52.50/47.50 for $1.55, which would put my breakevens at $49 and $50.95 respectively. The latter would be the best return and give me the higher delta.

I am more confident in this case, so I am going to choose the closer spread. Because I was okay with $10 to get more delta originally, I found it acceptable to tighten the width, but move the spread closer. Worst case scenario is that I lose $3.45. See Exhibit 7.30.

It says my spread should decrease to $.80, so if this is acceptable then that will be my target. If not, I run some more scenarios or select a new strategy. If I want to hold onto the trade longer, it might be a better idea to select a spread that is further away from the stock price.

Stops

Because the stock has a history of moving 7.75 percent, I will simulate an 8 percent drop with a 20 percent Ivol crush to get an idea of worst-case scenario. There I see that my spread will swell to $3.80, which will most likely be my stop-loss point unless the stock starts to bounce right away at which time I may hold. The reality is that

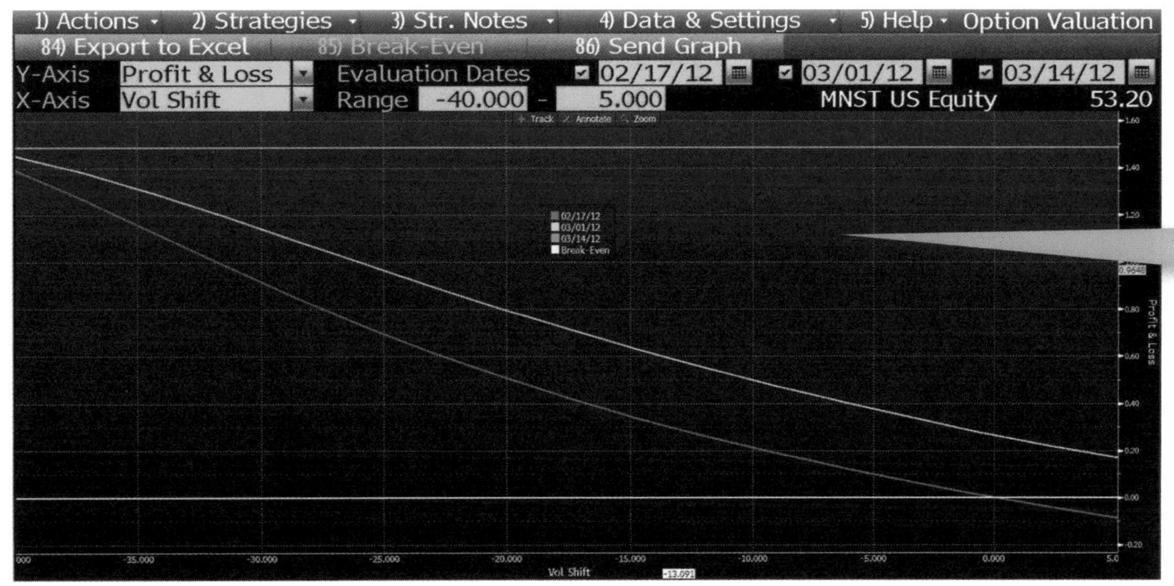

Let's run a quick scenario assuming a 20 percent Ivol crush and see what my spread's value would be; I also ran a scenario with the price of the stock jumping 5 percent, both of which have a high statistical probability of happening. I move time forward to simulate theta effects as well.

Exhibit 7.30

you should control your downside and stop the bleeding with an upside-down reward/risk strategy like this.

Outcome

My research paid off! MNST reported record sales and profits for quarter and full year! Gross sales for Q4 increased 28.4 percent; net sales for Q4 increased 28.7 percent to $410 million from $318.7 million a year ago.

Net sales for the year increased 30.6 percent to $1.703 billion from $1.304 billion, which sent shares higher in the days following the report. On the day after earnings were announced (4 P.M. 2/23) the stock moved only moved 3.7 percent from open to close and roughly 7 percent from the high to low of the day. The total move over the three days following the report was close to 8.6 percent. See Exhibits 7.31 and 7.32.

Overlaying alternative strategies: When it comes to earnings, the definitiveness of your research and reasoning should guide you to the most appropriate strategy. Test out several scenarios and find the one that feels the best and is most realistic, not the one that makes you the most money.

Here is a stock chart of the entry point and subsequent rally in the stock.

Exhibit 7.31

Overlay and test several strategies before selecting your final approach to the trade. It may also be beneficial to paper trade several techniques alongside one another to compare and contrast outcomes.

Fine-Tune Your Results

It pays to keep a detailed journal of your trades and strategies. The journal should detail your methods and data points for developing your thesis for a trade. You should also add brief commentary about your emotional state of mind and the overall tone of the market place.

Try to identify patterns for winning and losing trades with the goal of reducing the losing patterns and increasing the traits that were successful. This will take time and you must be objective.

Every month you should do a checkup on yourself; answer the following questions and drop the answers

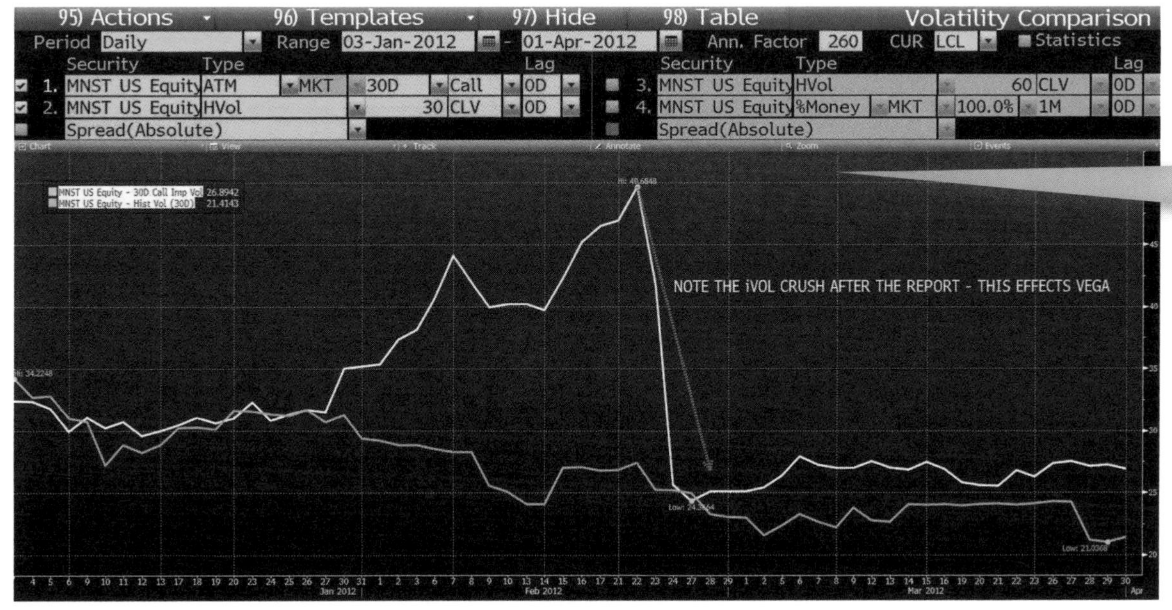

Ivol came in as expected, and I took the trade off for a $0.30 debit on Monday the 27th so I could capture some extra time decay over the weekend. That was a 36 percent profit in a weekend's time.

Exhibit 7.32

into a spread sheet. It will help you break bad habits and learn where you are going wrong. If you are winning all the time, still do the exercise—it can only refine your methods!

What Were the Common Elements of Your Losing Trades?

- What were their certain chart patterns or volume trends that typically led to a weak or losing trade?
- Is there a time of day (for entry or exit) where you found a majority of losing trades? Also look at the day of the week and how close you are to expiration and/or earnings events.
- Were there any common characteristics among the losing stocks? Volatility, volume, price, valuation (PEG, PE, etc.).
- Was there a particular sector that brought you more losing trades when you looked back? Were

DO IT YOURSELF

Find low-hanging fruit first. Assume that 80 percent of your losing trades were done 10 days before expiration; and 75 percent of your winners were on trades that had 30 or more days until expiration. This is an easy find. Targeting other traits may be more difficult.

the sectors in favor, out of favor at the time of the trade? Was your trade against the overall market climate?

- Was your mood compromised when you got into or out of losing trades? Stress at home, work? Were there other losing trades that made you feel like you had to get out?
- Does a certain method/strategy more often than not turn into a losing trade?
- Did you find more losers when you risked more (or less) money in a trade? Are you risking too much and overthinking the trade? Should you tone down the volatility by using a different strategy?
- How many exceptions did you make to the grading system? Did the trades with high exceptions end up as losers?

What Were the Common Elements of Your Winners? Also be sure and tally up your win/loss ratio:

- How many trades you executed and closed.
- Winning trades ÷ losing trades = win/loss ratio (hopefully this ratio is less than 1.7).

Now take all of the questions listed earlier and correlate them to your winning trades. Get as detailed as possible so that you can identify some of the smallest nuances that can have an effect on your outcomes.

You then want to compare and contrast your results in detail. You are looking for attributes that occurred frequently (+65 percent) to the winners and losers separately, but not to both. Those attributes that seem to "stick out" are the keys to unlocking more potential from your trades.

Look back as far as you can to gather as much data as possible.

Make one change at a time and test it for a month.

For the next month try not to enter any trades with less than 30 days until expiration. Reevaluate at the end of the month and run your analysis again on just those trades that occurred in the month. If you didn't trade much, stretch it out.

Once you make the change and you are comfortable with it, begin a new data set with your adjustment and see how it works moving forward. In a few weeks, make another change if you wish. The key is the constant reevaluation of performance. It's not just you that may need to change; the markets may be changing as well!

There is no "right way" in the markets, rather an evolving regimen of hypotheses, tests, and education of which the final objective is to provide you with a long-term method of making money consistently while keeping your losses under control. The process must always remain fluid, as must your willingness to adapt to new situations and technology.

Appendix: Bloomberg Functionality Cheat Sheet

BETA	beta analysis
CALL	call options
CEPR	directory of futures and options exchanges
CORR	correlation of equity to peers
EQS	equity search
ERN	earnings surprise analysis
EVTS	earnings and events calendar
GIV	graph intraday volatility
GPA	graph price average
GV	graph volatility
MOSO	most active options
NI OPTION	scrolling news: equity derivatives
OEM	option contract exchange menu
OGOP	oil options
OMON	options monitor
OMST	most active options
OSA	option scenario analysis
OSCH	intraday options search
OTM	option contract table menu
OV	options valuation (standard)
OVDV	volatility surface analysis screen
OVE	options valuation (est. price)
OVI	stocks with abnormal option volume
OVME	equity and index option valuation
OVT	options valuation total
PUT	put options
QRO	trade recaps for options

RV/VOL	volatility ranker
SCAN	scan option/equity markets
SECF	security finder
SKEW	option skew analysis
SYNS	synthetic options
TRMS	graph implied volatility across maturities
VML	currency and commodity option valuation

About the Author

Growing up in Philadelphia, Jared Levy spent his most of his adolescence and adult life immersed in the finance and options industries. Jared began his career as a retail stock broker, spending several years managing money and educating his clients on smart investing decisions, which included unconventional alternative derivative strategies, structured settlements, and unique real estate investments together with development, creative financing structures, and property management.

After creating his own stock and options trading strategy and algorithm in the 1990s, Jared went on to become a market maker and specialist on the Philadelphia Stock Exchange (PHLX), trading the largest volume issue on that exchange at the time, Dell (DELL). He then moved to the American Stock Exchange (AMEX), where he traded Cisco Systems (CSCO) options. Before the age of 25, Jared had been recruited by Equitec Proprietary Group to be one of the original market makers trading Nasdaq-100 Trust options ("Qubes"). During that time he successfully traded thousands of options contracts and shares daily, equating to millions of dollars in risk. Jared was also a member of the CSX.

In 2001, Jared returned to the PHLX to launch a new on-floor operation for his firm, serving as an options specialist for companies that included Krispy Kreme Doughnuts (KKD), Expedia.com (EXPE), Baxter Technologies, and Broadband and Semiconductor HOLDRS products.

After leaving the exchange, Levy traded distressed assets and consulted for Thomson Financial before relocating to Dallas to join Wizetrade and WTV as their chief options strategist and on-air options expert. He was known for his three-plus hours of daily, live, and unscripted market commentary and education. Jared dedicated his time with Wizetrade to enlighten investors worldwide about the mechanics of the market, risk management, and options trading, which is where he really found his passion for educating.

In 2004, Jared began his own live on-air career as an anchor/expert fielding questions and educating viewers from around the world, unscripted and raw.

Over the years he has been featured in many industry publications and won an Emmy for his daily video, "Trader Cast." He is regularly quoted by Reuters, the *Wall Street Journal*, and Yahoo! Finance, among many others.

In March 2009, he was recruited by CNBC to become a Fast Money contributor. Prior to that he had appeared on Bloomberg, Fox Business, CNN Radio, Wall Street Journal Radio, and many other financial and nonfinancial networks around the world and continues to appear on those networks regularly.

In 2008, Jared joined PEAK6, one of the world's largest option market makers as the Senior Derivatives Specialist, focusing on the Options News Network (ONN), where he hosted and was the resident expert on several shows.

There, Jared wrote a daily column called "The Practical Options Trader," a piece dedicated to education and strategy. He also managed ONN's options alerts service. During 2010, Jared also worked as the senior derivative strategist for OptionsHouse.com (a subsidiary of PEAK6).

For several years after, Jared published a daily financial e-letter called "Smart Investing Daily," along with Sara Nunnally.

His passion is teaching the public how to successfully and consistently trade and invest for a living, while keeping risk and portfolio volatility low but returns high through the use of option strategies and a wide variety of diverse instruments. He still actively invests in real estate around the U.S. and has held his real estate and insurance licenses in Pennsylvania as well as his Series 7 and 63.

Jared is also a pilot and enjoys collecting art, restoring cars, and motorcycles.

He is a managing partner of the alternatives division at Belpointe Capital LLC and also serves as Senior Equities Strategist for Zacks Investment Research where he manages the "Whisper Trader" earnings service.

Jared's first book, *Your Options Handbook*, was released in April 2011 by Wiley.

You can keep up-to-date with Jared and his option trading services and educational programs at his website www.jaredlevy.com

Index

A

B

C

D

E

F

G

H

I

P

R

S

T

W